The Posttraumatic Self

ROUTLEDGE PSYCHOSOCIAL STRESS SERIES
Charles R. Figley, Ph.D., Series Editor

The Posttraumatic Self

Restoring Meaning and Wholeness to Personality

Edited by John P. Wilson

Routledge
Taylor & Francis Group
New York   London

Published in 2006 by
Routledge
Taylor & Francis Group
270 Madison Avenue
New York, NY 10016

Published in Great Britain by
Routledge
Taylor & Francis Group
2 Park Square
Milton Park, Abingdon
Oxon OX14 4RN

© 2006 by Taylor & Francis Group, LLC
Routledge is an imprint of Taylor & Francis Group

Printed in the United States of America on acid-free paper
10 9 8 7 6 5 4 3 2 1

International Standard Book Number-10: 0-415-95017-1 (Softcover)
International Standard Book Number-13: 978-0-415-95017-6 (Softcover)

Library of Congress Cataloging-in-Publication Data

Catalog record is available from the Library of Congress

Taylor & Francis Group
is the Academic Division of Informa plc.

Visit the Taylor & Francis Web site at
http://www.taylorandfrancis.com

and the Routledge Web site at
http://www.routledge-ny.com

This book is dedicated to Zev Harel, a survivor of the Holocaust, friend, and colleague whose life exemplifies the virtues of human integrity, courage, and the capacity to transcend catastrophic stress and trauma to give to the world, his family and friends with generosity and altruism.

Contents

About the Editor

John P. Wilson, Ph.D., is professor of Psychology at Cleveland State University, a Fulbright scholar, and a widely recognized international expert on posttraumatic stress disorder (PTSD). He is co-founder and past president of the International Society for Traumatic Stress Studies (ISTSS), a Diplomate and Fellow of the American Academy of Experts in Traumatic Stress, and a Fellow of the American Institute of Stress. Dr. Wilson has been an international consultant to the United Nations, the World Health Organization, and many governmental agencies in the U.S., Europe and Australia. He helped create mental health services during the war in former Yugoslavia (1993–1995) and has lectured throughout the world on the effects of trauma and PTSD. Dr. Wilson is the author of *Broken Spirits: Empathy in the Treatment of Trauma and PTSD*, as well as many other books on psychological trauma. He has received many honors and awards for his work including the George Washington Honor Medal, the Vega Award from the American Red Cross (twice), and many distinguished service awards from nongovernmental agencies for his work with war victims, refugees, and war veterans.

Contributors

Christine Agaibi is a doctoral candidate in psychology at the University of Akron. She received her Master's Degree in Clinical Psychology from Cleveland State University, where she researched posttraumatic resilience in collaboration with Dr. John P. Wilson.

Boris Droždek, M.D., M.A., is psychiatrist at Outpatient and Day Treatment Centre for Asylum Seekers and Refugees/GGz's-Hertogenbosch, the Netherlands. He specializes in the treatment of asylum seekers and refugees/torture survivors, and initiated development of a treatment services network. He is also a teacher of social psychiatry, and international director of the Summer School of Psychotrauma in Dubrovnik, Croatia. He publishes in the field of psycho-traumatology, and teaches and gives training and workshops for different agencies on a regular basis in the Netherlands and abroad. He also works for different non-government organizations (NGOs) in post-war areas.

Brian J. Hall is an honors graduate of Cleveland State University, where he received his Bachelor's and Master's Degrees in Experimental Psychology. Currently, he is a clinical doctoral student at Kent State University, where he continues his research on posttraumatic stress disorder. His research interests include understanding the relationship of trauma to personality processes, resilience, and coping. Mr. Hall is a member of the International Society for Traumatic Stress Studies and a member of the American Academy of Experts in Traumatic Stress. He has presented his research findings at professional conferences in the United States and Canada.

Jacob D. Lindy, M.D., is training and supervising analyst and past director of the Cincinnati Psychoanalytic Institute in Cincinnati, Ohio. He is also co-director of the University of Cincinnati Traumatic Stress Study Center and has been a guest lecturer at Institute in Moscow and St. Petersburg, Russia. He is past president of the International Society for Traumatic Stress Studies.

Kathleen O. Nader, DSW, is a specialist in posttraumatic stress disorder in children. She currently resides in Cedar Park, Texas. She has served as an international consultant in Kuwait after the Gulf War in 1991 and in Croatia after the Balkans War. She is the author of numerous chapters and articles on PTSD in children and adolescents, and is the co-editor of *Honoring the Differences,* a book about ethno-cultural differences in PTSD published by Routledge Press.

Silvana Turkovic, Ph.D., is a psychologist/psychotherapist who has worked with migrants and refugees in the Netherlands since 1986. She was attached to the Centrum '45/De Vonk, Dutch National Centre for the treatment of war victims. Since 2000 she has been affiliated with the Day Treatment Centre for Asylum Seekers and Refugees at GGz's-Hertogenbosch and has been treating severely traumatized victims of war and political violence. She has also participated in the projects of Medecins sans Frontieres and other NGOs in different post-war areas.

Series Editor's Foreword

The Psychosocial Stress Book Series is happy to welcome this book to the series with a history dating back to the dawn of the modern age of traumatology. According to Bessel van der Kolk (2005), the publication of *Stress Disorders among Vietnam Veterans* (Figley, 1978) was the beginning of the field as we know it today. Yet this book marks an important turning point for both the series and the field itself.

Recognizing that the treatment of trauma can only help eliminate symptoms, *The Posttraumatic Self: Restoring Meaning and Wholeness to Personality* emphasizes the next steps in focusing on resiliency. This book represents what Marty Seligman in his American Psychological Association presidential speech in 1999 referred to as "positive psychology." He urged his fellow psychologists to look on the other side of the coin of human existence to hope, well-being, strength, and resiliency that seemed to be ignored; recognize that abnormality, problems, pathological illness, and symptoms have been the dominant focus of our field.

In the tradition of John P. Wilson books, including his first book that is part of this series (Wilson, 1989) and his most recent (Wilson & Thomas, 2004), Wilson has assembled an impressive group of scholars-practitioners who help map out this restorative piece for helping the traumatized, focusing on a vast but focused range of questions relevant to this restorative process. In this book Wilson goes back to his roots. Few people realize that before his interest in trauma in the mid-1970s, John's specialty was personality.

Among the goals of the book are to map the multitude of ways those exposed to trauma endure and transform their experience into stepping stones for human growth, rather than settle for mere stumbling blocks. Among the relevant questions are: How is it that human resilience occurs? What are the ways professionals help or hinder this process? How do ordinary people overcome extraordinarily stressful life-events? How does trauma potentially alter personality, the task of creating meaning and non-nihilistic philosophical views of life? How does the traumatized organism heal itself? How does self-transformation and ego-transcendence occur?

Any practitioner knows that change and restoration following exposure to trauma that debilitates requires hard work on the part of the client. This book serves as a road map for practitioners and clients alike in the process of "meaning making" (Neimeyer & Raskin, 2000) that can transform what was initially perceived as horror and evil that were major stumbling blocks in life into stepping stones to resiliency, strength, and wisdom—in other words, to help victims become survivors and survivors become prophets of change.

Therefore, I highly recommend this book. It will help shift the traumatology field toward what Seligman calls positive psychology and to balance our current emphasis on stress, loss, symptoms, and deficits with hope, wholeness, resiliency, and transformation.

Charles R. Figley, Ph.D.
Series Editor

REFERENCES

Figley, C. R. (1978). *Stress disorders among Vietnam veterans: Theory, research and treatment.* New York: Brunner/Mazel.

Neimeyer, R. A. & Raskin, J. D. (Eds.) (2000). *Constructions of disorder: Meaning-making frameworks for psychotherapy.* Washington, DC: American Psychiatric Association.

Raphael, B. & Wilson, J. P. (Eds.) (2000). *Stress debriefings: Theory, research, and applications.* Cambridge: Cambridge University Press.

van der Kolk, B. (2005). Introduction. Presented at the *Home from the War* preconference workshop at the Annual Boston University Medical School Trauma Conference, June 2, 2005.

Wilson, J. P. (1989). *Transformation and healing: An integrated approach to theory, research and posttraumatic therapy.* New York: Brunner/Mazel.

Wilson, J. P. & Thomas, R. B. (2004). *Empathy in the treatment of trauma and PTSD.* New York: Brunner-Routledge.

Preface

The Posttraumatic Self: Restoring Meaning and Wholeness to Personality is a book that is optimistic and positive in its focus. The contributors examine a wide range of questions about the nature of psychological trauma and the ways in which it is transformed into posttraumatic growth, self-integration, and optimal states of functioning or leads to trauma complexes and alterations in the basic structure of personality. Among the goals of the book is to explore the ways by which persons endure and transform extreme stress, psychological trauma, and the Abyss Experience of human suffering. How is it that human resilience occurs? How do ordinary people overcome extraordinarily stressful life-events? How does trauma potentially alter personality, the task of creating meaning and non-nihilistic philosophical views of life? How does the traumatized organism heal itself? How does self-transformation and ego-transcendence occur? Today, such questions are the province of the science of traumatology, which seeks to understand in balanced ways the answer to these questions.

In Chapter 1, an overview of the posttraumatic self is presented from the perspective of a positive psychology of trauma and posttraumatic stress disorder (PTSD). This introductory chapter outlines the critical issues facing the analysis of the posttraumatic self and how the self can be transformed by extreme stress and trauma. It is noted that the posttraumatic self is a complex phenomenon to understand and that the architecture of identity and self-processes can be radically altered by trauma in ways that crush the human spirit or give birth to forms of self-transcendence, posttraumatic resilience, and the transformation of the self.

In Chapter 2, a comprehensive overview of the posttraumatic self is presented. The chapter begins with a model of the posttraumatic self as it is shaped by traumatic impacts on organismic functioning. The model broadly lays out how trauma affects personality factors, the self-structure, identity, ego-processes, and systems of meaning and ideology. In this model, the posttraumatic self develops and evolves over time across 10 major dimensions of personality that are variably impacted by the experience of trauma (e.g., life-span epigenetic development; systems of morality; affect regulation, including states of posttraumatic shame and guilt; and the restructuring of the inner dimensions of the self). The nature of the posttraumatic self determines patterns of posttraumatic adaptation that range along a continuum from severe pathology (e.g., self-deintegration) to optimal health (e.g., self-actualizing capacities). The continuum of posttraumatic adaptations includes 11 distinct typologies of personality configurations and the formation of individually constellated trauma complexes.

In Chapter 3, trauma and the epigenesis of identity is discussed and expands Erik Erikson's theory of life-span development to examine the different ways that trauma affects specific stages of personality development as well as the trajectory of the life cycle itself. Specifically, 12 overarching questions are addressed by the chapter, which include the following:

- How do different types of traumatic events impact the process of the epigenesis of identity across the life cycle?
- How does trauma impact a specific stage of identity formation?
- How are the processes and structures of identity disrupted by trauma?
- How does trauma influence, shape, or alter the trajectory of epigenetic development?
- How does trauma cause regression, arrestation, intensification, or acceleration in the normative stages of psychosocial development?
- How does trauma cause dissociation at different stages of identity development?
- How does trauma cause dissociability in personality?
- How are different types of traumatic events associated with horizontal and vertical dissociative processes?
- How does trauma create links between early childhood alterations in identity functioning with later adult experiences of stress and trauma?
- How do dissociative processes become embedded with identity configuration and influence intrapsychic functioning?
- How are deficits in healing identity restored following traumatic injury to self-capacities?

The chapter includes a discussion of how transformations occur in the posttraumatic self through therapeutic recapitulation of epigenesis and the restoration of a healthy sense of self, and a coherent, integrated sense of ego-identity. Based on Erikson's conceptualization of normative crises of development as critical turning points in personality formation and the emergence of intrapsychic strength, the chapter examines how stage-specific impacts caused by trauma are reconfigured into new identity structures in the posttraumatic self.

In Chapter 4, Kathleen O. Nader presents a comprehensive overview of the effects of childhood trauma on the development of the self. To begin, she notes that there are a wide range of psychological effects produced by childhood trauma which include, but extend beyond, the diagnosis of PTSD. The effects of childhood trauma have differential and cascading effects on specific stages of development and those that follow in epigenetic development. The specific effects of childhood trauma are not only complex and often insidious in nature, they are multidimensional and generate consequences for thinking and cognitive style, affect regulation, and the organization of personality as a whole. In this regard, Nader emphasizes that the deeper wounds created by childhood traumatic experiences are to the self, the trajectory of academic and occupational development, and the person's outlook and views of human nature.

In her chapter, Nader lays out a framework by which to examine each of the central issues concerning childhood trauma and its effects. In a systematic fashion, there are separate sections on such topics as information processing and cognition; trust and attachment patterns; self-perception and locus of control; the sense of self; developmental disruptions and the long-term consequences to identity and the posttraumatic self as a whole. For each of the major sections in her chapter, Nader reviews the relevant literature and presents individual case histories to illustrate the questions under consideration. This chapter dovetails nicely with Chapter 3 to show how traumatic experiences at different points in epigenetic development cause stage-specific posttraumatic consequences and carry-over effects to later stages in adolescent and adult development.

Chapter 5 presents a discussion of Trauma Archetypes and Trauma Complexes. The Trauma Archetype represents universal forms of traumatic experience across time, cultures, and history. The Trauma Complex is the unique, individual constellation of the trauma experience in cognitive-affective structure located in the self. The Trauma Complex develops out of the Abyss, Inversion, and Transcendent Experiences as individual and collective modalities of traumatic encounters. The Trauma Complex has 10 defining characteristics that become constellated into a separate system of personality that contains autonomy, structural coherence, and motivational power. The Trauma Complex "cogwheels" dynamically with other psychic complexes and archetypal forms of experience. The Trauma Complex operates on the principles of living systems theory of Miller (1978) and is a more inclusive construct than PTSD, complex PTSD or PTSD plus Axis I or Axis II psychiatric diagnoses. The Trauma Complex contains parallels with, and comparable features to, dissociative disorders but is neither the same phenomenon nor necessarily pathological in nature. The Trauma Complex also has inherent motivational power which activates the Unity Archetype and the striving towards self-integration. As an organismically based process, the Trauma Complex is functionally related to Transcendent Experiences, precipitated by powerful traumatic episodes that include the following qualities: (1) awareness of higher levels of being, self-consciousness and the potential for unity in the self; (2) rapid transformational changes in value priorities in the meaning of one's existence; (3) awareness of illusions, deception, and other forms of perceptual and cognitive experiences; (4) personal consciousness of the numinous experience; (5) intuitive knowledge of the transformation of conscious at qualitatively higher levels of existence; and (6) an acute sense of death-in-life versus life-in-death paradigm of self existence. The chapter includes a discussion of the inner and outer worlds of traumatic experiences, how they relate to archetypal forms of trauma encounters, and their transformation and integration into personality.

In Chapter 6, the relationship between trauma, optimal experiences, and integrative psychological states is explored. This chapter examines the ways in which traumatic experiences are transformed into optimal states of integrated functioning. Specifically, five types of transformations are presented: (1) acute, epiphanous, conversion-like transformations; (2) epigenetically related transformations evoked by stages of life-course development; (3) transformations of chronic trauma-related pathology through treatment, spiritual experiences, or spontaneous remissions; (4) somatic transformations of traumatic states embedded in brain, body, and affective processes; and (5) combined patterns of the above.

The chapter presents a continuum of altered states of consciousness and integrative experience. At one end of the continuum are pathological self-organizational structures and complex dissociative phenomena. At the other end are optimal states of integration characterized by self-actualizing tendencies, peak experiences, and positive emotional states.

By establishing a continuum of integrative states of experience, it becomes possible to compare optimal versus pathological states in terms of normal and traumatic experiences across eight dimensions: (1) perception; (2) memory; (3) consciousness/awareness; (4) identity; (5) self-capacities; (6) motivation; (7) affect; and (8) somatic/motor behavior. In particular, peak (optimal) and dissociative experiences (deintegrative) can be compared using these eight dimensions to identify areas of convergence and divergence in psychological processes. Thus, a comparative analysis of pathogenic versus salutogenic qualities is possible for peak and dissociative states. This comparative analysis reveals that *optimal states of integrative experiences* enrich in positive ways the functions of consciousness, memory, identity, and perception of the environment. These same functions are diminished in dissociative states. In both peak and dissociative states there are significant alterations in time perception and motor activities. In peak experiences there is a loss of time/space perception but lucid and integratively useful memories of the experience. In dissociative states, the memory of time/space and action is missing, fragmented, or distorted. Through comparative analysis of deintegrated (e.g., dissociative) states and optimal integrative states (e.g., peak experiences), the mechanisms of transformation can be identified and specified in terms of their intrapsychic functions. This raises a critical question: What allows for unifying processes in external experiences and internal schemas of reality? It is suggested that the facilitation of conditions of optimal congruence helps restore balance between the outer and inner worlds of experience. Since traumatic experiences have the power to disrupt the normally integrative processes of adaptation and coping, it becomes possible to identify the mechanisms that restore optimal integrative states.

In Chapter 7, Brian Hall and John P. Wilson examine the question of trauma and alterations in the normal personality. How do different types of traumatic experiences impact the structure of personality as it exists at the time of the event? Do personality traits act as filters of trauma? Is there a direct causal relationship between age, type of trauma, and the proneness to developmental behavioral problems and the disposition to Axis II disorders? Do different types of traumatic experiences generate trauma-specific effects on personality traits and the manifestation of PTSD? These questions were explored in a study of urban university students from the perspective of the Five Factor Model (FFM) of personality.

First, Hall and Wilson used the FFM to develop predictions concerning trauma's impact on personality. Second, they reviewed and summarized the literature on personality characteristics and PTSD. Third, they used the 16 Personality Factors to assess personality traits, using the five second-order factors and the 16 bipolar personality trait measures. Fourth, they screened 326 university students and classified them into probable-PTSD (P-PTSD) and nonprobable PTSD (N-PTSD) groups based on their scores on PTSD screening measures. As predicted, the results showed that there were different patterns of personality traits associated with five different trauma categories used for a comparative analysis (sexual assault, motor vehicle accident, medical emergency, violent assault, September 11, 2001). Finally, it was also possible to differentiate the N-PTSD versus the P-PTSD groups on personality traits. Participants who scored higher on the PTSD measures were less stable and outgoing but evidenced higher levels of anxiety, self-reliance, and apprehension than did those without PTSD.

In Chapter 8, Jacob Lindy presents a richly complex examination of mutative transference and the restoration of the posttraumatic self. Using a modified psychoanalytic framework, Lindy reviews the history of mutative or "curing" transference reactions of patients with their therapist and then draws a distinction between them in terms of the classical neuroses and posttraumatic injuries to the self. Lindy correctly notes that trauma strikes psychic structure and produces alterations in intrapsychic processes which include rupture to ego-functions, perceptual processes, capacities for affect regulation, positive narcissistic balance, and the coherency of ego-identity. From a dynamic point of view, unconscious mechanisms seek to compensate for traumatically induced injuries to the inner functions of the self which form the nidus of PTSD and self-disorders. Especially in mutative transferences that occur in the spontaneous recovery from psychic trauma, or with the skilled assistance of a therapist, the nature of the mutative transference processes can be discerned in several ways. First, these are clearly discernible trauma-specific transference reactions (TST; Wilson & Lindy, 1994) in which the patient transfers and projects unconscious and unmetabolized information about their trauma experiences onto the person of the therapist and the context of treatment. Second, Lindy identifies three pathways or forms of mutative transference that occur during the course of treatment: (1) sequestering; (2) metabolizing; and (3) redefinition of the trauma experience. These three forms of transference expressions have their own unique character and structural properties. To organize and simplify these extraordinarily interesting and demonstrable processes, Lindy further classifies them as: (a) Lens Transference: Restoring Perception; (b) Prism Transference: Restoring Order; and (c) Existential or Mythic Transference: Restoring Meaning. These three forms of mutative transference are then analyzed and compared across 11 structural dimensions: (1) symptom picture; (2) damaged structure; (3) primary task; (4) ego-defense operations; (5) organizing metaphors; (6) modes of transference engagement; (7) primary curative activities; (8) specific therapeutic activities; (9) pro-plan interventions; (10) stabilizing factors; and (11) destabilizing factors. Thus, by creating a matrix of patient–therapist interaction during the course of treatment, it becomes possible to see how the mutative transference occurs and, by sufficient therapeutic response, restores the injured parts of the posttraumatic self.

There are many practical, theoretical, and clinical advantages to the analysis and understanding of mutative transferences in the context of posttraumatic treatment approaches. What Lindy has provided is a clinical lens of unusual clarity for examining what is unique and intrinsic to trauma-induced damages to the inner world of experience. As such, it is a clinical tool of high empathic potential (Wilson & Thomas, 2004) and an organizing conceptual framework of exceptional parsimony by which to understand the depth of the posttraumatic self in its many vicissitudes and protean manifestations.

In Chapter 9, Boris Droždek, Silvana Turkovic, and John P. Wilson present an elaborate discussion of posttraumatic shame and guilt as central elements in the posttraumatic self. The authors suggest that shame and guilt are Janus-faced companions following trauma that have different orientations. Posttraumatic shame concerns self-appraisals as to one's worth and moral virtue in relation to actions. Guilt, on the other hand, is more highly focused on self-recrimination for failed enactments and actions that were selfish, insufficient, or negative in their consequences for others. Moreover, posttraumatic shame and guilt are rooted in the nature of traumatic experiences and develop whether or not there are degrees of ego vulnerability, pre-existing personality problems or self-pathologies.

The authors propose that there are eight types of posttraumatic shame and seven forms of posttraumatic guilt. These different forms of shame and guilt are dynamically associated with dysregulated affects which include: (1) anger → rage; (2) anxiety → fear; (3) sadness → sorrow; (4) terror → horror; (5) loss → depression; (6) bereavement → grief; (7) humiliation → helplessness. Thus, by identifying the intrapsychic mechanisms of posttraumatic shame and guilt, it becomes possible to compare them across different psychological dimensions such as suicidality, defensiveness, PTSD-proneness, impact on personal identity, action appraisal, self-attribution processes, and emotional states. This comparative analysis is particularly valuable for purposes of assessment and clinical treatment. For example, in posttraumatic shame there is a high potential for suicide, a loss of self-worth and moral virtue, feelings of humiliation, rage and helplessness, a loss of face and inner identity, and tendencies for self-deintegration. In posttraumatic guilt, there is self-recrimination over one's behavior rather than negative self-attributions. There is relatively little loss of identity or self-dissolution but clear appraisals of failed actions or responsibilities. There is low suicidality and state-dependent emotions of guilt, remorse, and embarrassment. The comparative analysis of shame and guilt reveals that in posttraumatic shame the self-focus is inward to an evaluation of the goodness or badness of the self as an object of assessment. In posttraumatic guilt the self-focus and attributional processes are external to an evaluation of one's acting in the context of a traumatic experience.

These differences in intrapsychic and motivational dynamics are also evident in lexical analysis, which reflects differences for the two sets of affective states (i.e., shame vs. guilt). In posttraumatic shame, words of self-focus concern disgrace, dishonor, humiliation, hubris, and loss of self-respect. The corresponding emotional and verbal actions are reflected lexically in words such as: losing face, hiding face, poker face, red face, diminished posture, lowered head and eyes and withdrawal, isolation, avoidance, and secretiveness. In posttraumatic guilt, words of self-focus concern personal responsibility for actions: culpable, blamable, reproachable, censurable, impeachable, indicative, reprehensible, etc. Similarly, words of emotion and verbal action reference being exposed or held accountable for one's actions or inactions: caught-in-the-act, caught red-handed, being back-handed, hiding one's hands, looking or acting sheepish, or covering up deeds, evidence or clues to one's actions. In posttraumatic guilt, these lexical connotations reflect the seven types of guilt such as survivor guilt, bystander guilt, death guilt, moral guilt, situational guilt, and failed enactments.

The understanding of states of posttraumatic shame and guilt is most usefully analyzed in the context of cultural values, mores, and normative patterns of behavior. The authors note that there are both shame-based and guilt-based cultures that prescribe expected actions in terms of social behaviors. The chapter contains case histories to illustrate how cultural factors influence posttraumatic shame and guilt in traumatic situations that include torture, rape, ethnic cleansing, and warfare.

In Chapter 10, John P. Wilson and Christine E. Agaibi discuss the resilient trauma survivor. The question of how some survivors spring back following severe psychic trauma is integral to the full understanding of the posttraumatic self. What are the characteristics of resilient persons? What constitutes resilient behavior in different types of traumatic situations? Are there personality attributes that differentiate highly resilient trauma survivors from others?

Based on a comprehensive review of the literature on resilience, Wilson and Agaibi identify 20 specific attributes that characterize resilient trauma survivors. They note that these characteristics comprise a composite profile of highly resilient trauma survivors in terms of five dimensions: (1) personality characteristics and traits; (2) ego-defenses; (3) capacity for affect modulation; (4) the capacity for proactive, instrumental coping which includes the ability to mobilize social support mechanisms; and (5) trans-situational mastery of stress appraised processes which include the capacity to maintain a positive outlook on life and to find meaning in personal actions. Wilson and Agaibi suggest that resilience, including posttraumatic resilience, is best viewed as a complex behavioral repertoire that identifies patterns of perceiving, thinking, reasoning, and initiating actions that are manifest over time and across situations. Accurate portrayals of resilient trauma survivors specify "how they do what they do" at different points in time (e.g., peritraumatically and posttraumatically). The review of the literature, especially on PTSD and resilience, suggests that resilient survivors have very accurate stress appraisal processes; mature ego-defenses; a capacity to modulate fear responses; and the cognitive ability to formulate problem-solving actions across a wide range of situations (i.e., flexibility in coping). Resilient trauma survivors appear to manifest transitional consistency and flexibility in coping behaviors. These qualities of resilient coping can be learned through educational and training programs. Wilson and Agaibi discussed the fundamental objectives to facilitate posttraumatic resilience which include, among other things, the development of cognitive reframing techniques of stressor appraisal; strategies of affect regulation in the face of threat; education and interaction with highly resilient survivors; education about the nature and dynamics of the human stress response syndrome and the development of specific skills and competencies to deal with different types of traumatic stressors (e.g., physical assault, war-related trauma, political internment).

Chapter 11 discusses 12 principles that comprise the posttraumatic transformations in character and personality for trauma survivors. These 12 principles were derived from various sources which includes clinical and forensic work with trauma survivors, international humanitarian work under conditions of war and political strife, the accumulated research on PTSD with special emphasis on war veterans, torture victims, Holocaust and Hiroshima survivors, the mythological literature in anthropology on spiritual journeys, and the recent research on optimal states of human functioning. Based on this information, a composite personality profile is constructed that describes the psychodynamic functioning and philosophical views of transcendent survivors. In brief, the 12 principles of self-transformation that characterize the posttraumatic self are as follows:

- vulnerability and illusions,
- pain, suffering and transformation,
- acceptance: life's unequal playing field,
- limits to ego and humility,
- continuity versus discontinuity in life,
- connection to sources of meaning,
- balance and groundedness,
- empathy, compassion, and freshness of appreciation,
- honesty and gratitude,
- love and generosity,
- self-transformation and reinvention, and
- spiritual consciousness and altruism.

The chapter discusses each of these 12 principles of self-transformation and how they work together as a syndrome of personality functioning in transcendent trauma survivors.

In Chapter 12, transformational principles for healing and recovery are presented. Using a living systems approach to the analysis of how trauma impacts psychological functioning, 10 principles are discussed as transformative mechanisms of PTSD, Trauma Complexes, and states of traumatization: (1) restore optimal organismic integration; (2) attenuate maladaptive stress responses; (3) identify traumatic "mile markers" in life-span development; (4) unify Trauma Complexes in the self and personality; (5) restore optimal intrapsychic congruence; (6) transform and integrate dissociative states; (7) restore a sense of continuity and connection to meaningful sources of attachment; (8) facilitate the development of resilience; (9) facilitate peak experiences of optimal need gratification in the hierarchy of needs; and (10) facilitate optimal coping behavior and personality integration. Each of the 10 transformative principles corresponds to a dysregulated dimension of organismic functioning. Thus, the goal of recovery from the prolonged stress effects generated by psychological trauma targets a specific function that has been degraded, altered, or dysregulated. The chapter continues with a discussion of self-transcendent trauma survivors who exhibit high levels of autonomy, cultural transcendence, and healthy psychosocial development. Transcendent trauma survivors can be considered from a behavioral standpoint as "gold standards" of healthy adaptation since they have demonstrated by their history to have the capacity to overcome the hurdles and obstacles placed in their way by severe trauma and succeeded in living life fully with integrity. The chapter concludes with a comparative analysis of resilient and transcendent survivors by crossing the 20 dimensions of resilient trauma survivors with the 12 principles of posttraumatic self-transformation.

This final chapter echoes the overarching goal of the book, which is to explore the ways the posttraumatic self is shaped by the experience of trauma. Understanding how trauma leads to growth and transcendence represents a counterbalance to previous theories and research that focus narrowly on pathological outcomes. Trauma survivors strive for health not illness; they seek the restoration of meaning and wholeness to personality and the process of living.

REFERENCES

Miller, J. G. (1978). *Living systems.* New York: McGraw-Hill Publications.
Wilson, J. P. & Lindy, J. (1994). *Counter-transference in the treatment of PTSD.* New York: Guilford Publications.
Wilson, J. P. & Thomas, R. (2004). *Empathy in the treatment of trauma and PTSD.* New York: Brunner-Routledge.

Acknowledgments

There are many people I wish to acknowledge who helped shape this book and make it a reality. First, I thank the J. William Fulbright Foundation for the opportunity to serve as a Fulbright Scholar at the University of Zagreb Medical School where the idea for this book took root in its earliest form. Dr. Rudolf Gregurek of the medical school faculty and the clinic for psychological medicine was a wonderful Fulbright Sponsor and host while I was living in Zagreb, Croatia.

Professor Joel Aronoff of Michigan State University has provided many hours of useful conversation and eagle-eyed critiques of some of the early drafts of the book. Special thanks go to Joel and to Abraham H. Maslow, whose ideas and writings helped shape the ideas for the chapter on the relationship of trauma to optimal levels of personality functioning. Charles Figley, of Florida State University and editor of the Routledge Psychosocial Stress Series, has been most supportive of the idea for this book and has offered helpful editorial feedback. Special thanks are due also to Dana Bliss, associate editor at Routledge in New York, who has been most encouraging and enthusiastic about this project. His insightful comments and vision helped to shape the final direction and structure of the book.

Throughout the writing of the book, and in collaboration with the contributors, there have been many opportunities to share ideas with colleagues in the field of traumatology. I extend very special thanks to the following people: Mardi J. Horowitz, Mark Miller, Jon Conte, Yael Danieli, Robert Lifton, Allan Schore, Ray Scurfield, Jack Lindy, Mary Beth Williams, Erwin Parsons, Jim Chu, Donald Kalsched, Vamik Volkan, Matthew J. Friedman, Elliot Benay, Terry Keane, Steve Southwick, Andy Morgan, Bob Sollod, and Mark Ashcraft.

Finally, my personal assistant, Kathy Letizio, always makes sure that the writing process is smooth, orderly, and in the right direction. Her steadfast and tireless dedication to the ideas presented in this book, and to a deeper understanding of the importance of trauma in the lives of ordinary people, are Olympian in nature. Without her daily dedication, this book would not be a reality.

1

Introduction and Overview: A Positive Psychology of Trauma and PTSD

JOHN P. WILSON

The Posttraumatic Self: Restoring Meaning and Wholeness to Personality is a book that represents an attempt to provide a framework of a positive psychology of trauma and posttraumatic stress disorder (PTSD). At first glance the idea of a positive psychology of trauma and PTSD seems like a contradiction in terms and the opposite of the emotional reality for those who suffer. How can there be a positive psychology of horrific consequences of psychic trauma? After all, the word trauma originates from the ancient Greek word for "injury." Trauma, usually inflicted from an external source, causes damage, a loss of well-being, and a change in physical or mental status that is painful, aversive, and may result in a condition of prolonged traumatization. In this same mind set, we have traditionally spoken about the process of healing wounds, recovery, and the resumption of normal functioning. In medicine and psychology, the processes of healing and recovery meant that the victim of trauma overcame their illness and got better, assuming more control and autonomy in life, and experiencing fewer residual symptoms of their illness. In terms of PTSD, a recently codified stress disorder related to trauma (*DSM-III*, 1980), recovery from the illness usually implied that the symptoms dissipated, resolved, or no longer had the power to disrupt daily living (Wilson, Friedman, & Lindy, 2001). In fact, the official criterion for defining PTSD as a *disorder* is that: "the disturbance causes clinically significant distress or impairment in social, occupational or other important areas of functioning" (p. 468). By this logic, PTSD as a disorder can cause impairment in functioning which may be hidden, subtle, overt, covert or floridly dramatic, and evident for all to see in its maladaptive or unusual deviance from everyday behavior. When a PTSD illness gets "cured" or is no longer actively causing impairments in daily life, does that suggest that the person is healthy, fully-functioning and working at an optimal level of their human potential? Is the absence of psychopathology the same thing as optimal fitness and capacity for self-actualization? Is the reduction or amelioration of trauma-related symptoms of PTSD, anxiety, depression, phobias, substance dependence, etc., the same thing as positive, fully functioning behavior? When the symptoms of PTSD, such as nightmares, flashbacks, traumatic memories, hypervigilance, sleep disturbance, and social avoidance of others, dissipate in their power to cause painful emotional distress, has the person restored wholeness and become psychically integrated? When psychic trauma attacks the inner fabric of the self-structure, shredding it into pieces like a tattered and battle-torn uniform of an infantry soldier, how does it get put back together? How does the individual engage in a process of change, creating a new posttraumatic self, a reinvented architecture of oneself with a capacity to grow from the horrors and perils of trauma? How do resilient survivors find the pathways to meaning and wholeness in their lives? What does the inner world of a healthy and transcendent survivor look like in its rich tapestry of self-reinvention? What are the secrets to the success of such a survivor in living an authentic life, "in the moment," with humanity, courage, wisdom, knowledge, humility, forgiveness, a sense of justice, and the capacity for humanness that is awe-inspiring to others?

These and related questions form the nucleus of a positive psychology of trauma and PTSD. It is my belief, born from nearly four decades of experience in working with traumatized persons suffering from PTSD, that it is more important to study the healthy, self-transcendent survivors of trauma than those most dehumanized by it. By understanding the strong, resilient, self-transcendent survivor of extreme life-adversity, we can learn how it is that they found the pathway to healing, recovery, resilience, and the actualization of their innate human potentials. In this regard, Peterson and Seligman (2004), in their research on character strength and virtue, state that the strengths of transcendence,

> seem mixed, but the central theme running through these strengths of transcendence is that each allows individuals to forge connections to the larger universe and thereby provide meaning to their lives. Almost all of the positive traits in our classification reach outside the individual— character, after all, is social in nature but in the case of the transcendence

strengths, the reaching goes beyond other people per se to embrace part or all of the larger universe. The prototype of this strength is spirituality, variously defined but always referring to a belief in and commitment to the transcendent (nonmaterial) aspects of life whether they be called universal, ideal, sacred or divine. (p. 519)

Transcendence of self, I suggest, is among the cardinal characteristics of the posttraumatic self in which states of traumatization, including PTSD, have been overcome and integrated within a new identity structure as part of the architecture of the self and its six core components (i.e., continuity, coherence, connection, autonomy, vitality, energy). Indeed, understanding the posttraumatic self requires analysis and study of how personality processes and the self-structure is impacted by different types of traumatic experience. In the simplest formulation, we can ask: How is it that powerful traumatic experiences produces changes to inner self-processes and identity? How do overwhelming and adverse life-events affect the architectural integrity of the self? When trauma damages the tapestry of the self, identity, and basic psychological processes associated with them (i.e., perception, memory, consciousness, etc.), how do persons transform and rebuild themselves? Beyond a doubt, anecdotal accounts from those who have endured the Abyss Experience (Wilson, 2004a) of trauma and confronted the specter of their own death, the possibility of self-disintegration and loss of soul, report that afterwards their views of life and themselves change, often in profound ways. I have learned from war veterans, Holocaust survivors, torture victims, and those experiencing death encounters that they step back, sometimes way back, and reexamine their priorities in life, rearranging values and shedding nonessential things and patterns of living. They uniformly report being less materialistic and more concerned with authentic existence and the quality of life from a position that values life, kindness, justice, gratitude, hope, integrity, and simple pleasures.

A personal friend and Holocaust survivor of several Nazi death camps always remarked that his best "life insurance" policies were his few, close friends with whom he could enjoy life simply, honestly, and with the joy of their presence. My friend understood the gratitude of daily living and used to tell me to look in the mirror each morning upon awakening and meditate on life's goodness and what was going to be "good" about "today" without worrying about tomorrow or what would happen the rest of the week. After surviving the Holocaust as a young man who suffered from the devastating effects of typhus, he came to understand what Buddhists refer to as consciousness of living-in-the-moment. My friend taught me that so much of what we worry about is illusory and the product of a materialistic culture and has no ultimate meaning. After the Holocaust he had to reinvent himself, having lost family and friends to the death camps, and create a new sense of personal identity and a positive life-trajectory. He understood the fundamental existential choice—grow, change, and transcend the legacy of the death camps or remain frozen in time, bitter, and possessed by demonic memories. He found the pathways of self-reinvention and a new, positive posttraumatic self. It was a long and difficult journey but he manifest resilience and moral character, one battle at a time.

Since the beginning of the 21st century there has been a resurgence of interest in positive psychology which was referred to in the 1960s and 1970s as The Third Force after behaviorism and psychoanalysis as schools of thought (Maslow, 1968). Today, the study of positive psychology embraces in a more generic way what was previously classified as humanistic and transpersonal psychology. Martin E. P. Seligman (2002), one of the principal organizers of a new positive psychology, has stated that

> the aim of positive psychology is to catalog a change in psychology from a preoccupation only with repairing the worst things in life to also building the best qualities in life. To redress this imbalance, we must bring the building of strength to the forefront in the treatment of mental illness. (p.3)

Clearly, it is an important task for the field of traumatology to achieve balance in understanding the worst (i.e., lowest, pathological, destructive) and best (i.e., highest, growth-promoting, self-actualizing) consequences of psychic traumatization. Traumatic stressors and the phenomenon of PTSD are multidimensional in nature (Wilson, 2004b). Moreover, there is a continuum of posttraumatic impacts to human growth and development which range from severe states of psychic brutalization and the loss of humanness to transcendent self-actualizing modes of existence that represent the essence of all that is good in human character and virtue, irrespective of time, space, and culture.

In Chapters 11 and 12 I discuss the transformation of psychic trauma and that PTSD may result in different forms of self-transcendence and the farther reaches of human nature in terms of optimal states of functioning, consciousness, and enlightenment. Transcendent trauma survivors, who have reinvented the inner dimension of the self, exemplify and embody the deepest levels of compassion for others—an ultimate generative concern for the well-being of loved ones and the species as a whole. Their individual character structure contains most, if not all, the traits listed as strengths in Peterson's and Seligman's (2004) description of transcendent, high-order personality functioning: (1) wisdom and knowledge; (2) courage; (3) humanity; (4) sense of justice; (5) temperance; and (6) transcendence. Interestingly, the strength of transcendence as a trait includes the subdimensions of appreciation for beauty, awe, wonder, elation, gratitude, hope, humor, faith, and spirituality, all of which are positive aspects of resilient trauma survivors (see Chapter 10 for a discussion). Further, in terms of the transformed, posttraumatic self with a highly integrated cohesive identity structure, there are qualities of a grounded sense of self which has moved beyond the constraints imposed by PTSD and degraded organismic functioning to new and higher levels of human strength. A similar position has been expressed by Seligman (2002), who has discussed the positive preventive aspects of good mental health

> We have discovered that there are human strengths that act as buffers against mental illness: courage, future-mindedness, optimism, interpersonal skills, faith, hope, work ethic, honesty, perseverance, the capacity for flow and insight, to name several. Much of the task of prevention in this new century will be to create a science of human strength whose mission will be to understand and learn how to foster these virtues in young people. (p. 5)

I believe that knowledge of how individuals transform trauma, PTSD and comorbid states (e.g., depression, anxiety, substance abuse) is a critical task for a complete psychology of trauma. It is a fact that most people bounce back from trauma and resume the trajectories of their lives. And yet, many spend years and decades with the long-lasting effects of trauma. Recently, for example, an undergraduate student spoke to me of his concern for his aging grandfather, a survivor of World War II now in his eighties. The insightful 20-year-old said

> My grandpa is still bothered by what happened during WWII when he was a U.S. Marine who fought in the South Pacific against the Japanese. He still won't talk about what happened and my aunt said that he started drinking heavily right after the war [1945], had nightmares, sleep problems, and was real jumpy. He still is jumpy and gets upset when he watches war movies. I don't think the war ever ended for him.

Some trauma survivors remain frozen in time and unable to move beyond powerful experiences that seem to stop the natural progression of healthy development in life. When we encounter individuals whose lives are haunted by traumatic residues which continue to exude unresolved emotional pain after many years, we have to ask why healing, integration, and transformation did not occur. What is it that prevents or blocks persons from finding pathways to healing and the achievement of optimal states of functioning, affect balance, higher levels of self-awareness, and self-actualization? Clearly, these are central questions of a positive psychology of trauma.

This book has its goals and limitations in regard to furthering the understanding of the posttraumatic self and the restoration of meaning and wholeness to personality. There are many key points that will be addressed by the chapters in this book concerning a positive psychology of trauma and PTSD. These central focal points include:

- What is the nature of the posttraumatic self and its potential alteration by trauma and the existence of PTSD and self-pathologies?
- What are the impacts of trauma on the epigenesis of identity in the life-cycle?
- What are the stage-specific consequences of trauma in terms of growth, development, and defensive operations to guard against injury?
- How are optimal states of psychological functioning achieved following traumatization?
- How does the continuum of dissociation to integration function in the wake of trauma?
- What is the archetype of trauma across cultures throughout history?
- How does trauma impact normal personality states and traits?
- How are states of posttraumatic shame and guilt embedded in the self?
- What set of traits, personality processes, and behavioral tendencies characterize the resilient trauma survivor?
- What are the mutative transference processes in dynamic psychotherapy that lead to growth and mental health?
- What are the 12 sets of factors that characterize persons who have transformed extremely stressful life-events?
- How is posttraumatic resilience related to self-transcendence?
- What are the core principles for healing and recovery from psychic trauma?

A positive psychology of trauma and PTSD is one that contains a theoretical framework which provides insight into the polarities of illness and growth, traumatization and transformation, despair and transcendence. A positive psychology of trauma includes an understanding of the archetypes of trauma, trauma complexes and how they are shaped by individual experience, cultural embeddedness, and their place in history. A positive psychology of PTSD seeks to understand how persons create meaning and spring back from losses and the most horrible evils that humankind can inflict on the spirit, the striving towards unity integration and the will to thrive with dignity.

In undertaking an initial foray into analysis of the posttraumatic self, there are necessary limitations and constraints that need to be acknowledged. At present, we have a dearth of empirically based studies on the issues of posttraumatic resilience, growth, and what factors scientifically predict healthy mental health outcomes following a broad range of traumatic experiences. Second, many of the research studies that have examined the effects of trauma to personality processes were correlational and embedded in other studies of PTSD, rather than a direct examination of how trauma impacts personality traits or processes. Third, there are no longitudinal studies of a well-defined population of trauma survivors in order to carefully evaluate developmental, pathogenic and salutogenic pathways over time. Finally, there are no studies that have developed a set of criteria of the transcendent, optimally functional and resilient trauma survivor. As I argue in Chapter 12 on the principles of transformation, the study of the optimally functional, resilient trauma survivor is a "gold standard" approach to a positive psychology of trauma and PTSD. The study of the healthiest, strongest, most resilient and psychologically integrated survivor holds the key to understanding self-actualizing, transcendent persons as well as those who develop chronic PTSD self-pathologies and other psychological disorders. The "gold standard" survivor has jumped the toughest hurdles of life's adversity time and again with the best performance and outcome, much like the best Olympic athletes challenged by world-class records of performance.

In summary, the posttraumatic self contains many identities and architectural forms. A positive psychology of trauma and PTSD seeks to understand them, their structural variations and the dynamic processes of the psyche. Ultimately, a positive psychology of trauma and PTSD is the study of the highest virtues of human nature, as knowledge of that which can destroy spiritual essence becomes knowledge of that which permits self-transcendence and the evolution of consciousness.

REFERENCES

Maslow, A. H. (1968). *Towards a psychology of being.* New York: D. Van Nostrand.

Peterson, C. & Seligman, M. E. P. (2004). *Character strengths and virtues: A handbook and classification.* New York: Oxford University Press.

Seligman, M. E. P. (2002). Positive psychology, positive prevention and positive therapy. In C. R. Snyder & S. J. Lopez (Eds.), *Handbook of positive psychology* (pp. 3–13). New York: Oxford University Press.

Wilson, J. P. (2004a). Empathic strain, compassion fatigue and countertransference in the treatment of trauma and PTSD. In D. Knafo (Ed.), *Living with terror, working with trauma: A clinician's handbook* (pp. 121–143). Northvale: Jason Aaronson.

Wilson, J. P. (2004b). PTSD and complex PTSD: Symptoms, syndromes and diagnoses. In J. P. Wilson & T. M. Keane (Eds.), *Assessing psychological trauma and PTSD* (2nd ed.) (pp. 7–44). New York: Guilford Publications.

Wilson, J. P., Friedman, M., & Lindy, J. (2001). *Treating psychological trauma and PTSD.* New York: Guilford Publications.

2

The Posttraumatic Self

JOHN P. WILSON

1 INTRODUCTION

Taking care of the soul in its identities

(L. Wurmser, 1987, p. 96)

The posttraumatic self has many identities. The posttraumatic self is a profoundly challenging and multifaceted phenomenon that defines changes in the inner world of experience following trauma. The identity of the posttraumatic self reflects alterations and reconfigurations of its inner structural dimensions and the psychological processes they govern. The architecture of the self is altered by trauma and, in extreme cases, the entire infrastructure has to be rearranged, reconstructed, or reinvented with a new design. The survivor faces the reality of how emotionally infused traumatic exposure has altered their sense of well-being, values, and views of life. The nature of the posttraumatic self extends beyond knowledge of posttraumatic stress disorder (PTSD) to the entire human psyche as an integrated whole. It includes understanding transcendence and self-transformation, reaching the highest levels of human nature. The complexity of psychic traumatization is vast in scope and dimensionality, extending from neuropeptides in the brain (e.g., NPY) to complex behavioral forms of coping and adaptation (Friedman, 2001). In dynamic complexity, PTSD is to the posttraumatic self as the Earth is to the Solar System.

Understanding the nature and personality dynamics of the post-traumatic self is a critical task for the field of traumatology, knowledge of the vicissitudes of life-span personality development, PTSD, post-traumatic self-disorders (Parsons, 1988a), self-pathologies (Wolfe, 1990), and for the effective use of treatment approaches (Foa, Keane, & Friedman, 2001; Wilson, Friedman, & Lindy, 2001). The task of analyzing the architectural structure of the posttraumatic self is a daunting one because of the complex magnitude of integrated human behavior. Analyzing the structure of the posttraumatic self requires examination of its dimensions and how they work together in mastering experience and adaptive functioning. To undertake an analysis of the various ways that psychological trauma impacts the totality of organismic functioning requires a holistic perspective of behavior and raises important questions for future research and treatment innovations.

How does trauma affect personality, self-structure, identity, ego-processes, memory, perception, cognition, and integrative processes? How does trauma alter the architecture of the self? How does trauma disrupt systems of emotional regulation? How does trauma alter the balance between the inner and outer worlds of experience? How is trauma a catalyst for posttraumatic growth, emotional maturity and wisdom?

2 ORGANIZATION OF THE CHAPTER

This chapter is organized into nine sections that discuss different aspects of the posttraumatic self and personality processes. The purpose is to provide an overview of the key issues that will be presented throughout the book. The sections include: (1) a theoretical model of the posttraumatic self; (2) psycho formative paradigms; (3) the core dimensions of the self affected by trauma; (4) the effects of traumatic stress on the normal personality; (5) trauma and transformations of personality structures; (6) trauma and self-dissolution; (7) posttraumatic alterations in the self and the loss of structural integration; (8) identity coherence and self-continuity versus identity deintegration and discontinuity following trauma; and (9) trauma and the process of self-transfiguration and change.

3 A MODEL OF THE POSTTRAUMATIC SELF

The psyche, as a reflection of the world and men, is a thing of such infinite complexity that it can be observed and studied from a great many sides. Advp 1854.

(Jung, 1971, p. 23)

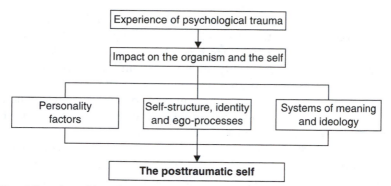

- Altered dimensions of the self (e.g., coherence, continuity, connection, autonomy, vitality, energy)
- Altered factors of personality (e.g., Five Factor Model, intrapsychic dynamics)
- Altered systems of affect regulation (e.g., anger, shame, anxiety, depression, rage)
- Altered ego-processes (e.g., constriction, flexibility, resilience, defense processes)
- Altered identity processes (e.g., sense of sameness and continuity, identity typologies)
- Altered trajectories of life-span development (e.g., patterns of epigenetic development)
- Altered systems of meaning and ideology (e.g., values, beliefs, attributional processes)
- Altered system of morality (e.g., moral reasoning and moral development)
- Formation of trauma complexes and PTSD (e.g., specific constellations of complexes)
- Posttraumatic resilience (e.g., rigidity vs. flexibility in coping)

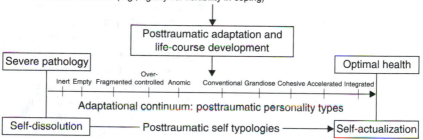

FIGURE 2.1. A model of the posttraumatic self. *Source:* ©2004 John P. Wilson.

To set the stage for analyzing the complexity and dimensions of the posttraumatic self, it is useful to have a conceptual overview of the phenomenon, much like a topographical map which highlights the key features and characteristics of the terrain. A model of the posttraumatic self is presented in Figure 2.1. The model is a general schema of how the experience of psychological trauma impacts on the organism. In varying degrees, psychological trauma "rattles" the organism and disturbs the equilibrium of the self. The effects of trauma have a psychobiological progression that occurs simultaneously at all levels of integrated organismic functioning (Schore, 2003b; Wilson, 2004a; Wilson, Friedman, & Lindy, 2001). *The impact of trauma on the organism is holistic in nature and produces allostasis, a disturbance in the homeostatic processes to integrated levels of psychic functioning* (McEwen, 2002; Wilson & Thomas, 2004). Allostasis refers to stress-response patterns that seek stability in functioning at a new baseline level after trauma (McEwen, 1998, 2002). Allostatic load refers to the residual stress effects produced by traumatic stressors to psychobiological systems and includes dysregulated affects, hyperarousal states, personality alterations, and adaptive failures of stress-response systems located in the sensory nervous system, and the "wear and tear" of coping generated by prolonged stress reactions (McEwen, 2002). Allostatic dysregulations caused by trauma effect all levels of integrated organismic functioning.

For purposes of clarity in presentation, Figure 2.1 shows that the various effects of trauma include: (1) impacts on personality processes and their psychological structure (e.g., Five Factor Model of personality characteristics); (2) ego-processes and identity configurations (e.g., sense of sameness and continuity); and (3) systems of meaning and ideology (e.g., beliefs, values). These superordinate domains of functioning each subsume basic processes of perception, learning, memory, emotion, cognition and development across the life-span (epigenetic processes, moral development, aging, etc.).

As a stress-related phenomenon, it is useful to consider posttraumatic impacts to the self as a complex set of factors that alter the integrated structural and functional components of personality processes as a whole. Trauma strikes at the structure of personality as it exists at the time of the event. Trauma strikes with varying degrees of force, directionally and precision. Trauma disrupts the functional quality of ego-processes, producing fluctuating ego-states, identity and self-configurations (Putnam, 1997; Wilson, 2004a; Lindy & Wilson, 2001). Trauma generates change to a person's schemas and alters adaptive patterns of inter-personal behavior (Horowitz, 1991). The effects of trauma are dynamic and reciprocal in nature, operating on the principles of living systems theory (Miller, 1978). For example, posttraumatic physiological pertur-bations disturb emotional balance and states of consciousness, often simultaneously. Trauma's impact on ego-processes and defensive sys-tems has, in turn, effects on perception, stress-appraisal processes, attributions of meaning and causality that influence systems of meaning and ideology (Lindy, 2001). Trauma's impact on system functioning can reprogram the command and control functions of the autonomic nervous system (LeDoux, 1996; Wilson, 2004a), generating a new disposition to response tendencies and interactions with the environment.

3.1 Posttraumatic Alterations in Personality Processes

As a part of personality, the posttraumatic self includes core dimen-sions of functioning that are altered by the experience of trauma: (1) altered dimensions of the self; (2) altered factors and trait characteristics of personality; (3) altered systems of emotional regulation; (4) altered ego-processes; (5) altered identity processes; (6) altered systems of meaning and ideology; (7) the formation of trauma complexes and PTSD; (8) altered patterns of posttraumatic resilience and coping; (9) altered trajectories of life-course development; and (10) altered systems of moral development and morality. *These 10 dimensions comprise areas of the posttraumatic self that manifest varying degrees of change from their pretraumatic baseline level.* Psychological assessment procedures can be utilized to examine the specific nature of change evident in these 10 domains of behavioral functioning (Wilson & Keane, 2004). Clearly, some areas of psychological and psychosocial functioning can be more severely affected than others, depending on the nature of trauma, age, constitutional, and characterological qualities of the person (Friedman, 2000a). Nevertheless, the residual "spill out" effects of extreme stress can be construed along a continuum of posttraumatic adaptation and life-course development. This conceptual continuum ranges from no significant changes in the pretraumatic baseline of organismic functioning to severe fragmentation of physical and psychological integrity. As Figure 2.1 illustrates, this continuum ranges from optimal health and self-actualization to severe pathology and self-dissolution. Throughout this book, each component of the model shown in Figure 2.1 will be discussed in detail.

4 DIMENSIONS OF PERSONALITY IMPACTED BY TRAUMA

What constitutes the nature of the posttraumatic self? The core questions concerning the dynamics of the posttraumatic self cannot be answered without first specifying the dimensions of personality and self capacities that are impacted by trauma. Trauma produces differentiated effects on each of these dimensions which are synergistically connected with trauma complexes, unconscious processes, and motivational dispositions (see Chapters 4 and 5). Table 2.1 lists 15 separate dimensions of personality that are potentially affected by extreme stress. Understanding the vicissitudes in the posttraumatic self requires an overview of how each of these 15 dimensions of personality can be adversely impacted by severe trauma. In Chapter 6 I will discuss how each of these dimensions can be transformed into optimal psychological states, higher levels of consciousness, and transcendent functioning.

4.1 Self-Structure

The self is an integrated system of structural dimensions that comprise reflective processes of personal awareness and contain motivational

TABLE 2.1
Dimensions of Personality and Self Processes Affected by Trauma

1. **Self-Structure** (dimensions: coherence, continuity, connection, autonomy, vitality, energy)
2. **Ego-Processes** (strength, weakness, resilience, defense)
3. **Identity** (sameness, continuity, typologies)
4. **Unconscious Processes** (dynamic repressed, collective unconscious, positive, regenerative unconscious)
5. **Trauma Complexes** (individually constellated complexes of trauma containing autonomy, motivational power that articulate with other complexes)
6. **Trauma Archetypes** (cross-cultural, universal forms of trauma experience)
7. **Moral Development** (impact of trauma on moral reasoning or moral development in the life-span)
8. **Systems of Meaning and Ideology** (values, beliefs, and ideological systems of meaning)
9. **Dissociative Processes** (states, traits, defenses, trauma complexes, identity related)
10. **Cognition and Information Processing** (memory, information processing, executive functioning, etc.)
11. **Memory** (encoding, processing, functioning, declarative vs. nondeclarative)
12. **Personality Development and Self-Transformation** (Five Factor Model [FFM], traits, motives, attitudes, characteristics, qualities of self transformation)
13. **Self-Monitoring Processes** (allostatic transformations in personal awareness)
14. **Spirituality** (Higher Power, ego-transcendence, self-in-the-world)
15. **Affect Regulation** (states of emotional dysregulation, including posttraumatic shame and guilt)

Source: ©2004 John P. Wilson.

power (Mischel & Morf, 2003). As noted by Stern (1985) and Wilson (2004a), the dimensions of the self-structure include: coherence, continuity, connection, autonomy, vitality, and energy. Each of these structural dimensions plays an important role in the architecture of the self and they are all interlinked. The dimensions of the self have specifically designed functions and reflect capacities that cross-cut basic mechanisms involved in perception, memory, cognition, intelligence, motivation, and emotional regulation. Trauma can produce damage to the integrated structure of the self or to any of its separate and interconnected dimensions. For example, clinicians have consistently noted that disrupted early childhood experiences caused by abuse, neglect, poor parenting, etc., can lead to ego-fragmentation, a loss of coherence in identity, and disrupted developmental patterns (Pynoos & Nader, 1993; Nader, 1997, 2004). Similarly, massive psychic trauma has been shown to cause a loss of self-continuity and radical changes in the perception of life-course development, including a loss of chronology as to the stability of the self over time (Niederland, 1964 ; Koenig, 1964; Krystal, 1968, 1988a; Lifton, 1976, 1979).

It is clinically and theoretically important to recognize that there can be differential effects of trauma to each of the six primary dimensions of the self (i.e., coherence, continuity, autonomy, etc.). In extreme situations, as noted by H. Krystal (1988a), the most severely damaging forms of trauma (e.g., abusive violence, political repression, internment, torture) can result in a total loss of the self—a dissolution of the internal structural components themselves—resulting in amorphous, catanoid states of extreme withdrawal, fear states, and ongoing intrapsychic brutalization (Lindy & Lifton, 2001). At the opposite end of the adaptation continuum, trauma can alter the normal personality structure, causing increases or decreases in specific personality attributes (see discussion later in this chapter).

4.2 Ego-Processes

Ego-processes refer to a complex set of cognitive functions and abilities. In a psychodynamic sense, ego-processes describe how persons act on the external world in attempting to master experience. The ego, as an agentic quality, seeks to master experience, maintain unity in the self and maximize need gratification. Similar to the self, the ego has its own processes and structural dimensions. The dimensions of the ego have been studied empirically and reveal qualities such as ego-strength, ego-resilience, ego-weakness, ego-rigidity, ego overcontrol, and ego undercontrol (Block & Kremen, 1996; Block, 1971). Ego functions involve security and defensive operations that include protection from threats to the organism from external or internal sources. As originally noted by Freud (1917a), ego-defenses primarily have the task of managing fear and anxiety states that could potentially interfere with intellectual and cognitive capacities needed for coping and goal-directed behavior.

The presence of trauma constitutes a clear and significant danger to organismic well-being and activates ego-defensive operations in a manner similar to the way radar screens detect foreign objects that enter into airspace. Depending on the nature, chronicity, and severity of the threat to organismic well-being, ego-defenses sustain optimal functioning or eventually become weakened, ineffective, and non-functional. When defenses lose their functionality, other dimensions of the ego may be at risk for failure or inadequate execution of their functional operations (e.g., memory, information processing, abstract thinking, affect regulation). Fragmentation in ego-processes can place the self-structure at risk for impaired functioning as well. The loss of ego-strength and the capacity to regulate internal systems of the self can result in states of extreme vulnerability, helplessness, and narcissistic injuries (Parson, 1988a). In a similar way, sustaining the constancy of ego functions is critical to the sense of self-sameness and continuity. Clinical research has shown that in the presence of powerful stressors, the ego can lose strength; the entire capacity of the ego-system to perform and integrate its constituent functions can degrade and lose vital energy (Erikson, 1968; Krystal, 1988a; Wilson & Drozdek, 2004; Dimsdale, 1980; Ulman & Brothers, 1988).

4.3 Identity

The concept of personal identity shares theoretical space with the self-structure and ego-processes. These personality dimensions are tripartite, interrelated aspects of intrapsychic life. At the heart of the construct of ego-identity is the idea of self-sameness and continuity in the way the person attempts to master personal experiences (see Chapter 3). Personal identity describes the uniqueness of personality, the "stamp of character" and behavioral style across different situations. It is the "stamp" of uniqueness that differentiates persons in terms of their style of ego-mastery and adaptive coping. In this sense, one can meaningfully speak of typologies of identity as defined by two conceptual axes: identity-diffusion vs. identity-integration and self-continuity vs. self-discontinuity. Using these sets of conceptual axes, it is possible to discern four distinct typologies of posttraumatic identity: (1) the amorphous self; (2) the unintegrated self; (3) the transitional self; and (4) the integrated self (Wilson, 2004a). These four typologies of individual identity formation are especially useful in understanding how psychic trauma can attack and tear apart identity configurations that exist at the time of trauma (see Chapter 3). It is theoretically parsimonious and clinically useful to understand that there are many possible posttraumatic configurations of personal identity which range from highly coherent, integrated structures to fragmented, unintegrated configurations. These structural configurations of identity may or may not include a sense of self-sameness and continuity in reference to ego-processes, self-appraisal, and one's subjective sense of personal identity (Wilson, 2004a).

4.4 Unconscious Processes

It is a truism to say that psychic trauma can produce lasting unconscious residues that have the power to influence human behavior (Freud, 1895, 1917a, 1928; Nemiah, 1998). Recognition of unconscious mental activity is one of the hallmark achievements of psychoanalytic research that extends back over a century to the astute seminal insights of Freud that traumatic experiences lead to repression and the rendering unconscious (i.e., excluded from ordinary awareness, memory, and recall) of emotionally distressing experiences that threaten the integrity and ability of the ego to sustain optimal reality orientation. Freud (1923) distinguished between dynamic (i.e., repressed) and descriptive (i.e., instinctual processes) forms of unconscious mental functioning. He reserved the term "dynamic unconscious" for repressed experiences of a threatening nature that were maintained by the forces of resistance as a part of the mechanisms of repression as an ego-defensive process. Indeed, Freud's original paradigm of neurosis was a posttraumatic stress model.

The unconscious refers to a more inclusive psychic vault of human experience that is out of reach by normal processes of introspection. The unconscious, especially with regard to traumatic experiences, includes the collective unconscious as described by Jung (1929). In brief, the collective unconscious is a transpersonal representation of universal human experiences in the primordial and potential forms of action and experiences (Wilson, 2004b). In terms of psychic trauma, the collective unconscious has pre-existing potentials with regard to the personal experience of trauma. The Trauma Archetype and the Trauma Complex have been described as aspects of the collective unconscious that develop following extremely stressful life-experiences (Wilson, 2004b). The Trauma Archetype represents the universal transcultural patterns of the trauma experience. The Trauma Complex characterizes how these experiences crystallize into highly differentiated psychic complexes that include PTSD, self-disorders and changes in ego-processes, identity configurations, and the structure of the self. The generic concept of the unconscious embraces the idea that there is a positive regenerative unconscious, one that contains the seeds of unrealized potential for personal growth and transformation. In terms of posttraumatic growth, psychic trauma can release greater self-actualizing tendencies at the same time as it institutes forms of dynamic repression, although this is an area of posttraumatic recovery that has received little theoretical or empirical attention (see Chapter 5).

4.5 Trauma Complex

The Trauma Complex refers to the intrapsychic constellation of factors that interact dynamically within the dimensions of the self, the collective unconscious, and the dynamic unconscious. The Trauma Complex is differentiated from complex PTSD and is a more parsimonious construct (Wilson, 2004a). The Trauma Complex represents a depth of intrapsychic experiences organized at unconscious levels around the trauma experiences. The Trauma Complex forms in conjunction with the Trauma Archetype and has its own qualities of autonomy, coherence, and motivational power. Wilson (2004b) has defined the 10 characteristics of the Trauma Complex and how they articulate with the archetypes of traumatic experiences (see Chapter 5).

4.6 Trauma Archetype

The Trauma Archetype represents universal forms of traumatic experiences. The Trauma Archetype is psychologically equivalent in form and subjective experience across cultures, time, and the evolution of humankind (Wilson, 2004b). The Trauma Archetype has 11 defining features: (1) universal forms of experience; (2) altered psychological states; (3) allostatic changes in psychobiological functioning; (4) experience of imminent threat to organismic well-being; (5) confrontation with actual or symbolic death; (6) the specter of self-dissolution; (7) a threat to personal identity; (8) an impetus to restructure attributional processes; (9) mobilization processes of defense, recovery, and healing; (10) a personal search for meaning in the trauma experience; and (11) potential spiritual transformations of the self. The Trauma Archetype articulates and has a "cogwheeling effect" with other archetypal forms of human experience (mother archetype, shadow archetype, wise old man, hero, etc.) and merges with them to set up enormously complex forms of intrapsychic mental processes (see Chapter 5). The Trauma Archetype is the primordial psychological "soil" in which trauma complexes take root and develop into individually constellated patterns of adaptive and maladaptive behavior.

4.7 Moral Development

Immersion in the depth of trauma has the power to change views on morality, ethics, and justice. Moral reasoning and moral development are related concepts. Moral reasoning and moral dilemmas concern the questions of ethical "rightness"; the "oughts" and "shoulds" of moral action when there exist competing claims on courses of action. Moral development (Kohlberg, 1973) is the progression and change in moral reasoning throughout the course of the life-span. As noted by Viktor Frankl (1984) and others, profoundly traumatic conditions force persons to reevaluate the nature of ultimate values and what constitutes "right" and "wrong" (see Chapter 9). For example, when interned in a concentration camp and subjected to brutal starvation, is it wrong to steal food in order to live? Is it wrong to lie about one's identity, education and skills if doing so promotes survival under coercive conditions that have life and death consequences? In other situations of trauma, the consequences of action may generate attitudinal changes about basic beliefs and values. For example, if one can escape and survive by immediate action, is it morally wrong not to help a fellow survivor who is trapped but pleading for assistance in an airline crash disaster? Is it morally wrong to carry out military orders to torture suspected terrorists being held as prisoners during wartime? Is it morally wrong to ignore the cries of fellow survivors and their excruciating screams for help when trapped in the inflamed, decimated and collapsing World Trade Center on September 11, 2001 if there is a very limited opportunity for escape and survival? These and many similar questions point to the reality that traumatic situations contain moral dilemmas about actions enacted and those that were not enacted and produced bad consequences for others. As part of self-processes, moral development, ethical principles, and moral actions are distinguishable qualities of personality. A comprehensive theory of the posttraumatic self involves an analysis of these dimensions of human functioning. The posttraumatic self does not exist in a moral vacuum in the aftermath of extremely stressful events that challenge the meaning of life and what constitutes ultimate human values. This is another way of inquiring as to how trauma alters views on the relativity of ethics and universal moral principles.

4.8 Systems of Meaning and Value

Traumatic events are aversive human experiences that frequently produce undesirable consequences for physical and psychological well-being. Traumatic experiences have the power to alter systems of meaning and values. The recovery from trauma often causes individuals to reassess and prioritize their lives and decide what is, and is not, defined as meaningful. Understanding how persons construct systems of meaning in the wake of trauma constitutes an important aspect of the posttraumatic self (see Chapter 11 for a discussion).

Baumeister and Vohs (2002) have reviewed the social-psychological literature on the nature of meaning. They note that there are four basic patterns involved in the process of creating systems of meaning. These four patterns are: (1) a sense of individual purpose; (2) values which are hierarchically organized and generate positive outcomes; (3) a sense of self-efficacy in the pursuit of purpose; and (4) a sense of self-worth in carrying out one's goals and responsibilities in life. According to Baumeister and Vohs (2002), the capacity to create systems of personal meaning is linked to appraisal processes:

> This reappraisal [process] often involves finding some positive aspect in a negative event. The transformation process from adversity to prosperity

has been referred to as the benefit-finding aspect of meaning-making ...
A second aspect of meaning-making involves looking for attributes in an
effort to understand the events. This aspect has been referred to as the
sense-making function of meaning-making ... Meaning-making also has
been defined as the search for significance. (p. 613)

The posttraumatic self faces the challenge of finding meaning in
traumatic experiences and personal suffering. Feelings of self-worth
and the basis of appraising self-efficacy may change in purpose, value,
and priority. This process of change from the pretrauma organization
of values, beliefs and ideology is, in itself, a transformational process
indigenous to survivorship. Viewed in this way, "meaning-making"
and personal identity are yoked processes. There is no inner sense of
identity without a system of meaning to guide value choices and
personal goals.

4.9 Dissociative Processes

Dissociative processes are innate forms of psychological defense
against the perception of threat to organismic well-being. Dissociation
can be pathological or adaptive in nature (Putnam, 1989). Depending on
the individual's personal history of coping with situations of threat,
trauma or abuse, dissociation has been conceptualized as a trait of
personality or as an acute state of stress-response patterns. Viewed in
a broader sense, dissociative processes are defensive mechanisms in the
service of preserving systems of meaning and the inner core of identity.
As described by Wilson, Friedman, and Lindy (2001), the types of
dissociation codified in *DSM-IV* (2000) are linked to intrinsic psychological processes (e.g., perception, memory, consciousness, information
processing). Dissociation is an important process in the formation of
trauma complexes in the posttraumatic self. Indeed, trauma complexes
represent dissociated aspects of the self that were formed in response to
extreme stress. Jung (1950) stated that "in regard to complexes [there
exists] this somewhat disquieting picture of the possibility of psychic
disintegration, for fundamentally there is no difference in principle
between a fragmenting personality and the complex" (CW8, para. 200-3).
In the posttraumatic self, dissociative processes are inextricably linked
to the dimensions of the self-structure (i.e., continuity, connection, coherence, autonomy, energy and vitality), ego-processes (i.e., strength, control,
resilience, etc.), identity (i.e., subjective sense of self-sameness and continuity in adaptive modalities), and the archetypal experiences of trauma
that give birth to individually constellated trauma complexes unique to
the person (see Chapter 5 for a discussion).

4.10 Cognition and Information Processing

Human cognition, memory and information processing are the bricks and mortar of basic psychological functions and the province of experimental psychology. Until the advent of PTSD as a diagnostic entity in 1980, there were no systematic studies of these basic psychological processes under controlled laboratory conditions in relation to diagnosable PTSD and associated conditions. Moreover, research ethics precluded the possibility of designing experimental paradigms to analyze the effects of trauma on human cognition and information processing. However, with the advent of PTSD as a diagnostic category, persons diagnosed with the disorder, or those who had endured life-threatening traumas, could be studied more systematically in terms of learning how trauma affects basic mental activities. Today, scientific technologies (e.g., MRI, PET scans, biological markers) allow for hypothesis testing in sophisticated and complex neuroimaging studies of PTSD (Kaufman, Aikins, & Krystal, 2004) and more traditional neuropsychological and psychophysiological studies of the effects of trauma on brain functioning, information processing, memory, and higher order cognitive complexes (Knight & Taft, 2004). These building blocks are the foundations to understanding their connections to all aspects of the posttraumatic self. To consider one possibility: Are there distinct differences in the brain processes of healthy, resilient survivors of psychological trauma in comparison with those with debilitating PTSD that was caused by the same traumatic event? Stated more broadly, can the personality typologies of the posttraumatic self be differentiated in terms of brain functions involving information processing, memory, and cognition?

4.11 Memory

Memory and remembrance lie at the heart of posttraumatic changes in the self. Memory is stored information about the unique and personal aspects of psychological trauma. Remembrance is the process of recalling and reliving different aspects of the trauma experience (Harel, Kahana, & Wilson, 1993). Without the capacity for emotionally infused memories of traumatic experiences, PTSD would not exist, although conditioned patterns of somatic reactivity might be demonstrable, reflecting learning mediated by more primitive brain functions (van der Kolk, van der Hart, & Marmar 1996).

Understanding the architecture of the posttraumatic self requires knowledge of memory and remembrance as it pertains to the essence of identity processes shaped by powerful traumatic experiences (Harel, Kahana & Wilson, 1993). The hallmark feature of PTSD as a psychiatric illness is traumatic memory and distressing forms of reliving, reexperiencing, or reenacting what happened in a traumatic situation (Wilson, 2004a). The memory of trauma is encoded in the brain and body in different ways (van der Kolk, van der Hart, & Marmar 1996). As part of normal and abnormal (i.e., PTSD) patterns of prolonged stress-response, persons reexperience, reenact, or relive elements of their trauma experience in "hard-wired" systems: perception, memory, affect, cognition, motivation, and attachment relationships (Schore, 2003b).

In terms of human memory, the encoding, processing, storage, and retrieval of traumatic memories occurs in two basic systems: declarative and nondeclarative (Tulving, 1972, 1983; Schacter, 1992). Declarative memory refers to reportable verbal memories that are consciously accessible (Kihlstrom & Hoyt, 1990). It is also characterized as explicit memory. Nondeclarative memory refers to other types of memory that are the product of psychological conditioning in forms of classical or operant learning that may not be available to conscious reflection or verbal reports. It is referred to as implicit memory (Erdelyi, 1990). Nondeclarative memories also refer to forms of nonconscious processes and include unconscious memories, unconscious "reenactment or flashback experiences" (Block, 1981) unconscious emotional states (e.g., guilt, anxiety, fear, shame), and unconscious behavioral dispositions (e.g., hypervigilance, conditioned response tendencies) and perceptual thresholds (i.e., thresholds for the unconscious recognition of trauma relevant stimuli, or trauma-specific cues (TSCs)) that are hierarchically woven into the matrices of memory (Wilson, Friedman, & Lindy, 2001; Wilson & Thomas, 2004).

In the architectural framework of the posttraumatic self, memories of trauma are connected to structural dimensions of the self (i.e., coherence, connection, continuity, autonomy, vitality, energy), ego-processes, and configurations of personal identity (i.e., a sense of continuity vs. discontinuity). Memories of trauma are integral and nuclear components of trauma complexes. Memories of trauma constitute the psychological substrata of all dissociative processes (Putnam, 1989). Memories of trauma are conscious and unconscious processes (Nijenhuis, 1992). Unconscious memories are nondeclarative in nature and stored in specifically designated vaults in the realm of the unconscious—like burial chambers in secret rooms hidden in the recesses of the pyramids of the pharaohs in ancient Egypt (Wilson, Friedman, & Lindy, 2001).

4.12 Personality Development

The study and analysis of the posttraumatic self and personality development across the life-span is a relatively new phenomenon

(Pynoos & Nader, 1993). The conceptualization of the Protean Self (Lifton, 1993), the posttraumatic self (Wilson, 2004a), and the posttraumatic growth of personality (Tedeschi, Park & Calhoun, 1998) are outside the domain of traditional academic approaches to the study of personality. Historically, research on the different aspects of personality has concerned understanding the structure and dynamics of personality as related to normal personality development and its vicissitudes during life-span development (Monte & Sollod, 2003). Moreover, very few theories of personality have specified how traumatic experiences influence the development of personality (e.g., needs, traits, motives, schemas, identity, life-tasks, values, moral character) or how trauma causes transformations in personality processes during the course of epigenetic development (see Chapter 3). In this regard, Tennen and Affleck (1998) state

> one's view of how personality influences transformative experiences, and how personality is in tune by those experiences turns on how both personality and the transformation process are construed. Current conceptions have relied explicitly on trait notions of personality and implicitly on an incremental model of transformation. (p. 90)

It is clear that Tennen and Affleck (1998) have identified the inherent "chicken and egg" problem of causal directionality. However, the larger and critically central theoretical questions concern more than causal directionality. There is abundant clinical evidence that extremely traumatic experiences causally influence: (1) existing ages and stages of personality development (Pynoos & Nader, 1993); (2) the development of personality characteristics and individual identity (Lindy & Lifton, 2001); (3) the development of coping styles and trauma-related traits of personality that originated in critical traumatic experiences (e.g., traits of secretiveness, personal guardedness, vagueness, hoarding or "putting on a good" face as related to the Holocaust death camp internment experiences) (Dimsdale, 1980); (4) a general orientation towards personal concerns as value priorities; (5) the long-term effects of critical nuclear life-episodes (McAdams, 1994); (z6) the potential of extremely stressful life-events to generate aspects of positive growth in personality (Tedeschi, Park, & Calhoun (1998); and (7) the delineation of which aspects of personality traits (Five Factor Model, FFM), are most strongly correlated with PTSD and other Axis I or Axis II disorders (Tedeschi, Park, & Calhoun, 1998). Therefore, the issues of causal directionality are important but less germane than defining the diverse pathways that characterize the impact of trauma on personality and integrated forms of holistic-dynamic functioning (see Chapter 5). Since traumatic experiences vary greatly in their stressor dimensions and impact on adaptive functioning (see Wilson & Lindy, 1994 for a discussion), the issue of which facet of personality is adversely or positively impacted requires specification of the interactive factors that exist at the time of the trauma (i.e., age, stage of personality development, trait profile, ego-strength, resilience factors, prior life-experiences, etc.). Personality processes operate in a dynamic and synergistic fashion, and therefore the analysis of the posttraumatic effects of powerful experiences requires an in-depth model of how perception influences affect regulation, evoked stress-response patterns and cognitive attributional processes which contribute to systems of meaning and values.

Is it possible to create typologies of posttraumatic personality functioning and their structural dimensions? If so, how do they relate to what is currently known about "normal" personality as studied from the five assessment paradigms discussed by Wiggins (2003): (1) psychodynamic, (2) interpersonal, (3) personological, (4) multivariate, and (5) empirical. Using each of these five approaches to personality assessment, what set of intrapsychic mechanisms and patterns of behavior differentiate the posttraumatic self from other forms of personality growth and development?

4.13 Self-Monitoring

PTSD involves complex forms of allostatic stress-response processes that are disrupted by trauma. Wilson, Friedman, and Lindy (2001) and Wilson and Thomas (2004) have discussed negative and positive allostatic changes in PTSD. The negative allostatic processes include: (1) altered thresholds of response; (2) hyperreactivity; (3) altered initial response patterns; (4) altered capacities for internal monitoring; (5) altered feedback based on distorted information; (6) altered continuous responses; (7) failure to habituate; and (8) new allostatic set points of baseline psychobiological functioning. In PTSD, there is a loss of accurate self-monitoring of internal states which precludes information-processing abilities, accurate signal detection, and executive functions. Altered self-monitoring capabilities include the *inability* to appreciate degrees of psychic numbing, emotional constriction and unresponsiveness, and loss of interpersonal sensitivity, depression and anxiety states. In positive allostasis, there is a restoration of the accurate ability to monitor internal psychological states. The encoding, processing and storage of information in memory is more efficient and productive. There is a strong improvement in the capacity to monitor internal and external cues without disturbing ego-defenses (Wilson & Thomas, 2004). The adverse behavioral and interpersonal consequences associated with negative allostasis and impaired self-monitoring abilities are diminished.

In the posttraumatic self, there exists a continuum of self-monitoring capabilities that is anchored at one end by optimal states of self-organization and, at the other end, by pathological self-organization (see Chapter 6). A continuum of altered states of consciousness and integrative psychological experiences embraces self-monitoring of internal psychological processes. In posttraumatic self-transformations reflecting optimal states of integration, there is strong synchrony between levels of consciousness (unconscious, preconscious, conscious), memory, higher order integrative processes in cognition and memory, and the experiences of positive emotions. In posttraumatic self-transformations characteristic of pathological self-organization, there is dysynchrony in mental processes that include dissociation, affect, memory cognition, and interpersonal patterns of affiliation in love and intimate relationships (Schore, 2003b; Wilson, Friedman, & Lindy, 2001).

4.14 Spirituality

Understanding the nature of the posttraumatic self would be incomplete without the inclusion of spiritual transformations that are commonly reported by survivors of life-threatening trauma. Tedeschi, Park, and Calhoun (1998), in their book *Posttraumatic Growth*, note that spiritual development and existential themes are related issues

> [M]any traumatic events raise the most fundamental assumptions about life that survivors of trauma previously may have considered only in a superficial fashion. These existential changes can be regarded as growth, but they are not always identified as pleasant by the individual who experiences them, because they are issues of the meaning and purpose of life and the inevitability of personal death. (p. 14)

While it is the case that not all survivors of trauma have epiphanous spiritual experiences, there is ample evidence that trauma can be a strong catalyst to religious and spiritual transformations (Sinclair, 1993). The spiritual transformation that occurs in the posttraumatic self is intimately related to core questions of identity, the conceptualization of the self, and the capacity to create meaning in the wake of life's most disturbing episodes as a human being.

4.15 Affect Regulation

The analysis and understanding of the posttraumatic self must include the central problems of affect regulation. As Allan Schore's (2003a, b) research has shown, the dysregulation of emotion is at the core of PTSD and self-disorders. As such, compound and complex affective states exist in the posttraumatic self, including specifically definable states of shame and guilt (see Chapter 9). These compound, dysregulated emotional states are intricately linked to processes of cognitive, ego-defensive, and self-attributional processes, especially those associated with self-appraisals as to self-esteem, moral virtue, belief systems, and world view.

5 TRANSFORMATIONS OF THE POSTTRAUMATIC SELF: PSYCHOFORMATIVE PARADIGMS

The concept of the posttraumatic self embraces many dimensions of personality. Central to the understanding of the posttraumatic self is the attempt to understand how basic self-processes are altered or influenced by stressful life-events. Among the few theories of "the self" to systematically explore the nature of changes in self-processes caused by trauma is that of Robert J. Lifton as discussed in his book *The Life of the Self* (1976). In this work, Lifton distinguishes psychoformative theory, which places emphasis of the processes of symbolic changes in the configuration of the self as a dynamic entity, from Freudian models of instincts and Erikson's model of ego-identity and self-continuity. Lifton's conceptual framework was strongly influenced by his work with Hiroshima survivors and others who had endured experiences of extreme stress and radical discontinuity in living. Lifton's theory emphasizes the power of death imagery, as well as the specter of one's own death, to planes of self-experience which he classifies into three sub-paradigms. To quote

> With this paradigm, absurd death and the discontinuity of life replace repressed and resisted sexuality and identity conflict as the major source of our psychological impairments. The result is not so much a problem of relegating unacceptable ideas to the unconscious, or the experience of identity confusion. The more basic difficulty is the impaired capacity to feel and give inner order to experience in general. (p. 81)

Lifton's three subparadigms by which individuals experience their psychoformative processes are: (1) connection vs. separation; (2) integrity vs. disintegration; and (3) movement vs. stasis (Figure 2.2). These three domains of self-processes have reference to intrapsychic mechanisms (e.g., having a sense of meaningful attachments; feelings of wholeness and personal integrity; and a sense of continued personal growth and development). The subparadigms refer to sociocultural relations as well, i.e., the creation and change in the self in a protean, shape-shifting way as forms of adaptation to important personal events and historical

Life vs. death
Connection vs. separation
Integrity vs. disintegration
Movement vs. stasis
Continuity (with/without sameness) vs. discontinuity
Proximate existential concerns vs. ultimate concerns of existence
Centering vs. decentering of self-experience
Grounding vs. ungrounding: balance and imbalance in self-experience

FIGURE 2.2. Symbolization of the self in life: subparadigms of experience and epigenesis (time, space, emotions, life-course). *Source:* After Lifton (1976); Wilson (1980).

circumstances. These subparadigms are considered a basic area of self in the relation to society and life-stage development. In this regard, Lifton (1976) proposes that the terms "centering" and "grounding" are useful in describing the relative degree of coherence, "flux" or dynamic change that is occurring in psychoformative processes. Lifton (1976) states that centering is "the ordering of experience by the self along the various dimensions that must be dealt with at any given moment—temporal, spatial, and emotional" (p. 72). A sense of psychological grounding "is the relationship of the self to its own history, individual and collective, as well as to its biology" (p. 72). Thus, centering and grounding are dynamically interlinked within the self. In this way, it is possible to speak meaningfully about the ungrounding and decentering of self processes as experienced through the subparadigms of the self. Trauma, therefore, can profoundly impact these processes. For example, trauma can cause decentering and ungrounding in the self so that survivors experience themselves as decentered and having a sense of separation (detachment), deintegration, and stasis—i.e., a lack of a positive sense of growth and ego-maturation.

6 PSYCHOFORMATIVE DIMENSIONS OF SELF-EXPERIENCE: BIOLOGICAL, SELF AND PSYCHOSOCIAL DIMENSIONS

In his work with different trauma survivors, Lifton (1976, 1979, 1993) found a convergence of themes in terms of the ways that psychoformative processes are effected. Table 2.2 presents an augmented summary of Lifton's (1976) sub-paradigms of psychoformative dimensions. Table 2.2 illustrates the bipolar qualities of the subparadigms in an expanded format for each dimension. In the posttraumatic self, all polarities of psychoformative processes are subject to change, depending on the nature of traumatic stressors experienced.

TABLE 2.2
Psychoformative Dimensions of Self-Experience: Biological, Self, and
Psychosocial Relations

Connection	**vs. Separation**
Bonding (mother/nurturant person, others)	Self-absorbed (withdrawal, disconnected)
Attachment (family/relations to others)	Detachment, distant, estrangement
Affiliation (group/social/culture)	Disaffiliation, isolation, alienation
Self-identity (ego-states)	Identity confusion
Eros: life-instinct (biological)—affirmation and growth	Thanatos (death instinct)—renunciation/death
Spiritual (theological, numinous)	Agnostic doubt, disavowal of God
Integration	**vs. Disintegration**
Physical intactness/wholeness	Fear of annihilation/deterioration/destruction
Ethical and moral intactness	Moral uncertainty
Personal integration and psychological integrity	Personality fragmentation/self-disintegration/ despair
Sense of completeness of life-course	Ennui/numbing/regression
Reconfiguration of positive self-identity, altruism	Identity diffusion/loss of self-integration
Movement/growth	**vs. Stasis**
Growth towards individuation and self-actualization	Cessation/arrestation/"soul" vs. death
Epigenesis, form and structure	Disruption of trajectory of life-course
Healthy development of personality and aging	Regression, arrestation
Animation, vitality, wholeness	Frozen states/depression, blocks, inanition
Recovery, healing, regeneration	Degeneration, decompensation
Expressiveness (creative)	Constriction (numbing)
Transformation/rebirth/reconfiguration	Desymbolization/formlessness/death

Source: ©2004 John P. Wilson.

6.1 Connection vs. Separation

The first subparadigm of self-processes is a sense of connection versus separation which has six aspects: (a) bonding; (b) attachment; (c) affiliation/social relations; (d) identity; (e) life-instinct, eros; and (f) spiritual relations to a Higher Power. The corresponding and polar opposite set of characteristics include: (a1) self-absorption, withdrawal, disconnection; (b2) detachment, distantiation, estrangement; (c3) disaffiliation, isolation, alienation; (d4) identity confusion; (e5) death-instinct, thanatos; and (f6) agnostic doubt and disavowal of God. Thus, for the trauma survivor, the polarities of connection vs. separation reflect degrees of change in these aspects of self-processes. For example, the severely traumatized may manifest extreme self-absorption, isolation, withdrawal, alienation, detachment, and problems in establishing or maintaining intimate relations. They can have a profound sense of identity confusion, spiritual disaffectation and the loss of will to thrive and continue living.

The subparadigms of self-experience, as active psychoformative qualities of existence, can be construed as a continuum as well as sets of bipolar dimensions. In this regard, Lifton (1976) states

> The subparadigm of connection–separation, movement–stasis, and integrity–disintegration, through which, from the beginning until the end of life, imagery of continuity and discontinuity is perceived and recast...A cardinal principle of the paradigm is that, at every moment, *the self is simultaneously involved with both proximate and ultimate matters.* (p. 62; emphasis original)

In this perspective then, the self has the capacity to redefine itself and change the elements that make up a sense of being centered and grounded (or their opposite) at any period of time, including in the trauma recovery period, which I will discuss in more detail later.

6.2 Integration vs. Disintegration

The sub-paradigm of integration vs. disintegration contains five domains of experience. The integration pole refers to: (1) physical (bodily) integrity, wholeness, intactness; (2) ethical and moral integrity; (3) personal (psychological) integration; (4) a sense of epigenetic (life-course) completeness; and (5) the formation of a positive self-identity with a capacity for altruism. In sharp contrast, the disintegration pole includes a fear of annihilation, moral uncertainty, self-deintegration, psychic numbing, and identity diffusion. As I will discuss, the negative polarity of a sense of deintegration characterized several typologies of the posttraumatic self (e.g., Inert Self, Empty Self, Fragmented Self).

6.3 Movement vs. Stasis

The subparadigm of movement vs. stasis has several elements that reflect the drive towards unity and organismic self-actualization. The processes of self-animation and growth are evidenced as follows: (1) growth towards self-individuation and self-actualization; (2) the unfolding of personality and identity across stages of epigenetic development; (3) the striving for healthy development in personality; (4) the presence on a consistent basis of animation, vitality, and wholeness; (5) the posttraumatic process of healing, recovery, and regeneration at all levels of functioning; (6) fluidity in creative expressiveness; and

(7) the capacity for self-transformation, rebirth, and the reconfiguration of identity. A strong sense of stasis in the striving for unity and self-individuation is seen in contrasting personality qualities. In this modality the trauma survivor has a strong, if not pathological sense of stasis. There is a consciousness of cessation in striving; a sense of being frozen in time; arrested, retrogressed, depressed, blocked, inhibited, constricted, and psychically numb. The psychoformative processes are associated with internal images of desymbolization, formlessness, and, ultimately, of dark images of the abyss and death. Such desymbolization is an overarching inner sense of loss of structure of the self as a whole; a psychic collapsing from within, accompanied by cessation in striving, goal-driven behavior and purpose to life.

7 THE ABYSS VERSUS TRANSCENDENCE IN
   SELF-EXPERIENCE: PSYCHOFORMATIVE PARADIGMS
   IN THE TRAUMA ARCHETYPE

The trauma archetype represents universal forms of traumatic experiences which is shaped by culture and historical forces (see Chapter 5). The Trauma Complex grows out of the archetypal experience of trauma and includes the Abyss, Inversion and Transcendent Experiences which are discussed in Chapter 4. The Trauma Complex represents individually constellated groups of emotion, thoughts, and fantasies that cohere around the nature of the trauma experience. As such, trauma complexes reflect changes in the nature of psychoformative experiences and alterations in the subparadigms of self-experience as well as degrees of groundedness and centeredness. Moreover, the Abyss Experience represents the nature of powerful traumatic stressors that attack positive polarities (integration, connection, movement) of self-experiences and can result in a loss of continuity, meaning, and striving towards unity in personality. In cases of traumatization, this results in pathogenic outcomes that include PTSD, personality reconfiguration, dissociative disorders, or Axis I or Axis II psychiatric disorders. On the other hand, the Transcendent Experience emerges from the confrontation with overwhelming life-stresses and leads to unification of opposites in a new form within the self. The transcendent quality evolves from the dialectic tension in the three subparadigms of self-processes (see Chapter 5 for an extended discussion).

We can conceptualize the dynamic interplay between the psychoformative polarities of self-experience by representing the structure of the self as a mandala (i.e., circle). As Figures 2.3 and 2.4 illustrate, the subparadigms can be "crossed" in a three-dimensional way along with the dimensions of the Abyss Experience (AE) and the Transcendent

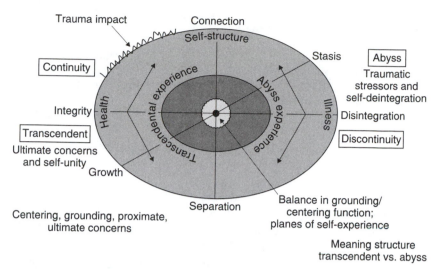

FIGURE 2.3. Abyss versus Transcendence in self-experience: basic psychoformative paradigms in the Trauma Archetype. *Source:* ©2002 John P. Wilson.

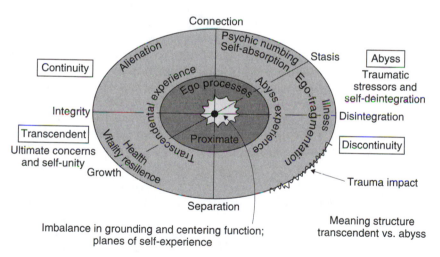

FIGURE 2.4. Self-experience: basic psychoformative paradigms in the Trauma Archetype. *Source:* ©2002 John P. Wilson.

Experience (TE). In Figure 2.3 in the center of the mandala representing the self as an integrated process is a circle which symbolically represents balance in the centering and grounding functions in planes of self-experience. In contrast, Figure 2.4 illustrates an imperfect, "warped" circle reflecting imbalance in the centering and grounding functions, leading to stasis, separation, disintegration, and pathogenic alterations in the self.

8 TRAUMA AND SELF-PROCESSES

The self develops through an interaction of biological maturation and a series of socialization experiences that while cross-culturally variable, still provide the evoking conditions necessary for the emergence of the sense of an autonomous, continuous, and internalized self.

(Froddy & Kashima, 2003)

Research on the structure of human personality characteristics highlights the important fact that there is an empirically measurable structure of traits that is cross-cultural and universal in nature. As an empirically derived model of personality, the phenotypic Five Factor Model (i.e., FFM) of personality (neuroticism, extraversion, openness, agreeableness, conscientiousness) has the scientific advantage of being clear and readily replicable (McCrae & Costa, 1996). It has the disadvantage of being atheoretical and therefore devoid of a larger conceptual framework by which to derive hypotheses about intrapsychic processes. However, the FFM model of stable personality traits enables us to consider in precise terms how psychological trauma attacks the structure of personality and its subcomponents (see discussion later in this chapter). By logical extension, therefore, we can discern how different types of trauma (e.g., war trauma, child abuse, natural disasters, physical injuries) impact the structure of the self and its six dimensions. The concept of the self is more fluid and dynamically modifiable than is the construct of personality traits as enduring dispositions of behavior. *The effects of trauma generate different types of alterations in their structural configurations and operational functions than is the case for personality traits.*

8.1 Trauma and Self-Processes

The damage caused by severe trauma to self-processes is transparent and readily observable, especially in premeditated acts of interpersonal violence and emotional abuse purposely designed to denigrate others (Friedman, 2000a; Breslau, 1998). Traumatic injury to the self is like a high-velocity bullet penetrating the body, tearing apart internal organs critical for survival. Similarly, whereas the brain and heart are critical organs of the body, the self and ego are core psychic organs of human personality. The self and ego are dynamically interrelated in mental health, psychological growth, and well-being, just as the brain and heart are organs with interrelated functions that are essential to integrated living systems.

The role of the self has been a major focus in many of the major theories of personality and psychopathology (Monte & Sollod, 2003).

Ulman and Brothers (1988) have reviewed theories and psychiatric conceptualizations of the self and the manner in which it may be damaged by trauma. The self may be shattered and result in dissociation, defensive constellations to protect narcissistic injuries and vulnerabilities or lead to more or less crystallized personality traits. These conclusions, of course, are consonant with many of the theories and clinical insights of Janet (1900), Freud (1917a), Jung (1963a), Kohut (1971), Rogers (1951), Stern (1985), Erikson (1968), Parsons (1988a), Putnam (1989), Kalsched (1996), and others. Common to these researchers is the idea that the construct of the self is central to internal organizing principles of psychological functioning. Studying the effects of trauma without a conceptually meaningful way to understand traumatic damage to the self is akin to trying to understand degenerative neurological disorders without understanding how the brain functions.

8.2 The Structure and Functions of the Self

To fully appreciate the internal injuries caused by trauma, it is useful to outline the structure and functions of the self. By understanding aspects of self-structure and its role in organizing behavior, especially posttraumatic adaptations, we can gain insight into the specific nature of injuries and psychic scars produced by trauma. The posttraumatic self is a temporary or enduring representation of how trauma has altered the inner workings of self-processes.

The self is an internal psychological structure that is organized in terms of its functions and designs. Daniel Stern (1985), in his detailed studies of the development of the self in infants stated: "they seem to approach interpersonal relatedness with an organizing perspective that makes it feel as if there is now an integrated sense of themselves as distinct and coherent bodies, with control over their activities, ownership of their affectivity, a sense of continuity, and a sense of other people as distinct and separate interactants" (p. 69). Stern's research shows that the self is an integral, organizing structural part of personality which establishes bases of self-worth (i.e., self-directed appraisals of the self as an object). As a psychological structure it provides a basis for self-esteem, a sense of well-being, and uniqueness to individual identity. The self is part of a self-object matrix in the world and establishes connections, relations, and investments of energy and value in others, whose worth is also appraised and "esteemed." The self-object matrix of significant others serves as a component of identity formation since others recognize and confirm the individuality, existence, and importance of the individual in a larger reference group, kinship network or community. In summary, the self is a central processing unit of personality which organizes experience and adaptation (Mischel & Morf, 2003).

The architectural framework of the self-structure contains ego and personal identity processes (Erikson, 1968) that can be considered an infrastructure of the self (see Chapter 2). As defined by Erikson (1968, p. 50), identity imparts a sense of self-sameness and continuity to the unique ways the ego masters experience, both in time (e.g., ontological epigenetic development) and space (e.g., culture and geographical location). The idea of identity is especially important in understanding damage to the self. Among the landmark studies of massive psychic trauma, Lifton (1967) found that many Hiroshima survivors lost their sense of self-sameness and continuity due to catastrophic devastation of every aspect of their lives, culture, and existence. Lifton spoke of "vacuum" states in which the vitality of the self was emptied. Survivors of the first atomic bomb referred to themselves as "the walking dead" serving penance in "hell." Lifton observed that prolonged psychic numbing was essential for survival for the Japanese survivors. These findings, along with those from Holocaust studies and studies on victims of totalitarian political regimes (Lindy & Lifton, 2001; Wilson, Harel, & Kahana, 1988; Krystal, 1968, 1988a), demonstrated that both the self and ego-processes could lose a sense of continuity. In *self-discontinuity*, whether radical or partial, the individual experiences a disruption, rupture, or severing of connection to self-objects and sources of psychic meaning and importance. Such survivors feel "cut off" or emotionally fragmented, torn away from the threads of continuity which give meaning and directionality to existence. Lifton (1976, 1979) termed this radical discontinuity the "broken connection" to underscore how psychoformative modes of self-experience were altered, often permanently, by catastrophic trauma.

9 THE ARCHITECTURE OF THE POSTTRAUMATIC SELF

The self system is an organized meaning system, guided and constructed by the organization of relationships among the person's self-relevant cognitions and affects ... the self is an organized dynamic cognitive-affective-action system and the self is an interpersonal self-construct system.

(*Mischel & Morf, 2003*)

There is an architecture to the self. It is a structure built from epigenetic life-span development that has form (identity), function and aesthetics (see Chapter 3). The self is shaped by culture and the forces of historical events. Although there is no consensus on the number of

Dimensions of self-structure: optimal function	Traumatic impact and altered function
1. **Coherency – Organized integration of function** (Functional integrity) Self–other boundaries; locus of control in degrees in unity in experience	**Fragmentation** – Loss of integrated coherence to functional capacity. Loss of locus of control, unity and boundary structures
2. **Connection – Planes of experience, physical and psychological** (Affectivity) Affective connectivity to self and others, symbolic connectivity to past and future	**Separation** – Loss of emotional ties to self, others, groups, and society. Loss of connection to self as object is psychic numbing
3. **Continuity – Time, space, self and others** (History) Personal history, experiential flow, enduring awareness	**Discontinuity** – Loss of an ongoing sense of self in time and space. Loss of continuity with past experience
4. **Energy – Drive and trajectory of striving** (Motivation) Motives, goal–directed behavior, purposeful striving	**Immobility; stasis** – Loss of physical and mental energy; generalized fatigue; malaise. Loss of motivation and goal directed behavior
5. **Autonomy – Self-regulation and control systems** (Agency) Capacity for self-regulation of physical and psychological processes	**Loss of autonomy, self-regulation** – A sense of self-esteem and capacity to freely self-regulate is lost or diminished. Feelings of shame, guilt and self-recrimination are present
6. **Vitality – Health and strength of organism** (Health) The degree of optimal physical health and psychological vitality to sustain self-functions	**Illness, loss of vigor** – Subjective or objective decrease in health status. Malaise. Experienced loss of psychic vigor. Loss of essential personal vitality may be entirely psychogenic

FIGURE 2.5. Core dimensions of the self affected by trauma. *Source:* ©2004 John P. Wilson.

elements that comprise the structure of the self, we can speak meaningfully about six core dimensions: (1) coherency, (2) connection, (3) continuity, (4) energy, (5) autonomy, and (6) vitality (Stern, 1985; Mischel & Morf, 2003; Leary & Tangney, 2003). It is important to have a clear definition of the dimensions of the self and their optimal function in personality in order to understand how trauma alters their efficacy in functioning. Figure 2.5 summarizes and defines these dimensions.

Trauma has the power to alter the structural and functional dimensions of the posttraumatic self in many different ways. Those who have studied forms of dissociation within the components of the self note that it may undergo changes which result in a loss of functional integrity, affectivity, motivation, agency, and health (e.g., Janet 1907; Kluft 1996; Nijenhuis & van der Hart, 1999; Goodwin & Attias 1999; Chu 1998; Kalsched, 1996). Within each of these dimensions, additional changes can occur to substructural components, for example, rendering changes in boundary permanence, self–other appraisals and sense of self-worth, loss of autonomy, decreased vitality and psychic energy, etc.

9.1 Trauma and the Architecture of Buildings and People

The way that severe trauma attacks the components of the self-structure can be compared to the terrorist attacks on the New York City

World Trade Centers in 2001. The Twin Towers lost their foundational supports after being attacked and waivered unsteadily before collapsing. The architectural integrity of the towers was permanently compromised. Steel girders, connecting rods, I-beams, steel joints, load-bearing walls, and supportive H-welded crossbeams come apart and detach from their designed function. The cables installed to transport elevator lifts to the 110 floors of the building snap, lose their mooring and give up their transport function. The power sources are damaged and so there is no energy to operate machinery or to provide heat, lighting, and air-conditioning. Without a source of power, the building becomes inert, stagnant, and nonfunctional. It cannot self-regulate when the controls of the engineering systems for power, transport, and maintenance are severely disrupted. The coherency, vitality, and energy of the structure have all been damaged or compromised, rendering its functional use severely limited, or nonexistent. Eventually, the structural damage caused by the terrorist attack destroyed the Twin Towers, which fell to the ground like a person shot in the head by a bullet.

Damage to the self-structure can result in different forms of posttraumatic self-disintegration, dissolution, fragmentation, narcissistic injury, and "implosive" self-destructiveness (Morrison, 1990; Kohut, 1971, 1977). On a world-wide basis, millions watched as the World Trade Centers initially withstood the impact of terrorist-commandeered air-liners, wondering and hoping that people inside would survive the attack. The buildings swayed, suddenly caught fire, buckled under the intense heat, broke apart, and ultimately collapsed into a massive pile of rubble. In the end, nothing remained of the towers; they were dead and nonexistent as were nearly 3,000 of their inhabitants. So, too, the self-structure can buckle, bend, break, shatter, and disintegrate in response to psychic trauma, especially that which is maliciously and purposely designed by humankind to inflict injury to the bases of self-functioning. If trauma is powerful enough, the self-structure can break apart (i.e., deintegrate), no matter what the pre-existing degree of ego-vulnerability. Torture, for example, is designed to attack the spirit, break individual will power and control it; to produce submission and surrender and denigrate and break the personhood of the victim (Vesti, Sonnier, & Kastrup, 1992).

We have learned through traumatic stress studies that there are many psychological equivalents of torture and ways to attack the self, destroy identity, and rape the soul (Simpson, 1993; Agger & Jensen, 1993; Jaranson & Popkin, 1998; Gerrity, Keane, & Tuma, 2001). Injury to the core self-dimensions can result in a loss of operational capacity. The "destructuring" of the dimensions of self-structure through trauma results in disunion, fissility, or disjoining of its interrelated dimensions (see Figure 2.5).

When the integrated self-structure pulls apart, it systematically begins to lose functional capacity. We know that depending on the age of developmental maturation in epigenesis (Stern, 1985; Erikson, 1968; Pynoos & Nader, 1993; Nader, 1997, 2004), the self-structure, personality, and the nature of adaptive ego-processes will reconfigure into new structures (see Chapter 3 for a discussion). These new structural configurations can be understood and conceived as posttraumatic typologies of the self with attendant modalities of ego-processes manifesting varying degrees of continuity and self-sameness (Wilson, 2004a; Erikson, 1968).

10 THE COHESION-FRAGMENTATION CONTINUUM
   IN THE POSTTRAUMATIC SELF

10.1 Structural Deintegration

It is theoretically possible to construct a continuum of integrative self-functioning and behavioral adaptation through identification of the critical dimensions of the self and by analysis of the FFM model of human personality (see later discussion). *We can speak, therefore, of a cohesion— fragmentation continuum as the experiential basis of the posttraumatic self.*

In severe trauma, the psychoformative planes of self-experience alter, leading to a sense of *separation, stasis,* and *disintegration* of, or a division within, the structure (see Chapter 5 for a discussion of the Abyss and Inversion Experience). In *structural deintegration processes,* the experiential planes of the self shift, much as internal tectonic plates shift and move under the force of gravity in an earthquake. If strong enough, an earthquake's tremors cause fissures in the earth's surface, generating damage from the shifting internal structural plates. Similarly, in the traumatized self, the conditions of worth, sense of stability, or orderliness in daily living are diminished or profoundly altered in ways associated with a sense of disequilibrium, flux, change, and alteration of what was once defined as "normal" living.

The posttraumatic change that accompanies a loss of continuity and self-sameness typically involves a loss of coherence of the self-structure—a crumbling of the structural components—much like that of a tall building disintegrating or imploding from explosive charges or the powerful tremors of an earthquake (Wolfe, 1990; Kohut, 1971, 1977). As the infrastructure of the building begins to come apart, the integrity of the entire structure is lost: it no longer manifests its original architectural form or functionality. The spatial and structural configuration has changed and that which once defined the identity of the building is gone, although parts may remain which contain elements of the former structure, such as the pillars of the Parthenon in Athens,

Greece or cross-hatched steel girders nested in the ruins of the World Trade Centers in New York before they were scraped away. Analogously, the structure of the self may be partially or totally injured or destroyed by trauma.

11 POSTTRAUMATIC TYPOLOGIES OF SELF-CONFIGURATIONS

A person is brought so completely to a stop by a traumatic event *which* shatters the foundation of his life *that he abandons all interest in the present and future and* remains permanently absorbed in mental concentration upon the past.

(Freud, 1916, p. 342; emphasis added)

Trauma's ability to injure the self and fractured its architectural design can cause an internal restructuring of its components. Figure 2.6 summarizes 11 typologies of posttraumatic self-configurations. These configurations grow out of the processes of coping with traumatic impacts on personality and crystallize (temporarily or permanently) as modalities of altered structural configurations. The derivation of these typologies was based on several sources of data: (1) the clinical and psychiatric literature on narcissism and self-disorders; (2) the research on massive psychic trauma; (3) research and treatment of dissociative disorders; and (4) modern personality research on the structure of personality (McCrae & Costa, 2003; Monte & Sollod, 2003). The trait constellations of the posttraumatic typologies are not to be construed as configurations of traditional personality disorders, although they may share many similarities in characteristics, symptoms and ego-defense dynamics. The posttraumatic self-structural configurations are not necessarily pathological in nature nor should be considered as a traditional psychiatric disorder, especially in the absence of documentable pretraumatic morbidity. The different configurations can be thought to exist on a continuum that ranges from dimensions of vacuous dispiritedness to transformative reintegration of the self in forms of self-actualization, individuation, and spiritual numinosity (see Chapter 6). It is possible to discern that each of the dimensions may be differentially affected, reflecting degrees of injury or impairment to the structure itself. Damage to the structure of the self results in lost functionality, which lessens its efficacy in coping with external demands of reality.

Some survivors report a loss of self-continuity and connection but retain a sense of autonomy, energy, vitality, and integral coherency. In extreme cases, as described lucidly by studies of Holocaust death camp survivors (Niederland, 1968; Krystal, 1988a), torture victims (Ortiz, 2001), and victims of ethnic genocide (Lindy & Lifton, 2001), the self may be destroyed, resulting in abject "psychological surrender," the cessation of striving and loss of the will to thrive. For such persons, posttraumatic self-configuration can be meaningfully characterized as inert, inanimate, lifeless, decimated, or annihilated. Such a profound form of alteration of the self is psychic collapsing—analogous to the demise of the World Trade Centers in New York. The structure of the self unravels, dismantles, and reverts to regressive forms of primitive ego-functioning at a rudimentary survival level (Morrison, 1990). When the psychic core of the self dissipates structure, there may be few internal resources remaining to facilitate the construction of a new configuration, which Wilson (1980) described as a process of retrogression among severely traumatized Vietnam War veterans. Individuals subjectively experience themselves as "gone," "frozen," "stuck in time and space," or "dead"; whoever they were before the trauma has disappeared, changed dramatically or has been diminished in stature (see Chapter 5 for illustrations). What remains are deintegrated or fragmented parts of the self which may be devoid of energy, hope, trust, and a viable system of meaning. Lifton (1967) and Frankl (1988) spoke of this posttraumatic condition as a "vacuum state" of existence—void of capacity for the creation of meaning and realizing a tangible future. In a "vacuum state" of emptiness, the person exists in the abyss of trauma, a kind of psychological "black hole" without end, which centripetally pulls in negative affect and experience (see Chapter 5). Such persons live with a broken spirit in the heart of darkness and despair, which I will discuss more extensively below.

We can conceptualize posttraumatic reconfiguration of the self as typologies of personality profiles. Figure 2.6 illustrates 11 typologies of self-reconfiguration following extreme trauma and key descriptions of ego-processes, personality and psychopathology associated with each form of posttraumatic structural reorganization. Figure 2.6 classifies the typologies from the most fragmented and damaged to the highest level of transformation, reintegration, and optimal functioning. The typologies can be considered to be arranged on a continuum from pathology to health; from broken spirits to transcendent ones; from loss of humanness to self-individuation and the capacity for the numinous connection to the existential meaning of life.

Based on the clinical literature on trauma and its impact on personality functioning (van der Kolk, McFarlane, & Weisaath, 1997; Goodwin & Attias, 1999; Wilson, 1980; Williams & Somer, 2002), we can define personality typologies and self-reconfigurations following powerful life experiences. Space limitations do not allow a full description of each posttraumatic typology summarized in Figure 2.6. A capsule summary is provided in Figure 2.9, which analyzes how optimal functioning is breached by trauma. The typological classification can be understood as

Post-trauma typology and alterations	Ego processes adaptational	Key descriptors	Forms of personality processes and psychopathology	
Continuum				
1. Inert self (soul death) pathology	Surrender	Regressed	Catanoid states: brief psychosis, PTSD	Severe
2. Empty self	Depression	Passive	Major depression: PTSD	
3. Fragmented self disorders	Diffusion	Mistrustful	Dissociation: PTSD	Borderline
4. Imbalanced self	Instability	Disconnected	Borderline PD: PTSD	
5. Overcontrolled self	Fixated anxiety disorders	Overcontrolled	Obsessive-compulsive	PTSD
6. Anomic self	Normlessness adjustment disorders	Nonattached	Dysthymia;	Anxiety: PTSD
7. Conventional self	Adjusted variations on Five-Factor Model of Personality (FFM)	Conforming	Generalized Adjustment disorder PTSD	Anxiety
8. Grandiose self	Exhibitionistic narcissistic disorders	Insolent	Narcissistic	PD: PTSD
9. Cohesive/vital self esteem and identity	Resilient	Flexible	Identity integration – prosocial	Self-
			Subclinical PTSD	
10. Psychosocial accelerated self individuation	Post-conventional	Existential	Individuation	Self-
			Partial PTSD	
11. Integrated-transcendent self-actualization	Actualized	Unified	Self-actualization	Self-

FIGURE 2.6. Trauma and reconfiguration of the "self-structure." *Source:* ©2004 John P. Wilson.

reflecting the dimension of motives, affect, self-organization, and ego-functioning. Moreover, the typologies presented bear resemblance to stage theories of ego and moral development as described by Loevinger (1976, 1983), Kohlberg (1973, 1978), and Erikson (1968). A review of these and other theories of ego development, from immature to mature levels of adaptation and functioning, can be found in Lapsley and Power (1988), who examined integrative approaches to self-processes.

12 TRAUMA AND TRANSFORMATIONS OF PERSONALITY STRUCTURES

12.1 Posttraumatic Typologies of Personality and Self-Processes

There are 11 posttraumatic typologies of personality that form unique configurations of self-processes and personality characteristics. A brief description will be given of each typology and its psychodynamic configuration.

12.1.1 Inert Self. The Inert Self typology consists of traits that characterize the most severely damaged person. The Inert Self is diminished in humanness and reduced to primitive ego-functioning. In these individuals trauma's impact on the self has broken their spirit and the will to thrive (Krystal, 1988a). Their self-structure has functionally dissolved. Their persona (i.e., facial mask) is unexpressive: blunt, blank, and withdrawn. Their motivational striving has ceased, even for safety, and they appear to manifest extreme helplessness, evidence of surrender, and the will to survive at the most basic level. They often have poor hygiene and unkempt domiciles. In previous studies (e.g., Krystal, 1968), they have been labeled as the "walking dead," the slave state of mind (e.g., musselman), or other terms indicating psychological stasis and near total surrender (Niederland, 1968). Their affective states are flat and nonexpressive: inert, lifeless, empty, vacuous, and numb. They manifest alexithymia. The personality processes and forms of psychopathology include catanoid states, brief psychosis, major depression, paranoid states, and PTSD. The Inert Self has regressed into a state of extreme helplessness and slid passively into autistic withdrawal which Krystal (1988a) described as the catanoid state. Key words: surrender, regressed.

12.1.2 Empty Self. The Empty Self typology consists of traits of passivity, depressiveness, and an exhausted sense of being depleted of energy (Wolfe, 1990). These individuals experience malaise, loss of interest in activities and relationships, and are isolated from others. They withdraw into themselves in self-absorbed ways, unable to actively initiate social relations. In the posttraumatic self, they manifest what Lifton (1976), Frankl (1984), and others have referred to as "vacuum states." They are insecure, dependent, safety-seeking; desiring structure, order, predictability, and guidance from others. They lack joy and a capacity for positive affect. They are frequently depressed and despairing. They feel as though there is a "hole" in the core part of themselves. They are chronically anxious and fearful, which they attempt to hide from others. They have strong traits of oral pessimism, doubt, and loss of trust in the world (Erikson, 1950). They have prevalent suicidal fantasies and ideation. Their personality processes and forms of psychopathology include major depression, dependency, schizoid states, and PTSD. Key words: depressive, passive.

12.1.3 Fragmented Self. The Fragmented Self typology consists of traits of identity diffusion, fragility, and strong feelings of discontinuity within the self and with others. In the posttraumatic self, these individuals experience themselves as "unglued," "not whole," "shattered," "falling apart," and "broken into pieces." They are chronically anxious and vacillate in attachments with strong emotional intensity. They manifest identity diffusion (see Chapter 3). Their ego-processes are diffuse and rigid. They are inconsistent in the adequacy of self-care. Their psychosocial functioning in work and affiliative relationships is often erratic. Under stress, they are especially prone to dissociation, as was typically experienced peritraumatically during trauma (Marmar, Weiss, & Metzler, 1997). Their personality processes and forms of psychopathology include dissociative disorders, dependent personality characteristics, and PTSD. Key words: diffusion, mistrustful.

12.1.4 Imbalanced Self. The Imbalanced Self typology consists of extreme emotional instability. These individuals fear abandonment and being left alone without others to rely on for nurturance, reassurance, love, and security. Ernest Wolfe (1990) described such persons as craving "external mirroring" from stable self-objects. They are chronically anxious and tense, states that they try to hide from others. They have a loss of internal coherency caused by trauma that expresses itself in severely disrupted interpersonal relationships. They are prone to idealize others perceived as strong and nurturant. They are emotionally labile, given to outbursts of anger or states of anxiety and agitation when they perceive a loss of connection of themselves, even temporarily, with others. They are extremely manipulative in secret and deceptive ways. Unlike the Inert Self and Empty Self, they mobilize disrupted affects to manipulate others to enhance self-mirroring. Their personality processes and forms of psychopathology include instability, manipulativeness, borderline personality disorder, PTSD, and transient depressive episodes. Key words: instability, disconnected.

12.1.5 Overcontrolled Self. The Overcontrolled Self is fixated to the trauma experience and over-defended with characterologically rigid traits. These individuals tend to be emotionally constricted and fear losing control. They use obsessive and compulsive behavior, rituals and rigid patterns of living to cope with a fundamental, pervasive anxiety which reflects fears that to "let go" will result in decompensation or agitated, overwhelming anxiety states (Shapiro, 1981). They typically have high energy levels which are employed to fortify and rigidify the damaged self-components of coherency, connection, and continuity. Behaviorally they overorganize their lives and transactions with others. The rigidity and compulsive stereotype of their behavior is unconsciously designed to protect self-dimensions and insure some sense of control over inner anxieties. They "ward off" the impact of trauma on their sense of vitality through denial, reversal of reality, and compensatory overactivity in work and efforts to maintain routine, discipline, and unswerving patterns of daily living. They can appear mechanical and inflexible in personal habits. Horowitz (1986a, 1999) observed that such persons "jam" attention by frenetic overwork to block traumatic memories. Their personality processes and forms of psychopathology include obsessive-compulsive disorders, adjustment disorders, characterological rigidity, and PTSD. Key words: fixated, overcontrolled.

12.1.6 Anomic Self. The Anomic Self is adrift and rootless in society. Trauma's impact has led these individuals to detach and isolate in self-contained, nonconventional and alienated ways from others. They experience normlessness which reflects the lack of internal coherency and connection within the component self-capacities. They are mistrusting of others and autonomously self-regulated by maintaining a controlled distance from conventional societal norms, which they scorn, reject or criticize. They mistrust, challenge, or sabotage authority. They often have unconventional, rebellious lifestyles. They are often hedonistic and impulsive. Their ego-processes are lacking in resiliency and strength, which is compensated by maintaining normlessness which serves defensively to quell episodes of dysthymia and anxiety. The Anomic Self characterizes a person who is a loner. The experience of trauma has caused them to be wary and suspicious of intimate involvement. They show tentativeness in making commitments which would require investments of their unsure sense of self-coherence and capacity for genuine connection to self and others. Frankl (1984) described such persons as existentially empty in meaning systems of belief. Their personality processes and forms of psychopathology include depressive episodes, anxiety states, antisocial or unconventional tendencies, and PTSD. Key words: normlessness, nonattached.

12.1.7 Conventional Self. The Conventional Self is adjusted to society following trauma. These individuals seek safety and affiliation with others to reassure normality to life (Wilson, 1980). They typically exhibit changes to their pretrauma baseline of adaptation as viewed by the Five Factor Model (FFM) of normal personality. The Conventional Self is able to maintain autonomy and vitality; to actively seek to enhance feelings of coherency and efficacy with others in affiliative, approval-seeking ways that reassure a meaningful sense of connection within themselves. They are overly conformist and group-oriented. They dogmatically adhere to in-group values and norms. They seek approval for adherence to values and behaviors which bring adulation or esteem from others who serve as reference points of traditional conventionality (Wilson, 1980). They are anxiety-ridden conformists. They are concerned with being liked by others and are anxious for praise, respect, and being seen as a good group-oriented person. Their personality processes and forms of psychopathology include generalized anxiety disorder and PTSD. Key words: adjusted, conforming.

12.1.8 Grandiose Self. The Grandiose Self represents a posttraumatic personality style in which the striving for recognition prevails. The striving for recognition from others is motivation for the attainment of depleted, injured, or lost self-esteem. These individuals seek external recognition that confirms self-worth. The Grandiose Self has high levels of energy and autonomy that fuel behaviors to achieve external acclaim, praise, and admiration from others who are seen as important and powerful icons of genuine success. Paradoxically, the Grandiose Self lacks true self-cohesion and continuity in identity. In the wake of trauma, their preexisting narcissistic tendencies are aggravated, leading to various defensive attempts to protect their denied inner vulnerabilities. Erwin Parsons (1988a) described war veterans with such psychological injuries as angry at the loss of appreciation for their suffering, and in turn demanding and manifest a sense of entitlement to special treatment. Their personality processes and forms of psychopathology include the spectrum of narcissistic traits, depressive episodes, and PTSD. Key words: exhibitionistic, indolent.

12.1.9 Cohesive Self. The Cohesive Self reflects resilience in ego-processes following trauma. Such individuals "spring back" from extreme stress and adversity; they regain their "shape" and functionality. Those manifesting the Cohesive Self have an internal locus of control, vitality, and security. Their identity reflects integration and continuity. Kahana, Harel, and Kahana (1988) described such persons as "resilient, hardy copers." They are prosocial in moral values and orientation to society. They evidence post-conventional adaptation, reflecting concerns with universal justice, fairness, ethics, and truth. Key words: resilient, flexible.

12.1.10 Accelerated Self. The Accelerated Self is an autonomous, individualistic outsider in society. These individuals are existential iconoclasts. They are highly individuated and autonomous. They live *without* strict adherence to social norms but are not antisocial in personality functioning. They are tough, resolute, resilient, morally principled, altruistic, and self-directed. They manifest self-individuation as a result of overcoming trauma. Their self-structure is coherent and flexible. They show positive affect and generativity (Erikson, 1968) on a consistent basis. As a consequence of trauma they have a discontinuity with the past, their former selves, and connectedness to others. They march to the beat of a different drum, whose rhythmical percussive cadence was born of trauma. Their self-metamorphosis is a shape-shifting, creative protean transformation of their inner resources, talents, and human personality propensities. The Accelerated Self reflects a "speeding up" in epigenetic ego-development as a result of trauma (Wilson, 1980). Normative age-related crises appear prematurely in personality. They are psychosocially accelerated or "fast-forwarded" ahead, dealing with critical life-stage issues in an advanced way before their usual or customary time in life-span development. They manifest creative patterns of coping and unusually high degrees of resilience. Wilson (1980) described such persons as having transformed traumatic impact into prosocial humanitarian modes of functioning. Key words: existential, individuation.

12.1.11 Integrated-Transcendent Self. The Integrated-Transcendent Self is characterized by structural integrity. The components of the self reflect optimal functioning in self-actualizing modalities. Frankl (1984), Lifton (1976, 1979, 1993), and Jung (1950) described such persons as transcendent in overcoming personal trauma. The Integrated-Transcendent Self has successfully overcome adversity, extreme stress and trauma in an optimal way (see Chapters 6 and 10). The self-structure of these individuals is configurationally integrated (see Chapter 5). It has transcended the pretraumatic self; evolving beyond self-individuation to the ability to function optimally in self-actualizing ways. Such persons seek growth and challenges that enrich the sense of vitality and autonomy of existence. Their personality processes include spiritual transcendence, the unity of self with wisdom, and a capacity to have peak experiences of the numinous (see Chapter 5). The Integrated-Transcendent Self is the apotheosis of spiritual transformation of personality into a unity of oneness (Jung, 1950). Erikson (1962) characterized the transcendent identity as "a post-narcissistic love of the human ego—not the self—as an experience which conveys some world order and spiritual sense" (p. 268). These individuals live in the present with consciousness attuned to a higher awareness of reality and cosmic order. They are altruistic by character structure. They have transformed trauma into an evolved self of actualized organismic potential. They manifest the personality characteristics of optimal integrative functioning (see Chapter 5). Key words: unified, self-actualizing.

In summary, the typologies represent a continuum of posttraumatic adaptational forms of personality processes which range from severe pathology (e.g., inert-self) to optimal mental health (e.g., self-actualization). Further, while the typologies are discrete personality syndromes, more than one pattern may be evident in the posttraumatic self.

13 TRAUMA AND SELF-DISSOLUTION: FRACTURES TO THE CORE OF PERSONALITY

Transformations of personality are by no means rare occasions ... the alteration of personality in the sense of iminution is furnished by what is known in primitive psychology as "loss of soul".

(Jung, 1950, p. 53, para. 213)

In an optimal structural configuration, the self is a unified whole and can be visualized graphically as a mandala, a circle of unity, or as various symbols of wholeness (see Chapter 5 for a discussion). Figure 2.7 presents a graphic representation of *primary forms* of self-dissolution following severe trauma: (1) the Inert Self; (2) the Empty Self, (3) the Anomic Self, (4) the Fragmented Self, (5) the Overcontrolled Self, and (6) the Imbalanced Self. The figure represents the fractures in the unity of the self. The key descriptors which characterize the respective ego-processes include surrender, depression, normlessness, diffusion, fixation, and instability. The figure shows a simplified way of visualizing how the self can fragment into new posttraumatic configurations. The wholeness of the self configuration is impacted by trauma, splintering into segregated parts. These descriptive characterizations are quite similar to forms of narcissistic injury to the self-described by Kohut (1977) and Wolfe (1990). Narcissistic injury, or damage to self-esteem and the functional integrity of the self, can be considered universal in post-traumatic self-reconfigurations, a fact observed by Freud (1920) in his last major theoretical analysis of traumatic neurosis presented in *Beyond*

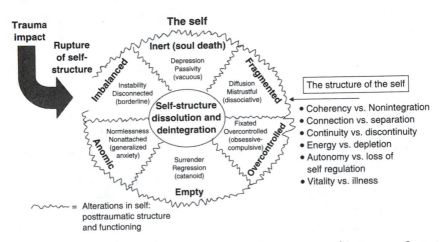

FIGURE 2.7. Primary forms of self-dissolution after severe psychic trauma. *Source:* ©2004 John P. Wilson.

the Pleasure Principle and earlier writings: *On Narcissism* (1911) and *Anxiety, Inhibition and Symptoms* (1912). More recently, Parsons (1988a) presented a model of how trauma leads to posttraumatic self-disorders, adapted from Kohut's work on forms of self-psychopathology, especially among severely traumatized Vietnam War veterans. Object relations theory, ego, and self-psychology are congruent with the depiction in Figure 2.7.

14 POSTTRAUMATIC ALTERATIONS IN THE SELF: THE LOSS OF STRUCTURAL INTEGRATION

The various forms of self-dissolution produced by trauma can readily be understood as a loss of structural cohesion. As such they represent changes in adaptation from optimal states of functioning. Trauma's impact on the self results in a loss of integrative complexity and function. Figure 2.8 illustrates the progression and pathways of self-alterations caused by trauma. These pathways characterize the structural deintegration of the self-structure which results in changes in personality, a reduction or alteration in ego-adaptive mechanisms, and reconfiguration of personal identity.

14.1 Structural Deintegration

The loss of structural cohesion precipitates defenses against anxiety and vulnerability to ego-adaptive processes in terms of need gratification and maintenance of selfhood. Regression can occur as the component parts of the self undergo dissolution, disunity and fragmentation. The intricate structural cohesion of personality breaks apart, unraveling and thus requiring more and more energy from defenses to guard the painful sense of annihilation, disintegration, and ineffectiveness in coping with external demands. It is as if the "organ" of the self shrinks or diminishes, filling up with the affect engendered by trauma which now occupies and encroaches on more conscious and unconscious ego-space. Krystal (1988a) reached a similar understanding: "I came to the conclusion that the final common path of traumatization was the development of overwhelming affects...the physical immobilization observable in the catanoid state is accompanied by a massive blocking of virtually all mental activity—not just affects, but all initiative, judgment, and other activity—to the point that "walking death" may ensue. This may serve as a model of an adult traumatic state" (pp. 142, 145).

The dissolution of the self can result in profound changes in psychological functioning which cuts across all the dimensions of the

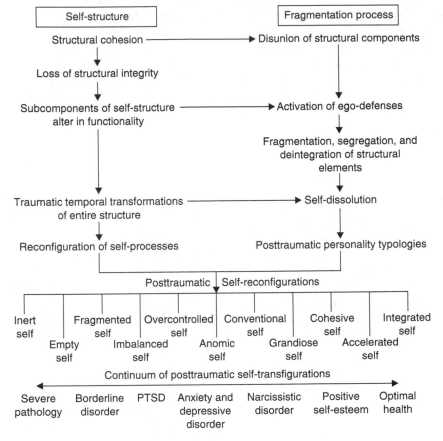

FIGURE 2.8. Trauma and the pathway of self-fragmentation. *Source:* ©2004 John P. Wilson.

self: coherency, connection, continuity, energy, autonomy, and organismic vitality. The personality reconfigures into clinically describable typologies as part of the Trauma Complex (see Chapter 5). Such posttraumatic states may become pathological and constitute forms of complex PTSD (Wilson, Friedman, & Lindy, 2001; Herman, 1992; Courtois, 1999) or severe mental illness. Trauma survivors nevertheless face the universal task of "protean" transformation and the rebuilding of a fragmented self. The reconstruction of the traumatized self is a process of gradual integration of the trauma experience; the reintegration of the "old" self into a new configuration of personality as a whole (Wilson, 1980, 1989).

It is possible to further understand the dynamics of posttraumatic self-typologies by examining how each of the core dimensions of the self is injured by traumatic experiences. *The core dimensions of the self, in their healthy developmental forms, reflect optimal levels of each dimension;*

Posttraumatic self-typologies (Self-dimensions)	Coherency	Connection	Continuity	Energy	Autonomy	Vitality
Inert ('dead') self (Surrender)	– – –	– – –	– – –	– – –	– – –	– – –
Empty self (Depressed)	–	– –	– –	– –	– –	– – –
Fragmented self (Diffusion)	– – –	– –	– –	+	–	– –
Imbalanced self (Instability)	– –	–	– –	+	– – –	–
Overcontrolled self (Fixated)	–	+	+	+	+	–
Anomic self (Normlessness)	– –	– –	–	+	+	– –
Conventional self (Adjusted)	+	++	++	+	–	+
Grandiose self (Exhibitionistic)	+	+	+++	+++	++	++
Cohesive/vital self (Resilient)	+++	+++	+++	++	++	++
Accelerated self (Post-conventional)	+++	++	+	+++	+++	+++
Integrated-transcendent self (Actualized)	+++	+++	+++	+++	+++	+++

Key: Optimal degrees of strength in dimensions of self
Weakness: (– – –) Pathological   Strength: (+)   Low
        (– –)   Very weak   (++)   Moderate
        (–)   Weak   (+++) Strong

FIGURE 2.9. Core dimensions of self injured by trauma. Degrees of strength in dimensions of the self: — — — — = pathologically weak; — — = very weak; — = weak; + = low strength; ++ = moderate strength; +++ = strong (optimal functioning). *Source:* ©2002 John P. Wilson.

all the parts of the architecture of the self are functionally integrated in the service of psychological health and efficacy in adaptive behavior. It is clinically and scientifically important to specify the strength and weakness of each posttraumatic typology. For each of the six dimensions of the self-structure, we can utilize a six-point rating scale of degrees of optimal function: pathological (– – –), very weak (– –), or weak (–); strong (+++), moderate (++), or low (+). This simple rating scale enables comparisons and contrasts of each dimension among the posttraumatic typologies.

15 ASSESSING POSTTRAUMATIC PERSONALITY RECONFIGURATIONS

The nature of how each dimension of the self-structure is damaged by severe trauma is shown in Figure 2.9, indicating the relative weakness or strength of the dimension following trauma and the degree of change from an optimal level of functioning[1]. For example, the Inert Self typology is pathologically weak in all dimensions, reflecting massive decentering and fragmentation of the self described by Krystal (1988a) as catanoid surrender. Psychic numbing is perfused throughout the ego. Despair and emptiness prevail. We can speak meaningfully of a "broken spirit." The Empty Self is also weak, helpless, and overwhelmed by depressive affects. Vitality is missing and victims/survivors are insecure, safety-seeking and profoundly mistrustful, lacking in autonomy and initiative. The Anomic Self is weak, alienated from social norms, but has some degree of continuity and the minimal capacity to mobilize energy for restorative purposes. The Anomic Self is rootless and adrift, seeking a source of attachment to provide grounding. The Fragmented Self has a profound loss of coherence, disrupted continuity, and identity diffusion. Such persons are prone to dissociation, anxiety, and have unstable self-object relations. The Overcontrolled Self is highly detached and fixated to trauma's impact on the self. However, there is more strength available in the form of energy, autonomy, connection (usually to fellow survivors) to form a sense of "survivor identity." The Overcontrolled Self often adapts by obsessive-compulsive behavioral defenses, compensatory action, and rigidified patterns of living. Similarly, the Imbalanced Self is emotionally labile and unstable, manifesting splitting and self-object deficits characteristic of borderline personality disorder. The components of the self-structure are nonarticulated. Such persons seek reassurance, nurturance, love, and security. They are anxious, agitated, and volatile. The Conventional Self is, in contrast, relatively adjusted to social norms and the capacity to carry out activation of daily living, albeit with compromises to the sense of vitality and well-being, experienced as free-floating or general anxiety disorders. Such persons are conforming, group-oriented, and approval seeking.

The Cohesive Self, Accelerated Self and Integrated Self represent different forms of integration and ego-synthesis for mastering experience, including resolution of trauma. The Integrated-Transcendent Self is transformative in nature and capable of utilizing (i.e., transforming) the negative energy (affect) from trauma to build a new, healthy identity hallmarked by individuation and self-actualization. In contrast, the Psychosocially Accelerated Self (Wilson, 1980) manifests alienation from norms, resistance to acculturation, and autonomy from

---

[1]The assessment of damage to self-configurations can be on a six-point scale which represents degrees of optimal strength or weakness in each of the six dimensions of the self. Optimal integration is scaled by three levels of optimal (positive) functioning. Deintegration is measured by three levels of weakness (negative) functioning.

social norms. In a descriptive sense, these individuals are iconoclastic "outsiders," "time-warped," accelerated in epigenetic development, and forge new identities congruent with strong drives towards self-reliance in a prosocial, humanitarian, and post-conventional orientation (Wilson, 1980).

The continuum of self-alterations is a way of analyzing the spectrum of self-disintegration, the loss of structural coherence and the subsequent manner in which restorative efforts reconfigure into healthier modalities of integration complexity. Wolfe (1990) has written that

> The person whose self-regresses from a state of cohesion to one of partial or total loss of structure experiences this as a loss of self-esteem, or a feeling of emptiness, depression, worthlessness, or anxiety. This change in the structured state of the self has been termed fragmentation. Fragmentation occurs in varying degrees and does not imply complete dissolution of the self...fragmentation is sometimes experienced as the terrifying certainty of imminent death, which signals a process of apparently irreversible dissolution of the self. The experience of a crumbling self is so unpleasant that people will do almost anything to escape the perception brought about by fragmentation...fragmentation means regression toward lessened cohesion, more permeable boundaries, diminished energy and vitality and disturbed harmonious balance. (p. 39; emphasis added)

The "disturbed harmonious balance" is psychic disequilibrium in the component dimensions of the self, which is produced by the allostatic load of trauma. The reversal of disturbed balance, affective dysregulation in posttraumatic ego-states, is a goal of treatment to facilitate the processes of self-reconstruction. The survivor has to reinvent himself or herself in order to resume life with a sense of vitality, connection, autonomy but, perhaps, without a sense of continuity to the past. In reinventing the posttraumatic self, the "old self" gets shed, like an exoskeleton, and is replaced with a more vital and functional one.

16 IDENTITY AND SELF-CONTINUITY FOLLOWING TRAUMA: RECONFIGURATION IN EGO-PROCESSES

Identity formation, thus, can be said to have a self aspect and ego aspect.
(Erik Erikson, 1968, p. 211)

It is impossible to understand the deleterious impact of trauma on the self without insight into the structure of identity. There is no psychological existence without a sense of personal identity. In semantic (i.e., psychological) connotation, the word identity is closest in meaning to "soul." Erik Erikson (1968), who wrote insightfully about identity in the life-course, spoke of identity as a sense of sameness and continuity to the ego's "synthesizing methods" in time and space (p. 50). Erikson's (1968) work with traumatized World War II veterans led him to understand self-dissolution and to use the term identity diffusion to characterize the loss in identity as a central agency of the self-structure (see Chapter 3 for a discussion).

It is useful and important to incorporate Erikson's seminal work into our analysis of the dissolution of the self. Using the concepts of continuity–discontinuity and identity integration-identity diffusion, we can construct two conceptual axes which reveal four modalities of identity: (1) Amorphous Self; (2) Transitional Self; (3) Integrated Self; and (4) Unintegrated Self. These relationships are illustrated in Figures 2.10 and 2.11, with the larger, outer figure representing the self and the smaller, central figure the style and form of ego-processes.

As derived from the conceptual axes, there are four dimensions of the self-structure and four qualities of ego-processes. The product of crossing Identity Diffusion and Self-Continuity represents the Unintegrated Self in which ego-processes are vulnerable, fragile, and unstable. The combination of Identity Diffusion and Self-Discontinuity illustrates the amorphous, disorganized self-structure and fragmented ego-processes. The Amorphous Self embraces the typologies described

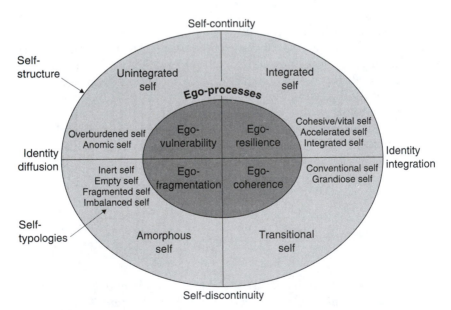

FIGURE 2.10. Identity and continuity in self-processes following trauma. *Source:* ©2002 John P. Wilson.

Posttraumatic self-typology	Characteristic ego-processes	Clinical descriptions
I. **Amorphous self clusters**: 1. Inert/dead self 2. Empty self 3. Fragmented self 4. Imbalanced self	**Ego-fragmentation** Identity diffusion Self-discontinuity	Surrender, catanoid, regressed, depression, vacuum state, passive, diffusion, disintegrated, mistrustful, borderline, unstable, nonarticulated
II. **Unintegrated self clusters**: 5. Overcontrolled self 6. Anomic self	**Ego-vulnerability** Identity diffusion Self-continuity	Fixated, rigid, overcontrolled, normless, alienated, nonattached
III. **Transitional self clusters**: 7. Conventional self 8. Grandiose self	**Ego-cohesion** Identity integration Self-discontinuity	Adjusted, conforming, approval-seeking, exhibitionistic, narcissistic, insolent
IV. **Integrated self clusters**: 9. Cohesive/vital self 10. Psychosocial/accelerated self 11. Reintegrated self	**Ego-resilience** Identity integration Self-continuity	Resilience, hardiness, flexible, spiritual, individuation, existential, transcendent, self-actualizing, unity

FIGURE 2.11. Ego-processes, self-coherence, and identity following trauma. *Source:* ©2004 John P. Wilson.

earlier as inert, empty and fragmented; the most severely disturbed and nonfunctional structure of the self-components. On the other hand, the conceptual axes of Identity Integration and Self-Discontinuity characterize the Transitional Self and discernible qualities of ego-coherency. Further, the quality of integrated identity in the Transitional Self provides stability but *without* a sense of continuity. The trauma survivor experiences changes in the planes of the self and a "broken connection" to the past. However, stability in identity integration enables ego-coherence in the transition of further differentiating the dimension of the self. We can see that the Integrated Self reflects both self-continuity and identity integration. The stability of the self-structure is associated with strong functional qualities to the dimensions of the self (i.e., continuity, vitality, energy, autonomy, coherence, affectivity), which, in turn, are associated with ego-resiliency, the capacity to maintain flexible and adaptive ego-processes.

In summary, these eight modalities of self-functioning are useful conceptual and clinical paradigms to understand the continuum of self-dissolution. Understanding identity structures and ego-space configurations is critical to all posttraumatic therapies since trauma "lives" inside these "chambers" of the psyche. These clinical phenomena are empirically verifiable by psychological testing and the understanding of how trauma gets embedded in organismic processes (Wilson, 2004a). The impact of trauma to the self results in injuries to psychic structures governing the structural integrity of the self and functional efficacy of ego-processes.

17 COHERENCE AND CONTINUITY IN THE
    POSTTRAUMATIC SELF

In a classificatory schema, we can combine the frameworks of understanding how trauma affects personality, self-processes, and identity to achieve more predictive, analytic power in clinical work and research programs. Figure 2.11 summarizes these relationships which are useful to clinical work. The classificatory schema represents a way of understanding the relative degrees of structural coherence of the self following trauma. Self-dissolution is not an "all or none" phenomenon. It represents degrees of disunion to the bases and functions of the self. Traumatic impact varies in terms of which dimensions of the structure are weakened, disjointed, or no longer functional. In massive trauma, the entire structure may collapse and crumble into fragments of what once existed much like a tall building that has been blown up. The posttraumatic self can be conceptualized in terms of relative degrees of coherence and experiential self-continuity. The Amorphous Self, for example, literally means incomplete, formless, unstructured, and inchoate. The opposite polarity, the Integrated Self, is complete, formed, structured, efficacious, and differentiated. Between the anchor points of the continuum of self-dissolution—integration, are the Unintegrated Self and the Transitional Self. Although these forms of self-configuration reflect traumatic injuries to components of self-functioning, they also represent interim points in the direction of healthier, integrated self-structure. As the self reconfigures, the trauma survivor experiences greater degrees of vitality, energy, connectedness to self and others, wholeness, well-being, a new continuity, sameness, and a sense of unity.

18 TRAUMATIC STRESS AND THE NORMAL PERSONALITY: THE
    FIVE FACTOR MODEL AND POSTTRAUMATIC CHANGES

Personality is the architecture of the whole, not just a list of adjectives of those parts or aspects which most impress observers.

(*Murray & Kluckhohn, 1953, p. 11*)

Analysis of the nature and dynamics of posttraumatic personality processes could start in many places of discovery. It is theoretically fruitful to examine the question of how trauma impacts the structure of normal personality characteristics. How does traumatic stress alter the configuration of personality structures? Digman (1994) reviewed the historical development and evolution of the Five Factor Model (FFM) of personality characteristics. His insightful review notes that, over five decades, there emerged a strong consensus of the number of discrete factors that comprise the empirically derived structure of human personality. In the last two decades, the application of the FFM has extended to the analysis of Axis I and Axis II mental disorders as classified by the Diagnostic and Statistical Manual of the American Psychiatric Association (e.g., *DSM-IV-TR*, 2000). For example, Costa and Widiger (1994) compiled representative research in a single volume dedicated to personality disorders and the FFM. Thus, the empirically defined existence of an FFM model of personality allows us to explore how traumatic experience could alter the different structural configurations of normal personality.

PTSD is not a personality disorder, but traumatized persons have personality characteristics that existed prior to their personal experiences of trauma. Consistent with the large body of research on the FFM (McCrae & Costa, 1996) we can assume that these dimensions of personality are normally distributed in the population of persons exposed to stressors that could cause PTSD (Kessler et al., 1995) or other (less pathological) forms of prolonged stress response. Stated simply, persons subjected to the psychological experience of trauma "bring" these attributes of character to the encounter with trauma. This being the case, we can ask several key questions as to how trauma impacts normal personality functioning.

18.1 Trauma and Normal Personality: The Core Questions

First, is there a general pattern of how trauma impacts human personality? Which dimensions of the FFM are increased or decreased in manifest behaviors and psychological processes as a result of trauma? Second, are some persons with higher scores on particular dimensions of the FFM more prone to develop PTSD? Third, do different types of traumatic experiences (e.g., combat in warfare versus a massive disaster) generate different effects on the structure of personality as measured by the FFM? Fourth, is it possible to predict changes in specific personality dimensions nested within each of the five factors as a function of exposure to traumatic stressors? Fifth, in terms of positive posttraumatic changes, how does the FFM alter in configuration and profile? Do some personality characteristics change a great deal (e.g., warmth, anxiety, achievement striving, openness to experience, straightforwardness, dutifulness) whereas others do not change at all or change in directions opposite to their pretrauma baseline level? These and related questions are empirically verifiable and important to studies of treatment outcomes (Foa, Keane, & Friedman, 2001; Wilson, Friedman, & Lindy, 2001).

Since the focus of this book is on understanding the nature, dynamics, and transformation of the posttraumatic self, a preliminary attempt will be made to delineate the transformations and permeations of personality using the FFM as it applies to the analysis of how traumatic stressors impact personality dimensions. In a rudimentary way, I will indicate the predicted direction of changes for the FFM in persons suffering from PTSD, and then the direction of positive changes associated with the metabolism of trauma. This conceptual approach is both heuristic and clinically valuable since it raises the fundamental question of how basic psychological processes (e.g., perception, memory, cognition, affect regulation) are affected by psychological trauma and how these mechanisms are manifest through the "lens of personality characteristics."

18.2 Personality and PTSD

Table 2.3 presents the FFM of personality and the personality characteristics that load statistically on each of the five factors. In total, the five factors (neuroticism [N], extraversion [E], openness to experience [O], agreeableness [A], conscientiousness [C]) contain 30 personality attributes. Table 2.3 indicates two sets of predictions regarding the nature of traumatic impacts to pretrauma personality processes: first, the direction of change predicted for each of the five factors in persons suffering from PTSD and/or prolonged stress-response patterns at a subclinical level; second, the direction of change associated with positive transformation, resolution and metabolism of posttraumatic states. Third, for each of the 30 personality attributes nested within the five factors, specific predictions are made as to whether there is: (1) no change in the personality characteristic; (2) an increase or decrease in the personality characteristic; and (3) the level of the personality change in positive transformation of trauma (level: low, medium, high, and variable degrees of change).

19 PERSONALITY CHANGES IN PTSD AND PROLONGED STRESS REACTIONS

The Big Five does not define any limits for personality research. Rather, the research leading to the Big Five structure simply constitutes a body of findings too powerful and critical to be ignored by anyone who seeks to understand personality.

(Saucier & Goldberg, 1996, p. 42)

TABLE 2.3
Traumatic Stress and the Five Factor Model (FFM) of Personality

Personality factor	Posttraumatic changes (PTSD)[a]	Positive transformations[b]
I. Neuroticism		
Anxiety	↑Increased	Low
Angry hostility	↑Increased	Low
Depression	↑Increased	Moderate
Self-consciousness	↑Increased	Moderate
Impulsiveness	↑Increased	Low
Vulnerability	↑Increased	Low
II. Extraversion		
Warmth	↓Decreased	Moderate
Gregariousness	↓Decreased	Moderate
Assertiveness	−Variable	Moderate
Activity	−Variable	Moderate
Excitement seeking	−Variable	Variable
Positive emotion	↓Decreased	High
III. Openness to Experience		
Fantasy	↓Decreased	High
Aesthetics	↓Decreased	High
Feelings	↓Decreased	Moderate
Actions	↓Decreased	High
Ideas	↓Decreased	High
Values	−Variable	Variable
IV. Agreeableness		
Trust	↓Decreased	Moderate
Straightforwardness	↓Increased	High
Altruism	↑Increased	High
Compliance	−Variable	High
Modesty	↑Increased	High
Tender mindedness	−Variable	High
V. Conscientiousness		
Competence	↓Decreased	Moderate
Order	−Variable	Variable
Dutifulness	−Variable	High
Achievement striving	↓Decreased	Variable
Self-discipline	−Variable	Variable
Deliberation	↑Increased	Moderate

Source: ©2004 John P. Wilson.
[a]↑, ↓ = Increased, Decreased.
[b]Level: low, medium, high, variable.

The predictions for changes in personality attributes caused by trauma for the FFM are presented in Table 2.3. The overall pattern of personality change for the five factors is quite variable but uniform in directionality for specific personality characteristics. For example, in Factor I,

Neuroticism, the six personality characteristics all show increases in directionality, indicating negative changes in well-being or increased levels of neuroticism. Specifically, anxiety, hostility, depression, self-consciousness, impulsiveness, and vulnerability show increased levels of dynamic activity in personality following extreme stress that causes PTSD or subclinical forms of prolonged stress reactions. As noted by McCrae and Costa (2003), fear and anxiety are the emotions which underlie the factor neuroticism and therefore conceptually overlap with PTSD as a prolonged stress pattern. In general, PTSD is associated with heightened levels of anxiety which are then expressed in different forms of emotions and behaviors.

Factor II, *Extraversion*, shows a more variable pattern of change in personality after trauma and the onset of PTSD. For example, the personality attributes commonly associated with sociability (i.e., warmth, gregariousness, and positive emotion) are significantly decreased following trauma, reflecting a constriction of ego-processes and a "pulling in" of friendly, outwardly engaging behaviors. In part, this "pulling in" of extraversion is underscored by the absence of positive emotions in PTSD and prolonged stress-response patterns at a subclinical (i.e., disparate) level. On the other hand, the other dimensions of extraversion (i.e., assertiveness, activity, and excitement-seeking) are quite variable in personality expressions after traumatic experiences. These differences in personality attributes reflect variability in coping patterns. For example, some individuals (e.g., rape victims, war veterans) become more energetic, assertive, dominant, and forcefully and vigilantly proactive in their coping efforts. Other survivors become timid, shy, withdrawn, isolated, and reclusive. These differences in personality functioning underscore the necessity of utilizing a person by situation interactional model of posttraumatic coping and resilience (Wilson & Prabucki, 1989), a position echoed by McCrae and Costa (2003) in their Five Factor Model of personality.

Factor III, *Openness to Experience*, shows a consistent pattern of reduction in the functional dimensions of these personality attributes. With the exception of the personality characteristic labeled "Values," there is a significant decrease for the entire factor, *Openness to Experience* (i.e., decreased levels of fantasy, aesthetics, feelings, actions and ideas). The decreases in this personality factor reflect the following PTSD symptoms: problems of concentration, attention, emotional constriction, detachment, diminished interest in significant activities and hobbies, and cognitive restriction in intellectual capacities (see Wilson, 2004a for a discussion). However, the variability in the direction of changes for the personality attributes "Values," underscores the fact that some traumatic experiences cause persons to reexamine their social, political and religious beliefs. Trauma may cause individuals to engage in a search for meaning in their involvement in a life-threatening or life-altering experience. In this regard, then, ideological systems of value and meaning can be reinforced, dissolved or transformed by the nature and quality of a traumatic experience.

Factor IV, *Agreeableness*, shows diversity in terms of potential changes in personality patterns following trauma and the onset of PTSD. The personality attributes of straightforwardness and modesty significantly increase in prominence. Many survivors are frank, open, sincere, and candid about themselves and how the trauma experience "shook up" their existence and situations in everyday life. The experience of trauma causes them to feel humble, small, vulnerable, and self-effacing. In many cases, this is associated with an increase in prosocial disposition and the willingness to engage in altruistic activities (i.e., to give back to others in helping ways). The negative changes associated with this factor are increased tendencies to be mistrustful, guarded, cynical, and vigilant to signs of danger in the world. Moreover, the characteristics of compliance and tendermindedness are likely to show a wide range of variability. Persons showing a posttraumatic increase in compliance will be more prone to forgive and forget; to acquiesce to others in passive, submissive ways which reflect states of insecurity, uncertainty and unsteadiness. Similarly, some persons will show increases in tendermindedness, concern for the well-being of others, empathy, sympathy, and concern for helping less fortunate individuals in society. Conversely, the characteristics of compliance and tendermindedness can calcify and result in increased levels of aggressiveness, self-absorption, "hardheadedness," and overly logical and rigidly rational problem-solving styles of coping and interpersonal behavior.

Factor V, *Conscientiousness*, contains six dimensions of personality, two of which are significantly decreased in posttraumatic states of functioning (i.e., competence and achievement striving). The decrease in these aspects of personality is associated with PTSD and prolonged stress-response patterns. As a result of trauma, various forms of competent functioning may be diminished, including executive functions, concentration, memory, attention, information processing, and feelings of competence and self-efficacy. Achievement striving may diminish after trauma and result in a loss of goal-directedness, ambition, and desire for excellence in task performance. Emotional dysregulations (i.e., affect imbalance) contribute to less focused self-discipline and difficulty beginning and completing tasks. Perhaps for this reason the quality of focused personal deliberation increases. In posttraumatic states, some persons with PTSD feel cautious, timid, reluctant, and fearful of initiating activities and prefer to err on the side of safety (i.e., the *DSM-IV* "C" cluster of avoidance symptoms). In contrast, the personality dimensions of order and dutifulness will likely show variability in posttraumatic states. For example, posttraumatic increases in dutifulness reflects concern with ethical standards, adherence to moral principles and commitment to personal and religious values. In contrast, some individuals with PTSD become obsessed with extreme degrees of organization and require high degrees of order in their lives. In some cases this appears obsessive and compulsive in nature (Horowitz, 1986a). They have difficulties tolerating uncertainty, ambiguity, vagueness, confusion, lack of clear rules, etc., and therefore impose high levels of orderliness on their daily lives. In this regard, order equals control. A sense of control and predictability equals safety, security and a means of reducing anxiety and fears.

The analysis of trauma and the FFM of personality suggest that structural dimensions of personality can be altered in acute or chronic ways. Research evidence (Foa, Keane, & Friedman, 2001) suggests that about one third of persons with PTSD, for example, restabilize and resume normal functioning within a year. In severe forms of psychological trauma, especially those that injure the bases of self-worth, identity, and the capacity to find meaning in suffering, the effects can last much longer. When the basic structure of personality is negatively altered in terms of the capacity for personal growth, the core dimensions of the self are likely to be altered in ways that have important clinical implications.

20 TRAUMA AND SELF-TRANSFIGURATION

A conceptual schema of trauma and self-transfigurations is presented in Figure 2.12. In understanding the posttraumatic self, it is useful to specify the pathways of self-transfiguration and how the core components of personality articulate with each other.

Trauma complexes produce a wide range of impacts to personality processes and life-span epigenetic development (see Chapter 5). Traumatic stressors impact ego-processes and the self-structure, producing alterations in their functional and structural abilities. These various reconfigurations of ego processes and identity structures result in the four principal typologies discussed previously: (1) the Amorphous Self; (2) the Unintegrated Self; (3) the Transitional Self; and (4) the Integrated Self. Each of these typologies of identity and self-configuration has subtypes: (a) ego-fragmentation; (b) ego-vulnerability; (c) ego-coherence; and (d) ego-resilience. Further, these subtypes of self-configuration contain distinct forms of self-reconfiguration that are unique and different from each other, although they share overlapping personality dynamics and characteristics. These subtypes of posttraumatic self-reconfigurations create a continuum of adaptational mental health.

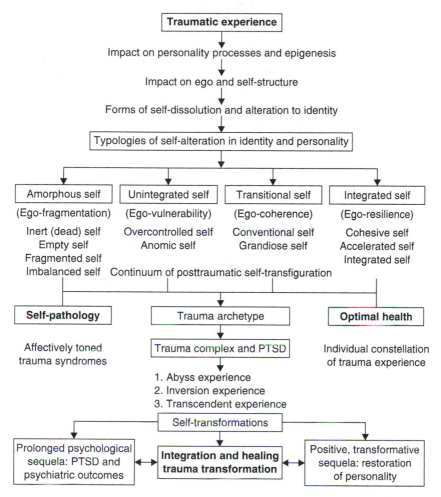

FIGURE 2.12. Trauma and self-transfigurations. *Source:* ©2003 John P. Wilson.

At the pathological end, there are severe forms of ego-fragmentation. At the healthy end, there are integrated forms of optimal functioning (see Chapter 6).

The conceptual continuum of posttraumatic self-reconfigurations provides an operationally definable way of delineating trauma archetypes and trauma complexes (see Chapter 5). Trauma archetypes represent universal ways in which trauma is experienced by the human psyche. Trauma complexes are defined by individually constellated modalities of the trauma experience and include PTSD, psychiatric disorders, and a depth of intrapsychic processes are manifest in dreams, fantasies, motives, emotional states, and personality characteristics. Building on

Jung's ideas of complexes, the Trauma Complex is an affectively toned syndrome that contains the unique and individually constellated nature of the trauma experience. As persons metabolize their traumatic experiences, self-transformations become evident and result in either positive transformational sequelae or prolonged, negative sequelae that include PTSD and distressing emotional states. In this regard, the processes of self-transformation result in various degrees of integration and healing and may be expressed in the Unity Archetype (see Chapter 5).

21 SUMMARY

In conclusion, traumatization is the resultant state of psychic injury inflicted from outside forces. Ultimately, traumatization is an organismic condition; it is injury to the whole of being. All parts of consciousness, executive function, memory, cognitive processing, and somatic expression of its impact are synergistically affected in discernible ways. Traumatic experiences do not stand alone in the mind. Nor is PTSD a unidimensional self-contained syndrome. Trauma and PTSD are twin processes nested in much larger components of organismic functioning. Nevertheless, our focus on trauma's impact on personality processes, the self, ego-processes, and identity has allowed discovery of forms of self-alteration and reintegration following resolution and the healing of traumatic injuries. The forms of self-dissolution have specific typologies associated with ego-processes (e.g., ego-fragmentation, ego-vulnerability, ego-coherence, and ego-resilience). The analysis of the forms of self-deintegration, their categories and typologies, has enabled us to construct a meaningful continuum from fragmentation to integration including specifications to how trauma alters normal personality functioning.

The dissolutions and alterations in the self are part of a larger matrix of psychological changes wrought by trauma. The Trauma Archetype and the Trauma Complex each have a defining set of interrelated characteristics. The Trauma Archetype and Trauma Complex are also twin processes with a nidus in the self. They include the Abyss, Inversion and Transcendent Experiences. The Trauma Archetype is a universal, transpersonal set of experiences, common to all cultures and human communities, which represents one form of archetypal experience. Due to the threat to existence contained in extreme stress experiences, the Trauma Complex may be a more powerful motivational phenomenon than other forms of experience. The Trauma Complex is an individually constellated set of memories, experiences, images and affects which are associated with the archetypal experience of trauma. The Trauma Complex is a construct which is superordinate to PTSD, but which includes the dynamics of the syndrome. It contains the psychobiological impact of trauma, damage to the self, PTSD, residues of the Abyss and Inversion Experiences. The Trauma Complex is a prototypical and mythological representation of reality, interweaving the images of the demonic versus the transcendent. Trauma experiences and their residues may become central in life-course trajectory. The posttraumatic self is the final product of such self-metamorphosis.

REFERENCES

Agger, I. & Jensen, S. (1993). The psychosocial trauma of torture. In J. P. Wilson & B. Raphael (Eds.), *International handbook of traumatic stress syndromes* (pp. 703–715). New York: Plenum Press.

Baumeister, R. F. & Vohs, K. D. (2002). The pursuit of meaningfulness in life. In C. R. Synder & S. Lopez (Eds.), *Handbook of positive psychology* (pp. 608–632). New York: Oxford University Press.

Block, J. (1971). *Lives through time*. California: Bancroft Books.

Block, J. (1981). Some enduring and consequential structures of personality. In A. I. Rabin, J. Aronoff, A. M. Barclay, & R. H. Zucker (Eds.), *Further explorations in personality,* (pp. 27–43). New York: Wiley.

Block, J. & Kremen, A. M. (1996). IQ and ego-resilience: Conceptual and empirical connections and separateness. *Journal of Personality and Social Psychology, 70,* 349–361.

Breslau, N. (1998). Epidemiology of trauma and posttraumatic stress disorder. In R. Yehuda (Ed.), *Psychological trauma* (pp. 1–27). Washington, DC: American Psychiatric Press.

Chu, J. A. (1998). *Rebuilding shattered lives: The responsible treatment of complex post-traumatic and dissociative disorders.* New York: Wiley.

Costa, P. T. & Widiger, T. A. (1994). *Personality disorders and the five factor model.* Washington, DC: American Psychological Association.

Courtois, C. (1999). *Recollections of sexual abuse.* New York: W. W. Norton.

Digman, J. M. (1994). Historical antecedents of the five factor model. In P. T. Costa & T. M. Widiger (Eds.), *Personality disorders and the five factor model* (pp. 13–19). Washington, DC: American Psychological Association.

Dimsdale, J. E. (1980). *Survivors, victims and perpetrators.* New York: Hemisphere.

Erdelyi, M. H. (1990). Repressions, reconstruction, and defense: History and integration of the psychoanalytic and experimental frameworks. In J. L. Singer (Ed.), *Repression and dissociation: Implications for personality theory, psychopathology and health* (pp. 1–31). Chicago, IL: University of Chicago Press.

Erikson, E. H. (1950). *Childhood and society.* New York: W. W. Norton.

Erikson, E. H. (1962). *The life cycle completed: A review.* New York: W. W. Norton.

Erikson, E. H. (1968). *Identity, youth & crisis.* New York: W. W. Norton.

Foa, E., Keane, T. M., & Friedman, M. J. (2001). *Effective treatments for PTSD.* New York: Guilford Press.

Frankl, V. E. (1984). *The will to meaning: Foundations and applications of logotherapy.* New York: Meridian Books.

Frankl, V. E. (1988). *The will to meaning: Foundations and applications of logotherapy.* New York: Meridian Books.

Freud, S. (1895) Project for a scientific psychology. In *Standard edition, 1* (pp. 27–42). London: Hogarth Press.

Freud, S. (1911). *On Narcissism.* New York: W. W. Norton.

Freud, S. (1912). Recommendations to physicians practicing psychoanalysis. In *Standard edition, 12* (pp. 111–120). London: Hogarth Press.

Freud, S. (1916). *The introductory lectures on psychoanalysis.* New York: W. W. Norton.

Freud, S. (1917a). *Introductory lecture on psychoanalysis.* New York: W. W. Norton.

Freud, S. (1917b). *New introductory lectures on psychoanalysis.* New York: W.W. Norton.

Freud, S. (1920). *Beyond the pleasure principle.* New York: W.W. Norton.

Freud, S. (1923). Ego and the id. In *Standard Edition, 19* (pp. 12–66). London: Hogarth Press .

Freud, S. (1928). *Beyond the pleasure principle.* New York: W. W. Norton.

Friedman, M. J. (1990). Interrelationships between biological mechanisms and pharmacotherapy of post-traumatic stress disorder. In M. E. Wolfe & A. D. Mosnian (Eds.), *Posttraumatic stress disorder: Etiology, phenomenology and treatment* (pp. 204–205). Washington, DC: American Psychiatric Press.

Friedman, M. J. (2000a). *Posttraumatic & acute stress disorders.* Kansas City: Compact Clinicals.

Friedman, M. J. (2000b). *Post-traumatic stress disorder: The latest assessment and treatment strategies.* Kansas City: Compact Clinicals.

Friedman, M. J. (2001). Allostatic versus empirical perspectives on pharmacotherapy. In J. P. Wilson, M. J. Friedman & J. D. Lindy (Eds.), *Treating psychological trauma and PTSD* (pp. 94–125). New York: Guilford Publications.

Froddy, M. & Kashima, Y. (2003). Self and identity: What is the conception of the persons assumed in the current literature? In Y. Kashima, M. Froddy, & M. Platow (Eds.), *Self and identity* (pp. 3–27). Hillsdale, NJ: Lawrence Erlbaum.

Gerrity, E., Keane, T. M., & Tuma, F. (2001). *The mental health consequence of torture.* New York: Klumer/Plenum Press.

Goodwin, J. M. & Attias, R. (Eds.) (1999). *Splintered reflections.* New York: Basic Books.

Harel, Z., Kahana, B., & Wilson, J. (1993). War and remembrance: The legacy of Pearl Harbor. In J. P. Wilson & B. Raphael (Eds.), *International handbook of traumatic stress syndromes* (pp. 263–275). New York: Plenum Press.

Herman, J. L. (1992). *Trauma and recovery.* New York: Basic Books.

Horowitz, M. (1986). *Stress response syndromes.* New Jersey: Jason Aronson.

Horowitz, M. (1986). *Stress response syndromes* (2nd ed.). New Jersey: Jason Aronson.

Horowitz, M. (1991). *Person schemas and maladaptive interpersonal patterns.* Chicago, IL: University of Chicago Press.

Horowitz, M. J. (1999). *Essential papers on posttraumatic stress disorder.* New York: New York University Press.

Janet, P. (1900). *L' automatisure psychologiqene.* Paris: Bailliere.

Janet, P. (1907). *The major symptoms of hysteria.* London: Macmillan.

Jaranson, J. & Popkin, M. (1998). *Caring for victims of torture.* Washington, DC. American Psychiatric Association Press.

Jung, C. G. (1929). The collected works (Bollingen series XX, 20 vols.). Trans. R. F. C. Hull. In H. Read, M. Fordham, & G. Adler (Eds.), *The therapeutic value of abreaction* (CW 16). Princeton, NJ: Princeton University Press.

Jung, C. G. (1950). The collected works (Bollingen series XX, 20 vols.). Trans. R. F. C. Hull. In H. Read, M. Fordham, & G. Adler (Eds.), *Four archetypes* (CW 8). Princeton, NJ: Princeton University Press.

Jung, C. G. (1963a). *Memories, dreams and reflections.* New York: Vintage Books.

Jung, C. G. (1963b). The collected works (Bollingen series XX, 20 vols.). Trans. R. F. C. Hull. In H. Read, M. Fordham, & G. Adler (Eds.), *Civilization in transition* (CW 10). Princeton, NJ: Princeton University Press.

Jung, C. G. (1971). The collected works (Bollingen series XX, 20 vols.). Trans. R. F. C. Hull. In H. Read, M. Fordham, & G. Adler (Eds.), *Psychological types* (CW 6). Princeton, NJ: Princeton University Press.

Kahana, B., Harel, Z., & Kahana, E. (1988). Predictors of psychological well being among survivors of the Holocaust. In J. P. Wilson, Z. Harel, & B. Kahana (Eds.), *Human adaptation: From the Holocaust to Vietnam* (pp. 171–192). New York: Plenum Press.

Kalsched, D. (1996). *The inner world of trauma: Archetypal defenses of the personal spirit.* London: Routledge.

Kaufman, J., Aikins, D., & Krystal, J. (2004). Neuroimaging studies in PTSD. In J. P. Wilson & T. M. Keane (Eds.), *Assessing psychological trauma and PTSD* (2nd ed., pp. 344–389). New York: Guilford Publications.

Kessler, R. C., Sonnega, A., Bromet, E., Hughes, M.H., & Nelson, C.B. (1995). Posttraumatic stress disorder in the national comorbidity survey. *Archives of General Psychiatry, 52,* 1048–1060.

Kihlstrom, J. F. & Hoyt, I. (1990). Repression, dissociation and hypnosis. In J. L. Singer (Ed.), *Repression and dissociation: Implications of personality theory, psychopathology, and health* (pp. 181–208). Chicago, IL: University of Chicago Press.

Kluft, R. P. (1996). MDD: A legacy of trauma. In C. R. Pfeffer (Ed.), *Severe stress and mental disturbances in children* (pp. 411–488). Washington, DC: American Psychiatric Association Press.

Knight, J. A., & Taft, C. T. (2004). Assessing neuropsychological concomitants of trauma and PTSD. In J. P. Wilson & T. M. Keane (Eds.), *Assessing psychological trauma and PTSD (2nd e.d)* (pp. 344–389). New York: Guilford Publications.

Koenig, W. (1964). Chronic or persisting identity diffusion. *American Journal of Psychiatry, 120,* 1081–1084.

Kohlberg, L. (1973). Continuities and discontinuities in childhood and adulthood moral development. In P. Baltes & K. W. Schaie (Eds.), *Life-span developmental psychology: Personality and socialization* (pp. 121–137). New York: Academic Press.

Kohlberg, L. (1978). Revisions in the theory and practice of moral development. In W. Damon (Ed.), *New directions in child development: Vol. 2. Moral development* (pp. 49–69). San Francisco, CA: Jossey-Bass.

Kohut, H. (1971). *The analysis of the self.* New York: International University Press.

Kohut, H. (1977). *The restoration of the self.* New York: International University Press.

Krystal, H. (1968). *Massive psychic trauma.* New York: International University Press.

Krystal, H. (1988a). *Integration and healing.* Hillsdale, New Jersey: The Analytic Press.

Krystal, H. (1988b). *Massive psychic trauma.* New York: International University Press.

Lapsley, D. K. & Power, F. C. (1988). *Self, ego and identity.* New York: Springer.

Leary, M. P. & Tangney, J. P. (Eds.). (2003). *Handbook of self and identity.* New York: Guilford Publications.

LeDoux, M. (1996). *The emotional brain.* New York: NYU Press.

Lifton, R. J. (1967). *Death in life: The survivors of Hiroshima.* New York: Simon & Schuster.

Lifton, R.J. (1976). *The life of the self.* New York: Simon & Schuster.

Lifton, R. J. (1979). *The broken connection: On death and the continuity of life.* New York: Basic Books.

Lifton, R. J. (1993). From Hiroshima to the Nazi doctors: The evolution of psychoformative approaches to understanding traumatic stress syndromes. In J. P. Wilson & B. Raphael (Eds.), *International handbook of traumatic stress syndromes* (pp. 11–25). New York: Plenum Press.

Lindy, J. D. (2001). An allostatic approach to the psychodynamic understanding for PTSD. In J. P. Wilson, M. J. Friedman & J. D. Lindy (Eds.), *Treating psychological trauma and PTSD (2nd Ed.)* (pp. 344–389). New York: Guilford Publications.

Lindy, J. D. & Lifton, R. J. (2001). *Beyond invisible walls.* New York: Brunner-Routledge.

Lindy, J. D. & Wilson, J. P. (2001). An allostatic approach to the psychodynamic understanding of PTSD. In J. P. Wilson, M. J. Friedman, & J. D. Lindy (Eds.), *Treating psychological trauma and PTSD* (pp. 125–139). New York: Guilford Publications.

Loevinger, J. (1976). *Ego-development: Conceptions and theories.* San Francisco, CA: Jossey-Bass.

Loevinger, J. (1983). On ego development and the structure of personality. *Developmental Review, 3,* 339–350.

Marmar, C. R., Weiss, D., & Metzler, T. J. (1997). The peritraumatic dissociative experiences scale. In J. P. Wilson & T. M. Keane (Eds.), *Assessing psychological trauma and PTSD* (pp. 412–429). New York: Guilford Publications.

McAdams, D. (1994). Can personality change? Levels of stability and growth in personality across the life span. In T. F. Heatherton & J. L. Weinberger (Eds.), *Can personality change?* (pp. 299–313). Washington, DC: American Psychological Association.

McCrae, R. R. & Costa, P. T. (1996). Towards a new generation of personality theories: Theoretical contexts for the five factor model. In J. Wiggins (Ed.), *The five factor model of personality* (pp. 51–88). New York: Guilford Publications.

McCrae, R. R. & Costa, P. T. (2003). *Personality in adulthood: A five factor item perspective.* New York: Guilford Publications.

McEwen, B. (1998). Protective and damaging effects of stress mediators. *Seminars of the Beth Israel Deaconess Medical Center, 338,* 171–179.

McEwen, B. S. (2002). *The end of stress as we know it.* Washington, D. C.: The Dana Press.

Miller, J. G. (1978). *Living systems.* New York: McGraw-Hill Publications.

Mischel, W. & Morf, C. (2003). The self as a psychosocial dynamic processing system: A meta-psychological perspective. In M. P. Leary & J. P. Tangney (Eds.), *Handbook of self and identity.* New York: Guilford Publications.

Monte, C. & Sollod, R. (2003). *Beneath the mask: Theories of personality* (7th ed.). New York: Wiley.

Morrison, A. (1990). Shame, ideal self and narcissism. In A. Morrison (Ed.), *Essential papers on narcissism* (pp. 348–373). New York: New York University Press.

Murray, H. A. & Klackhohn, C. (1953). Outline of a conception of personality. In C. Klackhohn & H. A. Murray (Eds.), Personality in nature, society and culture (pp. 11). New York: Knopf.

Nader, K. (1997). Assessing traumatic experiences in children. In J. P. Wilson & T. M. Keane (Eds.), *Assessing psychological trauma and PTSD* (pp. 291–349). New York: Guilford Publications.

Nader, K. O. (2004). Assessing traumatic experience in children and adolescents: Self-reports of DSM PTSD criteria B–D symptoms. In J. P. Wilson & T. M. Keane (Eds.), *Assessing psychological trauma and PTSD,* (pp. 513–538). New York: Guilford Publications.

Nemiah, J. C. (1998). Early concepts of trauma, dissociation and the unconscious. Their history and current implications. In J. D. Bremner & C. R. Marmar (Eds.), *Dissociation* (pp. 1–27). Washington, D.C.: American Psychiatric Association Press.

Niederland, W. G. (1964). Psychiatric disorders among persecution victims: A contribution to the understanding of concentration camp pathology and its aftermath. *Journal of Nervous and Mental Disorders, 139,* 458–474.

Niederland, W. G. (1968). Clinical observations of the survivor syndrome. *International Journal of Psycho-Analysis, 49,* 313–315.

Nijenhuis, E. R. S. (1992). Symposium hypnose, trauma en somal van de Nederlandse vereniging nur hypnotherapie. *Tijdschift voor Psychotherapie,* 18(1), 44–50.

Nijenhuis, E. R. S. & van der Hart, O. (1999). Somatoform dissociative phenomena: A Janetian perspective. In J. M. Goodwin & R. Attias (Eds.), *Splintered reflections* (pp. 89–129). New York: Basic Books.

Ortiz, D. (2001). The survivor perspective: voices from the center. In E. Gerrity, T. M. Keane, & F. Tuma (Eds.), *Mental health consequences of torture* (pp. 3–13). New York: Klumer/Plenum Press.

Parsons, E. (1988a). Post-traumatic self-disorders. In J. P. Wilson, Z. Harel, & B. Kahana (Eds.), *Human adaptation to extreme stress: From the Holocaust to Vietnam* (pp. 245–279). New York: Plenum Press.

Parsons, E. (1988b). Theoretical and practical considerations in psychotherapy of Vietnam war veterans. In J. P. Wilson, Z. Harel, & B. Kahana (Eds.), *Human adaptation to extreme stress* (pp. 245–261). New York: Plenum Press.

Putnam, F. (1989). *Diagnosis and treatment of multiple personality disorders.* New York: Guilford Publications.

Putnam, F. (1997). *Dissociation in children and adolescents.* New York: Guilford Press.

Pynoos, R. & Nader, K. (1993). Issues in the treatment of posttraumatic stress in children. In J. P. Wilson & B. Raphael (Eds.), *International handbook of traumatic stress syndromes* (pp. 527–535). New York: Plenum Press.

Rogers, C. (1951). *Client centered therapy.* New York: Houghton-Mifflin.

Saucier, G. & Gobberg, L. R. (1996). The language of personality: Lexical perspectives on the five factor model. In J. S. Wiggins (Ed.), *The five factor model of personality* (pp. 21–51). New York: Guilford Publications.

Schacter, D. L. (1992). Primary and multiple memory systems: Perceptual mechanisms of implicit memory. *Journal of Cognitive Neuroscience, 4,* 244–256.

Schore, A. N. (2003a). *Affect dysregulation and disorders of the self.* New York: W. W. Norton.

Schore, A. N. (2003b). *Affect dysregulation and the repair of the self.* New York: W. W. Norton.

Shapiro, D. (1981). *Autonomy and rigid character.* New York: Basic Books.

Simpson, M. (1993). Traumatic stress and the bruising of the soul: The effects of torture and coercive interrogation. In J. P. Wilson & B. Raphael (Eds.), *International handbook of traumatic stress syndromes* (pp. 667–685). New York: Plenum Press.

Sinclair, N.D., Fr. (1993). *Horrific traumata.* New York: Haworth Press.

Stern, D. (1985). *The interpersonal world of the infant.* New York: Basic Books.

Tedeschi, R. G., Park, C. L., & Calhoun, L. (1998). *Posttraumatic growth.* Hillsdale, NJ: Lawrence Erlbaum.

Tennen, H. & Affleck, A. (1998). Personality and transformation in the face of adversity. In R. G. Tedeschi, C. L. Park, & L. Calhoun (Eds.), *Posttraumatic growth* (pp. 65–99). Hillsdale. NJ: Lawrence Erlbaum.

Tulving, E. (1972). Episodic and semantic memory. In E. Tulving & W. Donaldson (Eds.), *Organization of memory* (pp. 381–403). New York: Academic Press.

Tulving, E. (1983). *Elements of episodic memory.* New York: Oxford University Press.

Ulman, R. B. & Brothers, D. (1988). *The shattered self.* Hillsdale, New Jersey: The Analytic Press.

van der Kolk, B., McFarlane, A. C. & Weisaeth, L. (1997). *Traumatic stress.* New York: Guilford Publications.

van der Kolk, B., van der Hart, O., & Marmar, C. (1996). Dissociation and information processing in PTSD. In B. van der Kolk, A. C. McFarlane, & L. Weisaeth (Eds.), *Traumatic stress* (pp. 303–331). New York: Guilford Publications.

Vesti, P., Sonnier, F., & Kastrup, M. (1992). *Psychotherapy with torture survivors.* Copenhagen: IRCT.

Wiggins, J. S. (1996). *The five factor model of personality.* New York: Guilford Publications.

Wiggins, J. S. (2003). *Paradigm of personality assessment.* New York: Guilford Publications.

Williams, M. B. & Somers, J. F. (2002). *Simple and complex PTSD.* New York: Haworth Press.

Wilson, J. P. (1980). Conflict, stress and growth: The effects of war on psychosocial development among Vietnam veterans. In C. R. Figley & K. S. Leventman (Eds.), *Strangers at home: Vietnam veterans since the war* (pp. 123–165). New York: Preager Press.

Wilson, J. P. (1989). *Trauma, transformation and healing.* New York: Brunner-Mazel.

Wilson, J. P. (1994). The historical evolution of PTSD diagnostic criteria: From Freud to DSM-IV. *Journal of Traumatic Stress, 7*, 681–689.

Wilson, J. P. (2004a) Broken spirits. In J. P.Wilson & B. Drozdek (Eds.), *Broken spirits: The treatment of traumatized asylum seekers, refugees and war and torture victims* (pp. 141–173). New York: Brunner-Routledge.

Wilson, J. P. (2004b). The broken spirit: Posttraumatic damage to the self. In J. P. Wilson & B. Drozdek (Eds.), *Broken spirits: Treating traumatized asylum seekers, refugees, war and torture victims* (Ch. 6, pp. 107–155). NewYork: Brunner-Routledge Press.

Wilson, J. P. & Drozdek, B. (2004). *Broken spirits. The treatment of traumatized asylum seekers, refugees and war and torture victims.* New York: Brunner-Routledge.

Wilson, J. P., Harel, Z., & Kahana, B. (1988). *Human adaptation to extreme stress: from Holocaust to Vietnam.* New York & London: Plenum Press.

Wilson, J. P. & Keane, T. M. (2004). *Assessing psychological trauma and PTSD* (2nd Edition). New York: Guilford Publications.

Wilson, J. P. & Lindy, J. (1994). *Counter-transference in the treatment of PTSD.* New York: Guilford Publications.

Wilson, J. P., Friedman, M. J., & Lindy, J. D. (2001). An overview of clinical consideration and principles in the treatment of PTSD. In J. P. Wilson, M. J. Friedman, & J. D. Lindy (Eds.), *Treating psychological trauma and PTSD* (pp. 59–94). New York: Guilford Publications.

Wilson, J. P. & Prabucki, K. (1989). Stress sensitivity and psychopathology. In J. P. Wilson (Ed.), *Trauma, transformation and healing: An integrative approach to theory, research and posttraumatic therapy* (pp. 75–111). New York: Brunner-Mazel.

Wilson, J. P. & Thomas, R. (2004). *Empathy in the treatment of trauma and PTSD.* New York: Brunner-Routledge.

Wolfe, E. (1990). *Treating the self.* New York: Guilford Publications.

Wurmser, L. (1987). Shame: The veiled companion of narcissism. In D. L. Nathanson (Ed.), *The many faces of shame* (pp. 64–92). New York: Guilford Press.

3

Trauma and the Epigenesis of Identity

JOHN P. WILSON

1 INTRODUCTION

Trauma and the transformation of identity is a universal theme in mythology and an existential reality for the survivor. In mythology, the protagonist Hero journeys into the abyss of dark forces, endures trials of spirit, soul, and body and emerges with transformed consciousness. In the experience of trauma, the survivor endures physical and psychic injuries that creates challenges to identity, the sanctity of spirit, and the strength of selfhood. Images of the Hero and survivor are powerful symbols of how adversity tests human resilience and character. In that regard, trauma and identity are inextricably interlinked in their consequences for human personality processes.

The posttraumatic self is a symbol of a new birth of identity and movement towards unification in personality and integrative organismic wholeness. The transformation of traumatized internal psychic states is a symbolizing process that balances the polarities of self-dimensions. The empowerment of the self through the active metabolism of trauma releases energy which is then utilized in the formation of new perceptions, images and forms of self-reconstruction. As the traumatized person achieves insight as to how his or her inner world of the self was injured by trauma, they become architects of self-reinvention.

Trauma impacts the existing structures of identity and personality organization with varying degrees of force and potential destructiveness. In extreme cases, the structure of identity has to be reconstructed from the ground to the top. The transformation of trauma is the process of reconnecting personal identity, the dimensions of the self and the organization of personality.

In a historical perspective, the analytic understanding of the relationship of traumatic experiences to identity and self-processes has roots which extend to the seminal works of Janet (1890, 1907), Freud (1895, 1917, 1920), Carl G. Jung (1912), and other psychodynamically oriented clinicians who focused attention on critical formative periods of attachment (e.g., Winnicott, M. Klein, Bowlby). John C. Nemiah (1998) reviewed early concepts of trauma, dissociation and unconscious processes and noted that Janet and Freud utilized traumatic and structural models of ego-processes to explain posttraumatic symptom manifestations; one emphasizing the role of dissociation (Janet) and the other repression (Freud). Nemiah (1998) concluded that there are lasting effects of childhood abuse and trauma-related dissociative processes: "the pathogenic effects... extend beyond its role in producing dissociative fragmentation of ego-function and results in severe developmental distortions of entire psychological structure that persist into adulthood as pathogenic conflicts leading to psychiatric disorders and pathological disturbances in behavior and personal relationships" (p. 22; emphasis added).

What are the pathogenic effects of trauma to states of consciousness, identity configuration, the trajectory of life's journey, and the intrapsychic reality of victims and survivors? In what ways does overcoming trauma lead to growth, personality change, and self-transformation? How do persons reinvent themselves in the wake of psychic trauma that alters the internal structures of the self?

Nemiah's thoughtful analysis suggests that there are a wide range of potentially pathogenic consequences generated by trauma. The fragmentation of ego-functions and their developmental sequelae to "psychological structure" can persist into adulthood with potentially pathogenic consequences to self-capacities. The expansive literature on posttraumatic stress disorder (PTSD) and dissociation has documented the diverse ways that traumatic events attack the integrity of functioning at different points in childhood and adult development (Putnam, 1997; Pynoos & Nader, 1993; Nader, 1997; Bremner & Marmar, 1998; Chu & Bowman, 2000). However, what is missing from this research is an explication of how the outer world of trauma impacts the inner world of psychic structure, unconscious processes and the capacity for self-transformation.

What are the dynamics of identity transformation in the posttraumatic self? How do we understand traumatogenesis within an ontogenetic framework? How does trauma produce normal and pathological transformations of ego-processes, identity and the self within an epigenetic life-span perspective? In analyzing traumatogenesis, Erik Erikson's (1950a, 1968) theory of identity formation is a useful framework that provides a way to examine posttraumatic pathways.

The nature of how traumatic events impact identity formation and self-development is a complex subject: it requires a conceptual framework that is parsimonious in order to understand the posttraumatic self. The heuristic value of an integrative model of traumatogenesis is that it permits theoretical and conceptual derivations that are directly applicable to understanding how traumatic experiences shape identity and self-development. Equally important is that these conceptual derivations can be operationalized and tested in empirical studies.

How do traumatic experiences impact specific stages of epigenetic development, the formation of identity during that stage, and the development of the self-structure across the life-span (i.e., ontogenetic development)? Taking a wide-angled look at this question, it is useful to note that Erikson believed that identity formation was a continuous process and changed in stage-related ways during the life-cycle including facing nonbeing and the end of life (Friedman, 2001). In a dynamic perspective, identity reconfigures with each normative crisis in epigenetic development. Traumatic events, therefore, impact stages of life-cycle development (e.g., infancy, childhood, adolescence, adulthood, old age) and influence the trajectory of subsequent phases of self-development.

While Erikson did not explore the nature of traumatic experiences and posttraumatic phenomenology, he did recognize their potential transformative power to emergent psychosocial stages that he identified as normative developmental "crises." Erikson's astute insights include understanding that war trauma could disrupt and change identity. In the 1940s, his clinical work discovered that traumatized war veterans lost their sense of self-sameness and continuity (1968, p. 17). Having experienced the loss of self-sameness and continuity in living, these repatriated combat veterans were described as feeling adrift and without the anchor of their former selves. They had lost a feeling of inner coherence and direction. Erikson (1950b, 1968) coined the term "identity confusion" to describe the altered configuration of identity produced by the stresses of World War II (WWII) to these former soldiers (1968, p. 17). In his career, Erikson examined (1968, p. 47–49) other forms of stressful life-experiences, such as the forced internment of Native Americans, and how coercive governmental policies caused changes in personal and cultural identity. He described identity loss in the formerly nomadic Sioux Indians who, starting in the late 19th century, were

72 The Posttraumatic Self

forced to live in restricted isolation on federal reservations by the dominant Anglo culture and its federal policies. To quote Erikson (1950a)

> The Sioux, under traumatic conditions, has lost the reality for which the last historical form of his communal integrity was fitted...step by step the Sioux have been deprived of the bases for a collective identity formation and with it that reservoir of collective integrity from which derive his status as a social being. (pp. 153–154)

The loss of identity in WWII combat veterans and in culturally displaced aboriginal Americans, illustrates Erikson's understanding of how different types of trauma impact identity formation in historical and culturally relevant ways. The stressors of combat depleted inner resources for coping and survival. The Sioux's loss of a nomadic and spiritual way of life depleted reservoirs of psychic strength built up over centuries of autonomous living in harmony with nature.

2 BACKGROUND TO THE CHAPTER

In developing the ideas on the relationship of traumatic experiences to identity formation throughout the life-cycle, it was necessary to review key reference sources on Erikson's works. First, I reviewed the seminal writings of Erikson's career which were published in books, journal publications, and monographs. Noteworthy among this substantial collection are *Childhood and Society* (1950a), *Insight and Responsibility* (1964), *Identity, Youth and Crisis* (1968), and *The Life-Cycle Completed: A Review* (1962). Critical clinical publications included "The Problem of Ego Identity" (*Journal of the American Psychoanalytical Association*, 1956), "The Nature of Clinical Evidence" (*Daedalus*, 1958), "Psychoanalysis and Ongoing History: Problems of Identity, Hatred and Non-Violence" (*American Journal of Psychiatry*, 1965), and "Growth and Crisis of the Healthy Personality" (White House Conference, 1950a).

To gain information and understanding of how Erikson formulated and evolved his ideas on the nature and vicissitudes of individual identity, two recent publications were valuable sources of his history. The first is a biography of Erikson's life, *Identity's Architect* (2000), by Lawrence J. Friedman. This is a comprehensive and detailed examination of Erikson's life and works and contains invaluable data from colleagues and associates who worked with Erikson throughout his career. As Friedman (2000) points out, Erikson's central concern with the formation and alteration of identity was the dominant theme of his career. Erikson recognized from his own work and that of his protégé, Robert Jay Lifton (1967), that extreme (traumatic) experiences could result in survivors struggling with issues of *continuity versus discontinuity* in their sense of identity. Lifton's (1967) work with Hiroshima survivors demonstrated that traumatic experiences impact stages of identity development and have the power to transform it in many directions with psychological and psychiatric consequences. These themes of identity and continuity in the life-cycle were discussed in the posthumous publication by Erikson's colleagues and associates: *Ideas and Identities: The Life and Work of Erik Erikson* by Robert Wallerstein and Leo Goldberger (1998).

3 TRAUMA AND IDENTITY TRANSFORMATIONS: THE CORE QUESTIONS

Drawing on the rich work of Erikson, it is possible to derive insights, ideas, hypotheses, and clinical applications relevant to the field of traumatology, which includes the spectrum of dissociative phenomena. A similar attempt was made with regard to Vietnam War veterans suffering from PTSD in which it was recognized, as Erikson had observed for WWII combat veterans, that the ego-identity of many Vietnam veterans was profoundly altered by the stressors of warfare at precisely the age (18–22 years) when identity forms to establish a coherent sense of continuity in preparation for an adult role in society (Wilson, 1980).

In the present chapter, questions of theoretical and clinical importance are addressed and their discussion is aided by the use of ten figures. Among the central questions posed by this chapter are the following:

- How do different types of traumatic events impact the *process* of epigenetic life-span development outlined by Erikson?
- How does trauma impact a *specific stage* of life-span development and identity formation?
- How are the processes and *structures of identity* disrupted by trauma?
- How does trauma affect the structure and *function* of ego-processes, identity and the *formation* of the self-structure?
- How does trauma influence, shape or *alter the trajectory* and the unfolding sequence in epigenetic development?
- How does trauma cause *regression, arrestation, intensification, or acceleration* in the normative stages of psychosocial development across the life-cycle? How does trauma affect ontogenesis?
- How does trauma cause dissociation at different stages of identity development? Are there stage-specific (i.e., horizontal) forms of dissociative processes? Are there *traumatic "mile markers"* of stage-specific dissociative processes?

- How does trauma cause *dissociation* in established identity structures in personality? Does childhood dissociation generate carryover effects into adulthood (i.e., vertical dissociation)?
- How are different types of traumatic events (e.g., childhood abuse, war trauma, catastrophic disasters, traumatic bereavement) associated with *horizontal* (within-stage) and *vertical* (between-stage) dissociative processes?
- How does trauma create *links* between early childhood alterations in identity functioning and later adult experiences of stress and trauma?
- How do dissociative experiences, especially repetitive pathogenic episodes, become *embedded within the identity* of the individual and subsequently influence intrapsychic functioning?
- How are deficits in healthy identity *restored* following traumatic injury to self-capacities?

4 ILLUSTRATIONS OF TRAUMATOGENIC EXPERIENCES WITHIN AN ONTOGENETIC FRAMEWORK OF SELF-METAMORPHOSIS

Figures 3.1 to 3.9 present capsule summaries of the material to be discussed. Figure 3.1 presents Erikson's model of the eight stages of identity formation and their basic alteration by traumatic experiences. Figure 3.2 summarizes how traumatic experiences adversely impact ego-processes, identity formation and the self-structure. Figure 3.3 illustrates how trauma influences both epigenetic and ontogenetic phases of identity development. Figure 3.4 indicates how trauma produces alteration in identity and symptom formation (e.g., PTSD, dissociation) for each of the eight stages of epigenesis. Figure 3.5 illustrates how trauma impacts the prepotent self dimensions (e.g., continuity, coherence, autonomy, connection, energy, vitality) associated with stages of epigenesis. Figure 3.6 illustrates stage-specific forms of horizontal and vertical dissociation in relation to traumatic experiences. Figures 3.7 and 3.8 list specific trauma-related changes which occur in identity and self-structures. Figure 3.9 illustrates the process by which de-integration and reintegration of identity and self-structures occur. These illustrations depict traumatogenic experiences within an ontogenetic framework of self-metamorphosis.

5 TRAUMA AND THE EPIGENESIS OF IDENTITY

An integrative understanding of psychological trauma requires a unifying theoretical framework by which to examine injuries to the self and ego-processes. In the most basic formulation, one must ask how trauma breaches the core dimensions of the self and optimal personality functioning. At present, there is not a comprehensive theory of trauma's impact on personality and the vicissitudes of the self. Erikson's theory of the epigenesis of identity provides us with a useful model by which to analyze different aspects of traumatic impact as embedded within stages of ego development throughout the natural history of the organism (see Wilson 2004a, b; 1980 for a discussion).

Understanding trauma's impact on the natural history of life-span development enables us to see the importance of Erikson's theory of ontogenesis to states of traumatization. To undertake such an analysis requires a framework of: (1) ego-development; (2) the evolution of the self-structure and its constituent components; (3) the formation of individual identity states or configurations that are associated with epigenetic and ontogenetic developmental processes; and (4) the onset of PTSD and dissociative processes as a manifestation of posttraumatic alterations in the self.

In terms of personality, the natural history of an organism has a progression and unfolding of life-stages and their associated processes of development, change and diminution. In a holistic theory of traumatogenesis, it is important to specify how trauma impacts intrapsychic and developmental processes. Trauma, as an external force, impacts this organismic ground plan of development at any point between birth and death for every phase and stage of the life-cycle (Wilson, 1980; Pynoos & Nader, 1993). *We may speak, therefore, of traumatogenic experiences within an ontogenetic framework of self-metamorphosis.*

Erikson's (1950a, 1964, 1968) formulation of personal identity rests on a foundation of stage-specific qualities of ego development. Central to Erikson's formulation are five principal concepts: (1) ego-identity formation, which includes the development of a clear sense of who and what one is within a cultural framework. To quote: "Ego-process is the organizational principle by which the individual maintains himself as a coherent personality with sameness and continuity both in his sameness and his actuality for others" (1968, p. 73). (2) The eight epigenetic stages of psychosocial development which emerge across the life-cycle as part of organismic maturation. (3) Ontogenetic development, which is the progression and trajectory of the human life-cycle from infancy to old age. (4) The ego-strengths, identity configurations, and emergent self-structures that are the product of the eight ontogenetic life-stages. (5) Forms of psychopathology, including PTSD, self-pathologies, and dissociative disorders, that may result from the lack of normal developmental progress or as the result of trauma which impacts specific developmental stages with their normative tasks (Erikson, 1968, pp. 66–68).

Age	Developmental crisis (stages)	Ego-strength acquired (virtues)	Traumatic impact and alterations in normative development
0–1 years	Trust vs. mistrust	Hope	Hopelessness, helplessness
2–3 years	Autonomy vs. shame, doubt	Will	Loss of self-regulation, excessive shame and guilt
3–5 years	Initiative vs. guilt	Purpose	Loss of initiative and striving
School age	Industry vs. inferiority	Competence	Futility, low self-esteem
Adolescence	Identity vs. role confusion	Fidelity	Identity confusion, fragmentation, negative identity, alienation
Early adulthood	Intimacy vs. isolation	Love	Isolation, estrangement, detachment
Middle age	Generativity vs. stagnation	Caring	Stasis, self-absorption, hostility
Old age	Integrity vs. despair	Wisdom	Despair, ennui, surrender

FIGURE 3.1. Epigenesis of identity in the life cycle and traumatic impacts. *Source:* Wilson (1980); John P. Wilson, 2003.

At the heart of Erikson's theory are the concepts of ego-identity and the emergent self (Friedman, 2000). Identity formation and self-development undergo transformations across the life cycle in conjunction with stage-specific developmental tasks. Erikson referred to stage-specific phases of development as turning points or "crises" in the trajectory of development. Similar to a clay sculpture of the human body, individual identity begins to cohere and "firm-up" in its early adult form by the end of adolescence. The molding of the clay substance of human identity is shaped by life-experiences within a cultural milieu. Erikson states: "One can then speak of ego-identity when one discusses ego-synthesizing power in light of its central psychosocial function, and of self-identity when the integration of the individual's self and role-images are under discussion" (1968, p. 211).

5.1 "A Distinct Loss of Ego-Identity"

Erikson's ideas about pathogenic alterations in identity originated, in part, from his work with repatriated WWII veterans who suffered from prolonged war stress. The exhausted, fractured egos of combat veterans led to the formulation of "identity crisis" and the loss of ego-identity. Erikson (1968) stated: "our patients had neither been 'shellshocked' or become malingers, but had through the exigencies of war lost a sense of personal sameness and historical continuity" (p. 17). To quote more specifically

What impressed me most was the loss in these men of a sense of identity. They knew who they were; they had a personal identity. *But it was as if, subjectively, their lives no longer hung together—and never would again. There was a central disturbance of what I then started to call ego-identity.* (1950a, p. 42; emphasis added)

In terms of work with veterans discharged from the armed forces...we become familiar with the recurring symptoms of a partial loss of ego synthesis...*the boundaries of their egos lost their shock-absorbing delineation.* Anxiety and anger were provoked by anything sudden or too intense, a sensory impression from outside, an impulse or a memory...insomnia hindered the nightly restoration of sensory screening by sleep and that of emotional rebinding by dreaming...somatic tension and social panic and ego-anxiety were always present...*the men felt that they did not know anymore who they were; there was a distinct loss of ego-identity.* (1968, pp. 66–68; emphasis added)

In reading these passages, it is evident that Erikson understood the phenomenonology of traumatic neurosis, PTSD symptoms, and the loss of ego-mastery in the face of overwhelming and prolonged stresses associated with military combat. In a simple phrase, "there was a distinct loss of ego-identity," Erikson established a theoretical link between the outer world of trauma and the inner world of experience.

Based on Erikson's seminal insights concerning the legacies of war trauma, it is possible to classify the vicissitudes of identity: (1) identity formation is developmentally sequential and a hierarchically integrated process; (2) identity formation is continuous throughout the life-cycle; (3) identity has age- and stage-related critical periods of differentiation; and (4) identity, as part of the self-structure, may be deintegrated and cause discontinuity in the self, especially as a result of severely traumatic experiences.

Identity and self-development is a fluid and continuous process in which the agentic ego confronts a series of psychosocial challenges. Erikson compared the way identity emerges and changes configurations across the life-cycle to embryological maturation, in which parts develop and differentiate in structure and function in an epigenetic manner to form the integrated organ systems of the body. But what if identity formation is injured? *What are the potential consequences of a traumatic experience to any achieved or emerging forms of self-development and identity formation?*

6 EGO-PROCESSES, IDENTITY AND SELF-STRUCTURE: THE NEED FOR DEFINITIONAL CLARITY

Identity formation and self-differentiation are yoked psychological processes. For purposes of clarity in terminology, I will define the inter-related terms of *ego-processes*, *ego-identity* and the *self-structure*. The differentiation between the concepts of the ego, personal identity and the self are resonant throughout Erikson's works. It is also apparent that he struggled to understand their similarities and differences in terms of intrapsychic functioning (1968, p. 211). In order to understand how trauma impacts epigenetic stages of development, it is important to understand the differences between and the interrelatedness of these terms.

6.1 The Agentic Function of the Ego

Erikson (1964, 1968) used the term "ego" in a manner similar to Freud (1923), who stated that "the functional importance of the ego is manifest in the fact that normally control over the approaches to motility devolves upon it" (p. 19). Erikson (1964) stated that "the ego unifies experiences on fronts seemingly remote from one another: awareness and attention, manipulation, verbalization, and locomotion" (p. 118). Erikson is referring to the *agentic function* of the ego: it acts on the external world as a cognitive processing system which attempts to "unify experience." Similarly, the term ego-strength refers to the capacity of the agentic ego to master experience. In Erikson's view, ego-strength grows in capacity and functionality and has an identifiable quality of strength associated with each stage of epigenetic development which he termed "virtue," referring to the integral strength of ego-processes.

6.2 Ego-Identity is Self-Sameness and Continuity in Life-Span Development

The concept of personal identity and ego-identity is central to much of Erikson's theory of identity transformation in the life-span. Erikson (1968) defines ego-identity in terms of its uniqueness of character and those features of agentic functioning that establish identity in mastering experience. He distinguished ego-identity from personal identity. Ego-identity refers to the subjective awareness of individuality and uniqueness as well as attempts to maintain self-sameness and continuity in striving throughout time and space (1968, p. 50). In contrast, personal identity was defined as the reality of the relative consistency of individual behavior in terms of sameness and continuity as recognized by others and oneself. Ego-identity and personal identity are twin processes, reflecting the perception and existence of a unique configuration of personality characteristics which have a "style" of mastery and coping that, in turn, serve to define the qualitative nature of identity. Erikson notes: "the term identity expresses such a mutual relation in that it connotes both a persistent sameness within oneself (self-sameness) and

a persistent sharing of some kind of essential character with others"
(1998, p. 174).

6.3 The Self-Structure is the Intrapsychic Configuration of
Identity Elements

In Erikson's view, the self contains ego-processes and identity
structures and is developed directly from them. The self is a superordinate concept that refers to the integrated structure of identity
elements and the ongoing agentic qualities of ego-processes.

In the most simplified way, we may speak of the ego as *process;*
identity as the *style* or *quality* of sameness and continuity in attempts
at ego-mastery;[1] and the self as the *structural configuration* of intrapsychic experiences, including identity. The self, however, is also an
active force of behavior which influences striving.

6.4 Traumatic Impact on the Agentic Ego, Identity, and
Self-Structure

Understanding the interrelations of ego-processes, identity, and the
structure of the self is particularly important when examining the ways
in which trauma impacts these processes. The aftermath of a traumatic
event can be analyzed in terms of levels of self-injury.

6.5 Altered Ego-Functions: Trauma, Repression,
Dissociation, Amnesia, and Psychic Complexes

As Nemiah (1998) summarized, the ideas of repression, dissociation,
amnesia, and constellated psychic complexes imply that the adaptive
function of the ego has been altered in terms of the capacity for mastery
and unifying personal experience. The resultant consequence of such
alterations is to produce personality changes and symptoms associated
with the intrapsychic organization of mental processes (e.g., perception,
memory, information processing, affect modulation). Freud (1917)
understood, for example, that traumatic experience could impact a
specific stage of psychosexual development and produce fixations,
repressions and tendencies towards regressive modes of coping during

---

[1]"It will appear to refer to conscious sense of individual identity;...to an
unconscious striving for continuity of personal character...[and] as a criterion
for the silent doings of ego-synthesis and ... as maintenance of an inner solidarity
with a group's ideals and identity" (1950a, 1998, p. 174).

episodes of stress. He wrote: "there remains the question of conflicts between the different identifications into which the ego is split up which cannot after all be described as primarily pathological" (1923 [SE], pp. 38–39). Freud's observation raises the interesting question of how the ego gets "split up" in the wake of trauma.

In the tradition of his psychoanalytic predecessors, Erikson looked for parsimonious ways to characterize the disparate aspects of intrapsychic dynamics. Ultimately, he settled on the importance of ego-identity as his central organizing principle and described its vicissitudes across ontogenetic development (Friedman, 2000). Erikson's ideas concerning ego-identity necessitates the explication of how ego-processes are associated with the formation of the self. Trauma's impacts to these intrapsychic *functions* and *structures* can be discerned by differentiating ego-processes, identity formation, and the structure of the self.

7 PSYCHOLOGICAL FRAGMENTATION IN THE AGENTIC EGO, IDENTITY PROCESSES AND THE SELF-STRUCTURE

What does ego-fragmentation mean in the wake of trauma? In the broadest sense, the functions of the ego lose efficacy and competence (see White, 1959 for a discussion for effectance motivation). The loss of efficacy and competence means that specific psychological functions (e.g., memory, information processing, affect regulation) are functionally diminished. In cases of extreme traumatization, the loss of ego-functions includes dysfunctional states characterized by cessation in striving, the loss of coping behaviors, helplessness, and narcissistic wounds to self-capacities. Consequently, the recovery from trauma and the restoration of ego-processes involves the transformation of traumatized states into healthier ones. Ego-functions are recalibrated, regain their optimal levels of functioning and once again act in the service of identity—that is, to restore a sense of continuity and sameness to individual experience. But what if this does not occur? What are the intrapsychic consequences of discontinuity in identity? What if trauma breaks the spirit of the person?

Traumatic experiences may cause a fragmentation in identity. Ego-identity may be fractured by trauma and result in identity confusion; a loss of continuity and self-sameness in terms of attempts at mastering experience (Erikson, 1968, pp. 17, 48, 50). In severe trauma, identity structures are fragmented, get "walled off," and encapsulate within the psyche as separate but coexisting parallel states (Putnam, 1997; Scharff & Scharff, 1994; Watkins & Watkins, 1997). There is a continuum of identity fragmentation that ranges from *transient* states of confusion and instability to periods of *normative* identity confusion to *dissociative identity disorders* characterized by encapsulated, alter personalities created in reaction to interpersonal assault (Chu, 1998; Putnam, 1997; Scharff & Scharff, 1994; Kluft, 1996, 1991). It is also possible to delineate *stage-specific dissociative processes* and their effects on the trajectory of life-course development including forms of horizontal and vertical dissociation (see Section 11.9).

Traumatic experiences impact the infrastructure of the self, producing fragmentation and dissolution of structural dimensions. Psychological trauma may cause ego-processes to dissociate and deintegrate; identity to alter and fragment; and the self to destructure in varying degrees. As noted by Mischel and Morf (2003), Stern (1985), and Wilson (2004a, b), the self-structure consists of interrelated dimensions: coherence, autonomy, energy, vitality, connection and continuity. These six dimensions of the self-structure are altered by traumatic impacts, leading to a destructuring of the individual parts or the entire structure, and may be associated with dissociation of the self.

When the self deintegrates (Knox, 2003), the structural foundation collapses, resulting in varying degrees of damage to the integrity of the structure and, consequently, its functional capacity. Restorative therapeutic efforts aim at repairing the foundations of the self-structure. *The resynthesis of personality processes subsequently includes restoring ego-coherence, identity integration and self-transfiguration.* Transformation of the posttraumatic self requires a recapitulation of identity formation throughout epigenesis. Traumatic impacts to ego-processes, identity formation, and self-capacities that result in pathology are summarized in Figure 3.2. These are basic intrapsychic

Trauma-related processes	Personality dimensions		
	Ego-processes	Identity	Self-structure
Alteration	Dissociation (Horizontal, vertical dissociation in developmental stages)	Alteration Alterations in self-constancy (transitional change in bases of identity)	Destructuring Alteration in dimensions of self (e.g., coherence, autonomy)
Transformation	Deintegration (Loss of efficacy in ego-functions)	Fragmentation Loss of continuity and sameness, identity confusion	Dissolution Loss of structural integrity and Developmental of Dimensions of Personality
Integration	Reconstitution (Restoration of efficacy in ego-functions and cognitive processes) Ego-coherence	Integration New sense of sameness and continuity Identity integration	Synthesis Reintegration of transformation of self-structural dimensions Self-transfigurations

FIGURE 3.2. Traumatic impacts to ego-processes, identity, and self-structure. *Source:* ©2003 John P. Wilson.

transformational processes in the dynamics of the posttraumatic self (see also Figure 3.9).

8 TRAUMATIC EVENTS AND INTERNAL ALTERATIONS IN PSYCHOLOGICAL PROCESSES

Erikson's theory of life-span development is among the few conceptual frameworks that attempt to identify how *internal* states (e.g., identity processes and self-capacities) are causally influenced by *external* events, including traumatic ones. Erikson wrote very little on psychological trauma per se. However, as noted, his clinical work with disturbed children, delinquent adolescents, WWII veterans, and culturally uprooted and displaced Native Americans shaped his thinking about the manner in which trauma is mediated by the ego and its impact on personal identity (1968, pp. 17, 63–68).

8.1 "...a Changing Self and Anticipated Self"

To speak analogically, ego-identity is to functions of the self as the brain is to the body. Healthy brain function is to organismic vitality as identity is to a sense of psychological integrity. Injury to the brain potentially has a range of consequences for health and optimal organismic capacities. Injury to the self and identity, especially by psychological trauma, potentially effects psychosocial functioning at any age and point in life-span development. To quote Erikson

> The ego, if understood as a central and potentially unconscious organizing agency must *at any given stage of life deal with a changing self* which demands to be synthesized with *abandoned* and *anticipated selves*. (1968, p. 211; emphasis added)

This passage is particularly interesting since Erikson observes that the agenetic ego organizes "abandoned selves" and plays a role in creating "anticipated selves." This being the case, the ego must master psychological trauma and find a way to reinvent a new, posttraumatic self, which I will discuss in a later section 11.9.

Understanding traumatic impact on the self is critical to the analysis of the inner world of traumatization (Kalsched, 1996; Knox, 2003). The impact of trauma to epigenetic and ontogenetic development is presented in Figure 3.3. These traumatic effects include: (1) *stage-specific* PTSD development; (2) *stage-specific* identity impacts and alterations; (3) *stage-specific* dissociative processes; (4) *stage-specific* acute and chronic psychiatric consequences; (5) *stage-specific* synthesis and reconfigurations

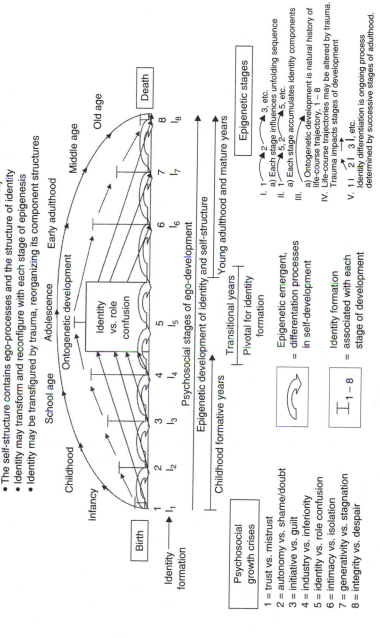

FIGURE 3.3. Erikson's theory of epigenetic development of identity and self-structure. *Source:* ©2003 John P. Wilson.

of identity within the self-structure; and (6) the transformation of trauma and the transfiguration of identity during the life-cycle.

9 THE PREPOTENCY PRINCIPLE AND ALTERATIONS IN IDENTITY AND SELF-DIMENSIONS FOLLOWING TRAUMA

The unfolding sequence in epigenesis means that each normative stage of development has a prepotent set of emergent capacities that includes differentiation of self-capacities. In the wake of trauma, emergent self-capacities can be adversely impacted or severely injured. The structural dimensions of the self (i.e., continuity, connection, coherence, autonomy, vitality, and energy) that are injured by traumatic experiences are presented in Figures 3.4 and 3.5.

9.1 Pathogenic Self-Alterations Caused by Trauma

The epigenetic nature of identity formation permits analysis of how trauma impacts *prepotent identity processes* associated with each stage of development. Each epigenetic stage also has a predominant "theme" and psychosocial modality reflecting degrees of self-differentiation processes. The dimensions of the self that are prepotent for the stages of identity development are presented in Figure 3.5 and illustrate the *primary pathogenic alterations* caused by trauma. I will abbreviate the prepotent stage of identity formation by the letter "I" (identity) and indicate, in a single word, the primary dimension of the self injured by trauma. Similarly, the primary structural dimension of the self will be designated by identifying the most critical component which may become functionally impaired.

In stage one (I_1), traumatic impact on a sense of trust versus mistrust results in disruptions in the *sense of self-continuity*. The emergence of discontinuity in identity and self-processes represents elements of the earliest operation of ego-processes and attempts at establishing mutuality in self-object relations. The earliest and most fragile forms of attachment experiences are disrupted leading to dissociative and detachment tendencies caused by fear, anxiety, threat, or loss. As developmental research has documented, early traumatic loss of critical attachments in self-object relations is among the most pathogenic experiences (Bowlby, 1969; Raphael, Woodling, & Martinale, 2004; Pynoos & Nader, 1993). Dimension of self-structure affected: continuity.

In stage two (I_2), the disruption to a sense of autonomy versus shame/doubt results in self-regulatory dyscontrol, thereby injuring the

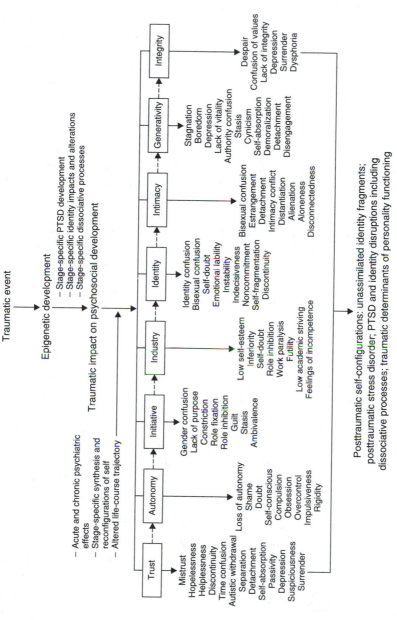

FIGURE 3.4. Trauma and the development of posttraumatic self-configurations in an epigenetic framework. *Source:* ©2004 John P. Wilson.

sense of healthy autonomy in early attempts at mastery over bodily, interpersonal transactions and affect regulations. Dimension of self-structure affected: autonomy.

In stage three (I_3), trauma impacts the stage of initiative and guilt, leading to a sense of separation and loss of connectedness to self and others. This is the childhood antecedent to alienation and estrangement in *intrapsychic* self-referents and detachment in *interpersonal* affiliative patterns which carry over to adult identity processes. Dimension of self-structure affected: connection.

In stage four (I_4), trauma strikes at the development of the sense of industry versus inferiority, leading to a loss of initiative, striving, self-esteem, and self-efficacy. The identity impact at this preadolescent stage is an *altered sense of purposeful striving* and the structural dimension of vitality; i.e., the overall sense of well-being. Dimension of self-structure affected: vitality.

In stage five (I_5), the critical transitional phase of early adult identity, trauma has the potential to cause a deintegration of the emergent identity structure, leading to identity confusion, loss of coherence, continuity, and fragmentation in the structure itself. A fractured sense of identity results a *loss of self-sameness and continuity*. When this occurs, identity confusion can adversely impact the subsequent trajectory of later adult stages. Dimension of self-structure affected: coherence.

In stage six (I_6), intimacy versus isolation, trauma can alter the self-structural component of *connection*, leading to a sense of separation, detachment, estrangement, and unconscious purposeful distantiation from others (Erikson, 1950a; Wilson, 1980). In this way, trauma rekindles earlier vulnerabilities associated with stage three (I_3) when childhood attachments were crystallizing during the oedipal stage of intensified object relations. Dimension of self-structure affected: connection.

In stage seven (I_7), generativity versus stagnation, trauma can cause a *loss of vitality*, leading to states of demoralization, stasis, and a loss of inner sense of aliveness and capacity for generative activity. The loss of vitality as a dimension of the self-structure is associated with depression, dysphoria, and a lack of motivation for career and personal interests. Dimension of self-structure affected: vitality.

In stage eight (I_8), integrity versus despair, trauma in later life can alter the individuals capacity for meaning and result in a sense of disconnectedness from life itself. The self-structural dimension affected is organismic energy; reflecting the disruption and *loss of spiritual vitality*, essence, and biological energy for continued striving. Dimension of self-structure affected: energy.

Epigenesis of identity formation (I)

Self Dimension[1]	I_1 Trust	I_2 Autonomy	I_3 Initiative	I_4 Industry	I_5 Identity	I_6 Intimacy	I_7 Generativity	I_8 Integrity
Continuity	+++	++	++	++	+++	++	++	0
Coherence	+++	++	++	++	+++	++	++	+
Connection	+++	++	+++	++	+++	+++	+	+
Autonomy	0	+++	+++	++	++	+	0	++
Vitality	+++	+++	+++	+++	++	++	+++	++
Energy	+	++	++	++	+	+	+++	+++

Trauma impact:

0	= None or not applicable
+	= Minimal
++	= Moderate
+++	= Maximal
☐	= Primary identity/self-dimension prepotently affected by trauma

Stage of identity formation:

I_1 = Trust/mistrust
I_2 = Autonomy/shame/doubt
I_3 = Initiative/guilt
I_4 = Industry/inferiority
I_5 = Identity/role confusion
I_6 = Intimacy/isolation
I_7 = Generativity/stagnation
I_8 = Integrity/despair

Primary trauma-related self-structural alterations in identity by epigenetic stages[2]

Epigenetic stage and
self-structure impacted — Primary alteration

Epigenetic stage and self-structure impacted	Primary alteration
I_1 Continuity	Discontinuity; trust in self-object reactions
I_2 Autonomy	Dyscontrol; over- and undercontrolled self-regulatory capacities
I_3 Connection	Separation; loss of initiative, purpose
I_4 Vitality	Loss of striving, self-esteem impairment
I_5 Coherence	Deintegration/confusion
I_6 Connection	Separation, detachment
I_7 Vitality	Demoralization, stasis
I_8 Energy	Meaning, disconnection

FIGURE 3.5. Alterations in identity and self-dimensions following psychological trauma. [1]Self-dimensions and PTSD (Wilson (2004a). [2]Self-structured dimensions may be dissociated in acute forms or as chronic dispositional traits. *Source:* ©2004 John P. Wilson.

10 TRAUMATIC IMPACTS TO ONTOGENETIC DEVELOPMENT

Ontogenesis refers to the natural history of an organism. Ontogenesis characterizes the pattern of growth, change and transformations between birth and death. The *critical phases* of ontogenetic development which are altered, transformed, or intensified by traumatic experiences include: (1) normative developmental stages; (2) trauma and regression, intensification of stages and accelerated development; (3) negative and positive polarities of identity formation; (4) acute and chronic effects of trauma on ego-strength; (5) reevocation of traumatic experiences; (6) continuity and discontinuity in self-processes; (7) life-course trajectory; (8) world view, ideology, and systems of meaning; and (9) horizontal and vertical dissociation in epigenesis. Each of these areas will be discussed under the conceptual umbrella of traumatogenesis.

11 TRAUMATOGENESIS

11.1 Trauma and Normative Developmental Processes, Psychosocial Stages, and Emergent Phases of Ego-Development

Traumatic life-events can and do strike all stages of life-span development (Pynoos & Nader, 1993; Nader, 2004, 1997). Traumatic impacts on a specific stage of identity development can have pathogenic or salutogenic consequences depending on the resolution of the crisis evoked by trauma. When trauma occurs, there is a normative and emergent stage of personality development in formation. Erikson (1968, p. 16) designated the term "crisis" to connotate a turning point in development, i.e., that various factors (family, historical propitiousness, trauma, etc.) shape the outcome of a specific stage of identity formation. *Traumatogenesis refers to the development of posttraumatic states.* It includes identity configurations which emerge in conjunction with a specific stage of development impacted by trauma. Traumatogenesis includes PTSD, dissociative disorders, self-pathologies, and alterations to personality processes which are not pathological in nature.

11.2 Trauma and the Intensification, Acceleration, or Regression in Personality Development

Trauma alters optimal functioning in many different ways: consciousness, memory, information processing, capacity for emotional regulation, and identity processes Trauma may cause *regression, intensify* a current developmental stage, or generate an *acceleration* in the rate at which emergent stages appear. Erikson (1950a, p. 78) wrote: *"what if this progress [epigenesis] is impeded, accelerated or arrested?"* The "fast-forwarding" of psychosocial development has been referred to as *psychosocial acceleration* since developmental tasks, moral values, ego-qualities, and ideological orientation emerge prematurely into consciousness and behavior (Wilson, 1980). In psychosocial acceleration, the individual confronts questions of meaning and identity in a manner that normatively would occur in later developmental stages. In psychosocial acceleration identity development skips forward, like fast-forwarding a videotape recording to later events and sequences. Trauma produces an acceleration effect on personality development especially for persons who seem to have innate resilience, independence, and autonomous personality traits (Elder & Clipp, 1988; Wilson, 1980, 1989).

11.3 Trauma and the Emergence of Salient Psychological Themes: The Negative and Positive Polarities of Identity Structures

Trauma impacts emergent identity structures and the configuration of the self-capacities which existed at the time of the stressful event. The effects of trauma on the emergent and existing identity structure have differential consequences for personality formation. These consequences include: (1) the optimal strength of ego-processes in terms of adaptive mastery; (2) the specific configuration of identity elements (e.g., a sense of self-coherence vs. fragmentation); and (3) "thematic" affective-cognitive dispositions regarding self-in-the-world (see later discussion).

Thematic material that results from coping with trauma reflects reconfiguration of stage-specific qualities of identity configuration. For example, *traumatic bereavement* may have radical consequences for an infant if early life-loss disrupts the development of a sense of trust in self, others, and the world, causing a breach in self-object relations and setting up fixed cognitive expectations, beliefs, and modes of information processing (Raphael, Wooding, & Martinek, 2004).

Traumatic bereavement is associated with related to themes of abandonment, dependency, insecurity, and schemas of an unsafe, dangerous, deceitful, and untrustworthy world (Sigman & Wilson, 1998). Each stage of self-development contains psychological control systems associated with levels of optimal functioning, self-efficacy and capacities for affect regulation. Trauma has the potential to disrupt these cognitive-affective control systems and those which are emerging epigenetically at the next stage of development (Nader, 1997; Pynoos & Nader, 1993; Knox, 2003; Bremner et al., 1998). I have referred to this process as the "cogwheeling" effects of trauma complexes (Wilson, 2004a, b).

Clinical assessment of the trauma patient reveals conscious and unconscious preoccupations that are expressed in themes of *trauma-specific saliency* (Wilson & Thomas, 2004; Lindy & Wilson, 2001; Wilson, Friedman, & Lindy, 2001a). The traumatized individual can describe their mistrust of persons, places, and situations; their feelings of self-doubt and confusion; the questioning of their own sense of identity; feelings of personal vulnerability in affective states of dysregulation, and the reevocation of "old [unresolved] issues" which are dynamically associated with changes in emotional well being. These trauma-related themes emerge not only from stressor impacts to a specific phase of identity development and personality, they may be dissociated, fragmented, or integrated within intrapsychic dynamics (see section on dissociation).

11.4 Trauma and Acute and Chronic Effects to Ego-Strength

The impact of traumatic stressors on the fabric of identity structures is akin to the effects of a large-scale disaster that damages the built and natural environment. After disaster strikes, signs of recovery emerge in the environment and the normal cycle of living and growth return. The disaster, too, may destroy existing structures or so altered them that they never regain their original forms of integrity or structural wholeness.

It is a truism to say that trauma has the power to diminish ego-strength and the capacity to master experience. Traumatic experience may drain organismic vitality and create depleted states of energy at all levels of functioning. Indeed, Freud (1917) noted that the ego contracts in the wake of trauma and becomes absorbed in the trauma material.

Trauma can mobilize and extract dormant qualities of ego-strength, resilience, and self-actualizing capacities that are rooted in constitution, character, and experience. Traumatic stressors can facilitate an awakening of consciousness concerning unrealized or denied aspects of identity and character strength (Campbell, 1988). The effects of trauma to self-efficacy vary in duration, severity, and degrees of impairment in coping with internal (self-regulatory) and external demands (coping, ego-defense, adaptation). Research indicates that severe, early traumatization and the loss of human attachments (Raphael, 1983; Putnam, 1997) has long-term consequences for adaptive behavior, proneness to psychiatric illness, expectable problems in motivation, cognitive development, memory, and information-processing systems (Bowlby, 1969; Raphael, Martinek, & Wooding, 2004; Pynoos & Nader, 1993; Nader, 1997, 2004; Schore, 2003a, b).

11.4a The Reversibility of Traumatic Impacts: Resynthesis, Reconfiguration, and ReIntegration of Ego-Identity

Erikson's theory of identity formation suggests that resynthesis, reconfiguration, and reintegration of inadequately resolved stages of development is possible at any point in the life-cycle (1968, p. 211). In this regard, traumatic stress effects, even if prolonged and chronic, are not irreversible nor necessarily pathological in nature. Trauma may evoke positive reconfigurations of identity, transforming structural weaknesses and solidifying them into greater strength of character. Trauma's differential impacts on the structure of the self include: (1) the formation of posttraumatic deficits in personality processes and character; (2) the activation of innate strengths (resiliency); and (3) the transitional and acute intensification of normatively occurring stages of identity formation.

11.5 Trauma and the Reevocation of Prior Life-Crises, Vulnerability and Memory Templates of Ego-States

In the wake of trauma, unresolved areas of conflict remain in memory and have the power to influence behavior and intrapsychic functioning (Putnam 1997; van der Kolk, 1999). Traumatic experiences create ego-states of varying complexity and simultaneously tap into stored memory templates of similar ego-states previously experienced, thereby activating repressed or dormant memory (Freud, 1920; van der Kolk, McFarlane, & Weisaeth, 1997; Nemiah, 1998; Watkins & Watkins, 1997). By definition, traumatic experiences are those located at the extreme end of the stress continuum and constitute threats to psychological and physical integrity. Traumatic stressors have the ability to evoke memory templates of prior states of vulnerability, uncertainty, doubt, fear, anxiety, helplessness, insecurity, confusion, and "feeling adrift." Traumatic memories rekindle states of consciousness associated with processes of encoding traumatic experiences into memory. Traumatic memories in themselves are altered forms of consciousness. As such, they have the power to disrupt the potential for optimal states of psychological being.

The experience of psychological trauma can re-evoke the affective distress and previously dissociated experiences associated with prior stages of development. As the processing of trauma occurs, emotions and cognitions associated with a specific stage of ego-differentiation can reappear. Dysregulated and painful affective states are connected to ego-states and maintain energy to influence thinking and behavior (Watkins & Watkins, 1997). When the effects of trauma induce dissociation, they may lead to trauma complexes as archetypal manifestations of trauma (see Chapter 5 and Wilson, 2004b).

11.6 Trauma and Alterations in the Organization of Ego-Processes, Identity and Self-Structures: Continuity vs. Discontinuity and Integration vs. Deintegration

Traumatic events disrupt the normalcy of daily living, destabilizing adaptive functioning (Wilson, Friedman, & Lindy, 2001a). Severe and prolonged trauma, especially that of an interpersonal nature (Schore, 2003b), alters the entire organization of the self (Goodwin & Attias, 1999). Chronic and repetitive episodes of altered ego-processes produce pathogenic consequences due to excessive allostatic load (Friedman & McEwen, 2004). The system overloads and creates repertoires of trauma-specific adaptive behavior (McEwen, 2002; Wilson, Friedman, & Lindy, 2001a). In this regard, it is meaningful to speak of the posttraumatic self as a unique state of being with its own properties and operating systems governing psychological functioning. The posttraumatic self is a transformed structural reconfiguration of the original structure that existed at the time of trauma.

11.6.1 Trauma and Posttraumatic Self-Typologies: Identity and Continuity of the Self. The posttraumatic self can be understood by analysis of how the intrapsychic processes of self-sameness and continuity are altered by traumatic experiences. Adapting the idea of *identity-diffusion* vs. *identity-integration* and *self-continuity* vs. *self-discontinuity*, four distinct modalities of posttraumatic self-typologies can be discerned (Wilson, 2004a, b). These modalities of posttraumatic self-reconfigurations are distinct styles of ego-processes classified as *ego-fragmentation, ego-vulnerability, ego-cohesion*, and *ego-resilience* (Wilson, 2004a).

There are four basic configurations of posttraumatic identity associated with these ego-styles. (I) *The Amorphous Self* reflects *ego-fragmentation, identity-diffusion*, and *self-discontinuity*. (II) *The Unintegrated Self* is characterized by *ego-vulnerability* and fluctuating internal states of *identity confusion, self-discontinuity*, and *emotional lability* (i.e., posttraumatic affective dysregulation). (III) *The Transitional Self* reflects posttraumatic cohesion and stability in *identity-integration* but with *self-discontinuity*. The dimensions of the self (e.g., coherency, connection, continuity, energy, autonomy, vitality) undergo *transitional transformations* caused by trauma's impact on core ego-processes, producing alterations in substructures of the self. In particular, the dimensions of continuity and connection are impaired and result in a sense of *loss* of self-continuity in time, space and culture as well as a disconnectedness to others, usually associated with psychic numbing (Lifton, 1976). (IV) The Integrated Self is characterized by resilience, vitality, energy, and feelings of wholeness. The integrated posttraumatic self is transcendent and self-actualizing, exhibiting individual creativity and synchronous "flow" in daily living. It is the healthiest form of posttraumatic adaptation.

11.7 Trauma's Impact on the Stages and Trajectories
of Life-Course Identity Development

The ways in which trauma impacts the stages and trajectory of life-course development are listed in brief below.

- Trauma influences stage-specific impacts on ego and identity processes, including regression, acceleration, or intensification.
- Trauma influences the pathways and trajectories of personality development and the formation of character traits.
- Trauma influences adaptive coping styles and ego-defenses leading to alternative forms of personality "trait" development, including those which are trauma-based personality styles which are often inaccurately labeled in psychiatric terms as "personality disorders."
- Trauma influences the reevocation of repressed and dissociated material at any age in the life-cycle.
- The stages of identity development may function as stressors with potential to evoke latent unmetabolized trauma.
- The residues of traumatic experience may fuse or combine with material from all stages of epigenetic development to form trauma complexes (Wilson, 2004a).
- Subsequent stages of epigenetic development present new challenges and opportunities for self-differentiation. These normative crises "open doors" to the past which may have been closed, illuminating new portals of posttraumatic self-discovery.

11.8 Trauma and Alterations in World View, Beliefs,
Ideology, Attitudes, Values and the Search for
Meaning

Monumental historical events and rapid cultural change have the power to produce discontinuities in the self. Lifton demonstrated that survivors of massive catastrophe undergo a transformation in their outlook on life (Lifton, 1967, 1976, 1993; Lindy & Lifton, 2001). To survivors, life just is not the same after trauma: how they feel about themselves, government, religion, and the meaning of life may have changed in significant ways. Trauma survivors say, "I'm not the same person I was before this [trauma] happened." This statement is always true because trauma alters the individual's personal history and adds another chapter to the book of their life's story. The critical clinical question is whether the traumatic residue spurns new growth or leaves unhealed scars.

Embedded within an epigenetic theory of identity and self-formation is the idea that the resolution (positive, negative, partial) of each crisis builds a segment of ego-identity. Ego-strength is a capacity to master experience, which includes an internal, differentiated cognitive structure which contains expectancies, beliefs, and motivational dispositions. These internal cognitive structures contain attitudinal orientations to reality. For example, the formation of the acquired ego-strength Erikson labels "hope" reflects an internalized belief that what is most essential for well-being will be possible to attain. Developmentally, it is among the earliest and most basic qualities of ego-strength which emanates from the stage of trust vs. mistrust. The concept of hope is a construct which includes the reinforcement history of needs, cognitive development, self-other distinctions, and capacity for emotional regulation.

Hope, in an Eriksonian sense, is a word which connotes a quality of ego-strength. It is a mental outlook of what constitutes goodness, trustworthiness, comfort, regularity, predictability and consistency in object relations. Hope is a dispositional attitude of expectancy for obtaining what is needed to sustain self-vitality. As a primordial cornerstone of identity, hope is a building block of attitudinal orientation about the meaning and purpose of life and the "self-in-the-world." In this regard, trauma may alter the sense of hope in the "outer world" in terms of trust of others, governments, agencies, culture or systems of faith, meaning, and ideology. Hope is a variable dimension in the posttraumatic self, reflecting the dual polarities of hope versus hopelessness. *Thus, we may say that faithful survivors never lose hope. Hopeless survivors lose faith and surrender to fate without purposeful striving and will.*

An epigenetic schema indicates that there are meaningful linkages between critical stages of identity development and their relationship to systems of meaning, values, moral reasoning, and ideological perspectives (Wilson, 1980). For example, posttraumatic impacts may create a loss of self-regulation and initiative. A person may lose the will to thrive and give up autonomy, purpose, aspirations, and life-goals (Stages 2, 3, 4, 5). The posttraumatic impacts can lead to a sense of futility, isolation, detachment, and estrangement in intimate relationships (Stages 6, 7). In extreme cases of psychic brutalization, identity deintegrates and results in the loss of selfhood, integrity, and a meaningful sense of self (Ortiz, 2001; Krystal, 1988). Traumatic events, too, impact the stage of generativity vs. stagnation (Stage 7), producing a loss of capacity to nurture, care for family and loved-ones, and find meaning in old age (Stage 8).

Taking a broad view, it can be seen that posttraumatic effects on stage-specific ego-processes and identity structures result in degrees of mistrust, shame, doubt, guilt, loss of initiative, purpose, and sense of connectedness with others. They include the potential loss of generativity, integrity, and the development of a range of psychiatric outcomes (see Figure 3.4). Trauma violates the inherent organismic ground plan of identity formation as a fluid, ongoing natural process in the life-cycle (i.e., continuity of experience) and contains the power to chip away the structural strengths that accrued from optimal developmental experiences. *When the foundation stones of identity are dislodged from their intricate interlocking structural scaffolding, the result is inevitably an alteration in the link between the inner world of traumatization and the perception of the outer world as a source of meaning, purpose and self-directed action.*

Erikson (1968, p. 109) noted that the ontogenetic source of a sense of free will emanates from the development of a sense of autonomy without a loss of self-esteem. The ontogenetic source of purpose is a capacity for self-initiative without disabling anxiety and guilt. For each dimension of ego-identity there is an ontogenetic source that is rooted in the natural history of experience. Traumatic experiences may damage these ontogenetic sources of ego-strength and human resilience.

Traumatic stressors, which strike at the foundations of the self-structure, can be toxic in their effects, damaging the pattern of growth and forcing alterations in the trajectory of self-differentiation in the life-cycle. These alterations in life-course trajectories and posttraumatic identity configurations rest on a continuum which ranges from severe fragmentation to optimal states of integration (Putnam, 1997; Chu, 1998; Goodwin & Attias, 1999; Steele, van der Hart, & Nijenhuis, 2001; Wilson, 2004a).

11.9 Dissociation and Identity: Trauma's "Mile Markers"

How is dissociation associated with the vicissitudes of identity development following trauma? The relationship of trauma to the dissociation of identity is critical to understanding the posttraumatic self. The relation of dissociative processes to core inner structures of identity is like looking at changing images in a kaleidoscope. Each twist of the kaleidoscope changes the view and configuration of identity images. Dissociation that occurs in association with a specific stage of identity formation can be considered as a traumatic "mile marker," as it "marks" the age, stage, and nature of traumatic injury.

The definition of dissociation in *DSM-IV-TR* (2000, p. 519) indicates that the major processes of the self are altered by traumatic experiences. The diagnostic and definitional words, "usually integrative functions of consciousness, memory and identity" implicitly recognize that ego-processes, information processing, memory, ego-defenses, and higher order executive functions can be affected by traumatic experiences, especially those of interpersonal abuse and violence (Chu, 1998; Putnam, 1997, 1989; Bremner & Marmar, 1998). The entire personality structure may be internally reorganized to bolster the capacities of the self to defend against severe trauma (Putnam, 1997; Bremner & Marmar, 1998; Chu & Bowman, 2000; Spiegel, 1994).

The psychological study of dissociative disorders has established that dissociation is a form of adaptive behavior to *external threats* to the self and to *intrapsychic conflicts* in which defenses retraumatized the self (Knox, 2003; Kalsched, 2003; Putnam, 1997). Dissociation can be normal or pathological. Dissociation is integral to trauma complexes (see Chapter 5 for a discussion) as constellated patterns of psychological patterns of unconscious processes (Kalsched, 2003; Knox, 2003; Steele, van der Hart, & Nijenhuis, 2001; Chu, 1998, Nemiah, 1998; Wilson, 2004a, b). *Dissociative trauma complexes contain psychologically nested structural configurations which hold elements of identity, repressed emotions, unprocessed memories, and dysregulated affects.*

12 STAGE-SPECIFIC FORMS OF DISSOCIATION IN EPIGENESIS

Trauma can cause dissociation to occur in different ways in the course of epigenesis. Dissociation and integration, as dynamically interrelated psychic processes, are mirror processes of each other (see Chapter 6 for a discussion). However, there are multiple pathways of dissociation in the unconscious. Ego-processes associated with a specific stage of development can be dissociated in response to overwhelming trauma (Watkins & Watkins, 1997) and therefore constitute *stage-specific consequences.* Moreover, the concept of stage-specific intrapsychic consequences generated by trauma include: (1) stage-specific PTSD development; (2) stage-specific psychiatric consequences (e.g., incubation of Axis II and depressive disorders); (3) stage-specific identity fragmentation; (4) stage-specific self-deintegration; (5) stage-specific reconfiguration of personality; and (6) stage-specific deficiencies in basic need gratification (see Chapter 6 for a discussion). The specific components of identity formation that are dissociated can be considered as *dissociated identity components* of an existing or newly forming identity structure. The dissociative fragmentation process constitutes *partial self-identity dissociation* in which dimensions of the self-structure are dissociated into segmented (fragmented) parts (e.g., segmented aspects of continuity, coherence, connection, autonomy, vitality, energy). Self-capacities can be dissociated in accordance with the prepotent structural dimension of the self being shaped by culture and maturational factors at any point in time (see Figures 3.5, 3.6, and 3.9).

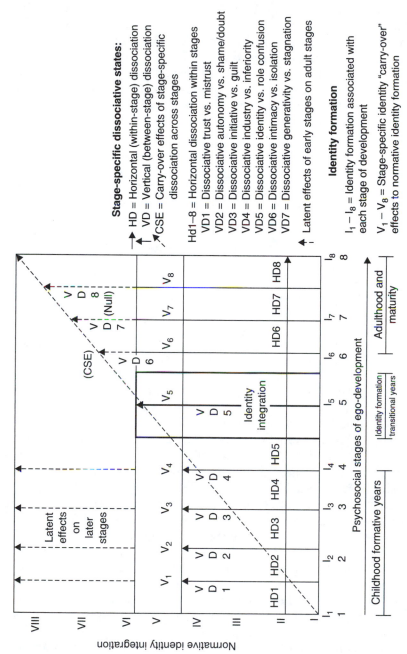

Stage-specific dissociative states:

HD = Horizontal (within-stage) dissociation
VD = Vertical (between-stage) dissociation
CSE = Carry-over effects of stage-specific dissociation across stages

Hd1–8 = Horizontal dissociation within stages
VD1 = Dissociative trust vs. mistrust
VD2 = Dissociative autonomy vs. shame/doubt
VD3 = Dissociative initiative vs. guilt
VD4 = Dissociative industry vs. inferiority
VD5 = Dissociative identity vs. role confusion
VD6 = Dissociative intimacy vs. isolation
VD7 = Dissociative generativity vs. stagnation

Latent effects of early stages on adult stages

Identity formation

$I_1 - I_8$ = Identity formation associated with each stage of development

$V_1 - V_8$ = Stage-specific identity "carry-over" effects to normative identity formation

FIGURE 3.6. Horizontal and vertical dissociative process: stage-specific dissociability in epigenesis. *Source:* ©2004 John P. Wilson.

Traumatic events and psychic dissociability are comparable to the impact of a projectile on a target. In a manner similar to a bullet striking its target, trauma can damage parts of the object or obliterate the entire mass, exploding it into splintered pieces of its former, structurally integrated design. Like a high-explosive hollow-point bullet, trauma produces splitting of ego-processes and elements of identity. And depending on the velocity and type of bullet, it may penetrate cleanly through the target or tear it into shredded pieces that fly into the air. The fragmented dimensions of the self include dissociated states of self-processes and identity (Knox, 2003; Kalsched, 2003; Watkins & Watkins, 1997; Putnam, 1997; Bremner, Vermutten, Southwick, Krystal, & Charney, 1998). The nature of dissociated states of identity resurrects Freud's (1923, p. 38) question of "conflicts between different identifications into which the ego is split up."

13 HORIZONTAL AND VERTICAL DISSOCIATION IN EPIGENESIS

Research shows that dissociative processes can exist as states or traits of personality (Putnam, 1997). Dissociative ego-states or enduring personality attributes can be evoked (e.g., as adaptive defenses) in response to perceived threats, situations of unusual stress or by stimuli that reactivate memory templates of past experience by trauma-specific cues (TSC) (Wilson, Friedman, & Lindy, 2001a). Once developed as intrapsychic mechanisms, dissociative processes can be integrated into the structure of the self or remain deintegrated outside the core self, like a satellite orbiting the earth (Knox, 2003; Putnam, 1997; Goodwin & Attias, 1999; Watkins & Watkins, 1997).

To illustrate the mechanisms of horizontal and vertical dissociation in epigenesis, consider the image of an eight-story building. Similar to an elevator lift rising through the floors of the building, each of the eight stages of epigenesis has a separate "floor" of identity elements with a collection of psychic objects and accumulated experiences stored in memory. The architecture of the building, like that of self-differentiation across epigenesis, has different "levels" that contain their unique properties that can be accessed through the entrance way to each "floor" of epigenesis and the experiences that occurred during that time. Each floor is unique but the floors all reside within the architectural identity of the building. Analyzed in this way, the role of dissociation in epigenesis has vertical (between-stages) and horizontal (within-stages) features that coexist in the architecture of the self.

It is possible to define horizontal and vertical dissociative processes more precisely using an epigenetic framework. Building on Erikson's (1950a) theory of infantile sexuality in which psychosexual and psychosocial modalities of development are described, it is possible to consider zones, modes, and modalities as arenas of ego-development in which dissociative processes can occur.

13.1 Linking Psychosexual Zones, Modes, and Modalities to Dissociation

In the way of summary, Erikson (1950a) distinguishes between zones, modes, and modalities of psychosexual functioning. There are *organismic zones* of the body (i.e., oral, anal, and genital). There are five *biologically based organ modes* (i.e., (I) incorporative passive, (II) incorporative active, (III) retentive, (IV) eliminative, and (V) intrusive) which have associated *psychobiological modalities* (e.g., (a) to get, to take; (b) to hold on, to let go; (c) to make, to pursue, (d) to make things, to learn industry; and (e) to establish individual identity) that emerge with physical and emotional maturation associated with each developmental stage. The psychosexual zones each have an epigenetic time of ascendance, time of maturation, and time of integration into developing structures of personality and ego-development, including the self-structure. Thus, each zone has a prepotent stage with a primary organ modality (e.g., incorporative, intrusive) associated with it. Erikson (1950a, p. 78) notes that there can be fixations that occur *within* a zone in any organ modality (i.e., primary or auxiliary modes). He characterizes deviation within a zone as a form of *zone fixation*. In contrast, a *vertical fixation* "represents a clinging to a mode which has proved satisfactory" (p. 78) and then carries over to the subsequent stages of epigenetic development and can appear later in adult mental functioning in all spheres of behavior (e.g., fantasy, dreams, wishes, sexuality, attachment behaviors, social relationships, coping styles). Thus, *horizontal and vertical fixation* occurs within a zone of organ development and a specific type of developing modality. As noted earlier, Erikson asks: "what if this progress is impeded, accelerated or arrested?" (1950a, p. 78).

13.2 Trauma, Fixations, and Proneness to Dissociation

In an analogous way, we can describe horizontal and vertical dissociative processes associated with each psychosexual zone, organ mode, and modality. Horizontal and vertical dissociative processes "piggyback" on horizontal and vertical fixations that occur in specific stages in life-course development. However, the most impactful and consequential of these dissociative processes occur during the first five stages of epigenesis, influencing the resultant initial structure of ego-identity in stage five (i.e., I_5, identity vs. role confusion).

13.3 Stage-Specific Dissociative Processes of Identity Formation

It is possible to see, then, that *horizontal dissociative processes* are stage-specific modalities of adaptive mechanisms that include common forms of dissociation (e.g., depersonalization, derealization, amnesia). *Horizontal dissociation occurs in response to trauma within the current prepotent stage of epigenetic and identity development.* It may occur, as well, for any organ modality (e.g., retention vs. elimination) in which a psychosocial modality becomes dissociated and takes on unconscious motivational power. *Vertical dissociation processes* are hierarchical integrations and "carry-over" effects of dissociation from a stage of epigenesis into those which follow sequentially (see Figure 3.6A). They may be expressed in adult behavior in conscious, unconscious or symbolic forms. For example, Dissociative Identity Disorder (DID) can be considered as a manifestation of *vertical synthesis* of dissociative processes within a larger framework of identity processes *and* the self-structure. The dissociative (i.e., encapsulated or "walled-off") components of identity become amalgamated into a superordinate structure of personality processes in DID (Putnam, 1997; Watkins & Watkins, 1997). Vertical dissociation occurs across stages in a sequential and hierarchical manner. Similarly, dissociated psychosocial modalities (e.g., to get, to take; to hold on, let go) may carry over to become personality traits as well as manifestations of fixations or "mile markers" of where traumatic experiences occurred.

14 ANALYTIC ARCHAEOLOGY: THE DISCOVERY OF HORIZONTAL AND VERTICAL DISSOCIATIVE ARTIFACTS

Analytic reconstruction of epigenetic development allows us to locate dissociated identity elements that were "walled-off" and encapsulated in psychic cocoons of safety. Dissociated memories, emotions, and motives are part of the interior of interconnected ego-space and their underlying neural networks, and they remain sequestered in encapsulated and protected areas of psychic life. The therapeutic reconstructive process is similar to an archaeologist uncovering artifacts of civilization that once existed as part of an ancient city. Archaeological discovery reveals that there are pieces of utilitarian objects, remnants of architectural structures, bone fragments, and decimated walls of buildings. By collecting and analyzing the archaeological fragments, the scientist is able to reconstruct

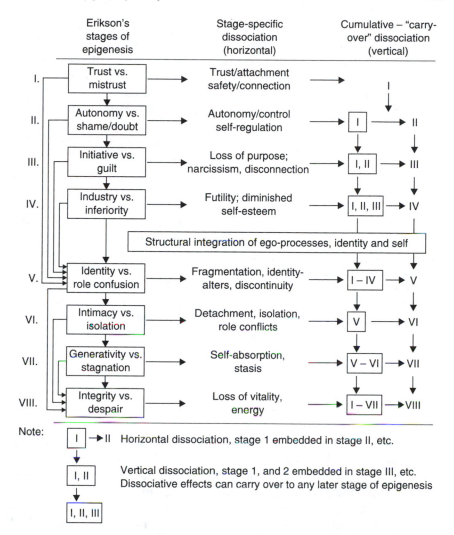

FIGURE 3.6A. Trauma and horizontal and vertical dissociative processes in epigenesis. *Source:* ©2004 John P. Wilson.

the nature of the ancient city and its patterns of daily activity. In doing so, he or she reconstructs the structural configuration that once existed and, by deduction, the processes it demanded for functioning.

Through analytic reconstruction, the therapist uncovers dissociated fragments of identity for stages of epigenetic development and their relation to trauma which, in turn, identifies points of fixation and the implementation of dissociative mechanisms. *Dissociation that occurs during a specific stage of development creates a horizontal axis of identity deintegration. The subsequent fragmentation of structural identity crystallizes into subidentities or remains split off and freely floating in ego-space, like debris upon the surface of the ocean.* As development progresses, these subidentities are incorporated into new identity configurations as part of the self-structure or coexist as discrete and encapsulated sectors of psychic functioning (Knox, 2003; Putnam, 1997; Kluft, 1991; Ross, 1989; Watkins & Watkins, 1997).

In an epigenetic sense, the hierarchical synthesis of dissociated identity elements is nearly complete by the resolution of the fifth stage of identity formation (see Figures 3.1 and 3.4). After stage 5 (I_5), the trajectory of self-development is subsequently shaped by the early adult identity structure that embeds dissociated elements from earlier stages that have the power to influence the trajectory of later growth (i.e., in stages 6 (I_6), 7 (I_7), and 8 (I_8)). I have termed this process the "cogwheeling effect" (see Chapter 5). Dissociative processes are *embedded epigenetically* and are conceptually inseparable from the self-structure and the basis of identity configuration. Once formed as adaptive mechanisms, dissociative processes "cogwheel" between stages in the life-cycle, generating psychic complexes that contain their own motivational power and appear in dreams, fantasies, unconscious motivation, and psychoformative processes (Knox, 2003).

14.1 Looking Backward: "Blind and Unpredictable Force of Trauma"

Configurations of identity that comprise the self are integral components of intrapsychic life. As noted, the role of the ego is that of "active mastery." Active mastery means protecting the self against threats, anxiety and harm; to bring libidinal need gratification that insures a sense of vitality and psychic wholeness. Erikson writes: "the ego thus is the guardian of meaningful experience, that is, of experience individual enough to guard the unity of the person; and it is adaptable enough to master a significant portion of reality with a sense, in this world of blind and unpredictable forces, of being in an active state" (1964, p. 148).

How does the ego master the "blind and unpredictable forces" of trauma? How does the ego master and integrate into the self the residues of traumatic experiences that threatened its very existence?

Looking backwards at the process of epigenesis, a partial answer to the question of ego mastery of "blind and unpredictable forces" begins to emerge and illuminate the processes by which the ego transforms trauma and integrates overwhelming experience into the self-structure.

The foundation stones of identity that have been attacked by trauma are rebuilt with the same ontogenetic sources of human courage, resilience, strength, and integrity. *The transfiguration of trauma requires a recapitulation of critical aspects of epigenesis that were injured by traumatic experiences and their transformation into a new structural configuration in the posttraumatic self.* The transfiguration of trauma also requires the restoration of optimal states of consciousness that are not disrupted intrusively by traumatic memory, affects, and perceptual processes. The rebuilding of a sense of safety and self-esteem serve as "guardians of meaningful experience," and sets in motion a drive towards intrapsychic unity.

The transfiguration of trauma requires the reestablishment of trust in oneself and faith in carefully selected others who will safeguard vulnerability and serve as foils against self-destruction, exploitation or the regressive withdraw into helplessness. The capacity to regain authentic control and autonomy restores self-esteem and self-determination (see Figure 3.8). The capacity to envision new purposes and goals, and to initiate meaningful pursuits is reestablished, further reinforcing trust in self and the free choice of pursuits. As a sense of trust, control of one's life, and the capacity to see a meaningful future uncompromised by shame, doubt, guilt, despair, and uncertainty develops, there is a gradual return of a sense of coherence and continuity within the self-structure. The core of the self-structure strengthens and solidifies (Kluft, 1991). The capacity to trust oneself now extends to others of personal significance as it did to the prototype of the maternal or nurturing person in the earliest years. Stable self-object relations contravene states of isolation, alienation, purposeful distantiation, and detachment from psychological intimacy (Wilson, 2004a, 1980). The world of social connections is reestablished, manifesting a capacity to care for oneself and others without fears of loss, self-annihilation, abandonment, or abusive relationships.

15 HIERARCHICAL INTEGRATION AND RESYNTHESIS OF IDENTITY IN THE POSTTRAUMATIC SELF

The process of transfiguring identity after trauma involves a hierarchical resynthesis of ego-strengths accrued from the previous stages which contributed to the level of optimal functioning present when trauma struck at the integrity of the self. The epigenetic cycle of identity formation recapitulates itself and sets the organism in motion for recovery. In this regard, it is possible to envision a set of nested boxes in which reside all the Eriksonian dimensions of ego-strength accumulated across life-span development. In reverse order: wisdom, care, love, fidelity, competence, purpose, will, and hope (see Figure 3.1). These elements of ego-strength are resynthesized and hierarchically integrated within the posttraumatic self. Trauma therapists have used the term

1. Trauma and normative developmental processes and psychosocial stages including emergent life-crises

2. Trauma and the epigenesis of personality, ego-identity and self-differentation.

3. Trauma and the emergence of salient psychological themes: the negative and positive polarities of identity structures

4. Trauma and acute and chronic effects on ego-strength and the structure of identity

5. Trauma and the reevocation of prior life crises, vulnerabilities and memory templates of ego-states

6. Trauma and alterations in the organization of ego-processes, identity and self-structures

7. Trauma and alterations in world view, beliefs, ideology, attitudes, values and systems of meaning and purpose

8. Trauma and the transfiguration of individual identity: Healing transformations by hierarchical recapitulation of epigenesis

FIGURE 3.7. Traumatic impacts to psychosocial development and to the self-structure. *Source:* ©2003 John P. Wilson.

"safe-sanctuary" to characterize a therapeutic environment in which transfigurations of the self can occur (Wilson & Lindy, 1994; Wilson, Friedman, & Lindy, 2001; Parsons, 1988; Ochberg, 1988, 1993). If nothing else, good posttraumatic therapies build relationships of trust and safety. In the context of the safe sanctuary and therapeutic alliance, the posttraumatic self can begin to reintegrate (Wilson, Friedman, & Lindy, 2001a). In varying degrees, the elements of ego-strength reemerge, like new spring growth in a plant which lay dormant during the harsh, inclement months of winter when covered by snow and ice (Figure 3.7).

16 TRAUMA-RELATED THEMES OF ALTERATIONS IN IDENTITY

Employing a panoramic perspective of the Eriksonian stages of development, a more universal classification of trauma-related themes of alterations in the self-structure becomes transparent. These trauma-related themes reflect organismic striving to formulate personal meaning as an outgrowth of powerful life experiences. This, then, is the task of self-transformation and the creation of a posttraumatic self.

Traumatic experiences impact the self-structure and its dimensions, attacking the infrastructure of the self, disrupting the intrapsychic and adaptive functions of continuity, connection, coherence, vitality, autonomy, and energy (Steele, van der Hart, & Nijenhuis, 2001). Understanding traumatogenic effects on the self allows specification of traumatic alterations in identity and their traumatic representations in consciousness and behaviors.

The concept of discontinuity in identity was explored by Lifton (1993) in his studies of Hiroshima survivors, Nazi doctors, Vietnam War veterans, victims of thought reform, and victims of terrorism (Lifton, 1967, 1976, 1979, 1993; Lindy & Lifton, 2001). His studies inform us that the critical dimensions of the self-structure can be acutely or chronically damaged. So pervasive and predictable are the effects of extreme stress on an individual's sense of continuity and wholeness that it is surprising severe mental illness does not result more often as a posttraumatic condition (Mueser & Rosenberg, 2001). Nevertheless, the alterations in self-structure associated with psychological trauma can be understood at different levels of intrapsychic and psychosocial functioning. Figure 3.8 summarizes the different forms and pathways of alteration in self-structure and are discussed below, beginning with loss of self-continuity and the onset of identity confusion.

17 IDENTITY CONFUSION AND THE LOSS OF CONTINUITY IN THE POSTTRAUMATIC SELF

An alteration in a sense of self-sameness and continuity is a prototypical form of identity confusion, reflecting a break in connection with esteem-enhancing experiences that preserve important parameters of individual identity. An alteration in identity characterized by degrees of discontinuity and lack of self-sameness is part of deintegration and ego-fragmentation (Knox, 2003). The dismantling of the component parts of the self creates a cascade of psychological effects, with rippling effects to the capacity for affect regulation, intimacy, nurturance, self-care, and social relations.

17.1 Continuity and Time Confusion

As the self undergoes a process of deintegration (Knox, 2003), the core structure of the self begins to change (Wilson, 2003a). *Time confusion* may permeate consciousness, with the recent past seeming like a lifetime ago from an estranged sense of one's life. The traumatized self experiences *a loss of time perspective* or confuses the perception of viable time left for having a meaningful future life. The personal sense of "time" and "space" and the role of the self within them may seem blunted, confused, distorted, or warped in perspective because of the prepotency

1. Identity alteration is a sense of loss, self-sameness, and continuity following trauma

2. Identity alteration is a sense of loss and self-coherence following trauma

3. Identity alteration is the experience of ego-fragmentation and self-dissolution following trauma

4. Identity alteration is the loss of, or confusion of, time perspective of the self-trajectory in the future following trauma

5. Identity alteration is self-consciousness characterized by uncertainty, doubt, self-recrimination, vulnerability, shame, guilt, and inadequacy following trauma

6. Identity alterations in a sense of meaning and system of values following trauma

7. Identity alterations result in a disrupted loss of capacity to modulate affective states and feelings evoked by trauma

8. Identity alterations result in a loss of capacity to trust self and others

9. Identity alterations result in "attachment-related trauma" in the capacity to identify with significant others, tasks of parenting, nurturance, work, and child-rearing

10. Identity alterations result in powerful distantiation, alienation, and detachment in intimate relations following trauma

11. Identity alterations may be dominated by psychic numbing and emotional anesthesia associated with the core aspects of the self-structure following trauma

12. Identity alterations may be characterized by stasis in psychological growth; traumatogenetic induced fixations, regressions, or arrestation in normal developmental processes

13. Identity alterations may be characterized by alienation and estrangement from culture, authority, and sources of perceived support following trauma

14. Identity alteration may be characterized by predominant, obsessive, self-destructive thoughts of suicidal self-annihilation following trauma

FIGURE 3.8. Trauma-related themes of identity alterations. *Source:* ©2003 John P. Wilson.

of trauma's imprint on "now" awareness and future orientation. Trauma survivors find it difficult to place the past into a viable time perspective when the immensities and consequences of trauma consume the reality of the moment. In the wake of immersion into the abyss of trauma, the distant future becomes a meaningless issue (Reis, 1995). From the survivor's perspective, what is the point of contemplating tomorrow when the reality of "now" in the posttraumatic ashes of trauma is the most "real" and tangible focus of daily living?

17.2 Trauma and Purposeful Distantiation

The cascade effects of identity alteration generated by psychic trauma flow into areas of psychosocial functioning and individual responsibilities. Trauma-induced identity alterations affect the capacity to work, parent, teach, care for oneself, and sustain emotional and sexual intimacy. The loss of trust in self and others in the wake of trauma extends to authority, government, organized religion, and other institutions or persons imbued with power. The destructuring of the self is, in itself, a loss of autonomy that makes it difficult to identify with others and roles in society. *Purposeful distantiation* (Wilson, 1980) and detachment from others reflects self-alienation and estrangements from the "old self" (Erikson, 1968, p. 136). The power of trauma, especially in extreme experiences such as terrorism, guerrilla warfare, torture, political internment, cultural dislocation and refugee status, repetitive abusive experiences, etc., may cause a reexamination of systems of meaning and future goals (Putnam, 1997; Wilson & Drozdek, 2004).

17.3 Alienation and Self-Estrangement

The posttraumatic experience of reappraising personal values and the meaning of existence is a correlate of the attempts to resynthesize the self-structure. Erikson (1968, 1964) recognized that alienation and estrangement from culture and authority are isomorphic with internal struggles with maintaining self-coherency and consistency (Friedman, 2000). A fragmented self that has experienced deintegration manifests psychological stasis (Lifton, 1976, 1967, 1993). For trauma survivors the painful process of self-renewal is an attempt to overcome a loss of coherence and self-discontinuity. The emotional core of the self is experienced as numb, fragile, vulnerable and a potential repository for guilt, shame, self-recrimination, self-doubt, and uncertainty (see Chapter 9 for a discussion).

17.4 Suicide as the Obliteration of Identity

In extreme cases, the dispirited, empty, and severely demoralized person experiences wishes to annihilate himself or herself. The desolate and vacuous posttraumatic self experiences a desire to end the numbing confusion, depression, pain, inner torment, self-fragmentation, and sense of nonbeing by taking the final step in fantasy or action of terminating their existence. Such actions can be an unconscious last act; a desperate attempt at self-control in the face of helplessness and hopelessness. Eckhart Tolle (1999), in an autobiographical voice, speaks of his depression, suicidal wishes, and the desire to obliterate himself

> The most loathsome thing of all, however, was my own existence. What was the point of continuing to live with this burden of misery? Why carry on with this continuous struggle? *I could feel that a deep longing for annihilation, for non-existence, was now becoming much stronger than the instinctive desire to continue to live*...Then I suddenly became aware of what a peculiar thought it was. Am I one or two? If I cannot live with myself, there must be two of me: the "I" and the "self" that "I" cannot live with. (p. 1; emphasis added).

Suicidal ideation, beyond concrete plans, contains psychoformative images of destroying an inner identity that is rejected, if not despised, because of its inert and confused quality. *States of profound despair and identity fragmentation in which the self is experienced as decimated in vitality, coherence, and continuity give birth to death imagery. In this regard, suicide is a self-willed act of total identity obliteration.* In killing oneself, the person furtively attempts to terminate the source of their pain; to end the persistent struggle to overcome their existence in the darkness of the abyss, the traumatic vortex with magnetic power that seems inescapable at the moment of suicide. In the darkness of existence, the magnetic power of the traumatic vortex is that it offers an illusion of a respite from despair and the tormenting of the soul. In the absence of hope, the "pulling" power of the dark, traumatic vortex grows in strength and its illusory appeal for serenity from pain and seemingly inescapable feelings of nothingness and meaninglessness.

18 SEAT OF THE SOUL: RENEWAL AND TRANSFORMATION IN THE POSTTRAUMATIC SELF

In their narratives, victims of trauma report the breakdown of trust, and the loss of autonomy, initiative, and self. They report a sense of loss, shame, anger, isolation, and an unclear sense of personal identity. They search for new sources of meaning in themselves and through relationships with others. A therapeutic milieu of support, constancy and authentic, accurate empathy provides a reference point in their confused and discordant experiences (Wilson & Thomas, 2004). A healing environment provides a directional vector to guide their treatment and recovery. In self-pathologies, damage to the structure of the self caused by relational trauma (e.g., childhood abuse, torture, interpersonal violence) is more deleterious to long-term readjustment than are other symptoms of PTSD, such as intrusive memories, startle responses, or acquired phobic reactions (Wilson, Friedman, & Lindy, 2001a; Goodwin & Attias, 1999; Courtois, 1999). This is so because the self contains the seat of the soul (Wilson, 2004a).

Posttraumatic interventions of a clinical nature involve a set of processes designed to restore a healthy sense of self, a coherent and integrated ego-identity (see Foa, Friedman, & Keane, 2001; Wilson, Friedman, & Lindy, 2001, for a review of posttraumatic treatment methods and objectives). Beyond understanding PTSD as a trauma complex, posttraumatic therapy aims to repair damage to self-processes; to facilitate the integration of the trauma experience into non-pathological modalities of functioning. The process involves a transfiguring of pretraumatic components of the self into a new synthesis and configuration (Wilson, 1989, 2001). The dynamics of such a synthesis are, of course, idiosyncratic and capitalize on areas of residual strengths, the amelioration of damaged components of the self-structure, and insight as to how trauma caused psychic injuries. In posttraumatic psychotherapy, the therapist is taking care of the soul in its various identities. Moreover, in a manner similar to a surgeon who repairs clogged arteries of the heart or potentially lethal aneurysms of the brain, posttraumatic therapy assesses how the "organs" of the self-structure and identity have been damaged. Clinical interventions require different modalities of treatment in order to mobilize the organism's natural striving towards optimal adaptive functioning following traumatic life-experiences (Wilson & Keane, 2004). *Transfiguring the self-structure and ego-identity involves a hierarchical resynthesis and recapitulation of individual identity functions throughout the life-cycle to the age and stage of traumatization.*

Posttraumatic traumatization in identity processes requires a reconfiguration of self-capacities since identity is embedded within the self. This structural reconfiguration is a complex and intricate process that occurs at all levels of consciousness. Unconscious defenses are erected to protect the vulnerable areas of identity and the functional capacities of the self (Knox, 2003; Kalsched, 1996; Watkins & Watkins, 1997; Chu, 1998). The self seeks to guard its own survival since there is no meaningful sense of being alive without an inner core of identity, no matter how it has been shaped, molded, or injured by trauma (Wilson, 2004).

18.1 Identity in the Posttraumatic Self: The Redefinition of "I Am"

As the traumatized self recovers vitality and energy, other structural dimensions begin to synthesize with greater coherency, continuity, connection, and true autonomy. Ego-processes now become the master architect of redesign and reconstruction. The emergent and transcendent posttraumatic self begins to establish a new center of grounding in a matrix of self-defined meanings. The posttraumatic identity referent, "I am," can come to represent an inner freedom from the limitations and restrictions imposed by trauma's impact on the individual's identity and self-structure. In the posttraumatic self the meaning of integration is ultimate consciousness of one's being and transcendent existential freedom.

19 SUMMARY

Traumatic life-experiences and their idiosyncratic stressors have the power to impact the ego and the process of identity formation and self-configuration at any stage of epigenetic development. The conceptual schema and "flow" of traumatic influences to these intrapsychic processes is shown in Figure 3.9.

Traumatic experiences, especially events of an abusive and violent interpersonal nature, are external forces which attack and impinge the functional integrity of ego-processes in terms of adaptive capacity for mastery (Schore, 2003b). The penetrating power of trauma produces alterations in the function of ego-processes and the self. The alterations in ego-processes directly influence the organization and functional integrity of the self which can be construed as an integrated intrapsychic structure consisting of six primary dimensions: coherence, continuity, connection, autonomy, vitality, and energy (Stern, 1985; Wilson, 2004). Ego-identity is a product of ego-processes in the service of learning a specific style of adaptive mastery which gives "color," "flavor" and uniqueness to individual behavior. *Ego-identity, therefore, encompasses two primary structural dimensions of the self: continuity and coherence. Traumatic impacts on these processes attack the infrastructure of the self, the functionality of ego-processes and the stability of identity components.* Trauma may produce differential impacts on: (1) dissociative tendencies; (2) identity fragmentation; (3) horizontal (within) and vertical (between) stage-specific dissociation; and (4) self-structural alterations (see Figure 3.9).

Trauma's impact on the self-structure mobilizes defensive and coping adaptations to master the overwhelming and threatening nature of

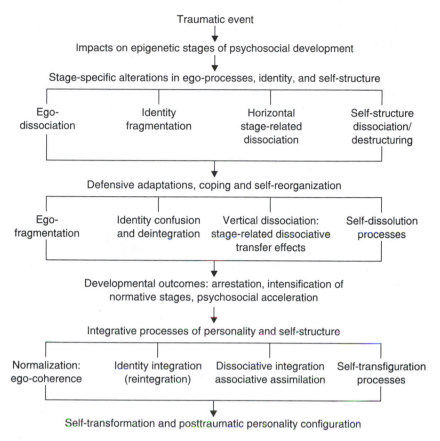

FIGURE 3.9. A psychodynamic model of traumatic impacts to Eriksonian life-stage development: ego-processes, identity, and self-structure. *Source:* ©2003 John P. Wilson.

traumatic experiences. These adaptive processes precipitate alterations in the structure of the self. They generate a series of cascade effects on the trajectory of epigenetic development—intensifying, compounding, disrupting, or accelerating the resolution and outcome of each stage. *Traumatogenic experiences occur within an ontogenetic framework of self-metamorphosis.* The posttraumatic self is a new configuration of identity that has been shaped by trauma.

There are developmental outcomes which emanate from traumatic experiences, depending on the age and stage of the person in the life-cycle (Pynoos & Nader, 1993; Nader, 2004). As part of the legacy of trauma to the natural history of epigenetic development, there may develop degrees of ego-fragmentation during a specific stage of development which carry over sequentially throughout the life-cycle.

Ego-fragmentation may be limited to a specific age and fracture identity formation through dissociation or alterations in the infrastructure of self-dimensions. When dissociation occurs in ego-processes *within* a specific stage of development, we may speak of *horizontal dissociative processes*. Prolonged or repetitive exposure to traumatic stressors may, in turn, perpetuate the use of dissociation, leading to states of identity confusion, self-dissolution and *vertical dissociative processes* in which there is a carry-over effect of dissociative processes across stages.

The task of reintegrating the shattered self is one of assimilation and resynthesis (Chu, 1998; Goodwin & Attias, 1999; Ulman & Brothers, 1988; Wilson, Friedman, & Lindy, 2001a). The restoration of effective ego-mastery, healthy coping and transformation of the structural bases of the self can be conceived as a logical and natural extension of the manner in which the levels of self-dismantling originally took place. Ego-coherence and resilience begin to replace ego-fragmentation. Identity integration refers to the reassimilation of part components, incorporating some dimensions and discarding others. Dissociative processes that alter the "usually integrative functions of consciousness, memory, identity or perception of the environment (*DSM-IV*, 2004)" are no longer useful or necessary for successful coping. Effective "associative" processes supplant "dissociative" ones. The self-structure undergoes transfiguration, and in some cases, transcendence. In self-transfiguration, the "figure and ground" perception and functions of the self are changed; the former traumatized, damaged or altered structure is "refigured." *Transfiguration means psychic transformation of the internal function of ego-processes and the structure of the self. In ego-transcendence, the old "self" is left behind, like an exoskeleton, and a new one emerges in self-metamorphosis.* As an organic psychic process, identity grows and reconfigures itself into a healthier whole.

Beyond doubt, traumatic experiences may shape the psychic landscape in the course of epigenetic development. The impact of trauma can be slight or catastrophic in terms of its effect on mental functioning. By carefully examining the relationship between ego-processes, ego-identity and the structure of the posttraumatic self, it is possible to discern a wide range of posttraumatic adaptive configurations, including the reconstruction of identity in the wake of trauma.

REFERENCES

American Psychiatric Association. (2000). *Diagnostic and statistical manual of mental disorders* (5th ed.). Washington, DC: American Psychiatric Association.
Bowlby, J. (1969). *Attachment and loss.* New York: Basic Books.
Bremner, J. D. & Marmar, C. R. (1998). *Dissociation.* New York: Guilford Publications.

Bremner, J. D., Vermutten, E., Southwick, S. M., Krystal, J., & Charney, D. (1998). Trauma, memory and dissociation: An integrative formulation. In J. D. Bremner & C. Marmar (Eds.), *Trauma, memory and dissociation* (pp. 329–346). Washington, DC: American Psychiatric Press.

Campbell, J. (1988). *The power of myth*. New York: Anchor Books.

Chu, J. A. (1998). *Rebuilding shattered lives: The responsible treatment of complex post-traumatic and dissociative disorders*. New York: Wiley.

Chu, J. A. & Bowman, E. S. (2000). Trauma and dissociation: 20 years of study and lessons. *Journal of Trauma and Dissociation, 1*(1), 5–21.

Courtois, C. (1999). *Recollections of sexual abuse*. New York: W. W. Norton.

Elder, G. & Clipp, E. (1988). Combat experiences, comradeship, and psychological health. In J. P. Wilson, Z. Harel, & B. Kahana (Eds.), *Human adaptation to extreme stress* (pp. 131–157). New York: Plenum Press.

Erikson, E. H. (1950a). *Childhood and society*. New York: W. W. Norton.

Erikson, E. H. (1950b). Growth and crisis of the healthy personality. White House Conference. Also found in M. J. E. Senn (Ed.), *Symposium on the healthy personality* (pp. 29–61). New York: Josiah Macy, Jr. Foundation.

Erikson, E. H. (1962). *The life cycle completed: A review*. New York: W. W. Norton.

Erikson, E. H. (1964). *Insight and responsibility*. New York: W. W. Norton.

Erikson, E. H. (1968). *Identity, youth & crisis*. New York: W. W. Norton.

Erikson, E. H. (1998). The problem of ego identity. In R. S. Wallerstein and L. Goldberger (Eds.), *Ideas and identities: The life and work of Eirk Erikson* (pp. 173–245). Madison, CT: International Universities Press, Inc.

Foa, E., Friedman, M. J., & Keane, T. M. (2001). *Effective treatments for PTSD*. New York: Guilford Press.

Freud, S. (1895). *Studies in hysteria*. London: Hogarth Press.

Freud, S. (1917). *New introductory lectures on psychoanalysis*. New York: W. W. Norton.

Freud, S. (1920). Beyond the pleasure principle. In *Standard edition, whole volume*. London: Hogarth Press.

Freud, S. (1923). Ego and the id. In *Standard Edition, 19* (pp. 12–66). London: Hogarth Press.

Friedman, L. J. (2000). *Identity's architect*. Cambridge, MA: Harvard University Press.

Friedman, M. J. (2001). Allostatic versus empirical perspectives on pharmacotherapy. In J. P. Wilson, M. J. Friedman & J. D. Lindy (Eds.), *Treating psychological trauma and PTSD* (pp. 94–125). New York: Guilford Publications.

Friedman, M. J. & McEwen, B. S. (2004). PTSD, allostatic load and medical illness. In P. P. Schnurr & B. L. Green (Eds.), Trauma and healing: Physical consequences of exposure to extreme stress (pp. 157–189). Washington, DC: American Psychological Association.

Goodwin, J. M. & Attias, R. (Eds.). (1999). *Splintered reflections*. New York: Basic Books.

Janet, P. (1890). *L' automatisme psychologique*. Paris: Felix Alcon.

Janet, P. (1907). *The major symptoms of hysteria*. London: Macmillan.

Jung, C. G. (1912). The collected works (Bollingen series XX, 20 vols.). Trans. R. F. C. Hull. In H. Read, M. Fordham, & G. Adler (Eds.), *The theory of psychoanalysis*. New Jersey: Princeton University Press.

Kalsched, D. (1996). *The inner world of trauma: Archetypal defenses of the personal spirit*. London: Routledge.

Kalsched, D. (2003). Daimonic elements in early trauma. *Journal of Analytical Psychology, 48*, 145–176.

Kluft, R. P. (1991). The hospital treatment of multiple personality disorders. *Psychiatric Clinics of North America, 14*, 695–719.

Kluft, R. P. (1996). MDD: A legacy of trauma. In C. R. Pfeffer (Ed.), *Severe stress and mental disturbances in children* (pp. 411–488). Washington, DC: American Psychiatric Association Press.

Knox, J. (2003). Trauma and defenses: their roots in relationship: An overview. *Journal of Analytical Psychology, 48,* 207–233.

Krystal, H. (1988). *Integration and healing.* Hillsdale, New Jersey: The Analytic Press.

Lifton, R. J. (1967). *Death in life: The survivors of Hiroshima.* New York: Simon & Schuster.

Lifton, R. J. (1976). *The life of the self.* New York: Simon & Schuster.

Lifton, R. J. (1979). *The broken connection: On death and the continuity of life.* New York: Basic Books, Inc.

Lifton, R. J. (1993). From Hiroshima to the Nazi doctors: The evolution of psychoformative approaches to understanding traumatic stress syndromes. In J. P. Wilson & B. Raphael (Eds.), *International handbook of traumatic stress syndromes* (pp. 11–25). New York: Plenum Press.

Lindy, J. D. & Lifton, R. J. (2001). *Beyond invisible walls.* New York: Brunner-Routledge.

Lindy, J. D. & Wilson, J. P. (2001). An allostatic approach to the psychodynamic understanding of PTSD. In J. P. Wilson, M. J. Friedman & J. D. Lindy (Eds.), *Treating psychological trauma and PTSD* (pp. 125–139). New York: Guilford Publications.

McEwen, B. S. (2002). *The end of stress as we know it.* Washington, D. C.: The Dana Press.

Mischel, W. & Morf, C. (2003). The self as a psychosocial dynamic processing system: A meta-psychological perspective. In M. P. Leary & J. P. Tangney (Eds.), *Handbook of self and identity.* New York: Guilford Publications.

Mueser, K. T. & Rosenberg, S. (2001). Treatment of PTSD in persons with severe mental illness. In J. P. Wilson, M. J. Friedman & J. D. Lindy (Eds.), *Treating psychological trauma and PTSD* (pp. 345–385). New York: Guilford Publications.

Nader, K. (1997). Assessing traumatic experiences in children. In J. P. Wilson & T. M. Keane (Eds.), *Assessing psychological trauma and PTSD* (pp. 291–349). New York: Guilford Publications.

Nader, K. (2004). Assessing traumatic experiences in children. In J. P. Wilson & T. M. Keane (Eds.), *Assessing psychological trauma and PTSD* (2nd ed., pp. 513–538). New York: Guilford Publications.

Nemiah, J. C. (1998). Early concepts of trauma, dissociation and the unconscious. Their history and current implications. In J. D. Bremner & C. R. Marmar (Eds.), *Dissociation* (pp. 1–27). Washington, DC: American Psychiatric Association Press.

Nijenhuis, E. R. S. (2001). *Traumatische Herinneringen: lichamelijk, emotioneel, gedissocieeerd.* presented at the study day Gedeelde Eenheid. Lichaam en Geest, Amsterdam, December 21, 2001.

Ochberg, F. (1988). *Post-traumatic therapy in victims of violence.* New York: Brunner/Mazel.

Ochberg, F. (1993). Posttraumatic therapy. In J. P. Wilson & B. Raphael (Eds.), *International handbook of traumatic stress syndromes* (pp. 773–785). New York: Plenum Press.

Ortiz, D. (2001). The survivor perspective: voices from the center. In E. Gerrity, T. M. Keane, & F. Tuma (Eds.), *Mental health consequences of torture* (pp. 3–13). New York: Klumer/Plenum Press.

Parsons, E. (1988). Post-traumatic self-disorders. In J. P. Wilson, Z. Harel, & B. Kahana (Eds.), *Human adaptation to extreme stress: From the Holocaust to Vietnam* (pp. 245–279). New York: Plenum Press.

Putnam, F. (1989). *Diagnosis and treatment of multiple personality disorders.* New York: Guilford Publications.

Putnam, F. (1997). *Dissociation in children and adolescents.* New York: Guilford Press.

Pynoos, R. & Nader, K. (1993). Issues in the treatment of posttraumatic stress in children. In J. P. Wilson & B. Raphael (Eds.), *International handbook of traumatic stress syndromes* (pp. 527–535). New York: Plenum Press.

Raphael, B. (1983). *When disaster strikes.* New York: Basic Books.

Raphael, B., Wooding, & Martinek (2004). Assessing traumatic bereavement. In J. P. Wilson & T. M. Keane (Eds.), *Assessing psychological trauma and PTSD* (pp. 492–513). New York: Guilford Publications.

Reis, B. E. (1995). Toward a psychoanalytic understanding of MPD. In J. G. Allen & W. H. Smith (Eds.), *Diagnosis and treatment of dissociative disorders* (pp. 25–35). New Jersey. Jason Aronson Inc.

Ross, C. (1989). *Multiple personality disorder: Diagnosis, clinical features, and treatment.* New York: Wiley.

Scharff, J. S. & Schaff, D. E. (1994). *Object relations therapy of physical and sexual abuse.* Northvale, New Jersey. Jason Aronson.

Schore, A. N. (2003a). *Affect dysregulation and disorders of the self.* New York: W. W. Norton.

Schore, A. N. (2003b). *Affect dysregulation and the repair of the self.* New York: W. W. Norton.

Sigman, M. & Wilson, J. P. (1998). *Traumatic bereavement: Posttraumatic stress disorder and prolonged grief in motherless daughters. Journal of Psychological Practice,* 4(1), 34–50.

Spiegel, D. E. (1994). *Dissociation.* Washington, D.C.: American Psychiatric Association Press.

Steele, K., van der Hart, O., & Nijenhuis, E. R. S. (2001). Dependency in the treatment of complex PTSD and dissociative disorders. *Journal of Trauma and Dissociation,* 2, 79–117.

Stern, D. (1985). *The interpersonal world of the infant.* New York: Basic Books.

Tolle, E. (1999). *The power of now.* California: New World Library.

Ulman, R. B. & Brothers, D. (1988). *The shattered self.* Hillsdale, New Jersey: The Analytic Press.

van der Kolk, B. (1999). The body keeps score: Memory and the evolving psychobiology of posttraumatic stress. In M. Horowitz (Ed.), *Essential papers on posttraumatic stress disorder* (pp. 301–327). New York: New York University Press.

van der Kolk, B., McFarlane, A. C., & Weisaeth, L. (1997). *Traumatic stress.* New York: Guilford Publications.

Wallerstein, R. S. & Goldberger, L. (1988). *Ideas and identities: The life and work of Erik Erikson.* Madison, Connecticut: International Universities Press.

Watkins, J. G. & Watkins, H. H. (1997). *Ego-states.* New York: W. W. Norton.

White, R. W. (1959). *The ego and reality in psychoanalytic theory.* New York: International University Press.

Wilson, J. P. (1980). Conflict, stress and growth: The effects of war on psychosocial development among Vietnam veterans. In C. R. Figley & K. S. Leventman (Eds.), *Strangers at home: Vietnam veterans since the war* (pp. 123–165). New York: Praeger Press.

Wilson, J. P. (1989). *Trauma, transformation and healing.* New York: Brunner-Mazel.

Wilson, J. P. (2001). An overview of clinical considerations and principles in the treatment of PTSD. In J. P. Wilson, M. J. Friedman, & J. D. Lindy (Eds.), *Treating psychological trauma and PTSD* (pp. 59–94). New York: Guilford Publications.

Wilson, J. P. (2003a). PTSD and complex PTSD: Symptoms, syndromes and diagnoses. In J. P. Wilson & T. M. Keane (Eds.), *Assessing psychological trauma and PTSD* (pp. 7–45). New York: Guilford Publications.

Wilson, J.P. (2003, February 16). *Target goals & interventions for PTSD: From trauma to the abyss experience.* Presentation at the International Critical Incident Stress Foundation's 7th World Congress on Stress, Trauma and Coping, Baltimore, Maryland.

Wilson, J. P. (2004a) Broken spirits. In J. P. Wilson & B. Drozdek (Eds.), *Broken spirits: The treatment of traumatized asylum seekers, refugees and war and torture victims* (pp. 141–173). New York: Brunner-Routledge.

Wilson, J. P. (2004b). The broken spirit: Posttraumatic damage to the self. In J. P. Wilson & B. Drozdek (Eds.), *Broken spirits: Treating traumatized asylum seekers, refugees, war and torture victims* (pp. 107–155). New York: Brunner-Routledge Press.

Wilson, J. P. & Drozdek, B. (2004). *Broken spirits: The treatment of traumatized asylum seekers, refugees and war and torture victims.* New York: Brunner-Routledge Press.

Wilson, J. P., Friedman, M., & Lindy, J. (2001a). *Treating psychological trauma and PTSD*. New York: Guilford Publications.

Wilson, J. P., Friedman, M. J., & Lindy, J. D. (2001b). An overview of clinical consideration and principles in the treatment of PTSD. In J. P. Wilson, M. J. Friedman, & J. D. Lindy (Eds.), *Treating psychological trauma and PTSD* (pp. 59–94). New York: Guilford Publications.

Wilson, J. P. & Keane, T. M. (2004). *Assessing psychological trauma and PTSD* (2nd Edition). New York: Guilford Publications.

Wilson, J. P. & Lindy, J. (1994). *Counter-transference in the treatment of PTSD*. New York: Guilford Publications.

Wilson, J. P. & Thomas, R. (2004). *Empathy in the treatment of trauma and PTSD*. New York: Brunner-Routledge.

4

Childhood Trauma: The Deeper Wound

KATHLEEN O. NADER

1 INTRODUCTION

Understanding the effects of trauma for children is a complex process. Children's reactions, including posttraumatic stress disorder (PTSD), may evolve or change over time or may appear years or months after an event (Fletcher, 2003; Greenwald, 2002; Yule et al., 2000). More importantly, the symptoms that follow childhood traumatic experiences may have cascading as well as direct effects (Ford, 2002). In addition to *DSM-IV* PTSD symptoms, a disruption to normal development and changes in patterns of thinking and behaving can affect each subsequent phase of development. Such alterations in functioning can have a cumulative effect on the youth's interactions with others, the inter-dependent relations among multiple levels of risk and protective factors, and the transactions between child and environment (Nader, in press; Yates, Egeland, & Sroufe, 2003). Trauma and its symptoms may exacerbate pre-existing symptoms or disorders, may be amplified by or create vulnerabilities, and may completely derail a youth from a personal life trajectory. Researchers and clinicians are beginning to look beyond *DSM* PTSD to examine, in addition, the deeper wound created by traumatic experiences: the damage to self and self-concept; the distortion of or interruption in a trajectory toward a meaningful purpose, career, relationships, and personal evolvement; as well as changes in how the psyche responds inwardly—the wound to the spirit, essence, or true self of the child (Kalsched, 1996; Nader, in press).

Alterations in a youth's interactional style, trust, self-view, confidence, information processing, neurochemistry and brain functioning, or academic performance will affect his or her ongoing opportunities, support systems and other relationships, goal setting, successes, failures, choices, and more (Nader, in press). In the U.S., abandoning, for example, extraverted or positive outlook qualities and taking on introverted or negative attitude traits can seriously change a youth's life and relationships. Loss of brain size and functioning or changed neurochemistry may alter achievement or increase a tendency toward aggressive reactivity (Schore, 2003). Experience activates, in the brain, specific neuronal connections. It permits the creation of new synapses and the strengthening of old ones. In some cases, lack of use results in diminished synaptic growth and a dying away process called pruning (Siegel, 2003). A major pruning process naturally occurs in the adolescent years. Trauma is likely to alter this process and to affect memory, attention, perception, emotion regulation, and patterns of thinking about self and others.

The experience and expression of mental health or psychopathology have physiological, affective, behavioral, and cognitive components (Mash & Dozois, 2003). Each of these areas may be affected by traumatic experiences. Dysfunction in any of these components may contribute to malfunction in the other areas. This chapter examines changes in patterns of thinking (information processing) and four of the traits that, when affected by trauma, may contribute to a disruption in a normal life-trajectory and to the deeper wound that traumatic experience can engender. Trust, self-esteem, sense of control, and their associated patterns of thought are among the qualities that impact the ability to adapt, cope, adjust, take reasonable risks toward goal achievement, and other aspects of normal functioning. As will be seen, these qualities are often interrelated or associated with one another as well as with the helplessness, disconnection from or doubt toward self and others, and/or humiliation/shame that are central to traumatization. This chapter concludes with a discussion of a few specific issues important to treatment and the recovery process.

1.1 The Developing Child

Children take into future situations and challenges the biological, social, cognitive, and emotional knowledge, skills, and other resources gained in earlier phases (Geiger & Crick, 2001; Price & Lento, 2001). At each phase of development, children must use internal and external resources to adapt to developmental demands. Successful adaptation to these demands—for example, to learn to regulate emotions, to establish desirable peer relationships—suggests a likely normative trajectory. Although failure at negotiating important developmental issues and tasks does not always signify pathology, it may indicate that a youth is on a deviant trajectory or at increased risk for maladaptive behavior. The longer an individual stays on a deviant pathway, the more difficult is a return to a normal developmental progression (Geiger & Crick, 2001; Yates et al., 2003). Major or minor life-events that disrupt physiology, emotion, and cognition represent a strain on an individual's adaptive capability and may interrupt habitual functioning (Ingram & Price, 2001). Stress may bring to realization a vulnerability to maladaption or pathology.

At any age, the diminishment of important developmental traits and qualities may have a major impact on life. Issues of trust, autonomy, self-concept, and cognitive processing, among others, are important at all ages. Because each stage of development is partially contingent upon the achievement of the preceding stages, disruption of these developing skills and tendencies at earlier ages may affect the rest of development in significant ways. Competence in one developmental period provides a foundation for success with subsequent developmental issues (Yates, Egeland, & Sroufe, 2003).

1.2 Cumulative Risk

In studies of resilience in youth, risk factors for problematic outcomes typically co-occur with other risk factors and usually include a sequence of stressful events rather than a single event (Fergusson & Horwood, 2003; Masten & Powell, 2003). In addition, single incidents and repeated traumas can induce vulnerability or sensitivity to other adverse events and experiences. In a longitudinal study in which adverse factors included (1) family economic: socioeconomic status, standard of living, and parent education; (2) parental relationship: single-parent, changes of parent, parental violence; (3) child abuse: excessive punishment or abuse or sexual assault; and (4) parental adjustment: parental alcoholism, criminality, or drug use, for New Zealand youth between ages 0 and 21 years ($n = 991$), Fergusson and Horwood found that youth exposed to six or more adverse factors had 2.4 times more externalizing and 1.8 times more internalizing disorders than youth with low adversity. With increases in childhood adversity, there were corresponding, significant increases in youths' property crimes, violent crimes, substance abuse, and conduct/antisocial disorders as well as in internalizing problems such as anxiety, depression, and suicidal ideation or attempts.

1.3 Helplessness and Humiliation

Fear, helplessness, and horror are required components of a traumatic experience in order for there to be a *DSM-IV* diagnosis of PTSD (APA, 1994). The association of these peritraumatic emotions with PTSD has been confirmed in studies of adults (Brewin, Andrews, & Rose, 2000). In addition to fear, helplessness, and horror, anger with others and shame are also strong predictors of adult PTSD (Andrews, Brewin, Rose, & Kirk, 2000). Brewin et al. found that fear, helplessness, horror, shame, and anger at others reported by adults 3 weeks after they were criminally assaulted were all associated with PTSD 6 months after the assaults. The few respondents with PTSD who had not experienced fear, helplessness, or horror during the event, had experienced high levels of shame or anger with others.

Traumatization is an experience of disempowerment that includes lack of control and reduced or inability to depend on self or others for protection (see Herman, 1992, 1997). It may result in disconnection from self and others, doubts about both, and humiliation or shame. The intensity of a youth's peri- and posttraumatic emotions reflect a combination of event, child, history, and other factors. The degree to which recovery is difficult is likely to be related to the depth, intensity, and lack of resolution of emotions such as helplessness, fear, humiliation or shame, and rage.

Childhood experiences such as severe assaults, abuse, relational aggression, and neglect often include extreme and/or repeated humiliation and helplessness. As described below (see Section 7.3), it is unbearable to feel that one is of no value, unlovable, or the object of hatred (Gilligan, 2003; Knox, 2003b). The traumatic fear, humiliation, and profound sense of helplessness that result (Crick et al., 2001; Knox, 2003b) are powerful emotions that may result in lashing out or lashing inward. Researchers have found among murderers, for example, frequent histories of repeated humiliations such as occur in violent or other intense traumatic experiences. Biblical stories, Homeric epics, war historians, and current analytic and forensic psychologists have recognized the path from rejection, disrespect, slighting, or embarrassment to shame/humiliation followed by anger or rage, then aggression (Gilligan, 2003; Scheff, 1997). Youths may try to fight their way out of helplessness, fight for respect, become self-destructive, or be functionally paralyzed by traumatic helplessness, humiliation, or rage.

Lack of trust, low self-esteem, and low perceived control can contribute to an ongoing sense of helplessness as well as being an expression of fear or helplessness—powerlessness to count on others, oneself, or one's value. Being unable to or not knowing when to trust suggests strong feelings of helplessness and fears of repeated victimization.

The experiences that lead to ongoing difficulties in trusting often cause humiliation or shame and a sense of betrayal. Herman (1992, 1997) states that posttraumatic shame is a response to helplessness, violation of bodily integrity, and the indignity suffered in the eyes of others. Shame or humiliation refers both to an experience of powerlessness and to one of relative powerlessness. Shame represents a perceived relationship, or a change in relationship, with other people (Leeming & Boyle, 2004).

1.3.1 Humiliation

Mortification = overwhelming humiliation (from the Latin roots mortis = dead and facere = to make—to make dead),

(Gilligan, 2003)

Allan Schore (1996) has made a distinction between shame and humiliation. A certain level of shame is essential for a child to learn to self-regulate states of mind and behavioral impulses (Siegel, 1999). Siegel explained that shame occurs when the aroused sympathetic nervous system is saying, "Let's go!" and the caregiver's protective "No!" activates the parasympathetic system to put on the brakes. This type of shame is not damaging and therefore is different from humiliation. Schore pointed out that it is when shame-inducing interactions are coupled with sustained caregiver anger and/or lack of repair of the disconnection between caregiver and child that it leads to humiliation. Peri- and posttraumatic shame and humiliation usually include feelings of intense degradation. In the study of trauma, the terms have been used interchangeably.

Gilligan (2003) has pointed out that there are many more synonyms for the word *shame* than for the word *pride*. Humiliation is synonymous with shame, degradation, embarrassment, indignity, dishonor, disgrace, debasement, abasement, and mortification (Morehead, 1962). Among the many meanings of shame are feelings of being slighted, insulted, demeaned, slandered; treated contemptuously, rejected, mocked, ridiculed; subjected to indignity or ignominy; being inadequate, incompetent, inferior, weak, a failure; losing face; and being treated as though unimportant, worthless, or insignificant. Any or many of these feelings may occur during traumatic experiences.

Acute emotional experiences in which a sense of shame comes vividly and painfully into awareness can be paralyzing in their intensity (Leeming & Boyle, 2004). Kaufman suggests that repeated experiences of shame, especially in childhood, become internalized as a part of a shame-based identity (cited in Leeming & Boyle, 2004). The youth develops a generalized sense of inferiority and unworthiness that persists into adulthood. Subtly different from an *internalized shame identity* is the idea of *shame-proneness*. H. Lewis (1971) observed that guilt implies the self is a relatively capable source of harm to others whereas shame intimates that the self is a helpless and inferior object of scorn (Gilligan, 2003; Leeming & Boyle, 2004). Lewis argued that shame-proneness was more strongly implicated than *guilt-proneness* in emotional problems such as depression, because of the negative focus on the entire self rather than merely on the self's actions. Research has found an association between shame and later adult psychopathology such as bulimia, PTSD, and depression (Andrews, Brewin, Rose, & Kirk, 2000).

1.3.2 Humiliation and Aggression

> *Those to whom evil is done/Do evil in return.*
> (W. H. Auden, quoted in Morrow, 2002, p. 64)

CASE OF THE VIOLENT INMATE (SEE GILLIGAN, 2003, PP. 1149–1151)

A cycle of assault and punishment (loss of privileges, isolation) developed for an inmate whose violence against the prison guards escalated each time they punished him. When asked what was so important to him that he was willing to risk everything in order to get it, the inmate said, "Pride. Dignity. Self-esteem." He added, "And I'll kill every motherf***er in that cell block if I have to in order to get it." He felt that the officers were trying to strip him of his last shred of dignity and self-esteem by disrespecting him. He was willing to die before he would humble himself to the guards' demands.

Although not all humiliation or shame leads to aggression, it is one possible outcome. Gilligan (2003) questioned inmates of prisons and prison mental health hospitals for 35 years. When he asked them why they had assaulted or killed someone, the most frequent response was that the individual had disrespected them or someone important to them. Many men told him that the reason restoring esteem was more important than preserving life was because they already felt dead inside—numb, empty, unable to feel physically or emotionally. Behaviors such as violent self-mutilation were performed to counteract the even more intolerable feelings of deadness and numbness. They experienced "the death of that fragile, vulnerable psychological construct, the self, as more tormenting than the death of the body could possibly be, with the implication that any act of violence by means of which they could attempt to resurrect their dead self, and bring it back to life—to become 'born again,' so to speak through an act of apocalyptic violence—would be more than worth the sacrifice of their body" (Gilligan, p. 1153).

In the Middle East, terror and humiliation have achieved a near-perfect circularity—*the tit for tat of almost war,* full war in all but the formalities (Morrow, 2002). Morrow describes humiliation as a "slower working explosive—a time bomb working in the brain and in the alleys of refugee camps: obsessive and enslaving in the way that all rage enslaves" (p. 64). Gilligan (2003), Scheff (1997), Volkan (2001) and other mental health, social, and political analysts have described how a sense of humiliation or victimization forms a fertile ground for the creation of suicide bombers and other terrorists. Posttrauma cultures are often characterized by fear, hatred, and rage. Scheff suggests that unacknowledged hatred and rage are generated by alienation and by cultural scripts for demonizing purported enemies. When anger's source is feelings of rejection or inadequacy, rage and aggression may mask a resulting shame or sense of humiliation. This composite of shame and anger result in the rage that generates violence. Gilligan explains that violent criminals and terrorist suicide killers appear to be tormented by feelings of shame and being disrespected by their enemies. They are willing to sacrifice their bodies/lives in order to replace those intolerable feelings with pride, self-respect, and honor from their allies. In "shame cultures," suicide is chosen when there is no other means of escaping personal, collective, or national humiliation.

1.3.3 Helplessness, Shame/Humiliation, and Trauma. Terr (1990) suggests that, following exposure to interpersonal violence, helplessness and terror typically turn into anger, rage, and shame. Following victimization, individuals have expressed shame over not being able to protect themselves, not having protected others, being a victim, loss of dignity during or after the event, being devalued (e.g., by a perpetrator's or rescuer's disregard), loss of skills and normal functioning, and damage to the self (Herman, 1992, 1997; Knox, 2003b; Schiraldi, 2000). Shame has been identified as a mediating variable between childhood trauma and adult psychopathology. In a study of adult victims of crime, Andrews, Brewin, Rose, and Kirk (2000) studied the role of previous child abuse, molestation, postcrime shame, and anger in the development of PTSD. They found that both shame and anger were associated with PTSD 1 month following the assaults. Anger with others was less potent than shame in predicting the persistence of PTSD symptoms 6 months after a crime. Although anger with others and shame independently predicted PTSD symptoms, the correlation between them was low. Shame was associated with reported childhood abuse and with anger with self. Childhood abuse was significantly associated with PTSD symptoms. As has been found for depression and bulimia, shame mediated the contribution of early victimization to later adult psychopathology.

2 INFORMATION PROCESSING

Faulty information processing may be related to attention, memory, interpretation, response search, and response selection. Fallacious information processing has been implicated in a number of childhood disorders and problems (Mash & Dozois, 2003). Cognitions interact with emotions and neurochemical reactions across time and contexts and result in specific enactment or inaction.

Internal *working models* (see Section 3.1) of self and relationships (Bowlby, 1969, 1982) "are based on a network of developing representations that emerge successively but interactively with age" (Thompson, 1999). This network includes social/relationship expectations derived from early relationships, event representations, autobiographical memories, and understanding of others and their psychological characteristics. Early attachments and ongoing experiences contribute to a child's personal data base. These working models are continuously revised and updated throughout development. They may have different time-tables and differing critical periods.

Cognitive thought patterns regarding the self (self-representations) and the world are directly associated with the way an individual acts and interacts in the world. These patterns of thinking may affect a youth's responses to traumatic events or may be a result of traumatic experiences. Trust or distrust, high or low self-esteem, and internal or external locus of control, among other represented models, have their individual and interrelated sets of cognitive thought processes.

Bowlby has suggested that imaginary fears in the course of early development can be viewed as defensive narratives constructed to define specific dangers so that they can be avoided (Knox, 2003). A traumatic experience is one during which the danger is actually or is perceived to be unavoidable. Trauma may overwhelm the capacity to cope (de Silva, 1999; Foa, Riggs, Massie, & Yarczower, 1995; Kirmayer, Young, & Hayton, 1995) and disrupt the normal progression of thinking about adults, peers, and self. Even a single traumatic experience may challenge, for example, a child's age-appropriate beliefs in adult (and Godly) wisdom and ability, may challenge beliefs in reasons for "being good," and may change the normal transition from reliance on parental guidelines to relying on peer and personal views as a moral compass (Nader, 2001). Early and traumatic experiences as well as temperamental characteristics may set up anticipatory attitudes that affect interactions and relationships (Caspi, 1998; Nader, in press). Youth with attributional biases may search a situation for fewer cues before making an attributional decision and find evidence for their biases through selective attention or biased interpretation (Caspi, 1998). When biases lead to aversive nonverbal, verbal, or behavioral expressions, they are likely to elicit reactions that reinforce them such as increased actual hostility and rejection from peers following aggression (Crick, 1995).

2.1 Posttraumatic Patterns of Thinking

Traumatic experiences can undermine judgment and introduce biases in attention, perception, and information processing (Nader, in press). Exposure to catastrophic events is likely to change youths' thinking to varying degrees. To some extent the variations in change may be attributed to age, child traits and temperaments, history and background, or aspects of the traumatic event (see case example of Trey, this chapter). Young children, for example, may lose a sense of protection by and faith in adults as well as the framework for resilience (competence, trust, control; Yates et al., 2003). Adolescents' sense of self and autonomy may be undermined.

Among the possible consequences of traumatization are anxiety, aggression, and depression. Youths who experience traumatic events may become selective in their attention to negative events and biased in their interpretations of others' behaviors (Dodge, Bates, & Pettit, 1990). Aggressive youths, for example, exhibit attributional biases (Crick & Dodge, 1996; Crick & Werner, 1998; de Castro, Slot, Bosch, Koops, & Veerman, 2003; Schippell, Vasey, Cravens-Brown, & Bretveld, 2003)—they perceive, interpret, and make decisions about social interactions that increase the likelihood of their aggressive acts. Dodge et al. (1995) found that a significant number of abused youths become defensively attuned to hostile cues and inattentive to relevant nonhostile cues. Their histories provide them with a repertoire of aggressive responses, the belief that aggression may lead to positive outcomes for the aggressor, and a sense of self-efficacy for aggressing.

Trauma may induce depression and patterns of thinking that include helplessness, a sense of futility, and negative expectations of the future. Research has shown an association between depressive symptoms and negative interpersonal expectations and perceptions, biased information processing regarding interpersonal interactions, and maladaptive relationship-oriented beliefs (Rosenbloom & Williams, 2002). Depressed individuals may evaluate themselves negatively, set unrealistic and perfectionistic goals for themselves, may believe that efforts to achieve goals are futile, or may feel hopeless or pessimistic about the future (Hammen & Rudolph, 2003).

For directly traumatized and other youths, anxiety often follows traumatic events. Research shows that anxious youths engage in more off-task thoughts, negative self-statements, and negative cognitive errors (e.g., more negative evaluations) (Malcarne & Hansdottir, 2001). Studies have demonstrated that anxious children engage in both depressive and anxious self-talk. These patterns of perception and information processing may be temporary or persistent. They may have a major impact on the youth's functioning, style, and quality of life.

3 TRUST

From the earliest models of trust provided by caregivers during infancy and young childhood to the ongoing patterns of trust that are affected by life experiences including trauma, the ability to trust is essential to all aspects of life and functioning. Early attachments set the stage for later relationships and assist the child to develop self-confidence, self-control, self-awareness, and awareness of the emotions of others. Trauma can disrupt or undermine attachments, trust, empathy, and relationship styles.

3.1 Early Attachments: Building Relationship Patterns

John Bowlby (1982) purported that genetic selection favored attachment behaviors that increased mother-child proximity. Proximity increased the likelihood of protection and survival. From an evolutionary perspective, infants that stayed close to their mothers were less likely to be killed by predators (Cassidy, 1999). For an infant, caregivers represent survival by providing physical and emotional nourishment, shelter from the elements, and protection from a variety of dangers. A child seeks security and comfort from the relationship with a caregiver to whom he or she is attached. With comfort and a sense of safety, the child explores the environment, develops competence, and acquires the qualities that lend to resilience (Luthar, 2003).

Bowlby (1969) suggested that early attachment styles become "working models" for significant social ties or interactions throughout life (Cassidy & Shaver, 1999; Rutter, 1997). The *patterns of relationship* established in early infancy, include defensive patterns of distance regulation that are internalized and stored as internal working models (Knox, 2003a). Knox suggests that these schematic patterns, stored in implicit memory and inaccessible to consciousness, are not merely *procedural "habits"* for interacting but are fully symbolic, representational and intrapsychic models, that exert a powerful organizing influence on conscious beliefs, attitudes, emotions, and desires as well as on behaviors.

The nature of the relationship with primary caregivers is of utmost importance to an infant and toddler (Cassidy & Shaver, 1999). Research has revealed that the early bonds established between caregiver and child may affect the rest of a child's life including physical and emotional health, coping, relationships, world view, personality, and personal choices (Cassidy & Shaver, 1999; Luthar, 2003). Youths who have internalized representations of available protection, self-worth, and sensitive care may be more responsive to the positive features of their environments and be better able to benefit from environmental resources (Yates et al., 2003). The capacity to trust based on early relationships may lead to the creation or selection of environments that sustain positive beliefs. Parent–youth relationships continue to be important across different phases of the youth's development. A positive relationship with parents and an adolescent's autonomy-seeking behaviors, for example, have tended to be highly correlated (Allen & Land, 1999; Crittenden, 1999). Data have consistently shown that supportive, responsive, structured, and affectively stimulating environments contribute to children's self-worth, social competence, empathic involvement with others, self-confidence, curiosity, and positive affective expression (Yates et al., 2003). Available care and positive self-regard foster the development of flexible problem-solving skills, emotion regulation patterns, and an expectation of success in the face of adversity. Situations that lead to disorganized attachments—abuse or the parents own unresolved trauma or loss—may undermine the development of these resilience factors.

Kalsched (1996) refers to the cumulative trauma of unmet dependency needs that may have a devastating effect on some children's development. This and other kinds of trauma often occur to infants before a coherent self-image and working defenses or coping mechanisms are formed. Kalsched says that the related anxiety "threatens the total annihilation of the human personality, the destruction of the personal spirit" (Kalsched, 1996, p. 1). As a result of this threat, primitive or dissociative defenses come into play. These defenses characterize and may cause severe psychopathology.

According to Fonagy, infantile internal working models contain images of oneself as both omnipotent and helpless (Knox, 2003b). Knox points out that trauma is bound to distort the developmental formation of internal working models including self-representations. Kalsched (1996) suggests that strong affect must be metabolized by symbolic processes, interpreted into language, and integrated into the *narrative identity* of the child. "'Not me' elements of experience must be distinguished from 'me' elements and must be rejected aggressively (outwardly) and repressed firmly (inwardly)" (Kalsched, 1996, p. 17). Kalsched suggests that the abused child cannot mobilize the aggression needed to expel the noxious, "bad," or "not-me" elements of experience. The child is unable to hate the loved parent and instead may identify with the parent as "good," take on the parent's aggression, and come to hate (and be rageful toward) itself and its personal needs.

3.1.1 Disturbed Attachments. It is generally agreed that infant character-istics such as temperament, parental attributes, cultural issues, family factors, and environmental factors interact in complex ways to affect relationship quality and interactive behaviors (Hesse, 1999; Nader, in press; Rosen & Rothbaum, 1993). Disturbances in attachments as well as the child's or parents' traumas may define or disrupt a youth's inter-actional patterns and relationships (Nader, in press). As described in Chapter 3, from infant–caregiver relationships are derived basic trust or security (Bowlby, 1969). Lack of responsive care as well as uncued, inconsistent, noncontingent, or frightening caregiving can warp a child's developing trust, self-worth, and social reciprocity (Yates et al., 2003). Attachment insecurity has been associated with a variety of problems, vulnerabilities, and disorders. Securely attached children have been found to be more competent, ego-resilient, happy, enthusiastic, popular with peers, and autonomous in adolescence than insecurely attached children (Atkinson, 1997; Rutter, 1997; Weinfield, Sroufe, Egeland, & Carlson, 1999). In contrast, insecure attachments are more often charac-terized by increased hostility, poorer social skills with peers, less qualitative and more romantic relationships, and ongoing problems with parents (Allen & Land, 1999).

Either a parent's own unresolved trauma or loss or child abuse by a parent may contribute to disturbed attachments. Fear of a caregiver is believed to lead to disorganized/disoriented attachments (Hesse et al., 2003). The infant's normal biological safe-haven becomes simultaneously the source of alarm. Maltreating caregivers' behaviors lead directly to this state of alarm or terror in infants. The nonmaltreating parent whose previous trauma or loss remains unresolved may exhibit frightened, absorbed or dissociative, sexualized, timid/deferential or protective, and unexplained or anomalous forms of frightening or threatening but not physically abusive behavior (Hesse et al., 2003; Siegel, 2003). Research has shown that some infants classified as disorganized do not have parents classified as "unresolved" on the Adult Attachment Inter-view, however, suggesting that there may be multiple pathways to disorganization (Lyons-Ruth, Yellin, Melnick, & Atwood, 2003). Studies have also found a differential effect of trauma or loss on parent–infant interactions and attachment. An Unresolved state of mind and the experience of childhood parental death contributed independently and additively to the prediction of infant disorganization at 12 months but not 18 months. At 18 months, the severity of a parent's trauma was related to the parent's Hostile-Helpless states of mind which in turn predicted infant disorganization.

Disorganized attachments in infants have been associated with aspects of psychopathology from middle childhood to late adolescence.

Although early disorganized attachments may contribute to intellectual, introspective, artistic, and other advantages, disorganized attachments have been linked with such problems as high levels of aggression; role inversion with the parent, response inhibition, dysfluent discourse, and narratives with catastrophic fantasies in 6-year-olds; and dissociative-like behaviors in elementary and high school students (Hesse, 1999; Hesse et al., 2003).

Youths (and adults) with insecure working models may expect less support from others and may deter supportive relationships by the distrust and uncertainty engendered by their expectations. In turn, people's negative responses to their hostility and distrust confirm and reinforce their expectations.

3.1.2 Trauma and Attachment. Insecure attachments have been linked to traumas in more than one way (Nader, in press). Significant major life-events can disrupt the continuity of attachments and attachment patterns and strategies (Allen & Land, 1999). Posttrauma behaviors of caregivers may reduce responsive care and disrupt attachments. Changes in the youth's interactional styles with peers, caretakers, and other adults may follow, for example posttraumatic increases in irritability, impulsiveness, aggressive reactivity, fears, or reactivity to reminders (Nader, 2002). Shared traumatic experiences may create traumatic attachments. As described above, children's traumas caused by caregivers or caregivers' unresolved traumas may produce disorganized attachments in infants or children which in turn result in vulnerabilities to traumas, traumatic reactions, and a variety of maladaptive behaviors and problems.

3.1.3 The Ability to Self Reflect. A caretaker's affective competence may provide a degree of protection against the damaging effects of abuse and other traumas and may reduce vulnerability to the transgenerational transmission of psychopathology (Fosha, 2003; Slade, 1999; Yates et al., 2003). From a primary attachment figure with the capacity to self-reflect, for example, a child gains a *reflective function*. Mary Main observed that an adult's ability to engage in a coherent and cohesive autobiographical narrative that includes the ability to consider one's own cognitive processes as objects of thought or reflection (*metacognitive monitoring*) is evidence of the adult's internally consistent working model of attachment (Fosha, 2003; Knox, 1999, 2003b; Slade, 1999). Fonagy and his colleagues concluded that this capacity for *metacognitive monitoring* or the *reflective self function* suggests the ability to perceive and understand one's own and others' behaviors in terms of mental or psychological states, i.e., to be aware of and to evaluate the meaning of one's own and others' emotions and reactions (Knox, 2003b; Slade, 1999). Knox has explained that failure to develop a reflective function results in a lack of the capacity to empathize with others and to place personal emotions in a meaningful context. Lack of empathy has been implicated in the development of aggression (Blair, Jones, Clark, & Smith, 1997; Nader, in press; Rothbart, Ahadi, Hershey, & Fisher, 2001). Knox (2003b) also has described the role of reflective function failure in an insufficiently developed sense of psychological separateness and in the development of pathology such as bulimia, self-harm, projective identification, and borderline personality disorder. The ability to self-reflect is essential to the capacity to learn from one's behaviors and experiences.

3.2 Trusting Others

Trust denotes an individual's expectations and beliefs about the reliability of self or others (Hardin, 2001; King, 2002; Rosenbloom & Williams, 2002). The fundamental bases of interpersonal trust are reliability (fulfillment of a word or promise), refraining from causing emotional harm (being receptive to disclosures, maintaining confidentiality about such disclosures, and avoiding acts that elicit embarrassment or harm), and the absence of deception (lack of dishonesty, maliciousness, and manipulating others for personal gain) (Rotenberg & Cerda, 1994). Trimble and Richardson (1982) found that interpersonal trust was strongly related to locus of control (Rotenberg & Cerda, 1994; see Section 5). Perhaps especially after trauma, lack of trust may include fear of others as well as lack of critical judgement of others (Regehr, 2001). For young children, trauma may undermine a normal progression from believing in the protection, knowledge and skill of adults (Stillwell, Galvin & Kopta, 1991) to more self reliance.

CASE OF BRANDY (NADER, IN PRESS)

Brandy had a good relationship with her parents. At the end of middle school, a boy whom her good friend liked began to pay more attention to Brandy than he paid to her enamored friend. In high school, Brandy experienced ongoing relational aggression (see Crick, 1995; Crick et al., 2001; Nader, in press) from her peers instigated by her former good friend. Girls who were her friends in elementary and middle school talked behind her back, made up stories about her, played tricks on her, used the personal information they knew about her against her, and excluded her from activities. She felt constantly humiliated, helpless, and persecuted. Sometimes her fellow students would pretend that they were going to include her again only to play an unpleasant trick on her. She contemplated suicide more than once, but someone had told her that people who commit suicide endured prolonged torment after death. She feared that even death would not provide relief. She felt trapped.

Brandy buried herself in her studies and made a few friends outside of school. She cried frequently. She lost faith in herself, her lovability, and her competence.

In college, Brandy was a good student. She did not experience the persecution that had been ongoing in high school. Although she remained a little guarded, she developed a few good relationships. She remained somewhat fearful about what people thought of her and what they were saying behind her back. In her first job after university, however, her old fears returned in full force. In her new position, she worked with other intelligent, ambitious young men and women. A strong competition for position seemed to generate some "back-biting" and exclusionary behaviors among the group. Brandy did not know whom to trust. She became cautious with others. She began to worry about sharing information and about delegating tasks when team-work was required. Almost every opportunity offered to her was suspect. She feared that people might be setting her up. Sometimes her fear seemed to paralyze her. In response to her behaviors, her coworkers were wary of her and began to withdraw from her.

As stated above, trust typically develops in infancy (from birth to 18 months) and is initially contingent on the quality of the infant's relationship with the caregiver (Congress, 2001; Erikson, 1950; Mitchell, 1990; Chapter 3, this volume). Interpersonal trust can be underdeveloped due to childhood experiences or undermined later in life. Research suggests that faulty development of trust may occur in response to a single trauma or to long-term environmental conditions (Mitchell, 1990). These environmental conditions may include emotionally distant, inconsistent, or abusive parenting; economic deprivation or conflict over needed resources; repeated disappointment by others who fail to behave in an anticipated positive manner; learning from parents and others who speak of people's unreliability; embarrassment from having trusted unwisely and disregarded the history or potential for betrayal or unreliability of another; being let down and then ridiculed for one's naivete or foolishness in having trusted; generalizing underconfidence in one's own trustworthiness to others; low self-concept and doubt about one's ability to survive disappointment; an overall negative and pessimistic attitude about another person's trustworthiness (and the satisfaction of being right); experiences of discrimination and prejudice; and rigidity and the need for control, especially when there is the perception of a lack of control (King, 2002; Mitchell, 1990; Rotenberg & Cerda, 1994). As demonstrated by Brandy's story, the disruption of trust at any point in life may hinder development or otherwise contribute to a less than desirable life.

Trust is essential for psychosocial competence, for stable social relationships, individual well-being, and adjustment to change (King, 2002; Mitchell, 1990; Rotenberg & Morgan, 1995). Lack of trust inter-feres with effective interpersonal functioning. Research suggests that individuals low in interpersonal trust are less confident, less popular with others, less satisfied with relationships, more lonely, more isolated, less happy, and have a negative self-concept (lower self-esteem). Major or enduring relationships can not exist happily and comfortably without trust. Without a foundation of trust, Mitchell suggests, cooperation, planning, caring, humor, and sharing are unlikely to develop. Failure to trust hinders growth of a relationship and may keep it at a superficial level; it nudges toward increased guardedness and lack of goodwill. The untrusting individual may already feel betrayed and rejected. A sense of rejection and isolation may even lead to paranoia. Verbal or nonverbal behavior may communicate lack of trust and may elicit untrustworthy behaviors in others. Andreou (2001) found that girls who scored high on Distrust also scored high on Victimization. Youths who were both bullies and victims had low faith in human nature, high expectations in others' untrustworthiness, and beliefs that others were manipulable in interpersonal circumstances.

As demonstrated by the case of Brandy, interpersonal trust is important in the workplace as well as in social settings. Fontaine and Lubow (1977) found that performance is mediated by the level of trust that occurs when an individual recognizes his or her dependence on others (Mitchell, 1990). Change in circumstances requires adjustment in interpersonal alliances and thus the need for new, continued, or stronger trust in others. The ability to delegate tasks is an act of trust. Trusting others elicits goodwill from them and encourages consistent trustworthiness, emphasizes their capabilities and desirabilities, and may increase support from them or performance in the work place (McGinnis, 1979; Mitchell, 1990). This is especially true when the one who trusts exudes strength and the ability to do well with or without the other's trustworthiness. The perception of vulnerability may increase vulnerability.

3.2.1 Trauma and Trust

CASE OF TREY

Trey, an 8-year-old, was sitting in the cafeteria of his school when a tornado hit. After a cafeteria wall began to collapse and bricks and glass started flying toward him, Trey experienced moments of intense indecision, not knowing whether to remain motionless, to hide under the table, or to run. He ran just before a large brick slammed into the place where he had been sitting, collapsing the table and crushing part of the bench. Among his other symptoms, Trey was very angry with his parents after the tornado. He explained that they had not prepared him to make a decision in that horrible moment when he could have been killed or badly injured. He no longer trusted their parenting. Trey was not so sure the teachers were preparing them well either. He joined other school children when they said, "Why should we be good, when you can die anyway?"

CASE OF MARY

Mary was a good student. In middle school, some of her classes were accelerated. She made mostly As and some Bs. By age 14, however, Mary had become depressed and withdrawn. She looked more sloppy and sometimes seemed angry and pessimistic. Her academic performance dropped significantly. Except in her favorite class (English), she made Cs, Ds and an occasional F (especially in classes she did not attend). Mary recalled how teachers began to describe her as a "slow achiever" and "not college material." Many teachers called her lazy, rebellious, and not smart. Some of them seemed to take it personally when she did not attend classes. A very few teachers told her she was not living up to her potential—an appreciated remark in comparison to the other teacher's comments.

At age 12, Mary's father had begun to molest her. When she was 16, the school principal asked Mary if she was doing drugs (she was not). He sent her to the school drug counselor. The counselor reviewed her records and asked her what had happened at age 12. Perhaps because the counselor was a man or perhaps because she no longer trusted adults, she did not tell him. She dropped out of school in the 12th grade.

After a broad range of traumas (natural disasters as well as violence), children can have trouble trusting those who are supposed to know best and to protect them. The capacity to trust can be seriously undermined by intra- or extrafamilial violence or other human-perpetrated traumatic experiences (Putnam, 1997). Damaged trust following traumas may lead to confused or biased expectations of others that affect behaviors, interactions, and choices. Ford (2002) has described how violently traumatized youths may adopt a generalized expectation of danger and betrayal and an unspoken belief that distrust and defiance are essential for self-protection or for coping. When the individuals a youth expects to rely upon the most are not trustworthy, when their goodwill cannot be counted upon, or, worse still, they inflict or allow injury, then it may become difficult to know whom or how to trust. The resulting inability to trust parents or a supreme being to provide protection may make it difficult to regain a sense of safety. When trust is damaged, basic assumptions about the world and other fundamental aspects of relationships are altered. Although distrust may at times be adaptive, intervention is required when it leads to interpersonal difficulties. Trust can be repaired but recovery may only occur in small increments over time (Mitchell, 1990; Putnam, 1997; Schiraldi, 2000).

4 SELF PERCEPTION

Traumatic events call into question basic human relationships...breach the
attachments of family, love, and community...shatter the construction of the self
that is formed and sustained in relation to others...undermine the belief systems
that give meaning to human experience ... violate the victims faith in a natural or
divine order and caste the victim into a state of existential crisis.

(Herman, 1992, 1997, p. 51)

4.1 Self-Esteem

Self-esteem is related to a broad area of adjustment and well-being including social relationships, school achievement, and resilience to stressful life-events. Self-evaluations begin to develop in early childhood. Theories of self-esteem suggest that self-esteem develops either through (1) one's feelings of competence which reflect the match or discrepancy between one's goal or ideal and one's performance or (2) social interactions and relationships especially mother–child attachment relationships (Heinonen, Räikönnen, & Keltikangas-Järvinen, 2003). Self-concepts may mirror those of parents as well (Geiger & Crick, 2001). During childhood, the parents' hopes and aspirations usually form the basis for what are perceived to be ideal self-representations (Heinonen et al., 2003). Normally, children's self-concepts become more negative, or less unrealistically positive, in middle childhood (between ages 7 and 8) and again in early adolescence followed by a slow increase in self-esteem in later adolescence (Geiger & Crick, 2001). Geiger and Crick have theorized that deviations in this normal pattern of development may indicate an increased risk for the distorted personality patterns and concepts of self characteristic of the adult personality disorders. Adult personality disorders have been associated with childhood traumas as well as with specific emotional and environmental characteristics (Krug, 1996).

The emotions and attitudes characteristic of low self-esteem may make it difficult for youths to get what they want out of life (Martin, 2003). Low self-esteem has been associated with psychopathology such as suicideality, substance abuse, personality disorders, posttraumatic stress disorders, childhood social withdrawal, and eating disorders (Fletcher, 2003; Heinonen et al., 2003; Rubin, Burgess, Kennedy, & Stewart, 2003). Low self-esteem has also resulted in vulnerability to criticism, self-destructive behaviors, negative feelings about self and others, and interference with relationships (Rosenbloom & Williams, 2002).

Kalsched (1996) describes defenses not only as avoidance mechanisms, but also as active constructions in the form of narratives, created in imagination and fantasy to support a positive sense of identity and personal worth (Knox, 2003b). Positive self-images are threatened by cruelty, hostility, or indifference from those who are loved and most depended upon. Youths' traumatic reactions have demonstrated that self-esteem may be injured by strangers who victimize as well as when loved ones cause harm.

4.1.1 Self-Esteem and Social Context.

Everyone has many different personalities which move like actors into the foreground in various situations.

(Radha, 1978, p. 107)

Turner, Brown, and Tajfel (1979) define an individual's social identity as "those aspects of his self-concept contributed by the social groups to which he perceives himself to belong" (p. 190). It is assumed that individuals are motivated to achieve a positive self-image. The search for positively valued distinctiveness in one's group (or beyond it) can lead to biased perceptions, evaluations, and behaviors. Discrepant comparisons in favor of one's own group promote a positive group identity which in turn enhances self-esteem.

The process of differentiation accelerates in adolescence with the proliferation of multiple selves that vary in different social contexts (Harter, Waters, & Whitesell, 1998). Research suggests that most adolescents' self-descriptions (about three quarters) vary across contexts—with parents, close friends, romantic partners, and classmates (Harter et al., 1998). Harter and her colleagues found that validation support (i.e., interest and respect in what the adolescent thinks, says, and feels) perceived within a specific context (e.g., parent, classmate) was predictive of self-worth in that context and was less predictive of self-worth in other contexts or of global self-worth. That is, validation from a specific group of significant others is most strongly associated with one's sense of self-worth with those particular others. Social support's link to fewer trauma symptoms following catastrophic events may be partly because of its connection to self-image (e.g., an increased need for validation) as well as its link to protection.

4.1.2 Self-Esteem and Trauma.

Low self-esteem can be a risk factor for increased trauma. Trauma can reduce self-esteem. Traumatic experiences can devastate how survivors feel about themselves including the ways they view, interpret, and judge themselves (Rosenbloom & Williams, 2002). Traumatic events that lead to demoralization and degradation (e.g., torture, violence, relationship aggression) are particularly damaging to self-esteem. Bolger and Patterson found that maltreated children have more difficulties with developing autonomy, emotional and behavioral self-regulation, self-esteem, and relationships with peers (Bolger & Patterson, 2003). Maltreated youths were more likely to be rejected by peers, less popular, and less likely to have a best friend. High-quality friendships, however, were associated with their greater increases in self-esteem over time.

5 LOCUS OF CONTROL

Like trust, high self-esteem has been significantly but modestly linked to an internal locus of control (Ozolins & Stenstrom, 2003). Belief that control over events, outcomes, behaviors, or emotions is internal (within the person) has been labeled an *internal locus of control* in contrast to the belief that control is external (outside of the child's control; *external locus of control*). Self-esteem and locus of control are presumed to be associated with parental practices and characteristics such as warmth, supportiveness, and encouragement of independence (Ozolins & Stenstrom, 2003). Both qualities have been found to be correlated with healthful behaviors and resilience in youth. Perceived control can play a moderating (increasing or decreasing outcome levels) as well as a mediating (as an intervening variable) role with regard to the development of internalizing problems (Bolger & Patterson, 2003). The positive effects of an internal locus of control in the outcomes of trauma assume that the youth does not feel responsible for the trauma.

5.1 Trauma and Locus of Control

Seligman's "learned helplessness" model purports that depression stems from experiencing uncontrollable, noncontingent events (Hammen & Rudolph, 2003). The revised model has evolved to attribute depression to the interaction between a "depressive attributional style" and exposure to negative events. A *depressive attributional style* includes a tendency to attribute negative outcomes to internal, global, and stable factors and to ascribe positive outcomes to external, specific, and unstable factors. Negative life-events may reduce a child's internal locus of control by inducing feelings of helplessness or impairing relationships (Haine et al., 2003). Experience with uncontrollable events may lead to the expectation that nothing a person does can control future outcomes (Deardorff, Gonzalez, & Sandler, 2003).

A number of researchers have found that a personal experience of mastery, control, or self-efficacy can attenuate the negative effects of traumatic experiences (Fletcher, 2003; Hammen & Rudolph, 2003; Nader, 1997). Moran & Eckenrode (1992) found that maltreated girls with high external locus of control and low self-esteem reported greater levels of depression than comparison girls or maltreated girls with internal locus of control and high self-esteem (Fletcher, 2003). Similarly, Bolger and Patterson's (2003) findings support the protective nature of an internal locus of control against internalizing symptoms for maltreated children. Studies have demonstrated that control beliefs mediate the relationship between stress and depressive symptoms in ethnically diverse, inner-city adolescents as well (Deardorff et al., 2003).

The effects of control beliefs may differ for different stressful contexts (Haine et al., 2003). Control beliefs have been shown to mediate the effects of negative life-events in some stressed youth populations— children of divorce, inner-city adolescents—but not others—children of alcoholics, bereaved children (Deardorff et al., 2003; Haine et al., 2003). Children with an internal locus of control may use more appropriate coping strategies or be less likely to appraise stressors as threatening, leading to a reduced negative impact of events (Haine et al., 2003). In contrast, maladaptive coping styles, depression, pessimism, anxiety, poor health habits, substance abuse, less involvement in school activities, and a high degree of societal estrangement—all possible results of trauma—have been linked to low levels of internal locus of control, strong belief in chance, and low self-esteem in adolescents.

6 SENSE OF SELF: THE PERSONAL SPIRIT

Although the search for the *True Self* can be traced back to ancient spiritual practices (Chidbhavananda, 1974; Holmes, 1938; M., 1942; Vivekananda, 1955), thoughts about the personal spirit may or may not include thoughts about religious or mystical beliefs (Tully, 1999). An individual's feelings and thoughts about his or her personal spirit or essence ("Who I am") are intuitive and intangible as well as a part of conscious and concrete assessment. In addition to thoughts about what one does, believes, is capable of, or is willing to do, the self includes a sense of who one is, an essence that expresses in distinct and unique individuality, a core self often including a spiritual essence. One's thoughts about oneself begin early in life, first responding to the image reflected by caregivers and influenced by personal biological and temperamental characteristics.

Followers of Jung have emphasized the self's "prescient 'unfolding' through the individuation process—its nudging the sometimes resistant ego toward its pre-specified 'plan' of individual wholeness" (Kalsched, 1996, p. 96). According to Jung, the self represents the psyche's totality (both conscious and unconscious), the ordering of the whole personality, whereas the ego represents the ordering of the conscious alone. The self is "a core of the individual's imperishable personal spirit" (Kalsched, 1996, p. 3).

> The violation of this inner core of the personality is unthinkable. When other defenses fail, archetypal defenses will go to any length to protect the Self—even to the point of killing the host personality in which this personal spirit is housed (suicide). (Kalsched, 1996, p. 3)

Preceding sections of this chapter describe some of the ways in which a youth's core self can be undermined. Trauma can wound the personal spirit by derailing an individual's life-trajectory (i.e., interrupting the life that would have been and the self that was), distorting and undermining the self concept and confidence, and altering the youth's relationships to others and the environment. Kalsched suggests that when the ego suffers severe trauma, the self is riddled with anxiety, fragile, and in a constant struggle to survive. Traumatized individuals live in a constant state of dread that the original traumatic state will return. Hypervigilance replaces play. The fear that everything will collapse is often confirmed. The *survival self* replaces the *individuating self* (see also Ford's comments in Section 3.2.1). Symptoms such as splitting affect from image are the survival self's misguided efforts to preserve the personal spirit from the unbearable trauma-related affects, which now seem to threaten at every turn.

6.1 Self in the World

CASE OF LANA

During the earthquake, Lana was not in the area of her school where part of the building collapsed killing several of her fellow students. She and her other schoolmates became very sensitive to the bad things that happened in the world following their exposure to this natural disaster. Lana noticed them more when little things went wrong and was more aware of the potential for things to go wrong. A few years after the disaster, her brother needed surgery for a medical condition. A few months after that, lightning struck her house entering through a window in her upstairs room. No one was injured by the lightning, damage was minimal, and her brother's surgery was successful. Nevertheless, Lana began to feel unlucky, and she developed migraine headaches that interfered with her school performance. She told the therapist that she thought it started when the school collapsed—that she had been jinxed and had become an unlucky person.

Trauma can change a youth's view of the world as well as of him- or herself in the world. In addition to the pessimistic outlook or reduced satisfaction that may follow a traumatic experience(s), one's concept of self in relation to others, the way one's personal world works, and one's ability to cope with or overcome adversity may be dramatically altered. When additional bad experiences or traumas occur, they reinforce negative expectations and patterns of thinking as well as symptoms such as reticence under certain circumstances, hypervigilance, and distrust.

6.2 World View and Life Satisfaction

An individual's world view (including core assumptions and expectations) is largely determined by his or her culture (including ethnic, religious, and peer culture) and experience (de Silva, 1999; Nader, in press; Terr, 1979). Suldo and Huebner (2004) found that, in contrast to youths who reported dissatisfaction with their lives, adolescents with positive life satisfaction scores were less likely to develop externalizing behavior problems after adverse life-events. Life satisfaction, then, may operate as a protective factor that buffers the effects of adverse life-events in adolescence. Traumatic experience, however, can reduce life satisfaction as well as change the way a youth views, greets, and interacts in the world.

Studies of traumatized adults have confirmed a marked decrease in multiple domains of life satisfaction after severe multiple traumas (Anke & Fugle-Meyer, 2003; Nader, in press). Studies of posttraumatic changes in youths' world views have suggested that a pessimistic attitude is more likely to occur for more extreme, chronic, or abusive stressors (Fletcher, 2003; Terr, 1991). Recently, some mental health professionals have stated that violence is the real trauma. Enduring repeated violence can create a deeper and more intense wound to the spirit. As demonstrated in the case example of Lana and others in this chapter, natural disasters and other nonviolent traumas may also be extreme stressors with significant consequences. They can disrupt development and wound the spirit.

Kalsched (1996, p. 3) has offered one explanation for the loss of spontaneity and positive outlook: "When trauma strikes the developing psyche of the child, a fragmentation of consciousness occurs … Typically, one part of the ego *regresses* to the infantile period, and another part *progresses*, i.e., grows up too fast and becomes precociously adapted to the outer world, often as a 'false self'. The *progressed part* of the personality then caretakes the regressed part. This dyadic structure has been independently discovered by clinicians of many different theoretical persuasions—a fact that indirectly supports its archetypal basis" (Kalsched, 1996, p. 3).

Kalsched (1996) explained that, following traumatic experience, in order to defend against additional trauma, the *progressed self* or *self-care system* screens all relations with the outside world resulting in major resistance to any unguarded, spontaneous expressions of self in the world. This Protector/Persecutor is not educable. It does not learn realistically about danger, but mistakenly sees each new life opportunity as a dangerous threat of retraumatization. It determines that the personal spirit will never again suffer this much or be this helpless in the face of cruel reality. As a result, a defensive pathology may develop, for example, to disperse the self into fragments (dissociation), to numb it (substance abuse), to encapsulate or soothe it with fantasy (schizoid withdrawal), or persecute it to keep it from hoping (depression).

6.3 View of Self and Personal Behaviors During
*   Traumatic Events*

CASE OF JANE

Jane was a good driver. Her parents trusted her with the car and allowed her to drive her younger siblings places. One day she came out of the store, threw her purse and bag of goodies on the floor, and started the car. She bent down to get her sunglasses out of her purse, then looked over her shoulder and started to back up. She hit something and slammed on her brakes. When she exited the car, she saw that she had hit a man who had bent down behind the car to tie his shoelaces. Jane was horrified. The man reassured her that it was his fault; that he should have waited until he was out of the parking lot to tie his shoe. He was not badly injured but had a fractured wrist and was bruised and sore. Her parents and friends also repeatedly reassured her that it was not her fault and that the man was okay. Jane was depressed, her chest ached, and she had nightmares. She went over and over the incident in her mind. She did not want to be around anyone and was anxious and shaky when driving. Jane called her friend who had moved away a few years earlier to tell her what had happened. The friend said, "Oh my God!" Jane said, "Yeah." Her friend, "Oh my God! It must ache in your soul to feel like you could hurt another human being like that." Jane began to cry. She said, "I knew you would understand."

CASE OF AHMED (NADER, IN PRESS)

Ahmed, now 17, had survived the ongoing horrors of war for more than a year without physical injury. Throughout most of his therapy session, Ahmed slumped in his chair, looked down at his hands, and mumbled while he described his experiences. An Iraqi soldier who patrolled their neighborhood during the occupation would make anyone outside of their homes watch while he tortured or killed someone. Ahmed heard how the soldier had sawed off someone's leg, gutted a cat, and made boys walk naked in front of their mothers before he shot them. One night, Ahmed was with an "older man" (aged 40) playing chess. The Iraqi soldier came in, accused the older man of working with the resistance, and began to beat him mercilessly. Ahmed wanted to defend the man but was so terrified that he could not speak. He started to move toward the man to help him, but the soldier warned him that, if he moved, he would be shot. Ahmed stood motionless and silent while the soldier beat the man to death. He did not know why the soldier had spared him. He wished he had died. He could not bear to be alive because he had let the soldier beat the man to death and had done nothing.

In addition to the deep injuries that result from being victimized, one's thoughts, actions, or inactions during a traumatic event can cause pain in the depths of oneself (Nader & Mello, 2001). Empathy may be a key factor related to the impact of hurting another. Experiences, such as intense helplessness and humiliation, that deflate the self-image can also be desolating. Behaviors or omissions that lead to guilt such as failing to rescue or doing something to injure or kill another person (even an enemy) can be personally devastating and can increase trauma symptoms (Herman, 1992, 1997; Nader, Pynoos, Fairbanks, Al-Ajeel, & Al-Asfour, 1993). Nader and colleagues found that youths who had injured someone else during the 1991 Gulf War had more trauma symptoms than traumatized youths who had not injured another. Young and older children sometimes overestimate what they should or could have done during an event. In addition to his other trauma symptoms, a 5-year-old boy remained distressed that he had not rescued his mother who was raped and stabbed to death. The boy had tried to stab the assailant with a kitchen knife but was unable to make the knife go in. He ran away when the rapist slapped him and yelled at him to get out.

7 RECOVERING FROM DEVELOPMENTAL DISRUPTION AND THE DEEPER WOUND

Multiple methods have been adapted to provide successful interventions for traumatized youth (Nader, 2001, 2002; Webb, 2002; Wilson, Friedman, & Lindy, 2001). It is likely that these methods work best when a youth, the method, and the clinician are well matched. Discussions of successful and proven methods of intervention can be found elsewhere (Cohen, Deblinger, & Mannarino, 1997; Nader, 2001, 2002; Silberg, 1998; Webb, 2002). This section underscores a few of the specific issues related to a youth's recovery from trauma's wounds to development and to the spirit. Maintaining flexibility, honoring individuality, providing a positive support system, and addressing the youth's needs in multiple contexts are essential to recovery from the helplessness and humiliation that can result from trauma and its symptoms.

The core experiences of psychological trauma are disempowerment and disconnection from others. Recovery, therefore, is based upon the empowerment of the survivor and the creation of new connections. . . . In her renewed connections with other people, the survivor re-creates the psychological faculties that were damaged or deformed by the traumatic experience. These faculties include the basic capacities for trust, autonomy, initiative, competence, identity, and intimacy (Herman, 1992, 1997, p. 133)

7.1 The Need for Flexibility

When it comes to funding and endorsement, there sometimes seems to be a war between methodologies. Combinations of methods are often included in successful treatment protocols, however, in order to remedy multiple symptoms and disparate courses in multiple contexts (March, Amaya-Jackson, Foa, & Treadwell, 1999; Nader, 2001; Terr, 2001). Youths vary in their personal traits, histories, and personal traumatic experiences. These differences sometimes call for variations and combinations of interventions.

As researchers and clinicians, we must first discover the full nature and impact of childhood traumatic reactions (in addition to the symptoms of PTSD) as well as the most accurate ways of assessing them before we can effectively evaluate the use of a variety of methods and their best applications. Moreover, it is important to discover the exceptions to a method's successes. Are they related to specific symptoms, personalities, personal experiences, or other aspects (and combinations of them) of the youth, the experience, the clinician, or the pre- and posttraumatic environment. How much individualization is important to effective treatment?

In addition to information about a youth's culture, background, and specific traumatic experiences, knowledge of specific personality styles can enhance and help to personalize interventions and assessments (Nader, in press). For example, in addition to those whose trust has been damaged, introverts (Myers & Myers, 1995) or those with a slow-to-warm personality style (Chess & Thomas, 1991) may need additional time to develop trust. A therapist's interpretation of a youth's silence or temporary "shutdown" may change if the therapist knows that an introvert needs to reflect on thoughts, feelings, and ideas before sharing them, tends to share them in bits and pieces, and may experience "shutdown" if deprived too long of "alone time" (Kurcinka, 1998). Each temperamental style has specific needs, values, and talents as well as particular stress styles, favored environments, and best-suited roles (Berens, 1998). Berens explains that idealists (emphasis: intuition and feeling) are particularly stressed by insincerity, betrayal, and lack of integrity. Rationals (emphasis: intuition and thinking/knowledge) are especially stressed by powerlessness, incompetence, and lack of knowledge. Research including data from clinical experience is needed to determine the importance to treatment of specific traits such as a youth's attunement to injustice, sensitivity to stimuli and the emotions of others, tendency to focus on the future or the past, or different paces at processing information.

7.1.1 Treating the Whole Child. PTSD describes a set of measurable symptoms common after trauma that is unlikely to delineate the entirety of trauma's impact on a child's life. In addition to its effects on development, self-concept, and relationships, a traumatic experience hypnotically engages the attention of multiple senses at multiple levels. Treating the multiple levels and the multiple impacts of trauma may be important to full recovery. Youths and adults have been found to become more concrete in their thinking following traumatization. Ignoring the less concrete and less overt aspects of response may result in treating only a part of the child and his or her reactions.

Effectual treatment of the more complex aspects of traumatic response often necessitates attending to the imaginative, intuitive, and unconscious as well as the overt cognitive and behavioral aspects of response. Trauma can impede a youth's creative, imaginative, and playful flow of ideas and actions. Engaging these aspects of the child within the treatment session can help to unblock this flow while providing protection from the overwhelming nature of any unleashed traumatic emotions. Research has demonstrated that imagining a reality or selectively forming a mental image(s) can bring about behavioral, affective, and physiological changes (Menzies & Taylor, 2004). Mental imagery dynamically involves the brain, the mind, and the body including the body's sensory mechanisms. Cognitive behavioral, play therapy, and analytic methods use imagery or respond to images that are conscious and below the consciousness threshold. They may enlist the child's imagination as well as cognitive skills by using or permitting, for example, games or imaginative enactments. By reactivating a representation, it can be modified and stored in modified form (Salvatore, Dimaggio, & Semerari, 2004).

Some views and evidence suggest that the right brain hemisphere more intensely experiences emotionally arousing states, mediates retrieval of autobiographical memories, and registers and regulates body states (Siegel, 2003). Left hemisphere processing uses syllogistic reasoning; it looks for cause-and-effect relationships that can explain the right and wrongness of things. Siegel suggests that the deeper healing process is the procurement of neural integration. "Trauma may induce separation of the hemispheres, impairing the capacity to achieve these complex, adaptive, self-regulatory states revealed in incoherent narratives" (Siegel, 2003, p. 15). Traumatized youths often respond to components of play or imaginative expression that can help to free them from immobilization or helplessness. Such creative depictions, repetitions of life or trauma issues and scenarios, and other engagements of the unconscious, imaginative, or right brain hemisphere provide useful methods to help work through potentially debilitating aspects of the trauma.

7.2 The Individual Child

Assisting youths to recover from trauma's disruptions to development and wounds to the spirit requires honoring their individuality as well as their functioning developmental age. In the normal course of childhood, youths are shaped by appropriate support, nurturance, limits, reinforcements, guidance, and opportunities/experiences. Play and imagination are a usual part of a young life. Successfully employing these normal aspects of childhood shaping and development into therapeutic practice (at home and in the therapist's office) requires understanding the youth's individual nature. Some but not all of what soothes the soul and restores normalcy is unique for different individuals. As has been demonstrated in earlier sections of this chapter, restoring trust, self-esteem, good support, and a reasonable sense of control is important to youth in general. The method of restoration and the manner and meaning of aspects of traumatic experience and response can be very individual.

To heal all aspects of traumatic injury means attending to developmental disruptions to relationships, skills, and the emerging self as well as to the whole child (conscious and unconscious; intuition, imagination, cognition, and behavior). This means understanding the child in context (e.g., cultural, familial, temperamental). Knowing even small details can aid rapport and repair. A clinician who worked with a depressed freckle-faced young girl with low self-esteem benefited from knowing the details of her family and culture. Cinnamon was a prized spice in this very religious family. In the process of establishing rapport, the clinician asked the child with delighted surprise at seeing her face, "Wow! How did you get so special that God sprinkled cinnamon all over your face?" The little girl seemed to be relieved as well as deeply touched by the comment.

7.2.1 Individuality. Although U.S. culture as a whole values independence and individual attainment, it does not always honor individuality. Honoring individuality can occur within a context of increased social support as well as in an independence-oriented society. In the U.S., extraversion, an easy-going nature, and a positive attitude are valued. Youths with negative emotionality, low sensory thresholds, or introverted traits have sometimes been found to be less resilient as well as less socially successful (Luthar, 2003). Inadequate emphasis has been placed on such youths' abilities to contribute through good analytic, empathic, and other skills. These and other individual traits can be recognized as important components of intervention planning. While working at the South Pole with a small group of researchers, Dr. Jerry Nielson discovered a lump on her breast (Boardman, 2002). Because of weather conditions, she was unable to leave to have medical treatment. Her well-publicized surgery at the South Pole occurred with the assistance of her fellow workers and long-distance instruction. In an interview after her return home, when asked what she had learned during her experience, Dr. Nielson reported that, in their small, isolated community, it became clear that there was a need for each personality type in order to make a community work successfully.

Knowing the details of a youth's personal history as well as his or her personality may make specific symptoms more recognizable or understandable. Following traumas, youths may regress, become more concrete, or function at more primitive levels in general. Children and adolescents may be regressed much of the time or may regress spontaneously in response to traumatic reminders of their experiences (Nader, 2001). When she was 5, Lupe loved to play with and take care of her 3-year-old brother. He was handsome even then with his long eyelashes and charming manner. At that age, Lupe loved to eat "beans and franks" and wanted them every day. Sometimes her mother allowed her to eat them a few days in a row. When they were both in high school, her little brother was beaten to death by a gang member whose sister he had spurned. Lupe found his badly beaten body. She tried without success to stop the bleeding, and then to breathe life back into him after he stopped breathing. His bruised and bloody face and his last gasps for breath haunted her. At first, she would not eat. Then she only wanted beans and franks. Knowing her history helped her therapist to understand that her food selection represented more than just her mother's loving indulgence. Unconsciously, beans and franks represented a happier, safer time during which she could protect and take care of her beloved brother.

7.3 Support Systems

Being victimized can make a youth feel less competent and devalued. Self-talk may include thoughts about being less worthwhile, unlovable, unlucky, helpless, and unable to take successful action during adversities. Irritability, reduced self-control, and other symptoms can disrupt relationships, make a youth less likeable or less tolerable, or otherwise change their interactions in ways that reinforce or materialize the negative feelings and thoughts about self. Adults may or may not understand the development of undesirable traits in loved ones following terrible experiences. When the traits persist over time, even understanding adults become intolerant, exhausted, or annoyed with the symptomatic traits. Children can be even less tolerant of such changes in personality. Following traumatic events youths have sometimes complained of a traumatized peer's irritability, jumpiness, or other strange or undesirable behaviors and have withdrawn from the traumatized youth. Although the terror of a traumatic experience may intensify the need for protective attachments (Herman, 1992, 1997), disruptions in trust and self-image may foster withdrawal. Right action from a youth's multiple environments can help to repair the damage caused by trauma and its reactions.

7.3.1 Validation Support. Respect and personal value by self and others may increase protection and the meeting of physical needs by self and the community. Thus, the needs for respect and a sense of personal value may be, like attachment behaviors, based in biological survival needs. Although some personalities require more alone time than others, the need for solitude does not negate the needs to be valued and respected by others. Knox (2003b) explains that it is unbearable to feel that one is of no value, unlovable, or the object of hatred. Fear, humiliation, and a profound sense of helplessness may result (Crick et al., 2001; Knox, 2003b). Knox suggests that, when engendered by feeling hated by a parent, these emotional reactions are likely to produce profound damage unless modified by a degree of omnipotent fantasy. In the case of maltreatment, a defensive fantasy that the child somehow caused the parent's violence, perhaps by some bad behavior, permits the hope that the parent will love the child again. Gilligan (2003) states that, although "adults who have attained internalized sources of pride can survive the withdrawal of love from others, up to a point, it appears to be difficult if not impossible for a child to gain the capacity for self-love without first having been loved by at least one parent, or parent-substitute. And when the self is not loved, by itself or by another, it dies, just as surely as the body dies without oxygen" (p. 1154).

7.3.2 Levels of Support. When he was 17, Jonah took woodshop at school. While he was using his father's table saw at home, he was distracted by a friend and was cut by the saw. Luckily the saw missed the artery but it badly injured flesh and tendons. The medical resident who bandaged his wrist and arm and put it in a foam-fortified sling told Jonah, "Perky little blood cells will rush into the area of your tendons and one at a time do their thing to help heal the tendons." Then the resident told Jonah that it was an amazing (although sometimes slow) process and that he should, "Praise those little cells for the great job they were doing." Jonah laughed. The resident told him that it was true. He commented, "Praise really helps, and not just for blood cells. All things respond to encouragement."

The documented positive impact of such practices as creative visualizations and prayer suggest that the usefulness of support may include silent as well as overt and self as well as other support. Medical studies have confirmed that prayer, faith, and rituals have strengthened health and healing perhaps by triggering emotions that influence the immune and cardiovascular systems (Walsh, 1998). Whether one is religious or not, knowing that others care enough to pray or engage in other supportive practices on one's behalf may register as validating. One study found that those prayed for showed greater improvement than the group who were not prayed for, even when those being prayed for were unaware they were in the prayed-for group. Other nonverbal communications besides prayer have an impact (negative or positive) on youths. This may be especially true for youths with enhanced sensitivity (low sensory threshold; see Chess & Thomas, 1991).

7.3.3 Family and Friends. As stated in Section 3 on trust, environments that are supportive, responsive, structured, and emotionally stimulating contribute to children's self-worth, social competence, empathic involvement with others, self-confidence, curiosity, and positive affective expression (Yates et al., 2003). A history of support; competent functioning; high parenting quality with high warmth, structure and monitoring, and involvement encourage the positive adaptation of youths exposed to adversity. Positive, reciprocal, and stable friendships also contribute to youths' well-being and their social development (Bolger & Patterson, 2003). They enhance emotional security and provide a setting for learning and practicing social skills, trust, and positive behaviors. These qualities, in turn, add to a youth's resilience.

The importance of support systems at home and at school following traumas has been well documented (de Silva, 1999; Nader, in press; Pole, Best, Metzler, & Marmar, 2005; Udwin et al., 2000). Children and adults respond to protective, physically and emotionally nurturant, validating, and approving support (Harter, Waters, & Whitesell, 1998; Rabalais, Ruggiero, & Scotti, 2002). Feeling protected, nurtured, approved, and validated becomes especially important for youths following traumatization. These forms of support help to restore a normal sense of safety, a positive self-image, and constructive self-talk. Creating environments that provide these forms of support in the individual ways that youths need them is essential at home and at school, among family and peers, and with other adults.

7.3.4 Society. Although specific traumatic reactions often have more than one contributing factor, what we teach our children lends to their responses. Survivor guilt is an example. The Viking warrior was taught that if he died bravely, he would find a desirable afterlife in Valhalla. The Roman soldier who died bravely was headed for the peace and beauty of the Elysian Fields. Honor to those who die in battle is also a current practice. Islamic suicide terrorists and other wartime martyrs are promised great rewards in the afterlife and benefits for their survivors. Clearly these beliefs shape cognitions, emotions, and behaviors.

Until recently less preparation has been given for those who survive violence or war. In times of war and terrorism, bravery is essential. Teaching bravery *and* the value and process of survival is more complicated. What of the child who successfully ran for safety but whose friend was shot? How can youth be prepared for such experiences in a way that prevents fears of being next (sometimes related to unacknowledged feelings of deserving it for deserting another), guilt over surviving when a friend was badly injured or died, or the depression about something that can never be resolved because someone died, without taking away from a normal childhood sense of safety or normal adolescent sense of invulnerability? In addition to addressing these reactions after the experience, children's texts and popular books provide an avenue for addressing these issues.

We are living in an era in the U.S. in which competition, self-centeredness, and independence are valued over interdependence and placing the group over the individual (Caspi & Roberts, 2001). We are less dependent upon one another for survival and foster increased individual accomplishment in our children. Although, over the last 40 to 50 years racial relationship aggression has become less and less accepted among the general U.S. population, recent news shows and books suggest that individually directed relational aggression within high schools has increased in the last 10 or 20 years (Simmons, 2002). Ideally mutually supportive behaviors would be encouraged and reinforced among youths at home and in schools from their earliest years. The terrorist attacks of September 11, 2001 at least temporarily increased supportive behavior in the New York area. Thoughtful consideration is needed to reinforce mutual support on an ongoing basis.

8 CONCLUSIONS

Although life-span studies are few, some evidence suggests that the intensity and duration of trauma symptoms is related to the intensity and/or duration of the traumatic experience itself, a youth's age at onset of trauma, personality factors, early symptoms, pretrauma circumstances and background, or the posttraumatic environment (Otis & Louks, 1997; Nader, in press; Udwin, Boyle, Yule, Bolton, & O'Ryan, 2000). It is likely that a number of elements combine to determine whether trauma resolves over time or persists. Some personality traits such as sensitivity, an enhanced behavioral inhibition system, or introversion, for example, may make youth more vulnerable to the deeper and more persistent wounds of trauma.

For traumatized children, there are deeper wounds beyond PTSD. Trauma's disruptions to development, relationships, self-view, and/or competence can diminish youths' effective functioning and evolvement. When the disempowerment and shame associated with a traumatic experience become evident in a youth's ongoing view of self and others, they may sabotage life and recovery. Persistent and intense posttraumatic troubles with trust, self-esteem, sense of control, and information processing are likely to undermine resilience and to create risk for ongoing problems that are difficult to resolve.

8.1 Resilience

The same factors that protect against stress may also help a child when traumatic stress occurs. They include good parenting, trust, self-esteem, control, human and material resources, intelligence, problem-solving skills, and self-regulation. The absence of these resilience factors or factor combinations has been associated with poorer outcomes across life and after traumatic stress.

In addition to the symptoms of PTSD, trauma can have a more complex effect on children. Each phase of development draws on the completion of the preceding phase and successful development of its associated transactional, adaptive, cognitive, emotional, and behavioral skills. Thus trauma's effects on children may be cascading and evolving. The earlier that trauma interrupts normal development and the longer the interruption, the greater potential trauma has to disrupt the youth's personal evolution. Nevertheless, some youths fare better than others following single or repeated traumatic exposures.

Secure early attachments and the trust that they engender, high self-esteem, and a sense of personal control have served as protective or resilience factors for youths exposed to adversities. These qualities are important, in general, for the development of psychosocial competence, stable social relationships, individual well-being, adjustment to change, and other desirable skills. They have provided a measure of protection against the effects of trauma.

Trauma can undermine resilience factors. It can reduce trust, self-esteem, control, self-regulation, and the capacity for empathy. Intense or repeated traumas may disrupt beliefs in self and others as well as in protection and protectors. Traumatic experiences can thwart judgment and introduce biases in attention, perception, and information processing. Thus, trauma may injure a child by derailing the youth's life trajectory, distorting and undermining his or her sense of self and personal spirit or core self, and disrupting the youth's relationships.

8.2 Life Disruption

Children need to feel valued, protected, and capable (able to do and accomplish, be, and express). Being valued is important to physical and emotional survival. When trauma (alone or combined with other factors) undermines the feelings of being valuable, valued, and protected, it can wound the personal spirit and may result in partial or extensive functional shutdown. Traits and beliefs such as a reduced ability to trust, unrealistic assessment of the locus of control, inability to assess a situation without automatic biased interpretations or reactions, and injured self-esteem contribute to helplessness and thwart functioning. It can be difficult to recover from these traumatic injuries because the resulting behaviors and attitudes impede accomplishment and elicit responses from others that confirm these traits and beliefs. Such wounds can cause a level of behavioral and emotional paralysis. Their hindrance to recovery may increase with elevations in the invoked levels of unresolved helplessness, humiliation, undermined held beliefs, and devaluation of the individual. Feelings and beliefs that a youth can no longer count on himself or others may make positive action and coping difficult. When a youth no longer knows what to expect and the youth's fears guide expectations, life is thwarted significantly.

8.3 Reparative Factors

To heal trauma's deeper wounds, it is important to combine and adapt therapeutic methods that address the individual child's needs; honor the youth's unique personality and personal history; recognize the youth's individual traumatic experiences; as well as provide validating, nurturing, and protecting support in multiple contexts. The healing process from traumas (and from faulty attachments) has been aided by the presence of supportive persons in a youth's life—friends or adults (Bolger & Patterson, 2003; Nader, in press; Yates et al., 2003). At the end of a diagnostic and therapeutic trauma interview with children following a sniper attack (Nader et al., 1990), in order to reorient the children from a focus on trauma symptoms to methods of effective coping, they were asked what helped them to feel better after the attack. Most of the children indicated that the most effective help came from having other people rally around them, to talk to, and to comfort them. Helping to reinstate a youth's personal value, feeling safe and protected, competence, sense of control, trust, and accurate assessment skills as well as validating his or her uniqueness can help to heal the difficult-to-resolve results of trauma.

REFERENCES

Allen, J. P. & Land, D. (1999). Attachment in adolescence. In J. Cassidy & P. R. Shaver (Eds.), *Handbook of Attachment: Theory, research, and clinical applications* (pp. 319–335). New York: Guilford Press.

American Psychiatric Association. (1994). *Diagnostic and statistical manual of mental disorders* (4th ed.). Washington, DC: American Psychiatric Association.

Andreou, E. (2001). Bully/victim problems and their association with coping behaviour in conflictual peer interactions among school-age children. *Educational Psychology, 21*, 59–66.

Andrews, B., Brewin, C. R., Rose, S., & Kirk, M. (2000). Predicting PTSD symptoms in victims of violent crime: The role of shame, anger, and childhood abuse. *Journal of Abnormal Psychology, 109*, 69–73.

Anke, A. G. W. & Fugle-Meyer, A. R. (2003). Life satisfaction several years after severe multiple trauma—A retrospective investigation. *Clinical Rehabilitation, 17*, 431–442.

Atkinson, L. (1997). Attachment and psychopathology: From laboratory to clinic. In L. Atkinson & K. Zucker (Eds.), *Attachment and Psychopathology* (pp. 3–16). New York: Guilford Press.

Berens, L. V. (1998). *Understanding yourself and others: An introduction to temperament.* Huntington Beach, CA: Telos Publications.

Blair, R. J., Jones, L., Clark, F., & Smith, M. (1997). The psychopathic individual: A lack of responsiveness to distress cues? *Psychophysiology, 34*, 192–198.

Boardman, E. M. (2002). Nielson, Dr. Jeri. Ice bound: a doctor's incredible battle for survival at the South Pole [book review]. Downloaded on November 18, 2004 from http://www.findarticles.com/p/mi_mOPX/is_107124225/print

Bolger, K. E. & Patterson, C. J. (2003). Sequelae of child maltreatment: Vulnerability and resilience. In S. S. Luthar (Ed.), *Resilience and vulnerability: Adaptation in the context of childhood adversities* (pp. 156–181). New York: Cambridge University Press.

Bowlby, J. (1969, 1982). *Attachment and loss: Volume I. Attachment.* New York: Basic Books.

Brewin, C. R., Andrews, B., & Rose, S. (2000). Fear, helplessness, and horror in Posttraumatic Stress Disorder: Investigating *DSM IV* Criterion A2 in victims of violent crime. *Journal of Traumatic Stress, 13*, 499–509.

Caspi, A. (1998). Personality development across the lifecourse. In W. Damon & N. Eisenberg (Eds.) *Handbook of child psychology, 5th ed.: Vol 3. Social, emotional, and personality development* (pp. 311–388). New York: Wiley & Sons.

Caspi, A. & Roberts, B. W. (2001). Personality development across the life course: The argument for change and continuity. *Psychological Inquiry, 12*, 49–66.

Cassidy, J. (1999). The nature of the child's ties. In J. Cassidy & P. R. Shaver (Eds.), *Handbook of Attachment: Theory, Research, and Clinical Applications* (pp. 3–20). New York: Guilford Press.

Cassidy, J. & Shaver, P. R. (Eds.) (1999). *Handbook of attachment: Theory, research, and clinical applications.* New York: Guilford Press.

Chess, S. & Thomas, A. (1991). Temperament. In M. Lewis (Ed.), *Child and adolescent psychiatry: A comprehensive textbook* (pp. 145–159). Baltimore, MD: Williams & Wilkins.

Chidbhavananda, S. (1974). *The Bhagavad Gita*. Tirupparaitturai, India: Sri Ramakrishna Tapovanam.

Cohen, J. A., Deblinger, E., & Mannarino, A. P. (1997). *Treatment of PTSD in sexually abused children*. Funded grant application, National Institute of Mental Health, 1R10 MH55963.

Congress, E. P. (2001). Individual and family development theory. In P. Lehmann & N. F. Coady (Eds.) *Theoretical perspectives for direct social work practice: A generalist-eclectic approach* (pp. 165–182). New York: Springer.

Crick, N. R. (1995). Relational aggression: The role of intent attributions, feelings of distress, and provocation type. *Development and Psychopathology, 7*, 313–322.

Crick, N. R. & Dodge, K. A. (1996). Social information-processing mechanisms in reactive and proactive aggression. *Child Development, 67*, 993–1002.

Crick, N. R., Nelson, D. A., Morales, J. R., Cullerton-Sen, C., Casas, J. F., & Hickman, S. E. (2001). Relational victimization in childhood and adolescence: I hurt you through the grapevine. In J. Juvonen & S. Graham (Eds.), *Peer harassment in school: The plight of the vulnerable and victimized* (pp. 196–214). New York: Guilford Press.

Crick, N. R. & Werner, N. E. (1998). Response decision processes in relational and overt aggression. *Child Development, 69*, 1630–1639.

Crittenden, P. M. (1999). Patterns of attachment and sexual behavior: Risk of dysfunction versus opportunity for creative integration. In L. Atkinson & K. Zucker (Eds.), *Attachment and psychopathology* (pp. 47–93). New York: Guilford Press.

de Castro, B. O., Slot, N. W., Bosch, J. D., Koops, W. & Veerman, J. W. (2003). Negative feelings exacerbate hostile attributions of intent in highly aggressive boys. *Journal of Clinical Child and Adolescent Psychology, 32*, 56–65.

de Silva, P. (1999). Cultural aspects of post-traumatic stress disorder. In W. Yule (Ed.), *Post-traumatic stress disorders: Concepts and therapy* (pp. 116–138). Chichester, UK: Wiley.

Deardorff, J., Gonzales, N. A., & Sandler, I. N. (2003). Control beliefs as a mediator of the relation between stress and depressive symptoms among inner-city adolescents. *Journal of Abnormal Child Psychology, 31*, 205–217.

Dodge, K. A., Bates, J. E., Pettit, G. S. (1990). Mechanisms in the cycle of violence. *Science, 250*, 1678–1683.

Dodge, K. A., Bates, J. E., Pettit, G. S., & Valente, E. (1995). Social information-processing patterns partially mediate the effect of early physical abuse on later conduct problems. *Journal of Abnormal Psychology, 104*, 632–643.

Erikson, E. H. (1950). *Childhood and society*. New York: W. W. Norton.

Fergusson, D. M. & Horwood, L. J. (2003). Resilience to childhood adversity: Results of a 21-year study. In S. S. Luthar (Ed.), *Resilience and vulnerability: Adaptation in the context of childhood adversities* (pp. 130–155). New York: Cambridge University Press.

Fletcher, K. E. (2003). Childhood posttraumatic stress disorder. In E. J. Mash & R. A. Barkley (Eds.), *Child psychopathology* (2nd ed., pp. 330–371). New York: Guilford Press.

Foa, E. B., Riggs, D. S., Massie, E. D., & Yarczower, M. (1995). The impact of fear activation and anger on the efficacy of exposure treatment for posttraumatic stress disorder. *Behavior Therapy, 26*, 487–499.

Ford, J. D. (2002). Traumatic victimization in childhood and persistent problems with oppositional-defiance. *Journal of Aggression, Maltreatment and Trauma, 6*, 25–58.

Fontaine, G. & Lubow, C. (1977). Causal attribution to other people and expected performance: The mediation role of interpersonal trust. *Psychological Reports, 40*, 763–766.

Fosha, D. (2003). Dyadic regulation and experiential work with emotion and relatedness in trauma and disorganized attachment. In M. Soloman & D. J. Siegel (Eds.), *Healing trauma* (pp. 221–281). New York: W. W. Norton.

Geiger, T. C. & Crick, N. R. (2001). A developmental psychopathology perspective on vulnerability to personality disorders. In R. E. Ingram & J. M. Price (Eds.), *Vulnerability to psychopathology: Risk across the lifespan* (pp. 57–102). New York: Guilford Press.

Gilligan, J. (2003). Shame, guilt, and violence. *Social Research, 70,* 1149–1180.

Greenwald, R. (Ed.) (2002). *Trauma and juvenile delinquency: Theory, research, and interventions.* New York: Haworth Press.

Hammen, C. & Rudolph, K. D. (2003). Childhood mood disorders. In E. J. Mash & R. A. Barkley (Eds.), *Child psychopathology* (2nd ed., pp. 233–278). New York: Guilford Press.

Haine, R. A., Ayers, T. S., Sandler, I. N., Wolchik, S. A., & Weyer, J. L. (2003). Locus of control and self-esteem as stress-moderators or stress-mediators in parentally bereaved children. *Death Studies, 27,* 619–640.

Hardin, R. (2001). Conceptions and explanations of trust: In K. S. Cook (Ed.), *Trust in society* (pp. 3–39). New York: Russell Sage.

Harter, S., Waters, P., & Whitesell, N. R. (1998). Relational self-worth: Differences in perceived worth as a person across interpersonal contexts among adolescents. *Child Development, 69,* 756–766.

Heinonen, K., Räikönnen, K., & Keltikangas-Järvinen, L. (2003). Maternal perceptions and adolescent self-esteem: A six-year longitudinal study. *Adolescence, 38,* 669–687.

Heinonen, K., Räikönnen, K., Keskivaara, P., & Keltikangas-Järvinen, L. (2002). Difficult temperament predicts self-esteem in adolescence. *European Journal of Personality, 16,* 439–455.

Herman, J. (1992, 1997). *Trauma and recovery.* New York: Basic Books.

Hesse, E. (1999). The adult attachment interview: Historical land current perspectives. In J. Cassidy & P. R. Shaver (Eds.), *Handbook of attachment: Theory, research, and clinical applications* (pp. 395–433). New York: Guilford Press.

Hesse, E., Main, M., Abrams, K. Y., & Rifkin, A. (2003). Unresolved states regarding loss or abuse can have "second-generation" effects: Disorganization, role inversion, and frightening ideation in the offspring of traumatized, non-maltreating parents. In M. Soloman & D. J. Siegel (Eds.), *Healing trauma* (pp. 57–106). New York: W. W. Norton.

Holmes, E. (1938). *The science of mind.* New York: Dodd, Mead, and Company.

Ingram, R. E. & Price, J. M. (2001). The role of vulnerability in understanding psychopathology. In R. E. Ingram & J. M. Price (Eds.), *Vulnerability to psychopathology: Risk across the lifespan* (pp. 3–19). New York: Guilford Press.

Kalsched, D. (1996). *The inner world of trauma: Archetypal defenses of the personal spirit.* London: Brunner-Routledge.

King, V. (2002). Parental divorce and interpersonal trust in adult offspring. *Journal of Marriage & the Family; 64,* 642–656.

Kirmayer, L. J., Young, A., & Hayton, B. C. (1995). The cultural context of anxiety disorders. *Psychiatric Clinics of North America, 18,* 503–521.

Knox, J. (1999). The relevance of attachment theory to a contemporary Jungian view of the internal world: Internal working models, implicit memory and internal objects. *Journal of Analytical Psychology, 44,* 511–530.

Knox, J. (2003a). Trauma and defenses: Their roots in relationship, an overview. *Journal of Analytical Psychology, 48,* 511–530.

Knox, J. (2003b). *Archetype, Attraction, Analysis: Jungian Psychology and the Emergent Mind.* New York: Brunner-Routledge.

Krug, R. (1996). Psychological effects of manmade disasters. *Oklahoma Dental Association, 86,* 40–44.

Kurcinka, M. S. (1998). *Raising your spirited child* (2nd ed.). New York: Harper Perennial.

Leeming, D. & Boyle, M. (2004). Shame as a social phenomenon: A critical analysis of the concept of dispositional shame. *Psychology and Psychotherapy: Theory, Research and Practice, 77,* 375–396.

Lewis, H. (1971). *Shame and guilt in neurosis.* New York: International Universities Press.

Luthar, S. S. (Ed.) (2003). *Resilience and vulnerability: Adaptation in the context of childhood adversities.* New York: Cambridge University Press.

Lyons-Ruth, K., Yellin, C., Melnick, S., & Atwood, G. (2003). Childhood experiences of trauma and loss have different relations to maternal unresolved and Hostile Helpless states of mind on the AAI. *Attachment & Human Development, 5*, 330–352.

M. (1942). *The Gospel of Sri Ramakrishna.* New York: Ramakrishna-Vivekananda Center.

Malcarne, V. L. & Hansdottir, I. (2001). Vulnerability to anxiety disorders in childhood and adolescence. In Ingram, R. E. & Price, J. M. (Eds.), *Vulnerability to psychopathology: Risk across the lifespan* (pp. 271–303). New York: Guilford Press.

March, J., Amaya-Jackson, L., Foa, E. & Treadwell, K. (1999). Trauma focused coping treatment of pediatric post-traumatic stress disorder after single-incident trauma. (Version 1.0). An unpublished protocol.

Martin, P. (2003). Taking control of your life: A brief journey and guide. *International Journal of Reality Therapy, 23*, 41–46.

Mash, E. J. & Dozois, D. (2003). Child psychopathology: A developmental systems perspective. In E. J. Mash & R. A. Barkley (Eds.), *Child psychopathology,* (2nd ed., pp. 3–71). New York: Guilford Press.

Masten, A. S. & Powell, J. L. (2003). A resilience framework for research, policy and practice. In S. S. Luthar (Ed.), *Resilience and vulnerability: Adaptation in the context of childhood adversities* (pp. 1–25). New York: Cambridge University Press.

McGinnis, A. (1979). *The friendship factor.* Minneapolis: Augsburg Publishing.

Menzies, V. & Taylor, A. G. (2004). The idea of imagination: An analysis of "imagery." *Advances, 20*, 4–10.

Mitchell, C. E. (1990). Development or restoration of trust in interpersonal relationships during adolescence and beyond. *Adolescence, 25*, 847–854.

Morehead, A. H. (1962). *Roget's college thesaurus.* London: The New American Library.

Moran, P. B. & Eckenrode, J. (1992). Protective personality characteristics among adolescent victims of maltreatment. *Child Abuse and Neglect, 16*, 743–754.

Morrow, L. (2002). How humiliation bites back. *Time South Pacific, 16*, 64 (April 29, 2002).

Myers, I. B., with Myers, P. B. (1995). *Gifts differing.* Palo Alto, CA: Davies Black Publishing.

Nader, K. (1997). Treating traumatic grief in systems. In C. R. Figley, B. E. Bride, & N. Mazza (Eds.), *Death and trauma: The traumatology of grieving* (pp. 159–192). London: Taylor and Francis.

Nader, K. (2001). Treatment methods for childhood trauma. In J. P. Wilson, M. Friedman, & J. Lindy (Eds.), *Treating psychological trauma and PTSD* (pp. 278–334). New York: Guilford Press.

Nader, K. (2002). Treating children after violence in schools and communities. In N. B. Webb (Ed.), *Helping bereaved children* (2nd ed., pp. 214–244). New York: Guilford Press.

Nader, K. (in press). *Assessing trauma in children and adolescents.* New York: Haworth Press.

Nader, K. & Mello, C. (2001). Interactive trauma/grief focused therapy. In P. Lehmann, & N. F. Coady (Eds.), *Theoretical perspectives for direct social work practice: A generalist-eclectic approach* (pp. 382–401). New York: Springer.

Nader, K., Pynoos, R., Fairbanks, L., Al-Ajeel, M., & Al-Asfour, A. (1993). A preliminary study of PTSD and grief among the children of Kuwait following the Gulf crisis. *British Journal of Clinical Psychology, 32*, 407–416.

Nader, K., Pynoos, R., Fairbanks, L., & Frederick, C. (1990). Children's PTSD reactions one year after a sniper attack at their school. *American Journal of Psychiatry, 147*, 1526–1530.

Otis, G. D. & Louks, J. L. (1997). Rebelliousness and psychological distress in a sample of introverted veterans. *Journal of Psychological Type, 40*, 20–30.

Ozolins, A. R. & Stenstrom, U. (2003). Validation of health locus of control patterns in Swedish adolescents. *Adolescence, 38*, 651–657.

Pole, N., Best, S. R., Metzler, T., & Marmar, C. R. (2005). Why are Hispanics at greater risk for PTSD? *Cultural Diversity and Ethnic Minority Psychology, 11*, 144–161.

Price, J. M. & Lento, J. (2001). The nature of child and adolescent vulnerability. In R. E. Ingram & J. M. Price (Eds.), *Vulnerability to psychopathology: Risk across the lifespan* (pp. 20–38). New York: Guilford Press.

Putnam, F. W. (1997). *Dissociation in children and adolescents: A developmental perspective.* New York: Guilford Press.

Rabalais, A. E., Ruggiero, J. K., & Scotti, J. R. (2002). Multicultural issues in the response of children to disasters. In A. M. La Greca, W. K. Silverman, E. M. Vernberg, & M. C. Roberts (Eds.), *Helping children cope with disasters and terrorism.* Washington, DC: American Psychiatric Association Press.

Radha, S. (1978). *Kundalini: Yoga for the West.* Spokane, WA: Timeless Book.

Regehr, C. (2001). Cognitive-behavioral theory. In P. Lehmann & N. F. Coady (Eds.), *Theoretical perspectives for direct social work practice: A generalist-eclectic approach* (pp. 165–182). New York: Springer.

Rosen, K. S. & Rothbaum, F. (1993). Quality of parental caregiving and security of attachment. *Developmental Psychology, 29,* 358–367.

Rosenbloom, D. & Williams, M. B. (2002). Life after trauma: Finding hope by challenging your beliefs and meeting your needs. In M. B. Williams & J. F. Sommer, (Eds.), *Simple and complex post-traumatic stress disorder* (pp. 119–133). New York: Haworth Maltreatment and Trauma Press.

Rotenberg, K. J. & Cerda, C. (1994). Racially based trust expectancies of Native American and Caucasian children. *Journal of Social Psychology; 134,* 621–631.

Rotenberg, K. J. & Morgan, C. J. (1995). Development of a scale to measure individual differences in children's trust-value basis of friendship. *Journal of Genetic Psychology, 156,* 489–502.

Rothbart, M. K., Ahadi, S. A., Hershey, K. L., & Fisher, P. (2001). Investigations of temperament at three to seven years: The Children's Behavior Questionnaire. *Child Development, 72,* 1394–1408.

Rubin, K. H., Burgess, K. B., Kennedy, A. E., & Stewart, S. L. (2003). Social withdrawal in childhood. In E. J. Mash & R. A. Barkley (Eds.), *Child psychopathology* (2nd ed., pp. 372–406). New York: Guilford Press.

Rutter, M. (1997). Clinical implications of attachment concepts: Retrospective and prospective. In L. Atkinson & K. Zucker (Eds.), *Attachment and psychopathology* (pp. 17–46). New York: Guilford Press.

Salvatore, G., Dimaggio, G., & Semerari, A. (2004). A model of narrative development: Implications for understanding psychotherapy and guiding therapy. *Psychology and Psychotherapy: Theory, Research and Practice, 77,* 231–254.

Scheff, T. (1997). Deconstructing rage [on-line]. Available from: http://www.soc.ucsb.edu/faculty/scheff/7.html (downloaded September 17, 2003).

Schiraldi, G. R. (2000). *The post-traumatic stress disorder sourcebook.* Los Angeles: Lowell House.

Schippell, P. L., Vasey, M. W., Cravens-Brown, L. M., & Bretveld, R. A. (2003). Suppressed attention to rejection, ridicule, and failure cues: A unique correlate of reactive but not proactive aggression in youth. *Journal of Clinical Child and Adolescent Psychology, 32,* 40–55.

Schore, A. N. (1996). The experience-dependent maturation of a regulatory system in the orbitofrontal cortex and the origin of developmental psychopathology: Social-environmental risk factors. *Pediatrics, 79,* 343–350.

Schore, A. N. (2003). Early relational trauma, disorganized attachment, and the development of a predisposition to violence. In M. Soloman & D. J. Siegel (Eds.), *Healing trauma* (pp. 107–167). New York: W. W. Norton.

Siegel, D. J. (1999). The developing mind: How relationships and the brain interact to shape who we are. New York: Guilford Press.

Siegel, D. J. (2003). An interpersonal neurobiology of psychotherapy: The developing mind and the resolution of trauma. In M. Soloman & D. J. Siegel (Eds.), *Healing trauma* (pp. 1–56). New York: W. W. Norton.

Silberg, J. L. (Ed.) (1998). *The dissociative child: Diagnosis, treatment, and management.* Baltimore: The Sidran Press.

Simmons, R. (2002). *Odd girl out.* New York: Harcourt.

Slade, A. (1999). Attachment theory and research: Implications for the theory and practice of individual psychotherapy with adults. In J. Cassidy & P. R. Shaver (Eds.), *Handbook of attachment: Theory, research, and clinical applications* (pp. 575–594). New York: Guilford Press.

Stilwell, B. M., Galvin, M., & Kopta, S. M. (1991). Conceptualization of conscience in normal children and adolescents, Ages 5 to 17. *Journal of the American Academy of Child and Adolescent Psychiatry, 30,* 16–21.

Suldo, S. M. & Huebner, E. S. (2004). Does life satisfaction moderate the effects of stressful life events on psychopathological behavior in adolescence? *School Psychology Quarterly, 19,* 93–105.

Terr, L. (1979). Children of Chowchilla: Study of psychic trauma. *Psychoanalytic Study of the Child, 34,* 547–623.

Terr, L. C. (1990). Too Scared to Cry. New York: HarperCollins.

Terr, L. C. (1991). Childhood traumas: An outline and overview. *American Journal of Psychiatry, 148,* 10–20.

Terr, L. C. (2001). Childhood posttraumatic stress disorder. In G. O. Gabbard (Ed.), *Treatment of psychiatric disorders* (3rd ed., Vol. 1, pp. 293–306). Washington, DC: American Psychiatric Press.

Thompson, R. A. (1999). Early attachment and later development. In J. Cassidy & P. R. Shaver (Eds.), *Handbook of attachment* (pp. 265–286). New York: Guilford Press.

Trimble, J. E. & Richardson, S. S. (1982). Locus of control measures among American Indians: Cluster structure analytic characteristics. *Journal of Cross-Cultural Psychology, 13,* 228–238.

Tully, M. (1999). Lifting our voices: African American cultural responses to trauma and loss. In K. Nader, N. Dubrow, & B. Stamm (Eds.), *Honoring differences: Cultural issues in the treatment of trauma and loss* (pp. 23–48). Philadelphia: Taylor and Francis.

Turner, J. C., Brown, R. J., & Tajfel, H. (1979). Social comparison and group interest in ingroup favoritism. *European Journal of Social Psychology, 9,* 187–204.

Udwin, O., Boyle, S., Yule, W., Bolton, D., & O'Ryan, D. (2000). Risk factors for long-term psychological effects of a disaster experienced in adolescence: Predictors of post-traumatic stress disorder. *Journal of Child Psychology and Psychiatry, 41,* 969–979.

Vivekananda, S. (1955). *Jnana-Yoga.* New York: Vedanta Press.

Volkan, V. D. (2001). September 11 and societal regression. *Mind and Human Interaction, 12,* 196–216.

Walsh, F. (1998). Beliefs, spirituality, and transcendence: Keys to family resilience. In McGoldrick, M. (ed.), *Re-visioning Family Therapy* (pp. 62–77). New York: Guilford Press.

Webb, N. B. (Ed.) (2002). *Helping bereaved children* (2nd ed.). New York: Guilford Press.

Weinfield, N. S., Sroufe, L. A., Egeland, B., & Carlson, E. A. (1999). The nature of individual differences in infant-caregiver attachment. In J. Cassidy & P. R. Shaver (Eds.), *Handbook of Attachment* (pp. 68–88). New York: Guilford Press.

Wilson, J. P., Friedman, M., & Lindy, J. (Eds.) (2002). *Treating psychological trauma and PTSD.* . New York: Guilford Press.

Yates, T. M., Egeland, B., & Sroufe, A. (2003). Rethinking resilience: A developmental process perspective. In S. S. Luthar (Ed.), *Resilience and vulnerability: Adaptation in the context of childhood adversities* (pp. 243–266). New York: Cambridge University Press.

Yule, W., Bolton, D., Udwin, O., Boyle, S., O'Ryan, D., & Nurrish, J. (2000). The long-term psychological effects of a disaster experienced in adolescence. I. The incidence and course of PTSD. *Journal of Child Psychology & Psychiatry & Allied Disciplines, 41,* 503–511.

5

Trauma Archetypes and Trauma Complexes

JOHN P. WILSON

1 INTRODUCTION

Trauma is an integral part of the natural history of humanity throughout the millennia. Knowledge of the posttraumatic self requires a comprehensive understanding of how traumatic experiences impact the human psyche in its totality. The matrices of the mind, the plasticity of adaptive behavior, and the capacity of consciousness to transform the contextual meaning of reality, requires perspective on the experience of trauma that extends beyond psychiatric classifications of posttraumatic stress disorder (PTSD) and self-pathologies. The Trauma Archetype and Trauma Complex are critical and little-understood aspects of the post-traumatic self. The Trauma Archetype represents universal forms of traumatic experiences across culture, time, and history. The Trauma Complex is the unique, individual constellation of the trauma experience in cognitive-affective structures located in the self and intrapsychic processes. The Trauma Complex is a suprasystem that is hierarchical in nature and embeds a wide range of phenomena including PTSD and alterations in personality. The Trauma Archetype and Trauma Complex are yoked psychological phenomena that have very distinct characteristics shaped by the nature of the trauma experience and the cultural context in which it occurs.

It is a truism that the experiences of trauma and situations of extreme stress are part of the human condition. For example, in the United States, despite its economic wealth and high standard of living, 60.7% of men and 51.2% of women experience exposure to stressful situations that could cause PTSD, or other psychological reactions (i.e., depression, anxiety) that could adversely effect emotional well-being (Bryant, 2004; Kessler, Sonnega, Bromet, Hughes, & Nelson, 1995). Epidemiological studies (Breslau, 1998) have documented over 20 categories of traumas common to everyday life that are associated with the prevalence of PTSD (1–49%) and its common comorbidity of depression, substance abuse, and generalized anxiety (21.5–58.1%). Moreover, "persons with PTSD are only a small fraction of those exposed to traumatic events" (Breslau, 1998, p. 25), a fact that underscores the ubiquity of trauma in the lives of ordinary people.

A retrospective look at the history of modern civilization, especially since the Middle Ages (500–1500 AD), shows that there are few periods of time that have not been marked by war, civil violence, political domination, the oppression of people, and genocidal and guerrilla warfare. At the international level, the 20th century saw global conflicts with two world wars, the first atomic bombing, mass genocide, multinational "ethnic cleansings," and the proliferation of nuclear weapons of mass destruction. The early 21st century has witnessed the onset and spread of terrorism that has threatened the existence of world peace. As a consequence of war and political disunions, there are currently over 40 million asylum seekers and refugees worldwide (Wilson & Drozdek, 2004). It can be stated unequivocally that the consequences of trauma are part of the awareness of ordinary people, especially since the attacks on the New York World Trade Centers in 2001. This global awareness includes personal knowledge of others who have been victims of traumatic experiences, small and large, whose lives have been altered by what they endured. The universality of trauma is imprinted in human consciousness in the same manner as the experiences of birth, death, marriage, and the aging process in the life-cycle. Stated simply, trauma is as primordial as injury to the organism and a common reality in the natural history of the life-cycle itself. At a higher level, cycles of trauma impact cultures, societies, and nation states, generating unique forms of posttraumatic injuries to the social fabrics and institutions that define civilization at a given period in history.

Our individual understanding of trauma is shaped by belief systems embedded within culture and personal experience that form individually constellated trauma complexes (Marsella, Friedman, Gerrity, & Scurfield, 1996). The universality of traumatic experiences are not only archetypal and part of the human condition, they give birth to trauma complexes of varied dimensions that contain structural coherence, motivational power, and autonomy of functioning within the psyche (Wilson, 2004c). Trauma complexes have the potential to interact dynamically with other archetypal forms of experience and dimensions of the self (e.g., coherence, continuity, connection, energy), qualities of personal identity (i.e., sense of self-sameness and continuity), the agentic function of the ego (e.g., ego-resilience, ego-control, ego-defenses), and major aspects of personality functioning (see Figure 5.7). These dynamic interactions have "cogwheeling" effects amongst archetypes, psychic complexes, and personality processes and will be discussed in this chapter.

2 THE TRAUMA ARCHETYPE,[1] TRAUMA COMPLEXES, AND THE DRIVE TOWARDS PSYCHIC UNITY

A model of the Trauma Archetype and its relation to Trauma Complexes, personality alterations, and the posttraumatic self as a phenomenological entity is presented in Figure 5.1. Examination of Figure 5.1 reveals a complex "flow" between the experience of trauma and its eventual integration into personality and the Unity Archetype, which will be described later. In the flow of the archetypal trauma experience, there are interrelated psychological processes that encapsulate the multidimensional nature of human responses to extreme and prolonged stress reactions. The left-hand side of the diagram identifies six generic, stress-related categories associated with the perception, encoding, and processing of the trauma experience: (1) universal forms of trauma exposure; (2) emotional regulation of stress response; (3) individual cognition and beliefs; (4) categories of extreme stress encounters; (5) complex and prolonged stress reaction patterns; and (6) archetypal manifestations of trauma experiences and the activation of other basic archetypes and psychic complexes. The generic stress-related categories are associated with individual dimensions of stress responses: (a) specific types of traumatic stressors; (b) posttraumatic affect dysregulations; (c) posttraumatic cognitive schemas; (d) individual and collective experiences of traumatic events; (e) posttraumatic personality constellations; and (f) posttraumatic cogwheeling effects among trauma archetypes and other psychic complexes. The correspondence between

---

[1]The Trauma Archetype and Trauma Complex are new concepts adapted from Jung's discussion of psychic complexes and archetypes and archetypal forms of experience. The terms are being used specifically in discussion of trauma and the development of complex forms of prolonged stress response syndromes.

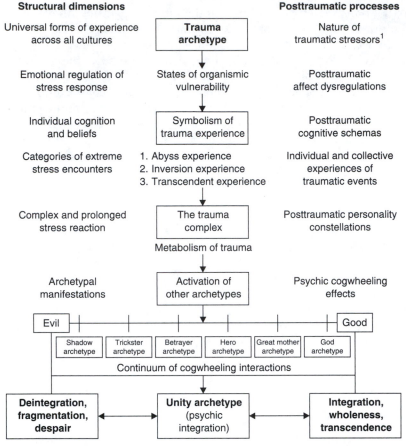

FIGURE 5.1. The Trauma Archetype, Trauma Complex, and the drive towards psychic unity. [1]See classification of 10 stressor categories in Wilson and Lindy (1994). *Source:* ©2004 John P. Wilson.

the *structural* and *process* dimensions of posttraumatic stress responses can be seen in the development of trauma complexes:

Universal Dimensions of Trauma	Individual Dimensions of Trauma
1. Universal forms of trauma experience	1. Specific nature of traumatic stressors
2. Emotional systems of stress Response	2. Posttraumatic affect dysregulations
3. Individual cognition and belief systems	3. Posttraumatic cognitive schemas
4. Abyss and inversion experiences	4. Individual and collective experiences
5. Complex and prolonged stress reactions	5. Posttraumatic personality constellations
6. Archetypal manifestations	6. Posttraumatic cogwheeling effects among archetypes

The Trauma Archetype (as the universal form of extreme stress across cultures, time, and space) leads directly to states of *organismic vulnerability* whose hallmark features are anxiety and a sense of uncertainty and unpredictability of events. Psychological states of vulnerability and the metabolism of the trauma experience are represented symbolically in psychoformative processes as filtered through the *Abyss, Inversion and Transcendent Experiences* that define specific categories of traumatic encounters. However, not all victims of extreme stress develop trauma complexes because of individual differences in the response to traumatic stressors and the nature of pretraumatic personality structure (see Chapter 10).

Trauma Complexes are suprasystems that are hierarchically organized and have psychological structure, boundaries, dimensions, dynamics, psychic energy, and motivational power. In plain words, they have their own character and identity. They activate and articulate with other archetypes and complexes that exist. In a unique way, the Trauma Complex cogwheels dynamically with other archetypes as determined by basic psychological needs, a phenomenon to be described more completely below. Specific forms of archetypes can symbolically represent the trauma experience (e.g., the Shadow, Betrayal, Trickster archetypes) and emotional needs made salient by traumatic stressors (e.g., arousal of needs for protection, rescue, love, safety, nurturance). The archetypes can be conceptualized to exist on a continuum from good (e.g., generative, growth-promoting) to evil (e.g., destructive, pathogenic). At one end, this continuum of archetypal forms of experience consists of states of deintegration, fragmentation, and despair (i.e., the demonic polarity). At the other end, are states of integration, wholeness, and transcendence (i.e., the transcendent polarity). Archetypes possess a duality of form and function that encompasses good and bad aspects of every archetypal experience, including traumatic ones. The healthy assimilation of the trauma experience into the posttraumatic self is represented in the Unity Archetype characterized by psychologically integrative experiences which include trauma-evoked transcendent experiences (see Chapter 6).

3 THE INNER AND OUTER WORLDS OF TRAUMA EXPERIENCE

In terms of theories about psychological trauma, it is important to clarify the different approaches used to analyze the nature of the trauma experience. The contrasting theoretical views place different emphasis and "weights" on the origin and causality of trauma experiences and the mechanisms by which they are encoded, stored in memory, and associated with dysregulated emotions (Schore, 2003b). For example,

Jean Knox (2003) noted the differences between conceptual and treatment approaches to psychological trauma. In analytic traditions, psychological trauma is conceptualized as originating from experiences that tax coping resources and ego-strength. By their nature, such emotionally strong experiences can be psychically traumatizing. The ego and self are vulnerable to rejection, loss of attachments, humiliation, and narcissistic injuries. As noted by Kalsched (1996, 2003), the defensive structures organized to deal with self-injuries retraumatize from within once set in motion. Conceptions of the inner world of trauma assume a model of causality in which the "traumatized psyche" is self-traumatizing, meaning that maladaptive defenses perpetuate the maintenance of the original trauma and its effects, setting up a reciprocal process of retraumatization like the proverbial dog chasing its tail (Kalsched, 1996).

It is possible to distinguish conceptual views regarding the inner and outer worlds of trauma experience. For example, Knox (2003) states

> This description of a polarized internal working model, containing omnipotent fantasies that defend against actual or feared rejection and humiliation, has considerable similarities, but some differences from the concept proposed by Kalsched (1996) of archetypal defenses which are activated by unbearable trauma. Kalsched highlights the vital protective role that dissociative defenses play when a person is threatened with intolerable trauma, psychic pain or anxiety, which are severe enough to bring about psychic disintegration, or the destruction of the personal spirit. (p. 222)

The polarized internal working model refers to intrapsychic defenses against the perception of intolerable trauma, no matter what its origin or magnitude. We can see, therefore, that an understanding of the complexities of psychological trauma varies depending on the type of conceptual model used to describe the inner working of the posttraumatic self. A model that emphasizes the stressor → response paradigm (i.e., *DSM-IV*) attempts to link trauma exposure to symptom formation with little, if any, delineation of how the self, attachments, and intrapsychic processes are simultaneously or sequentially affected by the perception of trauma as overpowering coping resources (Wilson, 2004b; Wilson, Friedman, & Lindy, 2001). On the other hand, external stressors of the type that define the *DSM-IV-TR* (2000) PTSD diagnostic criteria assume a "Big Bang" model of causality for the etiology of stress-evoked symptoms. It is a linear dose–response model of the effects of severe and prolonged stress reactions. In the analytic model of archetypal defenses, emphasis is on the "inner world of trauma": there is less concern with the magnitude of external stressor events but rather with the manner in which a range of life-experiences, including separation, loss, traumatic bereavement, rejection, humiliation, repetitive neglect, and abuse, impact on the intricate world of nascent ego and self-functions, leading to states of splitting, fragmentation (i.e., deintegration), dissociation, or alterations in the self (Kalsched, 1996, 2003). In this respect, it is germane to note that Jung used the term "dissociation" to refer to the formation of complexes which reference defensive, internal splitting of psychological processes. As Knox (2003) clarifies in her book *Archetype, Attachment, Analysis*, Jung's use of dissociation was different in meaning from the *DSM-IV* criteria of dissociative processes in which there are significant changes in the integrative processes of perception, identity, consciousness, and behavior. The analytic meaning of dissociability refers to the ways in which personality splits off and forms complexes embedded within personality.

Theoretically, the Trauma Complex is only one of many psychic complexes that can exist. The Trauma Complex is central to the functions of the posttraumatic self until transformed and integrated as part of the Unity Archetype. The tendency of the psyche to split into basic structural units, called *feeling-toned complexes*, is among the central axioms of Jung's psychology of personality. He (1972) stated

> Complexes are psychic fragments which have split off owing to *traumatic influences of certain incompatible tendencies* ... complexes interfere with the will and *disturb conscious* performance: they *produce disturbances of memory and blockages in the flow of association*; they can temporarily obsess consciousness, or *influence speech and action in an unconscious way* ... complexes behave like independent beings (CW 8, para. 253; emphasis added).

Jung (1972) considered the psyche's ability to split complexes into structural units as a natural form of differentiation in cognitive functioning, including dissociation. Jung was aware that, under traumatic conditions, complexes can split off and cause intrapsychic conflict (e.g., disorders such as hysteria and dissociative phenomena), or what he termed "states of possession" (Jung, 1968, CW 9.1, para. 224). However, it is noteworthy that Jung never postulated a specific form of trauma complex which, of course, would have followed logically from his definition of psychic complexes.

3.1 The Trauma Archetype, Posttraumatic Self, and Living Systems Theory

The Trauma Archetype and the Trauma Complex are an integral part of the posttraumatic self and personality processes. The Trauma

Archetype is a new term I am introducing based on an analysis of Jung's (1934) discussion of the universality of archetypes in personality (Wilson, 2004c). In terms of functional dynamics, the Trauma Archetype and Trauma Complex operate on the principle of living systems theory (Miller, 1978), which has as a premise that

> open systems [are] composed of subsystems which process inputs, throughputs, and outputs of various forms of matter, energy, and information . . . there are 19 critical subsystems whose processes are essential for life, some of which process matter or energy, some of which process information, and some of which process all three. (p. 1)

3.2 The Hierarchical Suprasystem of Trauma Complexes

In terms of psychological trauma, there are specific subsystems that are integral to the formation of Trauma Complexes, which include: (1) *input transducers,* which both filter and bring specific aspects of traumatic stressors into psychic constellations; (2) *internal transducers,* which receive from the sensory system the information about the nature and dimensions of the trauma experience; (3) *channels,* which indicate the routes by which traumatic impacts are transmitted through the organism (e.g., HPA-axis, memory systems, ego-defensive systems); (4) *decoders,* which alter the informational "meaning" of the trauma experience; and (5) *associators,* cognitive and memory processes that form linkages in terms of learning and information storage. In terms of memory and learning, emotionally infused traumatic memories become connected to other domains of knowledge and information. Viewed from the viewpoint of living systems theory, Trauma Complexes are the product of innate dispositional factors and learned cognitive-affective schemas that form trauma responses. Thus, they can be considered as *suprasystems* in a hierarchy of systems that exist within the organism in a synergistically interrelated fashion (Miller, 1978). The Trauma Complex is a suprasystem within the totality of psychic functioning in general, and personality processes in particular, primarily because of the power of fear and terror as primitive emotions linked to survival.

The Trauma Archetype is a universal form of stress reaction to experiences that evokes fear (including fear of annihilation) and generates the formation of Trauma Complexes. Trauma Archetypes meet the prime scientific criteria to define archetypal experiences: (1) they are universally present in psychological form in all cultures; (2) they are active dispositions to behaviors that influence thoughts, feelings, and actions; (3) they are primordial unconscious forms that are constellated with conscious material from traumatic experiences; and

(4) they are continuously present in human history and evolution (Stevens, 1994).[2]

Historically, the concept of complexes refers to intrapsychic processes that form as structural parts of personality: "[complexes], *each of which is linked to an archetype: for complexes are personifications of archetypes; they are the means through which the archetypes manifest themselves in the personal psyche*" (Stevens, 1994, p. 48; emphasis added). Complexes and archetypes are dynamically interactive with each other. Archetypes represent universal forms of human experiences as part of the collective unconscious. Trauma Complexes are individual constellations of stressful life-experiences which have "split off" and organized within the personal unconscious. Once formed as a suprasystem, they operate on the principles of living systems theory, with identifiable subsystems that include PTSD, affect regulation, personality processes, and cognitive schemas. The mechanisms of these subsystems will be discussed later.

In culture-specific ways, archetypes represent universal forms of traumatic experience embedded within the organism. Cultural forces shape the perception and symbolic meaning of individual trauma. The Trauma Archetype is species-specific because trauma exists in all cultures throughout history. Extreme experiences with life-altering consequences are found in all human communities and produce generic, injurious physical and mental effects to the organism. How the individual perceives and metabolizes trauma determines the outcome to the psyche, which may vary significantly by culture (Marsella, Friedman, Gerrity, & Scurfield, 1996). The characteristics of the Trauma Archetype are listed in Table 5.1.

The Trauma Archetype involves conscious and unconscious alterations in psychic states, allostatic changes in organismic functioning, disequilibration in states of meaning and belief, and impacts on the structure of the self and personality processes. As polarities of extreme experiences, the dialectic of the Trauma Archetype involves: (1) the integration of an ego-alien experience into personality; (2) the mobilization of energy for healing and recovery; and (3) the moral task of formulating prosocial dispositions versus the struggle with helplessness, anger, withdrawal, and self-absorption. In mythology, the Trauma Archetype comprises a psychological function of personal and spiritual transformation in a journey of self-discovery in which there is a confrontation with the darkness of existence, followed by the return from the

---

[2]See Stevens' (1994) discussion of the scientific criteria for defining archetypes and their similarity to innate releasing mechanisms (IRMs) in ethological studies of behavior.

TABLE 5.1
Dimensions of the Trauma Archetype (Universal Forms of Traumatic Experience)

1. The Trauma Archetype is a prototypical stress response pattern present in all human cultures, universal in its effects, and manifest in overt behavioral patterns and internal intrapsychic processes, especially the Trauma Complex

2. The Trauma Archetype evokes altered psychological states, which include changes in consciousness, memory, orientation to time, space, and person and appear in the Trauma Complex

3. The Trauma Archetype evokes allostatic changes in the organism (posttraumatic impacts, e.g., personality change, PTSD, allostatic dysregulation) which are expressed in common neurobiological pathways

4. The Trauma Archetype contains the experience of threat to psychological and physical well-being, typically manifest in the Abyss and Inversion Experiences

5. The Trauma Archetype involves confrontation with the fear of death

6. The Trauma Archetype evokes the specter of self-deintegration, dissolution and soul (psychic) death (i.e., loss of identity), and is expressed in the Trauma Complex

7. The Trauma Archetype is a manifestation of overwhelmingly stressful experience to the organization of self, identity, and belief systems and appears as part of the structure of the Trauma Complex

8. The Trauma Archetype stimulates cognitive attributions of meaning and causality for injury, suffering, loss, and death (i.e., altered core beliefs) which appear in the Trauma Complex

9. The Trauma Archetype energizes posttraumatic tasks of defense, recovery, healing, and growth, which include the development of PTSD as a Trauma Complex

10. The Trauma Archetype activates polarities of meaning attribution; the formulation of prosocial—humanitarian morality vs. abject despair and meaninglessness paradigm

11. The Trauma Archetype may evoke spiritual transformation: individual → journey/ "encounter with darkness" → return/transformation/re-emergence, healing (Campbell, 1949). The evocation of a "spiritual" transformation is manifest in the Trauma Complex as part of the Transcendent Experience and the drive toward unification

Source: ©2004 John P. Wilson.

trauma encounter and the processes of self-reconstruction, transformation, and healing.

3.3 States of Organismic Vulnerability

In the purest sense, the Trauma Archetype represents a state of *organismic vulnerability*. This state of organismic vulnerability has traditionally been characterized by the emotions of fear, terror, horror, anxiety, and behavioral states of uncertainty, doubt, shame, guilt, and helplessness. In the experimental and clinical literature, organismic states of vulnerability have been conceptualized as a loss of a sense of control over, and loss of predictability of, reinforcers of behavior (Seligman, 1975;

Aronoff & Wilson, 1985; LefCourt, 1982). In the traumatic stress literature, states of vulnerability have been conceptualized as disequilibrium, loss of homeostasis, allostasis, and loss of emotional balance and well-being (Friedman, 2000; Wilson, Friedman, & Lindy, 2001; Friedman & McEwen, 2004; McEwen, 1998, 2002).

In the primordial sense, the Trauma Archetype is *the* most profound state of organismic vulnerability. The Trauma Archetype contains levels of conscious awareness (LCA) of the existence of threat to organismic integrity that range on a continuum from minimal to imminent awareness of threat, danger, and self-annihilation. The accuracy of the perceptions of threat and danger exist on this same continuum, from accurate, realistic perceptions of threat (including intrapsychic threats) to degrees of inaccurate, distorted, or denied perceptions of traumatic stressors (Wilson, 1989, 2004c).

4 THE SYMBOLISM OF TRAUMATIC EXPERIENCES

The human capacity to create and use symbols extends to archetypal experiences of trauma and the formation of Trauma Complexes. The seminal works of Freud (1900, 1917) and Jung (1929) documented that symbols may be individualistic or universal in nature. Symbols stand for raw concrete forms of human experience and can be classified into a relatively small number of categories. Freud (1917) believed that symbols are largely unconscious and fall into 10 general categories: (1) the human body; (2) parental relations; (3) family and sibling relations; (4) domiciles; (5) gender; (6) birth; (7) death; (8) sexuality; (9) the human body (anatomy and physiology); and (10) aggression. Freud stated that the analysis of dream symbols would reveal these classifications and could be discerned on the basis of the symbol's structure (shape, design) and function (how it works).

The specific nature of a traumatic experience can be symbolized in a wide variety of ways in the Trauma Complex. Similar to Freudian dream symbols, the Trauma Archetype gets symbolized in unique ways that are manifested in symptoms, dreams, fantasies, and motivational vectors of striving in the Trauma Complex. In discussing the process of symbolization of experience, Sherry Salman (1997) states

> He [Jung] considered unconscious imagery to be symbolic, where a symbol is understood as something that compensates or rectifies the error of ego consciousness. *The symbol has a regulating function.* The essence of the teleological position is that (a) *all symptoms and complexes have a symbolic archetypal core,* and (b) the end result, purpose, or aim of a symptom, complex or defense mechanism is as important, if not more so, than its causes. A symptom develops not "because" of its prior history, but "in order to"

express a piece of psyche or accomplish its purpose. The clinical question is not reductive, but synthetic: *What is this symptom for?* (p. 62; emphasis added)

In this framework, symbols have meaning, purpose, and function. Symbols of the trauma experience are located within the Trauma Complex. Their ultimate purpose, in terms of maximizing optimal functioning, is to provide information to assist in their integration into personality without the requirement of maladaptive ego-defenses.

The Trauma Complex can activate other psychic complexes formed during psychosocial development (e.g., mother/oedipal complex). In this manner, psychic complexes of different types cogwheel with one another through conscious and unconscious dynamics. The Trauma Complex that grows out of the Trauma Archetype can activate basic needs for safety, nurturance, protection, affiliation, rescue, revenge, aggression, retaliation, or faith and hope in a Higher Power. Archetypes such as the nurturing Great Mother, The Wise Old Man, Hero, Trickster, Betrayer, or God may be activated at conscious and unconscious levels by the Trauma Archetype and generate cogwheeling effects among them, similar to how mechanical "tooth and spoke" wheels engage action to power functions of a machine (see Figure 5.9). In this sense, Jung (1929) believed that the self, as part of personality, was an archetypal form whose functions included balancing polarities and opposites that have a natural drive towards unity and integration. Jung described the integration or conjoining of polarities and opposite forces as the transcendent function. In terms of symbolic processes, intra-psychic tension among opposites and polarities in the self are capable of symbolic expression in nearly every aspect of mental life and creative endeavor. In the posttraumatic self, there will be evidence of Trauma Complexes that include other archetypal contents as well as residues of the trauma encounter, for example, PTSD, depressive states, and changes in identity and self-perceptions. However, the Trauma Complex itself is a process of continuous change and reconfiguration in the service of psychic integration. The assessment of the Trauma Complex and its symbolic content provides extraordinarily useful clues as to how the trauma experience was metabolized by the person. Analyzing the Trauma Complex opens the doors to integration and unification in personality in the direction of transcendence.

4.1 The Mandala of Trauma

Jung (1950) suggested that the mandala, or circle, was one form of symbolic representation of the self, as the core of personality, and its

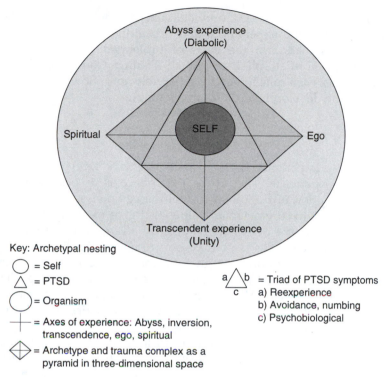

FIGURE 5.2. Trauma Archetype mandala. *Source:* ©2003 John P. Wilson.

constituent parts. The mandala represents wholeness and the projection of one's sense of inner unity. The mandala of the Trauma Archetype has been depicted as a large circle that contains an inner circle representing the self which, in turn, is nested within a triangle depicting the core triad of PTSD symptoms (i.e., reexperiencing, avoidance/numbing, hyperarousal). The symbol for the self is nested within a rotated square formed by two axes: (a) Abyss versus the Transcendent Experience and (b) Ego versus Spiritual Experience. The Trauma Archetype and Trauma Complex thus combine in geometric form (i.e., the rotated square and triangle) to create a three-dimensional psychic complex located in the nidus of the self (Wilson, 2004c). Figure 5.2 illustrates the symbol of the Trauma Archetype in mandala form.

5 THE ABYSS, INVERSION, AND TRANSCENDENT EXPERIENCES

Symbolism and deeper knowledge of the trauma experience in archetypal form and complexes cannot be fully understood without knowledge of the Abyss, Inversion, and Transcendent Experiences

(Wilson, 2004b, c). These terms characterize qualitatively different aspects of traumatic experiences and are indigenous to situations of extreme stress that form the basis of prolonged patterns of human stress, the primordial soil from which Trauma Complexes originate. I will discuss each phenomenon separately and how each, in turn, influences the development of Trauma Complex.

5.1 The Abyss Experience

The Abyss Experience is the vortex and dark foreboding space of the trauma experience. The Abyss Experience is associated with the realistic perception of the threat to life, the ego and self-structure, and imminent threat to core personal values that give meaning to existence. The Abyss Experience does not characterize all types of trauma experiences, although elements of it may be present in the lives of trauma survivors. These forms of threat include consequences to the organization of ego-processes and the structure of personal identity (see Chapter 2 for a discussion). The Abyss Experience involves three primary subsystems: (1) emotions, (2) self-dimensions and capacities, and (3) attachment relations. For example, it involves emotional states of extreme fear, the specter of nonbeing, death or physical annihilation. At the level of the self, it can precipitate dissolution, deintegration, dissociation, and fragmentation. At the subjective level of attachment behaviors and social relations, the Abyss Experience concerns the experience of abject ultimate aloneness in the universe and a sense of abandonment by God and humanity (Knox, 2003; Reis, 1995; Wilson, 2004c). Common to the Abyss Experience is the confronting of that which is life-threatening, evil, depraved, demonic, excruciating, vile, sinister, and the "darkness of being" (Knox, 2003; Wilson, 2002). The Abyss Experience can be construed as the negative polarity of the "peak experience" (see Chapter 6 for a discussion). As a subjective, negative emotional experience, the Abyss Experience is a psychological "black hole," analogous to an astronomical magnetic force, that sucks in negative experiences that are proximal in ego-space and interpersonal relationships.

In terms of psychic trauma, the Abyss Experience represents confrontations with different types of terror and horror. In religion, the Abyss Experience is construed as depictions of "Heaven and Hell." Ladner (2004) notes

> our projections about heaven and hell are rooted in and provide an *interesting window into our positive and negative emotions*... descriptions of hell in Western or Eastern religions ... are extreme magnifications of the very worst qualities of our human hearts. You can read of beings burning alive in the fires of rage and hate, which cause *intense pain,*

Dimensions of trauma abyss	Psychological phenomena
1. Confrontation with evil and death	Trauma experience
2. Experience of soul death and non-being	Self/identity
3. Abandonment by humanity	Loss of connection
4. Ultimate aloneness and despairing	Separation and isolation
5. Cosmic challenge of meaning	Spirituality/higher power (numinous)

FIGURE 5.3. Abyss Experience. *Source:* ©2004 John P. Wilson.

agitation, and breathless agony without allowing for escape into sleep or death. There are also descriptions of beings frozen in an infinite, icy tundra of utter isolation, entirely disconnected from all that lives and loves. Isolation, disconnection, rage, terror, envy, and hate are feelings that underlie the archetypal, psychological phenomenon of hell. (p. 265; emphasis added)

5.2 Dimensions of the Abyss Experience

The Abyss Experience is the metaphysical bottom of the seemingly endless chasm of emotional and spiritual darkness without relief from utter terror and fear during critical moments of the traumatic experience. During the Abyss Experience, the individual experiences excruciating terror and overpowering fear of annihilation. It is subjectively experienced as "the end" of life; the imminent end of existence. The Abyss Experience is an emotionally overwhelming force of immense power that threatens to darken the inner light of the soul. It is the sense of omnipotent anxiety, fear, and dread combined into a single phenomenon that foreshadow one's death. There can be a loss of identity, continuity, personal autonomy, meaningful connection to others, self-coherence, and extreme states of emotional lability both during and after the Abyss Experience. During the Abyss Experience, there is an awareness of the fragility of the self's architectural structure, that one's inner being, as previously known, could readily deintegrate, if not dissolve, into nothingness.

The Abyss Experience has five primary dimensions: (1) confrontation with evil and death; (2) the specter of nonbeing (annihilation) and soul-death; (3) sense of abandonment by God and humanity; (4) ultimate aloneness and despairing; and (5) cosmic challenge and meaning (see Figure 5.3). The dimensions of the Abyss Experience involve experiential components that correspond to the universality of the trauma experience and its impact on the structure and functions of the self as well as pre-existing personality factors. In terms of living systems theory, the intrapsychic dynamics of the Abyss Experiences are related to: (1) the nature of the trauma; (2) identity and the self-structure; (3) the loss of connection to self, others, and culture; (4) severe psychological separation and isolation (i.e., ultimate aloneness); and (5) spirituality, including the experience of God, Higher Power, the numinous and the confrontation with ultimate meaning.

The Abyss Experience "crosscuts" and impacts the potential actualization of archetypal requirements for human development described by Stevens

> ...an innate sequence of archetypal expectations, namely that the environment will provide the following: sufficient nourishment, warmth, and protection from predators and enemies to guarantee physical survival; a family consisting of a mother, father and peers; sufficient space for exploration and play; a community to supply language, myth, religion, ritual, values, stories, initiation and eventually, a mate; an economic role and/or vocational status. (1994, p. 74)

The archetypal basis for self-individuation and personal growth is attacked by severe trauma experiences. The Abyss Experience has the power to injure or permanently deprive archetypal expectations for healthy growth and maturation. The Abyss Experience is more than an encounter with powerful stressors; it represents traumatic impact on the innermost core of psychic functioning that defines personal identity.

The stressors associated with the Abyss Experience rapidly immerse the individual in the specter of nonbeing (imminent, potential, or symbolic death) or the witnessing of overwhelming and indescribable trauma to others such that it leads to a sense of impending demise or disintegration (see case vignettes). The Abyss Experience is subjectively experienced as a vast and painful emotional chasm of dark, empty, inner space, (Wilson, 2003). At the depth of the Abyss Experience there is little hope for relief, rescue, or salvation from the hands of destructive and catastrophic forces. The imminent fear of death or annihilation predominates consciousness (Kalsched, 1996, 2003; Knox, 2003; Wilson, 2004c).

6 CASE EXAMPLE: ON THE BANKS OF THE EUPHRATES RIVER

An example of the Abyss Experience can be seen in the following case history of a 30-year-old male torture survivor undergoing treatment as an asylum seeker and refugee. This case history is typical of many similar experiences reported by the survivors of Saddam Hussein's reign as dictator in Iraq until 2003. The fact that the victim survived, fled to another country, and reached out for help, speaks strongly to his desire for self-unification.

During his first arrest, "L." tried to commit suicide but was shot in the leg and taken directly to a notorious prison. There he was immediately beaten brutally over his entire body, and subjected to falanga. The torture continued and L. was forced to lick up blood from the floor. He was suspended on a cross, kicked over his entire body, and kept awake for days.

Not broken by the physical torture, L. was subjected to psychological torture. He was placed in a room between a mother and a daughter. The mother was whipped and ordered not to make a sound or the daughter would be [sexually] abused. He was subjected to mock execution several times; on one such occasion he was drenched with liters of petrol, and the torturers fumbled with matches in front of him. Threatened with homosexual rapes and beaten into unconsciousness, he also received electric torture around the ears. His nose was broken repeatedly, and he developed bleeding from the stomach and hemorrhagic vomiting. He was suspended both head up and feet up, and burned with cigarettes over his body . . . L. was isolated for about a year in a very small, completely barren cell . . . he was subjected to Russian Roulette and deprivation of food. (Vesti, Somnier, & Kastrup, 1992, p. 56)

L.'s experience is one of extreme torture and degradation. His torture was a sadistic attempt to destroy his human physical essence, spirit, and soul. One could correctly say that he visited the depths of the Abyss on many occasions of brutalization in which he confronted visions of his own disintegration and death.

The Abyss Experience, as a form of catastrophic trauma, can shatter the psyche to its core, rearranging its essential form but without destroying it completely, as occurred in L.'s case of torture. The Abyss Experience and the subsequent development of the Trauma Complex constitute a more comprehensive intrapsychic perspective of psychological trauma. As I will discuss, the Trauma Complex is a more inclusive term than PTSD. The Trauma Complex concerns the highly intricate inner world of individual experience. In his book *The Inner World of Trauma: Archetypal Defenses of the Personal Spirit*, Jungian analyst Donald Kalsched states

> For the person who has experienced unbearable pain, the psychological defense of dissociation allows external life to go on but at great internal cost. The outer trauma ends and its effects may be largely "forgotten," but the *psychological sequelae of the trauma continue to haunt the inner world*, and they do this, Jung discovered, in the form of certain images which cluster around a strong affect—what Jung called the *feeling-toned complexes*. (1996, p. 13; emphasis added)

The Abyss Experience connects memories, images, and conscious ruminations. It evokes unmetabolized and unmodulated emotions that bring about the dissociation of the psyche through formation of the Trauma Complex.

7 LEXICAL ANALYSIS OF THE ABYSS EXPERIENCE

It is useful to consider the meaning of the word "abyss" and its deeper lexical connection to intrapsychic processes. Words reflect meaning born of personal experiences. In the physical realm, an abyss is a deep, seemingly endless chasm of space, which may or may not be bordered, whirling, still, noisy (cacophonous), or silent. Abyss refers to depth and spatial dimensionality (e.g., bottomless gulf; endless, deep black hole; unfathomable void, shaft, vault, crevice, cavern; a whirling and descending vortex, etc.). Abyss, as a noun, is also used synonymously with the word "Hell" and a "place of evil darkness," to connote primal chaos, the infernal netherlands of perdition and purgatory, the world of sinister forces and depravity. The Hell of the abyss also refers to the diabolic, supernatural, wicked, demonic, shadowy foreboding space, psychological "black hole" of horrific pain; the realm of the damned. The Abyss represents dangerous, ungodly, ugly, cursed, and unimaginable sadistic, aggressive, and horrific torturous experiences.

7.1 The Abyss Experience and the Shadow Archetype

In Jungian (1972) theory, the Shadow Archetype characterizes the undesirable traits and typically disavowed and "shadowy" side of personality. It represents destructive impulses, aggressive, negative personality traits (e.g., dishonesty, unfaithfulness, deceptiveness, meanness) and salacious primary process thinking, raw urges, instinctual desires, unbounded libidinal wishes, and grandiose fantasies. As Anthony Stevens (1994) states: "the shadow tends to appear as a sinister force or threatening figure ... there is usually something alien or hostile about it, which gives rise to feelings of distrust, anger or fear. This is why Jung felt justified in regarding the shadow as a complex—a cluster of traits bound together by common affects—in this instance, the archetype of Energy, Predator or Evil Stranger (p. 64).

Once constellated as a Trauma Complex, the residue of the Abyss Experience can exist as a dynamic unconscious force, appearing, for example, in dreams, traumatic memories, PTSD reexperience phenomena, or as dissociated states which include memories and feelings. As a generic form of dissociation, the Trauma Complex incorporates and articulates with other archetypes. The Shadow Archetype, for example, can appear as an "alter personality" manifestation in dissociative identity disorder (DID), representing the split-off part of the trauma experience, as for example in cases of childhood sexual abuse (see Kalsched, 2003 for case history analyses from this perspective). The Shadow Archetype can also appear in PTSD, and in paranoid (PPD), borderline (BPD) and narcissistic personality disorders (NPD), as forms of self-pathology in which the disavowed sector of personality manifests itself in maladaptive transactions (e.g., deception, secretiveness, dishonesty, manipulation or suspiciousness of others, lying for personal gain, exploitation, indifference, and lack of genuine empathy).

8 HISTORICAL AND CULTURAL EXAMPLES OF THE ABYSS EXPERIENCE AND THE TRAUMA ARCHETYPE

The death encounter and the specter of self-annihilation are central elements of the Abyss Experience and the Trauma Archetype. These and related phenomena can be illustrated through case history vignettes. The following are quotes from survivors of the atomic bombing at Hiroshima (HR) and Nagasaki (NG); victims of the Nazi Holocaust; World War II (WWII) soldiers; the terrorist attacks on the World Trade Centers (WTC); survivors from the 1972 Buffalo Creek Dam disaster in West Virginia (BC); veterans of the Vietnam War (VN); victims of ethnic cleansing during the Balkans War; and victims of torture and other traumas.[3] Note that the italicized text is used to emphasize key aspects of the Abyss Experience

The people fleeing the [World] Trade Center were covered with debris ... they *looked unreal ... like ghosts in a fog.* (WTC)

The Tsunami (December 2004) seemed to come out of nowhere. The ocean got sucked out several hundred meters and then the waves came—four of them—10 to 30 feet tall—and hit the beach. *I ran and later there were dead bodies, fish, and destruction everywhere. It was terrifying and unreal.* (Thailand, 2004)

We went into the burning house, filled with smoke everywhere, knowing there were children inside. I went upstairs and found a 4-year-old girl lying on the floor of her bedroom. *I picked her up and her skin stuck to the floor and peeled off like a piece of charcoal-grilled fish skin.* (Firefighter, 1980)

Their clothes were all torn, their *skin was black from burning,* and pieces of shattered glass were stuck all over their bodies ... *It was hell in this living world.* (HR)

---

[3]See the works of Lifton (1967); Erikson (1972); Wilson and Thomas (2004); and Wilson and Drozdek (2004).

We entered Ohrdnuf-Nord forced labor camp, which was part of the Buchenwald camp. God, it was awful. *There were bodies everywhere, stacked up like cord wood in piles with freshly killed bodies that had been shot in the head after being tied up and blindfolded.* The bodies were burned on pyres. There were shallow graves, remains of crematories and dead, emaciated, starved bodies strewn about. *The survivors were walking skeletons who told us the story of what happened when General Patton and Omar Bradley came to visit* the camp early in May, 1945. That was 60 years ago, but it is still fresh in my mind. (WWII, anonymous soldier)

Like I say, they [the dead] was *black with muck and mud.* It was hard to distinguish who they was or anything about them. (BC)

Two young men. I don't know who they were. *They were burned black and bleeding on September 11, 2001.* (WTC)

All I could make out was his FDNY badge—*the rest was indescribable.* (WTC)

They was just black hulks. You couldn't tell who they were or what they were. *It was unreal.* (BC)

She was burnt in both the upper and lower limbs, in the face and on her breast . . . *On August 24, 1945 after vomiting black blood, she died.* (HR)

My best friend was crushed underneath a building and asked me for help; so I tried desperately to help her, but my efforts meant nothing, so I ran away with another friend. *I hear her voice even now, I'll never forget it.* (HR)

I went over and started taking pieces of wood and I found her body. I picked up the back of her hair, what hair she had left. She didn't have no clothes on, and *I turned her over and the blood and muck and water came out her eyes and nose and mouth and ears.* I had to go set down. (BC)

We were on duty in Thailand and received a call that an F-4 Phantom jet was on fire. It landed and we [paramedics] responded. We put out the fire and opened the cockpit. The smoke was still pouring out. *I took off the pilots' helmet and blood ran out of his eyes and mouth from his burnt, black face.* He was dead. It was his birthday and he was my best friend. We had planned to party that night. (VN)

I feel like I was in hell. It was so dreadful that I lost understanding and feeling. (HR)

I saw hell on earth: some people with their faces burnt black and their skin peeling and falling down and others injured by fragments of glass and bleeding all over their bodies; still others already dead and lying naked; and the completely flattened and burnt city. (HR)

Charred dead bodies scattered all over a burned out field that once was a residential area. *Bodies frozen in agony reaching up towards the sky.* Unidentified bodies left like that for days. (HR)

The Russian soldiers came into our village in Chechnya. *They raped me in front of my mother.* The soldiers took turns. I wanted to die right there, but couldn't. Later, I became pregnant and wanted to get rid of the baby inside me. (asylum seeker, The Netherlands)

I saw dreadful corpses in every corner of rooms, in rivers and every other place. *It was hell on earth.* (HR)

They thought perhaps that she was a black person. Come to find out later all the people looked like that, greasy and black, *and the look on their face was just horror.* (BC)

I can still smell the death of the WTC today. (WTC)

I can still smell death—the rotting, putrid, decomposing smell of human death in the jungle of Vietnam. (VN)

The smell of decomposing human bodies is unique. To this day, I can't stand the smell of cat food after smelling dead bodies in Vietnam. (VN)

Everything seemed dark, eerie and surreal on September 11, 2001. (WTC)

Big maggots were wiggling in his burns. All we could do is pick them off with tweezers and apply mercurochrome. There were few doctors and nurses. (NG)

The smell of death and burning of the [WTC] building was overwhelming. (WTC)

My body seemed all black, everything seemed dark, dark all over. (HR)

I can still smell ground zero in my mind—it won't go away. (WTC)

I saw the World Trade Center towers collapse—my God what is happening? *Is this the end—Am I going to die?* (WTC)

The feeling I had was that everyone was dead. The whole city was destroyed. *I thought this was the end of Hiroshima—of Japan—of humankind.* (HR)

Beyond these feelings was the sense that *the whole world was dying.* (HR)

I could not understand why *our surroundings had changed so greatly in one instant.* (HR)

I wake up in a sweat, *I can still see bodies falling from the towers*—it could have been me—I was on my way there [towers] to work. (WTC)

I wake up in a sweat, *I see a thousand eyes of North Vietnamese soldiers staring at me* through the elephant grass in the Plain of Jars. I know I am going to die. (VN, 1966)

I saw one woman—one corpse with the flesh removed from the bones ... then about one hundred people, mostly women and children, none of them with their clothes on, lying on the asphalt pleading for help—it was August 6, 1945. (HR)

We were operating out of An Khe when we came across an enemy soldier who was alive but badly injured and dying. He was hit in the gut by an M-16 ... the *Vietnamese pigs were eating his intestines and it smelled horrible.* (VN, 1969)

[On the Bataan death march] ... if people would fall down and couldn't go any further, the Japanese would either bayonet or shoot them. *They would also bayonet prisoners who couldn't keep up ... some American prisoners who couldn't keep up were run over by Japanese vehicles* ... As we walked along, we could see bodies of decomposing American soldiers and Filipino women who had been mutilated and obviously raped. *I'm sure the dogs in the area got fat.* (WWII, Alf Larsen in Gilpatrick)

I don't feel much [emotion] since September 11th—I'm kind of *a walking zombie*—I fake having emotions now. (WTC)

I'm just a *walking shell* of what I was before September 11th—there ain't nothing inside now. I'm still numb but don't talk about it for fear of people thinking I'm crazy. (WTC)

I hear many voices calling for help, voices calling for their father, voices of women and children. (HR)

I can still hear Rodriguez screaming for help. It was monsoon season in January of 1968 ... just before the TET offensive. We got hit on a search and destroy operation near Phu Bai. He was walking point man and hit a trip wire—it ripped him up real bad. His right leg was blown off but he didn't know it yet. *He was begging for God and his mother to come and help him.* (VN)

I walked by and looked at them and thought maybe I might recognize some of them, but couldn't ... One kid had all the hide tore off the top of his foot; toenails and all. Looked like about ten years old, hair all full of coal dirt. You couldn't recognize any of them because they was in such bad shape. *Their clothes was all tore off and they were skinned up and part of their scalps gone and it was a horrible thing,* I'll tell you it was. A man will never forget it. *If I live to be a hundred years old, I will never forget it.* (BC)

The bodies were black in color . . . most of them had a peculiar smell, and beyond thought this was from the bomb . . . the smell when they burned was caused by the fact their bodies were decayed . . . some of them having their internal organs decay even while the person was living. (HR)

My son was crushed up so bad, I went about four times trying to identify him. *His head was smashed to jelly. He had just a little piece of sideburn left, where you could tell it was him.* (BC)

The appearance of people was—well they all had skin blackened by burns . . . they had no hair because their hair was burned, *and at a glance you couldn't tell whether you were looking at them from in front or in back . . .* They held their arms bent [formed] like this . . . and their skin—not only on their hands, but on their faces and bodies too—hung down . . . *They didn't look like people of this world . . . they had a special way of walking—very slowly.* (HR)

Even now *I still hear their voices.* (HR)

I still hear the scream and sounds of the [World Trade Center] towers collapsing. When this happens at night, I drink scotch until it goes away. (WTC)

I believe I died there—a part of me is still there now—I don't know how I survived" (WTC)

I died that day in Vietnam [1968] *when my squad all got killed in the ambush by the NVA.* All I have done is occupy space since then until now. I've done nothing with my life since that moment in the A Shau Valley with the 101st Airborne. There isn't a day that goes by that I don't think about it. (VN)

The Serbian soldiers near Tuzla captured our village during the fall of 1995. The soldiers told me that I had to have sex with my 10-year-old daughter in front of my wife and 13-year-old son. *They told me if I refused, they would rape them and then kill me.* I had no choice so I did what they asked, holding my family at gunpoint. *Afterwards, they laughed at me and took turns raping my wife and children in front of me.* (Bosnia, 1995)

We had been running our PBR [small naval boat] up the rivers near the Cambodian border. We'd been ambushed many times from the mangrove swamp. On this day, we put in a team of Navy Seals who got wasted [killed] in an ambush. On the way down river, I stopped to buy beer at the usual stand from "Charlie" who worked for the enemy I'm sure. *On that day, I took my machete and whacked off his head as I bought the beer. His face still had a smile on it . . . I cut his head off so fast.* (VN, 1969)

Just then the USS *Arizona*'s forward magazine blew up with a tremendous explosion and large sheets of flame shot skyward, and I began to wonder about our magazines and whether they were being flooded ... large sheets of flame and several fires started aft. Burning fuel oil from the USS *Arizona* floated down on the stern of the ship. (USS *Arizona*, Pearl Harbor, 1941)

These case vignettes illustrate the universality of the Abyss Experience and the Trauma Archetype. Many of these events occurred a half-century apart in different cultures under different historical circumstances. The traumatic effects are virtually identical and set up complex posttraumatic sequelae. The survivors words are remarkably similar across time, space, and events: they are universal and archetypal in nature. The various sequelae of the Abyss Experience include: psychiatric illness, PTSD, anxiety, depression, ideological disillusionment, and spiritual transformations.

9 PSYCHOLOGICAL TRAUMA AND THE INVERSION EXPERIENCE

The Abyss Experience immerses the psyche into states of terror and darkness which may involve severe alterations in the perception of reality. Inversion Experiences are intrinsic to certain forms of trauma and generate Trauma Complexes that can defy rational, psychiatric understanding. Psychological Inversion Experiences have been defined (Wilson, 2004c) as the reversal of normal, consensual reality caused by the trauma experience and impact of excessive stress to the self (Figure 5.4). There are different types of psychological trauma that can induce Inversion Experiences. *Inversion Experiences are associated with altered states of awareness, perception, cognition, and motivation in which the understanding of reality inverts its order, function, and structural integrity.* In the Inversion Experience, the individual's understanding of reality inverts its order: "shape shifting," "inside out," "upside down," in transformative permutations, like looking at a kaleidoscope of changing patterns. The Inversion Experience is a palindromic psychological phenomenon. Each twist of trauma's kaleidoscope produces a new perceptual pattern, often overwhelming to the ego's capacity for processing its unusual stimulus field. The Inversion Experience inverts normal reality, so there are no customary schemas by which to process the experience.

There are different types of psychological Inversion Experiences—moral, political, social, interpersonal, and self—which are summarized in Figure 5.4. Several forms of inversion can be present at the same time,

Definition: – an alteration or change in awareness, perception, cognition and motivation in which the understanding of reality inverts its order, function, and structural integrity

Types of inversion

Moral inversion – inversion of normative moral order (e.g., good is bad; evil is good)
Political inversion – inversion of the political order of power
Social inversion – rapid shift in normal sociocultural order
Interpersonal inversion – inversion in attachments and self–object relationships
Self-inversion – inversion of the structural coherence of the self

Dimensions of inversion experience

1. Amodal and transmodal sensory, perceptual, and cognitive processes
2. Radical shift in time–space perspective and sudden shift of the normal order
3. Sense of "unreality"; disorientation (i.e., "abnormal vs. normal", "bad vs. good", "slavery vs. freedom", "abuse vs. affection", etc.)
4. Confusion of rules, order, procedures, laws, justice, fairness, etc.
5. Uncertainty as to appropriate action, initiative, coping
6. Fears of self-dissolution, self-annihilation or decompensation into mental illness
7. Absence of organizing framework – perception, cognitive encoding, classification, experienced cognitive disequilibrium
8. Loss of sense of grounding/centering to the self
9. Challenge to core beliefs, loss of meaning and the encounter of "ecological oddness" (i.e., a strange, alien world)
10. Appraisals of threat imposed by changes induced by Inversion Experience
11. Reversal of normal-expectable baseline with abnormal baseline expectations
12. Changed sense of self-in-world; existence and meaning of life
13. A subjective sense of free-falling into the abyss of nothingness, a vortex of the unknown or "psychological worm-hole" phenomena
14. Loss of symbolic integrity and meaning (i.e., non-functionality of value and meaning systems)
15. A temporary or prolonged decentering of the planes or subparadigms of self-experience

FIGURE 5.4. Psychological inversion reversal of normal reality caused by the experiences of traumatic stress. *Source:* ©2004 John P. Wilson.

depending on the nature of the trauma experience. Torture, for example, involves moral and political inversion (e.g., suffering = justice). Consider the following case history of a Bosnian woman, age 31, who was raped and tortured:

She was arrested in her home town together with her son (age 9) and daughter (age 12), and taken to the Manjača detention camp. She was beaten, humiliated and tortured by burning her thighs with hot iron, which left large scars. Together with other women she was raped many times every day. The rapes were performed by a group of soldiers. She was also present when other women were raped. Once she witnessed the death of a 9-year-old-girl after multiple rapes and torture ... She agreed [later] to make her testimony on a foreign television program ... after the interview her psychological condition deteriorated. (Arcel, Smale, Kovacić, & Marusić, 1995, p. 68)

Inversion Experiences may be transparent when experience shifts focus, meaning, and grounding, changing the experiential planes of existence, which results in psychic functioning in the vortex of trauma— a form of oscillatory immersion into an overwhelming world of unnatural order, an "odd ecology" with strange dimensions not previously experienced. When this occurs, psychological decompensation may occur at a very rapid rate, as was the case for the Bosnian torture victim.

9.1 Inversion Experience: Amodal and Transmodal Perceptual Processes

In the Inversion Experience, there is often a rapid and radical shift in time–space perspective. The continuity and flow of life alters, as if entering a twilight zone of a alien land at the first light of dawn. There is a sense of strangeness to individual perceptual processes (e.g., vision, hearing, smell, movement). The functions of *amodal perceptions* of reality have been studied in infant developmental processes. For example, Daniel Stern (1985) notes

> infants thus appear to have an innate general capacity, which can be called *amodal perceptions*, to take information received in one sensory modality and somehow translate it into another sensory modality ... the information is probably not experienced as belonging to any one sensory mode. More likely, it transcends mode or channel and exists in some unknown supramodal form. It is not, then, a simple issue of direct translation across modalities. Rather, it involves an encoding into still mysterious amodal representations, which can be recognized in any of the sensory modes. (p. 51; emphasis added)

9.2 Trauma-Induced Inversion Experiences

The concept of amodal perception is intrinsic to the trauma-induced Inversion Experience; a transmodal sensory-perceptual and cognitive experience. It is possible to see that traumatic experiences can cause a psychological recapitulation of infantile amodal perception—a return to earlier, less organized forms of environmental encounters. Trauma-induced disequilibrium leads the brain to search memory for prior patterns of amodal or transmodal perception, which it finds in memory archives of infantile modalities of perceptual experience. The Inversion Experience occurs because the experience cannot be matched through cognitive encoding to expectancies, i.e., there are no current cognitive schemas to assimilate the "oddness" of the experience nor is there a "ready-match" in existing cognitive schemas of past experiences. The absence of all but primitive infantile memories of amodal perceptions thus creates "lacunae" in pre-existing cognitive schematic structures of information processing. These cognitive lacunae are then experienced emotionally as fear, profound uncertainty, and confusion. An example of the Inversion Experience and amodal perceptual changes is described from the effects of torture

> Humanity is attacked when victims are guided through *surrealistic experiences*. Often the victims are forced to perceive that they are part of their own physical and mental destruction. Through all their humiliation and the *activity/passivity paradox*, the victims enter a *strange universe of surrealism. Suddenly, civil rules are no longer consistent*, and expectancies about other human beings behavior prove to be false. *There is absolutely no escape*, and in contrast to the outside world, nobody will arrive—*not even at the last moment*—victims are told: "You'll never be able to talk about this, or even if you do, nobody will believe you." (Vesti, Somnier, & Kastrup, 1992, p. 22; emphasis added)

How does the survivor metabolize such surrealistic and life-threatening experiences? What will be the dynamics and structure of their Trauma Complex as a result of such an experience when reality inverts itself and the abnormal becomes normal?

9.3 The Ecology of the Trauma Environment in the Inversion Experience

The question that emerges from our analysis is this: *What is the nature of the trauma environment associated with the Inversion Experience?* In this ecologically odd psychological environment, there is a confusion of rules, order, events, procedures, and expectancies. For example, this is especially characteristic of torture experiences (Ortiz, 2001). A radical shift in perspective occurs quickly and may persist for prolonged periods of time as a feeling or sense of unreality and uncertainty as to what actions and initiatives to take. The psychological unreality connected to the Abyss and Inversion Experiences is clearly evident in the following case history:

I cannot forget that one afternoon when my village was ambushed by rebels. I can see a little boy scurrying like a rabbit into the dead bushes, only to be shot in the back. And I remember my mother throwing herself on top of me and my 9-month-old sister to protect us. *Droplets of what I thought were my mother's tears fell on me. And I felt safe.* The next morning when everything was quiet, I tried to awaken my mother to tell her something I can never erase from my memory. My mother's body was covered with blood and *my sister's face was an ugly blue and her mouth was open as if she were gasping for air.* She had suffocated. I no longer have a family. *I am alone in this big world.* Sometimes I think about killing myself, then I wouldn't be alone, but my mother died to save my life. She wanted me to live. I live to remind them [rebels] that they didn't kill all of us. My mother, my sister, my village live in me. (Ortiz, 2001, p. 2; emphasis added).

In torture, sensory and sleep deprivation are techniques used to induce disorientation to time, space, and location. Physical torture is human intimacy sadistically inverted (i.e., affection, physical and sexual contact). Physical torture (i.e., burns, deprivation, beatings, electric shocks, suspensions, hanging, stretching, blindfolding, being hooded, etc.) is the inverted form of pleasure feelings and being able to experience sensual satisfaction. Psychological and emotional torture is the inversion of attachment, bonding, love, nurturance, and intimacy. Perpetrators create situations to induce dependency, pseudo-intimacy (e.g., traumatic bonding) and hopes for receiving relief from suffering, and to get basic need satisfaction (food, water, shelter, pain relief, clothing, light, toilets, medical treatment, reduction of fear, etc.). Psychological torture inverts intrapsychic ego-processes. Individual illusions of control, uniqueness, power, capacity to resist feelings of invulnerability are crushed, demolished, and destroyed by repetitive torture in the hands of the perpetrator who controls the environment of existence. Thus, for the world of torture, reality inverts itself in all areas of psychological functioning. The torture perpetrator experiences sadistic pleasure; the victim experiences horrific and undesirable pain.

9.4 The Loss of Psychological Orientation

In Inversion Experiences, the psychic compasses for orientation and direction are nonfunctional or of limited usefulness. There is an *Alice in Wonderland*-like construal of events; an absence of functional cognitive frameworks for coping and self-directed action. This amodal perception of "ecological oddness," the experience of *ineffable unreality* (i.e., loss of the natural order) diminishes emotional grounding, one's anchor point of being-in-the-world. When this occurs, the sense of the world itself becomes strange. Reality is supplanted with unreality; abnormality transposes normal reality. The "surreal" becomes real. Figure-and-ground perceptual processes reverse, flip-flopping like a tachistoscopic presentation of images in the minds' eye. As Stern (1985) described for early infantile perception, the transmodal perception seeks a way of assimilating the perceptions into a schema, which would include the adult transduction of the trauma experience in transmodal forms. The proprioception of the Inversion Experience is experienced in a transmodal way with the subjective feeling of being out of synchronization with everything in the environment.

While the Inversion Experience has aspects of dissociation, it is not the same thing as a dissociative disorder or dissociation per se in the face of threat. The Inversion Experience may not necessarily disrupt the normally integrative functions of conscious memory, identity, or capacity for self-reference. The Inversion Experience does not necessarily involve amnesia, fugue, depersonalization, or dissociative identity disorder. Rather, it is the subjective sense of self-separation, the loss of self-centering in experience without orienting mile-markers or distinct points of reference. Individual knowledge of time, space, and orientation seems nonexistent, inapparent, or suspended. The person feels as if they have experienced an astronomical tunnel between realities to another dimension in which time and space take on a new meaning. Stern (1985) refers to this phenomenon in infants as *supramodal perception*. It is beyond separate clear-channeled modes of perceptual experience. After extreme trauma, the individual feels as if they are looking at reality, as they knew it, upside down and free-falling into the abyss of the unknown accompanied by the terror of their spiritual essence evaporating into nothingness. Like an astronaut suddenly and unexpectedly untethered from his secure ties to the space shuttle, the person drifts aimlessly into the vastness of the trauma universe.

In mythology, the Inversion Experience, as well as the Abyss Experience, has been referred to as the demonic encounter with unknown forces of darkness and power (Kalsched, 1996; Campbell, 1949). It is precisely at such moments in the dread of nothingness and the fear of death, that the spirit emerges to confront death or begin a new journey of uncertainty. Thought of somewhat differently, amodal and transmodal perceptions give birth to the possibility of new modalities of self-configuration as a result of transduced and assimilated experiences which emerge out of the traumatic event. In the posttraumatic self, the metabolism of psychological trauma gives birth to new configurations of identity and selfhood. In this sense, the Trauma Complex undergoes a metamorphosis and evolves into a new structural configuration.

10 ANALOGS TO TRAUMA-INDUCED INVERSION EXPERIENCES

Analogs to trauma-induced Inversion Experiences have been scientifically studied in medicine, psychoanalysis, experimental psychology, psychophysiological research, and near death experiences (NDE) and accounts of abduction by extraterrestrial aliens. In medicine, for example, Hornsten (1974) and Steiner, Shanin, and Melamed (1987) described "inversion syndromes" and "inversion illusions" caused by disturbances of the otoliths in the inner ear. Research evidence suggests that the etiology is a malfunction in saccules and otoconia located in the utricle of the inner ear. Such malfunction of the inner ear occurs in medical disorders and healthy persons as well, and can result in the illusion that the world is upside down (e.g., seeing the ceiling as the floor; feeling upside down and other visual perceptive changes). Inversion illusions have been reported by stroke patients. In these cases evidence points to disease of the basilar arteries in the brain stem.

In experimental studies of human perception, Shore and Klein (2000) have examined the effects of visual scene inversion in perceptual and memory processes. Subjects were exposed to photographic images in a laboratory study which included inverting half of the image pairs they were required to view. In a variation of the study, these same images were modified by flickering displays to assess how the images were being processed in memory. The authors note that "there is an infinite amount of information in the visual world at any one instant, and we can process only a finite amount of it. Some information must remain relatively unprocessed. These two facts, rich subjective experience and the need for selecting, present something of a contradiction. How can we represent the entire visual scene and yet process only some of it?" (p. 1). The results of their experimentation suggest that "information from the visual environment is recalculated from scratch, upon each fixation" (p. 2). These findings point to the fact that changes in the visual field to be observed or understood can be changed by altering (inverting) or disturbing (e.g., "flickering displays") the nature of stimuli. Similar findings have been reported by Shipley (2003) who found that the accurate detection and recognition of a visual light stimulus was altered by physical inversion (e.g., walking on one's hands vs. feet). Shipley suggests that "event perception and recognition are based on spatiotemporal patterns of motion associated with the dynamics of the event" (p. 1).

Perhaps the closest phenomenological analog to traumatically induced Inversion Experiences is found in reports of *negative* Near Death Experiences (NDEs). In his research, Ring (1992) found that in contrast to positive descriptions of NDEs (i.e., salvation, tunnel experience, positive white light, religious messages, and numinous experiences) some persons reported negative NDEs which were classified into three categories: (1) inverted NDE; (2) hellish NDE; and (3) meaningless void NDE. In all three forms of negative NDEs there are reported degrees of fear of annihilation, soul death, or bizarre Abyss Experiences which include reports of hell, demons, satanic experiences, torture, pain, excruciating suffering, physical annihilation, intolerable trickery and illusions by hostile beings, bodily disintegration, and psychic trauma. Ring (1992) notes that the experience often reverts to a positive NDE as the sense of imminent death approaches.

A phenomenon related to NDEs in several important ways is anomalous traumatic experiences (Laibow & Laue, 1993), which include reports of alien abductions by extraterrestrial beings. Persons who report such experiences, which have been described by Mack (1999) and others, include most of the criteria for Inversion Experience. The abduction experiences invert reality as customarily known. They are ineffable and difficult to describe or disclose to others for fears of being seen as "crazy," lying, fabricating, or outright delusional. In the abduction experience, the individual typically experiences fear upon encountering small, short gray alien beings with black, almond-shaped eyes who possess nonhuman telepathic abilities and skills to psychically paralyze and immobilize the abductee. Reports of states of terror, fear, and helplessness are common as alien beings stand over the person and perform medical/scientific investigations, some described as torturous in nature, or transport them to spacecraft for evaluations or journeys to other worldly places. The abduction experience may include memories of the medical examinations, especially for women, being subjected to brain scans, and apocalyptic visions of the ecological destruction of the earth. Wilson (1990) described the difficulties in coping with the alien abduction phenomenon as resting primarily upon states of extreme psychological uncertainty because of the nonverifiability of such a phenomenon and lack of precise historical knowledge as to the past or future reoccurrence of such experiences. He proposed that the alien abduction phenomenon is similar in nature to the experience of persons who discover that they have had past exposure to chemicals of a dangerous and physically harmful nature and as a result have somatoform and PTSD symptoms. More recently, McNally, Lasko, Clancy, Macklin, Pitman, and Orr (2004) demonstrated in a psychophysiological study that persons claiming to have been victims of alien abductions respond to threat (i.e., trauma-specific stimuli) in exactly the same manner as do subjects suffering from PTSD (e.g., combat veterans). This study used the same experimental procedure employed in studies of patients suffering from PTSD. When exposed to scripts of a trauma-related nature versus a neutral story, abductee subjects show increased physiological arousal patterns congruent with traumatic memories and activity of autonomic nervous system arousal associated with heightened states of distress. As described subjectively, the experience of abduction by extraterrestrial aliens meets all 15 of the criteria for the Inversion Experience.

Finally, in a different area of psychological investigation, Keppe (2002) has described processes of inversion from a psychoanalytic perspective.

He suggests that inversion processes involve perceiving opposites or inverts in personal experience (e.g., love = pain; good = evil; reality = cause of abnormality).

Experimental, medical, and clinical research of Inversion Experiences suggests the following tentative conclusions. First, the phenomenon of "Inversion Experiences" has been observed in different areas of study of human perception and behavioral functioning. Second, there appear to be physiological and neurophsysiological bases for some types of Inversion Experiences (e.g., strokes, diseases of the inner ear, arterial malfunction, ketamine use in anesthesia mimicking NDE, etc.). Third, Jansen (2001) has demonstrated parallels between altered states of consciousness, NDEs, and dissociative experiences induced by administration of ketamine, an arylcyclohexylamine used for anesthesia. Fourth, the study of perceptual inversions has been a province of experimental psychology for over 50 years. Fifth, anecdotal accounts of Inversion Experience in NDEs, reported abductions by aliens, torture experiences, extremely stressful life-threatening situations, etc., show parallels in emotional and cognitive-affective reaction patterns that suggest a complex interaction between perceptual phenomena (i.e., capacity to recognize, codify, and process reality) and subsequent emotional reactions (e.g., fear, terror, horror) and their construal in cognitive terms (i.e., reality-orientation, meaning-context, phenomenological experiences, and "goodness of fit" to prior experience). Sixth, Inversion Experiences are typically described in negative emotional terms as subjectively unpleasant, disorienting, and confusing. Reality, as understood, suddenly shifts its orientation and framework, making coping and efficacious action difficult, confusing, and unpleasant. However, as discussed below, transformation of the stressful and overwhelming aspects of Inversion Experiences can lead to transcendent experiences in which new perspectives of self and reality are formed. In this sense, then, Transcendent Experience can emerge out of the Trauma Complex.

11 TRANSCENDENT EXPERIENCE IN TRAUMA COMPLEXES

Transcendent Experiences emanate from traumatic experiences, the struggle for meaning, and attributions of causality for suffering. They have direct links to the Abyss and Inversion Experiences. Transcendent Experiences have the potential power to release higher levels of integrative behavior (see Chapter 6). These states of integrated behavior typically involve higher consciousness; efficient and focused goal-directed behavior; emotional balance and a sense of serenity and quiescence accompanied by an awareness of creative potentialities within and beyond the self. Transcendent Experiences have parallels to Peak Experiences (see Chapter 6) but are different in form since they originate in trauma and become a structural dimension of the Trauma Complex. The connection between the Abyss Experience and the Transcendent Experience has been noted by Jaffe (1985)

> The dark night of the soul, the journey to a dark, painful world of struggle, is necessary for a certain level of development. It is only by going through this test that a person can be reborn. Struggle, according to the myth, is necessary to growth and the development of a certain level of self-awareness and wisdom. The extreme experience, the accounts of special people suggest, acts as just such an individuality test" (p. 102).

11.1 Dimensions of the Transcendent Experience

In contrast to the Abyss and Inversion Experiences, the Transcendent Experiences can emerge during a traumatic episode (i.e., peritraumatically) or at a later time as the metabolism of trauma occurs. The Transcendent Experience has operationally definable dimensions that include: (1) the awareness of higher levels of being, self-consciousness, and the possibility of unity in the self; (2) rapid transformational changes in value priorities and the meaning of one's existence; (3) the awareness of illusions, deceptions, and other forms of perceptual and cognitive "false" experiences; (4) personal consciousness of the numinous; (5) intuitive knowledge of the transformation of consciousness at a qualitatively higher level of existence that is beyond but not anathema to logical, analytical, and deductive modes of thinking; and (6) an acute sense of the death-in-life and life-in-death paradigm of self-existence that emerges in the specter of trauma, death, and dying (Figure 5.5).

1. Awareness of higher levels of being, self-consciousness and the possibility of unity in the self

2. Rapid transformative changes in value priorities in the meaning of one's existence

3. Awareness of illusions, deception, and other forms of perceptual and cognitive "false" experience

4. Personal consciousness of the numinous experience

5. Intuitive knowledge of the transformation of consciousness at qualitatively higher levels of existence

6. An acute sense of death-in-life vs. life-in-death paradigm of self-existence

FIGURE 5.5. The Transcendent Experience. *Source:* ©2004 John P. Wilson.

The qualitative nature of the Transcendent Experience creates a positive emotional basis for self-transformation.

11.2 Jung on Transcendence

In his work *The Structure and Dynamics of The Psyche*, Jung (1963) spoke of the transcendent function of the psyche in several ways

> There is nothing mysterious or metaphysical about the term "transcendent function"...The transcendent function arises from the *union of conscious and unconscious contents*...The shuttling to and fro of arguments and affects represents the transcendent function of opposites...The transcendent function manifests itself as a *quality of conjoined opposites*. (pp. 273, 298; emphasis added)

Jung stated that the conscious and unconscious act in complementary and reciprocal ways in terms of intrapsychic dynamics. He defines their relationship as follows

> (1) consciousness possesses *threshold intensity* which its contents must have attained, so that all elements that are too weak remain in the unconscious; (2) consciousness, because of its directed functions, exercises an inhibition (which Freud called censorship) on all the *incompatible material*, with the result that it sinks into the unconscious; (3) consciousness constitutes the momentary process of adaptation, whereas the unconscious contains not only all *the forgotten material of the individual's past*, but all the inherited behavior traces constituting the structure of the mind; (4) the unconscious *contains all the fantasy combinations* which have not yet attained the threshold intensity, but which in the course of time and under suitable condition will enter the light of consciousness. (p. 274; emphasis added)

These complementary processes of consciousness and unconsciousness have direct relevance to understanding the dynamics of the Trauma Archetype and Trauma Complex which, in themselves, contain juxtapositions of the Abyss Experience, the Inversion Experience, and the emergence of the Transcendent Experience. In a metaphorical sense, the Transcendent Experience emerges as the twin forces of the Abyss and Inversion Experiences come increasingly close together, like tectonic plates moving under the force of gravity beneath the surface of the Earth, squeezing the material lodged between them and pressuring changes to occur that may result in transformed landscapes on the surface.

In mythology the transcendent process involves the resolution of opposites in experience. In the journey of the participant, the mythic

Hero has to face the duality inherent in confrontation with disparate modes of encounters. In the experience of trauma, such encounters are inevitable. Campbell (1988) describes this process

> The hero is the one who comes to participate in life courageously and decently, in the way of nature, not in the way of personal rancor, disappointment or revenge ... the hero's sphere of action is not the transcendent but here, now, in the field of time, of good and evil—of the pairs of opposites. *Whereas one moves out of the transcendent, one comes into a field of opposites.* One has eaten of the tree of knowledge, not only of good and evil, but male and female, of right and wrong, of this and that, of light and dark. Everything in the field of time is dual: past and future, dead and alive, being and non-being. (p. 88; emphasis added)

In the Transcendent Experience that occurs in connection with trauma, the power of the experience is so great that it releases inhibitions, censorship, resistance, and ego-defenses against material that previously had been rendered unconscious. The relevance of old, previously unconscious material is now capable of being reappraised and reconstructed into new cognitive perspectives at a very rapid rate. It is capable of being "conjoined" with thoughts, emotions, and perspectives on the dimensions of the self (i.e., coherence, autonomy, connection, vitality, connection, energy) and identity (i.e., sense of continuity vs. discontinuity) in new configurations. The Transcendent Experience is part of the process of decentering planes of experience described by Lifton (1976). The decentering and ungrounding of the temporal, spatial, and emotional planes of the core structural dimensions of the self (i.e., autonomy, coherence, continuity, energy, etc.) enables new patterns to be configured and synthesized in terms of: (1) self-attributional processes (e.g., shame, self-esteem); (2) motivational vectors (e.g., goal priorities in daily life); (3) value and belief systems (e.g., personal ideologies, systems of valuing and meaning generation); and (4) the qualitative nature and experience of self-consciousness at higher levels of being. As Jung (1963) indicated, the transcendent function "arises from the union of conscious and unconscious contents ... the shuttling to and fro of arguments and affects [that] represent the transcendent function of opposites," a passage which illuminates the process by which emotion and thinking are actively resynthesized. The outcome of this dynamic process can be unity in the self. Viewed differently, the decentering and recentering of the subparadigms of the planes of self-experience potentially results in greater degrees of unity and integration. The ungrounded self becomes grounded; the decentered self becomes centered; the loss of ego-identity and a sense of continuity of the self in time, space, and culture, is reestablished in new ways. The fusion that occurs at conscious and unconscious levels in the Transcendent Experience is subjectively experienced as an acute and immediate sense of organismic strength that emanates from death-in-life versus life-in-death paradigms of self-existence. It is this process that establishes the identity of the Transcendent Experience in opposition to the Abyss Experience and the immersion into the realm of the demonic, "black hole" of traumatic experience in which the self and spirit are put to the test by fate or human malevolence.

12 A SCHEMATIC OVERVIEW OF THE TRAUMA COMPLEX

The Abyss, Inversion, and Transcendent Experiences are part of the Trauma Complex but do not make up its complete structure. This is because the Trauma Complex articulates in dynamic ways with the Trauma Archetype and other qualities of the posttraumatic self and personality. A schematic overview of the Trauma Complex as a dynamic intrapsychic phenomenon is presented in Figure 5.6. This conceptual overview illustrates the development of the Trauma Complex from the archetypal experience of trauma and how it articulates dynamically with other dimensions of identity, the self-structure, and systems of meaning and personality as a whole.

The Trauma Complex is a uniquely constellated psychic representation of the totality of the trauma experience. It functions in accordance with living systems theory and has suprasystems and subsystems that can be described. For example, it is logically necessary to discern how the stressors of the traumatic experience impact the pre-existing organismic processes that were operating at the time of the traumatic event. At the intrapsychic level, this includes: (1) the self-structure and its six dimensions (i.e., coherence, continuity, connection, autonomy, energy, vitality); (2) identity configurations; (3) systems of meaning (i.e., attribution processes; beliefs and values; ideological systems; faith and spirituality); (4) systems of affect regulation and their effects on consciousness; and (5) other personality and individual difference factors (e.g., temperament, intelligence).

The Trauma Complex encapsulates the self-structure, identity processes, and individual systems of meaning, beliefs, and values. The tripartite supradimensions of the Trauma Complex interact with mechanisms of perceptual processes, ego-defenses, affect regulation, and cognition at all levels of consciousness. The interactions among the tripartite supradimensions of the Trauma Complex activate other archetypes and psychic complexes in the unconscious which work with one another (i.e., cogwheel) and result in modifications of the posttraumatic self. Specifically, the structural and functional capacities of the

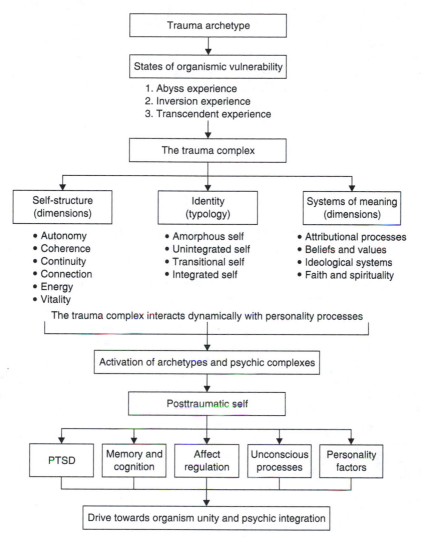

FIGURE 5.6. The Trauma Complex as a dynamic intrapsychic phenomenon. *Source:* ©2004 John P. Wilson.

posttraumatic self are altered (see Figure 1.1 in Chapter 1), as new "data" from extremely stressful life-experiences enter the system of organismic functioning. Allostasis, as a process of coping with extreme stress, resets the baseline functioning of the organism, recalibrating itself at multiple levels of functioning. Systems theory (Miller, 1978) shows that the organism is a hierarchically integrated set of psychobiological processes. Therefore, changes to one component of the system have the potential to alter subsystem functioning. The major subsystems that constitute the Trauma Complex suprasystem are: (i) memory and cognition; (ii) affect regulation; (iii) PTSD; (iv) unconscious processes; and (v) personality factors. These interrelated and overlapping subsystems of the Trauma Complex create powerful motives at the intrapsychic level that govern the striving towards unity and integration in the organism (see Figure 5.6).

13 THE TRAUMA COMPLEX AND PTSD

Clinical studies (Lindy, 2001, 1993; Lindy & Lifton, 2001) have demonstrated the role of unconscious mechanisms in PTSD and trauma response that include defensive attempts to protect areas of vulnerability, unconscious flashback (dissociative) episodes, repetition compulsion as reexperience, and risk-taking behaviors. Unconscious processes also include sensation-seeking as psychobiological reenactment as well as depressive suicidal syndromes (Blank, 1985; Chu, 1998; Kalsched, 2003; Lindy, 1993; Lindy & Lifton, 2001; Lindy & Wilson, 2001; Nijenhuis & van der Hart, 1999; Wilson & Ziegelbaum, 1986). The emotions of anxiety, fear, horror, posttraumatic shame and guilt, etc., are core elements that impact organismic attempts at homeostasis (Friedman, 2000; Friedman & McEwen, 2004; McEwen, 1998) and constitute the *DSM-IV-TR* criteria for PTSD (APA, 2000). It has been widely recognized that these negative emotions have the power to mobilize ego-defenses such as minimization, dissociation, repression, projection, and denial, and potentially cause a reorganization of the self and individual identity (Chu, 1998; Herman, 1999; Kalsched, 1996; Knox, 2003; Lindy & Lifton, 2001; Nijenhuis & van der Hart, 1999).

14 UNIVERSAL DIMENSIONS OF THE TRAUMA COMPLEX

The Trauma Complex represents a depth of intrapsychic experience, organized largely at unconscious levels, encapsulating the trauma experience which becomes a central and powerful motivational force in personality. The universal dimensions of Trauma Complexes: (1) develop in accordance with the Trauma Archetype; (2) are comprised of affects, images, and perceptions of the trauma experience; (3) are mythological in form, symbolic in nature, and shaped by culture; (4) contain the specter or images of the Abyss and Inversion Experience; (5) articulate with other psychic complexes; (6) may become central in the self-structure; (7) contain motivational power; (8) are expressed in personality; (9) are primarily unconscious phenomena; and (10) contain

1. The trauma complex is a feeling-toned complex which develops in accordance with the trauma archetype

2. The trauma complex is comprised of affects, images, perceptions, and cognitions associated with the trauma experience

3. The trauma complex is mythological in nature and takes form in accordance with culture and symbolic, mythological representations of reality

4. The trauma complex contains the affective responses of the Abyss Experience: fear, terror, horror, helplessness, dissociation

5. The trauma complex articulates with other psychological complexes and innate archetypes in a "cogwheeling" interactive manner. This includes the abyss, inversion and transcendent forms of traumatic encounters

6. The trauma complex may become central in the self-structure and reflect alterations in identity, ego-processes, the self-structure, and systems of personal meaning

7. The trauma complex contains motivational power and predisposition to behavior

8. The trauma complex is expressed in personality processes (e.g., traits, motives, altered personality characteristics, memory and cognition, etc.)

9. The trauma complex is primarily unconscious but discernible by posttraumatic alterations in the self and personality.

10. The trauma complex contains the polarities of the Abyss Experience, diabolic vs. transcendent, which are universal variants in the search for meaning in the trauma experience

FIGURE 5.7. The Trauma Complex. *Source:* ©2004 John P. Wilson.

residues of Inversion Experiences and the polarities of the Abyss Experience in terms of the diabolic vs. transcendent elements of consciousness which include images, affects, fantasies, and cognitions (Figure 5.7).

In 1934, Jung reviewed the nature and composition of various types of psychic complexes he postulated (Jung, 1972, CW 8). This analysis identified the psychodynamics of complexes and their constellation within the personal unconscious of the individual and how, in turn, they articulate with archetypes in the unconscious. Jung (1972) specified eight dimensions of constellated complexes, which are quoted verbatim here

(1) a disturbed state of consciousness; (2) unity of consciousness disrupted; (3) intentions of the will impeded or impaired; (4) memory noticeably affected; (5) energy [of complex] sometimes exceeds conscious intention; (6) active complex momentarily creates a state of duress; (7) compulsive thinking and acting; and (8) diminished judicial responsibility. (CW 8, paras. 200–3)

These universal dimensions of constellated complexes are important to identifying the central dimensions of the Trauma Complex as an unconscious dynamic that includes PTSD, dissociation, and anxiety states as well as articulating with other archetypal forms of experience. The Trauma Complex is more than an aggregate of symptoms which define PTSD, anxiety, and depressive and dissociative disorders. The Trauma Complex acts analogously to a perceptual prism, filtering light and experience. The Trauma Complex has the power to articulate and have a "cogwheeling" effect with other complexes and archetypes (Wilson, 2004b). To quote Jung

> this image [complex] has a powerful inner *coherence*, it has its own wholeness and, in addition, relatively *high degree of autonomy*, so that it is subject to the control of the conscious mind to only a limited extent, and therefore behaves like an *animated foreign body* in the sphere of consciousness. (Jung, 1972, CW 8, para. 201; emphasis added)

Once constellated, a psychic complex becomes an "animated" motivational force which is nested within the unconscious, containing energy (i.e., affects, cognitions, perceptual processes) which has structural coherence and a "high degree of autonomy" to influence behavior.

In a metaphorical sense, the Trauma Complex is similar to a hurricane, with high-velocity swirling winds and rain moving at different speeds. The Trauma Complex can combine and fuse with other, pre-existing complexes to set in motion (i.e., cogwheel) a vast array of intrapsychic processes. The Trauma Complex consumes psychic energy and activates other aspects of the personal unconscious in attempts to process the traumatic experience in an organismic drive towards unity (van der Kolk, van der Hart, & Marmar, 1996). This process of activation includes cogwheeling mechanisms in which different psychic *complexes interconnect* to set in motion a set of Archimedean processes in the realm of the unconscious.

15 CASE EXAMPLE: HELICOPTER MIND ASSAULT

Consider the following passage by a writer for *New Yorker Magazine* (Baum, 2004, p. 50) describing a combat veteran who continues to be haunted by his actions as a two-tour, Huey helicopter door gunner during the Vietnam War (1967–1969)

> Knox's infantry suffered huge casualties, but *what bothers him most*, more than three decades later, is not the fear, the carnage he witnessed, or the loss of friends but *the faces of people he killed while serving as a helicopter door gunner*. "If they told me to kill a whole village, that's what I'd do," he said. *"I still see images—a woman and her children rolling in the dust."* When I asked

Knox how often such images arise he thought for a moment and said, *"Really it's more like I'm always looking at a double image. I see you sitting there in that chair, and I'm watching this funeral party I gunned* [from the helicopter]. *In a few minutes, it will be a sampan on the river I gunned* [using an M-60 machine gun], *with a woman and her babies falling out of it into the water and kicking around as I shot them"* [repeatedly, pop, pop, pop with the M-60]. (p. 50; emphasis and clarifying interpolations added)

The former door gunner from Vietnam is haunted by his acts of senseless killing which established the nidus of his Trauma Complex. He continues to struggle with the meaning of his actions and the resultant PTSD and posttraumatic shame and guilt he feels (see Chapter 9). This case vignette helps illustrate that the manner in which a Trauma Complex becomes constellated varies significantly between persons and cultures because the experiences are diverse and caused by different types of traumatic stressors (Lewis-Fernandez, 1994).

15.1 Primordial Emotional Experiences and the Trauma Complex

Dysregulated affects are also an important part of the Trauma Complex (Schore, 2003a). Consistent with the research on emotional dysregulations in response to trauma, fear is the single most powerful emotion in the Abyss and Inversion Experiences and links up with primitive images of self and world annihilation (Schore, 2003b). The Trauma Complex activates images of the Abyss Experience that, in turn, evoke negative states of emotional dysregulation (Schore, 2003b). Jung observed that overwhelming experiences lead to changes in well-being: "So far as I can judge, these more severe forms of the complex occur . . . when something so *devastating happens* to the individual that his whole *previous attitude to life breaks down"* (Jung, 1972, CW 8, para. 594; emphasis added). It is necessary to consider the primordial emotional experiences that are structured in the form of affect-images typical of mythology and symbolic representations of the trauma experience within intrapsychic processes. Campbell (1990) notes that the predominant themes of the Trauma Complex exist in a universal form, confirming their archetypal form in mythology, which he discussed in rich detail in his book *Transformation of Myth Through Time* (1990).

16 STRUCTURAL PARALLELS BETWEEN PSYCHIC COMPLEXES, PTSD, AND DISSOCIATION

The relationship and parallels of the Jungian concept of complexes to the Trauma Complex, PTSD, and dissociation are shown in Figure 5.8.

Dimensions of constellated complex (Jung (1972) CW8, para. 200-3)	Dimensions of trauma complex[1] Parallels to PTSD and dissociation	Parallel *DSM-IV* criteria[2]
1. "A disturbed state of consciousness"	Psychological stress response: fear, helplessness, horror, dissociation.	A_2, Diss
2. "Unity of consciousness disrupted"	Normal integrative process of consciousness disrupted.	B_1, B_2, B_3, Diss
3. "Intentions of will impeded or made impossible"	Avoidance, psychic numbing, loss of motivation and interest in significant activities.	C_1, C_2, C_4 Diss
4. "Memory noticeably affected"	Traumatic memory, intrusive re-experiencing, amnesia, dissociation.	B_1, B_3, C_3, Diss
5. "Psychic energy exceeds conscious intention"	Affective dysregulation; hyperarousal; increased distress.	$D_1 - D_5$, $B_4 -$ B_5, Diss
6. "Active complex momentarily creates state of duress"	Physiological hyperarousal, emotional distress.	$D_1 - D_5$, Diss
7. "Compulsive thinking and acting"	Overdriven activity as manifestation of anxiety.	B_4, B_5, $D_1 -$ D_5, Diss
8. "Diminished judicial responsibility"	Unconscious or flashback forms of reenactment; dissociative states.	B_3, Diss

FIGURE 5.8. Constellation of a psychic complex (Jung, 1972) and the Trauma Complex (Wilson, 2002).[1]Wilson (2002, 2003, 2004b). [2]A, B, C, D = PTSD criteria. Diss = dissociative disorders.

In PTSD, for example, a disturbed state of consciousness is evident by its nature as a stress response syndrome, whose initial phase is characterized by fear. The integrative processes of cognition, personality, and behavior are disrupted by trauma, resulting in painful intrusive memories and coping adaptations that include avoidance behaviors, psychological numbing, and dissociation. Traumatic impacts in PTSD include altered psychobiological responses (e.g., sleep, startle, impaired concentration) leading to hyperarousal states that fluctuate in intensity, especially in terms of affective dysregulation. Affectively dysregulated states in PTSD (Schore, 2003b) include overdriven states of activity, obsessive thinking, and compulsive actions that are often defensive in nature, designed to "jam" attention from distressing, recurring thoughts, images, and perceptions associated with the trauma (Horowitz, 1986, 2003; Wilson, Friedman, & Lindy, 2001). The Trauma Complex includes the entire range of PTSD symptoms and dissociative phenomenology and extends beyond it. The Trauma Complex is located in the core of the self in the personal unconscious as a distinct, coherent set of affects, images, perceptions, and cognitions that are united by a common theme of association with the trauma (see Figure 5.11).

16.1 Beyond PTSD and Complex PTSD

The concept of the Trauma Complex as a central component of the posttraumatic self is more inclusive in breadth, depth, and scope than PTSD or complex PTSD (Herman, 1992; Wilson, 2004b; Williams & Somers, 2002). The Trauma Complex has the power to potentially dominate mental life, activating other unconscious materials and complexes, creating a massive psychic force that consumes energy and drive, and adversely impacts the internal struggle to maintain stability, balance, unity, and coherency within the psyche. In a metaphorical sense, the Trauma Complex may become an intrapsychic battleground that can be aided and abetted by other constellated psychic complexes.

The Trauma Complex is a hierarchical suprasystem that transcends the original concept of complex PTSD as proposed by Herman (1992). Herman correctly described phenomena of behavioral changes that extended beyond the *DSM-III-R* algorithmic criteria for PTSD and included: (1) somatization; (2) dissociation; (3) affect changes, i.e., states of dysregulated emotion; (4) changes in relationship and affiliative patterns; (5) changes in personal identity; and (6) the increased risk of repetitive harm. The Trauma Complex incorporates all the dimensions of complex PTSD described by Herman (1992) and as revised by Wilson, Friedman, and Lindy (2001) to 65 symptoms. It weaves them into a more parsimonious and intricate conceptual framework that ties the dimensions of the Trauma Complex (see Figure 5.7) to archetypal forms of experiences that are universal in nature and shaped by cultural forces unique to the person. In this regard, there are culture-specific manifestations of Trauma Complexes in patients afflicted with conditions that would be labeled in Western medicine as hysteria, somatoform disorders, trance-states, PTSD, anxiety disorders, mood disorders, brief reactive psychosis, etc. (see Lewis-Fernandez, 1994 for a discussion of cross-cultural perspectives on trauma and dissociation).

With the passage of time, the Trauma Complex may eventually function like a psychological "black hole" (Wilson, 2004b) that pulls in disparate experiences that may have little in common with the original complex itself (Kalsched, 1996, 2003). The Trauma Complex can intensify negative emotional experiences by interfering with the psyche's symbolic processes in such a way that they lose their transcendent, meaning-assigning function (Knox, 2003; Shalit, 2002; Stevens, 1994). Thus, the *pathological operation* of the Trauma Complex blocks the nature of, and potential for, Transcendent Experiences.

16.2 The Trauma Complex and Systems of Meaning

A unique and important feature of the Trauma Complex, which extends beyond diagnostic criteria for PTSD and dissociation, involves alterations in, or the collapse of systems of, meaning, belief, and ideology. For many traumatized persons, their system of personal meaning, values, and spiritual orientation are profoundly altered by trauma (Janoff-Bulman, 1992; Lindy & Lifton, 2001; Wilson & Moran, 1997; Wilson, Friedman, & Lindy, 2001). According to Kalsched: "to the psyche a negative meaning is preferable to no meaning at all; a negative fantasy better than no fantasy whatsoever" (1996, p. 95). The collapse of meaning in the wake of trauma can give birth to cognitive attributions of negative meaning, which may generalize to demoralized states. To protect the psyche's inner core from "experiencing the unthinkable," Kalsched (1996) suggests the archetypal self-care system comes into play to defend the inner psychic core against unbearable traumatic affect and demoralization. Similar observations have been made by Reis (1995)

> Severe dissociative states have been noted, however, which are understood to represent a *total cessation in the process of attributing meaning* to experience ... One patient with MPD referred to these latter experiences as falling into a *"black hole"* ... to describe a psychic space in which *meaning is obliterated*. (p. 31; emphasis added)

The ultimate result of action by the archetypal self-care system described by Kalsched (1996), is the "gradual amplification of the complex leading finally to severe psychopathology" (p. 95). In this perspective, the Trauma Complex is a central unit concerned with the psychic metabolism of trauma. The concept of the Trauma Complex, its inner activation of archetypal affects, and the Abyss Experience, is more inclusive in nature than PTSD as a psychiatric disorder.

17 POSTTRAUMATIC COGWHEELING: THE TRAUMA COMPLEX AND THE ACTIVATION OF OTHER ARCHETYPAL FORMS OF EXPERIENCE

In the posttraumatic flow of psychological experience, the Trauma Complex emerges and grows as the metabolism of trauma occurs (see Figure 5.1). The growth of the Trauma Complex is similar to cell division by mitosis at the biological level. The single cell divides, multiplies, divides again, and continues a process of differentiation until the genetically controlled process terminates. Once formed out of the nidus of the trauma experience, the Trauma Complex has its own unique character that, similar to a cell undergoing mitosis, grows, divides, and articulates with other parts of the psyche. It is an organic, dynamic intrapsychic process characterized by its dissociability.

The way in which trauma cogwheels with other archetypes is shown in Figures 5.9 and 5.10. Moreover, it is conceptually possible to organize archetypes along a continuum anchored at one end by experience of deintegration, fragmentation, and despair and at the other end by self-integration, wholeness, and transcendence. In the posttraumatic self, the healthy metabolism of trauma results in self-transformation (i.e., transcendence) and results in a new archetype, the Unity Archetype, which Jung (1971) referred to as Syzygy, a transcendent function of opposites into a new form.

To illustrate the dynamic nature of how the Trauma Archetype cogwheels with other psychic complexes and archetypes, we can refer to once again to Figure 5.1, which shows that the Trauma Archetype causes organismic states of *psychic vulnerability* to develop. These states of psychic vulnerability set in motion a wide range of posttraumatic

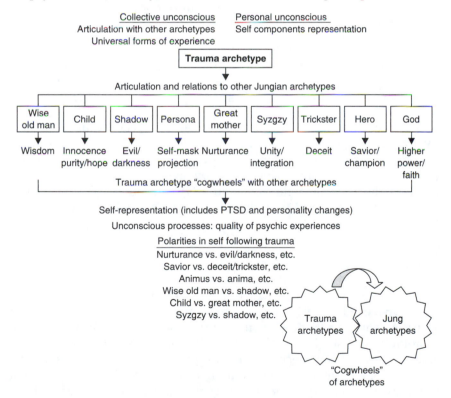

FIGURE 5.9. Trauma archetypal relations. *Source:* ©2004 John P. Wilson.

processes in terms of psychological functioning. For example, states of trauma-induced vulnerability intensify prepotent psychological need states and increase needs for survival, safety, love and belongingness, and self-esteem (see Chapter 6). Trauma-induced threats to basic psychological needs states may activate (through the Trauma Complex) the wish to be protected, nurtured, reassured, and calmed from the anxiety-residues of organismic disequilibrium. This being the case, the Trauma Archetype can activate the archetypes of nurturance (i.e., Good Mother), the protective hero (i.e., Hero or Wise Old Man archetype), or prayer to God to endure the travails of the trauma experience (i.e., the God archetype). It is equally possible that, depending on the specific nature of the trauma experience, archetypal forms of evil, danger, threat, the demonic and shadowy dark side of life will activate negative archetypes: the Trickster, the Shadow, Betrayal, and Crucifixion, among other possibilities. A similar psychodynamic conceptualization of the relationship of trauma to unresolved past conflicts from childhood has been described by Marmar, Weiss, & Pynoos (1996)

> Adult trauma may activate specific pre-oedipal or oedipal constellations, particularly those concerning *maternal protection and nurturance, control of emotions and bodily functions, and conflicts about potency, rivalry, aggression, and fear of retaliation.* The trauma activated themes are seen as *bridges* from current concerns to self-representations of other affect states, and concerns arising during early developmental periods" (p. 495, emphasis added)

It is interesting to note just how closely this psychodynamic perspective parallels a modified analytic perspective of the interplay between Trauma Archetypes and Trauma Complexes. Specifically, Marmar et al.'s (1996) reference to maternal protection and nurturance, etc. closely parallels the Jungian archetype of the Great Mother, Wise Old man, the Shadow, the Hero, and the drive towards unity in personality (i.e., Syzgzy archetype).

17.1 The Drive Towards Psychic Unity

The Trauma Complex, emanating from the template of the Trauma Archetype, can be considered an amalgam of the Abyss, Inversion, and Transcendent Experiences which are inherent in most types of profoundly stressful life-events. The posttraumatic self therefore includes a set of intrapsychic processes that are much larger in dimension than PTSD as one of many forms of human stress response. The Trauma Complex includes PTSD and its associated features, including what has been called complex PTSD (Herman, 1992; Wilson, 2004b), but is a more

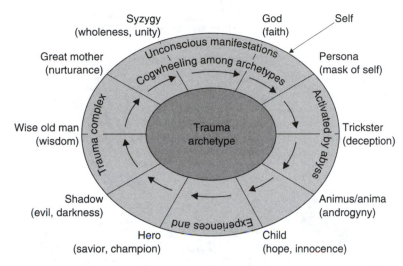

FIGURE 5.10. Trauma Archetype and its relation to Jungian archetypes. *Source:* ©2002 John P. Wilson.

central aspect of intrapsychic life because it necessarily articulates with the totality of personality at conscious and unconscious levels of functioning. The Trauma Complex, through its articulation with other archetypes, the dimensions of the self, identity, and ego-processes, enables analysis of the richness of mental processes in a systematic and thematic manner. The human propensity to strive towards self-integration balances the polarities of the self at multiple levels of integrated functioning as they exist at any point in time. As Jung (1971) noted, "the transcendent function manifests itself as a quality of conjoined opposites" (p. 298), a description which applies quite nicely to the dialectic tension between the Trauma Complex and the other dimensions of personality which are intensified by the power of human experience in the face of threat, adversity, and that which is intrinsically traumatic to existence itself.

18 THE MANDALA OF UNITY AND TRAUMA INTEGRATION

The holistic representation of the integrated Trauma Archetype and Trauma Complex is shown in Figure 5.11. It can be conceptualized as an integrated representation of the posttraumatic self, the mandala of unity and trauma integration.

To begin, the holistic nature of human psyche is represented by the large outer circle which symbolizes the organism. The qualitative nature of the Trauma Archetype and the Trauma Complex are indicated

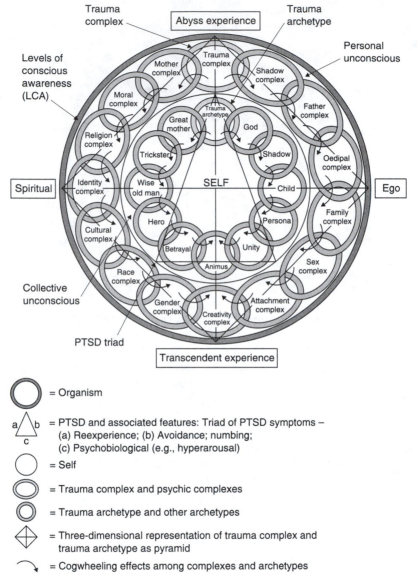

FIGURE 5.11. The Trauma Archetype, Trauma Complex, Jungian archetypes and the self. *Source:* ©2004 John P. Wilson and adapted from Stevens (1994).

by the two-dimensional axes of the Abyss Experience and the Transcendent Experience, and the Ego and Spiritual dimensions of conscious functioning. The Self, as conceptualized by Jung, rests within the center of the psyche and is located in the collective unconscious as a smaller circle. Nested within the Self is a triangle which represents the triad of

PTSD symptoms and its associated features. The Self also includes the Trauma Archetype as well as all other archetypal forms of experience. The archetypes articulate amongst themselves and are psychologically yoked to Trauma Complexes which are located in personality processes. The conceptual axes (Abyss vs. Transcendent and Ego vs. Spiritual) "cross-cut" the dimension of the Self, PTSD, archetypes, and psychic complexes. The Abyss, Inversion, and Transcendent Experience are present at different levels of conscious awareness within the organism (e.g., unconscious). Finally, the conceptual axes (Abyss vs. Transcendent; Ego vs. Spiritual) interact structurally within the Trauma Archetype, Trauma Complex, and PTSD to create a three-dimensional pyramidal structure which can be understood as the functional operation of psychic trauma within the organism.

18.1 Restoring Meaning and Wholeness to Personality

The representation of the integrated Trauma Archetype as a complex mandala has direct significance for restoring meaning and wholeness to personality. The image of the integrated Trauma Archetype represents the symbolic manifestation of transcendence and unity within personality. The transcendent function of the psyche is the union of conscious and unconscious contents, the conjoining of opposites which include positive and negative emotions, thoughts, and images connected to the experience of trauma. The process of "conjoining opposites" is another way of describing the metabolism and cognitive processing of powerful experiences that once threatened the well-being of personal existence. The Transcendent Experience is a natural outcome of the dialectical process of coming to grips with how a traumatic experience altered the sense of oneself as a person, i.e., one's sense of identity with its gyroscopic function in the stream of ongoing life-experience. Unity in the self emerges from the process of obtaining insight into the dynamic interplay between the Trauma Archetype and other archetypal forms of life-experiences that gave birth to psychic complexes, including the Trauma Complex. The Trauma Complex interlinks with other individually constellated complexes that formed during epigenetic development (see Figure 5.11). Past experiences, especially those with powerful emotional significance, have psychological connections to present-states of consciousness. Pre-existing psychological complexes, as nodules of memory storage, become associated with Trauma Complexes in highly selective ways based on their common emotional pathways that bind experiences together in the unconscious.

In the recovery from psychological trauma, there is a natural drive towards unifying experience in personality (Horowitz, 1986). In a broader, panoramic view of the ways that psychological trauma impacts personality, a fuller analysis of psychological functioning is possible. To this end, understanding the nature of the Trauma Archetype and the functioning of the Trauma Complex is important, parsimonious, and highly relevant to effective clinical treatment.

REFERENCES

American Psychiatric Association (2000). *Diagnostic and statistical manual of mental disorders* (5th ed.). Washington, DC: American Psychiatric Association.

Arcel, L. T., Smale, V. F., Kovacić, D. K., & Marusić, A. (1995). *Psychosocial help to war victims: Woman refugees and their families.* Copenhagen: IRCT.

Aronoff, J., & Wilson, J. P. (1985). *Personality in the social process.* New Jersey: Lawrence Erlbaum.

Baum, D. (2004). The price of valor. *New Yorker Magazine* [July 12 and 19], 44–51.

Blank, A.S. (1985). The unconscious flashback to the war in Vietnam veterans: Clinical mystery, legal defense, and community problem. In S. M. Sonnenberg, A. S. Blank, Jr., & J. A. Talbott (Eds.), *The trauma of war: Stress and recovery in Vietnam veterans* (pp. 293–309). Washington, DC: American Psychiatric Press.

Breslau, N. (1998). Epidemiology of trauma and posttraumatic stress disorder. In R. Yehuda (Ed.), *Psychological trauma* (pp. 1–27). Washington, DC: American Psychiatric Press.

Bryant, R. (2004). Acute stress disorders. In J. P. Wilson & T. M. Keane (Eds.), *Assessing psychological trauma and PTSD* (2nd edition), (pp. 46–56). New York: Guilford Publications.

Campbell, J. (1949). *Hero with a thousand faces.* New York. Penguin Books.

Campbell, J. (1988). *The power of myth.* New York: Anchor Books.

Campbell, J. (1990). *Transformation of myth through time.* New York: Harper.

Chu, J. A. (1998). *Rebuilding shattered lives: The responsible treatment of complex post-traumatic and dissociative disorders.* New York: Wiley.

Erikson, K. (1972). *Everything in its path.* New York: Simon & Schuster.

Freud, S. (1900). *The interpretation of dreams.* New York: W. W. Norton.

Freud, S. (1917). *Introductory lecture on psychoanalysis.* New York: W. W. Norton.

Friedman, M. J. (2000). *Post-traumatic stress disorder: The latest assessment and treatment strategies.* Kansas City: Compact Clinicals.

Friedman, M. J. & McEwen, B. S. (2004). PTSD, allostatic load and medical illness. In P. P. Schnurr & B. L. Green (Eds.), Trauma and healing: Physical consequences of exposure to extreme stress (pp. 157–189). Washington, DC: American Psychological Association.

Herman, J. L. (1992). *Trauma and recovery.* New York: Basic Books.

Herman, J. L. (1999). Complex PTSD. In M. Horowitz (Ed.), *Essential papers on post-traumatic stress disorder* (pp. 87–97). New York: New York University Press.

Hornsten, G. (1974). Wallenberg's syndrome. General symptomatology with special reference to visual disturbances and imbalances. *Acta Neurologica Scandinavica, 50,* 434–446.

Horowitz, M. (1986). *Stress response syndromes.* Northvale, New Jersey: Jason Aronson.

Horowitz, M. (2003). *Treating stress response syndromes.* Washington, D.C.: American Psychiatric Press.

Jaffe, D. T. (1995). Self-renewal: Personal transformation following extreme trauma. *Journal of Humanistic Psychology, 25,* 99–124.

Janoff-Bulman, R. (1992). *Shattered assumptions: Towards a new psychology of trauma.* New York: Free Press.

Jansen, K. (2001). *Ketamine: Dreams and realities*. New York: Multidisciplinary Association for Psychedelic Studies.

Jung, C. G. (1929). The collected works (Bollingen series XX, 20 vols.). Trans. R. F. C. Hull. In H. Read, M. Fordham, & G. Adler (Eds.), *The therapeutic value of abreaction* (CW 16). Princeton, NJ: Princeton University Press.

Jung, C. G. (1934). The collected works (Bollingen series XX, 20 vols.). Trans. R. F. C. Hull. In H. Read, M. Fordham, & G. Adler (Eds.), *A review of psychological complexes* (CW 8). Princeton, NJ: Princeton University Press.

Jung, C. G. (1950). The collected works (Bollingen series XX, 20 vols.). Trans. R. F. C. Hull. In H. Read, M. Fordham, & G. Adler (Eds.), *Four archetypes* (CW 8). Princeton, NJ: Princeton University Press.

Jung, C. G. (1957, 1972). The collected works (Bollingen series XX, 20 vols.). Trans. R. F. C. Hull. In H. Read, M. Fordham, & G. Adler (Eds.), *Recent thoughts on schizophrenia* (CW 3). Princeton, NJ: Princeton University Press.

Jung, C. G. (1959, 1968). The collected works (Bollingen series XX, 20 vols.). Trans. R. F. C. Hull. In H. Read, M. Fordham, & G. Adler (Eds.), *The archetypes and the collective unconscious* (CW 9i). Princeton, NJ: Princeton University Press.

Jung, C. G. (1963). *Memories, dreams and reflections*. New York: Vintage Books.

Jung, C. G. (1971). The collected works (Bollingen series XX, 20 vols.). Trans. R. F. C. Hull. In H. Read, M. Fordham, & G. Adler (Eds.), *Psychological types* (CW 6). Princeton, NJ: Princeton University Press.

Kalsched, D. (1996). *The inner world of trauma: Archetypal defenses of the personal spirit*. London: Routledge.

Kalsched, D. (2003). Daimonic elements in early trauma. *Journal of Analytical Psychology, 48*, 145–176.

Keppe, N. (2002). *The origin of illness: Psychological, physical, social*. Lisbon: Trilogy Press.

Kessler, R. C., Sonnega, A., Bromet, E., Hughes, M. H., & Nelson, C. B. (1995). Posttraumatic stress disorder in the national comorbidity survey. *Archives of General Psychiatry, 52*, 1048–1060.

Knox, J. (2003). Trauma and defenses: Their roots in relationship. An overview. *Journal of Analytical Psychology, 48*, 207–233.

Ladner, L. (2004). *The lost art of compassion*. Boston, MA: Harper.

Laibow, R. E. & Laue, C. S. (1993). PTSD in experienced anomalous trauma. In J. P. Wilson & B. Raphael (Eds.), *International handbook of traumatic stress syndromes* (pp. 93–105). New York: Plenum Press.

LefCourt, H. E. (1982). *Locus of control (2nd ed.)*. Hillsdale, NJ: Lawrence Erlbaum Publishers.

Lewis-Fernandez, R. (1994). Culture and dissociation: a comparison of Atagre de Nervios among Puerto Rican and possession syndrome in India. In D. Spiegel (Ed.), *Dissociation: Culture, mind and body* (pp. 123–167). Washington, DC: American Psychiatric Press.

Lifton, R. J. (1967). *Death in life: The survivors of Hiroshima*. New York: Simon & Schuster.

Lifton, R. J. (1976). *The life of the self*. New York: Simon & Schuster.

Lindy, J. D. (1993). Focal psychoanalytic psychotherapy of PTSD. In J. P. Wilson & B. Raphael (Eds.), *International handbook of traumatic stress syndromes* (pp. 803–811). New York: Plenum Press.

Lindy, J. D. (2001). An allostatic approach to the psychodynamic understanding for PTSD. In J. P. Wilson, M. J. Friedman & J. D. Lindy (Eds.), *Treating psychological trauma and PTSD (2nd Ed.)* (pp. 344–389). New York: Guilford Publications.

Lindy, J. D. & Lifton, R. J. (2001). *Beyond invisible walls*. New York: Brunner-Routledge.

Lindy, J. D. & Wilson, J. P. (2001). An allostatic approach to the psychodynamic understanding of PTSD. In J. P. Wilson, M. J. Friedman, & J. D. Lindy (Eds.), *Treating psychological trauma and PTSD* (pp. 125–139). New York: Guilford Publications.

Mack, J. D. (1999). *Passport to the cosmos*. New York: Crown Books.

Marmar, C. R., Weiss, D., & Pynoos, R. (1996). Dynamic psychotherapy of PTSD. *Boilliere's Clinical Psychiatry*, 2(2), 297–313.

Marsella, A .J., Friedman, M. J., Gerrity, E., & Scurfield, R. M. (Eds.). (1996). *Ethnocultural aspects of posttraumatic stress disorder: Issues, research and applications.* Washington, DC: American Psychological Associated Press.

McEwen, B. S. (1998). Seminars of the Beth Israel Deaconess Medical Center: Protective and damaging effects of stress mediators. *New England Journal of Medicine, 338,* 171–179.

McEwen, B. S. (2002). *The end of stress as we know it.* Washington, D. C.: The Dana Press.

McNally, R., Lasko, N., Clancy, S., Macklin, C., Pitman, R. K., & Orr, S. (2004). Psychophysiological responding during script driven imagery in people reporting abduction by space aliens. *Psychological Science, 15,* 493–498.

Miller, J. G. (1978). *Living systems.* New York: McGraw-Hill.

Nijenhuis, E. R. S. & van der Hart, O. (1999). Forgetting and re-experiencing trauma: From anesthesia to pain. In J. M. Goodwin & R. Attias (Eds.), *Splintered reflections* (pp. 9–39). New York: Basic Books.

Ortiz, D. (2001). The survivor perspective: voices from the center. In E. Gerrity, T. M. Keane, & F. Tuma (Eds.), *Mental health consequences of torture* (pp. 3–13). New York: Klumer/Plenum Press.

Reis, B. E. (1995). Toward a psychoanalytic understanding of MPD. In J .G. Allen & W. H. Smith (Eds.), *Diagnosis and treatment of dissociative disorders* (pp. 25–35). Hillsdale, New Jersey. Jason Aronson Inc.

Ring, K. (1992). *The Omega Project: Near death experiences, UFO encounters, mind at large.* New York: Morrow.

Salman, S. (1997). The creative psyche: Jung's major contributions. In P. Young-Eisendrath & T. Dawson (Eds.), *The Cambridge comparison to Jung* (pp. 52–70). Cambridge: Cambridge University Press.

Schore, A. N. (2003a). *Affect dysregulation and disorders of the self.* New York: W. W. Norton.

Schore, A. N. (2003b). *Affect dysregulation and the repair of the self.* New York: W. W. Norton.

Seligman, M. E. P. (1975). *Helplessness: On depression, development and death.* San Francisco, CA: Freeman.

Shalit, E. (2002). *The complex path of transformation from archetype to ego.* Toronto: Inner City Books.

Shipley, T. F. (2003). The effect of object and event orientation on perception of biological motion. *Psychological Science, 14,* 377–380.

Shore, D. I. & Klein, R. M. (2000). The effects of scene inversion on change blindness. *Journal of General Psychology, 1,* 1–12.

Steiner, I., Shanin, R., & Melamed, E. (1987). Acute upside down reversal of vision in vertebrobisilar ischemia. *Neurology, 37,* 1685–1686.

Stern, D. (1985). *The interpersonal world of the infant.* New York: Basic Books.

Stevens, A. (1994). *Jung: A very short introduction.* London: Oxford University Press.

Storr, A. (1999). *The essential Jung.* Princeton, NJ: Princeton University Press.

van der Kolk, B., van der Hart, O., & Marmar, C. (1996). Dissociation and information processing in PTSD. In B. van der Kolk, A. C. McFarlane, & L. Weisaeth (Eds.), *Traumatic stress* (pp. 303–331). New York: Guilford Publications.

Vesti, P., Somnier, F., & Kastrup, M. (1992). *Psychotherapy with torture survivors.* Copenhagen: IRCT.

Williams, M. B. & Somers, J. F. (2002). *Simple and complex PTSD.* New York: Haworth Press, Inc.

Wilson, J. P. (1989). *Trauma, transformation and healing.* New York: Brunner-Mazel.

Wilson, J. P. (1990). PTSD and experienced anomalous trauma: Similarities in reported UFO abductions and exposure to invisible toxic contaminants. *Journal of UFO Studies, 2,* 1–19.

Wilson, J. P. (2002). *An organismic, holistic model of complex PTSD.* Presentation at the International Society for Traumatic Stress Studies 18th annual meeting, Baltimore, Maryland, November 10, 2002.

Wilson, J. P. (2003). *PTSD and self-transformation.* Presentation at the International Institute of Psychotraumatology, Dubrovnik, Croatia, June 15, 2003.

Wilson, J. P. (2004a). PTSD and complex PTSD: Symptoms, syndromes and diagnoses. In J. P. Wilson & T. M. Keane (Eds.), *Assessing psychological trauma and PTSD* (pp. 1–46). New York: Guilford Publications.

Wilson, J. P. (2004b) Broken spirits. In J. P.Wilson & B. Drozdek (Eds.), *Broken spirits: The treatment of traumatized asylum seekers, refugees and war and torture victims* (pp. 141–173). New York: Brunner-Routledge.

Wilson, J. P. (2004c). The broken spirit: Posttraumatic damage to the self. In J. P. Wilson & B. Drozdek (Eds.), *Broken spirits: Treating traumatized asylum seekers, refugees, war and torture victims* (Ch. 6, pp. 107–155). NewYork: Brunner-Routledge Press.

Wilson, J. P. & Drozdek, B. (2004). *Broken spirits: The treatment of traumatized asylum seekers, refugees and war and torture victims.* New York: Brunner-Routledge Press.

Wilson, J. P., Friedman, M., & Lindy, J. (2001). *Treating psychological trauma and PTSD.* New York: Guilford Publications.

Wilson, J. P. & Moran, T. (1997). Psychological trauma: PTSD and spirituality. *Journal of Psychology and Theology, 26*(2), 168–178.

Wilson, J. P. & Thomas, R. (2004). *Empathy in the treatment of trauma and PTSD.* New York: Brunner-Routledge.

Wilson, J. P. & Ziegelbaum, S. D. (1986). PTSD and the disposition to criminal behavior. In C. R. Figley (Ed.), *Trauma and it's wake* (Vol. II) (Chapter 15, pp. 305–321). New York: Brunner/Mazel.

6

Trauma, Optimal Experiences, and Integrative Psychological States

JOHN P. WILSON

1 INTRODUCTION

The relation of psychological trauma to mental health, optimal functioning, and integrated states of personality functioning is critical to the complete analysis of psychopathology and human growth. How does trauma impact the structure of personality as it exists at the time of the experience? How do traumatic events adversely impact optimal levels of integrated functioning? How does the organism mobilize coping, adaptive, and security operations in the wake of trauma? How do traumatized psychic states become transformed into self-actualizing modes of optimal functioning? How do soul-injured spirits become vitally animated?

Theories of personality and clinical insights derived from the treatment of patients with posttraumatic stress disorder (PTSD) and self-pathologies have underscored the inherent propensity towards unity in personality and its dissolution by trauma (Schore, 2003). Unity in personality reflects a drive towards integration in consciousness, perceptual processes, identity, self-continuity, memory, and behavioral functioning. The psychological mechanisms associated with unity reflect a capacity for active mastery of experience, accurate perception of reality, and efficacy in adaptive behavior. Unity in personality facilitates organismic striving towards optimal adaptation in the environment that has been termed self-actualization, self-realization, optimal states, effectance motivation, fully functioning personality, and psychological health (e.g., Maslow, 1968, 1970; Rogers, 1951; White, 1959; Aronoff & Wilson, 1985). In contrast, disunity in personality has been described as fragmentation, the loss of self-coherence, and self-pathology in which there is deintegration of self-capacities and behavior (Wolfe, 1990; Knox, 2003a; Pearlman & Saatvikne, 1995). Traumatic experiences can lead to varying degrees of disunity in personality, disrupting the organismic drive towards optimal functioning.

In the field of mental health, it has long been observed that disunity in personality has been characterized by alterations in intrapsychic processes associated with normal and pathological forms of behavior (Freud, 1920; Janet, 1900, 1907; Wolfe, 1990; Nemiah, 1998; Lifton, 1993). Alterations in personality range from acute states of self-estrangement, ego-alienation, anxiety states, and identity confusion to severe forms of self-pathologies manifest in borderline personality disorders, dissociative disorders, and psychotic conditions. Degrees of unity and disunity in personality reflect organismic capacities associated with mastery of experience, coping, adaptation, and defensive functioning (Nemiah, 1998). *In a holistic sense, organismic processes exist on a continuum of unified self-processes and integrated forms of behavioral adaptation* (Lifton, 1993; Mischel & Morf, 2003; Wilson, 2004a).

The question of unity in self-capacities necessarily involves understanding disruptions to their inherent components and subsystems (Mischel & Morf, 2003). Personality processes are comprised of structural dimensions (e.g., traits, factors, individual differences, stable dispositions in motives) and process functions (e.g., perceptual accuracy, situational coping, interactional styles) which are attacked by the impact of trauma. How does an integrated, cohesive, and functional self-structure unravel and come apart? How does trauma potentially degrade optimal levels of functioning?

We begin by asking if the experience of severe psychological trauma is the universal paradigm of how optimal states of functioning become impaired and lead to deintegrated forms of behavior. At the analytic level, what does deintegration of optimal states mean? What defines trauma-related alterations in states of consciousness, self-awareness, identity, and the integrative processes of behavior? Does deintegration in psychological systems necessarily change operational functions in other organismic processes? Is there a threshold that delineates the point at which deintegrative psychological experience results in pathology (e.g., PTSD, depression, dissociation)? Is it possible to conceptualize a continuum of integrated states of experience that include optimal functioning versus deintegrated, pathological states of dissociated behavior? If so, is there a common set of psychological mechanisms that control integrative functioning? This chapter will address these and related questions and show how the understanding of deintegrated optimal states of functioning provides knowledge of how traumatized psychic states can be transformed into higher levels of integrated functioning.

2 A CONTINUUM OF INTEGRATED STATES OF PSYCHOLOGICAL EXPERIENCE

Our focus centers on the question of traumatic impacts on optimal and integrated states of psychological functioning. A continuum of integrated behavioral functioning is presented in Figure 6.1. In a conceptual context, peak experiences have been designated as the anchor point of optimal states since they are characteristic of psychologically healthy, fully functioning persons. Peak experiences are part of self-actualizing syndromes of personality and are the antithesis of dissociative states evoked by traumatic stressors. At the other end of the continuum are dissociative states since they are organismic reactions to trauma and threats to psychological and physical integrity. Simple and complex dissociative reactions to traumatic stressors are the immediate means used by the organism in the service of maintaining stability in adaptation. They are one of many defenses in a hierarchical repertoire of defensive processes available to protect against disequilibrium, threat,

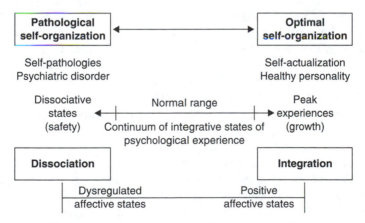

FIGURE 6.1. A continuum of altered states of consciousness and integrative psychological experiences. *Source:* ©2004 John P. Wilson.

and states of organismic vulnerability. These disparate forms of integrative psychic phenomena allow us to explore a broad range of issues concerning the processes by which traumatic states are transformed from pathology to health.

In *Towards a Psychology of Being* (1968) and *Motivation and Personality* (1970), Maslow stated that peak experiences are episodic events experienced by normal persons and a cardinal characteristic of self-actualizing persons as an epiphenomenal manifestation of self-actualizing states of being. Since self-actualizing behavior epitomizes healthy functioning, the question can be raised as to how traumatic experiences disrupt highly integrated, optimal states of coping and adaptation. What happens to the structural integrity of personality processes in fully functioning persons when catastrophic trauma impacts their capacity for effective coping? What happens to the vulnerable, fragile, and poorly integrated person when trauma "knocks at their door"? Does the self-structure deintegrate and unravel in the same way for strong and weak personality organizations? Does the unraveling of the self-structure have an analog in biological science in which pathogenic alterations of cell processes create illness?

In terms of a coherence–fragmentation continuum of self-processes (see Chapter 2), it may be seen that dissociative disorders anchor the pathogenic end of the integrative continuum of psychological experiences (Wilson, 2004a). Dissociative states are the antithesis of optimal and integrative states of consciousness (Sadock & Sadock, 2003). At the mid-range of the continuum are normally distributed forms of psychological functioning, reflecting coherence and stability of self-capacities (Pearlman & Saatvikne, 1995; Schore, 2003). By conceptualizing a continuum of integrated psychological states, it is possible to examine the ways in which trauma causes a reduction in healthy functioning, the loss of coherence, and self-deintegration.

Reviews of research evidence indicate that dissociative *disorders* are associated with childhood abuse and psychological trauma (Chu, 1998; Putnam, 1997). Dissociative *states*, on the other hand, are not necessarily pathological, but represent alterations in psychological systems (e.g., perception, memory, consciousness, identity, behavior) which are evoked by threat to the well-being of the organism and can be highly adaptive in nature (Putnam, 1997). The adaptations of mental processes evident in dissociative states and more severe forms of psychic alterations in dissociative disorders (e.g., perception, memory) reflect fundamental changes in cognition, information processing, and memory (see Putnam, 1997 for a review of the DBS (discrete behavioral states) model).

3 DIMENSIONS OF INTEGRATIVE EXPERIENCES

What characterizes the nature of integrative experiences in optimal psychological states of functioning? What are their forms and types? Are peak experiences the opposite of Abyss Experiences of despair, darkness, and immersion into the vortex of trauma (see Chapter 5)? If so, what can they tell us about the transformation of traumatized psychic states?

In essence, peak experiences are expressions of optimal states of integrated personality functioning and self-actualizing syndromes. Clinical research on peak experiences has identified the dimensions that define these optimal states: (1) perception; (2) memory; (3) levels of consciousness; (4) identity; (5) self-capacities; (6) motivational dispositions; (7) affect regulation; and (8) somatic/motor behavior (Maslow, 1968, 1970). In peak experiences these dimensions of psychic functioning are synergistic. They augment and intensify consciousness and capacity for performance.

In contrast, research on dissociative disorders has provided evidence (e.g., Chu, 1998; Bremner & Marmar, 1998; Putnam, 1997; Ross, Miller, Bjorns, Fraser, & Anderson, 1990) of how each of the dimensions of optimal functioning is altered in dissociative states and dissociative disorders (Putnam, 1997; Nijenhuis, 2000; Nijenhuis & van der Hart, 1999a). In a related way, the literature on the self-pathologies of borderline and narcissistic personality disorders (e.g., Goldberg, 1985; Wolfe, 1990; Aktar, 1983; Masterson, 1981; Kohut, 1971) has shown that there are significant deficits in self-functioning which reflect degrees of disunity in self-capacities, a lack of integrative ego-functions, and perceptual and interpersonal deficits in competence as a result of developmental insufficiencies in parent–child interactions, abusive and traumatic experiences (especially relational trauma), loss of attachments, and profoundly unstable family environments (Schore, 2003).

The data from seemingly diverse research on optimal states of psychological health and severe self-pathologies can be placed on a theoretically meaningful continuum of integrative psychological states. This continuum of integrative states of experience permits comparative analyses that reveal how core self-processes become arrested, altered, disrupted, transformed, and reorganized in response to demands imposed by: (1) traumatic life-experiences associated with epigenetic development; (2) disturbances in attachment and affiliative relationships; and (3) injuries to self-processes that cause shame, guilt, narcissistic damage, humiliation, and loss of regulatory processes associated with self-esteem and positive well-being (Wilson, 2004a; Wilson & Thomas, 2004; Ulman & Brothers, 1988; Schore, 2003).

4 A COMPARATIVE ANALYSIS OF OPTIMAL EXPERIENCES
   AND DISSOCIATIVE STATES

4.1 Peak Experiences and Optimal States

Peak experiences are epiphenomenal manifestations of healthy psychological functioning, optimal states of well-being, and states of self-actualizing functioning. Peak experiences are characterized as having specific qualitative dimensions of functioning that involve perceptions of time, space, and meaning; subjective feelings of joy, rapture, awe, wonder, ecstasy, and feeling fully at one's "peak" of power as a person. Maslow believed that peak experiences were more frequent among self-actualizing persons since they had "relatively permanent gratification" (1970, p. 18) of their basic needs for safety, love, affiliation, identity and self-esteem, and were able to function at higher motivational states of integrated activity. Maslow described higher levels of psychological functioning as B-motivation (i.e., B = Being), representing functioning at optimal states of integrated behavior.[1]

*4.2 The Reciprocity Principles of Deficiency Motivation
      and Need Gratification*

As a personality syndrome, self-actualization is an active, dynamic motivational process rather than an end state of personality development. In empirical research, it has been operationalized and assessed in different ways (Aronoff & Wilson, 1985). In terms of functional dynamics, prepotent needs, located lower in the hierarchy, cease to be motivators of action once they are gratified. Upon sufficient satisfaction, they simultaneously release higher order functioning of other needs in greater degrees of strength in the vector of motivational goals. The reciprocal principles of gratification and deficiency of basic needs induce changes in the dynamic configuration of prepotent motive states. For example, with relatively permanent gratification of the safety needs, behavior is motivated automatically by higher sets of needs. Given safety need gratification, the person's motivational goals orient automatically to affiliative, esteem, and self-actualizing needs in a progressive but simultaneous fashion. As each set of needs becomes increasingly satisfied, the

---

[1]Maslow's concept of peak experiences is similar to that of "flow" as optimal functioning as described by Csikszentmihalyi (1990): "Following the flow experience, the organization of the self is more complex than it had been before. It is by becoming increasingly complex that the self might be said to grow" (p. 41).

proportion or degree of self-actualizing behavior increases corresponding-ly since lower needs are less determining of goal-directed behavior and are less valued by the person. As the process of need gratification increases, more integrative experiences occur leading to greater strength in personality, identity, and active mastery unless thwarted by frustra-tion, blocks, deprivation, threat, trauma, or other types of experience that maintain focus on lower needs thereby preventing the development of more robust self-actualizing states (Maslow, 1970, p. 33).

In *Towards a Psychology of Being* (1968), Maslow analyzed the effects of peak experiences to optimal states of psychological functioning. Peak experiences serve as *acute identity experiences* (1968, pp. 103–115) and consequently enable individuals to experience more integrative and self-actualizing states of being. After the peak experience, mindful reflection empowers the individual to see self-actualizing potential "in the mirror," so to speak. As a form of optimal functioning, the peak experience is an inner glimpse of self-actualizing potentialities, like opening a door to a room full of hidden treasures that one did not know existed.

Acute identity episodes in peak experiences are a source of self-discovery. In a metaphorical sense, the organism is speaking to the person: "Look, this is the real you and how you can be when functioning fully with your highest potential." In this way acute identity episodes are positive in nature and can mobilize growth and personality development in self-actualizing directions. To quote Maslow (1968, p. 104)

> the person in the peak experiences feels more integrated (unified, whole, all of a piece) than at other times. He also looks (to the observer) more integrated in various ways, e.g., less split, dissociated, less fighting against himself, less split between experiencing self and observing self, more one-pointed, more harmoniously organized, more efficiently organized with all his parts functioning very nicely with each other, more synergic, with less internal friction, etc.

5 CHARACTERISTICS OF OPTIMAL INTEGRATIVE EXPERIENCES

5.1 Trauma and Optimal States

To understand how psychological trauma impacts optimal integrative states, it is useful and informative to contrast the central features of peak versus dissociative experiences. The central comparative features of peak experiences and dissociative states are presented in Figure 6.2.

Peak experiences are spontaneous, subjectively positive emotional experiences that occur without conscious intention, planning, or will. Individual accounts of peak experiences and optimal states of func-tioning are reported as effortless, fluid, natural, playful, egoless, and

Psychological dimensions	Peak experiences	Dissociative states
Perception	Vivid, clear, in-the-moment, centered, holistic, lucid, accurate, ego-transcending, unity, B-cognition, fulgent, detached, synchronicity, figure–ground unity, perspicacious, richer	Detached self-observation, disrupted, distorted, perceptually surreal, D-cognition, fuliginous, in and out of focus, outside self
Memory	Clear, total, continuous accurate recall, nondistorted, no amnesia, eidetic; desire repetition, intact	Amnesias, partial and fragmented, memory failure of recall, nonchronological recall, disrupted information processing
Consciousness/ awareness	Fluid, clear, resolute, acute, sharp, total attention, B-cognition, open to experience, oriented to person and place, disoriented to time and space, transcendent, mystical, ineffable	Clouded, opaque, disrupted, unreal, dream-like, daze, closed to new experience, time and space disorientation
Identity	Integrative, egoless, acute identity experience, identity enhancing, peak experience may alter self- and world view, sense of meaning and sharpened sense of continuity and sameness; fully functioning; here-now awareness	Confusion, identity deintegration, multiple identities, fragmented identity, disconnected, loss of sense of self-continuity and sameness
Self-capacities	Unified, whole, spontaneous, aware of potential, integrated, coherent, autonomous, connected, high energy, sense of vitality, synergistic self-function, positive self-reference	Fragmented, depersonalized, self-alienation, estrangement, split self-functions encapsulated in compartments, parallel ego-states, unstable self-capacities
Motivation	Effortless, intrinsic; self-directed, spontaneous, growth producing, need gratifying; releases and expresses creativity	Trance states, possession, pathogenic, deficiency need based, unconsciously driven by unmetabolized conflict
Affect	Positive, synchronized affects; subjectively pleasurable; increased positive arousal; experience intrinsically valued; no fear, anxiety, inhibition or negative self-reference; awe, wonder	Negative, dysregulated affects, anxiety producing, hyperarousal states, fear, terror, perceptions of harm, threat, damage, etc.
Somatic/motor	Sensitive, aware of sensory modalities, feelings of wholeness, heightened states of proprioception, effortless motor control, high states of tension or relaxation, peacefulness	Anesthesias, analgesias, hyperesthesias, involuntary motor movements, paralyses, tics, tremors, convulsions, stupor, somatoform dissociation

FIGURE 6.2. Comparative psychological dimensions of peak experiences and dissociative states. *Source:* ©2003 John P. Wilson.

automatically taking place. During the peak experience, the individual is actively or passively involved in activities such as exercise, athletics, sexuality, listening to music, viewing inspiring artistic productions, reading literature, walking in nature, giving birth to a child, or participating in a celebration of an accomplishment. In a more basic way, peak experiences may occur while looking at a magnificent ocean sunset with its orange hue descending below the Earth's horizon or taking a stroll on a resplendent spring day with opulent flowers in bloom and the redolent herbal smell of nitrogen-enriched earth and freshly cut grass.

Peak experiences are described as nonhabitual and effortless; being "in the flow," "natural," "just happening," and synchronous in multimodal sensory–perceptual channels (Maslow, 1968). During peak experiences, perceptual processes are characterized as holistic, "the big picture" and unifying, seeing figure and ground as one. In terms of emotional states, peak experiences are described as exciting or serene. As subjectively experienced, they are replete with a sense of acceptance of self, nature, and life itself as natural occurrences, without blocks, fear, or judgment as to its moral goodness.

Maslow (1968) believed peak experiences are intrinsically valuable and growth promoting, facilitating psychological health and feelings of well-being. However, his research subjects report *distortions in time and space perception*; i.e., losing track of time by being fully absorbed in the peak experience. Some individuals describe how during a peak experience they feel like an external observer or experience an "out-of-body" phenomenon that is emotionally positive and psychically fluid in nature. Hence, the term "being in the flow" of one's event. Unlike dissociative experiences, the memory of peak experiences is lucid, accurate, detailed, and recollected as important, sometimes leading to changes in personal identity, values, world view, and systems of meaning. A few individuals describe peak experiences in mystical terms and as transcendent in nature. They report experiencing unity with the "great chain of humanity." They have a capacity to look "backward" in time at significant events, persons, and accomplishments and feel a kinship, identification, and sense of connection to the past and others' lives. At the same time, they may envision future goals and aspirations and project themselves forward in time with anticipated achievements. Other subjects report physical and sensory qualities to their peak experiences, with heightened perceptual sensitivity and intense awareness of their internal states.

Peak experiences are universally reported in emotionally positive ways, a fact of great relevance to the transformation of traumatized psychic states as will be discussed later in this chapter. Individuals report states of heightened (positive) tension or extreme relaxation and peacefulness. Peak experiences are devoid of distress, anxiety, fear, and uncertainty. Maslow's subjects reported enhanced feelings of creativity during and after the peak experiences.

As optimal integrative experiences, the peak experience involves unifying cognitions of objects in-the-world in relation to self-as-process. Maslow (1968, p. 71) characterized such perceptual qualities as metacognition, or B-cognition, to describe functioning at Being levels of self-actualizing experience.

6 CHARACTERISTICS OF DISSOCIATIVE DEINTEGRATIVE EXPERIENCES

In nearly all respects, dissociative experiences are the polar opposite of peak experiences (Putnam, 1997; Chu, 1998; Wilson, 2003, 2004a). As research studies have shown, dissociative experiences are *deintegrative* in nature (Knox, 2003a; Chu, 1998; Schore, 2003; Kalsched, 2003; Nijenhuis & van der Hart, 1999a; Putnam, 1997). Dissociative states and disorders are reactions to threat and the perception of danger, harm, or injuries to physical integrity or psychological functioning. Dissociation occurs in multiple forms and has been classified into primary, secondary, tertiary, and somatic types (Nijenhuis & van der Hart, 1999a). The *DSM-IV-TR* of the American Psychiatric Association (2000, p. 519) defines dissociation and dissociative disorders as a "disruption in the usually integrative function of consciousness, memory, identity and perception of the environment." The *DSM-IV* definition indicates that the major processes and structures of the self can be altered by abuse, trauma, and perceived threats, which can result in alterations in personality, identity, memory, and basic psychological processes governing adaptive behavior. Knox (2003a) describes dissociative phenomena as deintegrative experiences which can occur outside of conscious awareness. As noted by Putnam (1997), dissociative experiences involve states and traits of personality processes which may vary in severity, frequency, periodicity, and intensity. In this regard, dissociative states may be highly adaptive in some situations and maladaptive in other situations, especially if dissociative behaviors impair functioning and adequate adaptation to external demands on the organism (Nijenhuis & van der Hart, 1999a).

A summary of dissociative characteristics is presented in Figure 6.2 with symptoms cross-cutting basic psychological processes associated with memory, perception, cognition, information processing, and self-capacities (Wilson, Friedman, & Lindy, 2001). The list of characteristics is adapted from recent research by Nijenhuis and van der Hart (1999a); Schore (2003); Steele, van der Hart, and Nijenhuis (2001); Lowenstein and Goodwin (1999); Chu (1998); Putnam (1997); van der Hart and Boon

(1997); van der Hart, van der Kolk, and Boon (1998); and Sadock and Sadock (2003).

Dissociative states and disorders are manifestations of alterations in basic psychological processes. In each of these systems of psychological functioning there are degrees of deintegration of normal functions associated with adaptive behaviors. There are forms of dissociated *sensations*: (e.g., anesthesias for sensory modalities of sight, smell, movement, hearing, touch); *perceptions* (e.g., perceptual distortions which enlarge or reduce the stimulus field; trauma-based hallucination experiences); *memory* (e.g., amnesia), *ego-functions* (e.g., altered conscious awareness, parallel ego-states, out-of-body observations of activity); *information processing* (e.g., state dependent learning), and *defenses* (e.g., unconscious flashbacks and acting out of repressed unmetabolized traumatic material).

Dissociative states, as acute or temporary alterations in mental functioning, are qualitatively different from dissociative disorders (Putnam, 1997). Studies have demonstrated, starting with Janet's (1907, p. 1558) observation, that "[traumas] produce their disintegrating effects in proportion to their intensity, duration and repetition." There is a direct causal relationship between exposure to traumatic events and the development of chronic dissociative disorders (Schore, 2003; Nijenhuis & van der Hart, 1999a).

Nosologically, dissociative disorders have been classified by a specific set of symptoms and their pathological effects on adaptive behavior (Sadock & Sadock, 2003). Dissociative amnesia, for example, reflects an inability to recall information, especially data connected to the experience of trauma. Dissociative fugue characterizes errant wandering, and confusion about personal identity. Dissociative identity disorder (DID) describes fragmented personality and self-processes with multiple encapsulated identities contained within one organizational system. Dissociative depersonalization is a manifestation of altered perception of self in relation to the world; perceiving situations or one's body as surreal, strange, dream-like, detached, removed, or perceptually altered in appearance. More recently, Nijenhuis and van der Hart (1999a), reviewing the seminal work of Janet, have proposed that there is also somatoform dissociation which "involves negative symptoms such as analgesia, anesthesia, as well as positive symptoms such as site-specific pain and changing preferences of taste and smell" (1999, p. 46). Nijenhuis and his associates have developed a psychometric measure, the SDQ-5 and SDQ-20, which discriminates patients with dissociative disorder from nonpatients in five somatic areas: kinesthetic anesthesia, visual anesthesia, analgesia, aphonia, and urological symptoms.

7 COMPARATIVE QUALITIES OF ALTERED STATES OF
PSYCHOLOGICAL INTEGRATION IN PEAK EXPERIENCES
AND DISSOCIATIVE STATES

As divergent psychological phenomena, peak and dissociative experiences involve alterations in the integrative functions of behavior. The scientific understanding of dissociative phenomena permits comparative analysis with peak experiences. This fact suggests that there may be similar psychological processes at work; one reflecting optimal states of well-being and the other reflecting organismic response to danger, harm, traumatic stressors, and threats to the unity of core inner processes of the self and personality, including intrapsychic threats generated by defensive systems (Kalsched, 1996). A comparative analysis can be made for different areas of integrative processes: (1) consciousness; (2) memory; (3) identity; (4) perception of the environment; and (5) time perception.

A comparative analysis reveals that peak experiences are *integrative, synergistic,* and *synchronous* in nature. Dissociative states are *deintegrating, fragmenting,* and *dysynchrous* experiences. Peak experiences reflect enriched, lucid sensory-perceptual experience, positive affective states, luminous memories, and recall. There are acute, intact bodily sensations and feelings of wholeness; a sense of self at optimal centeredness. Dissociative experiences, in contrast, represent distorted, sensory-perceptual and somatoform bodily processes. There are feelings of deintegration, oddness, unreality, fragmentation, and negative affective states that reflect a loss of centering in self-processes.

Peak experiences are growth-promoting, identity-enhancing, and reveal actual and unrealized human potentials (Maslow, 1968). Dissociative states and disorders are manifestations of defensive measures of protection and security in the face of threat to well-being. Prolonged, repetitive, or chronic dissociative processes adaptively or pathogenically alter the structure of personality (Putnam, 1997; Schore, 2003; Watkins & Watkins, 1997; Kluft, 1991).

Chronic dissociative processes reconfigure the internal architecture of the self and generate allostatic changes in behavior (Kalsched, 2003, 1997; Chu, 1998; Putnam, 1997; Wilson, Friedman, & Lindy, 2001). Dissociative allostasis refers to changes in baseline functioning in psychological systems during (i.e., peritraumatic) or after traumatic experiences (Marmar, Metzler, & Vries, 1997; Wilson, Friedman, & Lindy, 2001; Bremner & Marmar, 1998). Allostasis is the tendency of the organism to seek stability following stress-evoked alterations in baseline functions that do not return to homeostatic pretraumatic levels (McEwen, 2002). Dissociative allostasis characterizes changes in thresholds to activate dissociative mechanisms within the structure of intrapsychic processes

(Wilson, Friedman, & Lindy, 2001; Kalsched, 2003, 1996). Positive allostasis restores centeredness in self-capacities and the metabolism of psychic trauma (Wilson & Thomas, 2004).

In peak experiences, the subcomponents of the self fuse their functions in the service of optimal states. Peak experiences involve synergy in the structural components of the self: that is, autonomy, coherence, continuity, connection, vitality, and energy (Wilson, 2004a; Stern, 1985; Pearlman & Saatvikne, 1995). The usually integrative functions of consciousness and behavior combine in the service of maximizing adaptation. The synergistic functions of psychological processes were described by Maslow (1968) as an *altered psychological state* and a characteristic of B-motivation and cognition. Peak experiences salutogenically alter states of consciousness, memory, identity, and perception of the environment. Dissociative processes adaptively or pathologically alter basic psychological functions in response to threat and trauma. Peak experiences "illuminate" and integrate; dissociative experiences "blackout" and deintegrate.

Comparisons of the continuum of integrative peak experiences and deintegrative dissociative states shed light on their intrapsychic mechanisms, including the ones that govern the cognitive processing of traumatic experiences. At different levels of consciousness, psychological mechanisms are operating to control degrees of psychic integration. The architecture of the self is stratified into complex cognitive-affective systems, controlling the psychobiology of goal-directed actions. The operation of these subsystems of control has been described by Mischel and Morf (2003).

In terms of memory, peak experiences are lucidly recalled with brilliant and detailed accuracy. Memory for peak experiences is rich, fulgent, vitrified, transparent, and fully encoded. Peak experiences are recalled with precision, clarity, and accuracy because they are strong experiences with positive affective valence. The memory for peak experiences is continuous and without gaps, amnesia, distortion, or missing information. According to Maslow (1968), persons report unusual degrees of perceptual perspicuity and salience during the peak experience (i.e., unity, awe, wonder, deep absorption). Peak experiences are described in terms that emphasize perceptual luminosity and sharply heightened sensory experience involving touch, taste, smell, movement, and audition. It is as if extraneous noise in channels of sensory-perceptual experience is filtered out during the peak experience. The strength, clarity, and purity of the signal emanating from the peak experience is fully received in all modalities with similar frequency and amplitude and has maximal impact on consciousness. In a metaphorical sense, it is as if the peak experience emanates from the center of being, like light spreading outwards from its source, radiating a uniform energy pattern in all directions.

Dissociative perceptual and sensory experiences, in contrast, are reported as opaque, clouded, distorted, unreal, detached, dream-like, surreal, unusual, and out-of-body phenomena. For example, some dissociative patients describe states of depersonalization and derealization as if a dimmer switch was increasing or decreasing lighting on a theatrical stage set, alternating extremes of overly bright intense lighting with degrees of hazy darkness in which it was difficult to discern people, faces, situations, and events (Putnam, 1997; Kluft, 1991; Chu, 1998). In dissociative states, recall for emotionally strong experiences can be missing, partial, fragmented, repressed, or out of chronological sequence. In dissociation, the sharpness, clarity, crispness, and transparency of peak experiences is missing. The quality of precision about details and events is vague, confused, distorted, or muddled as to time, place, person, and chronology.

With regard to the stream of activity, peak experiences have continuity, flow, and naturalness in the stream of activities taking place. The synchronous flow in peak experiences is described as automatic or effortless with a disorientation to time and space, including experiences of being an external observer that are characterized as emotionally positive in nature. Unlike dissociative states, in which there are encapsulated forms of psychic experiences that coexist in parallel ego-states (Putnam, 1997; Watkins & Watkins, 1997), peak experiences reflect higher levels of integrative functions in cognition, memory and sensory-perceptual modalities.

Comparisons between dissociative states and peak experience extend to two additional areas: affect and somatic behaviors. Peak experiences involve powerful, positive emotional states (Maslow 1962, 1968, 1970, 1971). Peak experiences have a continuum of positive emotional arousal. At one extreme, are heightened states of positive arousal and expectations; at the other, are states of tranquility, calmness, quiescence, and passive contentment. These positive emotional states are expressions of increased sensory nervous system arousal. Subjects describe these states as rapture, ecstasy, joy, bliss, serenity, excitement, contentment, a sense of well-being, euphoria, transcendence, and free-flowing energy. There are reported states of relaxation, quiescence, and peacefulness.

The congruent strands of research on dissociation (e.g., Schore 2003; Nijenhuis & van der Hart, 1999a) document that dissociative disorders involve negative emotional states, fear, anxiety, and feelings of helplessness in response to perceived threat, physical, or psychological injury. Heightened states of autonomic nervous system arousal are manifestations of prolonged stress responses and allostatic dysregulations in coping and adaptation (Friedman, 2000a; McEwen, 1998, 2002; Schore 2003). As noted by Nijenhuis and van der Hart (1999a), when persons have traumatic memories with painful affect, they "will react to these events with chronic hyperarousal and concomitant cognitive symptoms of hypervigilance to trauma-related cues" (1999, p. 56). Dissociation "splits off" negative affects from traumatic memory, i.e., dissociating memories and affects to protect processes of adaptation. Moreover, while there are different patterns to dissociative states and disorders, "pathological dissociation also manifests itself in bodily symptoms, reactions and functions... which have labeled the phenomenon of somatoform dissociation" (Nijenhuis & van der Hart, 1999a, p. 46). In somatoform dissociation, anesthesias, analgesias, hyperesthesias, involuntary motor movements, paralysis, tics, tremors, convulsions, stupor, and other symptoms are conversions of dissociated psychic conflict into bodily form. Somatoform dissociation has trauma-specific meaning and significance (Nijenhuis & van der Hart, 1999a; Wilson, 2004a; Wilson & Thomas, 2004; Wilson, Friedman, & Lindy, 2001; Wilson & Lindy, 1994). The bodily symptoms manifest in somatoform dissociative disorders have a causal etiology in traumatic experiences and their meaning can be understood as a conditioned response generated in the context of the traumatic situation. As Wilson and Thomas (2004) have shown, PTSD symptoms are expressed in psychotherapy as trauma-specific transference (TST) behaviors in which the somatoform symptoms have interpretable meaning. Nijenhuis and van der Hart (1999a) have provided clinical case examples of analgesias, anesthesias, and somatic conversion reactions that illustrate the intrapsychic dynamics of dissociative somatoform disorders and their trauma-specific meaning during the course of treatment.

8 SALUTOGENIC AND PATHOGENIC ALTERATIONS IN THE INTEGRATIVE FUNCTIONS OF IDENTITY, CONSCIOUS MEMORY, PERCEPTION, AND TIME

A comparative analysis of peak and dissociative experiences permits a summary of key similarities and differences in the etiology, phenomenology, and internal organization of experiences within the self that reflect optimal integrating, growth-promoting consequences versus pathogenic alterations. A comparative perspective is presented in Figure 6.3. By utilizing the *DSM-IV-TR* (2000) operational criteria that dissociative disorders are pathogenic manifestations of disruptions in psychologically integrative functions, several conclusions emerge and raise questions pertaining to the mechanisms by which trauma leads to psychic deintegration.

First, in both peak experiences, as manifestations of salutogenesis and growth motivation, and dissociative states, as pathogenic reactions to trauma, there exist alterations in organismic functioning. In a convergent

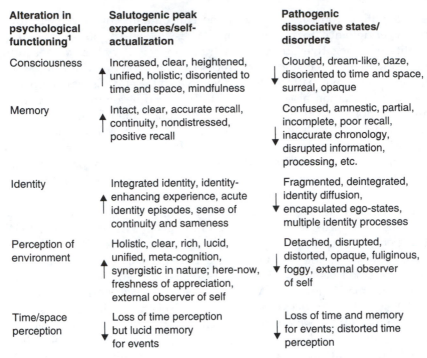

Alteration in psychological functioning[1]	Salutogenic peak experiences/self-actualization	Pathogenic dissociative states/ disorders
Consciousness	Increased, clear, heightened, unified, holistic; disoriented to time and space, mindfulness	Clouded, dream-like, daze, disoriented to time and space, surreal, opaque
Memory	Intact, clear, accurate recall, continuity, nondistressed, positive recall	Confused, amnestic, partial, incomplete, poor recall, inaccurate chronology, disrupted information, processing, etc.
Identity	Integrated identity, identity-enhancing experience, acute identity episodes, sense of continuity and sameness	Fragmented, deintegrated, identity diffusion, encapsulated ego-states, multiple identity processes
Perception of environment	Holistic, clear, rich, lucid, unified, meta-cognition, synergistic in nature; here-now, freshness of appreciation, external observer of self	Detached, disrupted, distorted, opaque, fuliginous, foggy, external observer of self
Time/space perception	Loss of time perception but lucid memory for events	Loss of time and memory for events; distorted time perception

FIGURE 6.3. Salutogenic and pathogenic alterations in the usually integrative functions of consciousness, memory, identity, and perception of the environment. [1]Area of integrative functioning defined by the *DSM-IV-TR* (2000) for dissociative disorders. *Source:* ©2003 John P. Wilson.

way, peak and dissociative experiences involve *altered forms* of psychological processes. In a divergent way, these alterations are *positive* in peak experience and lead to *increased* psychological integration. In dissociation these alterations are *negative* and *decrease* integrative processes, producing fragmentations, alterations, and disruptions in basic psychological processes (e.g., perception, memory, information-encoding) that result in changed ego-functions and behavioral tendencies.

Second, peak and dissociative experiences involve *alterations in time and space perception* with time being suspended or slowed down and mental stability of an altered pattern of cognitive processing of experiences. The person becomes absorbed in the peak experience but retains lucid memory for events, accurate recall of their actions, and positive feelings associated with heightened states of emotional arousal. In contrast, dissociative episodes separate the person from what they are experiencing and involve negative emotional states (e.g., fear, terror, helplessness, dread, horror, anticipatory anxiety). They have partial or impaired recall of experience. There are perceptual and sensory alterations in body image, feeling states or actions, the perception of external reality, and a loss of time and mental orientation.

Third, the nature of alterations in integrative psychological experiences can be discerned from the eight psychological dimensions shown in Figure 6.2. Peak experiences *augment, intensify, and increase* integrative processes. Peak experiences are growth promoting, need-gratifying, and associated with optimal states of adaptation and well-being. Dissociative experiences *reduce, intensify, and decrease* integrative processes and lead to deintegrated self-capacities and pathogenically altered sensory-perceptual, cognitive, and motivational qualities of behavior. Dissociative states may be pathogenic, need-depriving, and reduce effectance motivation, resulting in impaired functioning.

Fourth, the comparative analysis of peak and dissociative experiences poses questions as to the interrelationship between integrative and deintegrative experiences. For example, do the same intrapsychic and psychological processes govern both types of experience? Does understanding the positive, optimal and salutogenic aspects of peak experiences have implications for understanding the negative, pathogenic effects of dissociative states? Are peak experiences forms of positive adaptation to environmental demands on the organism whereas dissociative states are manifestations of negative allostatic reactions to threat, stress, and trauma (McEwen, 2002, 1998; Wilson, Friedman, & Lindy, 2001; Wilson & Thomas, 2004)? Do stability in self-object relationships, firm alliances, clear role delineation, and consistency in therapeutic relationships lead to the creation of secure, safe, predictable relationships that establish an external psychic structure that enables deintegrated states to reconfigure as more integrated and adaptive processes? Is a strong, resilient attachment relationship a necessary precondition to facilitate the reassimilation of deintegrated self-capacities? Does satisfaction of basic psychological needs for safety, trust, security, love, affiliation, and esteem lead to reductions in the operation of dissociative processes and result in transformed organismic states in which peak experience will occur more frequently as the pathogenic effects dissipate?

These questions suggest the possibility that optimal states of integrative experiences and dissociative states of self-fragmentation exist on a dynamically interrelated continuum of consciousness and organismic functioning.[2] Thus, traumatic experiences would have the power

---

[2]"One of the main forces that affects consciousness adversely is psychic disorder—that is, information that conflicts with intentions, or distracts us from carrying them out...Psychic energy becomes unwieldy and ineffective" (Csikszentmihalyi, 1990).

to impact this continuum of organismic functioning, much like an earthquake produces breaks in the surface and continuity of a highway designed for transportation. To further understand this set of complex questions requires analysis of the role of basic need gratification and *need-specific* forms of peak and dissociative experiences.

9 PEAK EXPERIENCES BASED ON NEED GRATIFICATION

Maslow's (1970) theory of motivation and personality includes two fundamental principles of the hierarchy of human needs. First, there is a hierarchy of needs in which lower needs take precedence over higher needs (cf. prepotency principle) until "relatively permanent" gratification changes the priority of need strength as determinants of goal-directed behavior (Maslow, 1970, p. 17). Second, gratification of the lower needs "releases" higher-need-level functioning in a progressive and dynamic manner so that, with greater need gratification, each of the other sets of needs (e.g., love, affiliation, esteem, self-actualization) will emerge more strongly as motivators of behavior (cf. gratification principle). An implication of this theory is that when lower needs are satisfied or partially satisfied, greater degrees of self-actualizing potential exist. Conversely, Maslow believed that thwarting, deprivation, frustration, or threats to the lower needs results in greater organismic preoccupation with obtaining satisfaction (1970, pp. 75–82).

10 NEED-SPECIFIC FORMS OF PEAK AND DISSOCIATIVE EXPERIENCES: IMPLICATIONS FOR ASSESSMENT AND TREATMENT OF TRAUMA AND PTSD

Need-specific forms of peak and dissociative experiences characterize different levels of integrated or deintegrated psychological experience with important implications for clinical assessment and treatment of trauma patients. Maslow (1970) stated that most persons have peak experiences during their lifetime and that self-actualizing individuals have them on a regular basis. His research revealed that they are experienced more frequently by self-actualizing persons because such people are functioning at higher need levels. The greater the degree of competence in mastery and adaptation, the greater the potential for peak experiences. Maslow's theoretical principles imply that peak experiences occur in relation to satisfaction of each need level in the hierarchy of needs. In other words, there are *need-specific forms of peak experiences*. Similarly, there are *need-specific forms of dissociation* that occur under conditions of threat, trauma, and abuse (Kluft, 1991;

Putnam, 1997). As I will discuss later, understanding the mechanisms that facilitate peak experiences and the restoration of optimal integrative states has profound implications for treatment and the recovery from PTSD and self-pathologies.

11 NEED-SPECIFIC PEAK EXPERIENCES AND TRAUMA

What are the characteristics of need-specific peak experiences? What is the relationship of need-specific peak and dissociative experiences to psychic trauma? As derived from Maslow's theory, need-specific forms of peak experiences share the generic properties of peak experiences listed in Figure 6.2 *and* stage-specific qualities associated with need satisfaction of every set of needs in the hierarchy (i.e., physiological, safety, love and belongingness, esteem, and self-actualization). As will be discussed later, need-specific gratifications and "mini" peak experiences have positive therapeutic implications for the treatment of PTSD and Trauma Complexes.

11.1 Physiological Peak Experiences

Peak experiences associated with physiological gratification involve feelings of optimal well-being. The organism as a whole has vitality and energy. There is satisfaction and pleasure that accompanies physiological gratification of thirst, hunger, sex, and tension relief from processes of retention and elimination. Physiological peak experiences extend beyond mere satisfaction with being sated or tension reduction; there is a sense that somatic processes are functioning extremely well and that one is healthy with good reserves of energy. Optimal physical (i.e., physiological) and mental vitality is not the same as the absence of disease or illness. Optimal states of psychological functioning are not the same as absence of psychopathology, neurosis, anxiety, or psychiatric disorders. In terms of traumatic states (e.g., PTSD), the transformation of trauma has been termed positive allostasis, reflecting a new baseline of organismic functioning (Wilson & Thomas, 2004) in which there is a healthy integration of the trauma experience.

11.2 Safety Peak Experiences

Peak experiences associated with safety-need gratification have specific qualities that include an inner sense of feeling safe, secure, comfortable, protected, free from ordinary worries, anxieties, fears, and perceived external or intrapsychic threats. Safety-need peak experiences include positive feelings that things are in proper order, "under control," running as they should be, and unlikely to be changed in unexpected ways that are anxiety-provoking. There is a fundamental comfort that one is safe and protected within one's home, work, and personal relationships. There is an inner sense that the world has predictability, structure, goodness, and trustworthiness as a result of the safety-need peak experience. Safety-need peak experiences significantly enhance subjective feelings that the world is a secure, nonthreatening place.

11.3 Love and Belongingness Peak Experiences

Peak experiences associated with gratification of love and belongingness needs include a sense of meaningful connection, affiliation, and attachments to others, family, groups, or culture. They include a positive perception of the world as a nurturing, warm, accepting, and caring place. Affiliative-need gratification includes having a sense of social identity within a meaningfully defined subculture, professional, ethnic, or reference group. Affiliative-need-based peak experiences embrace knowing that one has a defined place and role where mutually rewarding social interactions can occur. There is a strong sense that one "belongs" to a group and will experience positive relationships in it. There is an internal glow, warmth, and sense of intimacy associated with positive, anticipatory thoughts of being with others. Affiliative need peak experiences generate comfort that one has a place, "fits in," and has a capacity to affirm others in loving ways.

11.4 Esteem Peak Experiences

Esteem need peak experiences involve acceptance of oneself as coherent, unified, competent, and self-directing person with a sense of vitality and wholeness. Peak experiences for the esteem needs include feelings of having a clear sense of personal identity, self-sameness, and continuity. It is the sense that one has effective capacities for mastery of experience, despite frustration, threats, and challenges posed by situations. In esteem-need peak experiences, one feels autonomous self-control and a sense of competence in achieving personal goals. There is a sense of comfort that one's personhood is intrinsically (i.e., internally) valued and positively appraised without undue needs for external recognition by others. There is awareness of psychological autonomy and capacity for self-determined action. There is pleasure experienced at efficacy in motivational action.

Integration ◄————► Dissociation

Hierarchy of needs	Peak experiences: need specific-attributes	Dissociative states: dissociative need specific attributes
Self-actualization	Flow/optimal experience and organismic vitality	Organismic stasis, cessation in growth motivation
Esteem	Efficacious mastery	Self-deintegration, loss of bases of self-worth
Love and belongingness	Mutual affiliations in love and social relations	Detachment/estrangement/disengagement
Safety	Secure contentment	Defensive vigilance: mistrust, anxiety, fear, insecurity and withdrawal
Physiological	Optimal physical vitality	Somatoform dissociation

FIGURE 6.4. Need-specific peak experiences and dissociative states: primary attributes. *Source:* ©2004 John P. Wilson.

11.5 Need-Specific Peak Experiences and Dissociative States

The need-specific forms of peak experiences and dissociative states are presented in Figure 6.4. For each of the basic needs in the hierarchy of needs there is a corresponding set of primary attributes associated with peak experiences. Similarly, there is a set of primary dissociative attributes for each of the lower and higher needs in the hierarchy itself. By contrasting these two diverse and opposite sets of characteristics, it is possible to further define the continuum of integrative psychological experiences presented in Figure 6.1. Thus, the primary attributes associated with peak experiences and dissociative states are dimensions of: (1) continuum of integration versus dissociation and (2) optimal self-organization versus pathological self-organization.

12 PRIMARY ATTRIBUTES OF NEED-SPECIFIC PEAK AND DISSOCIATIVE EXPERIENCES

It is possible to summarize the consequences of peak experiences associated with the prepotency of need-directed behavior. First, there is a sense of optimal physical vitality, energy, and well-being associated with physiological need gratification. Second, a sense of secure contentment and freedom from anxiety, fear, worry, and threats to "basic" security is experienced with peak experiences for safety-need

gratification. Third, there is the subjective sense of mutually rewarding affiliative processes that emerge in peak experiences associated
with love and belongingness needs. Fourth, there is the awareness
of efficacious mastery in self-directed and personally valued task
pursuits for the esteem needs. Finally, in terms of the self-actualizing
need, there is a sense of flow of experience as evidenced in a variety
of optimal states of endeavor. As noted by Maslow (1970) self-
actualizing states are manifestations of organismic expressiveness versus
purely instrumental coping behavior. Moreover, when the need for self
actualization is prepotent, peak experiences become hierarchically
integrated; there is synergy and functional autonomy in forms of
motivated behavior (see section on functional autonomy and peak
experiences).

In a similar way to the specific attributes that define peak experiences
associated with lower and higher basic needs, the attributes of dissociative states for each need level can be specified as well.

13 NEED-SPECIFIC DISSOCIATIVE STATES

The specific attributes of dissociative phenomena associated with
each need level can be viewed as: (1) defensive reactions to fundamental threats to the deprivation of a basic need; (2) syndromes
of psychic encapsulation of dissociated experience to protect against
actual or perceived threats to a prepotent need state; (3) levels of unconscious psychic phenomena that may develop into Trauma Complexes
(see Chapter 5); and (4) fundamental disruptions of the organism's
striving towards optimal, fully functioning states of adaptive behavior.

In terms of dissociative attributes associated with threats to prepotent
need states, it may be seen that there can be somatoform symptoms
of dissociation; defensive vigilance and hypervigilance associated
with fear, anxiety, and withdrawal behaviors in response to threat to
safety needs; detachment, disengagement, and estrangement from
love and affiliative relations; evidence of self-deintegration and loss
of self-worth associated with threats to the basis of esteem-need
gratification, and the manifestation of organismic stasis in terms of the
overall pattern and directionality of self-actualization.

The research literature on dissociation indicates that threat, deprivation, trauma, and interpersonal abuse cause forms of dissociation to
occur (Putnam, 1997). *In that regard, dissociation can be viewed as an
organismic reaction to threats to the entire set of basic human needs, especially
those which are normatively prepotent early in childhood development
(i.e., physiological, safety, love and belongingness, and esteem needs).* However, residues of *need-specific dissociative processes* can be seen in both

dissociative disorders and self-pathologies (Schore, 2003). For example, a child whose basic needs for safety were chronically denied, threatened, or thwarted would be prone to dissociative reactions in later years when situations reactivate memories of earlier periods of safety deprivation, such as the sudden loss of a significant relationship, sources of security, protection or direct personal threats or physical assault. Similarly, the perceived threat to love, attachments, belongingness, and identity in groups would rekindle earlier dissociative episodes of threats to these basic needs, and so on for all the needs in the hierarchy.

14 CASE EXAMPLE: AUSCHWITZ HOLOCAUST SURVIVOR

Need-specific forms of dissociative episodes and peak experiences can be illustrated by a case history. In this case, previous trauma is reactivated by medical illness and precipitates dissociative episodes which originated in a Nazi concentration camp where the patient was a prisoner during World War II.

At the time she was admitted for surgical treatment, the patient was a 69-year-old Holocaust survivor who was hospitalized for a diabetes-related degeneration in vascular circulation in her right leg, which had developed sores, lesions, and ulcerations. After prolonged, unsuccessful outpatient treatment, it was decided that her leg would require amputation.

During the week-long course of hospitalization, it was discovered by the patient's adult daughter, also a Holocaust survivor as a young child, that the elderly woman had secretly hidden all the pills being given to her by the nurses as part of her treatment and preparation for surgery. The patient confided to her daughter that she thought that the staff physicians were Nazis who were plotting against her and that they were going to kill her in surgery. A psychiatric consultation was ordered and upon evaluation of her paranoia of the "Nazi doctors," the staff psychiatrist diagnosed her as experiencing an atypical psychosis and prescribed medication. Interestingly, however, the psychiatrist did not take a trauma history and learn of her experiences in the Auschwitz death camp where her sisters were killed in Nazi medical experiments. Had he done so, he might have diagnosed the patient with PTSD that was being rekindled by her state of helplessness, vulnerability, and the impending surgical loss of her leg and possibly her life. In fact, the patient requested that her daughter and son-in-law come to the hospital after midnight when the "Nazi doctors" were not around and help her escape from them, her fear being they would kill her in a surgical experiment in a similar way, a manner parallel to how her 24-year-old sister died in one of Dr. Joseph Mengele's death camp experiments in the mid-1940s. During the period of her hospital stay, the elderly woman told her beloved daughter, with whom she had lived in "closeted" isolation ever since the end of World War II, that while in the hospital everything seemed "as if it were not real," and that she was in a "bad dream" because she had left her daughter's home of safety and protection. The elderly patient had been agoraphobic, reclusive, and house-bound ever since immigrating to the U.S. with her only surviving child. Although she knew that she was hospitalized in a prestigious and internationally esteemed medical center, nothing about it felt real to her. She indicated that she could "see around her private hospital room from all angles, floor to ceiling," despite not being able to walk. She reported being able to observe hospital staff from a secret corner near the right-hand section of the ceiling in her private room where she could "look down" at the hospital personnel.

Her dissociative symptoms, as part of untreated, chronic PTSD, were a manifestation of her traumatic experiences during the Holocaust when she was in her mid-twenties. Her sense of safety-needs was profoundly threatened by her medical illness, need for surgery, and the impending amputation of her leg. To the elderly Holocaust survivor, the prospect of surgery and the possibility of death reactivated the memories of her concentration camp experiences and the daily struggle for survival in Auschwitz. Her anxiety-driven paranoia during her hospitalization was a reenactment of her life-threatening experiences as a Nazi prisoner during which her younger sister was murdered in medicalized experiments. Her fears associated with facing surgical amputation of her leg not only caused a reexperiencing of the earlier catastrophic anxiety and fear of annihilation, they reactivated the use of dissociative mechanisms that included states of depersonalization (i.e., being an external observer) and derealization (i.e., things seeming unreal or dream-like) which fused together distortions of her current medical situation with her (then) 45-year-old memories of trauma, internment, helplessness, utter vulnerability, and daily struggles for survival within the death camp environment of terror and human brutalization.

It is noteworthy that the patient successfully completed her surgery. Her paranoid fear of Nazi doctors dissipated when her PTSD symptoms were recognized and dealt with by an acute intervention by a PTSD specialist asked to consult on the case by her family. After discharge, she once again returned to the sheltered sanctuary of her daughter's home and resumed living with satisfaction and pleasure without any residual persecutory fears of Nazi doctors. As her sense of safety returned, so did her capacity to enjoy life and to experience her self-described "greatest happiness" as those times when her daughter, son-in-law, and grandchildren were together enjoying the ethnic foods of her Central European country of origin. Her peak experiences of joy, happiness, and deep sense of family well-being occurred in the safety of a protected home environment with the living offspring from her lifetime. Her parents, siblings, and extended family died in Nazi concentration camps. Her moments of peak experience came from the knowledge that she and her daughter survived the death camp and the realization, as a result of being with her two grandchildren (both of whom were successful lawyers), that life had continuity and meaning despite her irreplaceable losses of security, home, parents, and family during World War II. In this case example, dissociative and peak experiences were related to severe traumatic and life-threatening deprivations of safety needs, and the loss of family and emotional attachments during the Holocaust. Their restoration triggered peak moments of satisfaction with her post-Holocaust life and family.

15 TRANSFORMATIONS OF TRAUMATIC STATES INTO OPTIMAL STATES OF INTEGRATIVE EXPERIENCE

Can traumatic experiences be transformed into optimal experiences and higher states of consciousness, awareness, and intrapsychic integration? Psychological trauma, as seen in dissociation, has the power to transform the integrity of the organism at all levels of systemic functioning (Schore, 2003). Understanding the various ways that trauma can transform the integrative dimensions of psychological functioning is important to discovering the deeper psychic constellations of such experiences, including the seemingly odd connection between dissociative states and peak experiences.

The transformation of traumatized conditions into optimal and fully functional mental states involves two interrelated processes: first, restoring wholeness and functional capacity to the structural dimensions of the self (i.e., coherence, continuity, connection, vitality, autonomy, energy); second, empowering the individual to understand how they can bring congruence to internal and external modalities of experience. Congruence in self-functioning enables optimal organismic functioning. In contrast, trauma disrupts the internal equilibrium of self-processes producing degrees of allostatic change that may be acute or long-term in its effects (McEwen, 2002). More specifically, the dimensions of the self can be affected in different ways, injuring or damaging some structural dimensions more than others (e.g., coherence, continuity, autonomy). The transformation of internally damaged psychic states necessitates reparative experiences which restore healthy functioning.

Similar ideas were expressed over four decades ago by Ira Progroff (1963), who stated

> experience has shown increasingly that psychological illnesses do not behave like entities. They do not enter the life of the person and then leave. They rather are like the life of the person. They are even the destiny, or the channel by which an important aspect of the specific meaning of the individual's life unfolds... *When a person shows signs of internal stress, shall we interpret this stress in terms of the symptomatology of illness or shall we look into it to find the seeds of growth?* (p. 57; emphasis added)

What are the seeds of growth for psychically traumatized persons? What do posttraumatic symptoms and constellated psychic states tell us about injuries to core self-processes and their deintegration, dissolution, and dissociation? As observed by Freud (1917), symptoms have "a sense" (i.e., meaning) but they are also clues to the functional purpose of their existence. Symptoms of posttraumatic states do not exist in a vacuum; they typically have trauma specific meaning (Wilson & Thomas, 2004) which may be embedded within other psychic material. Viewed in this framework, symptoms can be regarded as nodules of psychically constituted information stored in memory in conscious or unconscious form. As Progroff (1963) observed, "constructive psychological work is to replace diagnostic analysis by a *method of evoking from the depths of the psyche the energy latent in the seeds of potentiality*" (p. 60; emphasis added).

15.1 Seeds of Psychological Growth and Dual Transformations

Progroff's (1963) metaphor of the "seeds of potentiality" is applicable to understanding the posttraumatic self and how it is transformed by extreme stress and trauma and then transformed again in the direction of psychological health and optimal states of functioning. Thus, there are dual transformations: the transformation of personality caused by trauma and the transformation back into optimal states of functioning. In terms of therapeutic relationships, Progroff suggests that the task

> is to establish in the person...a sensitivity to the inward process of the psyche...it is a feeling of a master cycle of life, which proceeds within the person and includes tensions and symptoms, doubts and dynamics of many kinds. *It involves a sense of time, an inward perspective...some continuity of personal psychological work* in order to develop an intuitive sense and familiarity with what is taking place at the depth of the psyche, and above all, to develop a sensitivity to the *symbolic style* in which the movement of the psyche are organized... *Only a unifying experience that establishes*

a new sense of wholeness as a principle working within the person can have a lasting healing effect. (pp. 61, 64; emphasis added)

15.2 Optimal Congruence: Unifying Processes in External Experiences and Internal Schemas

It is precisely the question of unifying experiences that it is critical to define in terms of recovery from PTSD and psychically traumatized states. Unifying experiences help restore balance and congruence between external reality and internal modalities of experience. Unifying experiences bring balance to the planes of self-experience, provide need gratification, and release higher levels of self-actualization.

How do integrative and deintegrative organismic states become transformed from one state of being into a different one? How do dissociative states become deencapsulated? How do traumatic, Abyss and Inversion Experiences become transformed into peak experiences and optimal psychological states? How does the psychic and spiritual encounter with the demonic, dark forces of existence, which involve the degradation or loss of the self, the specter of physical or psychic death, and being disconnected from critical human attachments, become transformed into a revitalized, autonomous self with the capacity for optimal states of psychological experience? In a holistic perspective, how does the traumatized organism, in all of its integrated complexity, transform its inherent energy, consciousness, and systems governing growth and entropy?

The transformations of traumatic states into peak experiences and optimal states of function are presented in Figure 6.5. Twenty representative dimensions of psychological functioning that are impacted by trauma are shown. The dimensions include self-capacities, ego-mechanisms, identity processes, and psychosocial aspects concerning basic needs, values, systems of meaning, and historical perspectives. The categorization identifies core intrapsychic and psychobiological processes of central significance to understanding how transformational processes occur from one state of organismic functioning to another.

16 UNIFYING MECHANISMS OF TRANSFORMATION

What are the unifying mechanisms of transformation from states of deintegrated psychological functioning to more functional and integrated ones? Are transformative processes isosynchronous in all subsystems of organismic functioning? Are transformative processes necessarily synergistic in nature? In transforming psychic trauma and PTSD, must there be a psychobiological change in brain hemispheric

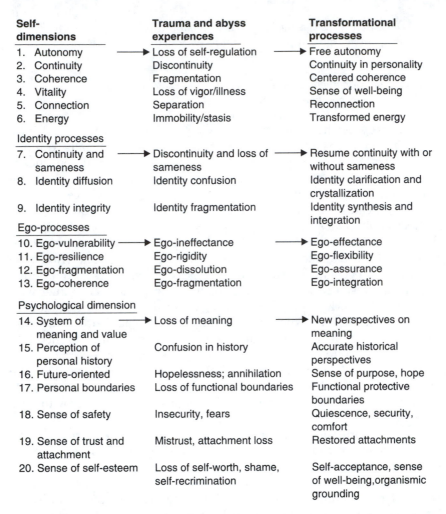

Self-dimensions	Trauma and abyss experiences	Transformational processes
1. Autonomy ⟶	Loss of self-regulation ⟶	Free autonomy
2. Continuity	Discontinuity	Continuity in personality
3. Coherence	Fragmentation	Centered coherence
4. Vitality	Loss of vigor/illness	Sense of well-being
5. Connection	Separation	Reconnection
6. Energy	Immobility/stasis	Transformed energy
Identity processes		
7. Continuity and ⟶ sameness	Discontinuity and loss of ⟶ sameness	Resume continuity with or without sameness
8. Identity diffusion	Identity confusion	Identity clarification and crystallization
9. Identity integrity	Identity fragmentation	Identity synthesis and integration
Ego-processes		
10. Ego-vulnerability ⟶	Ego-ineffectance ⟶	Ego-effectance
11. Ego-resilience	Ego-rigidity	Ego-flexibility
12. Ego-fragmentation	Ego-dissolution	Ego-assurance
13. Ego-coherence	Ego-fragmentation	Ego-integration
Psychological dimension		
14. System of ⟶ meaning and value	Loss of meaning ⟶	New perspectives on meaning
15. Perception of personal history	Confusion in history	Accurate historical perspectives
16. Future-oriented	Hopelessness; annihilation	Sense of purpose, hope
17. Personal boundaries	Loss of functional boundaries	Functional protective boundaries
18. Sense of safety	Insecurity, fears	Quiescence, security, comfort
19. Sense of trust and attachment	Mistrust, attachment loss	Restored attachments
20. Sense of self-esteem	Loss of self-worth, shame, self-recrimination	Self-acceptance, sense of well-being, organismic grounding

FIGURE 6.5. Transformation of traumatic experiences into peak experiences and optimal states of integrative psychological experience. *Source:* ©2003 John P. Wilson.

functioning (Schore, 2003) for transformation between states to occur? Is there a shift to right brain hemispheric dominance? Can alterations in meditative states of consciousness concerning traumatic experiences induce physiological changes in brain function? Can the positive alteration of dysregulated states of hemispheric brain function alter states of consciousness (Schore, 2003)? Does positive allostasis *reset* levels of organismic functioning following prolonged stress responses evoked by traumatic experiences (McEwen, 2002; Wilson & Thomas,

I. Acute, epiphanous, conversion-like transformations

II. Epigenetically related transformations triggered by stages of life-course development

III. Transformations of chronic trauma-related pathology through treatment, spiritual experiences or spontaneous remissions

IV. Somatic transformations of traumatic states embedded in brain, bodily and affective processes

V. Combined patterns of acute, somatic and epigenetic transformations

FIGURE 6.6. Transformations of traumatically deintegrated states to optimal psychologically integrative states. *Source:* ©2003 John P. Wilson.

2004)? How do dissociated ego-states become transformed into peak experiences?

The mechanisms of transforming psychological trauma are manifest in different forms, temporal sequences, and psychic and somatic configurations. Figure 6.6 presents five types of transformative processes in posttraumatic stress syndromes.

17 TEMPORAL FORMS, SEQUENCES, AND PATTERNS OF TRANSFORMATING TRAUMA AND PTSD

17.1 Acute, Epiphanous and Rapid Transformations

In temporal sequence, the usual (i.e., customary, normal, expected) process of transforming trauma for severe conditions of PTSD is gradual and occurs over many years (Foa, Keane, & Friedman 2001; Wilson & Drozdek, 2004; Friedman, 2000a; Wilson, Friedman, & Lindy, 2001; Kessler et al., 1995). It is a process like an oversized hourglass dripping ultrafine grains of sand from top to bottom through a narrow opening at an agonizingly slow rate. But in some cases there are spontaneous and rapid processes of recovery from acute or chronic states of traumatization.

Acute, epiphanous, and rapid transformations of PTSD occur, but under conditions that are not well understood. In acute epiphanous moments that resemble religious conversion experiences, the transformation of pathological, traumatic states occurs spontaneously, usually under conditions of safety, emotional calmness, and changes in thinking patterns of a holistic nature. In acute and spontaneous transformations, the individual has a new "vision" of themselves in a positive light, one that intuitively involves knowing that there is a different type of consciousness of being and organization of the self.

Acute changes of an epiphanous nature involve lucid insights as to the necessity of centering consciousness in the present moment rather than the past. When this occurs, there are acute and lasting transformative shifts in consciousness and the meaning of existence. Acute epiphanous transformations of trauma are not, however, dissociative conversion reactions of a neurotic type. They are qualitatively different phenomena since the origin of transformation is embedded in the trauma encounter, which is not the case for most religious conversions (James, 1958).

Acute transformation processes often begin in the Abyss or Inversion Experiences in which the perception of reality, as previously known, suddenly and dramatically changes (see Chapter 5 for a detailed discussion). This transformative phenomenon is a process of rapid cognitive disequilibration in which beliefs, attitudes, values, and systems of meaning are altered because of the overwhelming immensity and power of the trauma experience (Wilson, 2004a, 2003, 1980). In instances of acute transformation, systems of meaning and core values become clarified and sharply focused on a limited set of life-priorities which are critically important to the trauma survivor. It is as if extraneous, nonessential, and superficial aspects of daily living are seen in a different and less highly valued light. Rapid cognitive disequilibration occurs in the face of the death encounter, overwhelming catastrophe, the reality of human equality in pain, suffering, and the struggle to recover from injuries inflicted by malevolence or fate. Eckhart Tolle (1999) has commented similarly

> In life threatening emergency situations, the shift in consciousness from time [awareness] to presence sometimes happens naturally. The personality that has a past and a future momentarily recedes and is replaced by an *intense conscious presence, very still but very alert at the same time. Whatever response is needed then arises out of that state of consciousness.* (p. 42; emphasis added)

In acute transformative episodes, rapid cognitive disequilibration in systems of belief, meaning, and emotional balance causes a realignment of organismic valuing in the direction that Maslow (1968, p. 83) termed B-values (e.g., concern with justice, truth, higher morality, honesty, spontaneity, health, unity, transcendence, altruism, fairness). The B-value cluster is characterized by existential, authentic concerns for living at the level of Being (i.e., B-motivation). It is mindfulness and living in-the-moment without expectations relative to personal goals or the need to question the validity of experience. There is the release of old patterns of perception and meaning making (Baumeister & Vohs, 2003) to an acute awareness of the possibility of self-reinvention.

18 THE JOURNEY FROM PSYCHIATRIC IMPAIRMENT
TO SPIRITUAL RENEWAL

The transformation from traumatic experiences to optimally integrated states of psychological functioning involves a journey from profound states of dispiritedness and psychiatric illness to a restored sense of psychic vitality and well-being. In some cases, it is akin to a spiritual marathon of endurance, hardship, and soul-searching. In mythology, this is the journey of the hero who transverses a life-encounter of peril, danger, and spiritual challenge. These dangers are threats to physical and psychic existence; to the inner core of the soul. In the zone of darkness and danger of traumatic experience (cf. the Abyss Experience) the individual becomes traumatized and suffers spiritual consequences. The psychiatric consequences include the spectrum of anxiety, dissociative, and mood disorders, as well as forms of severe mental illness, and alterations in personality and character structure. The spiritual consequences include a loss of faith, hope, and a belief in God or Higher Power, demoralization, and challenge to one's inner soul. These losses result in states of dispiritedness, emptiness, despair, soul death, and feelings of living in a dark, sinister, unnatural, and unwanted psychological space. Trauma can mold personality into many variations, like an artist shaping a clay statue before casting it into permanent form. Thus, the identity of the statue may be molded by the forces of trauma, including the essence of its spiritual form.

In some typologies of the posttraumatic self (see Chapter 2), the inner soul may be experienced as defeated, exhausted, lost, tortured, dead, or simply "gone" (Krystal, 1988). The struggle with psychiatric illness and spiritual vacuity are parallel processes that run their course until a breakthrough, either from treatment, spiritually reconnecting experiences, or personal epiphany, ignites the inner mechanisms of organismic healing at a holistic level of functioning. Once these are set in motion, there is a natural drive towards unity and integration. The person heals and finds the pathway to restore meaning to life. A sense of wholeness is restored to personality. It is a process of self-reclamation which occurs at different rates for persons who have suffered from different types of trauma. In this regard, traumatic experiences produce more soul injury than other kinds of stressors or hassles of daily living.

To the trauma survivor, the process of transformation is experienced with discomfort, uncertainty, fear, and doubt. There is a strong and seemingly irrational wish to "hold on" to the traumatized self; to remain cast into a frozen state of psychological stasis; to resist growth and assume the "identity" of the traumatized victim. There are fears of letting go of psychic numbing as a protective emotional skin that develops after trauma. There are fears of feeling one's own true emotions and yet a strong unconscious desire to do so in healthier ways. For many persons, the experience of trauma is synonymous with the emotion of fear. Fear is a neurobiological reaction and a state of consciousness (LeDoux, 1996). Beyond primitive, neurohormonal-induced fear reactions, fear is a state of mind. In discussing the origin of fear, Tolle (1999) states

> The psychological condition of fear is divorced from any concrete and time-immediate danger. It comes in many forms: unease, worry, anxiety, nervousness, tension, dread, phobia, and so on. This kind of psychological fear is something that *might* happen, not something that is happening now. *You* are in the here and now, while your mind is in the future. This creates an anxiety gap. And if you are identified with your mind and have lost touch with the power and simplicity of now, that anxiety gap will be your constant companion. You can always cope with the present moment, but you cannot cope with something that is only a mind projection—you cannot cope with the future. (p. 35; emphasis added)

In self-unification a gradual process of reintegration takes place. The process of reconnection among the primary dimensions of the self (i.e., continuity, vitality, autonomy, energy, coherence, etc.) occurs automatically at multiple levels of consciousness. As self-fragmentation and dysregulated affective states decrease, there is an increase in positive well-being which is manifest in dreams, emotional coherence, and goal-directed striving.

The journey from pathology to spiritual transformation echoes the nascent inner voice that wants to know the freedom of vitality, energy, restoration of the spirit, self-coherence, and continuity with a past. The traumatized soul yearns for inner unity and serenity. As a sense of inner coherence and structural connection among the parts of the self occurs (e.g., more vitality, energy, day-to-day continuity of experience, etc.), the trauma survivor experiences the emergence of a new "self," spiritual revitalization and regains a sense of the future with meaning, hope, and capacity for simple enjoyment of daily living without false expectations. Sometimes it is a slow, step-by-step, day-by-day process until psychological energy mobilizes greater inner unity and coherence. As transformations of traumatic states occur in the posttraumatic self, there emerges a sense of feeling "anchored" in the capacity to live in the moment with clear consciousness and sensitive attunement to ultimate personal values. In many survivors, this transformation includes a sense of greater connectedness to ultimate sources of meaning, truth, and a Higher Power.

Leon Wurmser (1994) has vibrantly described the nature of self-transformation from the experience of being "gripped" by creative energy and insight

> phenomenologically, one experiences a breaking through of a wide variety of the most intense feelings. *The boundaries between self and parts of the outside world, between various objects, between different feelings, moods, images, and memories melt away. A heightened sense of being alive, of attaining the best within, the ultimate meaning of oneself, over an increasing feeling of bodily vitality* is accomplished by reaching out to others... At the same time this bursting through boundaries on so many levels, this glowing, warm infusion experience, stands against the dark finale of destruction. The old stale forms must be broken. (p. 293; emphasis added)

When the "old stale forms" of self-experience become broken, they must be supplanted with new ones—a task that can last a lifetime, especially when facing the task of creating meaning to contravene dispirited inner states of depression, emptiness, and nothingness.

19 SOMATIC TRANSFORMATIONS OF TRAUMATIC STATES

The human body encodes the trauma experience as sand absorbs water in the scorching heat of the desert. The transformation from a traumatized state to integrated organismic functioning also occurs through inductions that change somatic and physiological states. Psychic and somatic health are mirror reflections of an integral consciousness of being.

Transformations in the posttraumatic self-structure can be induced through somatic or bodily processes. Allan N. Schore's (2003) comprehensive review of the literature on trauma, PTSD, and dysregulated affective states has shown that trauma: (1) is encoded into somatic processes; (2) is powerfully associated with dysregulations in the right hemisphere of the brain; (3) is linked to complex dissociative processes and proneness to reenactments of traumatic experiences; (4) represents states of allostatically controlled organismic changes in baseline functioning. Given that traumatic states, especially PTSD, are manifestations of disturbed organismic states (van der Kolk, 1997, 1999; Schore, 2003) the issue of how they become recalibrated and restored to optimal levels through somatic treatments, clinical therapeutic procedures, or culturally based rituals, is important to understand (Marsella, Friedman, Gerrity, & Scurfield, 1996).

20 FROM HYPERAROUSAL STATES TO RELAXATION RESPONSE:
    RESETTING THE ORGANISMS BASELINE

Since trauma produces prolonged stress responses characterized by chronic hyperarousal states and dysregulated emotional systems (Schore, 2003; Friedman, 2000a), conditions that facilitate a reduction of hyperarousal states, especially if repeated on a regular basis, help to "reset" organismic levels to a new baseline. The deconditioning and extinction of hyperarousal states facilitates conscious awareness of differences between aroused and nonaroused emotional states. This awareness includes an intrusive understanding of the differences between "trauma-related" states of hyperarousal versus equilibrium and serenity. Once deconditioned, the trauma survivor learns to relax, stay calm, and experience positive states of well-being, including when thinking about their traumatizing experiences or experiencing unbidden flashbacks (Wilson, 1989a; Foa et al., 2001; Wilson & Thomas, 2004). Therapeutic treatments such as: (1) systematic desensitization (Jacobson, 1938), (2) progressive relaxation (Benson, 1975), (3) guided imagery (Achterberg, 1985), (4) eye movement desensitization and reprocessing, EMDR (Shapiro, 1996), (5) somatic bodily therapy (Wilson & Drozdek, 2004), (6) massage, (7) breathing exercises, (8) Native American Sweat Lodges (Wilson, 1989a); (9) cultural rituals (Silver & Wilson, 1988; Jilek, 1982; Marsella, Friedman, Gerrity, & Scurfield, 1996); and (10) pharmacotherapy (Friedman, 2001) focus individual awareness and attention on *internal bodily states*. These techniques and/or experiences help the trauma survivor discriminate between hyperaroused and non-hyperaroused states (Wilson, 1989a; Nijenhuis & van der Hart, 1999a). Over time and with repeated exposure, dysregulations in the right hemisphere of the brain undergo change, resetting themselves to new homeostatic levels (Wilson, 1989a; Schore, 2003). They cease to exercise command and control functions governing conditioned and prolonged neurophysiological responses evoked by traumatic stressors (Schore, 2003; Friedman, 2000a).

The transformative change from hyperarousal inherent in PTSD and prolonged forms of stress response, to a state of relaxed quiescence that allows new emotional and cognitive capacities of psychic functioning, has been described as follows

the therapeutic significance is that for a person with PTSD the awareness of the shifts in physical and psychological states may lead to the perception that there are then non-pathological states of being besides the chronic tension and hyperarousability associated with the anxiety disorder. Thus, the awareness and experience of the changed psychological state may be the beginning of organismically based healing. The person in the non-pathological state can begin to integrate and assimilate previously traumatic material in a new form. (Wilson, 1989a, p. 67)

20.1 Somatic Embedding of Trauma in
State-Dependent Forms

To understand the transformation of deintegrated psychological states produced by trauma, it is important to recognize that traumatic memories and affects are *state-dependent* in nature (van der Kolk, McFarlane, & Weisaeth, 1996; Putnam, 1997; Perry, 1999; Schore, 2003; Wilson, 1989a). Traumatic memories and emotions are encoded in hyperaroused states as part of the genetically governed stress-response pattern (Friedman, 2000a, 2001; Schore, 2003). Deconditioning of hyperaroused states enables the processing and reprocessing of traumatic memories in the right hemisphere, which involves holistic, verbal, and nonlinear forms of thinking (Schore, 2003; Foa, Keane, & Friedman, 2001). In a relaxed state, the person can revisit traumatic memories and metabolize them in a non-hyperaroused condition that is the antithesis of PTSD, mood disorders, and anxiety states. The healthy metabolism of traumatic memories occurs since neurophysiological processes associated with hyperarousal are no longer driving the system and impeding information processing, thinking, and cognitive reformulations of personal experiences. Cognitive processing improves in more efficient ways, including the capacity to reformulate the posttraumatic self (Schore, 2003).

21 EXPERIENCING THE POSTTRAUMATIC SELF
THROUGH THE BODY

As many trauma specialists have noted, self-capacities are impacted by traumatic life-experiences and cause changes in self-appraisal processes (Lifton, 1976; Ulman & Brothers, 1988; Herman, 1992; Wilson, 2004a; Wilson, Friedman, & Lindy, 2001; Pearlman & Saatvikne, 1995). These changes include the structural components of the self as detailed by Mischel and Morf (2003), Stern (1985), and Wilson (2004a): (1) autonomy; (2) coherence; (3) continuity; (4) connection; (5) vitality; and (6) energy.

21.1 The Body "Keeps Score" but Knows When the
"Game is Over!"

In traumatized states of deintegration, the dimensions of the self-structure are adversely affected and result in ego-fragmentation, identity diffusion, loss of vitality, and stasis in psychological growth (see Figure 6.5). In this regard, the self can be experienced in new ways once hyperaroused states dissipate and the body "lets go" of traumatically embedded states. The posttraumatic states of personality alterations can be experienced through the body. Research suggests that the body "keeps score" (van der Kolk, 1999) but it also knows when the "game is over" (Wilson, Friedman, & Lindy, 2001). When this occurs, the person experiences intrapsychic awareness in a nonaroused, emotionally positive state (Wilson, 1989a). I have termed this process positive allostasis, which is the opposite of trauma-evoked allostasis in which the organism seeks stability following the "shake-up" induced by overwhelming trauma (Wilson, 2004; Wilson & Thomas, 2004). In positive allostatic transformations of PTSD, the toxicity of trauma is extruded and healing restores well-being. Organismic processes reset themselves and strive to reach optimal adaptive functioning.

22 REINTEGRATION OF SELF-DIMENSIONS AND PEAK EXPERIENCES FOLLOWING TRAUMA

Does the reintegration of the traumatized self result in peak experiences? Is the process of self reintegration a peak experience in itself? Is reintegration of the self tantamount to basic lower-need gratification (i.e., physiological, safety, love, affiliate, esteem) that releases higher order functioning? Is reintegration of the self a precondition for organismic well-being and optimal states of functioning? Does reintegration of the dimensions of the self result in more fully functional persons? If patients suffering from PTSD and dissociative disorders have peak experiences as part of psychotherapy, would peak experiences *induce* positive allostasis and accelerate the potential for psychic integration? Can peak experiences be induced therapeutically? If so, what are need-specific forms of experience that would be associated with peak experiences? What types of therapeutic experiences could be structured to facilitate the induction of positive states of joy, wonder, awe, spontaneity, a relaxed sense of well-being, happiness, serenity, and other affective states typically associated with peak experiences? To the dispirited and traumatized person, "mini" peak experiences are windows to the future of a reinvented posttraumatic self. With the step-by-step accumulation of "mini" peak experiences, the awareness of an emergent healthy self begins to be experienced and realized as the usefulness of the old self is discarded. Peak experiences reflect changes in levels of conscious awareness and repeated "mini" peak experiences become new portals of conscious insight into the possibility of self-reinvention (see Chapter 5).

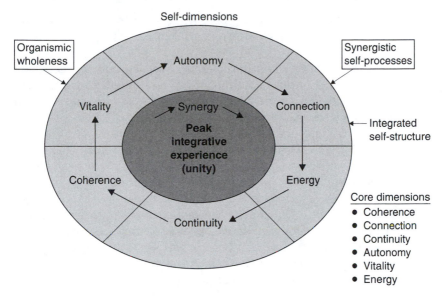

FIGURE 6.7. Unity in self-dimensions: integrative peak experiences. *Source:* ©2002 John P. Wilson.

22.1 Out-of-Body Experiences: Parallels to Peak and Dissociative Episodes

The potential benefit of peak experiences in facilitating recovery from trauma and PTSD can also be considered from research findings on out-of-body states (Gabbard & Twemblow, 1984). In a large-scale national survey of persons who reported an out-of-body experience (OBE), the authors analyzed the nature of reactions during, immediately afterwards, and the long-term effects of such experiences. During the OBE episode, the vast majority strongly experienced joy, sense of purpose, freedom, calmness, peacefulness, or quietude. Immediately after the OBE, the majority reported the episode as a spiritual experience; felt their life had changed, had new curiosity, and became interested in psychic phenomena. The long-term effects included a heightened awareness of reality and changes in beliefs about life after death.

Gabbard and Twemblow (1984) concluded that OBEs *"are quite reminiscent of categories used to describe peak experiences"*

Our subjects emphasize the heightened clarity and vividness of the real world as an increasing sense of logical *coherence*, an increased feeling of *harmony,* and a sensation of *being integrated with the real world*...the individual typically develops an increased sense of uniqueness and *autonomy* and begins an inner search for ways in which meaning can be assigned to the extraordinary experiences that seems to transcend ordinary paradigms of reality as we know it. (p. 25; emphasis added)

To place these conclusions into perspective, it must be recognized that traumatic experiences, especially those associated with the Abyss and Inversion Experiences, are always experienced as "outside the realm of ordinary experiences." By definition, traumatic experiences that lead to forms of PTSD are not ordinary, everyday events or daily hassles; they transcend the expectable stresses of life. In this regard, the subjectively reported qualities of OBEs are not only similar to peak experiences but generate similar, positive consequences that include increased autonomy, uniqueness, integration, clarity of perception, and enhance feelings of spirituality. The similar consequences of positive emotional and spiritual aspects for OBEs and peak experiences point to their potential to facilitate transformations of psychic states. In this regard, OBEs, peak experiences, and dissociative states share many common psychological properties with potentially positive or negative effects for adaptation and coping.

23 CONCLUSION

The considerations presented about the nature of peak experiences and dissociative states raise a final set of questions regarding the relationship of trauma and the continuum of integrative psychological experiences.

First, does psychological trauma impact all dimensions of the self in the same way? Does trauma generate differential consequences in terms of intrapsychic processes, defensive structures, and the functions of the ego? Second, are all dimensions of the self equally weighted in terms of intrapsychic processes? Do self-capacities unravel in the same pattern and with the same sequelae for all persons? For example, the loss of self-coherence results in various states of ego-fragmentation, dissociative and self-pathologies that have their own dynamic principles associated with internal schemas of reality (Knox, 2003a; Goodwin & Attias, 1999). Do different types of psychic trauma attack different self-capacities once they are formed into an integrated, structural whole? Third, how exactly does the self unravel in the wake of trauma? What are the specific mechanisms for each of its interlinked components?

Understanding how psychological trauma impacts epigenetic personality development and emergent growth processes of the self is critical to a complete analysis of self-integration and deintegration. For example, the early loss of autonomy due to trauma can have long-term pathogenic consequences, especially if the loss of capacity for free self-regulation occurs at a critical period of child development (Bowlby, 1969; Pynoos & Nader, 1993; Erikson, 1968). Attachment losses caused by trauma (i.e., traumatic bereavement associated with loss of parents or siblings) has consequences for the self-dimensions of connection, coherence, and continuity (Raphael & Martinek, 1997; Raphael et al., 1997, 2004).

Studies of adult trauma survivors indicate that some persons lose a sense of self-sameness and continuity after catastrophic trauma but later resume a new thread of continuity in the posttraumatic self (Lifton, 1967, 1976, 1993; Raphael, 1983; Wilson & Raphael, 1993; Wilson, 1980, 2004a). A loss of the self-dimension of "connection" (i.e., to self, identity, others, culture, ideas, etc.) results in alienation. However, is the loss of self-continuity and self-connectedness following trauma in adulthood as devastating to healthy personality processes as is the loss of a sense of coherency? Is the loss or diminution of a sense of vitality and energy a manifestation of self-fragmentation and/or symptomatic of a cessation in organismic striving? Is a loss of vitality and energy in the self an epiphenomenal expression of the organism as a whole, or merely a correlate of depression, surrender, and deanimation of psychic energy in the self? Are there stage-specific, differential consequences of damages wrought by trauma to the dimensions of the self? Do different parts of the self fragment in accordance with epigenetic maturational processes (see Chapter 3 for a discussion)? Does severe trauma cause the structural elements of the self to unravel and pull apart like two strands of the DNA double helix molecule in a destructuralized state?

Analysis of trauma-related intrapsychic mechanisms suggests that states of integrated psychological experience exist on a continuum. Dissociative states are expectable reactions to excessive stress in dangerous, assaultive situations, and highly adaptive to psychological survival in the face of threat (Putnam, 1997).

In a parallel way, peak experiences are normal and expectable. They may lead to growth, new insights about self-potentialities, or be enjoyed as optimal states of integrative experience. Peak experiences may emerge naturally and frequently with the metabolism of psychic trauma.

Peak experiences and dissociative states involve alterations in the usually integrative function of consciousness, memory, identity, and perception of the environment. The alterations that occur in peak and dissociative states anchor the two ends of the continuum of integrative capacities. Theoretically, they are interrelated phenomena which contain underlying mechanisms governing the internal operation of such phenomena which cross-cut major organismic processes starting with perception and ending with behavioral sequences of specifiable complexity (see Figures 6.2 and 6.3).

By understanding the mechanisms of peak and dissociative experiences, new insights into the posttraumatic self can be achieved and

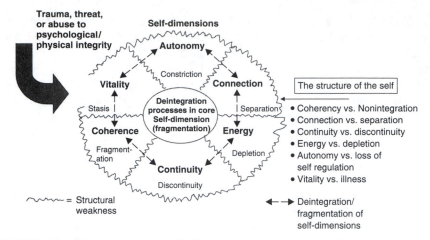

FIGURE 6.8. Deintegration in self-dimensions associated with dissociative states. *Source:* ©2002 John P. Wilson.

illuminate the inner workings of the self—much like a neurosurgeon viewing functional MRI scans of a patient's brain and localizing pathology, disease, and impairments to brain functions. Looking inwardly at the complexities of the self in its integrated and deintegrated states enables links to be established between intrapsychic states and their external representations in behavior. In this regard, understanding dissociative states in relation to peak experiences and self-actualization provides valuable clues to the transformation of pathological states into optimal states of integrative experiences. Understanding the relation of psychological trauma to resilience (see Chapter 10), optimal states, self-actualizing behaviors, and fully functioning personality may be more heuristically valuable that the analysis of PTSD phenomenology and the dynamics of posttraumatic pathologies.

REFERENCES

Achterberg, J. (1985). *Imagery and healing.* Boston, Massachusetts: Shambala.

Aktar, S. (1983). The syndrome of identity diffusion. *American Journal of Psychiatry, 141,* 1381–1385.

American Psychiatric Association. (2000). *Diagnostic and statistical manual of mental disorders* (5th ed.). Washington, DC: American Psychiatric Association.

Aronoff, J. & Wilson, J. P. (1985). *Personality in the social process.* Hillsdale, NJ: Lawrence Erlbaum.

Baumeister, R. F. & Vohs, K. D. (2003). The pursuit of meaningfulness in life. In C. R. Snyder & S. J. Lopez (Eds.), *Handbook of positive psychology* (pp. 608–632). New York: Oxford University Press.

Benson, H. (1975). *The relaxation response.* New York: Morrow.

Bowlby, J. (1969). *Attachment and loss.* New York: Basic Books.

Bremner, J. D. & Marmar, C. R. (1998). *Trauma, memory & dissociation (1ˢᵗ ed.).* Washington: American Psychiatric Press.

Chu, J. A. (1998). *Rebuilding shattered lives: The responsible treatment of complex post-traumatic and dissociative disorders.* New York: Wiley.

Csikszentmihalyi, M. (1990). *Flow: The psychology of optimal experience.* New York: Harper.

Erikson, E. H. (1968). *Identity, youth and crisis.* New York: W. W. Norton.

Foa, E., Keane, T. M., & Friedman, M. J. (2001). *Effective treatments for PTSD.* New York: Guilford Press.

Freud, S. (1917). *Introductory lecture on psychoanalysis.* New York: W. W. Norton.

Freud, S. (1920). *Beyond the pleasure principle.* New York: W. W. Norton.

Friedman, M. J. (2000a). *Posttraumatic and acute stress disorders.* Kansas City: Compact Clinicals.

Friedman, M. J. (2000b). *Post-traumatic stress disorder: The latest assessment and treatment strategies.* Kansas City: Compact Clinicals.

Friedman, M. J. (2001). Allostatic versus empirical perspectives on pharmacotherapy. In J. P. Wilson, M. J. Friedman, & J. D. Lindy (Eds.), *Treating psychological trauma and PTSD* (pp. 94–125). New York: Guilford Publications.

Gabbard, G. & Twemblow, S. (1984). *With the eyes of the mind: An empirical analysis of out-of-body states.* New York: Praeger.

Goldberg, A. (1985). *Progress in self psychology.* New York: Guilford Publications.

Goodwin, J. M. & Attias, R. (Eds.). (1999). *Splintered reflections.* New York: Basic Books.

Herman, J. L. (1992). *Trauma and recovery.* New York: Basic Books.

Jacobsen, F. (1938). *Progressive relaxation.* Chicago, IL: University of Chicago Press.

James, W. (1958). *The variety of religious experience.* Boston, MA: Harvard University Press.

Janet, P. (1900). *L' automatisure psychologiqene.* Paris: Bailliere.

Janet, P. (1907). *The major symptoms of hysteria.* London: Macmillan.

Jilek, W. (1982). *Indian healing: Shamanic ceremonies in the Pacific Northwest today.* Washington, DC: Hancock House.

Kalsched, D. (1996). *The inner world of trauma: Archetypal defenses of the personal spirit.* London: Routledge.

Kalsched, D. (2003). Daimonic elements in early trauma. *Journal of Analytical Psychology, 48*(2), 145–176.

Kessler, R. C., Sonnega, A., Bromet, E., Hughes, M. H., & Nelson, C. B. (1995). Posttraumatic stress disorder in the national comorbidity survey. *Archives of General Psychiatry, 52,* 1048–1060.

Kluft, R. P. (1991). The hospital treatment of multiple personality disorders. *Psychiatric Clinics of North America, 14,* 695–719.

Knox, J. (2003a). *Archetype, attachment, analysis.* London: Brunner-Routledge.

Knox, J. (2003b). Trauma and defenses: their roots in relationship: An overview. *Journal of Analytical Psychology, 48,* 207–233.

Kohut, H. (1971). *The analysis of the self.* New York: International Universities Press.

Krystal, H. (1988). *Integration and healing.* Hillsdale, New Jersey: The Analytic Press.

LeDoux, J. E. (1996). *The emotional brain.* New York: Simon & Schuster.

Lifton, R. J. (1967). *Death in life: The survivors of Hiroshima.* New York: Simon & Schuster.

Lifton, R. J. (1976). *The life of the self.* New York: Simon & Schuster.

Lifton, R. J. (1979). *The broken connection: On death and the continuity of life.* New York: Basic Books.

Lifton, R. J. (1993). From Hiroshima to the Nazi doctors: The evolution of psycho-formative approaches to understanding traumatic stress syndromes. In J. P. Wilson & B. Raphael (Eds.), *International handbook of traumatic stress syndromes* (pp. 11–25). New York: Plenum Press.

Lowenstein, R. J. & Goodwin, J. (1999). Assessment and management of somatoform symptoms in traumatized patients: Conceptual overview and practical guide.

In J. M. Goodwin & R. Attias (Eds.), *Splintered reflections: Images of the body in trauma* (pp. 67–89). New York: Basic Books.

Marmar, C. R., Weiss, D. S., & Metzler, T. M. (1997). The Peritraumatic Dissociative Experiences Questionnaire. In J. P. Wilson & T. M. Keane (Eds.), *Assessing psychological trauma and PTSD* (pp. 412–429). New York: Guilford Press.

Marsella, A. J., Friedman, M. J., Gerrity, E., & Scurfield, R. M. (Eds.). (1996). *Ethnocultural aspects of posttraumatic stress disorder: Issues, research and applications.* Washington, DC: American Psychological Association Press.

Maslow, A. H. (1962). *Towards a psychology of being (1st ed.).* New York: D. Van Nostrad.

Maslow, A. H. (1968). *Towards a psychology of being.* New York: D. Van Nostrand.

Maslow, A. H. (1970). *Motivation and personality.* New York: Harper.

Maslow, A. H. (1971). *The further reaches of human nature.* New York: Viking Press.

Masterson, J. F. (1981). *The narcissistic and borderline disorders: An integrated developmental approach.* New York: Brunner-Mazel.

McEwen, B. S. (1998). Seminars of the Beth Israel Deaconess Medical Center: Protective and damaging effects of stress mediators. *New England Journal of Medicine, 338*(3), 171–179.

McEwen, B. S. (2002). *The end of stress as we know it.* Washington, DC: The Dana Press.

Mischel, W. & Morf, C. (2003). The self as a psychosocial dynamic processing system: A meta-psychological perspective. In M. P. Leary & J. P. Tangney (Eds.), *Handbook of self and identity.* New York: Guilford Publications.

Nemiah, J. C. (1998). Early concepts of trauma, dissociation and the unconscious. Their history and current implications. In J. D. Bremner & C. R. Marmar (Eds.), *Trauma, memory and dissociation* (pp. 1–27). Washington, DC: American Psychiatric Association Press.

Nijenhuis, E. R. S. & van der Hart, O. (1999a). Forgetting and re-experiencing trauma: From anesthesia to pain. In J. M. Goodwin & R. Attias (Eds.), *Splintered reflections: Images of the body in trauma* (pp. 9–39). New York: Basic Books.

Nijenhuis, E. R. S. & van der Hart, O. (1999b). Somatoform dissociative phenomena: A Janetian perspective. In J. M. Goodwin & R. Attias (Eds.), *Splintered reflections: Images of the body in trauma* (pp. 89–129). New York: Basic Books.

Nijenhuis, E. R. S. (2000). Somatoform dissociation: Major symptoms of dissociative disorders. *Journal of Trauma and Dissociation, 1,* 7–32.

Pearlman, L. & Saakvitne, K. (1995). *Trauma and the therapist.* New York: W. W. Norton.

Perry, B. (1999). The memories of states: How the brain stores and retrieves traumatic experiences. In J. M. Goodwin & R. Attias (Eds.), *Splintered reflections: Images of the body in trauma* (pp. 9–39). New York: Basic Books.

Progroff, I. (1963). *The symbolic and the real.* New York: McGraw-Hill.

Putnam, F. (1997). *Dissociation in children and adolescents.* New York: Guilford Press.

Pynoos, R. & Nader, K. (1993). Issues in the treatment of posttraumatic stress in children. In J. P. Wilson & B. Raphael (Eds.), *International handbook of traumatic stress syndromes* (pp. 527–535). New York: Plenum Press.

Raphael, B. (1983). *When disaster strikes.* New York: Basic Books.

Raphael, B. & Martinek, N. (1997). Assessing traumatic bereavement and PTSD. In J. P. Wilson & T. M. Keane (Eds.), *Assessing psychological trauma and PTSD* (ch. 12, pp. 373–399). New York: Guilford Publications.

Raphael, B., Woodling, & Martinek (2004). Assessing traumatic bereavement. In J. P. Wilson & T. M. Keane (Eds.), *Assessing psychological trauma and PTSD* (pp. 492–513). New York: Guilford Publications.

Rogers, C. (1951). *Client centered therapy.* New York: Houghton-Mifflin.

Ross, G. A., Miller, S. D., Bjorns, R. P., Fraser, G. A., & Anderson, G. (1990). Structured interview data from 102 cases of multiple personality disorder from four centers. *American Journal of Psychiatry, 14,* 596–606.

Sadock, B. J., & Sadock, V. A. (2003). *Kaplan and Sadock's synopsis of psychiatry.* Philadelphia, PA: Lippincott, Williams & Wilkins.

Schore, A. N. (2003). *Affect regulation and repair of the self.* New York: W. W. Norton.

Shapiro, F. (1996). Eye movement desensitization and reprocessing (EMDR): Evaluation of controlled research. *Journal of Behavioral and Experimental Psychology* 27(3), 1–10.

Silver, S. M. & Wilson, J. P. (1988). Native American healing and purification rituals for war stress. In J. P. Wilson, Z. Harel, & B. Kahana (Eds.), *Human adaptation to extreme stress* (pp. 337–354). New York: Plenum Press.

Steele, K., van der Hart, O., & Nijenhuis, E. R. S. (2001). Dependency in the treatment of complex PTSD and dissociative disorders. *Journal of Trauma and Dissociation,* 2, 79–117.

Stern, D. (1985). *The interpersonal world of the infant.* New York: Basic Books.

Tolle, E. (1999). *The power of now.* Novato, California: New World Library.

Ulman, R. B. & Brothers, D. (1988). *The shattered self.* Northvale, New Jersey: The Analytic Press.

van der Hart, O. & Boon, S. (1997). Treatment strategies for complex dissociative disorder: Two Dutch case examples. *Dissociation,* 10, 157–165.

van der Kolk, B. (1997). Traumatic memories. In P. S. Applebaum, L. A. Uyehara, & M. R. Elin (Eds.), *Trauma and memory: Clinical and legal controversies* (pp. 243–260). New York: Oxford University.

van der Kolk, B. (1999). The body keeps score: Memory and the evolving psychobiology of posttraumatic stress. In M. Horowitz (Ed.), *Essential papers on posttraumatic stress disorder* (pp. 301–327). New York: New York University Press.

van der Kolk, B., McFarlane, A. C., & Weisaeth, L. (1996). *Traumatic stress.* New York: Guilford Publications.

Watkins, J. G. & Watkins, H. H. (1997). *Ego-states.* New York: W. W. Norton.

White, R. W. (1959). *The ego and reality in psychoanalytic theory.* New York: International University Press.

Wilson, J. P. (1980). Conflict, stress and growth: The effects of war on psychosocial development among Vietnam veterans. In C. R. Figley & K. S. Leventman (Eds.), *Strangers at home: Vietnam veterans since the war* (pp. 123–165). New York: Preager Press.

Wilson, J. P. (1989a). *Trauma, transformation and healing.* New York: Brunner-Mazel.

Wilson, J. P. (1989b). *Trauma, transformation and healing: An integration approval to theory, research and posttraumatic theory.* New York: Brunner/Mazel.

Wilson, J. P. (2003). *Empathic strain and post-traumatic therapy.* New York: Guilford Publications.

Wilson, J. P. (2004a). Broken spirits. In J. P. Wilson & B. Drozdek (Eds.), *Broken spirits: The treatment of traumatized asylum seekers, refugees and war and torture victims* (pp. 141–173). New York: Brunner-Routledge.

Wilson, J. P. (2004b). PTSD and complex PTSD: Symptoms, syndromes and diagnoses. In J. P. Wilson & T. M. Keane (Eds.), *Assessing psychological trauma and PTSD* (pp. 7–45). New York: Guilford Publications.

Wilson, J. P. & Drozdek, B. (2004). *Broken spirits: The treatment of traumatized asylum seekers, refugees and war and torture victims.* New York: Brunner-Routledge.

Wilson, J. P. & Lindy, J. (1994). *Counter-transference in the treatment of PTSD.* New York: Guilford Publications.

Wilson, J. P. & Raphael, B. (1993). *The international handbook of traumatic stress syndromes.* New York: Plenum Press.

Wilson, J. P. & Thomas, R. (2004). *Empathy in the treatment of trauma and PTSD.* New York: Brunner-Routledge.

Wilson, J. P., Friedman, M., & Lindy, J. (2001). *Treating psychological trauma and PTSD.* New York: Guilford Publications.

Wolfe, E. (1990). *Treating the self.* New York: Guilford Publications.

Wurmser, L. (1994). *The mask of shame.* Northvale, New Jersey: Jason Aaronson.

7

Trauma and Alterations in Normal Personality

BRIAN HALL AND JOHN P. WILSON

1 INTRODUCTION

Among the critical theoretical questions for the field of traumatology is the issue of how trauma affects the structure and dynamics of normal personality functioning. What types of trauma generate the most severe impact on the structure of personality as it exists at the time of the event? Is it possible to predict which types of traumatic stressors will cause the greatest changes in personality functioning? For example, we know from epidemiological studies (Breslau, 1998) that the stresses associated with interpersonal violence, sexual assault, and domestic trauma produce relatively high rates of PTSD and comorbidity (Kessler, Sonnega, Bromet, Hughes, & Nelson, 1995). These findings make sense and are expectable because the traumatic stressors associated with acts of interpersonal violence violate the physical and psychological integrity of the person, i.e., they are "frontal assaults" to integrated personality functioning. But what about other types of trauma that vary in their degree of psychological invasiveness? Would we expect to see significant alterations in the measurable dimensions of personality in survivors of a hurricane that destroyed their homes and property? A survivor of a frightening but noninjurious motor vehicle accident? An adolescent who lives in a home with abusive, chronic alcoholic parents? A spouse who had been repeatedly subjected to domestic violence? A person who witnessed from a safe distance the attack and collapse of the World Trade Centers on September 11, 2001 in New York City? A spouse, relative, or friend who witnessed a loved one being beheaded by terrorist extremists? A mother who watched her infant daughter starve to death in the genocidal warfare in the Darfur region of Sudan in 2004? A 20-year-old soldier who lost his arms and was severely wounded in a terrorist car-bomb attack in Baghdad during the Iraq war in 2004?

These considerations raise important questions regarding the relationship of trauma to personality development and functioning. First, are there universal pathways as to how traumatic experiences impact human personality as it exists at the time of trauma? Second, is there a causal relationship between age, type of trauma, and the proneness to developmental and personality disorders? Third, what is the relationship between a specific type of trauma and the phenotype of personality? Stated differently, is it possible to "tease out" the contributions to posttraumatic patterns of adaptation in terms of constitutional factors (referred to as basic tendencies of personality in the Five Factor Model of personality, FFM) and the magnitude of the traumatic stressor (McCrae & Costa, 2003)? This question relates to the diathesis concept that there are complex person–environment interactions that determine behavioral outcomes in posttraumatic coping and adaptation (Wilson, 1989). For example, what is the threshold point at which a traumatic stressor "overrides" basic personality dispositions to inflict acute or chronic damage to the structure and dynamics of personality? Are there, in fact, different thresholds of stress tolerance for different types of personality constellations? How do personality factors determine adaptive resilience and resumption of normal functioning? How does the profile of personality factors change in relation to specific types or classes of traumatic experiences? Is there a personality type that is at risk for the development of PTSD? Can personality act as a risk or protective factor in the development of PTSD?

In the ideal research protocol, it would be desirable to have a prospective and longitudinal study of the effects of psychological trauma across the life-cycle for a large group of normal persons (i.e., those without obvious psychopathology). By measuring pretraumatic characteristics of personality, it would be possible to discern patterns of change over time. In the area of personality research, such approaches have been employed by Jack Block (1971) in his landmark work, *Lives Through Time* and George Vaillant (1978) in his longitudinal study of Harvard University students in the book *Adaptation to Life*. These studies revealed important results that have direct relevance to the study of trauma and personality.

Block (1971) found there was great variability in the stability of personality as measured over time (four decades). Some characteristics changed very little; others changed a great deal. Second, the research identified a limited number of personality typologies (e.g., ego-resilience, unsettled undercontrollers, vulnerable overcontrollers, cognitive copers). Third, despite the consistency of measured personality characteristics over time intervals, there were clearly discernible patterns of continuity among personality types, which could wax and wane in salience across life-cycle development. A similar finding was found by Vaillant (1977) in his long-term study of psychological adjustment among elite college students. For example, Felsman and Vaillant (1987) found little evidence of a linear, uninterrupted sequence of personality development. There were periods of continuity and discontinuity in coping, adjustment, mental health, and psychosocial functioning. More recently, McCrae and Costa (2003) reviewed the empirical evidence for the stability of personality over time, especially for the Five Factor Model (FFM) of personality. They note that recent research challenges the notion of "concrete" stability to measurable personality factors. McCrae and Costa (2003) state: "more information from longitudinal, cross-sectional, and cross-cultural studies is now available, and the argument has become more measured. Newer studies confirm that stability is the predominant feature of personality in adulthood, but also documents predictable changes at certain ages in certain individuals" (p. 2). The authors further suggest that there may be different causes for changes in personality stability: "Perhaps a more likely candidate for a moderator of change is *some external event that alters one's life and thus personality traits* (p. 130; emphasis added). Beyond question, profoundly traumatic life experiences can alter the quality of life and personality in many different ways. If so, how is the underlying structure of personality altered by extreme stress? How do the fundamental characteristics of personality become altered, transformed, or remain unchanged by traumatic experiences?

In this chapter we will explore the relationship of traumatic stresses to normal personality and the symptoms of PTSD among university students. For practical purposes, it was decided to utilize the FFM of personality as a useful construct of normal personality. As Saucier and Goldberg (1996) state

> The Big Five does not define any limits to personality research. Rather, the research leading to the Big Five structure simply constitutes a body of findings too powerful and critical to be ignored by anyone who seeks to understand human personality... the Big Five appear to provide a set of highly replicable dimensions that parsimoniously and comprehensively describe most phenotypic individual differences. (pp. 37 and 42)

The Big Five factors of personality (i.e., the FFM) have a fairly long and interesting history of development, beginning with Allport and Odbert's (1936) ambitious early lexical study of trait personality through which they identified roughly 18,000 trait descriptors derived from *Webster's New International Dictionary*. This work followed the lexical hypothesis which holds that all relevant personality characteristics have been encoded in the natural language. Raymond Cattell further distilled Allport and Odbert's list to approximately 3,500, and through a series of factor analyses, refined this list further, which ultimately led to the development of the 16 Personality Factor (16PF) Questionnaire with its five second-order (i.e., Global) factors. McCrae and Costa (2003) continued the research on the FFM and incorporated it into their NEO (Neuroticism, Extraversion, and Openness to Experience). Subsequently, the factors Conscientiousness and Agreeableness were added to the revised version of their instrument, the NEO-PI-R. As Digman (1996) summarized, the heuristic significance of the FFM can be seen by the following quote

> with the Big Five, we have a model that has shown robustness across cultures, across media, across age groups, and which offers a model for unifying the field of personality attributes...the model has suggested use in fields as diverse as evolutionary psychology, clinical psychology and personal selection. (p. 16)

The cross-cultural and age-related stability of the FFM suggests that it might be a useful way to examine the impact of psychological trauma to personality. To this end, we will first present a model of traumatic stress and posttraumatic adaptations in the FFM, as well as the corresponding development of PTSD symptoms. Second, we will present the results of a research study using college students who were screened by self-reports of stressful life-experiences and administered the revised 16 Personality Factor questionnaire, fifth edition (Cattell, Cattell, & Cattell, 1993).

2 A MODEL OF TRAUMATIC STRESS, NORMAL PERSONALITY AND POSTTRAUMATIC ADAPTATIONS

Figure 7.1 represents a model of traumatic stress, normal personality (FFM), and predicted patterns of posttraumatic adaptation as well as their relation to PTSD symptoms (*DSM-IV-TR*, 2000). The model is a simplified version of Wilson's (1989) person–environment model of traumatic stress patterns and posttraumatic adaptations.

Examination of Figure 7.1 shows, in a purposely simplistic way, that traumatic stress impacts the structure of personality as it exists at the

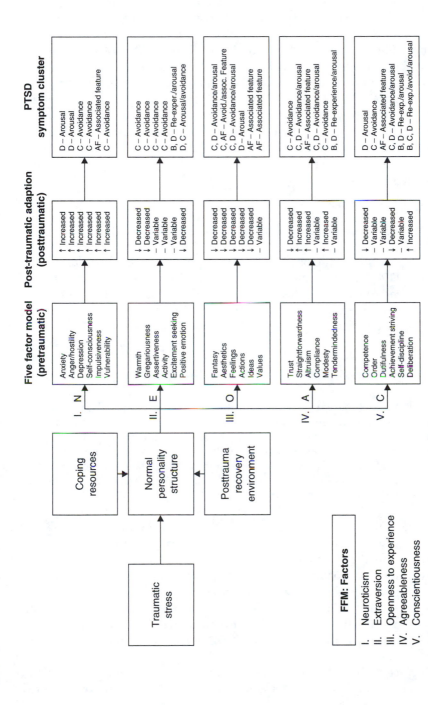

FIGURE 7.1. Traumatic stress, normal personality, and posttraumatic alterations. *Source:* ©2004 John P. Wilson.

time of the event. The outcome, in terms of posttraumatic adaptation, is moderated by two major functions: (1) coping resources (e.g., personal, social, economic) and (2) the nature of the posttrauma recovery environment (Green, Wilson, & Lindy, 1985; Wilson, 1989). As depicted in Figure 7.1, traumatic stressors have the potential to affect any or all of the Big Five factors of personality. Specifically, the predicted directions of posttraumatic adaptation are shown in Figure 7.1 for the subdimensions of the FFM. The specific rationale for the predictions was discussed in Chapter 3. The *DSM-IV* symptoms of PTSD and associated features are shown for the FFM (i.e., Neuroticism, Extraversion, Openness, Agreeableness, and Conscientiousness) and the 30 subdimensions, or facets, which define the five factors.

3 PREVIOUS RESEARCH ON PERSONALITY, STRESS AND PTSD

Since the inclusion of PTSD as a distinct mental disorder in the *DSM-III* (1980) of the American Psychiatric Association, the majority of clinical and research studies have focused on the anxiety disorder as a form of psychopathology. The nature of scientific discovery regarding PTSD as a phenomenon necessarily focused attention during the first two decades of research on questions related to etiology, prevalence, assessment, psychobiological processes, and clinical innovations (Wilson, Friedman, & Lindy, 2001). More recently, Miller (2004) stated

> Application of these developments to the study of PTSD has the potential to advance the understanding of one of the trauma fields most intriguing questions—why some individuals exposed to trauma develop significant pathology, while others do not. Research on the interface of personality and PTSD may also contribute to understanding factors that determine the course, behavioral expression, and patterns of comorbidity associated with the disorder. (p. 1)

These comments shed light on the necessity of understanding the manner in which personality factors are associated with different forms of posttraumatic adaptation and behavioral dispositions. Intuitively, many researchers have explored this question indirectly in relation to other hypotheses under evaluation in studies of PTSD. A few studies (Iris, Englehard, Marcel, van der Vout, & Kidt, 2003) have utilized prospective designs and evaluated premeasured aspects of personality (usually neuroticism) in relation to PTSD and other dependent variables of interest.

To place the relevant literature into an organizing framework, several issues are useful to consider. First, the majority of studies selected measures of personality that were convenient to use and generally tailored to the goals of the research study. Second, most studies utilized measures of personality that looked at the Big Five factors or their equivalents in personality questionnaires (e.g., 16PF). Third, most studies hypothesized or explored the relationship of neuroticism to PTSD since this dimension of personality has a long history of investigation in relation to dispositions to psychopathology (Hyer, Braswell, Albrecht, Boyd, Boudewyns, & Talbert, 1994). Fourth, studies have also explored the relationship between PTSD and the Axis I and Axis II mental disorders. Fifth, studies have attempted to map the empirical relationship between measures of personality with a pathological orientation (e.g., MMPI-2; MCMI-II) and PTSD symptoms. There are very few studies (Wilson & Keane, 2004) that have examined a wide range of personality characteristics from other measures of personality (e.g., California Personality Inventory; 16PF, NEO-PI-R, Thematic Appreciation Test; Self-Actualization; Dominance; Moral Reasoning; needs for intimacy, achievement, and power; Sense of Well Being). Sixth, there are even fewer studies of trauma and posttraumatic growth, resilience, mental health, positive coping, and personality. Seventh, the majority of these studies have limited focus on PTSD or other psychiatrically oriented outcome measures, rather than assessing psychosocial effects in the broadest context—social relationships, occupational functioning, parenting styles, self-esteem, life and marital satisfaction, adaptation to aging, etc. (Harkness, 1993, 2001).

Table 7.1 summarizes 21 studies that have examined the relationship of personality to PTSD in a variety of populations ranging from college students (Bunce, Larsen, & Peterson, 1993) to combat veterans of the Vietnam War (Wilson & Walker, 1989; Hyer et al., 1994; Talbert et al., 1993). Examination of the table shows that nearly all the studies found neuroticism related to PTSD and other aspects of behavioral functioning such as poor mental and physical health in aging (Lee, Vaillant, Torrey, & Elder, 1995).

3.1 Eysenck Personality Questionnaire

There are at least six studies that have analyzed the relationship between the Eysenck Personality Questionnaire (EPQ) and PTSD. In an early study, Davidson, Kudler, and Smith (1987) found that World War II, Korean War and Vietnam War veterans had higher neuroticism scores than controls, even after treatment. Bunce, Larsen, & Peterson (1993) studied 56 University of Michigan students throughout an academic semester. They ranked the male and female participants on traumatic events and asked them to keep a daily journal of daily

TABLE 7.1
Personality Studies and PTSD

Study	Year	Sample	Personality assessment	Results
Davidson, Kudler, & Smith	1985	World War I, Vietnam veterans	EPQ	High neuroticism and PTSD
Wilson & Walker	1989	Vietnam veterans	16 PF (A)	PTSD = Factors A, H, Q2, Q4, Extraversion
Bunce, Larsen, & Peterson	1993	College students	EPQ	Trauma group = higher neuroticism, intraverted, emotional instability
Kopriva, Kiyuna, & Farr	1993	College students	16 PF (A)	Abuse = Factors L, O, Q4
Talbert et al.	1993	Vietnam veterans	NEO-PI	High neuroticism and PTSD
Hyer et al.	1994	Vietnam veterans	NEO-PI	High neuroticism and PTSD
Trull & Sher	1994	College students	NEO-FFI	High neuroticism and PTSD
Clark, Watson, & Mineka	1994	N/A	Review of literature	Neuroticism (negative affectivity) = vulnerability to anxiety
Breslau, Davis, & Archewski	1995	Urban Detroit	EPQ	High neuroticism = higher risk for PTSD
Lee, Vaillant, Torrey, & Elder	1995	World War II veterans	NEO-PI	High Neuroticism and PTSD, poor mental health
Richman & Freuh	1997	Vietnam veteran	TPQ	Harm avoidance and novelty-seeking associated with PTSD
Kelly et al.	1998	HIV	EPQ	High neuroticism and PTSD
Nightingale & Williams	2000	Motor vehicle accident	NEO-PI	Self-disclosure, negative correlation with expressions
Paris	2000	Review	Various	High neuroticism and PTSD
Holeva & Tarrier	2001	Motor vehicle accident	EPQ	High neuroticism and PTSD
Lauterbach & Vrana	2001	College students	NEO-PI	High neuroticism and PTSD
Bennet et al.	2002	Heart patients	PANAS	Negative affect correlated with PTSD
Iris et al.	2003	Pregnant women	EPQ	High neuroticism and PTSD
Miller, Grief, & Smith	2003	Vietnam veterans	MPQ	PTSD and negative emotions
Quirk et al.	2003	College students	NEO-PI	High neuroticism and PTSD
Miller	2004	Vietnam veterans	MPQ	PTSD and negative emotions

Source: ©2004 John P. Wilson.

activities, emotions, and physical health. The group classified as having more traumatic events had higher neuroticism scores and lower scores on extraversion than the nontraumatized group. The traumatized group was also less emotionally stable and reported greater interpersonal withdrawal than the nontraumatized comparison group. In a prospective study conducted in the state of Michigan, Breslau and Davis (1992) sampled 1,200 participants from a health maintenance organization and used the Diagnostic Interview Schedule (DIS) for *DSM-III-R* diagnoses. They measured personality traits with the EPQ and found that extraversion and neuroticism were associated with risk factors for exposure to traumatic stressors and PTSD. In another sample of patients with health-related concerns, Kelly, Raphael, Judd, Kernatt, Burnett, and Burrows (1998) evaluated the relationship of neuroticism to PTSD in 61 patients suffering from HIV infection. The EPQ was administered along with measures of ego-defense, locus of control, and prior life-events. The results showed a moderately strong correlation (.50) between the 10-item neuroticism scale and PTSD as measured by the DIS-Version-III-R.

In a study of motor vehicle accidents, Holeva and Tarrier (2001) examined 265 victims on two occasions about 6 months apart. The Penn inventory was used to assess PTSD symptoms and results showed that PTSD patients had higher neuroticism scores and lower extraversion scores than those without PTSD. Somewhat similar results were obtained in a prospective study conducted in Holland with pregnant women who suffered the loss of their unborn child (Iris, Englehard, Marcel, van der Hout, & Kindt, 2003). A total of 126 women lost pregnancies and manifested PTSD symptoms within a month of miscarriage. Pretraumatic neuroticism as measured by the EPQ was significantly correlated with pregnancy loss and PTSD symptoms, especially hyperarousal symptoms (i.e., PTSD "D" cluster).

3.2 NEO-Personality Inventory of the Big Five Factors

There are at least six studies that have employed the NEO-Personality Inventory (PI) measure of the FFM model of personality and examined its relationship to PTSD. In two related studies on Vietnam War combat veterans (Talbert, Braswell, Albrecht, Hyer, & Boudewyns, 1993; Hyer, Braswell, Albrecht, Boyd, Boudewyns, & Talbert, 1994) high neuroticism scores were strongly associated with PTSD in two different samples of Vietnam veterans diagnosed with chronic combat-related PTSD. However, in the second study (Hyer et al., 1994) none of the other FFM factors of personality were significantly related to PTSD. Similar results were found by Trull and Sher (1994) in a sample of 468 nonclinical (i.e. normal) college students who were part of a larger longitudinal study on alcoholism. At a later phase in the study, a battery of personality measures was given and subjects were screened with the DIS-Version-III-R mental health interview. The results showed that PTSD was associated with higher scores on the NEO-PI dimension of neuroticism but not with any other factors. In a study of normal personality and clinical assessment, Quirk, Christiansen, Wagner, and McNulty (2003) found that persons with PTSD had higher levels of neuroticism and low levels of extraversion and conscientiousness.

In a study of aging World War II veterans, the trait of neuroticism was assessed by the NEO-PI and was found to be significantly associated with a wide range of postwar problems including PTSD, depression, alcoholism, and problems in psychosocial functioning (Lee, Vaillant, Torrey, & Elder, 1995).

3.3 Other Measures of Personality Characteristics and PTSD

There are several other studies that have examined personality factors related to PTSD. In a review article related to their tripartite model of anxiety and depression, Clark, Watson, and Mineka (1994) cited evidence that neuroticism (i.e., negative affectivity) represents a vulnerability to anxiety. In a study of 53 Vietnam veterans with combat-related PTSD, Richman and Freuh (1997) used the Tridimensional Personality Questionnaire (TPQ) and found that PTSD was associated with the variables of Harm Avoidance and Novelty Seeking. Similar findings were reported by Bennett, Owen, Stavrola, and Bisson (2002) who examined PTSD and affect dimensions using the PANAS scale. The results showed, consistent with other studies, that negative affect was associated with PTSD. More recently, in several large-scale studies of PTSD, Miller (2003, 2004) found that negative emotionality, as assessed by the Multidimensional Personality Questionnaire (MPQ), was significantly associated with PTSD.

Lauterbach and Vrana (2001) found that among university students, personality variation occurred as a function of the number of traumatic events reported. Those reporting a higher incidence of experiencing traumatic events were less sociable, warm, and outgoing (measured by the Gough Socialization Scale). Additionally, neuroticism was found to be related to PTSD. Symptoms of PTSD were found to correlate significantly with borderline and antisocial personality disorder symptoms.

In one study indirectly related to personality, PTSD, and adjustment, Nightengale and Williams (2000) found that persons who had negative attitudes towards expressing feelings were found to be more intraverted, less open, and less agreeable than those with positive attitudes to the personal disclosure of emotions.

Holmes, Williams, and Haines (2001) examined personality differences in those with PTSD, acute stress disorder (ASD), and subclinical responses related to motor vehicle accident trauma, using the Personality Assessment Inventory (PAI). Differences were found upon comparison of PTSD, ASD, and subclinical groups. Participants who had PTSD reported higher levels of somatic complaints, anxiety, anxiety-related disorders, and depression. They also reported significantly less warmth, more negative relationships, and lower levels of egocentricity.

Cherepon and Prinzhorn (1994) used the PAI to examine the relationship between child abuse and personality in a clinical sample of patients. Patients who reported abuse had significantly higher scores on the Anxiety Related cluster, Traumatic Stress Experiences, Phobia Tendencies, Obsessive Compulsive Tendencies, Paranoia and experiences of Persecution, Hypervigilance, Borderline Features, Instability, and Negative Relationships than those not reporting abusive experiences.

Wonderlich et al. (2001) compared childhood sexual abuse and adult rape victims on personality factors, as measured by the Dimensional Assessment of Personality Pathology (DAPP). When victims of sexual abuse were compared with controls, significantly higher levels of Suspiciousness, Intimacy Problems, and Restricted Expression were found on the DAPP. Those who had experienced childhood sexual abuse had elevated levels of Cognitive Dysregulation, Identity Problems, Affective Lability, Social Avoidance, and Self-Destructive Behavior. The authors suggest that these elevations point to a relationship between childhood sexual abuse and borderline personality disorder. Women who had both childhood sexual assault and adult rape had higher scores on Compulsivity and Anxiousness than control groups.

Moran and Shakespeare-Finch (2003) examined the relationship between personality and childhood maltreatment in a female adolescent population. The maltreated group differed from the control group on measures of depression, locus of control, and self-esteem. The maltreated group had higher external locus of control which moderated the effects of depression—higher in this group. Findings of other studies supported this relationship (Frye & Stockton, 1982; Solomon et al., 1998; Weiss et al., 1995; as cited in Schnurr & Vielhauer, 1999).

Kopriva and colleagues (1993) assessed several traumatic events—natural disaster, fire, auto injury, death, illness, and childhood abuse—and measured personality using the 16PF (Form A) across two groups: codependents (Codas) and adult children of alcoholics (ACA). Significant correlations were found between personality variables and the different traumatic events. Factor D (Dominance) was positively correlated with child abuse, Factor H (Social Boldness) was positively correlated with fire exposure, war injury, and physical abuse, Factor N (Privateness) was negatively correlated with abuse, Factor E (Liveliness) was negatively correlated with emotional and sexual abuse, and Factor C (Emotional Stability) was negatively correlated with sexual abuse but positively correlated with emotional abuse. Irrespective of Coda and ACA classifications, Factors L (Vigilance), O (Apprehension), and Q4 (Tension) were found to correlate positively with emotional and physical abuse, and Q4 (Tension) also correlated positively with sexual abuse.

In an early study of personality profiles and PTSD, Wilson and Walker (1989) found that the 16PF (Form A) differentiated Vietnam War veterans from nontraumatized persons. PTSD was strongly associated with being reserved, shy, self-sufficient, and tense (Factors A, H, Q2, Q4) and the second-order factor of extraversion.

We now turn to an empirical study which builds upon this previous literature and explores further the relationship between traumatic events and dimensions of normal personality.

4 METHOD

4.1 Research Participants

Participants were 326 university students (86 males, 240 females) recruited from a large urban university, ranging in age from 18 to 55 years with a mean age of 26.9 years, and a standard deviation of 7.5 years. Sixty-five percent of the sample was Caucasian, 23% were African American, 4% were Asian, and 3.4% were Latino. The remaining 4.6% identified themselves as Native American, Middle Eastern, or other (see Table 7.2).

4.2 Measures

Participants were given questionnaires to assess exposure to stressful life-events, PTSD symptoms, and personality characteristics. The questionnaire was ordered to elicit information regarding the participants' history of traumatic event exposure and included: demographics, Life Events Checklist (LEC) (Blake et al., 1995), Impact of Event Scale Revised (IES-R) (Weiss & Marmar, 1997), and the 16 Personality Factor Questionnaire (5th edition) (Cattell, Cattell, & Cattell, 1993).

4.3 Lifetime History of Traumatic Events Exposure

4.3.1 Life Events Checklist (LEC). The LEC was developed at the National Center for PTSD and is used as a screening measure for identifying Potentially Traumatic Events during clinical assessment of PTSD with the

TABLE 7.2
Participant Demographics

Characteristic	Frequency	Percentage
Gender	86	26.4
Male	240	73.6
Female		
Highest level of education	191	58.9
Some college, no degree	51	15.6
Associates degree	71	15.6
Bachelors degree	11	3.4
Masters degree	1	0.3
Professional degree		
Marital status	68	20.9
Married	13	4.0
Divorced/separated	68	20.9
Single, living with significant other	193	59.4
Single, not living with significant other	5	1.5
Other		
Other		
	74	23.1
$75,000 or more	48	15.0
$74,999–$50,000	76	23.8
$49,999–$30,000	56	17.5
$29,000–$15,000	29	9.1
$14,999–$8,000	37	11.6
$7,999 or less		
Individual or family income	14	4.3
Professional	14	4.3
Technical	30	9.2
Business	15	4.6
Blue collar	17	5.2
Sales	4	1.2
Unemployed	192	59.1
Student	41	12.6
Other		

Source: ©2004 Brian Hall.

Clinician Administered PTSD Scale (CAPS) (Blake et al., 1995). The checklist assesses lifetime exposure to traumatic life-events experienced, witnessed, or learned about. For the purpose of this study, an additional item was added to the end the checklist relating to the participant's experience during the events of September 11, 2001. The LEC has recently been shown to have adequate psychometric properties and to correlate well with a criterion measure of traumatic events history (Gray, Litz, Hsu, and Lombardo, 2004).

4.4 PTSD Symptoms

4.4.1 Impact of Event Scale–Revised (IES-R) (Weiss & Marmar, 1997). The IES-R was developed by Horowitz et al. (1979) and revised by Weiss and Marmar (1997) to include symptoms of hyperarousal not found in the original IES. The IES-R was used to elicit the most stressful event endorsed on the LEC and to specify the event and the date it occurred. If no event was reported, the subject entered "none" and they were classified as nontraumatic controls for purposes of the study. The 22 items of the IES-R are quantified on a 5-point scale (0 = not at all; 1 = a little bit; 2 = moderately; 3 = quite a bit; 4 = extremely). Based on the review by Weiss (2004), the IES-R has high internal consistency (Cronbach alpha for Intrusion = .89, Avoidance = .84, Hyperarousal = .82).

4.5 Personality Measures and their Correspondence to the FFM

4.5.1 The 16 Personality Factor Questionnaire, 5th edition (16PF). The 16PF (Cattell, Cattell, & Cattell, 1993) is a dimensional measure of normal trait personality characteristics. The questionnaire assesses 16 primary personality factors (i.e., (A) Warmth, (B) Reasoning, (C) Emotional Stability, (D) Dominance, (E) Liveliness, (G) Rule-Consciousness, (H) Social Boldness, (I) Sensitivity, (L) Vigilance, (M) Abstractedness, (N) Privateness, (O) Apprehension, (Q1) Openness to Change, (Q2) Self-Reliance, (Q3) Perfectionism, and (Q4) Tension), and five global (second-order) personality factors (i.e., (I) Extraversion, (II) Anxiety, (III) Tough-Mindedness, (IV) Independence, and (V) Self-Control)) derived from the primary factors. The use of the global factors also enables comparison with the FFM (McCrae & Costa, 2003).

The items consist of 185 true and false questions and a "(?) not sure" response option. Each of the primary factors is comprised of 10–15 test items. The responses of the 16PF are scaled as sten scores (range 0–10) arranged in bipolar fashion so that each scale score can be interpreted directionally based on the deviation from the scale mean of 5.5. The psychometric properties reported for the 16PF are quite sound. The average test–retest reliability for the global scales was .87 at 2 weeks and .78 at 2 months. The average test–retest reliability for the primary factors was .80 at 2 weeks and .70 at 2 months and the average internal consistency for the primary factors was .76 (Conn & Rieke, 1994).

4.6 Procedure

Research participants were recruited from undergraduate courses in psychology and were given research credit for participation in the study. Participants were told that they would be answering question-naires relating to stressful life-events and personality characteristics. After informed consent was obtained, each participant was given a packet of questionnaires. They first filled out a demographic sheet which was followed by the LEC, the IES-R, and the 16PF. Partici-pants also filled out additional questionnaires that are not the focus of the current study. The LEC was used to screen the participants for exposure to stressful events. Participants were asked to report their symptoms on the IES-R based on the most stressful event they recorded on the LEC and to specify that event and the date it occurred. If no event was reported, participants entered "none", did not complete the IES-R, and were classified as nontrauma controls.

4.7 Most Stressful Event and Criteria for Probable
PTSD Classification

The IES-R identified stressful life-events (e.g., motor vehicle accident, rape, assault) using the *DSM-IV* A_1 diagnostic criteria for PTSD. These events were then classified into categories for statistical comparisons. Similar to previous studies (e.g., Bernat et al., 1998), persons reporting the aggregated "A criteria" for traumatic events were designated as having *probable PTSD* if they reported the minimal diagnostic criteria for PTSD symptoms: Intrusion (1 symptom); Avoidance (3 symptoms); and Hyperarousal (2 symptoms). We realize that this may have artificially inflated the prevalence (i.e., base rate) of PTSD in this sample, but the purpose of this study was to examine differences between those who endorse symptoms of PTSD, not the degree of severity to which these symptoms are experienced.

Participants who did not report an "A criteria" traumatic event were used as controls. As found in other studies (Butler & Wolfner, 2000), some participants in our study identified as "most traumatic" events that did not meet the A_1 diagnostic criteria for PTSD (e.g., nontraumatic death of a loved one, divorce, etc.). We excluded these participants from the Probable PTSD group as they did not meet the explicit A_1 PTSD prime diagnostic criteria.

5 RESULTS

5.1 Comparison of Personality Factors for Probable
PTSD and Nonprobable PTSD

We hypothesized that differences between the probable and non-probable PTSD groups would be found with respect to the 16 Personality Factors and the Five Global Factors on the questionnaire. Two-tailed independent-samples *t*-tests were conducted to compare the 16PF scale scores for the probable PTSD and nonprobable PTSD groups. The control group consisted of individuals who reported no traumatic event and will be referred to as "controls."

Significant differences were found between probable PTSD ($n = 101$) and nonprobable PTSD groups ($n = 60$). The probable PTSD group had significantly lower scores on Factor C (Emotional Stability) and Factor H (Social Boldness); and higher scores on Factor I (Sensitivity), Factor O (Apprehension), and Factor Q2 (Self-Reliance) when compared with the nonprobable group (Figure 7.2 and Table 7.3).

In the second series of *t*-tests, the Five Global Personality Factors were used as dependent variables, and the two PTSD groups (probable vs. nonprobable) served as independent variables. The probable PTSD group was found to have significantly higher scores on Anxiety (Factor II)

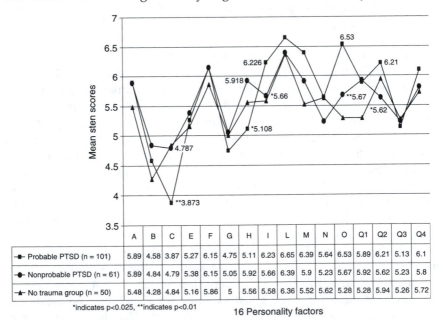

	A	B	C	E	F	G	H	I	L	M	N	O	Q1	Q2	Q3	Q4
Probable PTSD (n = 101)	5.89	4.58	3.87	5.27	6.15	4.75	5.11	6.23	6.65	6.39	5.64	6.53	5.89	6.21	5.13	6.1
Nonprobable PTSD (n = 61)	5.89	4.84	4.79	5.38	6.15	5.05	5.92	5.66	6.39	5.9	5.23	5.67	5.92	5.62	5.23	5.8
No trauma group (n = 50)	5.48	4.28	4.84	5.16	5.86	5	5.56	5.58	6.36	5.52	5.62	5.28	5.28	5.94	5.26	5.72

*indicates p<0.025, **indicates p<0.01　　　16 Personality factors

FIGURE 7.2. Profile of mean scores for probable PTSD, nonprobable PTSD, and no-trauma control groups on the 16 personality factors. *Source:* ©2004 Brian Hall.

TABLE 7.3

Results of Independent-Sample *t*-Tests for the Probable PTSD and Nonprobable PTSD Groups for the 16 Personality Factors

Personality factors	Probable PTSD group ($n = 101$) Mean (SD)	Nonprobable PTSD group ($n = 60$) Mean (SD)	$t(159)$
Factor A: Warmth	5.88 (1.78)	5.90 (1.58)	0.069
Factor B: Reasoning	4.58 (1.62)	4.88 (1.85)	1.036
Factor C: Emotional Stability	3.86 (1.23)	4.78 (1.52)	3.961**
Factor E: Dominance	5.22 (1.65)	5.40 (1.79)	0.606
Factor F: Liveliness	6.13 (1.90)	6.13 (1.67)	−0.018
Factor G: Rule-Consciousness	4.73 (1.56)	5.05 (1.47)	1.289
Factor H: Social Boldness	5.10 (1.99)	5.88 (1.80	2.532*
Factor I: Sensitivity	6.21 (1.54)	5.68 (1.22)	−2.419*
Factor L: Vigilance	6.64 (1.75)	6.41 (1.45)	−.885
Factor M: Abstractedness	6.41 (1.52)	5.91 (1.48)	−2.043
Factor N: Privateness	5.65 (1.62)	5.18 (1.67)	−1.742
Factor O: Apprehension	6.54 (1.65)	5.67 (1.57)	−3.352**
Factor Q1: Openness to Change	5.89 (1.57)	5.97 (1.72)	0.278
Factor Q2: Self-Reliance	6.22 (1.75)	5.62 (1.51)	−2.293*
Factor Q3: Perfectionism	5.10 (1.86)	5.25 (1.62)	0.539
Factor Q4: Tension	6.09 (1.61)	5.80 (1.29)	−1.247

Source: ©2004 Brian Hall.
*indicates $p < .05$; **indicates $p < .01$.

than the nonprobable group (Table 7.4). Figure 7.3 shows the profiles of the probable PTSD subjects, nonprobable PTSD subjects, and controls on the Five Global Personality Factors. Significant differences were found between the probable and nonprobable PTSD groups across personality dimensions.

We predicted that there would be 16PF personality profile differences for individuals experiencing different traumatic events, collapsed across PTSD classifications. For example, 16PF personality profile differences would exist among probable PTSD individuals experiencing *different* traumatic events. We also expected that there would be 16PF personality profile differences between different trauma groups with probable PTSD when compared with controls.

5.2 Comparative Analyses of Five Trauma Groups

One-way analyses of variance (ANOVAs) were conducted to explore the relationship between personality and trauma exposure as measured by the mean scores on the 16 Personality Factors and the Five Global

TABLE 7.4
Results of Independent Samples *t*-tests for Probable PTSD and
Nonprobable PTSD Groups for the Five Global Personality Factors

Personality factors	Probable PTSD group (*n* = 101) Mean (SD)	Nonprobable PTSD group (*n* = 60) Mean (SD)	*t*(159)
Extraversion	5.465 (1.56)	5.945 (1.85)	1.753
Anxiety	7.085 (1.47)	6.198 (1.74)	−3.444*
Tough-Mindedness	4.648 (1.28)	5.020 (1.53)	1.649
Independence	5.565 (1.58)	5.878 (1.49)	1.234
Self-Control	4.580 (1.38)	4.918 (1.40)	1.494

Source: ©2004 Brian Hall.
*indicates $p < .01$.

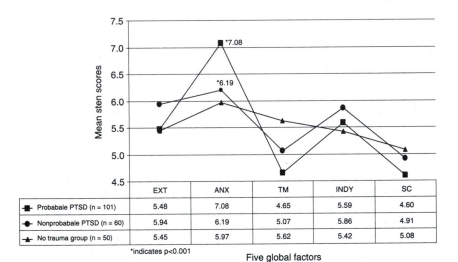

FIGURE 7.3. Profile of mean scores for probable PTSD, nonprobable PTSD, and no-trauma control groups on the five global personality factors. *Source:* ©2004 Brian Hall.

Factors (Extraversion (I), Anxiety (II), Tough-Mindedness (III), Independence (IV), and Self-Control (V)). Participants were classified into five groups: Medical Emergency (ME), Motor Vehicle Accident (MVA), Sexual Assault (SA), the September 11, 2001 Terrorist Attacks (TA), and Violent Assault (VA). It was hypothesized that group differences would be found across dimensions of personality between different trauma groups.

Significant differences were found between the five trauma groups on Factor I (Sensitivity), Factor O (Apprehension), and Global Factor Tough-Mindedness(III). Post-hoc comparisons for the 16 Personality Factors, using the Tukey HSD test, indicated that the mean for Factor I (Sensitivity), was significantly lower for the MVA group than for the TA group. The TA group scored significantly higher on Factor O (Apprehension) than did the VA group (Table 7.5). Post-hoc comparisons for the Five Global Factors, using the Tukey HSD test, indicated that the means for Tough-Mindedness (III) were significantly higher for the MVA group compared with the SA and TA groups (Table 7.6).

5.3 Comparative Analysis of the Five Trauma Groups Versus Control Groups

Independent-sample *t*-tests were conducted to examine differences among the five trauma groups and controls. These analyses examined the differences between those who experienced the traumatic event, irrespective of whether they also had probable PTSD. The 16 Personality Factors and Five Global Factors were used as dependent variables (two separate series of analyses), and the five traumatic event groups served as independent variables. It was hypothesized that individuals in the trauma groups would report different patterns of personality compared with controls.

The ME group was found to have significantly higher scores on Factor M (Abstractedness) and significantly lower scores on Tough-Mindedness (III) compared with controls (Figures 7.4 and 7.5).

Significant mean differences were also found between the MVA group and controls. The MVA group scored significantly higher on Factor B (Reasoning) than controls (Figure 7.6).

The SA group scored significantly higher on Factor A (Warmth), Factor M (Abstractedness), Factor O (Apprehension), and Factor Q1 (Openness to Change); and lower on Factor C (Emotional Stability), Tough-Mindedness (III) and Self-Control (V) compared with controls (Figures 7.7 and 7.8).

Significant mean differences were also found between the TA group and controls. The TA group scored significantly lower on Factor C (Emotional Stability) and Tough-Mindedness (III); and higher on Factor I (Sensitivity), Factor O (Apprehension), and Anxiety (II) compared with controls (Figures 7.9 and 7.10).

In summary, Tables 7.7 and 7.8 show the personality factors for which significant differences were observed among the groups that had been involved in each of the five different types of traumatic event.

TABLE 7.5
Results of ANOVA for Different Traumatic Event Groups on the 16 Personality Factors

Personality factors	Medical emergency (n=21) Mean (SD)	Motor vehicle accident (n=26) Mean (SD)	Sexual assault (n=20) Mean (SD)	Events of 9/11/01 (n=19) Mean (SD)	Violent assault (n=18) Mean (SD)	$F(4,99)$
Factor A: Warmth	5.67 (1.85)	5.85 (1.78)	6.30 (1.30)	6.05 (1.12)	5.94 (1.92)	0.429
Factor B: Reasoning	4.71 (1.67)	5.31 (1.46)	4.35 (1.56)	4.68 (1.94)	4.11 (2.02)	1.537
Factor C: Emotional Stability	4.52 (1.16)	4.69 (1.40)	3.95 (2.03)	3.74 (1.44)	4.39 (1.50)	1.459
Factor E: Dominance	5.10 (1.17)	5.04 (1.63)	5.35 (1.59)	5.00 (1.56)	6.00 (1.94)	1.294
Factor F: Liveliness	6.09 (1.97)	6.46 (1.82)	6.10 (1.86)	5.74 (1.72)	6.72 (1.70)	0.834
Factor G: Rule-Consciousness	4.90 (1.41)	5.46 (1.63)	4.50 (1.50)	4.73 (1.04)	4.66 (1.18)	1.652
Factor H: Social Boldness	5.52 (1.80)	4.92 (1.89)	5.60 (1.98)	5.37 (1.80)	5.94 (1.89)	0.870
Factor I: Sensitivity	5.76 (1.04)	5.65 (1.46)	6.10 (1.33)	6.95 (1.43)	5.78 (1.55)	2.957*
Factor L: Vigilance	6.43 (1.28)	6.50 (1.50)	6.80 (1.96)	6.53 (1.77)	5.833 (1.46)	0.913
Factor M: Abstractedness	6.47 (1.40)	5.34 (1.41)	6.55 (1.53)	6.05 (1.54)	6.00 (1.60)	2.434
Factor N: Privateness	5.62 (1.58)	5.62 (1.13)	5.10 (2.31)	5.32 (1.76)	5.06 (2.04)	0.519
Factor O: Apprehension	5.67 (1.58)	6.08 (1.74)	6.40 (1.93)	7.00 (1.45)	5.39 (1.61)	2.716*
Factor Q1: Openness to Change	6.05 (2.02)	5.00 (1.09)	6.35 (1.56)	5.74 (1.36)	5.78 (1.89)	2.324
Factor Q2: Self-Reliance	5.86 (1.76)	5.85 (1.22)	6.00 (1.97)	6.00 (1.24)	5.39 (1.75)	0.453
Factor Q3: Perfectionism	4.62 (1.68)	5.38 (1.92)	4.85 (1.75)	5.63 (1.25)	5.50 (1.75)	1.336
Factor Q4: Tension	5.67 (1.35)	5.69 (1.46)	5.60 (.88)	6.47 (1.42)	5.67 (1.23)	1.619

Source: ©2004 Brian Hall.
**indicates $p < .05$.

TABLE 7.6
Results of ANOVA for Different Traumatic Event Groups on the Five Global Factors

Personality factors	Medical emergency (n = 21)	Motor vehicle accident (n = 26)	Sexual assault (n = 20)	Events of 9/11/01 (n = 19)	Violent assault (n = 18)	F(4,99)
Extraversion	5.59 (1.83)	5.63 (1.28)	5.91 (1.78)	5.62 (1.42)	6.25 (1.78)	0.581
Anxiety	6.25 (1.45)	6.38 (1.74)	6.86 (1.96)	7.36 (1.59)	6.02 (1.39)	2.030
Tough-Mindedness	4.81 (1.27)	5.70 (1.40)	4.37 (1.43)	4.43 (1.17)	5.03 (1.25)	3.854*
Independence	5.61 (1.39)	5.10 (1.56)	5.96 (1.68)	5.44 (1.29)	6.08 (1.54)	1.512
Self-Control	4.44 (1.30)	5.24 (1.62)	4.36 (1.15)	4.98 (1.22)	4.72 (1.45)	1.619

©2004 Source: Brian Hall.
*indicates $p < 01$.

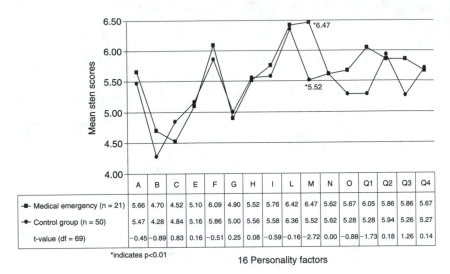

FIGURE 7.4. Profile of mean scores for the medical emergency and no-trauma control groups on the 16 personality factors. *Source:* ©2004 Brian Hall.

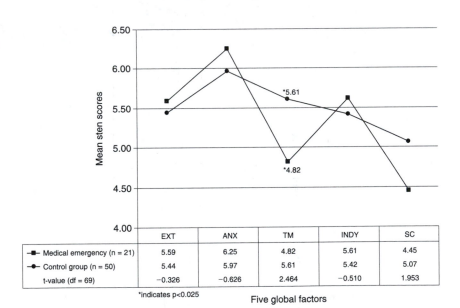

FIGURE 7.5. Profile of mean scores for the medical emergency and no-trauma control groups on the five global personality factors. *Source:* ©2004 Brian Hall.

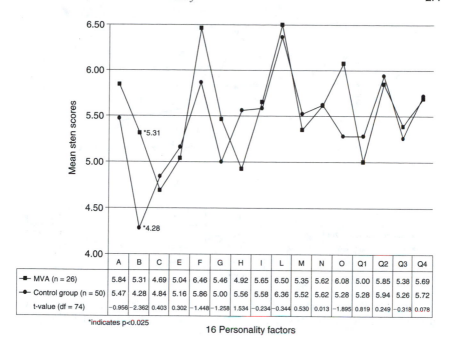

FIGURE 7.6. Profile of mean scores for the motor vehicle accident (MVA) and no-trauma control groups on the 16 personality factors. *Source:* ©2004 Brian Hall.

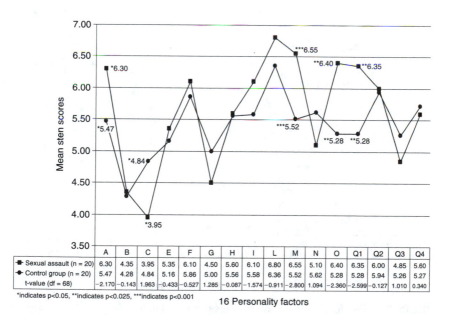

FIGURE 7.7. Profile of mean scores for the sexual assault and no-trauma control groups on the 16 personality factors. *Source:* ©2004 Brian Hall.

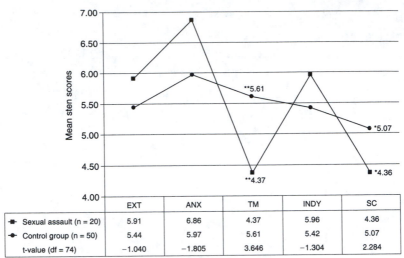

	EXT	ANX	TM	INDY	SC
Sexual assault (n = 20)	5.91	6.86	4.37	5.96	4.36
Control group (n = 50)	5.44	5.97	5.61	5.42	5.07
t-value (df = 74)	−1.040	−1.805	3.646	−1.304	2.284

*indicates p<0.025, **indicates p<0.001

Five global factors

FIGURE 7.8. Profile of mean scores for the sexual assault and no trauma control groups on the five global personality factors. *Source:* ©2004 Brian Hall.

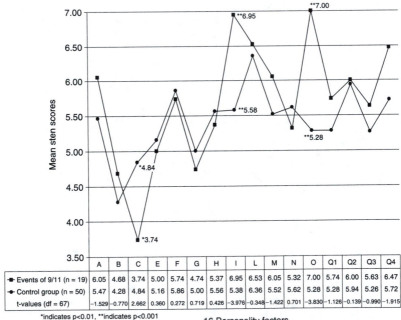

	A	B	C	E	F	G	H	I	L	M	N	O	Q1	Q2	Q3	Q4
Events of 9/11 (n = 19)	6.05	4.68	3.74	5.00	5.74	4.74	5.37	6.95	6.53	6.05	5.32	7.00	5.74	6.00	5.63	6.47
Control group (n = 50)	5.47	4.28	4.84	5.16	5.86	5.00	5.56	5.38	6.36	5.52	5.62	5.28	5.28	5.94	5.26	5.72
t-values (df = 67)	−1.529	−0.770	2.662	0.360	0.272	0.719	0.426	−3.976	−0.348	−1.422	0.701	−3.830	−1.126	−0.139	−0.990	−1.915

*indicates p<0.01, **indicates p<0.001

16 Personality factors

FIGURE 7.9. Profile of mean scores for those involved in the events of September 11, 2001 and the no-trauma control groups on the 16 personality factors. *Source:* ©2004 Brian Hall.

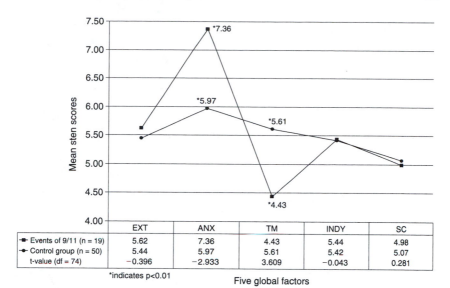

	EXT	ANX	TM	INDY	SC
Events of 9/11 (n = 19)	5.62	7.36	4.43	5.44	4.98
Control group (n = 50)	5.44	5.97	5.61	5.42	5.07
t-value (df = 74)	−0.396	−2.933	3.609	−0.043	0.281

*indicates p<0.01

Five global factors

FIGURE 7.10. Profile of mean scores for those involved in the events of September 11, 2001 and the no-trauma control group on the five global personality factors. *Source:* ©2004 Brian Hall.

5.3a *Comparative Analysis of Participants with Probable PTSD across Five Trauma Groups versus Control Groups*

Independent-sample *t*-tests were conducted to examine differences between those who satisfied the criteria for probable PTSD and experienced exposure to different traumatic events and controls. The 16 Personality Factors and Five Global Factors were dependent variables (two separate series of analyses), and the trauma groups with probable PTSD were used as independent variables. It was hypothesized that individuals in the trauma groups with PTSD would report different patterns of personality compared with controls than would those who experienced the traumatic event without meeting the criteria for probable PTSD.

Using two-tailed independent-sample *t*-tests, no significant mean differences were found between the ME group with probable PTSD and the control group. However, significant mean differences were found between the MVA group with probable PTSD and controls. The MVAMVA group scored significantly higher on Factor B (Reasoning), Factor O (Apprehension), and Factor A (Warmth) compared with controls (Figure 7.11).

TABLE 7.7
Significant Factors for the Five Traumatic Event Groups Compared to the No Trauma Control Group on the 16 Personality Factors

Personality factors	Medical emergency (n = 21)	Motor vehicle accident (n = 26)	Sexual assault (n = 20)	Events of 9/11/01 (n = 19)	Violent assault (n = 18)
Factor A: Warmth	–	–	–	–	–
Factor B: Reasoning	–	X	–	–	–
Factor C: Emotional Stability	–	–	–	XX	–
Factor E: Dominance	–	–	–	–	–
Factor F: Liveliness	–	–	–	–	–
Factor G: Rule-Consciousness	–	–	–	–	–
Factor H: Social Boldness	–	–	–	–	–
Factor I: Sensitivity	–	–	–	XXX	–
Factor L: Vigilance	–	–	–	–	–
Factor M: Abstractedness	XX	–	XX	–	–
Factor N: Privateness	–	–	–	XXX	–
Factor O: Apprehension	–	–	X	–	–
Factor Q1: Openness to Change	–	–	XX	–	–
Factor Q2: Self-Reliance	–	–	–	–	–
Factor Q3: Perfectionism	–	–	–	–	–
Factor Q4: Tension	–	–	–	–	–

Source: 2004 Brian Hall, 2004©
X indicates $p < .05$; XX indicates $p < .01$; XXX indicates $p < .001$; – indicates nonsignificance.

TABLE 7.8
Significant Factors for the Five Traumatic Event Groups Compared with the No Trauma Control Group on the Five Global Personality Factors

Personality factors	Medical emergency (n = 21)	Motor vehicle accident (n = 26)	Sexual assault (n = 20)	Events of 9/11/01 (n = 19)	Violent assault (n = 18)
Extraversion	–	–	–	–	–
Anxiety	–	–	–	XX	–
Tough-Mindedness	X	–	XXX	XXX	–
Independence	–	–	–	–	–
Self-Control	–	–	X	–	–

Source: ©2004 Brian Hall.
X indicates $p < .025$; XX indicates $p < .01$; XXX indicates $p < .001$; – indicates nonsignificance.

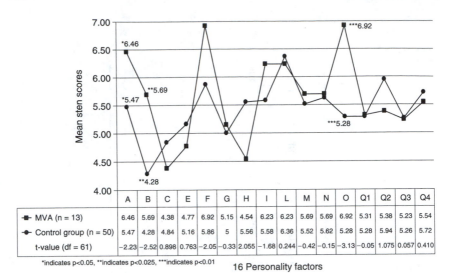

FIGURE 7.11. Profile of mean scores for the motor vehicle accident (MVA) with probable PTSD and the no-trauma control groups on the 16 personality factors. *Source:* ©2004 Brian Hall.

Significant mean differences were found between the SA group with probable PTSD and controls. The SA group scored significantly lower on Factor C (Emotional Stability), Tough-Mindedness (III), and Self Control (V); and higher on Factor O (Apprehension), Factor Q1 (Openness to Change), and Global Factor Anxiety (II) compared with controls (Figures 7.12 and 7.13).

Significant mean differences were found between the TA group with probable PTSD and controls. The TA group scored significantly lower on Factor C (Emotional Stability) and Tough Mindedness (III); and higher on Factor I (Sensitivity), Factor O (Apprehension), and Anxiety (II) (Figures 7.14 and 7.15).

No significant mean differences were found between the VA group and controls.

Tables 7.9 and 7.10 summarize the significant personality factors associated with the trauma groups analyzed in this study.

6 DISCUSSION

The results of our study indicate that the 16PF can be used to identify personality traits associated with PTSD in a nonclinical population. Examining differences between the probable PTSD and the nonprobable

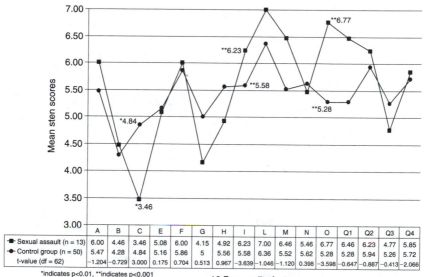

FIGURE 7.12. Profile of mean scores for the sexual assault with probable PTSD and no-trauma control groups on the 16 personality factors. *Source:* ©2004 Brian Hall.

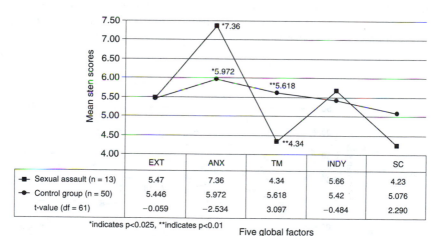

FIGURE 7.13. Profile of mean scores for the sexual assault with probable PTSD and no-trauma control groups on the five global personality factors. *Source:* ©2004 Brian Hall.

PTSD groups, differences were found among the 16 Personality Factors and Five Global Factors. Compared with the nonprobable group, the probable PTSD participants presented themselves as Reactive and Emotionally Unstable (low Factor C), Shy and Threat-Sensitive (low Factor H), Sensitive (high Factor I), Worried and Apprehensive (high Factor O),

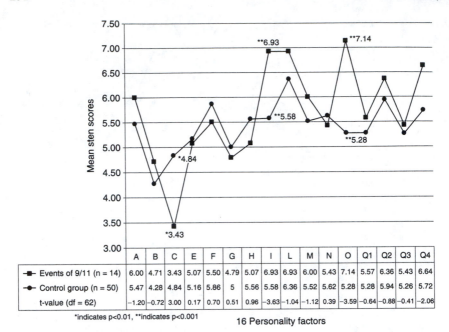

FIGURE 7.14. Profile of mean scores for those involved in the events of September 11, 2001 with probable PTSD and the no-trauma control group on the 16 personality factors. *Source:* ©2004 Brian Hall.

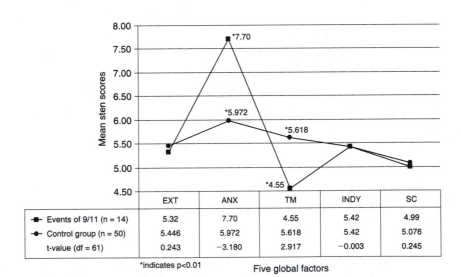

FIGURE 7.15. Profile of mean scores for those involved in the events of September 11, 2001 with probable PTSD and the no-trauma control group on the five global personality factors. *Source:* ©2004 Brian Hall.

TABLE 7.9

Significant Factors for the Five Traumatic Event Groups with Probable PTSD Compared with the No Trauma Control Group on the 16 Personality Factors

Personality factors	Medical emergency (n=9)	Motor vehicle accident (n=13)	Sexual assault (n=14)	Events of 9/11/01 (n=14)	Violent assault (n=13)
Factor A: Warmth	–	X	–	–	–
Factor B: Reasoning	–	XX	–	–	–
Factor C: Emotional Stability	–	–	XX	XXX	–
Factor E: Dominance	–	–	–	–	–
Factor F: Liveliness	–	–	–	–	–
Factor G: Rule-Consciousness	–	–	–	–	–
Factor H: Social Boldness	–	–	–	–	–
Factor I: Sensitivity	–	–	–	XXX	–
Factor L: Vigilance	–	–	–	–	–
Factor M: Abstractedness	–	–	X	–	–
Factor N: Privateness	–	–	–	–	–
Factor O: Apprehension	–	XX	XX	XXX	–
Factor Q1: Openness to Change	–	–	XX	–	–
Factor Q2: Self-Reliance	–	–	–	–	–
Factor Q3: Perfectionism	–	–	–	–	–
Factor Q4: Tension	–	–	–	–	–

Source: ©2004 Brian Hall.

X indicates $p < .05$; XX indicates $p < .01$; XXX indicates $p < .001$; – indicates nonsignificance.

TABLE 7.10
Significant Factors for the Five Traumatic Event Groups with Probable PTSD Compared to the No Trauma Control Group on the Five Global Personality Factors

Personality factors	Medical emergency (n = 9)	Motor vehicle accident (n = 13)	Sexual assault (n = 14)	Events of 9/11/01 (n = 14)	Violent assault (n = 13)
Extraversion	—	—	—	—	—
Anxiety	—	—	X	XX	—
Tough-Mindedness	—	—	XX	XX	—
Independence	—	—	—	—	—
Self-Control	—	—	X	—	—

Source: ©2004 Brian Hall.
X indicates $p < .05$; XX indicates $p < .01$; — indicates nonsignificance.

and Self-Reliant (high Factor Q2). The probable PTSD group reported higher levels of anxiety (high Global Factor Anxiety (II)), being emotionally reactive, untrusting, apprehensive and tense compared with the nonprobable group (Schuerger, 2000; Karson, Karson, & O'Dell 1997).

The differences between the probable PTSD and nonprobable groups on Factors C (Emotional Stability), H (Social Boldness), O (Apprehension), Q2 (Self-Reliance), and Global Factor Anxiety (II), are all consistent with previous studies using the 16PF (Hyer et al., 1990; Kopriva et al., 1993; Wilson & Walker, 1989). However, our study demonstrates differences on Factor I (Sensitivity) not previously reported in the literature. Additionally, we did not find significant differences on Factors A (Warmth), F (Liveliness), G (Rule Consciousness), Q3 (Perfectionism), Factors L (Vigilance), and Q4 (Tension), or on Global Factor Extraversion, in the probable PTSD group, as was previously reported.

The traits differentiating the probable and nonprobable PTSD groups are consistent with the diagnostic symptoms for PTSD. Factor C (Emotional Stability) is a measure of ego-strength and when reported in the negative direction may indicate a diminished capacity to cope with stress, becoming easily upset, and being disconnected from one's feelings (Cattell, 1989). These personality factors correlate with denial of emotions, feeling irritable, and experiencing strained interpersonal relationships which, in turn, may be related to PTSD avoidance symptoms (i.e., PTSD "C" cluster). From a psychodynamic perspective, this trait has been associated with one's ability to mobilize energy to manage stress (Cattell, 1989). Moreover, low levels of Factor H (Social Boldness) reflect shyness and being emotionally cautious. As noted in Chapter 3 and in Figure 7.1, low scores on this personality dimension relate to the avoidance cluster of PTSD, given that such persons have a low tolerance for fear and excessive arousal. They are vigilant and self-protective in regard to places and situations that can evoke anxiety and distress.

Factor I (Sensitivity), when elevated in the positive direction, suggests one who is insecure, has an imaginative inner life, and feels anxious about themselves (Cattell, 1989). Persons who score high on Factor I demonstrate an emotional response style and being attuned to personal vulnerabilities. This trait may be related to the PTSD symptoms due to vulnerability in affective states as a result of their stressful life-events.

High Factor O (Apprehension) is associated with feelings of low self-worth, excessive worry, depression, moodiness, and phobic symptoms. It is also associated with low self-esteem. It is also one of the major indicators on the 16PF of psychological pain (Cattell, 1989). This personality factor also appears associated with the avoidant symptoms of PTSD and negative emotional states, i.e., avoiding the psychological experience of distressing traumatic memories.

Factor Q1 (Openness to Change), is associated with openness to new experiences. Persons with high scores on this factor make frequent environmental changes. In terms of PTSD this factor may also be related to PTSD avoidance symptoms (C cluster), manifested as a need to significantly alter aspects of one's environment following a traumatic experience—for example, moving residence and relocation, geographic isolation, social withdrawal.

When the different trauma groups (those experiencing specific events with and without probable PTSD) were compared with the controls, some personality factors overlapped while others remained dependent on the traumatic event that had been reported. This may reflect the relationship between dispositional factors or more general patterns of adaptation. For example, personality Factor B (Reasoning) was associated with the Motor Vehicle Accident (MVA) group, suggesting possible post-event cognitive alterations. Comparing persons with probable PTSD and the same event, scores on Factors A (high Warmth) and O (high Apprehension) were statistically different from controls. This suggests that probable PTSD may be related to increased levels of affiliation and worry among those experiencing motor vehicle accidents. A similar difference was found for the Sexual Assault (SA) group. Factors M (Abstractedness), O (Apprehension), and Q1 (Openness to Change) and Global Factors Tough-Mindedness (IV) and Self-Control (V) were statistically different compared with controls. However, when probable PTSD was examined, only Factor C (Emotional Stability) and the Global Factor Anxiety (II) were shown to be significantly different between the two groups. This suggests that the effects of the trauma in this group are evidenced by increased emotionality and a lack of ego-strength.

When considering the Terrorist Attack (TA) group, a different pattern emerges. No significant differences were shown between the TA group and the probable PTSD TA group across the personality factors. In both groups, Factors C (Emotional Stability), I (Sensitivity), O (Apprehension), Global Factors Anxiety (II), and Tough-Mindedness (III) remained significantly associated within each group. The lack of difference in profiles between the TA group and the probable PTSD TA group suggests that the events of September 11, 2001 may be qualitatively different from the other trauma categories in relation to personality factors.

The prevalent theme that emerges from the analysis of the TA group is one of emotional instability, empathy, excessive worry, high levels of anxiety, and being especially emotional. Today, the maintenance of anxiety and worry associated with the events of September 11, 2001, is present among many individuals, given the continued exposure to threats associated with terrorism in Iraq, and many parts of the world, especially the perceived threat of terrorist activities in the U.S. and to U.S. interests abroad.

7 CONCLUSION

Taking a broad overview of the significant findings, there is clear evidence for the predictions derived from the Five Factor Model in Chapter 2 (see Table 2.2) and as summarized in Figure 7.2. In comparing the probable PTSD (P-PTSD) with the nonprobable PTSD group (N-PTSD), major differences were found for four of the five FFM factor clusters. In terms of Factor I (Sensitivity), the results from the corresponding 16PF measures indicated that the P-PTSD group showed higher states of anxiety, apprehension, sensitivity, and emotional instability. The P-PTSD group showed introverted features (evidenced by low Social Boldness, Factor H) which can be matched to the Extraversion factor on the FFM. In terms of FFM factor V, C (conscientiousness), the P-PTSD group was higher on self-reliance, which corresponds to the FFM characteristic of self-discipline. Table 7.11 summarizes these results and shows comparisons between the FFM and 16PF for the P-PTSD group and N-PTSD groups.

Table 7.12 presents a summary analysis for the five comparative trauma groups versus controls for the 16PF personality factors, classified by the FFM in terms of predicted changes. As Table 7.12 shows, there were significant differences on eight variables between the five trauma groups and controls. In general, the pattern of results shows higher degrees of anxiety, emotional instability, and apprehension for the trauma groups (FFM, Factor N). Similarly, the trauma group showed decreased Tough-Mindedness, reflecting a lower level of FFM Factor II, E, Assertiveness. However, there were two findings that did not match our predicted outcome for the trauma group. Higher abstractedness (FFM Factor C, Competence) was found for subjects reporting medical emergencies and sexual assaults. Moreover, victims of sexual assault also

---

TABLE 7.11

Differences Between Probable PTSD and Nonprobable PTSD Groups on 16PF Personality Factors, Classified by the FFM

Probable PTSD vs. nonprobable PTSD groups	16PF variable	FFM dimension	Prediction confirmed (?)
Lower emotional stability	C	N (Vulnerability)	Yes
Lower social boldness	H	E (Assertive)	Yes
Higher sensitivity	I	N (Self-conscious)	Yes
Higher apprehension	O	N (Anxiety)	Yes
Higher self-reliance	Q_2	C (Self-discipline)	Yes
Higher anxiety	II	N (Anxiety)	Yes

Source: ©2004 John P. Wilson.

TABLE 7.12
Differences Between Trauma Groups and Controls on 16PF Factors, Classified by the FFM

Trauma group vs. controls 16PF personality factor	16PF factor	FFM dimension	Prediction confirmed (?)
Higher abstractedness (ME/SA)	M	C (Competence)	No
Lower tough-mindedness (ME/TA)	III	E (Assertiveness)	Yes
Higher reasoning (MVA)	B	C (Delineation)	Yes
Higher openness to change (SA)	Q_1	O (Action)	No
Higher apprehension (SA/TA)	O	N (Anxiety)	Yes
Lower emotional stability (TA)	C	N (Vulnerability)	Yes
Lower self-control (SA)	Q_2	C (Self-Discipline)	Yes
Higher anxiety (TA)	II	N (Anxiety)	Yes

Source: ©2004 John P. Wilson.
MVA = motor vehicle accident; ME = medical emergency; SA = sexual assault; TA = terrorist attack; VA = violent assault.

scored higher than controls on Openness to Change, perhaps reflecting a tendency to be open to making changes in life-style to guard against the fear of reoccurrence of another attack.

While there are limitations to the present study (e.g., its cross sectional nature, elevated base rates, threat of Type I error), the results warrant some conclusions in terms of the issues posed in the introduction to this chapter. First, it is important to study personality profiles in normal populations and to examine differences among and between individuals who have experienced traumatic events. Identifying persons with probable PTSD (P-PTSD) versus nonprobable PTSD (N-PTSD) permits comparative analysis and begins to shed light as to how different traumas impact personality functioning. Second, comparative analysis of personality characteristics and profiles for persons who have endured different types of traumatic events is also valuable, highlighting personality changes that may be related to the specific nature of the event (e.g., terrorist attack vs. sexual assault vs. motor vehicle accident). Third, using hypotheses derived from the FFM, it was possible to predict the direction of personality changes. In this study, 12 of 14 predicted changes were substantiated. These findings raise the intriguing possibility that using a personality measure such as the NEO-PI-R it may be possible to predict with even greater precision changes in all 30 subdimensions of the FFM as well as the *interactive effects* among personality variables with a given factor (e.g., Neuroticism) and between factors (e.g., Openness). If so, this would be especially important to understanding the intrapsychic dynamics which underlie these more complex forms of personality traits. Fourth, the results of this study reinforce the need for prospective studies of normal populations to discern the person–environment interactions (Wilson, 1989) in terms of the outcome of exposure to traumatic events that meet the A_1 prime criteria for the diagnosis of PTSD. Prospective and longitudinal studies of personality and subsequent exposure of the participants to naturally occurring traumatic events would do much to clarify the dispositional role of personality traits as risk factors or resilience buffers to powerful life-events at different points in the life-cycle. Knowledge of these effects on personality and epigenetic development would be useful to: (1) clinical treatment approaches; (2) the identification of "at risk" persons; and (3) age and developmental vicissitudes in the nature of human personality as a structural dimension and as a complex set of intrapsychic processes.

REFERENCES

American Psychiatric Association. (1994). *Diagnostic and statistical manual of mental disorders* (4th ed.). Washington, DC: American Psychiatric Association.

Allport, G. W. & Odbert, H. S. (1936). Traitnames. A psycho-lexical study. *Psychological Monographs 47*, 171.

Bennett, P., Owen, R. L., Stavoula, K., & Bisson, J. (2002). Personality, social context and cognitive predictions of PTSD in myocardial infarction patients. *Psychology and Health, 17*, 489–500.

Bernat, J. A., Ronfeldt, H. M., Calhoun, K. S., & Arias, I. (1998). Prevalence of traumatic events and peritraumatic predictors of posttraumatic stress symptoms in a non-clinical sample of college students. *Journal of Traumatic Stress 11*, 645–664.

Blake, D. D., Weathers, F. W., Nagy, L. M., Kaloupek, D. G., Gusman, F. D., Charney, D. S., et al. (1995). The development of a clinician-administrated PTSD scale. *Journal of Traumatic Stress 8*, 75–90.

Block, J. (1971). *Lives through time*. Berkeley, CA: Bancroft Books.

Breslau, N. (1998). Epidemiology of trauma and posttraumatic stress disorder. In R. Yehuda (Ed.), *Psychological trauma* (pp. 1–27). Washington, DC: American Psychiatric Press.

Breslau, N. & Davis, G. C. (1992). Posttraumatic stress disorder in an urban population of young adults: Risk factors of chronicity. *American Journal of Psychiatry, 149*(5), 671–675.

Breslau, N., Davis, G., & Adreski, P. (1995). Risk factors for PTSD related traumatic events: A prospective analysis. *American Journal of Psychiatry, 152*, 529–536.

Bunce, S. C., Larsen, R. J., & Peterson, C. (1993). Life after trauma: Personality and daily life experiences of traumatized people. *Journal of Personality 63*, 165–188.

Butler, L. D. & Wolfner, A. L. (2000). Some characteristics of positive and negative ("most traumatic") event memories in a college sample. *Journal of Trauma and Dissociation 1*, 45–68.

Cattell, R. B., Cattell, A. K., & Cattell, H. B. (1993). *Sixteen personality factor questionnaire* (5th ed.). Champaign, Illinois: Institute for Personality and Ability Testing.

Cattell, H. B. (1989). *The 16PF personality in depth*. Champaign, Illinois: Institute for Personality and Ability Testing.

Cherepon, J. A. & Prinzhorn, B. (1994). Personality assessment inventory (PAI) profiles of adult female abuse survivors. *Assessment 1*, 393–399.

Clark, L. A., Watson, D., & Mineka, S. (1994). Temperament, personality and the mood and anxiety disorders. *Journal of Abnormal Psychology, 103*, 103–116.

Conn, S. R. & Rieke, M. L. (1994). *The 16PF fifth edition technical manual*. Champaign, Illinois: Institute for Personality and Ability Testing.

Davidson, J. R., Kudler, H., & Smith, R. (1987). Personality in chronic PTSD: A study of the Eysenck inventory. *Journal of Anxiety Disorders, 1*, 295–300.

Digman, J. M. (1996). The curious history of the five factor model. In J. S. Wiggins (Ed.), *The five factor model* (pp. 1–21). New York: Guilford Publications.

Felsman, J. K. & Vaillant, G. (1987). Resilient children as adults: A 40-year study. In E. J. Anthony & B. J. Cohen (Eds.), *The invulnerable child* (pp. 284–315). New York: Guilford Publications.

Frye, J. S., & Stockton, R. A. (1982). Discriminant analysis of posttraumatic stress disorder among a group of Vietnam veterans. *American Journal of Psychiatry, 139*(1), 52–56.

Gray, M. J., Litz, B. T., Hsu, J. L., & Lombardo, T. W. (2004). Psychometric properties of the Life Events Checklist. *Assessment* 11, 330–341.

Green, B. L., Wilson, J. P., & Lindy, J. (1985). Conceptualizing post-traumatic stress disorder: A psychosocial framework. In C.R. Figley (Ed.), *Trauma and it's wake: The study and treatment of post-traumatic stress disorders* (Vol. I, pp. 53–69). New York: Brunner/Mazel.

Hall, B. J. (2004). *Life stress and personality correlates of trauma*. Master's Thesis, Cleveland State University, Cleveland, OH.

Harkness, L. L. (1993). Transgenerational transmission of war-related trauma. In J. P. Wilson & B. Raphael (Eds.), *International handbook of traumatic stress syndromes* (pp. 635–643). New York: Plenum Press.

Harkness, L. & Zador, N. (2001). Treatment of PTSD in families and couples. In J. Wilson, M. Friedman, & J. D. Lindy (Eds.), *Treating psychological trauma and PTSD* (pp. 339–340). New York: Guilford Press.

Holeva, V. & Tarrier, N. (2001). Personality and peritraumatic dissociation in the prediction of PTSD in victims of road traffic accidents. *Journal of Psychosomatic Research 51*, 687–692.

Holmes, G. E., Williams, C. L., & Haines, J. (2001). Motor vehicle accident trauma exposure: Personality profiles associated with posttraumatic diagnoses. *Anxiety, Stress, and Coping 14*, 301–313.

Horowitz, M. J., Wilner, N., & Alvarez, W. (1979). Impact of event scale: A measure of subjective stress. *Psychosomatic Medicine 41*, 209–218.

Hyer, L. A. L., Woods, M. G., Boudewyns, P. A., Harrison, W. R., & Tamkin, A. S. (1990). MCMI and 16-PF with Vietnam veterans: Profiles and concurrent validation of MCMI. *Journal of Personality Disorders 4*, 391–401.

Hyer, L. A. L., Braswell, L. C., Albrecht, J. W., Boyd, S., Boudewyns, P. A., & Talbert, F. S. (1994). Relationship of NEO-PI to personality styles and severity of trauma in chronic PTSD victims. *Journal of Clinical Psychology 50*, 699–707.

Iris, I. M., Englehard, M., Marcel, M., van der Hout, A., & Kindt, M. (2003). The relationship between neuroticism, pre-traumatic stress, and post-traumatic stress: A prospective study. *Personality and Individual Differences, 35*, 381–388.

Karson, M., Karson, S., & O'Dell, J. (1997). *16PF interpretation in clinical practice: A guide to the fifth edition*. Champaign, Illinois: Institute for Personality and Ability Testing.

Kelly, B., Raphael, B., Judd, F., Perdices, M., Kernitt, G., Burnett, P., et al. (1998). Post-traumatic stress disorder in response to HIV infection. *General Hospital Psychiatry, 20*, 345–352.

Kessler, R. C., Sonnega, A., Bromet, E., Hughes, M., & Nelson, C. B. (1995). Post-traumatic stress disorder in the national comorbidity survey. *Archives of General Psychiatry 52*, 1048–1063.

Kopriva, R. J., Kiyuna, R. S., & Farr, S. J. (1993). A study of the interactive elements of personality structure and early traumatizing events in alcohol related support group members. *Journal of Social Behavior and Personality 8*, 437–460.

Lauterbach, D. & Vrana, S. R. (2001). The relationship among personality variables, exposure to traumatic events, and severity of posttraumatic stress symptoms. *Journal of Traumatic Stress 14*, 29–45.

Lee, K. A., Vaillant, G. E., Torrey, W., & Elder, G. K. (1995). A 50-year prospective study of the psychological sequela of World War II. *American Journal of Psychiatry, 152*, 516–523.

McCrae, R. R. & Costa, P. T. (2003). *Personality in adulthood: A five factor item perspective.* New York: Guilford Publications.

Miller, M. W. (2003). Personality and the etiology and expression of PTSD: A three factor model perspective. *Clinical Science, 10*, 373–393.

Miller, M. W. (2004). Personality and the development and expression of PTSD. *PTSD Research Quarterly, 15*, 1–7.

Miller, M. W., Grief, J. L., & Smith, A. (2003). Multidimensional personality questionnaire profiles of veterans with traumatic combat exposure: Externalizing and internalizing subtypes. *Psychological Assessment, 15*, 205–215.

Moran, C. C. & Shakespeare-Finch, J. (2003). A trait approach to post trauma vulnerability and growth. In D. Paton, L. M. Smith, & J. M. Violanti (Eds.), *Promoting capabilities to manage posttraumatic stress: Perspectives on resilience* (pp. 27–42). Springfield, IL: Charles C. Thomas.

Nightengale, J. & Williams, R. M. (2000). Attitudes to emotional expressions and personality in predicting PTSD. *British Journal of Clinical Psychology, 39*, 243–254.

Paris, J. (2000). Predispositions, personality traits, and posttraumatic stress disorder. *Harvard Review of Psychiatry 8*, 175–183.

Quirk, S. W., Christiansen, N. D., Wagner, S. H., & McNulty, J. L. (2003). On the usefulness of measures of normal personality for clinical assessment. *Psychological Assessment 15*, 311–325.

Richman, H. & Freuh, C. (1997). Personality and PTSD. II. Personality assessment of PTD-diagnosed Vietnam veterans using the Cloninger tridimensional personality questionnaire (TPQ). *Depression and Anxiety, 6*, 70–77.

Saucier, G. & Goldberg, L. R. (1996). The language of personality: Lexical perspectives on the five factor model. In J. S. Wiggins (Ed.), *The five factor model of personality* (pp. 21–51). New York: Guilford Publications.

Schnurr, P. & Vielhauer, M. (1999). Personality as a risk factor for PTSD. In R. Yehuda (Ed.), *Risk factors for posttraumatic stress disorder* (pp. 191–222). Washington, DC: American Psychiatric Press.

Schuerger, J. M. (2000). The sixteen personality factor questionnaire (16PF). In J. C. Watkins, & V. L. Campbell (Eds.), *Testing and assessment in counseling practice* (pp. 73–110). HIllsdale, NJ: Lawrence Erlbaum.

Solomon, Z, Mikulincer, M.M & Avitzu, E. (1998). Coping, locus of control, social support, and combat-related posttraumatic stress disorder: A prospective study. *Journal of Personality and Social Psychology, 55*, 279–285.

Talbert, F., Braswell, L. C., Albrecht, J. W., Hyer, L., & Boudewyns, P. A. (1993). PI profiles in PTSD as a function of trauma. *Journal of Clinical Psychology, 49*, 663–669.

Trull, T. J. & Sher, K. J. (1994). Relationship between the five-factor model of personality and Axis I disorders in a nonclinical sample. *Journal of Abnormal Psychology 103*, 350–360.

Vaillant, G. (1978). *Adaptation to life.* Massachusetts: Little Brown.

Weiss, D. S. & Marmar, C. R. (1997). The impact of event scale–revised. In J. P. Wilson & T. M. Keane (Eds.), *Assessing psychological trauma and PTSD* (pp. 399–411). New York: The Guilford Press.

Weiss, D. S., Marmar, C. R., Metzler, T. J., & Ronfeldt, H. M. (1995, June). Predicting symptomatic distress in emergency services personnel. *Journal of Consulting and Clinical Psychology, 63*(3), pp. 361–368.

Weiss, D. S. (2004). The impact of event scale-revised. In J. P. Wilson & T. M. Keane (Eds.), *Assessing psychological trauma and PTSD,* (2nd ed., pp. 169–189). New York: The Guilford Press.

Wilson, J. P. (1989). Trauma, transformation and healing: An integrative approach to theory, research and posttraumatic theory. New York: Brunner/Mazel.

Wilson, J. P. (2004). Broken spirits. In J. P. Wilson & B. Drozdek (Eds.), *Broken spirits: The treatment of traumatized asylum seekers, refugees and war and torture victims* (pp. 141–173). New York: Brunner-Routledge.

Wilson, J. P., Friedman, M. J., & Lindy, J. D. (2001). An overview of clinial consideration and principles in the treatment of PTSD. In J. P. Wilson, M. J. Friedman & J. D. Lindy (Eds.), *Treating psychological trauma and PTSD* (Ch. 3., pp. 59–94). New York: Guilford Press.

Wilson, J. P. & Keane, T. M. (2004). *Assessing psychological trauma and PTSD* (2nd Edition). New York: Guilford Publications.

Wilson, J. P. & Walker, A. J. (1989). In the arms of justice. In J. P. Wilson (Ed.), *Trauma, transformation, and healing: An integrative approach to theory, research, and post-traumatic therapy* (pp. 217–260). New York: Brunner/Mazel.

Wonderlich, S. A., Crosby, R. D., Mitchell, J. E., Thompson, K. M., Smyth, J. M., Redlin, J., et al. (2001). Sexual trauma and personality: Developmental vulnerability and additive effects. *Journal of Personality Disorders 15,* 496–504.

8

Mutative Transference and the Restoration of the Posttraumatic Self

JACOB D. LINDY

I procured me a Triangular glass-Prisme, to try therewith the celebrated Phenomena of Colors. And in order thereto having darkened my chamber, and made a small hole in my window-shuts, to let in a convenient quantity of the Suns light, I placed my Prisme at its entrance, that it might be thereby refracted to the opposite wall. It was at first a very pleasing divertissement to view the intense colors produced thereby.

Isaac Newton

1 THEORETICAL BACKGROUND

1.1 History of Mutative Transference in Psychoanalytic Theory

Major psychoanalytic theorists, such as Sigmund Freud (1923) and James Strachey (1934), Melanie Klein (1957) and Otto Kernberg (1971), Heinz Kohut (1966) and Anna and Paul Ornstein (1985), Weiss and Sampson (1986) have based their models of psychic structure on the transferences they and their colleagues observed. Working closely over many years, *especially with patients in a particular range of psychopathology,* each described carefully the contours of their patients' neurotic, narcissistic, and borderline problems as they impinged on the doctor–patient relationship. The transferences they describe are of two types: negative transferences which vividly repeat the pathogenic problems of the past onto the present circumstances of the doctor–patient relationship and, more pertinent for this chapter, the positive, "curative" or mutative transferences which when stable enough over time fill in missing, damaged, or distorted elements in psychic structure so that enduring therapeutic change can occur. The positive or mutative transference acts as a hold so that the repetitions of pathology onto the present doctor–patient relationship can be withstood without the familiar negative interaction of self and other which have characterized pathogenic relationships in the past and in the external present; in its place, the therapist offers containment, empathy, interpretation, and the time and safety in which the patient can work through the meanings and applications of insights related to the pathogenic problems.

In specifying the details of these positive or mutative transferences, these major theorists define specific healing functions of the therapeutic relationship, as applied especially to patients in the range of pathology within which they are working. These elements then constitute the unique silent components in the therapist's bearing that facilitate cure especially for patients in that diagnostic category. They provide the substance for modeling, identification, and internalization Such structural conceptualizations have been most useful to clinicians, because they offer an orienting point, a specifically therapeutic attitude, position, and technique. When such a mutative transference is in place, the patient better tolerates the inherent frustrations in the treatment situation and in his or her external life-circumstances and works more effectively with the interpretations designed to master them. When the curative transference becomes inadvertently disrupted, this smoother work abruptly stops, but even such derailments in the presence of the theory give clinicians a roadmap to better understand why regression has occurred and why some of their interventions were, at that moment, off the mark. Recognizing the temporary destabilizing of such positive transferences, and understanding which elements in the patient's experience of the clinician have gone awry, often allows the clinician a range of subsequent interventions and behaviors to help get the treatment back on track.

"Curative" or "mutative" transferences in this sense are necessary components within the treatment relationship affording the patient new opportunities to grapple with healthier versions of pathogenically damaged structures than the ones which exist in themselves or object choices currently, or in themselves or the objects of early childhood. When the classically neurotic patient expresses guilt in the transference by assuming the analyst will be critical of him for competing, Strachey (1934) argues that it is the patient's engaging over time with the analyst's relatively benign superego (the mutative transference), which allows him or her, after interpretation, to see the neurotic fantasy as a distortion, and in this way the patient can renegotiate the tension between his or her drives and harsh superego from childhood. When patients with narcissistic personality disorder assume that the therapist will humiliate them for revealing a grandiose wish, Kohut (1966) argues that it is the ongoing capacity of the analyst's taking on the empathic gleam in the mother's eye, the instituting of the stabilizing (and mutative) mirror transference, which permits patients to renegotiate through interpretation the deficits in development and ultimate taming and maturation of their grandiose selves. Similarly it is the analyst's willingness to accept without challenge the patients' need to idealize him or her that allows patients the room to develop and work with a stable (and curative or mutative) idealizing transference. With this backdrop, when the patient correctly identifies flaws in the analyst, the traumatizing de-idealization of childhood has the potential for transformation. More optimal frustration of idealization in the treatment relationship, accompanied by interpretation, permit the growth of healthy ideals, values, and ambition.

Winnicott (1963) and Mahler (1972) worked with adults and children who had failed to negotiate the separation individuation stages of childhood. In order to accomplish their goal of differentiation, they found that their patients needed them to provide a holding and containing environment, one which would tolerate the expression of regressive infantile hostility toward them (wishes, for example, that the analyst be hurt or die) without crumbling or retaliating. The curative space between patient and therapist becomes a play space where the dangerous emotional risks of childhood can be replayed on safer ground. Klein's work with psychotic children (1957) and Kernberg's with borderline adults (1971) led them to appreciate the value of the firm and clearly differentiated analyst, one with self-knowledge who maintained clear predictable boundaries between patient and therapist, one who could understand projective identification and splitting without getting caught up in it, offering interpretive understanding rather than retaliatory attacks. When such a patient threatens the therapist that frustrating their wishes to attach will "draw blood", it is the presence of those firm boundaries, which enables sufficient safety for the interpretations and working through of separation and individuation to take hold.

Weiss and Sampson (1986) declare that it is the therapist's foremost task to pass a series of unconscious tests which their patients direct at them, and having done so, to encourage the patient's curiosity and boldness in exploring the roots of such wishes (mutative transference). On the other hand, giving in to the patient's demands, for example to extend the hour or reduce the fee, may reproduce the pathogenic pathology of childhood (negative transference); whereas being able to withstand pressures to comply with demands by their patients to stretch the therapeutic frame may indeed pass the test. By behaving so as to maintain reasonable limits, acceptingly yet curiously, not succumbing to these repetitive responses from childhood figures, the analyst in fact passes the unconscious test set by the patient and permits integration of understanding, becoming a new figure in the present who is cooperating in the patient's wish to master the past pathological pattern. Paul and Anna Ornstein (1985) argue that the patient enters therapy with a specific "curative fantasy" (or positive mutative transference). Thus the major task for the therapist is to diagnose or read the unconscious plan of the patient for recovery and to behave in a manner relatively consistent with the patient's curative fantasy.

For each theorist, different aspects of the silent components in the therapist's posture (a nonjudgmental superego, the gleam in the therapist's eye, the firmness of the therapist's management of boundaries) make huge differences for those individuals with pathology in a given spectrum of illnesses. The models these theorists have offered us give us the opportunity to evaluate a given treatment chronologically to determine the presence or absence of these curative or mutative positive transferences and thereby help us understand the peaks and valleys of our work.

Have we, in the field of posttraumatic stress, accumulated sufficient experience in working with the positive and negative transferences of patients with posttraumatic stress disorder (PTSD), to describe in some detail the contours of positive and negative transferences which characterize treatments with patients with PTSD? If so, what does the curative or mutative transference look like? Is it stable throughout treatment or does it take different forms depending on the nature of the work? How does it act to stabilize the treatment and to give the kind of backdrop which allows interpretation of negative transference to be effective? In this chapter, I shall be arguing that we know a great deal about these transferences. They are in important ways different from those of the classical neurotic, the narcissistic personality disorder, and the borderline patient. Further, the borrowing—lock, stock, and barrel—of theoretical constructs from work based on transference phenomena with other patient populations is misleading, and at times not helpful to the clinician on the line treating the survivor with PTSD.

Trauma ruptures structure; it does not simply set elements of the ego into conflict with each other as in neuroses, nor reveal deficits in self as in the narcissistic pathologies, nor induces regressive ego mechanisms such as projective identification and splitting as in borderline pathology. The ruptures appear in ego functions such as perception and affect regulation, and in self-functions such as self-soothing, positive narcissistic balance, identity, and continuity. Unconscious psychic mechanisms attempt to bridge this ruptured structure even as the mind tries to cope with continuing intrusive imagery: emergency defenses such as denial, disavowal, and dissociation, and altered posttraumatic self configurations form. Chronically, these altered ego and self states evoke new patterns of object relations, leading to a more or less stable but allostatic system. Resultant identity is a far cry from the ego and self structure which preceded trauma.

The language of trauma transference, by definition, should differ from the language derived from the neurotic, narcissistic, and borderline patient because trauma, as an etiological agent in structural change, may occur anywhere in the life-cycle; it is not limited to the years of early childhood; and as a corollary, the clinical language of transference in PTSD should not be confused with the language of damaged psychic structure whose origins are necessarily infantile.

At the end of the chapter I shall review these two issues in more detail, but first we should ask: What is the nature of the restoration of function in PTSD as a natural phenomenon and what mutative or positive transference in the treatment of PTSD parallel these natural forces?

While the dimensions and characteristics of the self as they relate to the many posttraumatic states considered in this book are broadly based (engineering cohesiveness, psychoanalytic psychology of narcissism, other psychologies of self including spiritual ones), we are limiting the field of investigation in this chapter to concepts of self that arise in reported spontaneous improvements in individuals with diagnosed PTSD and in successful reported therapeutic transferences with patients with PTSD. We further limit the range of our considerations here to types of transferences which seem to relate specifically to restoration of the posttraumatic self as opposed to other injuries to self. As such the reported paths of spontaneous recovery and mutative transferences are narrower than the larger domain of possible ones.

2 THREE PATHS TO SPONTANEOUS RESTORATION OF SELF IN PTSD

We do not yet know enough about the physiological and psychosocial conditions under which spontaneous restoration of function in survivors afflicted with PTSD occurs—the natural history, as it were, of recovery from the disorder. Were we to have more data on this, perhaps we could deduce how certain elements of psychopathology are repaired, how movement along certain spontaneous pathways would facilitate recovery, and how certain processing mechanisms might define a given path. Then we could ask of the clinical situation: Do such mechanisms and pathways afford themselves to the patient and to the patient–therapist matrix, and might understanding of these pathways contribute to a better understanding of how the doctor–patient relationship works in PTSD? Such an orientation might help us in better aligning the survivor's positive or mutative transference wishes with the treatment experience itself.

In this section I shall present brief case studies on survivors with PTSD whose improvements seemed to occur largely outside the clinical situation. In the course of our work we came upon these survivors in several ways: they are nontreatment subjects in various trauma populations under study, treatment cases reported by us and others in the literature whose course was strongly related to psychosocial interventions other than the therapist's, and patients in psychoanalysis whose traumas had been unknown to the analyst and whose improvement seemed to occur independent of a clinical focus on them.

2.1 The First Spontaneous Path: Sequestering

Louise was a subject in a 20 year follow-up of children who had experienced the Buffalo Creek Dam Collapse. She was 12 at the time of the disaster and 32 at follow-up. Extensive psychiatric interviews had been carried out in her temporary home soon after the flood, and the data collated with others in her family. She had signs and symptoms of PTSD. In addition there was a particularly gruesome detail of her experience: the traumatic image of a truncated body of a mud-encrusted infant which she had seen and reacted to while going up the mountain to safety. When examined two decades later she was essentially clear of symptoms and signs of PTSD. At the time of her follow-up she initially had no memory of the traumatic detail above. She was pleased to see the interviewer who reminded her of those who had come to the valley in the aftermath of the flood and helped her become aware of a wider world than her immediate hollow. She believed these contacts encouraged her to think of living outside the valley as an adult. She narrated the events of the flood, recalling the supportive roles that her grandmother and uncle had taken during the hurried evacuation from the valley as the waters rose. At the time, she was in a cast from a broken ankle and needed to be carried up the mountainside. Upon rejoining her other family members her grandmother had insisted that everyone discuss what had happened in the flood, how it had started, what its consequences had been, and how and why they were now safe. She then explained that all the cousins would be living together in another valley during the period in which they would be rebuilding their homes. Louise narrated this in a positive tone, happy to share the story of her experience, without affectively reliving the trauma. The story of her broken ankle, the cast, and her being carried up the mountain by her uncle was familiar and comfortable. However, when, while following the directions of the follow-up protocol she drew a picture of the flood, as she had done in her initial interview, she spontaneously recognized an unsettling feeling. It came over her as she drew her location at a particular spot coming up the mountain. As she ground her pen onto the paper, she became agitated, recalling coming in contact with the blanket her uncle had used in carrying her up the mountain. At the time of the exposure to the gruesome traumatic image, her uncle handed her to her grandmother as he examined and picked up the dead infant. Grandmother then shielded her from the gruesome sight, turning her head away and shielding her with the blanket. Louise had successfully sequestered and suppressed her trauma using a variety of basic ego defenses such as condensation, displacement and symbolization.

It was as if Louise had built an unconscious filter protecting herself against reminders of the trauma. Rather than flashbacks of the anxiety of the flood and the grotesqueness of the image, she experienced only a vague somatic discomfort as if her face was coming in contact with a particular type of rough wool. Only at the end of the 20-year follow-up interview, with the sensory-laden act of drawing the picture of the trauma did the traumatic image reappear. Sequestering, for Louise, was a supportive-suppressive activity, that is, a highly supportive emotional presence acted in concert with internal mechanisms to shield her from her traumatic memory. Many distressing parts of the experience, danger to her own life, loss of friends and relatives, months of displacement in temporary quarters, fright associated with rain and water, were condensed into a single grotesque image; and that in turn was literally and figuratively covered by a loving blanket, discomfort registering only in its rough texture. Her grandmother's efforts acted like the shutter on a lens, keeping out traumatic image.

Such a case report is consistent with less successful but similarly structured sequestration which Lenore Terr (1994) describes in forensic patients and study subjects who long after childhood trauma experience a breakthrough of previously sequestered traumatic memory. For example, her subject, Gary, for many years, when he felt he just could not go further, described himself being "up against a cold dark wall." He later understood that this somatic condensation actually sequestered the repressed traumatic childhood memory of being locked in the refrigerator by his mother. Additionally Gary had been ominously intrigued with a silvery reflective light which turned out to be the condensation of another memory of being nearly drowned by his mother in an irrigation ditch.

In sequestration, it is as though the mind pulls the blinds over reality. Emergency defense operations and the energy necessary to keep them in place serve the purpose of disbelief, reassuring the survivor that for practical purposes the world is essentially safe and unchanged; the trauma is as if it were only a dream. Trauma, better left forgotten, caused and continues to cause some distress but one can readapt to this now-changed world as though it is as rational or as irrational as it has always been. Trauma, through disavowal, has hopefully become relegated to the arena of inattention.

For Louise, her psychosocial environment helped her create an alternative view of the trauma, one that was under control, and hidden by laughter and anticipated fun with her cousins—indeed, the affects with which she greeted the follow-up interviewer many years later. The dominant metaphor of the sequestering process is sensory and in this case visual and tactile. Because of a potential tear in the stimulus barrier caused by the trauma, light threatens to break through not as a single manageable perception, but as a force which is too bright, and therefore overwhelming. It cannot be thought about and coped with appropriately in the current circumstances. The light source somehow needs additional filtering or shielding functions, in Louise's case amply picked up by her sensitive grandmother and uncle. Here the survivor needs help at the site of perceptual filtration.

I have earlier used the term "trauma membrane" to speak of this function in terms of biological metaphor, i.e., an organically formed protective barrier. We offer here another metaphor to grasp the problem of limiting traumatic overstimulation and the role of the therapist in it. This metaphor is to invoke Sir Isaac Newton's famous experiment on the nature of light in which he first had to limit the light to a single beam or source to enter a room, a metaphor which we shall expand below otherwise it would not lend itself to an examination of its content.

2.2 The Second Spontaneous Path, Metabolizing (Type 1): Finding the Phrase that Fits

Laurie Harkness and Noka Zador (Wilson, Friedman, & Lindy, 2001) describe a traumatized Vietnam War veteran, part of a school-family intervention study, among whose injuries was the "loss" of one eye. Bart's 4-year-old daughter had alarmed her nursery school teacher by spending inordinate time crawling under the furniture. At a conference with the teacher and parents the child clarified that she was looking for her daddy's missing eye from Vietnam, so she could give it to him. When the father heard his daughter's words "looking for daddy's lost eye" in their concrete expression, he also glimpsed the spontaneous expression of empathy which the child showed for him, and he was moved to tears. While she was concretely looking for a lost eye/marble, her empathic tone pierced her father's alienation in a way that adult efforts had failed to do. He came to understand how the painful nature of his irritability came across to others when emotions from the day overwhelmed him and he complained of his "lost" eye. He also understood via his daughter's game, some of the symbolic meanings of his lost vision, hopes, capacity to see the future, of his struggle over looking or not looking when traumatic memory of his war experience intruded. He also saw how much his small daughter and indeed his whole immediate family loved him and wanted to help. The child's play and her innocent words gave shape to a sequence which he recognized in his own life: hard work followed seemingly inevitably by trauma, loss, pain and the search for restoration. While the sequence had its traumatic origin in Vietnam in its residual form, the sequence encapsulated in the phrase, "I'm looking for daddy's lost eye" became a crucial organizer for how he was living or rather not living his everyday life. The phrase seemed to metabolize trauma into more manageable working segments and augmented significant recovery.

2.2.1 Metabolizing (Type 2): Finding a Parallel but Mastered Childhood Experience

Maggie, was interviewed as part of an emergency room study of survivors of rape, and followed up clinically several months later. Maggie, 28 years old at the time, was jogging on a city street deserted because of rain. Her assailant tripped her, attacked and beat her (breaking her jaw), threw her to the ground, dragged her away from the street, threatened to maim her with a broken bottle, and raped her. Considering herself well trained in the martial arts, she was nonetheless, over-whelmed, and dangerously assaulted by her rapist. Her instinct as a fighter only worsened her beating, and the brutality of the rape. PTSD was marked. At 6 months she was concerned with protracted symptoms, especially episodes of feeling over-whelmed, and sought a therapist associated with the study. Over several weeks her dreams took a dramatic turn. Initially, the dreams were exact replications of her being forced to the ground and being overwhelmed physically in the rape situation. Then, without any clear provocation by the follow-up clinician, the dreams changed. Now she was on the floor of her childhood apartment growing up; she was struggling with her older brothers with whom she was wrestling, but unable to subdue them. Father watched the sometimes brutal wrestling matches without intervening on her behalf, as if to say that life is often unfair and you have to make the best of it. After her rape her fiancé was as understanding as he could be, as was the male follow-up therapist, while she complained that neither was helpful enough nor in the right way. The term "unfair wrestling match" came to capture much of her rape experience.

Spontaneously, she began speaking of the tensions in her household of child-hood, in which being female exposed one to physical danger but required active confrontation rather than passivity. She experienced the rape now as some-thing psychologically familiar, rather than totally alien from her life experience. She had survived her brothers' power in childhood; perhaps she could now survive the trauma. Trauma now fell intrapsychically along the same alignment as her childhood conflicts around favored stronger brothers winning father's allegiance while mother looked on helplessly. But this was now familiar ground which she felt she had mastered. Gradually, the rape lost much of its ongoing traumatizing impact and could be subsumed under a variety of experiences involving struggles with men, conflicts which she had integrated in an earlier treatment. She was metabolizing the trauma. Not only did symptoms decrease, but she now found renewed energy which she directed into forming a women's running group which promoted women running together as a prevention against such attacks. She knew she had to continue to work hard, to refuse to give in to passivity, and seize initiative herself—as in representing the new running group's contact with community organizations.

When trauma aligns itself with earlier childhood anxieties *which have been to some extent mastered*, it may be metabolized by moving from the vertical split of disavowal to the horizontal split of neurotic conflict. Helplessness in the presence of unfair violence in Maggie's case converted the present trauma to a past pattern where it could be metabolized like other neurotic conflicts. (Note: see the case of Brick later, to illustrate overlapping adult and childhood trauma where there has been no mastery of the earlier trauma.)

In both forms of spontaneous metabolizing, the dominant instrument of the metabolizing path is verbal: a particular word or phrase like "looking for daddy's lost eye" or "I'm losing the unfair wrestling match" permits the breaking down of the overwhelming into ordered and usable segments. The ordering is sequential, it is causal, it explains catastrophic physical and biochemical workings, and it is psychological with both conscious and unconscious components. Finally, it is characteristic of these fortuitous words or phrases that the survivor hears them empathically.

It is useful here to return for a moment to the metaphor of Newton's light experiment. After he had narrowed his lens to a single point of light entering his experimental space, Newton positioned a prism so that the poorly understood white light could be broken down into a distinct sequence or bands of color. For Maggie it was as if the phrase "unfair wrestling match" functioned as a prism which clarified into distinct bands of color the complex and overly condensed affects she was feeling: the unfairness of the attack, frustration that even with all the practice she had endured her strength would not defeat her accoster, the pain and mortification that defeat and bodily intrusion occurred anyhow, and the shame until she could avenge her indignation. With the use of this "prism" she could align the sequence of condensed affects in a sequential psychological manner.

The causal sequence in self and others which is uncovered as the metabolizing occurs is both conscious/rational and unconscious/ irrational. Both paths are present. The world is not so benevolent, nor the trauma not so disavowed, as in sequestration, but then again the forces necessary to explain the causal sequence in the trauma, while including humankind's most primitive and denied ones, are of the same quality as they have always been.

2.3 The Third Spontaneous Pathway: Redefining

Mike, a 19-year-old who was seen as part of a community outreach trauma project, saw his best friend, Joe, jump into a small lighted (and electrified) pond at night at a public park, where, despite being a good swimmer, Joe struggled in the water and drowned. As Mike saw his friend writhing he jumped in to help. Almost as immediately he allowed himself to be pulled out of the pool, only then aware that Joe had been electrocuted and he badly shocked. In his posttraumatic dreams, his drowned friend Joe, who had been horsing around on the bridge over the park pond before he fell, was clearly waving to him under the water in a gesture of asking for help. In the dream Mike became panic-stricken at his own state under the water, leading him to reject his friend's plea for help and reach for safety for himself. He awoke from traumatic nightmares amazed that he was alive, but with unremitting guilt for his self-preservative behavior which he saw as self-centered. Later, after meeting with his pastor, this repetitive dream underwent a spontaneous transformation. In the new dream he recognized in Joe's gesture a signal, understanding that he (Joe) was about to die, and the hand movement now indicated to Mike the instruction to save his own life from the dangerous water. Mike had transformed and redefined Joe's troubling gesture: originally a guilt-invoking trauma symbol (help me), it was now a new sign instructing him that he must exit the life-endangering water immediately, that his life had special meaning, and that his friend had given him a symbolic command: "leave and live."

When a trauma gains positive redefinition, elements in the trauma experience itself transform from indicators of personal failure to symbols of personal meaning in survival. Behaviors within the trauma are placed in a new context which manages paradox, forgives guilt, ameliorates blame and revenge; trauma elements now accentuate the significance of and direction for new life. Redefinition is an existential, philosophical, spiritual activity which connects the pretrauma self with the posttraumatic self.

With redefining and myth formation, there is an effort to explain fundamental paradoxes in how the universe works. Mike's world had become chaos; with his friend's death and his inability to save him, it had turned against the stars (disaster). An individual myth, in this case a signal from the Almighty constructed jointly by his pastor and himself, would take these forces into account and lead the survivor to new ground onto which myth now narrates the story of survival.

Here Mike spontaneously sought a wise person; a person holding a repository of personal, group, and cultural mythology; a believer in the value of new perspectives—in this case his family pastor.

With redefining and myth formation, there is an effort to explain in new and often spiritual ways, the fundamental paradoxes in how the universe works. It is chaos which is primal, it is that which is against the stars (disaster) which is now fundamental. The new myth must take these forces into account and lead the survivor to new ground on which myth now narrates a new story of survival.

3 THREE MUTATIVE TRANSFERENCES IN PTSD

Case reports of spontaneous restoration of function, occurring external to clear interventions within a treatment situation, suggest that psychopathology in three spheres—perceptual, affect processing, and symbolic meaning—seems capable of repair and restoration under certain psychosocial circumstances. We have termed these paths sequestering, metabolizing, and redefining. Perhaps similar pathways exist in treatment. When silently present in the therapist–survivor relationship, certain reparative and restorative work goes on unimpeded. Such a balance of needed and provided functions constitutes the positive, mutative, or curative transferences in the psychoanalytic psychotherapy of PTSD. Linking them to their nontreatment analogues, we are terming these three positive transferences: the *perception-sequestering or lens transference* which helps create safety by filtering, shuttering, or refracting the intrusive light of trauma; the *metabolizing or prism transference*, which breaks down the white light of overwhelming traumatic affect into discrete, empathically understood, and causally related steps; and the redefining, *existential or mythic transference*, which establishes insight into the continuity of self in a fundamentally changed universe. Here, the survivor projects necessary, curative attributes onto the therapist–survivor matrix, depending on the stage and focus of the treatment.

The three transference configurations become stabilizing axes in the treatment; such that the therapist may orient his or her action in alignment with the dominant transference, coming to recognize its presence or sudden absence. The names of these more or less stable transferences are intended to invoke the image of Isaac Newton's experiment on the properties of light such that the first step sequesters the light to a manageable dose, the second refracts the light into colors which arrange themselves in a lawful manner, and the third uses that same light in a transcendental way to establish meaning. In the sections below we will discuss these three positive or mutative transferences in PTSD, examining what tends to stabilize them, and what may interfere with their stable functioning. In the clinical vignettes we wish to illustrate how the particular transference works, how misalignments in the transference–countertransference matrix cause derailments in the mutative transference, and how the therapist may realign the therapy once an understanding of the difficulty is clear.

3.1 The Lens Transference: Restoring Perception

In the perceptual or lens transference, the therapist maintains a position as though alongside the damaged stimulus barrier of the survivor. The therapist is asked to fill in missing, damaged, or distorted perceptual functions. In response to the survivor's requests, the therapist tries to shield, protect, refract, filter, buffer, and dose traumatic stimuli. Interactive tensions exist where the survivor oscillates between withholding and asking, and where the therapist hesitates to clarify distortion and then does so. Such tensions are inevitably about the safety or lack of safety to share thoughts and feelings within the confines of the treatment space. The process, like the opening phase in any form of psychotherapy is about trust, but the area of content is, uniquely, about perception. The therapist's job during the period of the mutative lens transference is to stay attuned to the dialectic within the survivor regarding this simple question: Is too little or too much (of trauma stimulus) getting through?

When the follow-up clinician asked Vince, a Vietnam War veteran whose severe PTSD had improved notably as a result of his therapy, in what ways the treatment had helped, Vince's words describe how he thinks about an internalization of the therapist's function that worked for him. Vince explained that now, when he hears the rotor noise of a particular helicopter (a sound associated with life-endangering trauma in Vietnam and dissociative reactions at the time treatment began), he catches himself before he completely "goes back" to a particular Vietnam catastrophe: "It's like Doc T. is still in my head, saying, 'Vince, it's many years later now; that is not the same helicopter which was part of your trauma.'"

In the treatment itself helping the survivor's processing of such here-and-now perceptual distortions is often the business of early hours, even as the survivor is otherwise acquainting his therapist with the remembered trauma events.

Mr. L., a survivor of the Beverly Hills Supper Club fire (Southgate, Kentucky) arrived at his third session anxious and perspiring. On the way to his appointment he had seen from his car window several boys pushing and shoving on the side-walk. They appeared to be "fighting dangerously" he thought to himself. Mr. L. was uncertain if he should have stopped to try to break up the fight, felt panicky at the thought and then, hurrying away, tried to put it out of his mind. His therapist pointed out empathically that his perception of the boys, like his description in the previous session, was of "dangerous pushing and shoving". When he saw such pushing and shoving next to the exit during the fire it indeed was evidence of catastrophe (nearly 125 dead bodies were found at that site later). Mr. L.'s attention continued to be riveted on feelings associated with his frightening and guilty exit from the fire. Later in the session he revised his description of the boys: "I guess they were pushing and shoving the way kids do; maybe they weren't really hurting each other, it wasn't quite so dangerous after all." The therapist had contextualized the perception of the boys in the traumatic context of the fire, enabling Mr. L to refract his current image as one less dangerous than he first registered.

For Mark it was difficult for him to understand how he had so clearly mistaken clinicians, members of the Vet Center team who had come to his home, as enemy, holding them hostage for many hours. His doctor understood that the frightening stand-off in which he threatened to fire his loaded weapon at those who were trying to help him was a trauma reenactment in reverse form, a dissociative reaction set off by the misperception that they were VietCong coming to hold him hostage. As Mark came to trust his therapist they pieced together how the scene paralleled, but was also different from his actual capture by the VietCong.

Indeed, a survivor's dangerously distorted perceptions may suddenly turn against the treating doctor creating a temporary misalignment in perception. In this circumstance, to restore the positive perceptual or lens transference, the therapist needs to find a specific, empathic but firm way to communicate to his patient that the details of this traumatic perception have important reality in past memory but do not directly transpose to the current situation.

Marshall suddenly rose from his chair during a diagnostic interview, towered over the seated clinician and pointed his extended finger at the forehead of the therapist, saying, "You have no idea of what it's like to have to pull a trigger and kill a child." His doctor recalled that a few moments earlier Marshall had referred to this interview as an "interrogation." He thought that it was the false perception of this interview as an interrogation which had triggered the current enactment, reversing roles so that Marshall now had to, as it were, put the interviewer "under the gun." The doctor responded, "I believe there was a time in Vietnam when someone interrogated you threateningly, putting you under the gun." Marshall regained his composure and explained that many units at this point in the war, operating in Laos, were carrying out their own missions, with no compliance to the Geneva Convention, and that such interrogations about atrocities did occur.

Jeb, well into his treatment, suddenly presented a similar problem. He entered his doctor's office suspiciously. He looked along the floorboards and under the doctor's desk. "You've started recording these sessions," he said, with a paranoid certainty. "Well, you can forget about my saying anything, or continuing the therapy." The therapist, genuinely alarmed by the paranoid intensity but also realizing that Jeb had traveled a long way to be present and on time for his visit, recalled that in the past several sessions there had been allusions to a My Lai type event (massacre of innocent civilians). He said, "While you were in Vietnam, were there people who tried to spy on you?" "Yes," Jeb said, going on to describe ways in which soldiers from the legal affairs office infiltrated the unit to learn if there was evidence of atrocity. Affirming the actual perception of being spied on within the trauma story, allowed Jeb to filter out his false perception in the present, that the doctor too was engaged in such activity.

The positive perceptual transference centers on trust. In this transference, trust in the validity of trauma perceptions. The opposite reaction to trust, in this dimension, is disbelief. When the therapist reacts to reports with disbelief the alliance can come into acute danger.

Vince had shared many terrifying images and experiences from Vietnam with his doctor, and a positive perceptual transference was very much in place. However, one day he mentioned almost in passing that there had been 50,000 suicides among Vietnam veterans. The doctor's facial expression registered disbelief at this large number. The following session, Vince was strikingly distrustful; it was as if many months of work had disappeared in a flash. The doctor had also registered Vince's displeasure at his not believing the figure of 50,000 suicides. By clarifying that his skeptical response had set off a striking change, the doctor acknowledged that he had been unaware of this figure, that it might be true, but more importantly that his not believing it had set an obstacle in their path. Aware of the temporary derailment, Vince's doctor acted to realign the axis.

3.1.1 Summarizing the more or less stable lens transference. Posttraumatically, the survivor is plagued with unbidden reminders of the traumatic event (see Table 8.1). Stimuli which are similar enough to sensory stimuli which have become omens of the event, or which in fact preceded or were part of the trauma itself, break through a tear in the stimulus barrier created by the trauma, leaving the survivor vulnerable to repetitions of the traumatic response and affective overreactions to it.

TABLE 8.1

Factor	Perceptual or lens transference	Metabolizing or prism transference	Existential or mythic transference
Symptom picture	Intrusions	Affect dyscontrol, dissociation	Numbing, alienation
Damaged structure	Torn stimulus barrier	Impaired affect regulation	Damaged self/world-view interaction
Primary task	Sequester/limit perceptual field	Regulate affect, new cognitive schema of trauma sequence; construct new cognitive pathways	Redefine meaning
Defenses	Hypervigilant, paranoid, disavowal, denial	Dissociation, allostatic adaptation, denial of symbol	Psychic constriction, impaired energy, pessimism
Organizing metaphor	Sensory: visual, auditory, etc.	Word or phrase	Symbol, religious, spiritual
Mode of transference engagement	Sensory: visual, spatial, temporal	Reflection on condensed affects	Ennui; hope for renewed meaning, continuity of experience
Primary curative activity within stable transference	Limiting the perceptual field of trauma, shielding, protecting, neutralizing perceptual stimulus overload	Finding words for and then schematizing and sequencing condensed affect state; constructing metaphor	Exploration of symbol, myth-making, constructing new symbolic stories
Pro-plan interventions	Engender safety, trust, support, tests, educate re: primacy of trauma situation	Setting prism in place, creating setting in treatment where affect dyscontrol can be understood, empathized with and mastered	Searching for symbolic order within cultural context

Stabilizing factors	Appropriate medication, dosing manageable sensory segments within alliance, confidence that sensory overload can be cut to manageable size	Empathy with state of potential dyscontrol, setting the prism in place; order, sequence, and crop trauma; maintain confidence within alliance that "we" will be able to figure this out; medication where indicated	Wisdom, thinking outside the box, intimate knowledge of this disaster, wide range of scientific and human knowledge, unafraid to challenge conventional wisdom, maintains bearings in world of evil intentions and actions in others and self
Destabilizing factors	Therapist dismisses, denies or greets with disbelief trauma-specific perception and its effects	Lack of empathy with shame or guilt, diagnostic ambivalence, countertransference, overmedication	Disavowal of wise person role: denying, exploiting, or disillusioning idealization

Here the survivor is seeking from his therapist ways to shield his inner self from faulty perceptions close to the trauma experience and all too ready to pour through the hole in the stimulus barrier. He wishes to hold, sequester, and neutralize such a stimulus. He seeks from the therapist the missing or impaired perception-regulating function which under other circumstances might more effectively reality-test the current danger. Within this perceptual or lens transference, the therapist is first a protecting or shielding presence, one who helps the survivor limit the sensory field to segments that are more manageable. Such filtering may call for finding a particular word or phrase that captures a single component of the traumatic stimulus, allowing only that fragment of the experience in for further consideration. Later, the survivor may call on the therapist to act as a correcting lens, reinforcing his own clues that the stimulus is less dangerous than it initially appeared. The survivor asks the therapist to reality-test given input (Is it potentially dangerous?) and to refract, as it were, the otherwise distorted perception that the trauma is about to repeat itself. During this period the therapist must empathize with the survivor's wish to suppress his traumatic overreactions, physiologically or psychologically, to have a supportive environment which will function as a protective shield. He must also understand that in the absence of such shielding, the survivor is apt to develop hypervigilant or paranoid defenses. Alternatively, and perhaps more dangerously, avoidant and numbing defenses may take over as the threat is denied and disavowed. All these defenses in turn negatively affect current relationships and are likely to be repeated in the therapeutic one. Until a stabilizing positive perceptual transference forms, the therapeutic space itself is dangerous, full of sensory, spatial and temporal clues to potential catastrophe. Veterans in one treatment study had anxiety attacks when landscaping was changed (potential bomb sites), when unfamiliar cars were in the parking lot (infiltrators), when the sound of helicopters could be heard as patients were being delivered to the nearby hospital (gun ships). Thus negative transferences of perception are common, and need to be understood as plausible within the trauma context.

Gradually, through careful attention to potential danger points within the hour, by passing tests of trustworthiness, by focusing on the sensory primacy of the trauma situation, by finding the right words and phrases to limit and contain traumatic exposure, and by effective interpretation of negative perceptual transference reactions, a more positive, curative, or mutative perceptual or lens transference emerges. Here a stabilizing transference–countertransference matrix forms: one in which appropriate medication is matched with a dosing manageable sensory segments within the alliance, and the survivor begins to express hope for restoration of some significant functions. But the positive transference may be both unstable and fragile with dramatic regressions when it is broken.

Therapists may help realign the perceptual axis of repair in several ways: pharmacological, supportive/suppressive, and interpretive. Therapists may interfere with the recovery process by ignoring, or misreading the relative primacy of perceptual dangers, and by not understanding that suppressive mechanisms are at times most useful.

3.1.2 Managing Misalignment in the Lens Transference. As the above cases demonstrate, challenges to the lens transference are common. It is really the working through of these challenges which characterizes this portion of the treatment. But sometimes difficulties in perception remain central for long periods. The persistence of flashbacks in the presence of appropriate medication and support indicates that the physiological-psychological impact of the trauma has not been sequestered. This may have both physiological and psychological meanings.

Intrusive symptoms of PTSD can be persistent, and letting the doctor see what the survivor sees can be most troubling.

Bobby continued, almost nightly, to relive the moment of his being caught in a chemical fire which set him and his clothes on fire resulting in third degree burns to his face and 70% of his body. Twenty years later he had mastered much in the metabolizing of his trauma, and in redefining its significance, and as a result was able to manage a healthy marriage and excellent relations with his teenage children. But Bobby could not integrate the "monster" image he had found when he prematurely removed his bandages and looked at the mirror while his facial burns and skin grafts were far from healed. He now read in the eyes of those who saw him for the first time, the reaction he himself had had in response to that traumatic image. Even with his therapist's empathy at that self-image, he remained humiliated and bitter when he caught the facial expressions, especially of those who stared at him. The reciprocal of successful sequestering is persistent flashback.

While not usually recognized as such, difficulties arise in the therapeutic alliance in nonanalytic forms of treatment of PTSD when the trauma survivor perceives her therapist as unnecessarily exposing her to excessive traumatic stimuli. It may be useful to include these cases as a disruption of this positive perceptual transference. The illustrations below are from a cognitive behavioral treatment and a psychopharmacological treatment. In the case of H.G. the therapist was able to realign the perceptual axis; in the case of Rebecca he was not.

H.G., a Vietnam War veteran with intrusive PTSD, responded favorably to increasing his dosage of the beta blocker metoprolol during daylight hours. However, he refused the medication at nighttime. Upon the query of his psychiatrist, H.G.

explained that it was during the night that the most dangerous events occurred; that being obtunded by medication only frightened him more, since the lack of alertness to potential sounds of danger interfered with his capacity to discriminate more dangerous sounds from less dangerous ones. Here, the doctor's attention to the patient's need for perceptual clarity during potential trigger times effectively overrode a rule-of-thumb pharmacological prescription and in this way he reestablished the lens transference pharmacologically.

Rebecca had been nearly fatally assaulted in a dark alley by a man who was still at large. When her male therapist insisted that she enter a dark closet with him, as a step in the therapeutic schema for behavioral desensitization, Rebecca became terribly frightened, fearing that the dark space would repeat the near fatal assault of her recent trauma. She left her treatment. It did not occur to her therapist that his intended desensitization technique could disrupt the positive lens transference and be seen as repetition of the trauma in the treatment. Treatment was disrupted because a protecting, shielding transference had been disrupted; misperception carried the day.

3.2 The Prism Transference: Restoring Order

Once a trigger stimulus (sensory or psychological) sets off an automatic condensed and highly complex traumatic psychophysiological state, the survivor experiences being out of control. He feels overwhelmed, sometimes even more so than during his experience at the time of the trauma. He is confused and ashamed of actions that are irrational in the present, and notes how this sudden unbidden highly complex affective state interferes with competent functioning. The experience of affective dyscontrol provides one more reason to feel disconnected with his pretrauma view of himself.

As the survivor grapples with the embarrassing consequences of these complex affect states in the posttraumatic situation he looks upon the therapist as someone who will help him understand what is happening to him and help him regulate affect more effectively. The therapist responds to this need not only by dosing trauma, as in the lens transference, but by taking on the task of breaking down an indescribable whole into describable parts. The therapist finds the right space and angle, as in Newton's experiment, to refract with a psychological prism the hot, blinding light of trauma into a comprehensible spectrum of colors, each band falling into predictable and lawful sequence. In this way the therapist–survivor pair learn to explain empathically the internal logic or trauma-specific plausibility of such behaviors. The ways in which one subjective step in the trauma sequence precedes the other falls into place with an elegance that matches the distinct bands of color in the spectrum. Successful work in the prism transference may occur as doctor and survivor look at an episode of dyscontrol in the survivor's external life or an event which transpires within the shared space of survivor and therapist. Insight here is a useful tool in the restoration of function.

While Tom's earlier treatment was along the axis of the perceptual or lens transference, a later event occurred requiring a prism for understanding. Tom explained to his therapist without affect that he and his fellow paratroopers were captured by the VietCong. There he witnessed his comrades being chosen for hanging one at a time. Between sessions, an affective breakthrough took him unawares, and set off prolonged crying spell, sadness, and shame. The event started innocently. He had called his children and their friends for lunch. When the children rushed into the kitchen he became aware, too late, that there was one more child than there were seats. The last child looked forlorn as there was no place for him. Inexplicably to Tom, he felt a rush of remorse, left the kitchen and, closing the bedroom door behind himself, sobbed uncontrollably. As he told the event in his session, the therapist thought silently of the childhood game of "musical chairs," which seemed to describe both the scene in the kitchen and, more importantly, Tom's experience of how his comrades learned they were to be killed. The therapist explained that as in the childhood game the "winner" is left with guilt, remorse, and grief at being spared. The forlorn child represented the fellow prisoner chosen for death; the guilt, remorse, and grief at being spared were the unmentionable and suppressed parts of Tom's reaction.

While for Tom and his therapist the condensed moment of dissociative affect dyscontrol, appeared in the therapy as an after-the-fact description, from within the protected space of the doctor's office (discovering the prism effect of the childhood game "musical chairs"), such condensed moments of overwhelming affect can also present themselves within the transference with the doctor. Such an event occurred when Mr. K. was nearly at his doctor's office.

Mr. K. had barely survived being trapped in the lethal Beverly Hills Supper Club fire. He dreaded the repetition of such an experience with his doctor. In the previous hour Mr. K. had reported a dream where he was passenger in a plane moving very swiftly, seated next to the pilot who was taking the plane dangerously low to the ground. He awoke fearing the plane would crash. On his way up in the elevator to the doctor's office for this session he sensed the elevator was getting warm. Touching the wall of the elevator he found his perception confirmed, abruptly got out of the elevator, ran down the stairs and outside the building, imagining the building was on fire. There, he became so agitated that he was taken to the nearby hospital emergency room. His doctor was called, and met him there. Once it was clear that the doctor's office had not been on fire, the doctor and patient attended to the details of the dissociative reaction. Together they were able to lay out in sequence the critical events of the trauma: sensing the fire's presence early; turning quickly to leave (he leaped over tables at the club to get to the exit early); then, finding himself safely outside the building, realizing that in his reflexive effort to save his life he had given no attention to his wife, who was still in the Supper Club (and doctor in the reenactment); and finally being overcome with the condensed affects of relief at survival, and relentless guilt for not saving the person close to him.

In the session in which he reported the dream of the low-flying plane, Mr. K. was sharing his fear that the treatment was coming dangerously close to an overwhelming collision with the fire. Mr. K.'s doctor later regretted that he had missed this clue, a cry that the stimulus barrier was about to be breached. While the trauma reenactment in the next session broke through the protective lens or perception apparatus, the alliance was strong enough for the dissociation to be refracted as though by a prism as both patient and therapist pieced together previously forgotten and central details of the trauma sequence. The prism transference was now in place.

Finding the site at which to place the prism is not always an easy matter. Sometimes the dysphoric affect or blinding traumatic light is hidden from immediate view; rather it sits at the periphery of the survivor–therapist space.

Chip, an air traffic controller who had been termed a hero for saving many lives in an emergency landing, suffered nonetheless from PTSD with a heavy sense of shame and guilt for his own role in the deaths that did occur. In his treatment he had insisted that his doctor act as a judge to determine his guilt for his failings. Despite the doctor's protests, Chip systematically presented evidence on both sides regarding the causes of the emergency landing and the tragic consequences of the landing being only partially successful. His therapist was at a loss as to where to place the prism so that they could see how this vivid retrial was telling the patient's own subjective PTSD story. At the height of the affect stirred in the room, Chip asked, like a prosecuting attorney, if the doctor had been aware why the patient was significantly behind in his bill; in short, was he, the doctor, following closely enough the details of the hand-off of insurance payments for the treatment. Bitterly he accused the therapist of being inattentive to the "hand-off" between insurance carriers. Using the prism, the therapist was now able to understand how unconsciously in the "trial" in the office, Chip had reversed roles with his doctor. Chip now accused the doctor of "missing the hand-off" just as he felt accused by his own superego for "missing the hand-off" from the previous radar control person who had been following an unexpected blip on the radar screen earlier, a blip that turned out to be the troubled aircraft. Now the traumatic sequence, conscientiousness at the center of a crisis with inattention to the periphery, was alive in the room. Even though the therapist was doing his best he had missed something on the periphery. In the process, the phrase "missing the hand-off" became a way for the therapist to orient himself to the patient's subjective experience of his trauma.

Here, finding the right location at which to place the prism for the survivor and therapist meant finding the hidden transference event which was just out of sight, namely "tracking the hand-off" from the insurance company.

Sometimes, it is only the survivor who can fill in the important details of a given sequence. That is, the therapist may be clear about the dissociative behavior which needs explaining but may have little idea what the explanation is.

Jonah expected his therapist to be furious with him for sleeping outside the office in his parked truck for 30 minutes of his session. Not only had he done this once, but he repeated it twice on a single day. He anticipated the response, "You idiot, what did you do that for!!" a reaction he frequently received while growing up and while serving in Vietnam. But the therapist's thoughts were different, searching for the place to put his prism. Jonah was heavily invested in his treatment. The parking lot had become his one safe place. He sometimes parked there at dawn, the most dangerous part of the day. This day after he was too late for his first appointment the doctor gave him a second one, during an hour which another patient had cancelled. So the second exactly 30 minute delay was striking. Piecing this fragment together with those events Jonah had been trying to narrate in the previous several sessions, the doctor established that the 30 minutes repeated a particular traumatic delay which he was trying to keep from awareness. Now, with all but the content in place, Jonah filled in the pieces, as though they had been available to him throughout. In Vietnam, after he had turned the watch tower over to the next soldier and returned to headquarters, the tower was overrun. He desperately sought to get relief to his successor, but was being ignored. Indeed, there had been a 30 minute delay in his officer delivering help to his comrade isolated at that watch tower as it was being overrun by the enemy. What appeared as Jonah's 30 minute irresponsibility, in fact was a specific dissociative reaction with particular meaning. Understanding the event in the transference in this light allowed the "30 minutes asleep in the truck" to function not as a threat to the working alliance but as a prism through which to see trauma. Jonah could now outline with clarity a series of interrelated traumas in Vietnam and the affective states and emergency decisions that went with them. And he could see how this same sequence disturbed him in the present. The moment of "You idiot" turned into the reversal of an empathically understandable trauma sequence: "How dare you [the officer in charge] not order relief to the men in the watch tower for 30 minutes!"

3.2.1 Summary of the More or Less Stable Prism Transference. In summary, the primary symptoms under consideration during the prism transference are dissociative. The mode of engagement or organizing metaphor is verbal, the mutual discovery of the right words or phrase which break down overwhelming affect into ordered and usable segments. It is the discovery of these special words that organizes meaning from chaos and in turn alters traumatic reliving into masterable memory. These newly found words explain catastrophic physical, physiological, and psychological events in causal and sequential form. And it is the empathic effect of these words which is necessary for the prism transference to work. In the postmodern sense, this is a mutual construction of the trauma by the survivor and therapist in the present. The words, phrases, or metaphors may originate from the therapist (such as "musical chairs") or the patient ("watching for the hand-off"), or a nonverbal reaction ("you idiot, keeping me waiting for 30 minutes"), but they must resonate mutually between the two in the interconnected psychological space formed by the survivor–therapist relationship. Most important, this newly defined order to previously experienced chaos is both encompassing and empathic to the survivor.

When the prism transference is stable, there is ongoing hope within the alliance that survivor and therapist together will be able to break down any currently distressing affect into its component, understandable, sequentially linked, and empathically understood parts. Words, including metaphors, take on a more integrating function within the mind, turning an enigmatic puzzle into the predictable solution. As Tom said to his doctor, "This treatment is like trying to solve a Rubik cube. What seems like randomness on the outside is actually organized along several rotating axes." In his final session he gave the doctor a Rubik cube along with the diagrams to solve it, as a way of saying thank you.

Recognizing misalignment, countertransference, and resistance are central difficulties in negotiating the prism transference. Returning for a moment to the metaphor of Newton's prism experiment, while the therapist may function temporarily as the primary wordsmith along this path, it is also critical that the survivor learn to set the prism on his own.

3.2.2 Managing Misalignment in the Prism Transference. The prism transference, like the perceptual one, is open to derailments. When it is lost, the survivor's ego state is prone to severe regression. Words lose their metaphoric and symbolic integrating function. Dissociation, far from providing the raw material for insight, becomes highly destructive. The working alliance vanishes. Misalignment may come from misreading, misdiagnosing, or ignoring the patient's desperate cry for help in regulating affect. Countertransference is a common offender in such situations. In this situation the therapeutic space is not safe enough to set the prism.

Jim was explaining to his therapist the events associated with an assault on a hill in Vietnam when the terrifying image of a headless, legless torso of an American soldier propped against a tree, stopped his narrative. Because this image stirred a countertransference trauma from the therapist's childhood, one which he thought he had put behind him, the therapist momentarily lapsed into his own dysphoria, and disconnected from the clinical situation in the room. Invoking the affective state of his own trauma and the effort to cope with it at the time, namely, to proceed ahead no matter what the cost, he told the patient to continue the story, that is "Go back to the hill" (despite internal messages that both patient and doctor needed to remain safe). Jim's dissociative reaction became complete, his behaviors dangerous and seemingly psychotic, and required hospitalization. The regressive experience in response to this momentary derailment was a powerful dissociative state. The patient had let through to awareness and shared with his therapist an unnamed traumatic image requiring metabolizing. Unable to find words for the complex affect state or to place it in meaningful sequence, the therapist substituted a directive motivated from his own unconscious. Asked by the patient to function in the affect regulating, holding, wording sequencing, and metabolizing roles, the therapist was temporarily unable to fulfill his task as a result of having a child-hood trauma of his own activated by the image. An unstable transference counter-transference matrix supervened, and the patient fell out of the hold of the positive transference and into the regression of a dissociative state. Unwittingly the instruction of "Go back to the hill" repeated the lieutenant's actual trauma instruc-tions in Vietnam. The idea of such a phrase might later in the treatment have become a useful and empathically understood organizer or prism for the trauma, but in this instance the dissociation occurred in the midst of a countertransference reac-tion, before a stable enough working alliance was in place, and before the therapist and survivor had built a safe space together.

Alternatively patients may be delayed in recovery even though the prism may be placed in the right spot. For example, in the case below, the trauma coexists with the physiology of recovery.

Renee had experienced a sense of competence with her enthusiasm and energy; it was a characteristic which people noted about her. Then one day, having recovered from an episode of depression, she energetically raced down stairs and through a stuck glass door, the fragments lacerating her radial artery. She continued to be aware of heightened excitement as her body continued to pour out adrenaline, but she rapidly lost blood, fainted, and by the time she was found and taken to the hospital she was close to death. The familiar sense of excitement that went with enthusiasm, hopefulness, and restored strength, was now the trigger of a new trauma configuration binding the phenomenon of energy and enthusiasm in her work and relationships with death. To improve, to return to her pretrauma excitement was to exacerbate the trauma configuration calling for more extended working through.

Treatments may also become fixated at the prism transference because uncovering the traumatic sequence does not bring empathic relief but only confirms faulty self-judgments derived from *unresolved* conflicts from childhood. Brick's case is the reciprocal of the situation with Maggie, whose trauma configuration overlapped with a childhood one, and whose earlier successful work on these conflicts of childhood permitted rapid and spontaneous restoration of function after the trauma (see Section 2.2.1).

"Brick" had been an effective sergeant in the Kurdish region of Iraq during the period of the American pull-back after the 1991 Gulf War. He was entrusted with ensuring the safety of the few who were authorized to evacuate from American-supported positions, and keeping back the many who also wished to leave and were frightened lest they remain and be subjected to slaughter by forces loyal to Saddam Hussein. Brick negotiated an impossible situation with energy, courage, and loyalty to his fellow soldiers. He clearly saved many lives. But officers, not exposing themselves to the circumstances and dangers on the ground, greeted Brick's independent judgment with contempt blaming him for the impossible situation. In his treatment Brick and his therapist soon discovered his affective vulnerability to situations calling for quick judgment that "others will see differently." Setting the prism was not difficult. But working through the conflict was lengthy because it was exactly the same as the traumatic situation that he had not mastered from childhood.

The world constructed during the prism transference for Brick, Renee, Jonah, and Tom is not so benevolent as the one pictured in spontaneous sequestration of Maggie. It is the tension created by as yet unsolved paradoxes and contradiction to the new universe of trauma that leads us to our final positive transference, one which allows us to use the metaphor of light in yet one more way: the existential or mythic transference.

3.3 The Existential or Mythic Transference:
Restoring Meaning

Whereas distorted perception heralds the lens transference and dissociation heralds the prism transference it is continuing ennui or alienation which are signs that the survivor still feels discontinuous with himself, and cut off from connection with a meaningful world.

Trauma, that which is against the stars, confronts the survivor, the therapist, and society at large with contradictions and paradoxes that challenge the assumption of well-meaning people in a relatively benign universe. The world of the ideal is shattered. The questions: How could this have happened? Why did they die? Why have I lost so much? Why am I still alive? become paramount. Survivors are confronted with a terrifying reality: the ordering principles of the universe, as they had known it, are gone. Their sense of self has been shattered. While the problem of affect regulation reminded them daily that the self was not continuous, the problem of alienation reminds them that their place in the universe is no longer a meaningful and secure one.

All this sets the stage for the survivor to view the therapist in one more hopeful light: as the one who might assist them in restoring renewed meaning and continuity of self in a universe that is forever changed. Now, the primary task in treatment is redefining meaning: of self and of self in relation to the world. On the one hand this calls on the diad to be not only stable but to gain sufficient distance from the traumatic events so as to see them, and one's decisions from within the trauma, from a new perspective. It is as if the light beams broaden through time to take in the larger drama of human struggle through history in the context of the epic poems, the wisdom and laments of the ages, in the context of myth itself. On the other hand, during the mythic transference both patient and therapist are sometimes able to see that, in small behaviors embedded within the traumatic events, contrary to the survivor's predominantly self-condemning views, some of the most valued traits persevered even in the midst of trauma itself. Here it is as if the light beams narrow like a microscope under the highest power, so that clarity and connection come in the detail rather than the chaos. Both perspectives help to reshape the survivor's sense of meaning of the trauma and connection to the world in its aftermath.

In the treatment the survivor may yearn to expiate guilt, to relinquish blame, to ameliorate the need for revenge, and to integrate as human the behaviors of others and self: problems that otherwise the survivor can not imagine synthesizing on his own.

Our first clear exposure to this mythic transference occurred with Mr. K., described above. Mr. K., having failed to take action to save his wife in the Beverly Hills Supper Club fire, condemned himself to a life of guilt for his lack of altruism when his own life was endangered during trauma. But in the reenactment described earlier in this chapter, the therapist had been neutral and nonjudgmental and empathic as he replayed the scene in the transference. During the termination of his therapy, Mr. K. dreamt that his therapist appeared as an accepting grace-giving Christ-like figure. Within the dream there was a sense of forgiveness for his behavior at the fire in which his precipitous exit might have endangered his wife.

The healing transference had moved to a mythic dimension which found a home in this fundamentalist Christian survivor.

In "naming" his patient "Abraham" his therapist became aware of the powerful story which had guided his perception during the final period of the treatment. Abraham blamed himself for sacrificing the life of an innocent Vietnamese boy and assumed he must pay for this for the rest of his life. Abraham lay in a field in Vietnam all night with a Vietnamese boy whom he had shot in a free fire zone dying in his arms. The dead boy remained a delusional presence attached to his shoulder even as he tried to relate to his own son, now a youngster about the same age. He struggled mightily with the tensions of permitting himself to love his own son when he had already killed another "son" in Vietnam. It was the Old Testament story of Abraham and Isaac, and the anguish Abraham must have felt for a lifetime after he had agreed to sacrifice Isaac at God's command, that gave his therapist a wider and accepting perspective on the trauma. Abraham's struggle and his therapist's comparable struggle was one of aligning the transference–countertransference matrix along a shared or common myth, one which would permit integration of the pretrauma self (heavily committed to looking after younger sibs), the trauma self (who had killed the Vietnamese boy), and the posttrauma self (who identified with the Abraham of a Bible story).

For Jonah and his therapist the search for myth took each in separate yet parallel directions. Jonah could find no redeeming value in his existence after he had radioed naval bombings onto coordinates he understood to be enemy hospitals. He expected damnation and his life had become just that. His therapist saw Jonah as a relatively unassuming and relatively naïve teenager, the high-school drop-out/pool hall youngster, the one who overreacts to crisis, and the one who gets caught, always in trouble and never having had solid guidance. Once the sequence of Jonah's trauma experiences had been clarified within a positive prism transference (see above), the task became one of realigning his self-image and view of the world. During this mythic transference, his therapist came to think of his patient as the Jonah of the Old Testament. Finding himself far from home, having carried out distasteful duties, Jonah could not bear to see his enemies survive. The Jonah of the Old Testament, he thought, would have called in naval bombings onto Ninevah, had the instruments been available to him. While his therapist was silently engaged as above, Jonah himself settled on his own new symbol, a tie-dyed shirt, long hair, and a head-band. Jonah reframed his experience by joining with rather than separating himself from his fellow Vietnam veterans. Like his therapist, he found a new image for his past although a different one from his Old Testament oriented doctor—one he could now wear with pride.

In Lee's case, the patient and therapist discovered together an element in the trauma which Lee had suppressed and which gave a new light on it. Here it is as if light becomes sharply focused as in the microscope under high power. Lee had thought of himself as one who did what he could to protect others. He had looked after his sick mother as a child, and protected his weaker friends. After multiple traumas in the Vietnam War his self-image had changed. He now thought if he cared for people they would die. He ceased thinking of himself as one who could ever again protect. He and his therapist discovered a previously forgotten movement within a trauma sequence. Describing how he had spotted a dynamited knapsack moving in a crowd, Lee gestured as though pushing the therapist away. The nonverbal transference gesture allowed a reconstruction which was confirmed by memory: that just prior to firing he discovered that he had pushed away his friend so that he would fall away from the explosion which was about to occur. Never forgiving himself for killing the child who carried the knapsack, he nonetheless received some solace from knowing his instincts were that of protecting his friend. Therapy allowed him to reconnect with the trait of protecting others, a trait that endured before during and after the trauma.

The dominant mode of communication during mythic transference is symbolic. Like the simultaneous presence of good and evil forces as in the yin and yang of eastern religion, or the Chinese symbol for crisis which condenses the pictographs of danger and opportunity, it is in the world of symbol that Abraham and his therapist and Jonah and his therapist worked. It is symbol that unites contradiction. It is the freshly constructed spiritual, existential story within the treatment alliance that signifies wholeness.

3.3.1 Summarizing the More or Less Stable Mythic Transference. The light beam which avails itself to the mythic transference is one which is initially very dim indeed. It is present beneath an exterior of numbing and alienation. It is present beneath a damaged self and a damaged self–world view interaction. It is best understood as the survivor's wish to redefine meaning in his life given the reality of the trauma. In the evolution of this mutative transference, the dominant defensive roles of psychic constriction, impaired energy, and pessimism give way only gradually to a slim hope for renewed meaning. In the therapeutic interaction which coincides with the early development of the mythic transference the therapist becomes ill with the survivor's burden. A gradual but striking shift occurs within the survivor–therapist field. The survivor, up till now slumped in posture carrying the weight of trauma and crushed ideals on his shoulders, begins to find a lilt in his walk and spontaneous expression in his face. The therapist, on the other hand, absorbing what the two have learned about the trauma, now bends under the vicarious weight of the trauma experience. It is as though the survivor has temporary relief in this existential transference, as the therapist bears the weight of pondering the contradictions and paradoxes in the trauma events.

Gradually and in unexpected ways elements of the transference–countertransference matrix become charged with the opportunity for a changed outlook regarding self and universe. Exploration of a symbolic transference gesture, an unusual piece of clothing, a dream symbol, a career shift, may contain within it the substance of a new symbolic or mythic life story which now contains the potential for renewed energy and hope.

In this endeavor the therapist is called upon by the survivor-patient to think outside the box, to be unafraid to challenge conventional wisdom. The therapist is expected to bring to the therapeutic situation a wide range of scientific and human knowledge as well as to become intimately aware of the specificity of this particular traumatic situation. The therapist must also understand how human beings comport themselves in a world of evil actions where the evil-doer may even be oneself. The therapist facilitates work along this axis by remaining non-judgmental, reflective concerning existential and spiritual aspects of disaster, and hopeful about the survivor's finding a perspective from which he can go forward.

There are many ways in which therapists excuse themselves from allowing themselves to being drawn into the mythic transference. They may disavow the role of wise person. They may become uncomfortable with being idealized, and in that discomfort deny its legitimacy in the patient; they may avoid the role altogether and thereby disillusion the survivor; or even in an unwitting countertransference may exploit the survivor, repeating the trauma rather than letting the treatment give it new form.

Therapists interfere with work along this axis when they excuse themselves from such reflection as being beyond the range of the treatment, when they retreat from the vicarious challenge placed on their shoulders, or when they project their own solution or myth onto the patient irrespective of the patient's self and world definitions.

3.3.2 Managing Misalignment in the Mythic Transference. Therapists prefer not to engage in the world of inexplicable tragedy. They prefer the well-worn paths of early childhood, for example, to the world of existential despair.

Emmanuel recognized that his therapist was backing away from appreciating the full impact of his trauma in Auschwitz as a child, when she interpreted the survivor's feelings about working in the latrines (actually a life-saving assignment) with anal disgust rather than linking the experience with the mythic hope that he might (with the relative safety of this despised assignment) survive. It was as if she was coaching Emmanuel to speak of early childhood rather than engage in the more profound, existential, and mythic dimensions of his trauma experience, as though the task ahead would be one of metabolizing a childhood struggle rather than redefining meaning, and hope in the midst of existential despair.

Where trauma has come from earliest childhood, and faulty efforts to reach resolution by an immature ego have left scarred ego fragments each with its own dissociated history, work at the level of the existential or mythic transference is difficult because it has so many layers.

As a small child, Tina had defensively tried to overcome the impact of incest by splitting into an "angel of death" self and a "whore" self. These represented faulty early childhood efforts to explain to herself her interaction with the terrifying world around her. The two selves represented two myths. In one, she retained the power to help her troubled parents like an angel, but reserved the right to destroy them if she wished. In the second myth she possessed the capacity to seduce any male of her choosing including her needy father. But continuing to view her complex affect states through these two prisms as an adult only led to more complex allostatic difficulties. As repeated in the treatment the therapist, in the negative transference, was dangerous like her parents, certainly incapable of helping her to find more mature forms of meaning in her current relationships. Having come to treatment in adulthood to find meaning in the sudden death of her child, this current work could only be fully engaged after the earlier faulty myths from childhood had been addressed.

Some patients present years after trauma as though it is *only* work in the area of existential or mythic transference which is needed while, in fact, there may be incomplete working through in other areas which continues to block their way.

Pete's PTSD was severe and disabling, 9 years after he, in the line of duty, shot and killed at point blank range a threatening man who had raised a gun towards him. The problem for this former policeman was less the continuing intrusive images or nightmares, but rather the preoccupation that the restorative posttraumatic goal he had set for himself after the shooting, his personal myth which would redefine meaning in his life, namely to teach other law enforcement personnel about confrontation tactics and PTSD, had proven impossible for him to carry out. In treatment Pete's PTSD and its severity improved as he learned that other outlets for his passion for teaching about law enforcement were possible.

Many factors may throw the therapist off course during the existential or mythic transference. In the illustration below a countertransference temporarily derailed an otherwise stable transference.

Bobby, many years after a chemical burn affecting 70% of his body and nearly all of his face, insisted on learning about his Jewish therapist's reaction to Mel Gibson's film The Passion, which highlights the suffering of Jesus prior to and during his crucifixion. The therapist had been disturbed by the film, finding in it stereotypic anti-Semitic elements of greed and betrayal among Jews. The great suffering of the protagonist at the hand of Jews, he felt were, at core, anti-Semitic. The therapist, in a countertransference reaction, felt defensive about his being Jewish and uncomfortable knowing how important Bobby's Protestant fundamentalist beliefs were to him. Bobby patiently listened, but rejected his therapist's observations about the film. Bobby realigned the transference himself. He explained that the film had accurately captured the sight of his torso with the permanent disfiguring marks of torture along with the cries of scorn from the crowd, not motivated by empathy or love but by pleasure in the suffering of the other. In short, he had found comfort in the portrayal of Christ's suffering, educating his therapist so that he could realign the mythic transference, an identification with Christ. This survivor would not let his therapist derail the alignment between them.

4 CONCLUSIONS

4.1 Summary of Three Paths Towards Restoration of the Posttraumatic Self

Spontaneous pathways to the restoring of self function in PTSD parallel three curative or mutative positive transferences that we find in the treatment of the disorder. The first spontaneous pathway, sequestration, parallels the lens transference. It reduces the quantity and intensity of the blinding light of traumatic intrusion via conscious suppressive supportive and unconscious repressive activity. Community-based programs and culturally sensitive group settings which are non-uncovering, and medication all assist the suppressive path. Respect for defenses such as condensation, displacement and symbol formation assist the unconscious path. The overly aggressive uncovering-driven therapist, inattentive to defensive needs of the survivor, can undo sequestering by prematurely challenging these defenses. The analytic psychotherapist addresses sequestration only when its adaptive function is no longer working. In this way, it is the survivor who invites the therapist to serve a specific intrapsychic function, alongside the perceptive apparatus, a perceptual assistant as it were, who doses, filtrates, and refracts sensory input into more manageable and understandable segments.

The second spontaneous pathway, metabolizing, parallels the prism transference. In this activity the survivor finds words and phrases that help to break down complex affective states into sequentially arranged and empathically grasped component parts. Here, in the parallel action of psychotherapy, the therapist is invited to hold a prism against a defined segment of the otherwise blinding light of traumatic reenactment, helping the survivor refract dissociation into its component and sequential parts. Interpretations, so derived, are trauma reconstructions. They identify the special configuration of the traumatic events and promote the survivor's recognizing and working through parallel dynamics in other current-day experiences.

The third spontaneous pathway, redefining meaning, parallels the mythic transference. Here the survivor engages others in his culture in the search for a symbolic expression for his individual traumatic experiences, restoring meaning out of chaos, continuity of the pre- and posttrauma self, and reconnection to the world. In the parallel mythic or existential transference the survivor–therapist team reframes the trauma experience with integrity in new ways. Here, the survivor places onto the shoulders of the therapist some of the affective load of living with the contradictions and paradoxes inherent in the trauma itself. The two together, survivor and therapist, transform and expand the interfaces of paradoxical bands of light in the trauma spectrum to resonate with the wisdom stories and laments of human history and myth.

4.2 A Word About the Words We Use: Above All Do No Harm

We return briefly at the end of this chapter to our theoretical discussion in Section 1 and the language we use to describe those mutative transferences we see in the human and clinical situations before us. Two characteristics of transferences born of traumatic repetition compel us to distinguish the language of clinical constructs derived from transference work with survivors of trauma in adulthood, from the language of clinical constructs gained through transference experiences with neurotic, narcissistic, and borderline patients. The first characteristic is that trauma disturbs already formed psychic structure (perceptual, affect-regulating, and self-continuity). Those underlying structures may or may not have been damaged before the trauma. Second, trauma occurs at all points in the life-cycle, arresting function at that most advanced epigenetic phase, the time of trauma, as well as regressing to earlier phases. Failing to make these distinctions leads the clinician to misunderstand the developmental level at which the therapist serves mutative functions as restorative object in the positive transference and may lead to an inappropriate infantilizing of the trauma survivor.

While occupying the positive transference or new object position in PTSD, the therapist is more properly in the role of structural splint rather than representing the totally new object required to fill a deficit as in new internalization. The splint's goal is to allow the reknitting of damaged structure, whether perceptive, affect-regulating, adaptive, self-regulating, or existential. The survivor is taking advantage of the safety of the therapeutic space to borrow from the therapist a function he once had; he is not acquiring it anew. There is an important assumption here: that the survivor has not always been in this state of duress; that there existed in the past a smoother, more integrated self-regulating and effective psyche. It is the restoration of that psyche within the context of the known trauma which is the therapeutic goal. The mutative transferences in PTSD restore function; they do not build it anew.

Among other factors this may affect rate of improvement. In some cases, return of function during treatment can be much more rapid than in the neurotic, narcissistic, and borderline conditions.

On the other hand, traumatic conditions may resonate with incompletely resolved developmental stages in the past; where structure may be previously deformed, conflicted, or absent. Here the splint is insufficient. In these situations comprehensive treatment requires more thorough-going working through and may be lengthy.

As we have seen it is childhood with its microscope on the conflicts, deficits, and distortions of earliest years which informs the developmentally based constructs of psychoanalytic model-makers: Freud and Strachey, Klein and Kernberg, Kohut and Ornstein, all use language of archaic childhood wishes, fears, and deficits. Within those systems, the positive transference or the new or curative object which the therapist fills is, by definition, an object rooted in early childhood, not located temporally in the aftermath of trauma in any phase of development. We believe the language of these infantile models deflects therapist empathy away from the trauma patient and does disservice to the trauma survivor.

For example, given the language of theoretical constructs from earliest years: paranoid reactions to the therapist in the transference can be seen as difficulty in basic trust, i.e. damage in the oral phase of development, the inability of the early psyche to form symbiotic attachments, or healthy infant–mother and self–object ties, rather than specific dangers in trauma-specific situations; i.e. distrust of specific objects usually considered trustworthy in the nontraumatized general public. Distancing and difficulty with authority in the transference may be seen as conflict at the anal phase, generic problems with autonomy, rather than trauma-specific danger situations with those who abuse authority. Insecurity around interpersonal boundaries in the transference may be seen as residue of absent self–object boundaries from childhood, rather than the result of trauma-specific sexual transgressions. From the point of view of the survivor, such infantilizing constructs may distance the therapist from the survivor and from immersion in the trauma experience itself. The therapist mistakenly imagines that the needed positive or mutative transference, the new object, is the trusting mother of infancy rather than the sufficiently watchful protector in an adult situation of danger; or the therapist may think that the patient requires parental tolerance in the face of the willful child rather than the ability to pass tests of reliability and integrity which are specific to the traumas endured.

Dissociative phenomena occurring in the consulting room with the therapist can be mistakenly clustered with the psychotic disorders. Such frightening dramatic clinical events may lead the therapist to abandon whatever positive or mutative transference may have been in place, and to treat the patient as though these breaks with reality indicate an underlying psychosis with its roots perhaps in biological or earliest infancy. Heavy medication and suppression often follow, conveying loss of hope. It is then as though there is no use in remaining curious about subsequent dissociation in the hopes of understanding the origins of the trauma and restabilizing the prism transference. Instead, in all these cases, the words we use carry the risk of leading to misdiagnosis and a derailing of the positive transference. Indeed, all of the above situations have been reported to me in supervisory or conference settings.

The new terminology would name damaged psychic structure in PTSD in trauma-specific language such as perceptual, affect-regulating, and existential, and would name the new mutative transferences in language respectful of yet different from that of Freud, Kernberg, and Kohut—such as lens, prism, and myth. Through terms such as these the clinician would seek to align trauma therapy along axes which promote specific healing paths for patients living in the aftermath of trauma and, most importantly, when treatment becomes temporarily derailed would look to one of these organizing transference–countertransference matrices along which to realign the work.

APPENDIX. CASE STUDIES CITED

Of the 21 cases referred to in this chapter which lend support to the mutative transferences in the analytic psychotherapy of PTSD, many are also reported elsewhere in the trauma literature where these same cases have illustrated other clinical aspects of PTSD. Below, these cases are ordered alphabetically with their original reference noted. Cases not previously referenced in the literature are at the end.

PREVIOUSLY REPORTED CASES

Abraham (Lindy, J. D., with MacLeod, J., Spitz, L., Green, B., & Grace, M. (1988). *Vietnam: A casebook* (pp. 7–31). New York: Brunner Mazel.)

Bart (Harkness, L. & Zador, N. (2001). Treatment of PTSD in families and couples. In J. Wilson, M. Friedman, & J. D. Lindy (Eds.), *Treating psychological trauma and PTSD* (pp. 339–340). New York: Guilford Press.)

Chip (Lindy, J. D. (1993). Focal psychoanalytic psychotherapy of PTSD. In J. Wilson & B. Raphael (Eds.), *International handbook of traumatic stress syndromes* (pp. 805–806). New York: Plenum Press.)

H. G. (Friedman, M. (2001). Allostasis vs. empirical perspectives on pharmacotherapy for PTSD. In J. Wilson, M. Friedman, & J. D. Lindy (Eds.), *Treating psychological trauma and PTSD* (pp. 117–118). New York: Guilford Press.)

Jeb (Lindy, J. D., with MacLeod, J., Spitz, L., Green, B., & Grace, M. (1988). *Vietnam: A casebook* (pp. 121–148). New York: Brunner Mazel.)

Jim (Lindy, J. D., with MacLeod, J., Spitz, L., Green, B., & Grace, M. (1988). *Vietnam: A casebook* (pp. 244–262). New York: Brunner Mazel.)

Jonah (Lindy, J. D., with MacLeod, J., Spitz, L., Green, B., & Grace, M. (1988). *Vietnam: A casebook* (pp. 179–208). New York: Brunner Mazel.)

Mr. K. (Lindy, J. D., Green, B., & Titchener, J. (1983). Psychotherapy with survivors of the Beverly Supper Club Fire. *American Journal of Psychotherapy, 27,* 593–608.)

Mr. L. (Lindy, J. D., Green, B., & Titchener, J. (1983). Psychotherapy with survivors of the Beverly Hills Supper Club Fire. *American Journal of Psychotherapy, 27,* 593–608.)

Lee (Lindy, J. D. (1993). Focal psychoanalytic psychotherapy of PTSD. In Wilson & B. Raphael (Eds.), *International handbook of traumatic stress syndromes* (pp. 805–806). New York: Plenum Press.)

Louise (Lindy, J. D. (1996). Psychoanalytic psychotherapy of PTSD. In B. van der Kolk, A. McFarlane, & L. Weisaeth (Eds.), *Traumatic Stress: The effects of overwhelming experiences on mind, body and society.* New York: Guilford Press.)

Marshall (Lindy, J. D., with MacLeod, J., Spitz, L., Green, B., & Grace, M. (1988). *Vietnam: A casebook* (pp. 234–235). New York: Brunner Mazel.)

Rebecca (Zoellner, L., Fitzgibbons, L., & Foa, E. (2001). Cognitive behavioral approaches to PTSD. In J. Wilson, M. Friedman, & J. D. Lindy (Eds.), *Treating psychological trauma and PTSD* (pp. 174–177). New York: Guilford Press.)

Tina (Lindy, J. & Wilson, J. (2001). Allostasis and the psychodynamics of PTSD. In J. Wilson, M. Friedman, & J. D. Lindy (Eds.), *Treating psychological trauma and PTSD* (pp. 133–134). New York: Guilford Press.)

Tom (Lindy, J. D. (1985). The trauma membrane and other clinical concepts derived from psychotherapeutic work with survivors of natural disasters. *Psychiatric Annals, 15,* 153–160.

Vince (Lindy, J. D., with MacLeod, J., Spitz, L., Green, B., & Grace, M. (1988). *Vietnam: A casebook* (pp. 35–52). New York: Brunner Mazel.)

Cases Not Previously Reported

Bobby
Brick
Emmanuel
Maggie
Mark

Mike
Pete
Renee

REFERENCES

Freud, S. (1923). *The ego and the id.* (standard edition, Vol. 29, pp. 12–59). London: Hogarth Press.

Harkness, L. & Zador, N. (2001). Treatment of PTSD in families and couples. In J. Wilson, M. Friedman, & J. D. Lindy (Eds.), *Treating psychological trauma and PTSD* (pp. 339–340). New York: Guilford Press.

Kernberg, O. (1971). Prognostic considerations regarding borderline personality disorder organization. *Journal of the American Psychoanalytic Association, 19,* 595–635.

Klein, M. (1957). *Envy and gratitude.* London: Tavistock.

Kohut, H. (1966). Forms and transformations of narcissism. *Journal of the American Psychoanalytic Association, 14,* 243–272.

Mahler, M. S. (1972) On the first three subphases of the separation–individuation process. *International Journal of Psychoanalysis, 53,* 333–338.

Ornstein, A. & Ornstein, P. (1985). Survival and recovery. *Psychoanalytic Inquiry, 5,* 99–130.

Strachey, J. (1934). The nature of the therapeutic action of psychoanalysis. *International Journal of Psychoanalysis, 15,* 126–159.

Terr, L. (1994). *Unchained memories* (pp. 96–119). New York: Basic Books.

Weiss, J. & Sampson, H. (1986). Testing alternative psychoanalytic explanations of the therapeutic process. In J. Masling (Ed.), *Empirical studies of psychoanalytic theories* (Vol. II) (pp. 68–83). Analytic Free Press.

Winnicott, D. D. W. (1963). *The maturational processes and the facilitating environment.* London: Hogarth Press.

9

Posttraumatic Shame and Guilt: Culture and the Posttraumatic Self

BORIS DROŽĐEK, SILVANA TURKOVIC, AND JOHN P. WILSON

1 INTRODUCTION

Ibrahim is a Bosnian refugee and asylum-seeker in the Netherlands. He survived the ethnic genocide in former Yugoslavia (1991–1995) and speaks of his experiences:

I had a good life, and did nothing else except taking care of my family and trying to do my work as good as possible. Suddenly times changed. Not only time but mentality of people changed, too. The war started. Strangers came into our town. One day they caught me and brought to a concentration camp. I used to read Dante, but I did not know that devil really existed. I can't tell you everything what I saw, because I am ashamed of and I don't think that talking about it is going to help me. But I can tell you briefly about what has changed my life.

It was the day that seven of them took me out of the room where I was kept in together with other prisoners. All seven of them raped me. Their age was between 14 and 17. This went on for days; it was terrible. I thought that God never existed. But when I was released from the camp it went even worse. I had two children, a daughter of 12 and a son of 15. So when I saw my son again I just couldn't stand him. I could actually kill him, because he made me remember of what I have been through in the camp. From that moment on I did not live any more; I just existed. No priest, nor another holy man, could give me absolution. I am deeply ashamed of having being raped, and not being a good father any more, hating my own son. Everybody tries to comfort me, but it is my secret and my nightmare that makes me feel ashamed. From that moment on I have accepted the fact that I do not live any more.

Shame is a secret; something one always carries with oneself, something so difficult to deal with or to share. It is something that destroys all those things that one has learned about good people, good husbands, and good family. Shame is an experience that does not fit into the world I was raised in. It is a secret in which I am alone. This has nothing to do with my past, or the way my parents have raised me. It is worse. It is the destruction of everything I have ever learned.

2 THEORETICAL PERSPECTIVES OF SHAME AND GUILT

Shame and guilt are Janus-faced partners in the human psyche. Shame is a more complex intrapsychic process than guilt because it involves attributes concerning the core dimensions of the self, identity, ego-processes, and personality. Guilt, on the other hand, concerns different forms of self-recrimination about responsibility for personal actions. In the posttraumatic self, shame and guilt may coexist depending on the critical incidents that the survivor endured during trauma. Shame and guilt possess unique psychological dimensions (see Table 9.3) that differentiate them from each other. Posttraumatic shame and guilt are complex forms of intense affect and negative cognitions, especially in posttraumatic stress disorder (PTSD) and trauma complexes. Posttraumatic shame and guilt have consequences for proneness to PTSD, suicidality, ego-defenses, psychopathology, and other aspects of psychosocial functioning which we shall discuss in this chapter. Posttraumatic shame and guilt exist whether or not there are degrees of pretraumatic ego vulnerability, including self-pathologies and narcissistic shame (Morrison, 1990). Posttraumatic shame and guilt can be coupled with a broad range of affects (including pre-existing shame and guilt) to form complex states of intrapsychic tension as part of PTSD, depression, generalized anxiety disorder, and psychosis.

3 POSTTRAUMATIC SHAME

Shame is on the face, on the front of the soul.

(R. Stoller, 1987, p. 304)

A turning away of the face, avoidance of contact, downcast eyes, slumped posture, blushing, mind going blank, and arrested behavior— these are some signals of the ashamed. Clark and Wells (1995) label these actions as "safety behaviors" with desire of the ashamed to escape, disappear, and submit. Wurmser (1987) remarked that "the eye is the organ of shame par excellence" (p. 67). The analyst Fenichel (1945) wrote, "I feel ashamed" means "I do not want to be seen" (p. 139). These expressions of shame are universally understood and present across cultures.

There are a spectrum of experiences that include shame or interact with it in a dynamic manner. This continuum ranges from mild embarrassment to severe humiliation. Embarrassment, feeling "undone," and uncomfortably visible, has multiple meanings and personal consequences in terms of the posttraumatic self. Shame can be experienced with or without an audience present. It requires an inarticulate sense of one's shame becoming visible to others (Miller, 1985). Humiliation arises, for example, from torture experiences where the victim is abused, dehumanized, and made an exhibition for others, as in Ibrahim's case history. Victims may not blame themselves for what has happened but experience a profound loss of dignity and power. These types of experiences may later evolve into posttraumatic shame and guilt. As Broucek (1982) and Wilson (2004) describe, experiences of extreme humiliation lead to "soul-death" and "soul-murder."

In its extreme forms, shame is a painful and debilitating experience. Shame is a deeply rooted sense of having violated one's true nature, no matter how accurately or inaccurately perceived. It arises out of a tension between the ego and the ego ideal and can be viewed as a state of tension (Miller, 1985). The ego ideal consists primarily of internalized and idealized parental and cultural values (Hanly, 1984). In psychodynamic terms, the ego ideal is a psychic structure that includes fantasies of one's perfection, grandiosity, and images of moral virtue.

Gilbert (1997, 1998) distinguished between external and internal shame. External shame is associated with social anxiety and is related to one's preoccupations about how others appraise and judge actions. The shamed self feels inferior, flawed, disgusting, weak, unattractive, and inadequate. Similarly, Wurmser (1994) distinguishes "negative" and "positive" forms of shame. The negative forms result in shame anxiety and depressive affect as a reaction pattern, while the positive form serves as a protective attitude, a guardian of values and ideals, prevention against dangerous self-exposure (exhibition) and curiosity (voyeurism). Shame anxiety is fear of disgrace and being looked at by others with contempt. Depressive affect in shame is a result of feeling "under the glare of the mind's eye" or the eyes of the others. Depressive shame is demoralization and a feeling that one's true integrity has been badly damaged or lost. Various researchers suggest that core states of shame reside in a preoccupation and near-obsessive concern with the real or imagined evaluation of others (Gramzow & Tangney, 1992).

In the experience of posttraumatic shame and guilt, mechanisms are mobilized to protect the structural dimensions of the self (i.e., coherence, continuity, connection, autonomy, vitality, energy). The most archaic defense is a kind of a stupor-like, frozen state, wherein the subject forgets parts of his or her own life-history or personality (see Chapter 3). A more differentiated form of defense is an alteration of the mask of personality, as seen in the "poker face" that protects against shame in a very rigid way. Counterphobic forms of shamelessness also develop in the posttraumatic self to stave off fear, vulnerability, and feeling humiliated. A variation on counterphobic reactions is omnipotence, in which there is an attempt to restore intrapsychic balance by developing narcissistic rage, anger, and hostility (van der Zwaal, 1988; Tangney et al., 1992). While clinical theory (Lewis, 1981, 1987a) suggests that narcissistic individuals are more vulnerable to shame than others, research findings (Gramzow & Tangney, 1992) indicate that shame-proneness is negatively correlated with narcissism and positively associated with the risk of psychopathology (Tangney & Dearing, 2003).

The eight dimensions of posttraumatic shame that develop after trauma are presented in Table 9.1. We will discuss each of these dimensions separately and then establish a comparative analysis with posttraumatic guilt (see Tables 9.2 and 9.3).

TABLE 9.1
Dimensions of Posttraumatic Shame

1. Loss of self-worth, virtue, self-esteem, wholeness, goodness, moral integrity
2. Loss of sense of self-continuity in upholding culturally defined values, norms, and respected patterns of behavior
3. Feelings of worthlessness, powerlessness, inadequacy, failure, humiliation, smallness
4. Perception of shame in the eyes of others: condemnation and failure
5. Suicidality in fantasy or action; self-obliteration, desire for escape, isolation, withdrawal, self-imposed exile and alienation
6. Self-consciousness over disappointing others, letting down kinship, family, friends, fellow survivors, etc.
7. Devalued self-appraisal; "loss of moral goodness"
8. Loss of self-respect within culturally defined roles, status, expectations

Source: ©2004 John P. Wilson.

TABLE 9.2
Dimensions of Posttraumatic Guilt

1. Self-recrimination for failed personal enactments
2. Survivor guilt over surviving perils of trauma
3. Death guilt over being alive when others died or were injured
4. Bystander guilt for failure to help others in need
5. Personal guilt for acts of transgressions with negative consequences for others
6. Situational guilt for acting contrary to personal values under coercive processes
7. Moral guilt for failed enactments inconsistent with personal ethics and moral responsibility

Source: ©2004 John P. Wilson.

TABLE 9.3
Posttraumatic Shame Versus Guilt

Psychological dimension	Posttraumatic shame	Posttraumatic guilt
Self-attribution processes	Loss of self-worth, moral virtue, self-esteem, sense of failure	Self-recrimination over behavior rather than self-as-object of appraisal
Emotional states	Humiliation, powerlessness, helplessness, sadness, anger, rage	State-dependent guilt, remorse, regret, apologetic, embarrassment
Action appraisal	I did something to cause it; therefore I am shameful/bad	I failed to act properly or I acted badly
Impact on personal identity	"Loss of face," loss of self-continuity and self-sameness, ego-fragmentation, self-dissolution	No "loss of face," no loss of identity
Suicidality	High potential	Low potential
Defensiveness	Repression, avoidance, suppression, denial	Denial, rationalization, minimization
PTSD-proneness	High	Variable
Dimensions of self-structure negatively affected	All ↓ (for example, decreased sense of continuity, coherence connection, vitality, autonomy, energy)	Part ↓(for example, vitality, connection)

Source: ©2004 John P. Wilson.

4 THE DIMENSIONS OF POSTTRAUMATIC SHAME

4.1 Loss of "Face," Self-Worth, Virtue, and Moral Integrity

Shame is the deep-seated feelings of "losing face" to others important in one's life and the world at large. In simple, spontaneous acts, shame is experienced as losing one's "persona" in the eyes of others, often

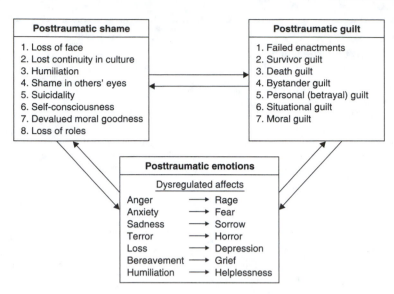

FIGURE 9.1. Affect dysregulation in states of posttraumatic shame and guilt. *Source:* ©2004 John P. Wilson.

manifest by hiding one's face and avoidance behaviors (see Figure 9.1). Shame is closely related to humiliation. Stoller (1987) states

> shame connotes a more fierce, flaming (as in a blush), face manifested, exhibiting and publicly broadcast set of qualities than does humiliation and its humbling...Humiliation is deeper, more hidden in muscle, bone and mind; often more dangerous to others (as in paranoidness), more likely to provoke retaliation; and lower, in the body where enteron becomes humus. (p. 304)

In Greek mythology, the "persona" is the mask of personality as projected to others. The persona of the self, its unique identity and virtue, is an outer "mask" and symbol of selfhood. The true personality resides beneath the mask. In the experience of shame, the individual loses their cherished sense of self-worth. Their persona is tarnished. Virtue, wholeness, and moral integrity are temporarily or permanently lost. In the posttraumatic self, shame develops from traumatic experiences that render the victim powerless, helpless, and unable to act congruently with moral values.

4.2 Loss of Continuity in Upholding Cultural Values

A second aspect of shame is the sense of loss of self-continuity in upholding culturally defined values, norms, and respected patterns of behavior. The loss of self-continuity in synchrony with cultural values is the feeling of having "slipped downwards" from doing the "right thing" according to cultural norms. It is the sense that one has violated the internalized expectations of others about proper behavior. The inner feeling of failure to uphold internalized societal values is one of transgression and having fallen from grace and living with continuity and goodness of character as a person, a quality recognized and positively affirmed by others.

4.3 Humiliation, Feelings of Powerlessness, Worthlessness, Inadequacy, Failure and Smallness

The perceived loss of "face" in the eyes of the world, the internal devaluing of oneself for the failure to sustain culturally important values and expected patterns of actions, results in feelings of humiliation and "smallness." The feeling of "smallness" is similar to being a naive child who has been forcefully scolded by irate parents. The child shows a red face of embarrassment for acting improperly and disappointing its parents. Humiliation is the sense of having been exposed and rendered childlike in stature; diminished in power, status, worth, and importance.

In the posttraumatic self, being subjected to extraordinary stressors (e.g., rape, acts of interpersonal violence, witnessing killings, being coerced at gunpoint to commit unsavory acts, etc.) renders the victim powerless, helpless, and personally inadequate to reverse the course of aversive experiences. In situations of interpersonal violence, the perpetrator exploits these psychological states of vulnerability to their own advantage. As a consequence, shame, including irrational shame, can result.

In the posttraumatic self, shame and psychic numbing are emotional cousins in a family of PTSD symptoms. Insight into this relationship has been made by Wurmser (1987) who stated

> The blank stare and the mask-like face express the global denial of traumatically intense acute feelings (traumatic because they arouse anxiety, e.g., of castration or abandonment). "I don't want to respond to what I have witnessed by feelings." I believe it is such severely traumatogenic shame that underlies what is now often dubbed alexithymia. (p. 82)

The relationship between shame and psychic numbing illustrates that shame is a complex affect rather than a unidimensional emotion. As Wurmser (1994) notes,

> in its complexity, it [shame] resembles emotions like jealousy, envy, and spite, love and hatred, elation and depression, and its own counterpart,

pride, and then belongs to the group of compound affects—highly complex compositions of cognitive emotional structures. (p. 69)

4.4 Perceptions of Shame in the Eyes of Others: Condemnation and Failure

As a psychological phenomenon, shame is comprised of emotions, cognitive attributes, and ego-defensive processes to protect areas of the self. Shame is an overly self-conscious sense of oneself as having been exposed in undesirable ways that conflict with ideal self-images and the bases of self-esteem. The exquisitely attuned pain of shameful self-consciousness is due, in part, to the perception of being actively shamed "in the eyes of others." Hence the English language expression, "Damn your eyes!" This perception may be based on comments or actions taken by others that reflect their disapproval or moral judgments about the behaviors that led to a sense of shame. The idea of being shamed in the eyes of others has been conceptualized as related to estrangement, derealization, and processes of dissociation. Wurmser (1994) states

> The wish inherent in the feeling of shame is, "I want to disappear as the person I have shown myself to be"...in depersonalization the patient indicates, "I'm not this, this is someone else, not I"...this being different once again entails a dichotomy, "I want to be looked at as a different person. I am afraid to be exposed as what I am." (p. 232)

Similarly, the perception of being judged and shamed by others can be a form of externalized projections of one's own self-condemnation and hatred. Self-condemnation is an attribution of personal failure and implies a moral imperative that one "ought" to have acted in a different manner. In the posttraumatic self, harsh self-condemnation is associated with suicidal ideation and the fantasy of obliterating the self completely (see Chapter 3 for a discussion). In suicidal ideation and fantasies of self-annihilation, the unspoken logic is that: If I kill my "self," then I will no longer have to experience the humiliation of shame and the perceived condemnation of others.

4.5 Suicidality in Fantasy or Action: The Desire for Escape, Isolation, Withdrawal, Self-Imposed Exile, and Alienation

Shame and suicidal thinking are yoked thought processes which share the same emotional center. Suicidal ideation is a wish to obliterate the self as an object. If the self does not exist, neither does shame. Suicidal fantasies are manifestations of the desire to escape the pain of losing face and the feared condemnation and outright rejection by others. In the presence of unremitting states of shame, the individual may impose exile, isolation, and alienation to further protect themselves from the experience of public shame and humiliation.

In the posttraumatic self afflicted with PTSD, trauma complexes, or other distressing emotional consequences of trauma, shame can increase the strength of suicidal ideation, especially if there is no foreseeable escape from haunting, intrusive memories of trauma, severe affect dysregulation, and an overwhelming sense of being rendered helpless and powerless. The presence of PTSD, depression, and a shameful appraisal of the worth of the self is a potentially lethal combination.

4.6 Self-Consciousness over Disappointing others and Kinship Networks Embedded within one's Culture

Shame is a multifaceted phenomenon in which self-consciousness associated with negative self-appraisals extends outwards and inwards at the same time. The feeling of having "lost face" is intensified through sources of attachment, affiliation, and interpersonal relationships. The experience of shame reflects a loss of global self-esteem and heightened self-consciousness over disappointing others in kinship networks and important personal relationships.

In the posttraumatic self, shame over what happened during the traumatic experience can be internalized through incorrect and inaccurate appraisals of responsibility (e.g., "it was my fault the enemy soldiers raped me as part of ethnic cleansing;" "it was my fault that I was tortured, or captured, or interrogated," etc.). In clinical assessment, the shameful victim reports feeling small, dirty, a loss of innocence, diminished self-virtue, or a loss of being respected by others because of what happened to them. Shameful states of anxiety-ridden self-consciousness get projected outwards by the internal perception of how they, as a person, are being viewed within the context of role and cultural values that are esteemed by others.

In a psychoanalytic perspective, Wurmser (1987) notes that shame reflects discrepancy between one's self-appraisals of the virtue of the self in comparison with external conflicts of a compliant and aversive emotional behavior

> shame is a faulty defined affect, conscious or unconscious, caused by a discrepancy between expectation and realization, an inner and outer

discrepancy, an inner or an outer conflict. It is the polarity, the tension, between how I want to be seen and how I am. In its internalized version, shame is thus the outcome of a very specific tension between the super-ego and ego-function of self-perception. (p. 76)

As we will discuss, this discrepancy between inner and outer forms of self-experience give rise to defensive measures to quell the anxiety, tension, and self-recrimination that accompany posttraumatic states of shame and guilt.

4.7 De-valued Self-Appraisal: The Loss of Moral Goodness

The experience of shame inevitably involves self-appraisal and negative affects as to personal worth and goodness (Tangney & Dearing, 2003). In states of shamefulness, the person loses their previously enjoyed feeling of goodness and integrity. The loss of face is the perceived loss of being able to present a favorable persona to the world, a "mask" of an unblemished virtuous character.

In the posttraumatic self, shame is negative appraisal of the self that extends to future prospects of restoring a sense of self-esteem and integrity to one's value as a person. Shame can operate unconsciously in trauma complexes and initiate self-destructive and self-defeating modalities of behavior. The internalization of a shameful sense of personal identity sets up a wide range of possibilities by which to create self-fulfilling prophecies of unworthiness. In extreme cases of PTSD, the profoundly shamed person may recreate the conditions in their current lives that attempt to reenact, repeat, or symbolically recapitulate what occurred during a traumatic experience, sometimes as an aborted or belated sense of repetition compulsion (Freud, 1917). Stated differently, internalizing shame and incorporating it into the structure of personal identity can cause a reconfiguration of the self as a whole. The persistent experience of shame in self-conscious states infused with anxiety may ultimately lead to the choice of a negative identity ("I am shamed therefore I am bad and undeserving"), which is the antithesis of optimal states of integrative experiences following trauma.

4.8 Loss of Self-Respect within Culturally Defined Roles and Values

It is theoretically interesting to ponder the question as to whether or not shame would exist if there were no cultures to shape human development. If there were no contextualized cultural norms regarding moral behavior, would shame exist? If social comparison processes were absent due to anomic societies, would shame and guilt exist? If there were no mutually beneficial patterns of hedonic regulation or restrictions on antisocial behaviors aversive to the common good of society, would shame exist?

The fact is that humans have long lived in cultures that shape patterns of living, traditions, and expectations regarding moral behavior. In the experience of shame, it is the transgression of values deemed culturally important and enforced by the authority of law that leads to shame. The perceived act of transgressing culturally defined norms, beliefs, and patterns of behavior forms the basis of self-repudiation. The shame of transgression is the feeling of having failed to conform to the expectations of others; to uphold the values that form the foundation of social structures embedded in the culture (i.e., family, marriage, religion, kinship patterns, etc.). There can be no self-appraisal associated with states of shame if there are no internalized standards by which to judge one's actions.

5 POSTTRAUMATIC GUILT

In Roman mythology, Janus is a God with two faces that look in opposite directions. As a mythological symbol, Janus represents vigilance, faithfulness, and new beginnings. Janus was the guardian of the door to Heaven who had to maintain vigilance in two directions, front and back, to protect the entranceway to the eternal sanctity of goodness. In considering the role of guilt in the posttraumatic self, the opposing, side-by-side faces of shame and guilt look in different directions, left and right. Shame looks away from negative self-appraisal towards guilt, which focuses on action and self-recrimination for failed enactments. In trauma, failed enactments are embedded in the matrix of traumatic stressors and the responses the individual makes to them. In the posttraumatic self, guilt is self-recrimination for failed actions that the individual believes would have created a more salutary outcome. These beliefs can be rational or irrational, correct or incorrect, and are filtered through the prism of ego-defenses.

While shame transforms, guilt motivates remorse and regret (Andrews, 1995). In guilt, there is tension present because one tries to set things right and repair the damage. In posttraumatic guilt, there are self-appraisals of bad conduct since the transgression could have been prevented by acting differently (Lindsay-Hartz, 1984). In our view, posttraumatic guilt is less incapacitating and painful than shame. As Piers and Singer (1953) wrote, the relationship between shame and guilt can be reciprocal and both can coexist in posttraumatic stress disorder following trauma. Moreover, guilt-laden memories focus on a desire to confess wrongdoing (whether actual or imagined) in an attempt to make amends (Lee, Scragg, & Turner, 2001). Although unpleasant, guilt supports and enforces life-sustaining personal values (Lindsay-Hartz, 1984). Guilt highlights moral standards and creates a sense of control by supporting the idea that there is order and meaning in the world, while strengthening the value of reconciling with others and being forgiven for improper actions and failed enactments in traumatic situations.

Table 9.2 presents seven dimensions of posttraumatic guilt that develop during or after traumatic experiences. These seven dimensions are distinct forms of posttraumatic states of guilt that overlap with one another depending on the complexity and demands of the traumatic situation.

6 THE DIMENSIONS OF POSTTRAUMATIC GUILT

6.1 Self-Recrimination for Failed Personal Enactments

In a generic and broadly encompassing way, states of posttraumatic guilt concern failed personal enactments. These failed personal enactments lead to self-recrimination about behaviors manifest in relation to the stressors that require action in terms of coping (Lifton, 1993). Fundamentally, self-recrimination is a form of state-dependent guilt, acute or prolonged in nature, in which the survivor feels remorse, regret, embarrassment, or condemning self-judgments concerning manifest behavior. Unlike shame, guilt does not necessarily involve internal appraisal processes about the self and its "goodness" or "badness" (Tangney & Dearing, 2003).

6.2 Survivor Guilt Associated with Surviving the Perils of Trauma

Living through the perils of trauma that claim the lives of others is among the most common form of survivor guilt. The universal question posed by the survivors is, "Why me? Why did I live when others died or had to suffer losses, injury or the death of loved ones?" The unspoken thought connected to survivor guilt is the feeling of relief and happiness at being spared while others had to die or were painfully injured.

6.3 Death Guilt

Death guilt was a term initially coined by Lifton (1967) in his studies of Hiroshima survivors. In death guilt, the survivor struggles to create a sense of immediate meaning to their survival in the face of death. As Lifton (1979, p. 143) notes, there is a "sensitivity to the dead" and acute awareness of what the survivor had to endure during the traumatic experience. He states

> At the heart of traumatic syndromes—and the overall human struggle with pain—is the diminished capacity to feel, or psychic numbing. There is a close relationship between psychic numbing (including its acute form, "psychic closing off") and death-linked images of denial ("If I feel nothing, then death is not taking place") and interruption of identification ("I see you dying, but I am not related to you or to your death") . . . [the survivor] undergoes a reversible form of symbolic death in order to avoid a permanent physical or psychic death. (p. 173)

Thus, it can be seen that survivor guilt and death guilt are interlinked phenomena. In the specter of one's own death, psychic numbing serves to shut-down powerful emotions that have generated shock to the psyche and the construal of reality. Once the acute stress effects dissipate, self-recrimination for failed personal enactments begin to surface in consciousness, memory and the attempts to process the events that were traumatically disturbing.

6.4 Bystander Guilt for Failure to Help Others in Need

Bystander guilt is another form of posttraumatic guilt that contains self-recrimination for failed enactments (Danieli, 1988). In bystander guilt, the survivor feels regret, remorse or self-condemnation over the failure to help fellow survivors during or after the trauma. Bystander guilt can be rational or irrational in nature. In rational bystander guilt, the survivors know, often correctly, that they could have taken actions to help others but failed to do so. In irrational bystander guilt, the survivors feel that they "should have," "could have," or "might have" been able to generate prosocial behavior during the traumatic experience but failed to do so. In irrational bystander guilt, reconstruction and assessment of the choice-point scenarios (i.e., alternative courses of action) reveals that their feelings of failure are unfounded and mired in psychic confusion that existed at the time of critical incidents, often with very narrow windows of opportunity for any type of prosocial behavior that would have been beneficial to less fortunate survivors or those who perished.

6.5 Personal Guilt for Acts of Transgressions with
Negative Consequences for Others

Another form of posttraumatic guilt pertains directly to acts of transgression that generated negative consequences for others. This form of posttraumatic guilt could also be characterized as "betrayal guilt" since the survivor may have engaged in selfish actions that resulted in personal gain at the expense of others (e.g., stealing, lying, informing on persons, bargaining, deal-making, false accusations, deception, falsifying documents, murder, sexual exploitation). Although the motivational dynamics vary between personal guilt and betrayal guilt, there is a similarity in that both involve moral dilemmas and options for pro-social behavior versus selfish action. In order to understand betrayal guilt, it is necessary to examine the power of situational determinants of behavior and how they were perceived during the traumatic experience. If the perception and assessment of limited degrees of choice or degrees of freedom exist, the intensity of fear may lead to constricted cognitive processes and regressive actions in the service of self-survival above all else (see Krystal, 1968; 1988 for a discussion).

6.6 Guilt for Acting Contrary to Personal Values
Under Coercive Situational Pressures

By definition, traumatic situations are extraordinarily stressful and contain demands for coping that supersede the ordinary stresses of daily living. Under the duress of coercive situational pressures, persons may act in ways that are atypical of their personality characteristics, customary patterns of coping, and moral values. For example, under the "right" confluence of environmental and situational factors, soldiers in combat may adopt an attitude of "revenge," "payback," and "retribution" after suffering heavy losses of fellow soldiers. Such an event was the 1968 My Lai massacre during the Vietnam War. In the context of jungle warfare, tired, angry, and demoralized soldiers killed Vietnamese civilians from My Lai, a small village of "suspected" enemy (old men, women, children) in a "free-fire" war zone. This atrocity took place after the U.S. Army unit, commanded by Lt. William (Rusty) L. Calley, Jr., had incurred significant losses during the preceding days.

The gruesomeness of the My Lai massacre is archetypal in nature as primitive emotional forces were unleashed by military authority that provided rationale to eliminate suspected enemy forces in a geographical area defined as a free-fire zone. At My Lai there existed a confluence of situational factors (e.g., casualties, fatigue, free-fire zones, authorized orders, hierarchical military command structure, ideological justification) that led to the atrocity. Afterwards, as the true and horrific reality of the situation unfolds (e.g., there was no real enemy threat at My Lai), guilt may be experienced as the realization that the actions taken were not morally justifiable or excusable. The dissonance between actions during the stressful situation and their inhuman consequences generates the potential for guilt, despite the opportunity to blame the situational conditions that existed and coercive psychological pressures to initiate the actions that took place. The example of My Lai characterizes many traumatic situations wherein coercive and powerful situational factors exert pressure on survivors to act in ways that may violate their own moral code of conduct.

6.7 Moral Guilt for Failed Enactments Inconsistent with Personal Ethics and Moral Responsibility

In the posttraumatic self, moral guilt is an internal struggle within the self that can produce seeds of self-destruction or, alternatively, self-transformation and personal growth. Moral guilt is a form of self-recrimination for the failure to act authentically in congruence with one's capacity for higher levels of moral reasoning and the yoked behavioral capacity or disposition for moral behavior.

Moral guilt has also been discussed as existential guilt—i.e., guilt connected with the responsibility for making choices regarding moral responsibility for personal actions including those that occur under conditions that produce traumatic injuries. According to Lifton (1979): "The pain of existential guilt...stems directly from a specific act, which can neither be undone, attributed to prior experience, nor erased by social or religious confession. That irresponsibility has a temporal dimension, is in fact bound up with time irreversibility, so that recognizing the one means recognizing the other along with ultimate individual consequence, one's own inevitable death" (p. 138). We can see, then, that moral guilt concerns the struggle of living with acceptance of the irreversibility of action. Viewed differently, moral guilt and the problem of meaning are inseparable since the self is the arbitrator of truth versus deception, i.e., the core dilemma of living without self-derision and debilitating shame.

7 A COMPARATIVE ANALYSIS OF POSTTRAUMATIC SHAME VERSUS GUILT

In their review of the literature on shame and guilt, Tangney and Dearing (2003) attempted to classify early distinctions between shame

and guilt derived from clinical work and specific schools of psychotherapy. In particular, they highlighted the analytical work of Helen B.
Lewis (1971, 1987a, 1987b, 1981) who suggested that shame and guilt
are different concepts. Consistent with our analysis of posttraumatic
shame versus guilt, Lewis (1971) and Tangney and Dearing (2003)
suggest that shame concerns self-appraisal and evaluation of actions and
their worth, goodness, and moral integrity whereas guilt reflects
personal assessments about inappropriate actions for which one feels
remorse, regret, or sorrow. Based on these fundamental distinctions
between shame and guilt, Tangney and Dearing (2003) attempted to
compare the two constructs across several dimensions (e.g., degree of
distress, focus of evaluation, impact on self) to differentiate their
dynamics in psychological functioning. They also noted that shame
and guilt share features which include: (1) responses to negative events
involving moral failures or transgressions; (2) self-appraisals and self-
consciousness about certain types of behavior; (3) negative affects; (4)
cognitive attributions about behavior; (5) interpersonal contexts of
occurrence; and (6) moral actions and moral judgments.

Building on the work of Tangney and Dearing (2003), we have constructed a comparative analysis of posttraumatic shame versus guilt
which is presented in Table 9.3. Examination of Table 9.3 enables comparisons between psychological states of posttraumatic shame versus
guilt. A comparative analysis is useful because it allows hypothesis
testing and clinical application in the treatment of trauma survivors.
To facilitate a comparative analysis, we will examine posttraumatic
shame versus guilt across eight dimensions: (1) self-attribution processes; (2) emotional states; (3) action appraisal; (4) impact on personal
identity; (5) suicidality; (6) defensiveness; (7) PTSD proneness; and
(8) dimensions of self-structure negatively affected by shame or guilt.

In states of posttraumatic shame, self-attribution processes involve
negative cognitions of the self and personally generated attributions of
loss of self-worth and self-esteem, and judgments of moral failure. As
part of negative self-attributional processes, the trauma survivor experiences humiliation, powerlessness, helplessness, sadness, anger, rage, and
hopelessness. These powerful and deep-seated emotions are directly
linked to personal appraisals of moral responsibility: "I did something
bad to cause this to happen; therefore I am shameful and bad person."
As a consequence of these cognitive-affective processes, there are impacts
on personal identity resulting in a "loss of face," loss of a sense of
self-continuity, and feelings of ego-fragmentation and "coming apart"
in terms of moral integrity. The inner conflict associated with states
of posttraumatic shame activates ego-defense mechanisms of repression,
denial, suppression, and strong avoidance behaviors. In the wake of
traumatic experiences, these dysregulated psychobiological states of

affect, identity, and ego-processes increase the proneness to develop psychopathology (Tangney and Dearing, 2003) and PTSD.

In our view, the intensity and severity of shame are directly correlated with high suicide potential and fantasies of killing oneself to obliterate the inner experience of shame and the changes experienced in wholeness, integrity, and moral virtue. In this regard, all dimensions of the self-structure (i.e., continuity, coherence, connection, autonomy, energy, vitality) can be adversely affected, leading to rapid disequilibrium in these planes of self-functioning. In extreme cases of shame, the essential vitality of the self feels drained, with little or no psychic energy to mobilize the other dimensions to govern efficacious action. Moreover, shame is experienced as the loosening (i.e., deintegration) of the dimensions of the self-structure. Shame is loss of boundaries in fine-tuned functioning among dimensions of the self. It is the subjective sense of "I" being diminished, lost, dissolved, broken apart, and exposed in a vulnerable state of being. Therapeutically, then, transcendence of shame is creative self-reinvention and resynthesis of personal experience. It is freeing the ego from super-ego condemnation. The dimensions of the self regain integrity and, when this occurs, there is a reexamination of the self with new meaning and wholeness.

In comparison with states of posttraumatic shame, the experience of posttraumatic guilt tends to be less severe and damaging in its effects to psychological functioning. As Tangney and Dearing (2003) found in their research guilt-proneness is not as strongly predictive of social pathology (e.g., drug and alcohol use, high risk sexual behavior, suicide, arrests, disciplining problems in school) as is shame-proneness. Similarly, in posttraumatic guilt, the survivor has self-recrimination over failed enactments of behavior rather than failed judgments of the self. Accordingly, the attendant emotion is guilt, remorse, regret, and apologetic embarrassment for one's actions which are appraised as "acting badly." Moreover, because cognitive-attributional processes tend to focus on actions rather than the "goodness" of the self, there is relatively little impact on the core dimensions of the self (i.e., continuity, coherence, connection, autonomy, vitality, energy). And while ego-defenses of rationalization, denial, and minimization are utilized in the service of adaptive functioning, the suicide potential is low and the proneness to PTSD is variable (i.e., low to high) depending on the severity of the traumatic situation and the degree of threat to organismic integrity.

While guilt was identified as an associated symptom of PTSD in *DSM-IV* (APA, 1994), the relationship between shame and PTSD is much less clearly defined. Stone (1992) hypothesized that individuals with PTSD suffer from both shame and guilt. Guilt was primarily conceptualized as "survivor guilt," because many survivors reported such feelings as being exempted. As a consequence of core beliefs, shame was described as a feeling of doubting the right to exist (Janoff-Bulman, 1985). Traumatized individuals often feel detached from others, lose trust, and may not perceive life as predictable and controllable. Wong and Cook (1992) suggest that feelings of shame, inferiority, and alienation are part of the PTSD symptom cluster. In the context of traumatic events, shame can be a primary emotion arising at the time of trauma (peritraumatic) and a secondary emotion emerging in the aftermath of trauma when the individual seeks to understand the meaning of the event via attributional processes (Lee, Scragg, & Turner, 2001). Other researchers (Leskela, Dieperink, & Thuras, 2002) suggest that the measure of shame-proneness is positively correlated with PTSD symptom severity, whereas guilt-proneness is not. Empirical evidence (Tangney et al., 1992) indicates that shame-proneness is strongly correlated with characterological self-blame. Andrews et al. (2000) examined the role of shame as a mediator between childhood abuse and adult psychopathology, and found that shame can be considered an independent predictor of PTSD. Kubany, Haynes, Abueg, Manke, Brennan, and Stahura (1996) developed the Trauma-Related Guilt Inventory (TRGI) and identified four primary factors of guilt: emotional distress; hindsight-bias/responsibility; wrongdoing-violation of personal standards; and lack of justification for actions. In validity studies using university students, Vietnam War veterans and battered women, the TRGI was significantly correlated with PTSD, depression, and maladjustment. Kubany (2003) has proposed a multidimensional model of guilt and identified eight contextual variables related to distress over attributes about behavior. A similar analysis and review of the literature was conducted by Baumeister, Stillwell, and Heatherton (1994) who concluded that guilt, in general, is associated with transgression of behavior in interpersonal contexts and is strongest in intensity in tightly knit communal situations where expectations and monitoring of behavior are highest.

7.1 Premorbidity and Shame-Proneness

In our view, shame generated from war or torture is a phenomenon beyond psychoanalytic conceptualization, which focuses on the processes of bonding, attachment, separation, and individual self-development. Development of shame in adult survivors of war violence has direct impact on persons with and without shame-proneness. The dynamics of shame-proneness in these two groups appear to be different. Based on our collective clinical experience, individuals who had an impaired development before being exposed to trauma as adults, integrate shame more easily because war violence is congruent with their assumptions of the world being "mean" and "bad." For example, a patient from Azerbaijan was diagnosed with transitory reactive psychotic episodes. At an early age he was traumatized by family violence and maltreatment. In the course of treatment as a refugee, he stated that during the siege of his city he felt the happiest in his life. The killings, rapes, and the war matched his internalized picture of the world and confirmed that external reality was as bad as his internal world. The stressors of war that surrounded him made him feel healthy since everything suddenly fell into place in a meaningful way. When he came to the Netherlands as an asylum seeker, the cultural context changed and he suffered identity confusion, feeling out of place in the host culture.

8 SHAME AND AFFECT REGULATION IN THE POSTTRAUMATIC SELF

The experience of shame and guilt in the posttraumatic self can be coupled with a broad range of emotional states. Shame and guilt originate in interpersonal transactions that affect others in negative ways, through acts of either omission or commission. Posttraumatic states of shame and guilt can be triggered by trauma-specific cues (TSCs; Wilson & Lindy, 1994) or through stimulus generalization and conditioned learning (Wilson, Friedman, & Lindy, 2001a). Figure 9.1 illustrates the synergistic and reciprocal effects between states of posttraumatic shame and guilt and dysregulated affects (e.g., anger, rage, anxiety, fear, terror, grief, sadness). Thus, compound affective states can fuse in states of posttraumatic shame or guilt. For example, a survivor may have bystander guilt and rage at others who hindered their ability to respond in prosocial ways to help others, or inwardly directed anger at themselves for failed enactments. In other cases, for example, a person may experience intense anxiety at being exposed by others for their failure to act in ways expected by cultural norms in a situation involving rape in a war of ethnic genocide. Moreover, it is possible for a complex state of posttraumatic shame and guilt to coexist and be accompanied by multiple negative, affective states. Fear, anxiety, anger, and rage can function in different ways in terms of motivation and behavioral dispositions. For example, posttraumatic shame associated with profound humiliation, ridicule, and feelings of betrayal, can lead to aggression and attacks on the perceived sources of being "shamed by others." On the other hand, posttraumatic shame or guilt associated with intense anxiety feelings can lead to depressive withdrawal and isolation from others. Moreover, posttraumatic shame and guilt can exist in persons without pre-existing ego-vulnerability of self-pathologies (Kohut, 1971, 1977). Morrison (1990) noted that

> When considered in the context of self-psychology, must the experience of shame be relegated only to those patients suffering from the (relatively serious) personality disorder of narcissism? Certainly, we know that all individuals, including the relatively healthy (possessors of a firmly cohesive "nuclear self") suffer at times from the affect of shame...I suggest that shame in healthy people can also be understood in terms of micro-failures of the (relatively undifferentiated) ideal self. (p. 365)

Considered from the perspective of psychic trauma, the core emotional element which appears to cross-cut all compound affective-cognitive states embedded in the posttraumatic self is fear. The affect of fear in posttraumatic shame and guilt is the fear of losing self-virtue and identity because of failed enactments (i.e., guilt) or attributions of failed moral virtue and character (i.e., shame). In the posttraumatic self, the emotions of anxiety and fear, especially in states of shame and guilt, are powerfully linked to unconscious processes and concerned with self-deintegration and the specter of annihilation. Subjectively, this is manifest in diffuse anxiety states and fears of "falling apart."

9 LEXICAL ANALYSIS OF POSTTRAUMATIC SHAME VERSUS GUILT

Insight and understanding into the nature of posttraumatic states of shame and guilt can be achieved by lexical analysis of the meaning of these emotional states as embedded within posttraumatic conditions and Trauma Complexes (Wilson, 2004).

Figure 9.2 contains a comparative lexical analysis of posttraumatic shame versus guilt. The figure is organized into two sections. First, the key words that describe posttraumatic shame and guilt are presented. Second, words that depict emotional states and nonverbal actions that accompany these psychological states are described. A careful comparison of states of posttraumatic shame versus guilt illustrates the major differences between them, as we have noted above. To clarify, in posttraumatic shame the self-focus and major attributional processes are *inward*, to an evaluation of the "goodness" or "badness" of the self as *the object* of assessment. In contrast, in posttraumatic guilt, the self-focus and attributional processes are *external*, to an evaluation of action. Building on these fundamental differences in psychological processes (i.e., self-focus, attributional processes, and emotion) it may be seen that the two states have attendant nonverbal and emotional qualities.

Posttraumatic states of shame

Words of self-focus (WSF)	Words of emotion and verbal action (WEVA)
Disgrace, dishonor, disesteem	Red-faced, blushing
Degradation, debasement, scorned	Lost face, hide face, "poker" face, blank stare
Descend, fall, come-down, dirty	Hang head, lower head, cover head
Humiliation, embarrassment, weak	Bite tongue
Loss of countenance, transgressions	Isolate, disappear, inanimate
Impaired pride, tarnished hubris, self-respect	Avoidance, shyness
Contempt, mortification, chagrin	Withdrawal, hidden, secretive
Stigma, aspersion, personal flaw	Detachment, stoic appearance
Put down, come down, let down, lowered	Feel small, childlike, "don't look at me"

Posttraumatic states of guilt

Words of self-focus (WSF)	Words of emotion and verbal action (WEVA)
Culpable	Red-handed, black-handed, back-handed
Blamable	Bloody handed
Reproachable	Hiding one's hands
Censurable	On one's hands
Impeachable	Flatfooted
Indictable	Caught in the act
Peccancy	Caught with pants down
Malefactor	Sheepish
Malfeasance	Looking guilty
Misdeed, wrongdoing	Stammering, uneven speech
Faulty	Nervousness and uneasiness
Failure to act	Sweating, darting eyes
Guilty	Covering up deeds
Reprehensible	Hiding evidence

FIGURE 9.2. Lexical analysis of posttraumatic shame versus guilt. *Source:* ©2004 John P. Wilson.

However, because human emotions share common pathways of expression there are overlaps in some areas and important differences in other areas. Further, it is clear that over generations of human experience, the lexical connotations have evolved to accurately "tell the story" and meaning of these emotional states which are universal in nature and readily transparent across cultures.

10 WORDS OF SHAME: APPRAISALS OF SELF

The words of shame reflect negative self-appraisal, loss of self-worth, and a perceived loss of status and reputation in the eyes of others. The Janus face looks to the left. The core emotion in shame is the painful feeling of humiliation and embarrassment (see Figure 9.2). The feeling of humiliation is likewise associated with a sense of disgrace, dishonor, and the fall from one's previous state of grace and goodness. In posttraumatic shame, there is a loss of countenance, a feeling that one has lost virtue, wholeness, integrity, and élan. In some cases, it is the feeling of loss of soul, spirit, identity, human essence, and vitality—as if the seeds of psychic life have been sucked out of the body. In shame, feelings of self-contempt, stigma, debasement, injured pride, tarnished hubris, and a sense of having been "lowered" in status, prominence, importance, or "standing" dominate personal awareness and contribute to self-consciousness and fears of being judged by others.

The lexical connotations associated with states of posttraumatic shame include increased emotional distress: anxiety, fear, tension, apprehensive worry about other's judgments, and phobic anxieties. In terms of observable action, states of shame are evident in being "red-faced" or in attempts to hide or cover up one's face from others. The head, as the seat of the soul and personality, is an important symbol of internalized shame. The face, in the mask of personality or persona of the self, feels "shamed," "lost," or desires to be "hidden" or "covered" by stoic nonexpressiveness (i.e., blank stare, vacuity, etc.). A "lowered head," "hung head," or "covered head" is an act of submission, surrender, and passivity. The "lowered" or "hung head" represents a primordial act of submission and loss of power to assert the self with integrity and strength. A "lowered head" reflects a loss of standing in the social hierarchy; a diminished status among peers and a sense of ostracism. In the animal kingdom, a lowered head signifies submission to a more dominant animal or member of one's species. A similar perspective has been offered by Wurmser (1994) who states

> The power sphere around a person resembles territory in animals. There is an inner limit covering this intimate area that one does not want to show. Yet, there is also an outer limit beyond which one should not expand one's power. The inner limit may be called the "boundary of privacy," the outer limit the "boundary of power expansion." If one crosses another's outer limits, he violates the other's integrity, social prestige, and power, injuring him and causing pain. The transgressor feels guilty. (p. 62)

The powerful emotions of posttraumatic shame and guilt are associated with a broad range of avoidance behaviors: isolation, detachment, withdrawal, hiding, nonappearance, self-imposed exile, cancellation of appointments, surrender of responsibilities, emotional constriction, psychic numbing, affective flatness, and nonconfrontation of others. Beneath the anxiety, fear, and shame that motivate forms of avoidance, the person feels small and childlike, reflecting a sense of having been diminished in stature. At the same time, the feeling of smallness and humiliation may be expressions of sadomasochistic feelings or regressive wishes to return to less stressful times in life and the innocence of childhood.

11 WORDS OF GUILT: APPRAISALS OF ACTIONS

In states of posttraumatic guilt there is a shift of focus away from shame and appraisals of the worth of the self to appraisals of action. The Janus face looks to the right. The lexical connotations associated with words of guilt concern responsibility for behavior. The words of guilt reflect judgments of the "correctness" of action as determined by the actor or others (see Figure 9.2). Hence the lexical connotations of words like culpable, reproachable, indictable, censurable, impeachable, and shameable implicitly define assessments of personal responsibility. Indeed, the suffix "able" suggests the specific meaning of potential acts that can be rendered. Thus, one is "able" to be indicted, reproached, blamed, censured, impeached, and held accountable for malfeasance, misdeeds, failures, wrongdoing, unlawful acts, and peccancy. In essence, guilt is a form of failure to act in a manner deemed appropriate by oneself, others, society, or the law.

In states of posttraumatic guilt there is self-recrimination for failed enactments that occur in the context of traumatic situations. The nonverbal and emotional elements of posttraumatic guilt are reflected in common language. The guilty party has "blood on their hands" or acted in a "backhanded" or "bloody handed" way. The attempt to cover up misdeeds is found in subtle actions—"sitting on one's hands," "hiding one's face," "looking sheepish," acting guilty, or showing cues of increased arousal such as sweating, nervousness, stammering, or darting eyes that avoid contact. Other linguistic expressions refer to acts of detection of one's transgressions by others: "being caught in the act," "being caught with one's pants down," "being caught flat-footed," and thus unable to escape scrutiny. However, unlike states of shame, states of guilt have less emotional distress because the focus of evaluation is the act, not the "self-worth" of the person. The appraisals of the "goodness" or badness of "acts" versus the "self" have significantly different consequences. In this sense, shame is to guilt as punishment is to reprimand. In punishment, there are consequences of temporal duration, privation, and loss of privileges. In reprimand, there are short-lived effects that are forgotten with minimal long-term emotional and psychological consequences. Posttraumatic shame is connected to depression, anxiety, self-dissolution, ego-fragmentation, identity confusion, and alteration in personality processes. In severe cases of posttraumatic shame, the proneness to suicide and PTSD is very high.

In contrast, states of posttraumatic guilt are readily modified by cognitive reframing and reappraisal with a low potential for lethality and the wish to obliterate the self.

12 CULTURE AND SHAME

In terms of history, cultures can be divided into "shame-cultures" and "guilt-cultures" (Dodds, 1951). Shame-cultures utilize external sanctions whereas guilt-cultures employ internal sanctions of conscience. An example of the shame-culture is classical Greek society where the highest goal of an individual was taking care of a good reputation, one's own pride, and enjoying social prestige. Sanctions against those who could not meet the highest goals were social isolation, expulsion, and public contempt.

12.1 The Posttraumatic Self in Cultures of Shame
Versus Guilt

Today, good examples of the shame-culture are seen in the traditional layers of the Islamic societies in the Middle East, Caucasus region, and North Africa. An Arabic proverb says: "A hidden sin is for two thirds forgiven" (from Stroeken, 1988). A sin becomes a sin only at the moment of public revelation. As long as it remains hidden, it does not have to be considered a sin. The cause of a sin must be found outside the person of a sinner, who is considered partially responsible for his deeds. The Djin, a ghost, can be responsible, and sinner must be reconciled with it, by following instructions from the Koran given by traditional healers.

In other cultures, the connection between shame and retribution is governed by tradition. An example of "social balancing" (i.e., justice) after a shameful incident is blood feud (vendetta). In traditional Chechen society, after a crime has been publicly disclosed and a dark layer of shame has fallen onto the perpetrator and his family, it is the responsibility of the family to catch and deliver the perpetrator to the victim's family. By tradition, the guilty perpetrator has to be dressed in black clothes and must wear a beard. According to custom, the victim's family may decide to kill him or to shave his beard and give him his life back (i.e., symbolic forgiveness and an opportunity for rebirth).

Guilt-cultures developed later in history. Religious orientations changed from a shame to a guilt religion. Crime and punishment, guilt and penance became important issues. In the beginning guilt was not internalized and was linked to something one had done wrong.

A motive for doing something bad was considered less important. Later the issue of sin started to exist. In its more extreme forms this led to a collective Christian guilt neurosis (Stroeken, 1988), with Victorian morality and Calvinism as examples. According to Protestant morality, one is born as a sinner, and penance does not help to remove a sin. In Islam guilt is an important issue. One has to pray several times a day in order to prove devotion to God, and plead freedom from sins.

In guilt-cultures, values of individual reality, individual identity, and individual responsibility as ethical principles are propagated (Mansfield, 1981). In addition, family structure may be different in shame- and guilt-cultures. Unlike the patriarchal family in shame-cultures, a guilt-culture family is less authoritarian. Society is different too, veering in guilt-cultures in the direction of individualism. Western societies are good and, in some aspects, extreme examples of this development of a guilt-culture.

In a guilt-culture, moral virtue rests on personal responsibility for action. Our work (Wilson & Drozdek, 2004) with asylum seekers, refugees, and war and torture victims has uncovered complex problems of adaptation for persons who relocate from a shame-culture to a guilt-culture. In some cases, one's cultural identity does not transform and the refugee cherishes the values and personal identity of the culture of origin. In other situations, one's cultural identity undergoes a process of transformation, typically accompanied by confusion, as new cultural values are assimilated. A variation of this phenomenon may be seen with a population of second or third generation migrants in West European countries. They lose connections with a culture of origin of their migrant parents. When this occurs, shame and social control no longer play an important role in their lives. When they introject values of Western guilt-culture, the gap between personal and parental values becomes broader and leads to conflicts. In cases where introjection of the host culture values has not taken place, there is chaos, "culture bereavement," and the forming of a "lost generation," with potentially negative consequences for future generations.

Clinical experience with treatment of migrants suggests that society and religion are two variables that determine whether an individual is prone to shame or to guilt. For example, a Persian family from Teheran may have more in common with an American family living in Los Angeles than with a Persian family from a village in the east of Iran. In addition, having Arab roots and worshiping Allah will not always result in the same identity structure in someone living in Paris as it will in an inhabitant of Riyadh.

Wurmser (1994) discussed the mirroring of the shame- and guilt-culture dichotomy in politics. Conservative political movements are associated with a shame-oriented philosophy, focused on avoiding shame and employing values like pride, honor, strength, power, and independence in body, spirit, and money. On the other hand, liberal movements are associated with guilt-oriented philosophy, promoting justice and fairness and avoiding guilt in the sense of suffering under inequitable regimes that suppress freedom of choice and individual liberty.

Shame is often unacknowledged or neglected as an issue in treatment because it is something to hide and painfully difficult to talk about. Stone (1992) offered suggestions for treatment of the complications of shame in PTSD that include identification, assessment, normalization, and the opportunity to reconceptualize the basis of shame formation.

13 CASE ILLUSTRATION

13.1 Do I Have to Kill my Raped Daughter? The Dilemma of a Chechen Father, Masoud

Masoud is a 48-year-old Chechen man who has lived for 2 years in a west European country as an asylum-seeker with his two sons. His wife and daughter remained in the home country where the war rages on today (2004). They are afraid for their lives as there is a clear and present danger for females to be raped by Russian soldiers as a part of ethnic cleansing. Masoud left Chechnya with his sons because his mother begged him to do so. She told him to leave and save her grandsons from being conscripted. She stated that she could not bear any tragedy happening to them. Masoud immigrated because the wish of the elderly has to be respected and obeyed in his culture. However, he left his wife and daughter behind as there was not enough money for the entire family. His daughter was engaged to be married. Masoud's wife, however, wanted to stay in Chechnya in the hope that the war would end. She found it difficult to leave the tattered ruins of their family house.

Upon arrival in Western Europe, Masoud and his sons entered a procedure of seeking asylum. By law, they had no right to work and moved from one reception center to another. After a year in Europe, Masoud entered treatment because he suffered from symptoms of PTSD and depression. He was exhausted and disappointed in life. He felt guilty because he had left his wife and daughter behind. He believed he was not a good husband and father. He felt he was a good son obeying his mother's orders, and yet felt guilty because he could not be a better father for his sons nor protect his family. He was unemployed, without economic resources, and demoralized. His sons respected him the way a father should be respected in the Chechen culture (i.e., a patriarchal, authoritarian family organization). He was proud of them because they learned the language of the host country and their teachers told him that the boys were very clever and would succeed in the host culture.

One day Masoud spoke with his wife on the phone. She angrily informed him in disguised terms that their daughter had been raped by Russian soldiers. After the sexual assault, the daughter tried to commit suicide by hanging but was saved by neighbors at the last moment. Due to her shame, the daughter did not want to speak with her father. Their conversation lasted only for a couple of minutes and was the first contact in a year. Masoud could not return the telephone call, as his wife was in hiding. At that time, phone connections with Chechnya were poor and unavailable. Masoud was psychologically devastated by the report of his daughter's rape and afraid that his sons would learn of it. He felt guilty because he could not protect his daughter. He was furious and felt blocked because he could not avenge her death. However, having lived outside Chechnya for almost 2 years, he questioned whether or not he wanted to meet the expectations of his native culture.

In accordance with Chechen tradition, Masoud was supposed to kill his daughter since a raped woman brings shame on a family. As a father, he was supposed to kill the perpetrator, seek revenge, and cleanse his family's name.[1] Finding the rapist was impossible and Masoud did not want to kill his daughter because he loved her very much. He told his therapist that he found vendetta an inappropriate solution to a crime but that it was the expectation in his home country. As a protector, he felt guilty of failing but not ashamed because in the host Western country nobody knew what had happened to his daughter. For this reason he was afraid that his sons might hear the story and eventually seek revenge themselves or expect him to act according to the Chechen tradition. If his sons discovered their sisters' rape, he would not only feel guilty but shameful as well. He feared feeling ashamed in the eyes of friends and family in Chechnya who were far away. Masoud collected enough money to pay somebody to smuggle his daughter out of Chechnya, and she eventually joined him in the Netherlands.

Masoud immigrated from a shame-based culture and was forced to migrate to a guilt-oriented culture. Outside of his native culture he was partially freed of shame but experienced guilt for failing as a father.

---

[1] As this chapter was being written nearly 1,000 school children, teachers, and civilians were killed in Beslan, Chechnya by Muslim militants and Russian soldiers in a local elementary school. Terrorists booby-trapped the interior of the school, selectively murdered teachers and students and then detonated explosive devices, creating havoc, mass destruction, and senselessly killing innocent children.

His identity was in transition. He started questioning expectations his native culture had for him and by rationalizing his choices by using the norms of the host culture. He hoped that the incident would remain secret and he would not have to feel ashamed or act in revenge to sustain his pride and that of his family.

14 Case Histories: Aisha and Neris

14.1 The Story of Aisha, an Expelled Bosnian Woman

The war began in May 1992 for Aisha. It came suddenly. Here is her story:

The soldiers came, destroyed the mosque and a number of houses, and left again. They settled not far from our village and one day they collected all the men between the age of 16 and 66. My father was also taken then. That day I was alone at home. My mother had left together with my brother and sister a week before. My brother had to have an operation and that was the reason for them leaving. Two days later the soldiers came to pick me up, too. I was 17 years old at the time. I screamed: "Where are we going?" They said: "Hold on, we're bringing you to your father." They brought me to the local prison and put me in a cell. They said: "If your father won't pay then somebody must pay, and that someone is you." For six days I heard nothing. Then a soldier came in and ordered me to undress, which I didn't want to do. He began to beat me and said that if I didn't do it he would undress me. He tore off my clothes, while swearing and beating me. Then another soldier came. I fainted. After a while when I woke up, my whole body hurt. I was alone in the cell and covered with something that looked like a shirt. I couldn't move. In front of me there was a bowl with water, but I was so weak that I couldn't pick it up. Then I fell asleep. Every now and then I woke up and I was always alone. Once I could stand up I took the shirt and looked around me. Very high up there was a window. I stood on a chair, knotted the shirt on the bars and the other end around my neck. I wanted to die. I believe that the guards heard me. They appeared at once, I jumped from the chair, but it didn't work. They found me and pulled me off. Then they said: "If you do this one more time we'll put you naked into the prison courtyard and you know what's going to happen then." I told the guards that they must kill me immediately. They answered that I would have to wait for that. So they left me there alone again. The next day another soldier came to rape me, followed by another one, and another one. They said that I knew what was going to happen with me and that I wouldn't survive that. After that they took three of us girls out of the cells and they took us with a truck in an unknown direction. After a while we had to get out. We stopped by a building that looked like a hangar. We slept there one night. The following evening they came back and said that we had to leave again. We drove endlessly. From time to time they took one of the girls off the truck, and

I never saw her back again. I was the last one left. Then they brought me back to my house.

On arrival I saw that the people of the village gathered in a few houses. There I found my aunt and her children. She was happy to see me. We continued to live in the village like in a concentration camp. The soldiers came every now and then to pick up people who never came back. Day in, day out we sat there waiting to see whom they would take next. At a certain point everyone who could walk was made to do forced labor. They came with trucks to pick us up and forced us to do hard labor in the fields. In the evenings they brought us back to the village, and every evening I asked myself where I would be taken to the next day.

Then I began to experience ugly things from the people of my village. They asked me how it came about that I had survived. How it was that I was brought back alive? What had I given to the enemy or said to them? Why did they let me live? They said that I was a traitor, a collaborator. I don't know how I have survived those days. The only thing I wanted was to be dead.

One day the International Red Cross team found us by accident. They registered us and said that they would come back to free us, but they never came back again. In June the soldiers gathered us all together and took us away. They didn't tell us where we were going. They brought us to a nearby city and from there to the mountains. They told us that our people were waiting there for us. If they wanted to receive us we would be free and could go. They ordered us to get out of the trucks. Soldiers again selected the young women and didn't let them go. There was screaming and crying and mothers begged the soldiers to leave their daughters alone. All at once the soldiers were in a hurry. Then shooting began. There were shots from every side. Then the soldiers disappeared, and the UNPROFOR trucks came and took us away to another city. That was a city where my mother was at the time. When I met my mother I didn't tell her what had happened to me. I only said that the very worst thing that happened to me is that I am still alive. She tried to help me. She sacrificed herself completely. She followed me everywhere, and even wanted to follow me when I went to the toilet. She was afraid that I would do something to myself. At a certain moment I couldn't take it any more and looked for help by an international humanitarian organization in the city. I wanted to talk with somebody. There I just got some tablets from a doctor. I returned to my mother.

At that time bad things started to happen again. The other women I knew (those were all women who had lost someone or had someone missing) started asking me why I had survived. I didn't any longer dare to leave my house. I believed that after some time people would forget me and leave me in peace. But this didn't happen. Then the men began to insult me, too. They called out that I was a traitor, a whore, and they threatened me. My family was also threatened. My brother had difficulties at school. Then my mother suggested that I should leave. But at that time this was not possible. However, I couldn't stay at home either. One day my mother came home with the proposal that I should go to The Netherlands. I had to decide very quickly. Not only to protect myself, but the whole family. They were all under pressure because of me. I had the feeling that if I went everyone would be relieved. I got a visa through a person who organized the journey and left for The Netherlands.

14.2 Did Neris Really Survive the Fall of Srebrenica?

The war came to Neris where she lived in Kravica, in the Bratunac region of Bosnia. She was 9 1/2 years old when war broke out. The war began with gunshots. Her family fled from their village to a safer place but fighting broke out there too. A long process of moving from one place to another began and as soon as the family arrived somewhere that place would come under siege.

At the end of their flight they arrived in the city of Srebrenica in Eastern Bosnia. Once there, the family looked for a place to stay. In the meantime Srebrenica was surrounded. In the city daily life went on in the midst of war. Neris and other children were required to go to school. The route to school was very difficult because bombs would fall and there was fighting. Neris remembers that when she was going to school, shells fell on a place where many people gathered. An atrocity of war had commenced. She remembers people screaming and the body parts flying around her. Today, she can still see hands, legs, and other parts of dismembered human bodies in front of her eyes. Her brother lived near the school Neris and her sister ran to his place and waited until shelling was over. Eventually they ran home but fighting and shelling started again. Neris lived in a house without a roof and she and her sister went to school without shoes and in tattered clothing. In the fall of 1995, the weather was extremely cold and they had very little to eat. Here is her story:

On July 10th at first it was quiet, and then we saw lots of people fleeing. People felt that something bad was going to happen. Suddenly we heard sounds and there was a terrible fear. There was shooting from all sides. The next morning, masses of people were leaving. Some were shouting that Srebrenica was going to fall. My mother, five other sisters, and me joined this mass of people. We walked to Potocari, about 5 or 6 kilometers away from the town. Then shooting began from every direction. We didn't have any bread or water with us. We reached Potocari around midnight. Then they packed us all together in a sort of factory. We were there with hundreds of people; there was no place to sleep. We found a place to sleep on the concrete, my father, mother, brother, and sisters. When night fell we heard screaming and noise. Then they came, wearing black bands round their heads and sunglasses. They began to beat people with sticks and took young girls and women out of the crowd. They took one of my sisters with them. Then they raped her. My sister screamed for help but we couldn't do anything. We had to watch with our hands tied behind our heads. This lasted for 1 or 2 hours. I tried to shut my eyes but I couldn't. When they had finished with my sister they let her go. My sister was naked and broken. As soon as they let her go she fell down unconscious. Afterwards they did the same thing with other girls and young women.

The night fell. My father sat in the dark, and my brother was next to him. Then four of them came again. They were wearing UNPROFOR uniforms. They took older men and children out of the crowd. They slammed the children against the wall. After that they kicked the men with their boots in the stomach, head, and wherever they could. Some men didn't get up any more. We sat in a corner. Then two of them approached us. They took my father out. They asked: "What are you doing here with all the women, come here!" My sisters and me screamed to leave him alone. Then they took out a rifle. We shut our eyes. On the barrel of the rifle a big knife was tied. They stabbed my father in the hands, then in his stomach, and then in his neck. Finally, they cut his throat. Then they put his head in one bag and his body in another. They threw everything out of the room, I don't know where. After that they came to get my brother. He had problems with his leg. They murdered my brother the same way as they did my father. Then they continued killing other people. We all began to scream. My mother went to fetch some rainwater, she took a bottle with her and went to the door. We stayed sitting in the corner, with hands behind our heads. I saw that someone took off my mother's headscarf and pulled her by the hair. I ran to my mother and tried to defend her. He yelled at me: "Bitch, what do you want? Do you want to be left without your mother as well?" I began to cry and then he gave me a terrible kick. That's how I lost all my front teeth. I fainted. When I woke up, I was completely covered with blood, and I called to my mother. She was covered with blood, too. She was beaten, and lying next to me. That night we stayed in the factory.

The next day we were forced to leave the building and get into buses. We waited for hours, until we could get a place on one of the buses. The street was cordoned off with ribbons. They began to spray water on us. They threw pieces of bread at us. Then the UNPROFOR vehicles arrived. The first couple of buses left, but we were waiting until it was our turn to go. We saw the next row of buses coming towards us. There were trucks and buses. They let them come in one by one. Around midday we could leave, too. We ran as fast as possible to get on the bus. Women with children, young and older women. The door of the bus was open. We all crowded in. There was fighting to get on the buses, everyone wanted to get on. When the bus was completely packed we left towards Bratunac. We passed Kravica, my village, and Konjevic Polje. Then the buses had to stop; soldiers were looking for gold and money. They pointed their rifles at the women and told them to give them all their money and gold. Whoever had some gave it to them. Then they hauled young women out of the buses. These women never came back. After that we drove further for a very long time. When we arrived in Kladanj, they ordered us to go out of the bus as quickly as possible. They beat us wherever they could. We all thought that they were going to murder us. Then we had to continue walking for a long time. We were frightened. We passed their bunkers. They laughed and spat at us. At a certain point it was said that we were on a free territory.

Some months later, my sister who was raped discovered that she was pregnant. My mother at first wanted to distance herself from her, because she was ashamed of her pregnancy. Other sisters and I said that it was not her fault. My sister gave birth and immediately gave the child away. Throughout her pregnancy we couldn't stand her. Her stomach disgusted us.

Later on, I went to Sarajevo to visit my other sister who was married there. There I got to know a guy who was a friend of my sister's husband. I fell in love and married him. I didn't know that he had problems with some people. I knew nothing about these people and also nothing of what my husband did. I only knew that he had to hide. He found a home for me and I sat there always alone.

I was pregnant for four months. One evening somebody was knocking at my door. I opened it and there stood two men with tights over their heads. They were looking for my husband, and I said that I didn't know where he was. Then they attacked me. One of them tried to strangle me with a plastic bag, and kept asking me questions about my husband. Then they started to hit me. They swore at me. One of them took out a knife and pushed it at my stomach. He said that he would cut my stomach open if I don't tell him where my husband is.

They threw me against the wall and I fell on the floor. Then one of them tore my clothes off. I began to scream and they gagged my mouth with paper. They beat me very hard and I fainted. When I came to they had already gone. I was completely covered with blood. After that my neighbor took me to the hospital. I lay there for 10 days with drips in both arms and on an artificial respirator. My husband knows nothing about this incident. A doctor came to me and told me that I had been raped, but that I'd kept the baby. After everything that had happened I couldn't stay in Sarajevo any longer. I went to my mother's place, but my husband came looking after me. Finally, he found me and told me that we must leave Bosnia. I was afraid to leave because I was frightened of him, but I had no choice. I was pregnant and married to this man, and what becomes of a woman without a husband and what becomes of a child without a father? I didn't want my child to be a bastard.

When I arrived in The Netherlands in December that year I felt really bad. Our child got sick when it was 6 months old, and had to stay in a hospital. I don't know what's wrong with my child. Doctors say that it suffers from an unknown viral infection. I'm exhausted, I don't know how I'm going to manage my life. I have to keep going to the hospital for the little one. My husband doesn't go with me to the hospital, and does not support me. I am alone again.

Aisha and Neris came to the Netherlands driven by the need for safety. They were deeply ashamed of the experiences they had during the war in Bosnia (1992–1995). Neris never understood how her mother could desert her daughter who was raped in front of the village and became pregnant. She never disclosed the story of her rape to her husband. And though many people from Srebrenica were witnessing rapes, killings, and deportations, they could not accept that their spouse was one of the victims. The secret of rape stood in the way of intimate relationships. Aisha and Neris were profoundly emotionally damaged and wanted to die to end their suffering.

In the counseling process, the feelings of shame and death fantasies were strongly present and blocked Aisha and Neris from telling their life stories. Both women went into psychotherapy and received psychoeducation (Drozdek & Wilson, 2004). As time passed, psychotherapy and adaptation to forced migration brought positive changes. Aisha and Neris discovered the host culture with its norms and values, especially democracy and respect for the individual. They stated that it helped them to make progress and feel more relieved. In Bosnia it is not common for a woman to divorce following ethnic cleansing and rape. Divorce means breaking up a family and being a "bad woman." The invisible pressure that Aisha and Neris felt was an informal way of social control that made them feel stigmatized as individuals in the native community. Aisha and Neris felt that the host culture accepted them the way they were, with all their abusive and violent experiences. Living in new surroundings and receiving posttraumatic treatment made them feel that many of their problems could be solved. However, the feelings of shame and rejection remained. Bad memories and nightmares continue as part of unmetabollized war trauma. Despite treatment and the disappearance of stigma caused by rape in the host society, the feeling of shame remains present. The Janus-faced emotions of shame and guilt are still active and alternate in the persona of the self. The power of war trauma can be authenticated by psychotherapy but it cannot be erased from memory.

15 THE TRANSFORMATION OF POSTTRAUMATIC SHAME AND GUILT

The transformation of posttraumatic shame can occur with the passage of time, psychological treatment, or by spiritual epiphany. However, unresolved posttraumatic shame continues to have the power to influence behaviors, and to generate fuel for Trauma Complexes, PTSD and self-destructive patterns of coping. As Wurmser (1987) observed

> the careful analysis of shame requires great tact and patience. We have to respect the patient's need to hide behind layers of silence, evasion, omission, intellectualization as dictated by such anxiety about exposure. We have to understand his need to assume a mask of hauteur and arrogance ... we have to respect it as rooted in anxiety, not in sinful self-indulgence. To attack these protective tactics as narcissism or just to

accept them as legitimate modes of self-expression, may be expedient, but neither is part of an optimal psychoanalytic approach. With both eventually we may have to pay a heavy price in negative transference, in acting out, and in stagnation. (p. 90)

This passage by Wurmser crystalizes a basic truth that shame inevitably leads to needs to protect posttraumatic injuries to the self in all its constituent dimensions. Stated differently, shame damages the soul of the person, their most cherished inner sense of identity and humanity. Damage to the sanctity of the self, especially rending it vulnerable and in danger of symbolically dying, is a primordial fear at the deepest level of the psyche. Hence, it is not surprising that narcissistic defenses will be instituted to protect the fragility of the self. In the posttraumatic self, these areas of injury and defense against them will be transferred to the therapist in trauma-specific ways (TST, Wilson & Lindy, 1994; TSTT, Wilson & Thomas, 2004). In our view, effective posttraumatic therapy must recognize the significance of TST (i.e., trauma specific transference modalities) during treatment. We agree with Wurmser (1987) that there will exist "negative transference" and that it will unfold during the therapeutic process of metabolizing psychological trauma. However, what Wurmser did not describe is that there will be equally strong countertransference reactions manifest by the therapist (Wilson & Lindy, 1994; Wilson & Thomas, 2004). These countertransference reactions include empathic strains and strong tendencies to become over involved with the turmoils of the patient or desires to unconsciously escape through avoidance, distancing, and detachment reactions upon confronting the horrific realization of suffering from PTSD, Trauma Complexes, and severe damage to the self. In this regard, shame and guilt are a two-way street: they will exist in the patient and therapist at the same time in different intrapsychic configurations. The narcissistic injuries in the patient make salient the narcissistic vulnerabilities in the therapist. Working with the complexities of shame and guilt in the posttraumatic self, patient and therapist share a common ground of human vulnerability whose management likely determines the quality of outcome.

REFERENCES

American Psychiatric Association. (1994). *Diagnostic and statistical manual of mental disorders* (4th ed.). Washington, DC: American Psychiatric Association.

Andrews, B. (1995). Bodily shame as a mediator between abusive experiences and depression. *Journal of Abnormal Psychology, 104,* 277–285.

Andrews, B., et al. (2000). Predicting PTSD symptoms in victims of violent crime: The role of shame, anger, and childhood abuse. *Journal of Abnormal Psychology, 109,* 69–73.

Baumeister, R. F., Stillwell, J., & Heatherton, C. (1994). Guilt: An interpersonal approach. *Psychological Bulletin, 115,* 243–267.

Broucek, F. J. (1982). Shame and its relationship to early narcissistic developments. *International Journal of Psychoanalysis, 63,* 369–378.

Clark, D. M. & Wells, A. (1995). A cognitive model of social phobia. In R. Heimberg et al. (Eds.), *Social phobia: Diagnosis, assessment and treatment* (pp. 69–93). New York: Guilford Press.

Danieli, Y. (1988). Confronting the unimaginable: Psychotherapists' reactions to victims of the Nazi Holocaust. In J. P. Wilson, Z. Harel & B. Kahana (Eds.), *Human adaptation to extreme stress* (pp. 219-237). New York: Plenum Press, Inc.

Dodds, E. R. (1951). *The Greeks and the irrational.* Berkeley, California: University of California Press.

Drozdek, B. & Wilson, J. P. (2004). Uncovering: trauma focused treatment approaches for war veterans and refugees. In J. P. Wilson & B. Drozdek (Eds.), *Broken spirits: Treating traumatized asylum seekers, refugees, war and torture victims* (Ch. 10, pp. 241–274). New York: Brunner-Routledge Press.

Fenichel, O. (1945). *The psychoanalytic theory of neurosis.* London: Routledge & Kegan Paul.

Freud, S. (1917). *Introductory lecture on psychoanalysis.* New York: W. W. Norton.

Gilbert, P. (1997). The evolution of social attractiveness and its role in shame, humiliation, guilt and therapy. *British Journal of Medical Psychology, 70,* 113–147.

Gilbert, P. (1998). What is shame? Some core issues and controversies. In P. Gilbert & B. Andrews (Eds.), *Shame: Interpersonal behavior, psychopathology, and culture* (pp. 39–45). New York: Oxford University Press.

Gramzow, R. & Tangney, J. P. (1992). Proneness to shame and narcissistic personality. *Personality and Social Psychology Bulletin, 18,* 369–376.

Hanly, C. (1984). Ego ideal and ideal ego. *International Journal of Psychoanalysis, 65,* 253–261.

Janoff-Bulman, R. (1985). The aftermath of victimization: Rebuilding shattered assumptions. In C. R. Figley (Ed.), *Trauma and its wake: The study and treatment of post-traumatic stress disorder* (pp. 15–35). New York: Brunner/Mazel.

Kohut, H. (1971). *The analysis of the self.* New York: International Universities Press.

Kohut, H. (1977). *The restoration of the self.* New York: International University Press.

Krystal, H. (1968). *Massive psychic trauma.* New York: International University Press.

Krystal, H. (1988). *Integration and healing.* Hillsdale, New Jersey: The Analytic Press.

Kubany, E. (2003). *Trauma related guilt inventory.* Hawaii: National Center for PTSD Publication.

Kubany, E., Haynes, S. N., Abueg, F., Manke, F. P., Brennan, J. M., & Stahura, C. (1996). Development and validation of the trauma-related guilt inventory. *Psychological Assessment, 8,* 428–444.

Lee, D. A., Scragg, P., & Turner, S. (2001). The role of shame and guilt in traumatic events: A clinical model of shame-based and guilt-based PTSD. *British Journal of Medical Psychology, 74,* 451–466.

Leskela, J., Dieperink, M., & Thuras, P. (2002). Shame and posttraumatic stress disorder. *Journal of Traumatic Stress, 15,* 223–226.

Lewis, H. B. (1971). *Shame and guilt in neurosis.* New York: International University Press.

Lewis, H. B. (1981). *Freud and modern psychology* (Vol. 1). New York: Plenum Press.

Lewis, H. B. (1987a). Shame and narcissistic personality. In D. Nathanson (Ed.), *The many faces of shame* (pp. 93–133). New York: Guilford Publications.

Lewis, H. B. (1987b). *The role of shame in symptom formation.* Hillsdale, NJ: Lawrence Erlbaum.

Lifton, R. J. (1967). *Death in life: The survivors of Hiroshima.* New York: Simon & Schuster.

Lifton, R. J. (1979). The broken connection: On death and the continuity of life. New York: Basic Books.

Lifton, R. J. (1993). From Hiroshima to the Nazi doctors: The evolution of psychoformative approaches to understanding traumatic stress syndromes. In J. P. Wilson & B. Raphael (Eds.), *International handbook of traumatic stress syndromes* (pp. 11–25). New York: Plenum Press.

Lindsay-Hartz, J. (1984). Contrasting experiences of shame and guilt. *American Behavioral Scientist, 27,* 689–704.

Mansfeld, J. (1981). Protagoras on epistemological obstacles and persons. In G. B. Kerferd (Ed.), *The sophists and their legacy* (pp. 38–53). Wiesbaden: Franz Steiner.

Miller, S. (1985). *The shame experience* (pp. 4–140). London: The Analytic Press.

Morrison, A. (1990). Shame, ideal self and narcissism. In A. Morrison (Ed.), *Essential papers on narcissism* (pp. 348–373). New York: New York University Press.

Piers, G. & Singer, A. (1953). *Shame and guilt.* Springfield, IL: Charles C. Thomas.

Stoller, R. J. (1987). Pornography: Daydreams cure humiliation. In D. Nathanson (Ed.), *The many faces of shame* (pp. 292–308). New York: Guilford Publications.

Stone, A. M. (1992). The role of shame in post-traumatic stress disorder. *American Journal of Orthopsychiatry, 62,* 131–136.

Stroeken, H. P. J. (1988). Cultuur zonder schuld en schaamte? In P. J. G. Mettrop, M. L. van Thiel, & E. M. Wiersema (Eds.), *Schuld en schaamte: Psychoanalytische opstellen* (pp. 31–44). Meppel/Amsterdam: Boom.

Tangney, J. P., et al. (1992). Shamed into anger? The relation of shame and guilt to anger and self-reported aggression. *Journal of Personality and Social Psychology, 62,* 669–675.

Tangney, J. P. & Dearing, R. (2003). *Shame and guilt.* New York: Guilford Publications.

Wilson, J. P. (2004) Broken spirits. In J. P.Wilson & B. Drozdek (Eds.), *Broken spirits: The treatment of traumatized asylum seekers, refugees and war and torture victims* (pp. 141–173). New York: Brunner-Routledge.

Wilson, J. P. & Drozdek, B. (2004). Broken spirits: The treatment of traumatized asylum seekers, refugees and war and torture victims. New York: Brunner-Routledge.

Wilson, J. P. & Lindy, J. (1994). *Counter-transference in the treatment of PTSD.* New York: Guilford Publications.

Wilson, J. P. & Thomas, R. (2004). *Empathy in the treatment of trauma and PTSD.* New York: Brunner-Routledge.

Wilson, J. P., Friedman, M., & Lindy, J. (2001a). *Treating psychological trauma and PTSD.* New York: Guilford Publications.

Wilson, J. P., Friedman, M. J., & Lindy, J. D. (2001b). An overview of clinical consideration and principles in the treatment of PTSD. In J. P. Wilson, M. J. Friedman, & J. D. Lindy (Eds.), *Treating psychological trauma and PTSD* (pp. 59–94). New York: Guilford Publications.

Wurmser, L. (1987). Shame: The veiled companion of narcissism. In D. L. Nathanson (Ed.), *The many faces of shame* (pp. 64–92). New York: Guilford Press.

Wurmser, L. (1994). *The mask of shame.* New Jersey: Jason Aaronson.

Wong, M. R. & Cook, D. (1992). Shame and its contribution to PTSD. *Journal of Traumatic Stress, 5,* 557–562.

van der Zwaal, P. (1988). Verzwijgen en bekenn, en: de oorsprong van twee houdingen. In P. J. G. Mettrop, M. L. van Thiel, & E. M. Wiersema (Eds.), *Schuld en schaamte: Psychoanalytische opstellen* (pp. 15–30). Meppel/Amsterdam: Boom.

10

The Resilient Trauma Survivor

JOHN P. WILSON AND CHRISTINE E. AGAIBI

1 INTRODUCTION

The nature and complexity of the posttraumatic self compels analysis of how resilience results after emotionally significant and life-changing traumatic experiences. How do some survivors "spring back" following life-threatening trauma and manifest healthy and optimal levels of psychological functioning? Anecdotal clinical evidence has documented case histories of war veterans, torture victims, survivors of ethnic cleansing, genocide, terrorist attacks and others who have endured unimaginable, horrific trauma and gone on to live healthy, productive lives (e.g., Wiesel, 1969; Dimsdale, 1980; Wilson, Harel, & Kahana, 1988; Harel, Kahana, & Wilson, 1993; Krystal, 1968; Eitinger, 1961; Lifton, 1993; Ulman & Brothers, 1988). The remarkable lives of resilient survivors lead us to ask: What are the factors that enable some persons to overcome and transform profoundly traumatic life-events? What differentiates them from their cohorts who develop chronic posttraumatic stress syndrome (PTSD), depressive states and post-traumatic self-disorders (Parsons, 1988)?

Theoretical models of traumatic stress syndromes and the literature on PTSD have established that there is a wide range of outcomes in how persons cope with traumatic experiences (Bonnano, 2004; Wilson & Drozdek, 2004; Wilson, Friedman, & Lindy, 2001; Wilson, 1995; Zeidner & Endler, 1996; Wilson & Raphael, 1993). The conceptual models of traumatic stress (Wilson, 2004a; Wilson, Friedman, & Lindy, 2001; Wilson & Thomas, 2004; Wilson, 1989a) and adaptive coping processes (Folkman, 1997) are useful paradigms by which to examine the question of resiliency, i.e.: How do persons recover from psychological trauma? What are the psychobiological factors that are associated with resiliency and effective coping? What are the mechanisms of resilience that allow for plasticity in coping?

In this chapter we will explore the question of trauma and resiliency. We will present a conceptual model of trauma and resilience based on a review of the literature. To undertake such an analysis requires definitional clarity on the meaning of resilience. As a construct, resilience is generally viewed as a quality of character, personality, and coping ability. Resiliency connotes strength and flexibility; a capacity for mastery and resumption of normal functioning after excessive stress that challenges individual coping skills (Richardson, 2002; Lazarus & Folkman, 1984). In the context of extreme stress, resilience refers to an ability to overcome the demands posed by hardship (e.g., trauma, bereavement, economic loss, disaster, political upheaval, and cultural changes) and maintain psychological vitality and mental health (Bonnano, 2004; Wilson, 2004a; Wilson & Drozdek, 2004; Harel, Kahana, & Kahana, 1988; Yehuda, 1998; Harel, Kahana, & Wilson, 1993).

In experimental studies, resilience has been used as an independent and dependent variable. In this regard, it is meaningful to speak of *resilient persons, resilient behavioral adaptations,* and *resilient outcomes* in different situations. A "person by situation" interactional model of resilience is conceptually advantageous to the analysis of resilience as a posttraumatic phenomenon (see Wilson, 1989a; Aronoff & Wilson, 1985; Zeidner & Endler, 1996 for a review). Employing an interactionists' framework we can ask: What are the characteristics of resilient persons that distinguish them from less resilient persons? What constitutes resilient behavior in different types of traumatic situations with varying stressor demands, adversity, or the complexity of problems to be solved? These questions have been examined in a comprehensive review of the literature (Agaibi & Wilson, 2005) and enable us to identify 20 distinct characteristics of highly resilient trauma survivors. We will first present a theoretical model of resilience and then discuss the characteristics of the resilient trauma survivor.

2 A MODEL OF RESILIENCE IN RESPONSE TO PSYCHOLOGICAL TRAUMA

Figure 10.1 presents a model of resilience in response to psychological trauma. The model identifies key variables that interact dynamically in the determination of resilient behavior evoked by traumatic life-experiences. The figure is a simplification of the various pathways

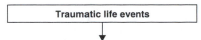

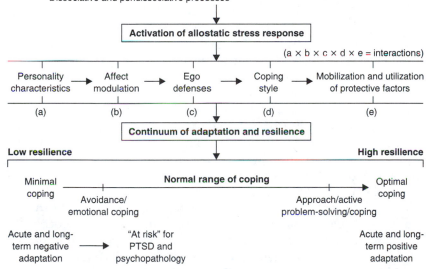

FIGURE 10.1. A model of resilience in response to psychological trauma. *Source:* ©2001, 2004 John P. Wilson.

by which resilience results from exposure to different types of traumatic events (see Wilson & Lindy, 1994 for a discussion).

The model is integrative in nature and is implicitly a person–environment paradigm of resiliency in relation to the perception, processing, and adaptation to traumatic stress. As such, it incorporates the earlier models presented by Green, Wilson, and Lindy (1985), Wilson (1989a), Wilson, Friedman, and Lindy (2001), Maddi (1999), and

Richardson (2002). The integrative nature of the model helps to identify the complex levels of interaction among variables that work together to produce a continuum of adaptive behavior and different degrees of resilient behavior in the wake of psychological trauma. The model of resiliency in response to trauma serves to clarify which aspects of the resilience puzzle have been investigated empirically and which ones have not been studied at all, or systematically analyzed within the context of an interactional model that attempts to specify how traumatic events impact psychological processes at multiple levels of psychological functioning.

To understand the plasticity of behavior in response to traumatic life-events, it is necessary to recognize the multidimensional nature of traumatic experiences. First, traumas are not equal in their impact to the psyche and vary greatly in their stressor dimensions (Wilson, 1989a, 2004a; Wilson & Lindy, 1994). Second, there are individual subjective responses evoked by trauma which set in motion a cascade of internal psychological processes (Wilson, 2004b). Third, there are different types of stressor events (e.g., single vs. multiple, simple vs. complex, individual vs. collective) that vary in their severity of impact and resultant states of allostatic load (McEwen, 1998, 2002; Wilson, Friedman, & Lindy, 2001). Moreover, as an intrinsic part of allostatic load phenomena, there are degrees of affect dysregulation that are directly related to the cognitive processing of traumatic experiences (Schore, 2003a, b). In brief, there are at least five distinct patterns of allostatic load caused by trauma that result in different baseline levels of organismic functioning following trauma (McEwen, 2002). In other words, there is a new "set point" of stress-response patterns (Wilson, Friedman, & Lindy, 2001; Wilson & Thomas, 2004).

Traumatic events impact pre-existing personality traits (i.e., structure, dynamics, defenses, competencies, self-structure, and ego-processes) in multifaceted ways. As Figure 10.1 shows, there are potential impacts on personality, ego-states, identity configurations, and cognitive schemas of self, others, and situations (Wilson, 2004b). Moreover, extremely stressful experiences have the power to evoke peritraumatic dissociation (Marmar, Weiss, & Metzler, 1997) and full-blown dissociative states (Wilson, Friedman, & Lindy, 2001). Considered from a holistic perspective, trauma's impact on the organism not only has the power to attack personality and self-processes, it automatically activates allostatic stress-response patterns that are part of the sensory nervous system's (SNS) neurohormonal engineering system governing acute and prolonged forms of human stress-response (Wilson, 2004b; Friedman, 2000; McEwen, 2002).

The activation of allostatic stress-response patterns include at least five interrelated areas of functioning: (1) coping styles, (2) personality characteristics (e.g., hardiness, locus of control, assertiveness), (3) affect modulation and degrees of affect balance, (4) ego-defensive processes, and (5) the mobilization and utilization of protective factors that may exist in the repertoire of coping behaviors.

The outcome of the response patterns triggered by a traumatic life-event is the generation of a continuum of adaptation and resilience. Viewed in this way, the positive end of the continuum reflects optimal coping with trauma. This includes acute and long-term patterns of adaptation and resilience that result from the mastery of excessive stress by: (1) the operation of specific personality variables (e.g., hardiness) that moderate the perception, appraisal, and effects of traumatic stressors; (2) the function of ego-defenses and protective factors that are part of ego-states, identity configuration, and coping styles; (3) the capacity for affect modulation (i.e., affect balance); (4) the capacity to maintain a positive outlook and create a positive sense of meaning from the trauma experience that may be aided by mobilizing social support mechanisms; and (5) the manifestation of resilient forms of behavior as required by specific stressors that evoke stress-response syndromes.

3 PSYCHOLOGICAL CHARACTERISTICS OF THE RESILIENT TRAUMA SURVIVOR

What is the psychological profile of a resilient trauma survivor? What are the commonalities in personality and behavior that are shared among survivors of extreme stress and trauma? How do they appraise their experiences during (i.e., peritraumatic) and after traumatic experiences? How do they utilize different types of resources to facilitate coping? What cognitive processes enable them to transcend the primary stressors of trauma and the secondary stressors that follow and generate cascade effects in the problems of daily living? How do they perceive themselves in relation to culture and systems that regulate government and social intercourse? What factors distinguish their capacity to modulate emotions in the face of trauma and subsequent life-stressors? How do they transcend trauma and create personal systems of meaning? These are some of the central questions that are important to raise when analyzing the resilient survivor. Table 10.1 lists 20 distinct attributes of resilient trauma survivors derived from Agaibi and Wilson's (2005) review of the literature on trauma and resilience.

TABLE 10.1
Psychological Characteristics of the Resilient Trauma Survivor

1. Personality characteristics: high self-esteem, hardiness, locus of control, autonomy, assertiveness, humor, etc.
2. Sense of positive identity as a survivor
3. Sense of group identity and connection (attachment) to others as a survivor
4. Prosocial and altruistic behaviors
5. Mature ego-defenses and post-conventional levels of moral development.
6. Positive emotional states (affect balance)
7. Autonomy, freedom from enculturation, prosocial dispositions
8. Accurate assessment and appraisal of stressors
9. Efficient information processing, executive functions, and cognitive framing of experiences
10. Sense of human kinship as a survivor
11. Humor and ability to see light side of dark situations
12. Capacity to generate meaning from trauma experiences
13. Psychological flexibility in short- and long-term coping
14. Ego transcendence and healthy self-detachment
15. Problem-solving, proactive coping style
16. Positive ideology and world view
17. Lack of personalizing bad experience
18. Absence or minimal levels of guilt (i.e., survivor guilt, bystander guilt)
19. Capacity to effectively mobilize personal and social resources
20. High energy and persistence in problem-solving

Source: © 2004 John P. Wilson.

3.1 Resilience is a Complex Repertoire of Behavioral Tendencies

It is conceptually advantageous to consider resilience as a complex repertoire of behavioral tendencies. Resilience defines specific types of response tendencies for persons faced with challenging situations, stressful circumstances, and traumatic events. Resilience characterizes a style of behavior with identifiable patterns of perceiving, thinking, reasoning (e.g., evaluating alternatives), and taking actions that are manifest over time and across situations. Accurate descriptions of resilient trauma survivors specify how they cope in different situations; i.e., "how they do what they do" that constitutes resilient behavior. This discernible style of mastering experience reflects a quality of character that is the product of genetics, social learning, and overcoming the adverse effects of extreme stress and trauma (Wilson & Thomas, 2004). Psychological resilience is *not* the same thing as having immunity from life stressors. While it is the case that resilient persons possess identifiable personality factors, characterological virtues, and psychological capacities to modulate stress and nervous system arousal, they can and do develop stress-related symptoms and disorders, including PTSD. Resilience as a psychological process can be learned, modeled, imitated, and analyzed in terms of its component dimensions (see discussion in this chapter). This fact is critically important since the understanding of the factors that comprise resilient coping can be taught in preventative ways and as posttraumatic education and formation of debriefings (Raphael & Wilson, 2000).

At present there is no definitive set of personality characteristics that characterizes resilient survivors. However, there is a convergence of data that points to a set of motives, traits, and personality attributes that typify persons with high degrees of resiliency. A "crow's nest" view of these personality processes reveals that resilient personalities are characterized by high self-esteem, autonomy, assertiveness, tenacity, energy, flexibility, and self-efficacy across traumatic situations that vary in complexity, difficulty, ambiguity, and stressor loads that challenge coping abilities and resource utilization. *Resilient persons manifest trans-situational consistency and flexibility in coping behaviors and adaptational outcomes.* However, as Hewitt and Flett (1996) have noted, not all classes of personality variables have been subjected to experimental analysis in relation to resilience. For example, one would not expect personality attributes associated with insecurity, intraversion, passivity, dependency, anxiety, fearfulness, neuroticism, low frustration tolerance, depression, or lack of tolerance for uncertainty, order, structure or ambiguity, etc. to be linked to the processes of resiliency. In fact, researchers have selected personality variables for the study of resilience from the extraversion and self-esteem cluster of variables (Aronoff & Wilson, 1985). This cluster includes the factors of hardiness, ego-strength, dominance, assertiveness, sociability, flexibility, optimism, self-confidence, and an internal locus of control. These personality dimensions are conceptually linked to the Five Factor Model (FFM) of personality traits and correspond to the first-order factors of extraversion and openness (McCrae & Costa, 2003).[1]

The accumulated research evidence (Agaibi & Wilson, 2005) strongly supports the finding of a moderate correlation between variables associated with self-esteem (e.g., nurturance, achievement, dominance, recognition, hardiness, extraversion) and resilient behavior in the aftermath of trauma. As we will discuss, individuals with personality characteristics associated with a strong sense of self-efficacy manifest higher levels of mental health, well-being, life satisfaction, and a tendency to be proactive and self-initiating in situations requiring problem-solving

---

[1]The personality characteristics associated with the FFM for extraversion and openness are as follows: Extraversion (warmth, gregariousness, assertiveness, activity, excitement-seeking, positive emotions); Openness (fantasy, aesthetics, feelings, actions, ideas, values).

actions of different kinds (Aronoff & Wilson, 1985). Moreover, research on attachment-behavior has shown that persons with secure attachment relationships in childhood are more likely to develop good self-esteem, an internal locus of control, and capacity to relate well to others (see McCrae & Costa, 2003; Cassidy & Shaver, 1999). The relationship between early childhood experiences and personality has indirect linkages to the propensity for resilient behavior across different situations. It is also possible that persons with a history of insecure attachments may be "high" risk takers in some traumatic situations since attachment relations may not be important to them, enabling forms of detachment that can be highly adaptive under the right circumstances (e.g., being prisoner of war; political group internment; self-oriented survivor actions). Thus, there exists configurations of personality typologies with admixtures of personality trait combinations such as (1) high self-esteem, secure and strong attachment histories or (2) high self-esteem, insecure and weak attachment histories that will predispose different patterns of coping and adaptation in the face of trauma. For example, high self-esteem persons with secure attachments (HSE-SA) will likely be assertive, warm, gregarious, extraverted, and actively engaging of others. In contrast, high self-esteem individuals with insecure attachments (HSE-IA) would manifest arrogance, aloofness, and a calculated detached stance towards others. In predicting forms of resilient behaviors, these different configurations of personality characteristics might be equally effective in mobilizing persons and resources under distinctly different traumatic situations (e.g., group vs. individual survival actions). However, having a strong internal locus of control, hardiness, self-esteem, dominance, extraversion, openness, or assertiveness does not exist in a vacuum. These attributes of personality are dynamically related to other psychological processes in important ways. In terms of coping with psychological trauma, these processes include perception, ego-defenses, cognitive appraisal, intelligence, prior learning history, and capacity to regulate emotions (i.e., affect balance).

As found by Agaibi and Wilson (2005), the resilient survivor has the capacity to successfully manage the stress-appraisal process before, during, and after the occurrence of trauma (i.e., pre-, peri-, and posttraumatic stress appraisal). The resilient personality has a capacity to maintain balance and equilibrium and not get "rattled." Such people tend to be "cool under pressure" and recover quickly from excessive emotional arousal (see Southwick et al., 2004 for a discussion). Those with a resilient personality are good at "sizing up" the big picture of things in very accurate and realistic ways with minimal ego-defenses of suppression, denial, or distortion. They are less prone to dissociation in response to fear or anxiety-provoking percepts. They quickly see things as they are, not as they want them to be, even if unpleasant, dangerous, and foreboding. Their actions are unclouded by personal needs, overwhelming emotional states, materialistic, or socioemotional attachments. They quickly identify the nature of the challenge, threat, the parameters of the problems to be solved, and formulate a course of action. Their personality characteristics of autonomy, freedom from the forces of enculturation, and a capacity for self-directed action enable them to initiate a set of responses aimed at mastery of the trauma situation. They mobilize the available resources of a personal (i.e., self-competencies) or environmental nature. Resilient survivors have the ability to engage in healthy self-detachment that allows them to rise above the powerful impact of traumatic situations. They are able to assess quickly the challenges of traumatic situations through the observant lens of healthy self-detachment that places value on the primacy of survival above all else. It is as if they are fully in-the-moment of the trauma situation in such a way as to realize the insignificance of materialistic attachments or nonsignificant matters in contrast to the priority of maximizing options necessary to meet challenges or to sustain the basis of life as a survivor. They have an eagle-eyed view of that which has high survival value and utility. The attitude of healthy detachment is that of: "things can be replaced; life and the basis of creating a meaningful existence, cannot."

In terms of coping style, there is ample evidence that resilient trauma survivors utilize problem-solving rather than emotion-focused coping (e.g., Agaibi & Wilson, 2005; Solomon, Mikulincer, & Avitzu, 1998). Problem-solving coping entails several dimensions of mastering the peritraumatic stresses of trauma or the posttraumatic strains of adaptation that include: (1) accurate perception, recognition, and definition of the threats, problems, or situational challenges posed by traumatic events; (2) formulation of a solution-focused plan of action; (3) capacity to modulate emotions, especially reactions of fear, anxiety, feeling overwhelmed, and potentially helpless; (4) initiation of a sequence of action to confront the challenges, demands, and problems to be solved during (i.e., peritraumatic) or after trauma; (5) mobilization of personality, social, economic, or environmental resources to cope with the demands inherent in the situation; and (6) a superior capacity to reduce allostatic stress loads intrinsic to extremely stressful situations (Wilson, Friedman, & Lindy, 2001; Friedman & McEwen, 2004; McEwen, 2002). *These interrelated aspects of problem-solving coping (Folkman & Lazarus, 1988) are trans-situational qualities of the resilient trauma survivor and associated with flexibility in short- and long-term coping processes.* As such, they reflect both personological attributes (e.g., locus of control, hardiness, extraversion) and cognitive-style factors in terms of capacity to encode, store, and process information (Aronoff & Wilson, 1985). As Block & Kremen (1996) found, persons with high levels of ego-resilience were characterized as active, energetic, autonomous, calm, outgoing, assertive, and internally consistent in functioning. Trauma survivors with good ego-resilience utilize these capacities in the service of coping and adaptation. More importantly, perhaps, they tend not to personalize bad experiences, interpersonal encounters, challenges and threats, including those of a confrontational and demeaning nature. In this limited sense, problem-solving coping is the ability to have ego-transcendence; to avoid getting caught up in confusion, chaos, assaults on the ego and personal conflicts. Healthy self-detachment includes the ability, when needed, to rise above the "fray" by depersonalizing the situation and staying in-the-moment by ego-transcendence of one's importance relative to the pressing needs for a positive outcome that will enable more genuine freedom of choice in the immediate future. By being in-the-moment, accurately focused, ego-transcendent and detached from self, the resilient survivor is able to maximize: (1) their native intelligence; (2) capacities for information processing; (3) executive functioning and problem-focused coping activities as described above; and (4) gain a clear and coherent sense of what needs to be done to achieve a positive outcome. This positive orientation to problem-solving coping styles involves a capacity for humor; to see the "lighter" side of "dark" situations. Humor, as a personal characteristic, serves not only to relieve stress and tension but cements emotional bonds with others. Indeed, the esteemed linguist Paul Watzlawick (1983) wrote: "the situation may be hopeless but it's not serious." This lexical anomaly points out a fundamental truth about many situations of extreme stress and trauma, namely that accurate appraisal and assessment may reveal a limited set of alternatives for finding solutions. Yet, it is precisely at such moments that resilient survivors have the capacity to self-detach and find solutions in an array of limited choices through active information processing. They exhibit calm, steady emotions, ego-transcendence, and the ability to let go of material and nonsignificant personal attachments. This capacity appears to be associated with the use of mature ego-defenses (Felsman & Vaillant, 1987). Perhaps for this reason they appear to be *less* affected by survivor guilt, bystander guilt, or death guilt. This is not to say that they do not experience episodes of survivor guilt or states of posttraumatic shame, since the capacity to experience trauma-related emotions is the polar opposite of psychic numbing and emotional constriction. Resilient survivors tend to be compassionate, tolerant, and empathic. The presence of survivor and bystander guilt negatively impacts appraisal processes and attributions for failed behavioral enactments (Lifton, 1993). What resilient survivors do feel guilty about are honest shortcomings and failures that could have produced better consequences for themselves and others. However, since guilt, especially survivor guilt, is a form of self-recrimination, the resilient trauma survivor is *less* affected by such feelings since their actions tend to reflect: (1) efficacious striving; (2) goal-directed attempts at finding solutions; (3) realistic assessment of options and alternative paths of actions; and (4) a recognition and acceptance of the inherent limitations of the traumatic situation. This may be another way of saying that they have an acceptance of fate, historical circumstance, or divine ordination without moral or neurotic conflicts and psychological resistance.

In terms of self-processes, the resilient trauma survivor forms a clear and coherent sense of their posttraumatic identity. As discussed in Chapter 3, they may or may not have a sense of self-sameness and continuity in identity and selfhood. They understand that by fate or historical propitiousness they are survivors in important ways that include a deep appreciation and sense of human kinship; i.e., being a part of the great chain of humanity from the past to the present. Having a broader, more species-wide identification as a survivor, the resilient individual bonds with fellow survivors to form an enclave of support. Group identification with other survivors represents an outer and inner sense of continuity and connection to shared sources of meaning and values. Group identification as a survivor maintains historical continuity and coherence (Wilson, 2001, 1995; Lifton, 1976). A shared sense of group identity contravenes alienation, isolation, and detachment through active involvement with others whose lives reinforce group membership and functional patterns of living. Having a sense of group identification with other survivors preserves relations to sources of meaning and is an arena for trusted self-disclosure about bad and good aspects of the trauma experience and survivorship.

Prosocial and altruistic actions are important and salutary character-istics of resilient trauma survivors (Wilson, 1995). After trauma, they engage in prosocial forms of behavior that generate a sense of meaning and positive emotional states. Resilient survivors inherently understand the need to "reach out" to others. By helping others, they help them-selves maintain a continuous self-transformative process. They manifest generativity in attitude and behavior (Wilson & Thomas, 2004) and give of themselves in nurturing ways without expectations for immediate benefits. As a part of posttraumatic adaptation, acting in prosocial and altruistic ways reflects trauma-induced changes in beliefs, attitudes, and values. By nature, resilient survivors are empathic and compassionate, having overcome pain, suffering, and loss. They tend to exhibit higher stages (i.e., 4, 5, 6) of moral reasoning as described by Lawrence Kohlberg (Wilson, 1980). They understand that traumatic experiences produce injuries, suffering, and disillusionment about the meaning of life and the trustworthiness of persons. Resilient survivors have a deep capacity to generate meaning in the face of overwhelming personal vulnerability. They intuitively understand that self-transformation and reinvention, as well as spiritual consciousness and altruism, are mirror processes of each other. Resilient survivors are admired by others because of their uniform capacity to manifest psychological and spiritual strength by "letting go" in the face of adversity while maintaining a positive orientation to others, life, and the meaning of existence. The virtue of human integrity and self-transcendence is manifest in the face of loss, injury, and death. They are frank, self-effacing, honest, humble, and genuine in social interactions. Through higher consciousness they transcend the limits imposed by the oppressive forces of psychic trauma to psychical freedom. True resilience is one facet of freedom of being at the highest level of consciousness as an autonomous person.

4 A BRIEF HISTORY OF THE CONCEPT OF RESILIENCE

To facilitate a review of the literature on trauma and resilience, this chapter will first discuss the history of early studies on resilience in children and then shift to the study of trauma survivors and PTSD, reflecting the evolution of research studies on the topic.

Current definitions of resilience vary from absence of psychopathology in a child of a severely mentally ill parent, to the recovery of a brain-injured patient, to the resumption of healthy functioning in survivors of extreme trauma (Wilson & Drozdek, 2004; Wilson & Raphael, 1993; Harel, Kahana, & Wilson, 1993; Folkman, 1997; Garmezy, 1996). In this regard, it is helpful to study resilience longitudinally, examining positive versus negative adaptation, coping, and the operation of personality variables in different traumatic contexts. For example, is resilience a stable characteristic of personality or a variable dimension of behavioral adaptation under situational pressures? Is the study of resilience in relation to trauma a universal paradigm by which to understand all forms of resilient behavior?

In a meta-theory of resilience, Richardson (2002) proposed that the history of research on resilience can be classified into three waves: (1) identifying the unique characteristics of *persons* who cope well in the face of adversity; (2) identifying the *processes* by which resiliency is attained through developmental and life-experiences; and (3) identifying the *cognitive mechanisms* that govern resilient adaptations. Previous research on the phenomenon of resilience has examined a substantial domain of factors thought to be associated with resilience, including: genetics, neurobiological factors, childhood development, type of trauma or stressful life-event, personality characteristics, cognitive style, prior history of exposure to stressful events, gender, age, capacity for affect regulation, social support, and ego-defenses (Agaibi, 2003; Zuckerman,

1999; Schore, 2003b; Zeidner & Endler, 1996; Wilson, 1995; Fredrickson, 2002; Southwick, Morgan, Vythilingham, Krystal, & Charney, 2004).

The most basic definition of resiliency is that it is the ability to adapt and cope successfully, despite threatening or challenging situations. Resilience is a good outcome regardless of high demands, costs, stress, or risk (Lazarus & Folkman, 1984). Resilience is sustained competence in response to demands that tax coping resources (Garmezy, 1991). Resilience is healthy recovery from extreme stress and trauma (Wilson & Drozdek, 2004). Resilience has been linked conceptually with curiosity and intellectual mastery, the ability to detach, and conceptualize problems (Block & Kremen, 1996). Resilience has been postulated to include strong extraverted personality characteristics (e.g., hardiness, ego-resilience, self-esteem, assertiveness, locus of control), the capacity to mobilize resources, and learned helpfulness versus learned helplessness (Hewitt & Flett, 1996; Agaibi, 2003).

Richardson (2002) states that "from a historical view, the first wave of resiliency inquiry focused on the paradigm shift from looking at the risk factors that led to psychosocial problems to the identification of strengths of an individual" (p. 309). Indeed, prior to the onset of systematic research on PTSD in 1980 (Wilson & Raphael, 1993; Wilson, 1994; Wilson, Friedman, & Lindy, 2001) studies looked at how children subjected to harsh developmental experiences emerged psychologically healthy rather than impaired. In his review, Richardson (2002) highlights the research of Werner and Smith (1992), Michael Rutter (1990), and Norman Garmezy (1991), who studied children thought to be "at risk" because of economic poverty, severely mentally ill parents, or developmental deprivations of different types (e.g., neglect, abuse, poverty, social class). Among the classic, pioneering studies of psychological resiliency, Garmezy (1981) and Cicchetti and Garmezy (1993) noted that in the study of resilient persons one should not select extremes for study. At one end of the spectrum is the "spun glass theory of mind" that suggests children are so vulnerable that even minor criticism or rejection could traumatize them and lead them to psychopathology. On the other end of the spectrum, caution is advised in portraying invulnerable children as psychologically immune to stress. Cicchetti and Garmezy (1993) opt for a middle ground in this continuum, studying successful adaptation in the context of unusually adverse life circumstances.

Researchers studying resilience recognize the multifaceted task of understanding the different forms of adaptation that characterize resilient behaviors (Caffo & Belaise, 2003). Multi-risk situations as well as psychobiological (Southwick et al., 2004) and sociocultural (Mikulciner & Florian, 1996) influences have been analyzed to understand the nature and dynamics of resiliency. Similarly, in regard to psychological trauma, Weisaeth (1995) has identified the nature of high-risk persons, situations, and reactions to traumatic stressors and proposes a matrix analysis of their interactive effects in coping and adaptation.

In studies of trauma, PTSD and coping with stress, an internal locus of control has been associated with effective adaptation to stress (Harel, Kahana, & Kahana, 1988; Wilson, Harel, & Kahana, 1989; Wilson, 1989; Harel, Kahana, & Wilson, 1993). Persons with an internal locus of control tend to exhibit less PTSD, psychopathology, and have better overall adjustment than persons with an external locus of control. For example, Elder and Clipp (1988), using the Oakland Growth studies longitudinal data bank, were able to evaluate personality variables evident in childhood that predicted PTSD symptoms in Korean War and World War II veterans. Prior to military service, men who were sensitive, introspective, obsessive, and intraverted were more likely to manifest psychiatric morbidity (i.e., PTSD, depression) than were men who were extraverted, dominant, assertive, and self-assured. While risk factors include traumatic life stressors, protective factors are significantly related to positive family and peer relationships. Pre-existing psychopathology tends to be a risk factor for negative psychosocial consequences, including the development of PTSD following trauma (Garmezy & Masten, 1991; Friedman, 2000; Yehuda, 1998; Wilson & Drozdek, 2004). In this regard, Rutter (1990), defines three broad variables as protective factors: (1) personality coherence, (2) family cohesion, and (3) social support. Personality factors include level of autonomy, self-esteem and self-efficacy, good temperament, and positive social outlook. In the area of traumatic stress research, Wilson and Raphael (1993) and Wilson (1995) identified similar factors associated with resilience, which include internal locus of control, altruism, the perception of social and economic resources, self-disclosure, and the formation of a clear sense of identity as a survivor. Family cohesion, warmth, and lack of discord or tension have been identified as protective factors (Garmezy & Masten, 1991). External support systems, whether perceived or utilized, promote good coping.

In a 40-year longitudinal study of Harvard University students, Felsman and Vaillant (1987) attempted to identify the factors in childhood and adolescence associated with resiliency in later adulthood. This study has direct relevance to understanding psychological trauma and resiliency because of its longitudinal nature and the wide domain of personal characteristics assessed throughout the course of the study (e.g., Eriksonian life-stages; maturity of ego-defenses; IQ; boyhood competence; family background; socioeconomic status).

The results produced an interesting set of findings which tend to "dove-tail" with the findings on studies of trauma, PTSD, and resilience. First, IQ and boyhood competence (a measure of active involvement in activities and a good childhood environment) were positively correlated with current mental health, the attainment of ego-maturity (i.e., generativity), good object relations, and the use of mature ego-defenses (e.g., altruism, sublimation). Conversely, their measure of childhood emotional problems was negatively correlated with these same variables but significantly associated with sociopathy. Second, there was considerable variability in psychosocial development across early adult development for the more resilient members of the study. There was little evidence for a linear, uninterrupted pattern of life-span development that led to successful achievements later in life. There were periods of discontinuity and regression. However, what seemed to distinguish the resilient adults was "a clear pattern of recovery, restoration and gradual mastery" (p. 311). In terms of resilience, this would suggest that there were identifiable periods of rest, recuperation, and recovery that facilitated a restoration of competence, active coping, and striving which "gradually" culminated in the mastery of challenging personal experiences. In terms of personological variables, the data suggests that men who came from relatively stable childhood backgrounds and positive early learning periods developed more functional and mature ego-defenses that, in turn, may have moderated the development of self-esteem, locus of control, and prosocial behavior. This being the case, we would expect that persons suffering from psychological trauma and PTSD would manifest patterns of adaptation, coping, and resilience that would wax and wane over time, marked by periods of continuity versus discontinuity, ego-coherence versus fragmentation, good versus poor object relations, and gradual assimilation and mastery of the impairment of trauma into their sense of well-being (see Wilson, 2004a for a discussion).

5 PARADIGM SHIFT: FROM "AT RISK" CHILDREN TO TRAUMA SURVIVORS AND THE STUDY OF PTSD

With the advent of PTSD as a diagnostic entity in 1980, the study of resilience moved away from traditional social-psychological and developmental studies to more in-depth studies of trauma survivors. Studies of trauma and resilience have tended to examine resilience as pre- and posttrauma areas of adaptive competence among different trauma populations, including those who do and do not develop PTSD.

Zuckerman (1999) reviewed the literature on vulnerability and the development of PTSD. In terms of PTSD, vulnerability and resilience are related concepts, as they characterize twin sides of trauma and the responses to it. In his summary analysis, Zuckerman notes that there are clearly identifiable vulnerability factors to the psychiatric sequelae of PTSD which include genetics (True, Rice, Eisen, Heath, Goldberg, Lyons, & Nowak, 1993), individual risk factors (e.g., family background), personality (e.g., types of ego-defense, extraversion), biological factors (e.g., alterations in brain function), cognitive style, and information processing. While these findings do not directly address the issues of resiliency in the face of trauma, they do suggest that there are an interrelated set of psychobiological processes at work which influence: (1) the genetic predisposition to trauma; (2) the probable protective factors from childhood development; (3) the operation and moderating functions of personality processes; and (4) the nature and cause of prolonged stress response patterns in the central nervous system, i.e., the active psychobiological metabolism of the trauma experience, including traumatic memories (see Southwick et al., for a review, 2004).

In a review of studies concerned with war trauma, natural and technological disasters, torture, the Holocaust, and duty-related trauma, Wilson & Raphael (1993) and Wilson (1995) identified seven factors associated with resilience. Wilson (1995) found that there were similar constellations of predictors of current well-being, positive mental health, and manifestations of resilience in these survivor populations which included: (1) locus of control (i.e., a sense of efficacy and determination; (2) self-disclosure of the trauma experience to significant others, (3) a sense of group identity and sense of self as a positive survivor; (4) the perception of personal and social resources to aid in coping in the posttrauma recovery environment; (5) altruistic or prosocial behaviors; (6) the capacity to find meaning in the traumatic experience and life afterwards; and (7) connection, bonding, and social interaction within a significant community of friends and fellow survivors. Viewed from the perspective of resilience, these seven factors appear to be identifying important classes of variables that interact in generating resilience. These dimensions include factors within the *person* (i.e., locus of control, cognitive attributions of being a strong survivor, a firm sense of personal identity as a survivor) as well as specific forms of *coping* (i.e., perception of personal and social resources to aid coping, capacity to find meaning) and *behavioral activities* in the recovery environment (e.g., appropriate self-disclosure, altruism, prosocial behaviors, bonding and fellowship with other survivors) that promote resilient functioning. Thus, persons who have an internal locus of control who can find meaning in their trauma experiences may be able to initiate a set of processes that enables them to shape a personal sense of identity by being bonded and attached to fellow survivors who, in turn, are perceived as resources for coping with emotional, social and economic needs (see Zakin, Solomon, & Neva, 2003). Further, within a trusted enclave of fellow survivors, the bonding and networks formed may facilitate healthy self-disclosure and the opportunity to enact prosocial behaviors and positive emotional states as part of the natural transformation process of dealing with individual trauma experiences. In this way, too, prosocial enactments reinforce personal systems of meaning and validate the strengths of survivorship. Similar conclusions were found by Hendin and Hass (1984) who found that Vietnam combat veterans with high resilience were characterized by six factors: (1) calmness under pressure; (2) acceptance of fear in self and others; (3) low levels of excessive violence in the war zone; (4) the importance of understanding and good judgment; (5) absence of guilt; and (6) humor.

It is a truism to say that not everyone develops PTSD following trauma, a fact that makes the study of resilience both interesting and important. Clearly, it is necessary to understand vulnerability and resiliency factors in order to meaningfully interpret the adaptation to trauma. Yehuda (1998) clarifies the difference between chronic, non-life-threatening stress and acute, life-threatening stress. She indicates that while acute stress reactions have mental and physical health consequences, it has been assumed that these consequences would lift once the stressor terminated (Bryant, 2004). While chronic stress effects developed over a period of time, acute stress effects were sudden and immediately impactful. In chronic stress, physiological and emotional processes degrade over time (McEwen, 2002; Friedman, 2000). In acute stress there is a rapid and sudden change in these physiological and mental processes (Friedman, 2000; Friedman & McEwen, 2004). In chronic stress the individual experiences feelings of being overwhelmed and has to cope with the long-term consequences of prolonged stress-related symptoms. Traumatic stress results in feelings of fear that can activate complex allostatic psychological responses (McEwen, 2002; Wilson, Friedman, & Lindy, 2001; Wilson, 2004a; Wilson & Thomas, 2004; Thomas & Wilson, 2004).

5.1 War Trauma, Terrorism, Prisoners of War, Internment, and Civil Violence

In terms of trauma and PTSD, there are several studies that have examined resilience in relation to war trauma, internment, civil violence, and terrorism. In terms of war trauma, King, King, Fairbank, Keane, and Adams (1998) studied resiliency associated with PTSD among Vietnam veterans in relation to hardiness, social support, and stressful life-events. King et al. (1998) predicted that hardy war veterans would cope better with life stresses than less hardy veterans. They suggested that hardy veterans would utilize social supports in their environment to overcome a stress. They predicted that veterans exposed to extreme war stressors who had strong, current social support would display fewer PTSD symptoms than veterans with less support. They argued that when war stressors were measured at low levels, there would be a weak relationship between social support and the development of PTSD.

The results indicated that male and female veterans who scored high on the hardiness dimensions of control, commitment, and challenge showed fewer PTSD symptoms. Hardiness was associated with fewer PTSD symptoms and appears to help the individual establish relationships that aid coping with PTSD symptoms when present. Contrary to King et al.'s hypothesis, hardiness did not seem to protect veterans from PTSD symptoms if these individuals experienced heavy combat, a finding replicated in studies of prisoners of war (Zeiss & Dickman, 1989). However, the amount of social support received did predict the extent of PTSD symptoms. King et al. (1998) concurred with Solomon, Mikulincer, and Avitzu (1998) who stated that negative life-events tend to be negatively correlated with prevalence of intact social support. Stressful events can deplete social networks that, in turn, increase PTSD symptoms. Similar findings were reported by Sutker, Davis, Uddo, and Ditta (1995) in a study of war-zone stress, personal resources, and PTSD in veterans of the 1991 Gulf War. From a sample of 775 military veterans, 97 with diagnosed PTSD were compared with 484 who did not show pathological signs of distress. The results indicated that veterans with PTSD scored lower on Kobasa's measure of hardiness (i.e., commitment, control, challenge) and had less social support and family cohesion as well as avoidant coping styles with strong tendencies to self-blame. These results illustrate the interaction between personality characteristics, coping styles, and utilization of social support.

There are several studies that have examined stress, coping, and the presence of PTSD among veterans of the 1991 Gulf War. They share a similar pattern of results showing that, as a personality dimension, hardiness moderates the effects of war-zone stress and postwar coping with civilian stressors. Bartone (1999) studied six Army National Guard and reserve medical units about a year after the end of the Gulf War. A sample of 787 subjects were given the Kobasa Hardiness scale, the Brief Symptom Inventory, the Holmes-Rahe Stress scale, a 20-item measure of current health status, and a 15-item Gulf War zone stressor assessment scale. The results supported a person by situation model of resilience. Using a regression analysis, hardiness interacted with combat stress in predicting the global severity psychiatric index for low and high hardiness subjects. Persons with high hardiness had fewer psychological and health-related symptoms than did those with low hardiness. Similar findings were reported by Benotsch, Brailey, Vasterling, Uddo, Constans, and Sutker (2000) who examined 348 Gulf War veterans at two different time intervals after repatriation. The authors measured PTSD, dispositional resilience, coping styles, personal resources, and social support. At the first time interval after repatriation, those with more severe PTSD symptoms were characterized by avoidance coping styles and lack of family cohesion. At the second time interval, conducted about 2 years after the war, avoidance coping and a decrease in perceived social support resources predicted PTSD symptoms. In a related study, Sharkansky, King, King, Wolfe, Erikson, and Stokes (2000), examined 2,949 Gulf War veterans and measured combat exposure, coping styles, PTSD, life-stressors, and depression. Results showed that when comparing postwar adjustment at two different intervals within 2 years of repatriation, veterans who used approach (i.e., active) coping styles had fewer PTSD symptoms than men who utilized avoidant forms of coping. However, those with the highest levels of combat exposure had more PTSD and depressive symptoms, irrespective of coping styles.

In another study, Zakin, Solomon, and Neva (2003), examined the relationship between hardiness, attachment style, and long-term distress among Israeli prisoners of war (POWs) and combat veterans of the Yom Kippur War in 1973. Using Israeli POWs and matched combat controls, the former soldiers were administered the SCL-90, a measure of attachment styles, the Kobasa Hardiness scale, and a measure of PTSD based on the *DSM-III-R* diagnostic criteria. The results showed that hardiness was associated with low levels of symptoms reported. Using a hierarchical regression analysis, the interaction between hardiness and attachment style accounted for 20–40% of the measured variance in depression, anxiety, somatization, and present and past PTSD symptoms. These results are consistent with the findings on hardiness as a personality dimension that is correlated with resilience in the form of fewer manifest symptoms of psychiatric distress associated with exposure to war-zone stressors.

In a study by Gold, Engdahl, Eberly, Blake, Page, and Frueh (2000), PTSD symptoms and recovery were studied in World War II and Korean War former POWs. Former POWs whose exposure to trauma was severe were at high risk for experiencing psychological problems such as PTSD, depression, anxiety, or cognitive deficits (Beebe, 1975; Eberly and Engdahl, 1991; Engdahl et al., 1997; Page et al., 1991; Tennant et al., 1986; Sutker et al., 1990). While combat veterans have a lifetime occurrence of PTSD of 30%, POWs have a lifetime occurrence of PTSD of 67% (Kulka et al., 1990; Khuznik, 1986). Gold et al. (2000) suggest that the greater the torture and weight loss experienced while imprisoned, the greater the PTSD symptoms. They noted that premilitary trauma, personality, age, and postmilitary social support played a role in determining the severity of the PTSD symptoms.

The predictors for the severity of PTSD symptoms were thought to include severity of trauma during imprisonment, factors of resilience, and postwar social support. It was found that the severity of the trauma experienced during imprisonment was related to distress experienced

40–50 years later. The level of distress was inversely associated with education and age at the time of the trauma. There was a significant correlation between reexperiencing the trauma and the initial coping response (i.e., peritraumatic coping) of avoiding triggers that reminded veterans of their POW experience. Contrary to other studies, the presence of social support did *not* moderate the level of PTSD symptoms.

In a 40-year follow-up study of former POWs, Zeiss and Dickman (1989) assessed factors associated with PTSD among World War II veterans who were captured as POWs in Europe and the South Pacific war zones. They employed a person by situation interactional analysis of the variables significantly associated with the persistence of PTSD symptoms across four decades. The results revealed that 55.7% reported PTSD symptoms using the *DSM-III* (APA, 1980) diagnostic criteria. They note, however, that PTSD symptoms waxed and waned during this time. In terms of person variables, higher military status (rank) and education predicted better outcomes in terms of PTSD and postwar adaptation. Duration of interment and age at capture did not correlate significantly with assessments of PTSD over time. The authors suggest that "personal characteristics, such as greater self-efficacy, emotional maturity, intelligence, interpersonal skill, educational level, commitment to the war effort, or locus of control may be mediating variables that resulted in both promotion in rank and relative ease of adjustment to stresses of POW life and repatriation" (p. 86). These findings match well Block and Kremen's (1996) findings of the personality characteristics of ego-resilient persons.

The concept of hardiness has also been used to study coping among POWs in Israel. Waysman, Schwarzwald, and Solomon (2001) studied Israeli POWs of the 1973 Yom Kippur War. Hardiness was viewed as either a direct or a moderating effect leading to long-term positive or negative change as a result of exposure to war trauma. Consistent with the theoretical work of Antonovsky (1979), Waysman et al. (2001) looked at the role of hardiness in protecting POWs from long-term negative consequences. They developed two models in their study. In the first model, hardiness acts in a direct manner. In the second model, hardiness has direct and moderating effects. In the direct model, hardiness is a constant variable. Moderating effects, on the other hand, are assumed to exist during times of trauma or crisis. The results revealed that hardiness was beneficial for people who were exposed to extreme stressors compared with those who were exposed to lower levels of stress. Hardiness as a stress moderator exerted an effect on stress-related symptoms in POWs but not on controls who fought in the same war but experienced less exposure to stress. An inverse relationship was found between hardiness and negative changes in both the POW and non-POW groups. It was found that the *higher* the hardiness score, the fewer negative changes experienced. POWs generally reported more negative changes in their lives following the trauma of war than their non-POW counterparts. Hardy POWs were less adversely impacted by postwar negative life-changes than less hardy former internees.

In a study of survivors of the Holocaust who were children at the time of their internment, Cohen, Dekel, and Solomon (2002) examined the role of attachment as a variable associated with PTSD symptoms and patterns of adjustment. In comparison with non-Holocaust controls, the survivor group manifest more symptoms of PTSD. However, treatment-seeking survivors showed higher levels of anxiety, avoidant attachment, and current symptoms of PTSD than did the untreated survivors and matched controls. However, the authors note that as a cohort, Holocaust survivors show a wide range of variability in their scores for PTSD, coping styles, and issues related to attachment. These findings parallel those reported by Kahana, Harel, and Kahana, (1988), Eitinger (1980), and Harel, Kahana, and Kahana (1993).

As an independent variable, resilience has been conceptualized as a personality characteristic (e.g., hardiness, locus of control) and in terms of ego-processes. Block and Kremen (1996) studied the relationship between intelligence and ego-resiliency using Block's measure of ego-resilience as an independent variable (Block, 1981). The subjects were participants in the Longitudinal Study of Cognitive and Ego-Development who were administered measures of intelligence, a 14-item scale to assess ego-resilience, and the California Adult Q-Sort of personality measurement. The study generated a wide set of findings which included descriptions of persons with high levels of ego-resilience who were characterized on dimensions that included flexibility, challenge, confidence, curiosity, assertiveness, control, sociability, energy, and prosocial dispositions. When the effects of intelligence were controlled, resilient men and women were found to be outgoing, warm, assertive, calm, energetic, autonomous, active, productive, internally consistent, poised, and responsive to humor. In summarizing their findings, Block and Kremen (1996) state: "the biosocial problem of the individual is adaptation. *Insufficiencies of adaptation are signaled to the individual by the intrusion of affect. Yet, current expanded conceptions of intelligence have remained 'cognitive' and still largely ignore affective and motivational aspects of behavior*" (p. 359; emphasis added). Thus, it would appear that ego-resilience reflects qualities of personality and their use in adaptation, but also a capacity to modulate stress response, an important issue in the dynamics of PTSD. Consistent with Fredrickson's (2001) formulation that positive emotions establish a "broaden and build" domain of effective behaviors with regard to stress modulation, ego-resilience appears to reflect an interrelated set of cognitive and personality variables that work in harmony to promote resilient behavior. These findings match conclusions by Siebert (1996) who studied the traits of survivors of extreme environmental hardship and threats to life. Siebert indicated that survivor personalities were characterized by optimism, acceptance of their situational fate, creative problem-solving, and integration of the right-brain abilities of intuition and holistic thinking with left-brain analytical thinking. These characteristics of survivor personality traits are quite similar to the attributes of ego-resiliency as described by Block and Kremen (1996).

In two related studies, Connor and Davidson (2003) and Connor, Davidson, and Lee (2003) reported findings on the development of a scale to measure resilience as a concept. In the first study, the 25-item Connor–Davidson Resilience scale (CD-RISC) was developed to measure dimensions thought to be associated with resilience (e.g., #1: able to adapt to change; #6: see the human side of things; #12: when things look hopeless, I don't give up). Five groups of subjects were selected for study: (1) general population, (2) psychiatric outpatients, (3) participants in a generalized anxiety disorder study, (4) patients in private practice, and (5) participants in a study of PTSD. The 25-item CD-RISC, when administered to all five groups and subjected to a factor analysis, revealed five factors: (1) personal competence, (2) affect tolerance, (3) acceptance of change, (4) sense of internal control, and (5) spirituality. The CD-RISC scale was also cross-validated in this study with the Kobasa hardiness measure, the Perceived Stress Scale, and the Stress Vulnerability Scale. The results show that measured resilience was significantly correlated with high levels of hardiness and low levels of perceived stress vulnerability.

Connor, Davidson, and Lee (2003) used the CD-RISC in a study of survivors of violent trauma who completed an online computer survey that assessed spirituality, anger, health, PTSD, and trauma-related distress. As predicted, resilience was associated with more positive outcomes in terms of current physical and mental health status and fewer PTSD symptoms. The results suggest that while the relationship between trauma and psychological distress is complex, resilience is strongly associated with positive outcomes in terms of affect balance (i.e., less anger), fewer PTSD symptoms, and better overall health status.

6 CONCLUSION

Our truncated review of the literature on trauma, PTSD, and resilience has identified a core set of findings which fit well within the model illustrated in Figure 10.1. In summary, these results show that researchers have implicitly used a person by situation interactional model in formulating hypotheses about the factors that influence different forms of resilient behavior for different survivor populations (Agaibi & Wilson, 2005). However, the task of predicting resiliency is further complicated because there is no universally defined concept of what constitutes resilient behavior. In some cases, resiliency is defined by the absence of psychopathology, prolonged stress response patterns (e.g., PTSD), or maladaptive coping usually defined by the avoidance of aversive outcomes. In other cases, resilience is defined by having superior coping over a longitudinal course of life-span development (Felsman & Vaillant, 1987). In some studies, resilience is defined as a personality variable (e.g., locus of control, ego-resilience, hardiness) which is presumed to moderate outcome variables such as resilient behavior patterns. As a personality variable, resilience has been examined in terms of how it affects thinking, perception, affect modulation, and disposition to behavior. Personality processes (e.g., hardiness, locus of control, self-esteem, assertiveness) are one side of the person–environment equation that subjectively determines the stress appraisal process and, by implication, the level of emotional arousal experienced and the capacity to modulate affect (Hewitt & Flett, 1996; Block & Kremen, 1996). Personality processes, including intelligence and cognitive styles of information processing, are correlated with coping styles (e.g., avoidance, approach, problem-solving, emotional) and the types of ego-defenses utilized under anxiety-provoking situations (Felsman & Vaillant, 1987; Vaillant, 1977). Moreover, there is some evidence that coping style and ego-defense are related to the capacity to mobilize and utilize protective factors to master overwhelmingly stressful situations. In this regard, researchers have identified protective factors such as social and personal support mechanisms, mobilizing aid, and initiating instrumental actions directed at finding solutions to the problems embedded within the stressful situation.

TABLE 10.2
Factors that Distinguish Highly Resilient Trauma Survivors

1. Sufficient childhood environments for general competence
2. Secure attachment relationships in childhood
3. Good affect modulation/positive emotions
4. Ability to see the "big picture" of situations
5. Spring-back personality factors (e.g., autonomy, hardiness, esteem, assertiveness)
6. Lack of personalizing bad events/experiences
7. Continuity in identity and connection to survivors
8. Mature ego-defenses (e.g., altruism, sublimation)
9. Healthy self-disclosure

Source: ©2005 John P. Wilson.

It is important to define a conceptually meaningful continuum of adaptation and resilience as pertains to normal, acute and prolonged forms of human stress response (Wilson, Friedman, & Lindy, 2001; McEwen, 2002; Friedman, 2000). Optimal coping and adaptation defines highly resilient behaviors in terms of acute and long-term positive adaptation. At the other end of the continuum, minimal coping defines acutely maladaptive and long-term negative adaptation and represents significant risk factors for the development of PTSD and psychopathology. Table 10.2 summarizes the factors that distinguish the highly resilient trauma survivor. Factors that seem to distinguish highly resilient survivors of trauma include the following: (1) they tend to have childhood environments that promote a general level of competence, social skills, and adequate self-esteem that, in turn, is associated with a positive, problem-solving orientation; (2) they tend to have more secure attachments; (3) they are able to effectively modulate emotions, employing positive emotions to cope with adversity and maintaining affect balance; (4) they have cognitive abilities to place trauma and stress within the "big picture" of life and to create meaning from their trauma experiences; (5) they possess a "spring-back" factor associated with personality variables such as self-esteem, hardiness, internal locus of control, dominance, assertiveness, and autonomy that enables them to utilize proactive mechanisms of coping, and resource utilization; (6) they tend not to overly personalize bad events and life-stresses but maintain an active, problem-solving coping style; (7) they exhibit a capacity to sustain identity and find meaning as a survivor who maintains continuity and connection with other survivors; (8) they tend to have more mature ego-defenses as adults, which are correlated with altruistic and prosocial behaviors; and (9) they have outlets for healthy self-disclosure with trusted others of the bad and good aspects of the trauma experience and its aftermath.

7 THE DEVELOPMENT OF POSTTRAUMATIC RESILIENCE

Is it possible to learn posttraumatic resilience? Can effective coping and adaptation to extreme stress be learned? Patton, Violenti, and Smith (2003) suggest that resilient capabilities can be promoted, especially among first responders. In a recent review article, Masten and Reed (2002) present an overview of the factors that promote resilience in children and discuss the mechanisms of learning that promote resilient behaviors. Masten and Reed identify three domains that can be targeted for promoting resilience in children: (1) risk-focused strategies, (2) asset-focused strategies, and (3) process-focused strategies. Masten and Reed propose that within each domain, new behaviors can be learned to increase problem-solving coping, improve access to resources, and mobilize effective behavioral strategies of adaptation to stressful situations.

The extensive research on promoting resilient coping in children has direct relevance to the development of posttraumatic resilience in trauma survivors. As noted above, there are at least nine categories that distinguish resilient trauma survivors from their less resilient cohorts. By examining these nine categories derived from research studies, it becomes possible to identify specific areas of posttraumatic functioning that can be bolstered by (1) clinical interventions, (2) educational and specifically "tailored" stress-management programs designed to improve personal competencies, coping skills, and resource utilization, and (3) cognitive strategies for effective coping with situations of extreme stress. In the way of a summary, these nine areas and their social-learning applications are as follows:

7.1 Programmatic Objectives to Facilitate Posttraumatic Resilience

- Identification of areas of competence and skill development, especially to deal with traumatic stressors and their specific dimensions and how they challenge coping repertoires.
- Teaching of attachment skills and building social connections to fellow survivors and others.
- Teaching of strategies of emotional regulation and the generation of positive emotions following trauma (i.e., teach effective means of affect modulation).
- Teaching of cognitive-behavioral reframing perspectives by which to place stress and trauma in a comparative "big picture" framework.
- Teaching of skills and the development of programs to promote hardiness, internal locus of control, assertiveness, a sense of efficacy and autonomy, prosocial dispositions, etc.
- Education about the factors and qualities of highly resilient survivors.
- Teaching of strategies for learning how to mobilize resources to aid in coping following trauma.
- Exposure to and interaction with resilient survivors of different types of trauma (e.g., war veterans, civilian catastrophe).
- Education about the nature, dynamics, and processes of coping with trauma and PTSD.
- Teaching and model examples of healthy self-disclosure, role-play effective coping under situations of adversity.

- Education and exposure to survivors who manifest prosocial and altruistic behaviors.
- Education about systems of meaning and values that characterize trauma survivors.
- Involvement in rituals or the development of cultural rituals to promote a sense of collective transformation of the trauma experience.

The 12 areas identified above provide arenas in which new forms of social learning can take place to aid recovery from psychic trauma and develop a broad range of cognitive, emotional, and behavioral competencies associated with resilient coping. Specific training and educational goals can be developed through: (1) specially designed clinical intervention programs, (2) risk reduction identification, (3) education that occurs before and after potential trauma exposure, (4) stress inoculation and preventive classes in the immediate wake of trauma, and (5) group-based, collectively experienced programs, or cultural rituals to transform the adverse effects of the trauma experience and promote a positive sense of self with group identity as a survivor who has generated positive meaning from the trauma experience.

REFERENCES

Agaibi, C. (2003). *Understanding resilience to the effects of traumatic stress.* Masters thesis, Cleveland State University, Ohio.

Agaibi, C. & Wilson, J. P. (2005). Trauma, PTSD and resilience: A review of the literature. *Journal of Trauma, Abuse and Violence, 6,* 195–216.

Antonovsky, A. (1979). *Health, stress and coping.* San Francisco, California: Jossey-Boss.

Aronoff, J. & Wilson, J. P. (1985). *Personality in the social process.* Hillsdale, NJ: Lawrence Erlbaum.

Bartone, P. T. (1999). Hardiness protects against war-related stress in Army reserves. *Consulting Psychology Journal: Practice and Research, 51,* 72–82.

Beebe, G. W. (1975). Follow up study of WWII and Korean War prisoners. II. Morbidity, disability and maladjustment. *American Journal of Epidemiology, 101,* 400–422.

Benotsch, E. G., Brailey, B., Vasterling, J. J., Uddo, M., Constans, J. I., & Sutker, P. (2000). War zone stress, personal and environmental resources, and PTSD symptoms in Gulf War veterans: A longitudinal perspective. *Journal of Abnormal Psychology 109,* 205–213.

Block, J. (1981). Some enduring and consequential structures of personality. In A. I. Rabin, J. Aronoff, A. M. Barclay, & R. H. Zucker (Eds.), *Further explorations in personality,* (pp. 27–43). New York: Wiley.

Block, J. & Kremen, A. M. (1996). IQ and ego-resilience: Conceptual and empirical connections and separateness. *Journal of Personality and Social Psychology, 70,* 349–361.

Bonnano, G. A. (2004). Loss, trauma and human resilience. *American Psychologist, 59,* 20–28.

Bryant, R. (2004). Acute stress disorders. In J. P. Wilson & T. M. Keane (Eds.), *Assessing psychological trauma and PTSD* (2nd ed., pp. 46–56). New York: Guilford Publications.

Caffo, E. & Belaise, C. (2003). Psychological aspects of traumatic injury in children and adolescents. *Child and Adolescent Psychiatric Clinics of North America, 12*, 493–535.

Cassidy, J. & Shaver, P. R. (1999). *Handbook of attachment*. New York: Guilford Publications.

Cicchetti, D. & Garmezy, N. (1993). Prospects and promises in the study of resilience. *Development and Psychopathology, 5*, 497–502.

Cohen, E., Dekel, R., & Solomon, Z. (2002). Long-term adjustment and the role of attachment among Holocaust child survivors. *Personality and Individual Differences, 33*, 299–310.

Connor, K. M. & Davidson, J. R. T. (2003). Development of a new resilience scale: The Connor–Davidson resilience scale (CD-RISC). *Depression and Anxiety, 18*, 76–82.

Connor, K. M., Davidson, J. R. T., & Lee, L. C. (2003). Spirituality, resilience and anger in survivors of violent trauma: A community survey. *Journal of Traumatic Stress, 16*, 487–494.

Dimsdale, J. E. (1980). *Survivors, victims and perpetrators*. New York: Hemisphere.

Eberly, R. E. & Engdahl, B. E. (1991). Problem of somatic and psychiatric disorder among former POWs. *Hospital and Community Psychiatry, 42*, 807–813.

Eitinger, C. (1961). Pathology in the concentration camp syndrome: Preliminary report. *Archives of General Psychiatry, 5*, 371–379.

Eitinger, C. (1980). The concentration camp syndrome and its late sequelae. In J. E. Dimsdale (Ed.), *Survivors, victims and perpetrators* (pp. 127–161). New York: Hemisphere Publishing.

Elder, G. & Clipp, E. (1988). Combat experiences, comradeship, and psychological health. In J. P. Wilson, Z. Harel, & B. Kahana (Eds.), *Human adaptation to extreme stress* (pp. 131–157). New York: Plenum Press.

Engdahl, B. E., Dikel, T. S., Eberly, R. E., & Blank, A. (1997). PTSD in a community group of former POWs: A narrative response to severe trauma. *American Journal of Psychiatry, 154*, 1576–1581.

Felsman, J. K. & Vaillant, G. (1987). Resilient children as adults: A 40-year study. In E. J. Anthony & B. J. Cohen (Eds.), *The invulnerable child* (pp. 284–315). New York: Guilford Publications.

Folkman, S. (1997). Positive psychological states and coping with severe stress. *Social Science and Medicine, 45*, 1207–1221.

Folkman, S. & Lazarus, R. S. (1988). *The ways of coping questionnaire*. New York: Consulting Psychologists Press.

Fredrickson, B. L. (2001). The role of positive emotions in positive psychology. The broaden and build theory of positive emotions. *American Psychologist, 56*, 218–226.

Fredrickson, B. L. (2002). Positive emotions. In C. R. Snyder & S. J. Lopez (Eds.), *Handbook of positive psychology* (pp. 120–134). New York: Oxford University Press.

Friedman, M. J. (2000). *Posttraumatic and acute stress disorders*. Kansas City: Compact Clinicals.

Friedman, M. J. & McEwen, B. S. (2004). PTSD, allostatic load and medical illness. In P. P. Schnurr & B. L. Green (Eds.), *Trauma and healing: Physical consequences of exposure to extreme stress* (pp. 157–189). Washington, DC: American Psychological Association.

Garmezy, N. (1981). Children under stress: Perspectives on the antecedents and correlates of vulnerability to psychopathology. In A. I. Rabin, J. Aronoff, A. A. Barclay, & R. H. Zucker (Eds.), *Further explorations in personality* (pp. 123–144). New York: Wiley Interscience.

Garmezy, N. (1991). Resiliency and vulnerability to adverse developmental outcomes associated with poverty. *American Behavior Scientist, 34*, 416–430.

Garmezy, N. (1996). Reflections and commentary on risk, resilience, and development. In R. J. Haggerty, L. R. Sherrod, N. Garmezy, & M. Rutter (Eds.), *Stress, risk, and resilience in children and adolescents* (pp. 1–18). New York: Cambridge University Press.

Garmezy, N. & Masten, A. S. (1991). The protective role of competence indicators in children at risk. In E. M. Cummings, A. L. Greene, & K. H. Karraker (Eds.), *Life-span developmental psychology: Perspectives on stress and coping* (pp. 151–174). Hillsdale, NJ: Lawrence Erlbaum.

Gold, P. B., Engdahl, B. E., Eberly, R. E., Blake, R. J., Page, W. F., & Frueh, B. C. (2000). Trauma exposure, resilience, social support, and PTSD construct validity among former prisoners of war. *Social Psychiatry and Psychiatric Epidemiology, 35,* 36–42.

Green, B. L., Wilson, J. P., & Lindy, J. (1985). Conceptualizing post-traumatic stress disorder: A psychosocial framework. In C. R. Figley (Ed.), *Trauma and its wake: The study and treatment of post-traumatic stress disorders* (Vol. I, pp. 53–69). New York: Brunner/Mazel.

Harel, Z., Kahana, B., & Kahana, E. (1988). Psychological well-being among Holocaust survivors and immigrants in Israel. *Journal of Traumatic Stress, 11,* 145–193.

Harel, Z., Kahana, B., & Kahana, E. (1993). Social resources and mental health of aging Nazi Holocaust survivors and immigrants. In J. P. Wilson & B. Raphael (Eds.), *International handbook of traumatic stress syndromes* (pp. 241–252). New York: Plenum Press.

Harel, Z., Kahana, B., & Wilson, J. (1993). War and remembrance: The legacy of Pearl Harbor. In J. P. Wilson & B. Raphael (Eds.), *International handbook of traumatic stress syndromes* (pp. 263–275). New York: Plenum Press.

Hendin, H. & Hass, H. (1984). *Wounds of war.* New York: Basic Books.

Hewitt, P. L. & Flett, G. L. (1996). Personality traits and the coping process. In M. Zeidner & N. S. Endler (Eds.), *Handbook of coping* (pp. 410–433). New York: Wiley.

Kahana, B., Harel, Z., & Kahana, E. (1988). Predictors of psychological well-being among survivors of the Holocaust. In J. P. Wilson, Z. Harel & B. Kahana (Eds.), *Human adaptation: From the Holocaust to Vietnam* (pp. 171–192). New York: Plenum Press.

Khuznik, J. G., Speed, N., VanVelkenberg, C. & MacGraw, R. (1986). Forty-year follow-up of U.S. prisoners of war. *American Journal of Psychiatry, 143,* 1443–1446.

King, L. A., King, D. W., Fairbank, J. A., Keane, T. M., & Adams, G. A. (1998). Resilience-recovery factors in post-traumatic stress disorder among female and male Vietnam veterans: Hardiness, postwar social support, and additional stressful life events. *Journal of Personality and Social Psychology, 74,* 420–434.

Krystal, H. (1968). *Massive psychic trauma.* New York: International University Press.

Kulka, R., Schlenger, W., Fairbank, J., Hough, R., Jordan, B. D., Marmar, C. R., et al. (1990). *Trauma and the Vietnam war generation.* New York: Brunner/Mazel.

Lazarus, R. & Folkman, S. (1984). *Stress, appraisal and coping.* New York: Springer.

Lifton, R. J. (1976). *The life of the self.* New York: Simon & Schuster.

Lifton, R. J. (1979). *The broken connection: On death and the continuity of life.* New York: Basic Books, Inc.

Lifton, R. J. (1993). From Hiroshima to the Nazi doctors: The evolution of psychoformative approaches to understanding traumatic stress syndromes. In J. P. Wilson & B. Raphael (Eds.), *International handbook of traumatic stress syndromes* (pp. 11–25). New York: Plenum Press.

Maddi, S. R. (1999). Hardiness and optimism as expressed in coping patterns. *Consulting Psychology Journal: Practice and Research, 51,* 95–105.

Marmar, C. R., Weiss, D., & Metzler, T. J. (1997). The peritraumatic dissociative experiences scale. In J. P. Wilson & T. M. Keane (Eds.), *Assessing psychological trauma and PTSD* (pp. 412–429). New York: Guilford Publications.

Masten, A. S. & Reed, M. G. J. (2002). Resilience in development. In C. R. Snyder & S. J. Lopez (Eds.), *Handbook of positive psychology* (pp. 74–88). New York: Oxford University Press.

McCrae, R. R. & Costa, P. T. (2003). *Personality in adulthood: A five factor item perspective.* New York: Guilford Publications.

McEwen, B. (1998). Protective and damaging effects of stress mediators. *Seminars of the Beth Israel Deaconess Medical Center, 338,* 171–179.

McEwen, B. S. (2002). *The end of stress as we know it.* Washington, DC: The Dana Press.

Mikulincer, M. & Florian, V. (1996). Coping and adaptation to trauma and loss. In M. Zeidner & N. S. Endler (Eds.), *Handbook of coping* (pp. ?????). New York: Wiley.

Moskowitz, J., Acree, M., & Folkman, S. (1998). The association of positive emotion, negative emotion and clinical depression in a longitudinal study of caregiving partners of men with AIDS. Cited in S. Folkman & T. Moskowitz. (2000). Positive affect and the other side of coping. *American Psychologist, 55*, 647–654.

Page, W. F., Engdahl, G. E., & Eberly, R. E. (1991). Prevalence and correlates of depressive symptoms among former POWs. *Journal of Nervous and Mental Disorders, 179*, 670–677.

Parsons, E. (1988). Post-traumatic self-disorders. In J. P. Wilson, Z. Harel, & B. Kahana (Eds.), *Human adaptation to extreme stress: From the Holocaust to Vietnam* (pp. 245–279). New York: Plenum Press.

Patton, D., Violanti, J. M., & Smith, L. M. (2003). *Promoting capabilities to manage posttraumatic stress.* Springfield, IL: Charles C. Thomas.

Raphael, B. & Wilson, J. P. (2000). *Psychological debriefing: Theory, practice, evidence.* Cambridge, UK: Cambridge University Press.

Richardson, G. E. (2002). The metatheory of resilience and resiliency. *Journal of Clinical Psychology, 58*, 307–321.

Rutter, M. (1990). Competence under stress: risk and protective factors. In J. Rolf, A. S. Masten, D. Cicchetti, K.H. Nuechterlein, & S. Weintraub (Eds.), *Risk and protective factors in the development of psychopathology* (pp. 181–214). New York: Cambridge University Press.

Schore, A. N. (2003a). *Affect dysregulation and disorders of the self.* New York: W. W. Norton.

Schore, A. N. (2003b). *Affect dysregulation and the repair of the self.* New York: W. W. Norton.

Sharkansky, E. J., King. D., King, L., Wolfe, J., Erikson, D. J., & Stokes, L. R. (2000). Coping with Gulf War combat stress: Mediating and moderating effects. *Journal of Abnormal Psychology, 109*, 188–197.

Siebert, A. (1996). *The survivor personality.* New York: Pedigree Books.

Solomon, Z., Mikulincer, M., & Avitzu, E. (1998). Coping, locus of control, social support, and combat-related posttraumatic stress disorder: A prospective study. *Journal of Personality and Social Psychology, 55*, 279–285.

Southwick, S. M., Morgan, C. A., Vythilingam, M., Krystal, J. H., & Charney, D. S. (2004). Emerging neurobiological factors in stress resilience. *PTSD Research Quarterly, 14*, 1–6.

Sutker, P. B., Davis, J. M., Uddo, M., & Ditta, S. R. (1995). War zone stress, personal resources, and PTSD in Persian Gulf War returnees. *Journal of Abnormal Psychology, 104*, 444–452.

Sutker, P., Winsted, D. K., Galina, Z. H., & Allain, A. N. (1990). Assessment of long-term psychosocial sequela among POW survivors: The Korean conflict. *Journal of Personality Assessment, 54*, 171–180.

Tennant, C. C., Goulston, K. J., & Dent. O. F. (1986). Clinical psychiatric illness in POWs of Japan: Forty years after release. *Psychological Medicine, 16*, 833–839.

Thomas, R. B. & Wilson, J. P. (2004). Issues and controversies in the understanding and diagnosis of compassion fatigue, vicarious traumatization, and secondary traumatic stress disorder. *International Journal of Emergency Mental Health, 6*, 1–12.

True, W. R., Rice, J., Eisen, S. A., Heath, A. C., Goldberg, J., Lyons, M. J., et al. (1993). A twin study of genetic and environmental contributions to liability for posttraumatic stress symptoms. *Archives of General Psychiatry, 50*, 257–264.

Ulman, R. B. & Brothers, D. (1988). *The shattered self.* Northvale, New Jersey: The Analytic Press.

Vaillant, G. (1977). *Adaptation to life.* Boston, MA: Little, Brown.

Watzlawick, P. (1983). *The situation is hopeless, but not serious.* New York: W. W. Norton.

Waysman, M., Schwarzwald, J., & Solomon, Z. (2001). Hardiness: an examination of its relationship with positive and negative long term changes following trauma. *Journal of Traumatic Stress, 14*, 531–548.

Weisaeth, L. (1995). Disaster: Risk and prevention intervention. In B. Raphael & G. Burrows (Eds.), *Handbook of preventative psychiatry* (pp. 301–332). Amsterdam: Elsevier.

Werner, E. & Smith, R. (1992). *Overcoming the odds: High-risk children from birth to adulthood.* New York: Cornell University Press.

Wiesel, E. (1969). *Night.* New York: Hill and Wang.

Wilson, J. P. (1980). Conflict, stress and growth: The effects of war on psychosocial development among Vietnam veterans. In C. R. Figley & K. S. Leventman (Eds.), *Strangers at home: Vietnam veterans since the war* (pp. 123–165). New York: Preager Press.

Wilson, J. P. (1989a). *Trauma, transformation and healing.* New York: Brunner-Mazel.

Wilson, J. P. (1989b) *Trauma, transformation and healing: An integration approval to theory, research and posttraumatic theory.* New York: Brunner/Mazel.

Wilson, J. P. (1994). The historical evolution of PTSD diagnostic criteria: From Freud to DSM-IV. *Journal of Traumatic Stress, 7,* 681–689.

Wilson, J. P. (1995). Traumatic events and PTSD prevention. In B. Raphael & E. D. Barrows (Eds.), *The handbook of preventative psychiatry* (pp. 281–296). Amsterdam: Elsevier.

Wilson, J. P. (2001). An overview of clinical considerations and principles in the treatment of PTSD. In J. P. Wilson, M. J. Friedman, & J. D. Lindy (Eds.), *Treating psychological trauma and PTSD* (pp. 59–94). New York: Guilford Publications.

Wilson, J. P. (2004a). Broken spirits. In J. P. Wilson & B. Drozdek (Eds.), *Broken spirits: The treatment of traumatized asylum seekers, refugees and war and torture victims* (pp. 141–173). New York: Brunner-Routledge.

Wilson, J. P. (2004b). The broken spirit: Posttraumatic damage to the self. In J. P. Wilson & B. Drozdek (Eds.), *Broken spirits: Treating traumatized asylum seekers, refugees, war and torture victims* (Ch. 6, pp. 107–155). New York: Brunner-Routledge Press.

Wilson, J. P. & Drozdek, B. (2004). *Broken spirits: The treatment of traumatized asylum seekers, refugees and war and torture victims.* New York: Brunner-Routledge.

Wilson, J. P., Harel, Z., & Kahana, B. (1988). *Human adaptation to extreme stress: from Holocaust to Vietnam.* New York & London: Plenum Press.

Wilson, J. P., Harel, Z. & Kahana, B. (1989). The day of infamy: The legacy of Pearl Harbor. In J. P. Wilson (Ed.), *Trauma, transformation and healing* (Ch. 6, pp. 129–159). New York: Brunner/Mazel.

Wilson, J. P. & Lindy, J. (1994). *Counter-transference in the treatment of PTSD.* New York: Guilford Publications.

Wilson, J. P. & Raphael, B. (1993). *The international handbook of traumatic stress syndromes.* New York: Plenum Press.

Wilson, J. P. & Thomas, R. (2004). *Empathy in the treatment of trauma and PTSD.* New York: Brunner-Routledge.

Wilson, J. P., Friedman, M. J., & Lindy, J. D. (2001). An overview of clinical consideration and principles in the treatment of PTSD. In J. P. Wilson, M. J. Friedman, & J. D. Lindy (Eds.), *Treating psychological trauma and PTSD* (pp. 59–94). New York: Guilford Publications.

Yehuda, R. (1998). Resilience and vulnerability factors in the course of adaptation to trauma. *Clinical Quarterly, 8,* 3–6.

Zakin, G., Solomon, Z, & Neva, Y. (2003). Hardiness, attachment style, and long-term psychological distress among Israeli POWs and combat veterans. *Personality and Individual Differences, 34,* 819–829.

Zeidner, M. & Endler, N. S. (1996). *Handbook of coping.* New York: Wiley.

Zeiss, R. A. & Dickman, H. R. (1989). PTSD 40 years later: Incidence and person–situation correlations in former POWs. *Journal of Clinical Psychology, 45,* 80–87.

Zuckerman, M. (1999). *Vulnerability to psychopathology.* Washington, DC: American Psychological Association.

11

Trauma and Transformation of the Self: Restoring Meaning and Wholeness to Personality

JOHN P. WILSON

1 TRAUMA AND THE TRANSFORMATION OF THE SELF

There are causes for all human suffering, and there is a way by which they may be ended, because everything in the world is the result of a vast concurrence of causes and conditions, and everything disappears as these causes and conditions change and pass away.

(The Teachings of Buddha)

The experience of personal trauma can lead to immensely valuable growth. Those who find the way to transform profoundly difficult life-experiences often exhibit character strengths and virtues that define full humanness and give authentic meaning to integrity, wisdom, generativity, capacity for irony, and self-transcendence. Understanding how experiences of psychological trauma are transformed into character strength and integrated forms of psychological functioning is critically important to psychological theories of behavior and innovative treatment approaches for those who suffer the adverse effects of extreme stress. What is it that we know about the experience of trauma and the transformation of the self leading to growth and the actualization of human potential? What are the character strengths, virtues, and attributes of the psychologically healthy and self-transcendent trauma survivor? This chapter is about the awe-engendering and transforming potential of human character after the abyss of trauma.

Since the advent of PTSD as a classification in *DSM-III* (APA, 1980), research has focused on studying the etiology, prevalence, comorbidity, and developmental processes affected by trauma (Friedman, 2000; Wilson, 2004). Comparatively less attention has been focused on the phenomenology of prolonged stress-response syndromes as innate, preprogrammed organismic responses to trauma, with the notable exception of McEwen's research on allostasis (McEwen, 2002, 1998; Friedman & McEwen, 2004). Moreover, research and clinical studies have not attempted to analyze how positive transformations in the self occur which may lead to personal growth and increased character strength (Wilson & Thomas, 2004; Tedeschi, Park, & Calhoun, 1998). Since trauma has the power to cause widespread physical and psychological injuries, it is understandable that the majority of research catalogued in the international database on traumatic stress studies (i.e., P.I.L.O.T.S.@ncptsd.org) has examined pathological aspects of posttraumatic stress disorder (PTSD) or made comparisons between trauma populations with the disorder and those without it. In contrast, little, if any, empirical research has determined the mechanisms by which persons transform psychic trauma (Aldwin, 1994).

Prior to the existence of PTSD as an anxiety disorder, studies of trauma survivors had focused primarily on pathogenic outcomes and how they relate to psychiatric symptoms, social pathology, and disruption of normal patterns of daily living (Raphael, 1993; Grinker & Spiegel, 1945; Gleser, Green, & Winget, 1981; Eitinger, 1975; Wilson & Raphael, 1983; K. Erikson, 1974; Dimsdale, 1980; Lifton, 1979; Barton, 1969; Quarantelli & Dynes, 1973). Analysis of post-1980 studies of PTSD in trauma populations reveals similar and parallel patterns in research to the pre-1980 studies of survivor populations. Specifically, the progression of studies and resultant knowledge evolved from *phenomenological descriptions* of posttraumatic patterns of adaptation and symptom formation (e.g., traumatic neurosis, K-Z syndrome; A-bomb syndrome; shellshock; battle fatigue; railway spine; post-Vietnam syndrome; delayed stress syndrome; rape trauma syndrome; battered women syndrome) to *empirical studies* of medical and psychological sequelae, including the psychiatric and psychosocial effects of trauma in *comparative analyses* of survivors with control groups constructed for research purposes. This evolutionary progression and parallel in research approaches (i.e., before and after the 1980 advent of PTSD as a diagnostic entity) was expectable and quite interesting from the history of science viewpoint. In these studies, research hypotheses were largely empirically driven, derived from existing theories of personality, human development, the general adaptation syndrome, and behavioral medicine (Wilson, Friedman, & Lindy, 2001). Major theories of personality and empirical research were utilized to examine the pathological aspects of human adaptation to extreme stress, usually within nosological classifications of the *Diagnostic and Statistical Manuals* (DSM, 1952–2000) of the American Psychiatric Association (i.e., *DSM-I* to *DSM-IV-TR*).

In the twentieth century, the study of the pathological effects of trauma was necessitated by the sheer number of catastrophic events and the urgent need to care for millions of trauma victims on a worldwide basis, including children, civilians, military veterans, political prisoners, disaster victims, asylum-seekers, refugees, and war and torture victims (Wilson & Drozdek, 2004). However, beyond the important need to provide health care to trauma survivors, the history of research on trauma and PTSD reflects a skewed emphasis on studying psychopathology rather than the full range of behavioral adaptation: pathological, normal, optimal, and transformative. In this regard, it is important to place in perspective that clinical psychology and psychiatry has been dominated by an illness model of functioning that views human adaptation through the lens of pathology rather than health. James E. Maddux (2002), in a review of positive psychology and the deconstruction of the illness ideology and the *DSM*, wrote:

> the language of clinical psychology remains the language of medicine and pathology—what may be called the language of illness ideology. Terms such as symptom, disorder, patient, clinic, clinical and clinician are all consistent with the four assumptions noted previously. These terms emphasize abnormality and sickness over health. They promote dichotomy between normal and abnormal behaviors, clinical and non-clinical problems, and clinical and non-clinical populations. They locate human adjustment and maladjustment inside the person rather than in the person's interactions with the environment or sociocultural values and sociocultural forces such as prejudice and openness. Finally, these terms portray the people who are seeking help as passive victims of intrapsychic and biologic forces beyond their direct control and therefore should be the passive recipients of an expert's care and cure. (p. 14)

This passage is directly relevant to the issues of trauma, PTSD, and self-transformation. The theoretical and research perspectives of a positive psychology (Snyder & Lopez, 2002) suggest that the study of posttraumatic adaptation must be able to account for pathological and healthy forms of coping and adaptation. The primary focus on trauma and psychopathology limits knowledge about human resilience, self-actualization, psychological health, positive emotions, and the mechanisms by which persons transform the adverse effects of trauma and, in the process, transform themselves as persons. While this set of research priorities was understandable given the widespread human suffering produced by the massive prevalence of traumatic events that dominated the twentieth century, the critical question of how such experiences were integrated into the consciousness and dynamics of the human psyche were less well understood or examined in experimental research.

The core questions of a positive trauma psychology are: How do trauma survivors transform powerful and life-threatening experiences in healthy ways? What are the qualities, character traits, and virtues of individuals who have overcome the adverse effects of massive psychic trauma (Krystal, 1968, 1988)? What are the pathways to health by which ordinary people move on with their lives after trauma? What set of characteristics define the intrapsychic functioning of trauma survivors who have transcended and transformed the powerful impact of trauma on organismic functioning? How has trauma affected the way in which they view life, create systems of meaning, and maintain a positive attitude in daily living? How do their person schemas function in integrated relations (Horowitz, 1991)? Is the capacity to transform psychological trauma correlated with self-actualizing behaviors and optimal states of integrated organismic functioning? This question has also been raised by Carolyn M. Aldwin (1994) in her research studies on stress, coping, and development. She states

> the key to understanding the *positive aspects* of stress lies in how individuals (or individuals within a culture) cope with a given stressor. Rather than simply homeostatic functioning, the more important role of coping may be *transformation*. Unfortunately, *the transformational aspects of coping have received little attention in the stress and coping literature*. Clearly, we need more information on how individuals *transform themselves* through the process of coping with stress, including inward mastery, self-knowledge, and the ability to take a different perspective on stress. *The ability to transform a situation is also of extreme importance*—to be able to perceive and act upon opportunity in crises. *Thus, transformational coping may be the key to preventative mental health*. (p. 270; emphasis added)

This chapter will explore these and related questions in an attempt to develop a description of how individuals undergo a transformation of the self and personality in the wake of trauma. The description includes a psychological analysis of the healthy and transformed trauma survivor. It is a characterization of the posttraumatic self in a highly integrated form of functioning which draws on clinical insight, scientific

research on optimal and positive states of mental health, and a substantial literature on the qualities of human resiliency (see Chapter 10).

2 PRINCIPLES OF SELF-TRANSFORMATION IN THE POSTTRAUMATIC SELF

2.1 Source Materials

Table 11.1 presents 12 principles that characterize transformations
of personality in trauma survivors. These 12 principles were developed
from the following sources: (a) the expansive literature on PTSD
(Friedman, 2000); (b) clinical treatment approaches and their limitations in psychotherapy with trauma survivors (Foa, Keane, & Friedman,
2001); (c) anecdotal accounts of trauma survivors and patients from
momentous historical events (e.g., World War II, Hiroshima, the Vietnam
War, the Balkans War (1991–1995); September 11, 2001 terrorist
attacks; civilian catastrophes; and victims of childhood abuse); (d) novels
and biographical writings by trauma survivors (e.g., Caputo, 1977);
(e) the mythological literature found in anthropology and literary forms
(Campbell, 1990); (f) the literature on self-psychology and narcissistic
personality processes (Kohut, 1965; Wolfe, 1990); (g) recent research
on optimal states of functioning (Sheldon, 2004); and (h) personal
interviews from 1973 to 2005 with thousands of trauma survivors
(e.g., war veterans, refugees, torture victims, disaster victims), most of
whom suffered from anxiety, depression, substance abuse, PTSD and
posttraumatic self-disorders (Parsons, 1988). These trauma survivors
were involved in treatment, forensic settings, inpatient hospitalization,
asylum-seeking, or receiving assistance from governmental and nongovernmental agencies in the U.S., Europe, and Asia (Wilson, in press).

2.2 The Composite Personality Profile

The qualities of personality and behavioral functioning of psychologically healthy trauma survivors reflect intrapsychic transformations
of the ways that traumatic and life-altering experiences were metabolized
and resulted in new configurations of self-dimensions. These transformations represent adaptive responses to pain, suffering, and states of
traumatization. The descriptions that follow are a composite personality
profile of the integrated posttraumatic self built primarily upon the
typologies described in Chapter 2: the Cohesive Self; the Accelerated
Self; the Integrated Self, and the empirical research on resilient trauma
survivors (Agaibi & Wilson, 2005). Specifically, these typologies and their

TABLE 11.1
Principles of Self-Transformation in the Postraumatic Self

1. Vulnerability and illusions
2. Pain, suffering, and transformation
3. Acceptance: life's unequal playing field
4. Limits to ego and humility
5. Continuity to discontinuity in life
6. Connection and sources of meaning
7. Balance and groundedness
8. Empathy, compassion, and freshness of appreciation
9. Honesty and gratitude
10. Love and generosity
11. Self-transformation and reinvention
12. Spiritual consciousness and altruism

Source: ©2004 John P. Wilson.

various combinations are higher order characteristics of self-dimensions, configurations of personal identity, ego-processes, and factorial dimensions of personality (McCrae & Costa, 2003). As resilient and psychologically healthy survivors, these persons could be viewed as having optimal, integrated levels of psychic functioning. The closest analogy in the literature on personality and mental health is Maslow's (1970) description of self-actualizing people and Csikszentmihalyi's (1990) characterization of flow and optimal states of functioning. More recently, the renewed interest and zeitgeist of "positive psychology" has opened doors of inquiry as to character strength, virtue, and optimal states of functioning (Peterson & Seligman, 2004). In this genre, Sheldon's (2004) work on optimal human beings is relevant. In self-psychology, Kohut's (1965) paper on forms and transformations of narcissism is highly informative and applicable to the analysis of posttraumatic injuries to the self. In religious traditions, the "best fit" for understanding transcendence and personal growth stems from Buddhism (Thurman, 2004; Campbell, 1990).

3 TRAUMA MESSAGES

Transcendence refers to the very highest and most inclusive or holistic levels of human consciousness, behaving and relating, as ends rather than as means, to oneself, to significant others, to human beings in general, to other species, to nature, and to the cosmos.

(A. H. Maslow, 1971, p. 279)

The 12 characteristics that form the substrata of self-transformation can be considered trauma messages: they resonate from the heart and soul of survivors. The personality profile was derived from personal interviews with a broad cross-section of survivors (e.g., disaster survivors, accident victims, child abuse victims, torture victims, rape victims, asylum-seekers and refugees, and veterans from different wars [World War II, Korea, Vietnam, Iraq, Bosnia, Croatia, Persian Gulf]). The messages are actual, symbolic, and metaphorical expressions of inner voices and spiritual essence that have emerged through the gradual assimilation of the trauma experience through the decentering and recentering of core self-processes. They reflect states of psychic pain and emotional wounds that have been healed and transformed. The messages are universal and archetypal in nature. The qualities of character, moral virtue, and uniqueness were shaped and reshaped across different stages of the life-cycle. The psychic energy of traumatization has been transformed and evolved into new constellations of ego-states, consciousness, personality, identity, personal values, ideology, views of morality, and systems of meaning.

The 12 characteristics represent the transformation of Trauma Complexes and archetypal experiences of trauma into unified transcendent modalities of intrapsychic functioning. The characteristics also contain universal themes embedded in the archetype of trauma and Trauma Complexes throughout the history of humankind. They are manifestations of unconscious expressions of how the totality of mental functioning can be injured by psychic trauma and then transformed in healthy ways. As unconscious phenomena, they are epiphenomenal expressions of transformed ego-states, identity configurations, and the structure of the self and personality. In discussing the concept of transcendence as a positive personality trait reflective of character and virtue, Peterson and Seligman (2004) state: "Almost all of the positive traits in our classification reach outside the individual—character, after all, is social in nature—*but in the case of the transcendence strengths, the reaching goes beyond other people per se to embrace part or all of the larger universe*" (p. 519; emphasis added). Thus, the transformations that have occurred through the metabolism of psychic trauma result in a reinvented self, one that is more grounded, centered, and connected to ultimate values, higher states of consciousness, and Being-in-the-world[1] (Maslow, 1968). In many respects, the personality characteristics of trauma survivors reflect the psychosocially accelerated and optimally

---

[1]Eckhart Tolle (1999) defined Being as follows: "Being is the eternal, ever present One Life beyond myriad forms of life that are subject to birth and death" (p. 10). In a more existential-psychological sense, Being is authentic functioning at the highest level of one's potential with transformed narcissism.

integrated personality described in Chapter 2. The healthy transformation of trauma and integration into personality results in many
of the characteristics of self-actualizing persons described by Maslow
(1970).

4 THE CHARACTERISTICS OF SELF-TRANSFORMATION IN TRAUMA SURVIVORS

The characteristics of self-transformation in trauma survivors all
involve knowledge and actualization of 12 principles or core themes
that dominate the organization of personal values (Table 11.1).

The 12 principles comprise a syndrome of positive self-transformation
that personifies some trauma survivors more fully than others. The 12
principles are common if not universal characteristics of resilient
survivors. Clearly, some individuals embrace the principles and personal
attributes of self-transformation more strongly than others. The 12
principles represent resultant states of personality functioning and
reflect higher levels of integrative organismic functioning. The 12
principles of self-transformation in trauma survivors have a great
deal in common with the characteristics of self-actualizing persons as
described by Maslow (1970) (e.g., autonomy; realistic perception of
self, others and nature; spontaneity; humor; human kinship; freedom
from enculturation; higher ethical principles; freshness of appreciation;
problem-solving orientation; peak experiences; creativity; resolution of
dichotomies). The overlap in characteristics between self-actualizing
persons and the personality attributes of trauma survivors is not
coincidental. Both phenomena reflect optimal levels of integrative
functioning.

4.1 Vulnerability and Illusions

> *Everything in this life is transitory and filled with uncertainty.*
> *(The Teachings of Buddha)*

In his studies of Hiroshima survivors, Robert J. Lifton (1967) pointed
out that the innocent Japanese victims of the first atomic bomb lost
forever their *sense of invulnerability.* The loss of invulnerability means
many things, ranging from the acute awareness of one's finite stature
in the big picture of life, to the omnipresence of trauma in the lives
of ordinary people. Trauma renders one vulnerable and forces a confrontation with the specter of death, dying, injury, or the overwhelming fear
of physical or soul death. Trauma produces *deillusionment* (i.e., the

loss of illusions about self, others, life, systems of belief and meaning) and *dis-illusionment* (i.e., loss of faith or confusion about the nature of things and reality). Trauma survivors instinctively know that much of life is illusory; that the creation of meaning is an existential choice between personal growth and self-deception. Trauma survivors know that material attachments are ephemeral and elusive. Trauma survivors know that ultimate truths contain paradox and confusion. The specter of actual or imagined self-annihilation causes a massive reevaluation and reordering of life's priorities. Aldwin (1994) notes that "undergoing stressful experiences, especially threatening ones, may change both an individual's perspective on problems and his or her value hierarchy" (p. 261). The loss of one's identity, soul, inner sense of being, and self-continuity forces a rapid *disequilibration* in systems of meaning, value, and the perception of reality in all of its human matrices. Trauma survivors know that, as stated in the teachings of Buddha, what constitutes reality is illusory, fleeting, and subject to change. Personal meaning is created through active mindfulness of being centered in oneself with consciousness invested in the reality of the moment, free from anxious, obsessive ruminations about the past or what might happen in the future. Thus, the paradox: trauma immerses consciousness into the reality of fear, terror, and the necessity for survival. Transformation of trauma is mindfulness of the existential freedom to create meaning through consciousness of one's being through self-directed choices.

4.2 Pain, Suffering and Transformation

Birth and death are found in each moment. Nothing persists at all.
(S. Hagen, 1996, p. 42)

Psychic trauma involves pain, suffering, and states of vulnerability. Exposure to traumatic stressors threatens bodily and psychological integrity. Immersion into the heart of the trauma experience is gut-wrenching, overwhelming, and anxiety-provoking. It can be terrifying and cause profound fears of annihilation. Immersion into the dark abyss of traumatization is temporarily a form of being spiritually uprooted, alone, and adrift in a sea of confusion as to the meaning of the experience. It is a painful, lonely, soul-searching experience in which the world, as previously known, suddenly changes forever. It is a journey that may last a short time or a lifetime until the self regains a center and feels meaningfully grounded, with or without a sense of continuity. As Lifton (1967) found for the survivors of Hiroshima, the transformation of pain, suffering, and vulnerability is a universal task. It is an unavoidable and gradual process that, once begun, generates its own momentum within the organism which has psychobiological, moral, and spiritual consequences in behavior.

4.3 Acceptance and Surrender: Life's Unequal Playing Field

> *We are foolish to think we can have mastery over what is not ours to master.*
> *(S. Hagen, 1996, p. 31)*

The deillusionments caused by trauma include the realization that life is an unequal playing field. In many traumatic situations, the expectations for fairness, justice, compassion, equality, care, respect, and civility are destroyed. Liberty and freedom are psychological ideals that are missing in the lives of many victims of human oppression. Traumatic experiences can crush beliefs that life is fair, just, and equitable in its consequences. For some survivors, the scales of justice simply do not exist. Figley (1985) noted that survivors ask a common set of questions, which include: Why me? Why now? Why this way? Why was I spared? For what purpose and meaning? Why this consequence of harm, injury or suffering?

In self-transformation, survivors universally face the task of answering such questions and placing them into a perspective of meaning in relation to systems of belief, God, and the universe. There are no readily available guidebooks or reference sources to provide answers to these difficult questions. In this sense, there are no absolute truths. The answers emerge with the struggle to find meaning and often are facilitated by maintaining connection and continuity with fellow survivors. The acceptance that comes with the realization that life can be an unequal playing field involves the principle of surrender. The deep soul acceptance of one's fate, during or after trauma, is related to surrender and the capacity of the self to find a higher purpose. As Tolle (1999) states: "surrender is the single but profound wisdom of *yielding to* rather than opposing the flow of life ... acceptance of what is *immediately frees you from mind identification* and thus reconnects you with Being" (pp. 171–172; emphasis added). Viewed in this way, acceptance and surrender are related processes in higher states of consciousness. Though seemingly paradoxical, true surrender is self-affirmation rather than resignation, cessation in striving or passivity. Acceptance and surrender recognize the inherent wisdom of letting go of things that are beyond one's capacity to control. Acceptance and surrender in the recognition of superior forces and events is healthy acknowledgment of the limits of ego.

4.4 Ego-Transcendence and Humility

Joyful participation in the sorrows of the world.

(J. Campbell, 1990, p. 117)

The experience of trauma is paradoxically similar to awe-inspiring personal experiences of the vastness of nature, i.e., one is rendered humble, small, and insignificant. The specter of harm to the self and existence produces changes to ego-states and one's appraised sense of importance in work, love, and family relationships, as well as the "big picture" of life. Trauma teaches lessons of humility and smallness. Trauma teaches that life is finite and can terminate at any moment in time, depending on the whims of fate. The emotional state of being rendered small by overwhelming trauma is one of humility. Similar to the experience of the vastness of nature or viewing the expanse of the universe on a clear night sky with its brilliant stars, black holes, and swirling celestial galaxies located millions of light years away, profoundly traumatic experiences place in perspective one's finite nature and brief period of existence on Earth. Ego-transcendence, therefore, is a matter of accurate self-knowledge in the larger scheme of reality and earthly existence. Transcendence of one's ego—i.e., moving beyond egoism and narcissism—sows seeds of humility. Ego-transcendence and humility are closely related to each other as concepts and rest on the principles of surrender and acceptance.

In a review of the concept of humility, June Tangney (2003) stated that "the key elements seem to include:

- an accurate assessment of one's abilities and achievements (not low self-esteem, self-depression);
- an ability to acknowledge one's mistakes, imperfections, gaps in knowledge, and limitations (often vis-à-vis a Higher Power);
- openness to new ideas, contradictory information and advice;
- keeping one's abilities and accomplishments—one's place in the world—in perspective (e.g., seeing oneself as just one person in the larger scheme of things);
- an appreciation of the value of all things, as well as the many ways that people and things can contribute to the world." (p. 413)

These five sets of characteristics are common to psychologically healthy survivors who have transformed their painful ordeals. They have a clear sense of themselves and their importance in life without distortion or grandiose inflation. In the wake of trauma, they have a new sense of ultimate values and priorities and are open to new experiences, especially those that maintain a sense of centeredness in the self and promote organismic well-being. As Tangney (2003) notes, a sense of humility includes knowing one's place in the world and possessing sanguine perspectives of one's station in life. Psychic trauma teaches that many dichotomies coexist in life—good vs. evil, justice vs. unfairness, love vs. hate, luck vs. fate, head vs. heart, narcissism vs. humility, vulnerability vs. strength, autonomy vs. connectedness, trust vs. mistrust, despair vs. hope, compassion vs. indifference, etc.—that contain sources of wisdom and directionality in terms of living by higher moral principles. Traumatic experiences function as a magnifying glass in terms of the polarities intrinsic to human dichotomies in living. They magnify the qualitative nature of such dilemmas, which appear mean-ingless in the face of life-threatening events and the subjective fear of one's psychological annihilation or physical death. Among the posttrau-matic consequences is disequilibrium in the experience of self—the feeling of smallness and humility in comparison to the vast diversity of human existence and long history of humankind. The acquisition and understanding of humility enables ego-transcendence to trans-form previous modes of egocentric orientation and self-absorption into a wider acceptance of one's limitations and imperfections and, at the same time, broaden one's identification with the species as a whole. In Buddhist tradition, this is known as joyful participation in the sorrows of the world, according to mythologist Joseph Campbell (1990).

4.5 Continuity and Discontinuity in Life

> *Life is full of stops and starts, sometimes in different directions.*
> *(J. P. Wilson, unpublished)*

Trauma teaches that people get injured, killed, and psychically scarred. Trauma teaches that life goes on and that those not directly involved in the stresses of the experience may quickly forget about its prolonged effects and resume their personal lives as if little has changed. The unaffected kin of trauma survivors often expect that the survivor will return to normal in a relatively short period of time. But what *does* "normal" mean after a life-altering trauma?

Trauma teaches that life and death have continuities and discon-tinuities. Insight about life's discontinuities that accompany trans-formational healing is acceptance of the limitations of ego, a genuine sense of gratitude and humility for being alive, albeit with a different perspective on the meaning of life itself.

The changes wrought by trauma to the survivor's sense of well-being and psychic integrity include changes in the sense of self-continuity and the continuity of life. Trauma disrupts the continuity of one's sense of self-sameness and the ongoing flow and trajectory of the life-course. Trauma can cause a radical shift in the experiential planes and dimensions of the self (i.e., connection, coherence, continuity, autonomy, vitality, energy) and lead to a sense of being ungrounded, uncentered, and without an emotional anchor (Lifton, 1967, 1976; K. Erikson, 1974). Trauma survivors may feel a personal loss of their past; a broken connection to sources of meaning and kinship communities. The subjective experience of loss of self-continuity evoked by trauma is typically expressed in feelings of fragmentation, loss of coherence, loss of connection to others, diminished personal autonomy, and an emotional sense of vulnerability that is similar to the loss felt in bereavement, the death of a loved one or valued friend, and states of shame. As posttraumatic self-transformation and reinvention progresses, a new sense of continuity with the past can be established. In other cases, a new start point is created, marking the beginning of a different baseline of self-continuity and sameness, although transmuted in form and essence in comparison with the pretraumatic self and personality structure.

4.6 Connection to Sources of Meaning

> *The fact is that we are always in and a part of Totality ... we cannot remove ourselves from it.*
>
> (S. Hagen, 1996, p. 14)

Traumatic experiences have the power to disrupt the flow of life and one's connection to sources of meaning, including a relationship with a Higher Power. The term "sources of meaning" has wide reference that includes religion, philosophy, ideology, political beliefs, and personally created systems of meaning and value. The transformational process of establishing meaning after trauma involves reestablishing, affirming, or developing connections that are important to maintaining a sense of posttraumatic self-continuity. In this regard, the affirmation and maintenance of connection to sources of meaning has direct relations to the inner dimensions of the self (i.e., continuity, coherence, connection, autonomy, vitality, energy). The congruence between *outer* sources of connection that create meaning to *intrapsychic* connections among the components of the self is critical to an overall sense of well-being. There is a direct relationship between a sense of connectedness to *external* sources of meaning (e.g., one's culture, group membership, religion, nature, beliefs in a Higher Power), and an *inner* sense of continuity and self-sameness.

4.6.1 A Sense of Continuity and Connection: The Past Was, The Present Is! In a simplified formula, a sense of continuity and connection to significant others, including fellow trauma survivors, serves to reinforce the sanctity of the trauma experience while sustaining existential meaning of life on a daily basis. Awareness and consciousness shifts: The past was, the present is! An inner sense of continuity and connection reinforces a sense of personal identity because the connections to tangible sources of meaning have continuity in time and space. Viktor Frankl (1984), himself a Holocaust survivor, stated that the creation of meaning is a core task of survivorship

> man's search for meaning may arouse *inner tension rather than equilibrium.* However, precisely *such tension is an indispensable prerequisite of mental health* . . . what man actually needs is not a tension state but rather the striving and struggling for a worthwhile goal, a freely chosen task. (p. 109; emphasis added)

He continues

> We must never forget that we may find meaning in life when confronted with a hopeless situation, when facing a fate that cannot be changed. For what then matters is to bear witness to the uniquely human potential at its best, which is to *transform a personal tragedy into a triumph,* to turn one's predicament into human achievement. (p. 116; emphasis added)

Finally, in terms of existential freedom, Frankl (1984) states

> By the same token, every human being has the *freedom to change at any instant* . . . one of the main features of human existence is the capacity to rise above such conditions, to grow beyond them. (p. 133; emphasis added)

4.7 Balance and Groundedness

> *you have these moments of ecstasy . . . and living in those moments of ecstasy is the difference between being outside and inside the garden. You go past fear and desire, past the pain of opposition.*
>
> (Joseph Campbell, 1988, p. 34)

The psychic disequilibrium caused by trauma alters the survivor's sense of being grounded to reality and centered within the self. The concept of centering in self-dimensions and phenomenal experiences extends to emotional, temporal, and spatial places of existence (Lifton, 1976)

> On the temporal plane centering consists of bringing to bear upon the immediate encounter older images and forces in a way that can

anticipate future encounters. On the spatial plane, centering means unifying immediate (proximate) exposure, including bodily movement, with "distant," "ultimate," "abstract," "immortalizing" meanings. A third aspect of centering is that of making discriminations in emotional value between our most compassioned images and forms (what we call the "core" of the self) and those that are less impassioned and therefore more peripheral. (p. 71)

In contrast to the processes that constitute the centering of self-experiences, especially in terms of trauma's disruptional aspect, grounding is a "fraternal twin" concept. Lifton (1976) notes

Grounding in turn is the relationship of the self to its own history, individual and collective, as well as to its biology. Ordinary grounding permits *decentering and separation or alteration* of the existing involvements of the self necessary for growth and change. (p. 72, emphasis added)

Centering and grounding are related aspects of self-processes and occur for every structural dimension of the self (i.e., continuity, connection, coherence, autonomy, vitality, and energy). The dimensions of the self can be centered and grounded in terms of time, space, and emotional balance. Psychological trauma generates psychic disequilibrium and produces relative degrees of decentering and ungrounding of these self-dimensions. Moreover, massive psychic trauma causes radical decentering and ungrounding of the self—i.e., the structure unravels and the self begins to fragment and lose its integrated coherence. In order to restore vitality and wholeness, the aspects of the self that have become decentered and ungrounded must be restored through transformational processes, including reconceptualizing, reinventing, and symbolizing the nature of the self as a whole. On this point, Lifton (1976) writes

Decentering inevitably involves the possibility that the self will become un-centered, will not cohere and will be unable to make the *symbolic transformation* necessary to assimilate new experiences. Every movement away from centeredness, every encounter with significant novelty ... entails anxiety and risk, after guilt, rage, and a sense of inner chaos where there is grounding, decentering can exist in healthy tension with centering, and its accompanying pain and confusion can be experienced in the service of recentering—achieving a new mode of still-flexible ordering. *Where there is no such equilibrium, both centering and decentering are inevitably impaired, and un-centering becomes a perpetual threat.* (p. 73; emphasis added)

In the posttraumatic self, then, the processes of centering and grounding planes of experience are dynamic, fluid, and ongoing processes within each dimension of the self. There are processes of centering and decentering, grounding and ungrounding, for the self-dimensions of coherence, continuity, connection, autonomy, vitality, and energy. Thus, there are dialectic polarities in the posttraumatic self: coherence vs. fragmentation; continuity vs. discontinuity; connection vs. separation; autonomy vs. over-control, vitality vs. lethargy; and energy vs. fatigue. The dialectic process between temporal, spatial, and emotional planes of self-experiences are paramount with decentering and ungrounding processes. The resilient trauma survivor instinctively knows this fact and maintains an attitude of openness to new experiences that facilitates the healthy decentering–recentering process that maintains a sense of continuity to personal identity.

4.8 Empathy, Compassion, and Freshness of Appreciation

Empathy requires the bravery to face others' suffering.

(Ladner, 2004, p. 127)

The immersion into psychic trauma and its later metabolism through processes of centering and decentering typically produces a freshness of appreciation for the beauty of life. This freshness of appreciation is similar to a swimmer who holds his or her breath as long as possible under water and then rapidly emerges through the smooth, silvery surface of the water to inhale clean, fresh air into aching lungs filled with carbon dioxide. As refreshing, clean air fills the lungs, there is a relief of tension, quelling the fear of drowning and not having enough air to breathe. So, too, the trauma survivor inhales the freshness of life upon recovery from physical or psychic injuries. There is a sense of goodness to being alive, feeling well, and realizing that a tangible future exists that holds opportunities for self-actualization that were unrecognized prior to the trauma experience.

In self-transformation, the trauma survivor automatically possesses a greater capacity for empathy, compassion, and the ability to appreciate life in the most basic ways (Wilson & Thomas, 2004). The capriciousness of trauma makes salient that it can occur to anyone, anywhere, at any time under the right circumstances and whims of fate. Eckhart Tolle (1999) describes his personal self-transformation after episodes of depression and suicidality. Noteworthy is his characterization of the freshness of appreciation of his immediate environment:

The first light of dawn was filtering through the curtains. Without any thought, I felt, I knew, that there is infinitely more to light than we realize. That soft luminosity filtering through the curtains was love itself.

Tears came to my eyes. I got up and walked around the room. I recognized the room and yet I knew that I had never truly seen it before. *Everything was fresh and pristine, as if it had just come into existence.* I picked up things, a pencil, an empty bottle, *marveling at the beauty and aliveness of it all.* (p. 2; emphasis added)

In the process of recovery from traumatic stress, PTSD, self-pathologies, or other forms of psychological distress, the preoccupation with one's self and the quality of existence sensitizes awareness to the vulnerability and emotional states of others. Through self-recovery and the transformation of trauma, gratitude and humility generalize and widen the circle of experiential modalities of empathy and compassion. Similarly, the circle of personal identification with others, and humanity in general, widens in scope. There is a strongly felt sense of belonging to the great chain of humanity. The heightened development of empathy and compassion for others relates to the principle that life is an "unequal playing field." Traumatic experiences often increase awareness of unfairness, injustice, inequity, and cruel suffering. For the survivor, the reality of having been dealt a "trauma playing card" in the "big game of life" sensitizes them to the vulnerability of others and to their areas of emotional angst. Empathy, as a form of knowing another's inner state of being, and compassion, as to the ability to "be with" others in their moments of despair, are twin sides of being centered and grounded in the dimensions of the self (Wilson & Thomas, 2004). Ladner (2004) notes that in Buddhist traditions there are different meanings and levels of compassion as a state of mind: "The most Tibetan word is nying-je. Nying means heart and je means the foremost exalted. So compassion is the most exalted of all states of the heart of mind ... Buddhism defines compassion as a mental state of wishing others may be free from suffering" (pp. 10–14). While there is no direct correspondence in the English language to the Buddhist connotation, the word compassion seems to combine empathy and nonjudgmental acceptance as reflected in words such as kind, tolerant, magnanimous, dispassionate, generous, unbiased, gracious, merciful, goodhearted, and sympathetic. In overcoming death anxiety, the fear of annihilation, and exposure to the painful sorrow and suffering of others, the transformed trauma survivor often manifests human compassion and transcendent detachment in states of mindfulness with others.

4.9 Honesty and Gratitude

Gratitude is the opposite feeling of being depleted; it predisposes us to a positive state of mind.

(Ladner, 2004, p. 167)

The power of the trauma experience is like a cascading stream of water that flows downwards at different speeds. The ripple effects of the cascading water generate changes in the current and direction of the water's path. Similarly, the universality of trauma's ripple effects on the psyche include deillusionment; the loss of a sense of invulnerability; the experience of fear and the specter of death; decentering and ungrounding of the self; the experience of humility, smallness, shame, and guilt; and a temporary or permanent loss of continuity with the planes of self-experience. In extreme cases of traumatization, the trauma survivor becomes immersed in the Abyss and Inversion Experiences in which reality suddenly and rapidly changes its recognizable quality. The surreal becomes real and the fear of death becomes a tangible emotional reality.

In the healthy posttraumatic self, characterological honesty is a fundamental principle for self-transformation. The sterling quality of honesty appears to originate in the trauma experience and the confrontation with the specter of death, the limits of one's ego, and the sense of powerlessness over many aspects of life. Characterological honesty involves candid self-effacement. Trauma has the power to shatter ego-defenses and strip the survivor psychically naked. As a dimension of characterological honesty, posttraumatic self-effacement is a fundamental principle of authentic existence. The resilient survivor seeks to maintain a healthy sense of centering and grounding within the dimensions of the self and to do so requires honesty, mindfulness, and self-awareness of emotions and values. Authentic existence and the capacity to love with full consciousness of choice, freedom, and the potential for higher degrees of self-actualization, necessarily involves a grounded sense of honesty. It is paradoxical that the deillusionment in systems of belief caused by severe trauma precipitates opportunities for more accurate, realistic, and honest self-assessments.

Characterological honesty and the ability to self-efface in grounded ways is directly connected with a sense of gratitude at being alive. Gratitude is also correlated with the posttraumatic characteristic of freshness of appreciation. Feeling alive, grounded, and centered in themselves and systems of personal meaning, healthy survivors manifest gratitude at the beauty of life at all levels of daily existence—from seeing the rising sun in the morning to the inner beauty of others. Gratitude and humility are companions in ego-space. As an inner schema of the self, gratitude not only serves to maintain psychic equilibrium, it counterbalances a sense of humility, like the two sides of balanced weighing scales. Persons who have overcome the adverse effects of psychic and physical trauma intuitively know that being alive calls for an attitude of humility and gratefulness. In the posttraumatic self, these qualities are embedded in consciousness and constitute a principle for living.

4.10 Love and Generosity

Freeing ourselves from narcissism allows us to find real joy in compassion for others and to avoid drowning in our own illusions.

(Ladner, 2004, p. 252)

As a consequence of self-transformation resulting from traumatization, resilient trauma survivors develop a deep capacity for love and generosity. As survivor attributes, these qualities of character are principles for living that are closely related to empathy, compassion, and freshness of appreciation. Moreover, with good centering and grounding that emerges as part of honest self-effacement, the trauma survivor experiences love for themselves and others without fears of loss, abandonment, detachment, conflict, or rejection. Having a sense of humility, humor, and realization of finite limitations, the transformed posttraumatic self can extend itself and its ego-boundaries to others without undue needs for self-protective defenses or behavioral security measures designed to ward off rejection. Ego-extension to wider circles of human identification involves capacities for generativity and nurturance (Erikson, 1968; Aronoff & Wilson, 1985). In a similar manner, the positive survivor exhibits generosity of spirit, energy, and resources. The act of manifesting generosity, kindness, compassion, etc., is a symbolic expression of generative caring, rather than an attempt to please others for purposes of recognition or ego-gratification.[2]

To the resilient and transcendent survivor, the value of loving and being loved is a paramount virtue which has been shaped by the stark confrontation with traumatic experiences, especially those that threaten one's existence. When one faces the fear of death or has witnessed the death, dying or profound suffering of others, radical changes in perspectives concerning the meaning of life may occur. In this sense, the capacity to be loving is also self-affirmation of one's existence. The capacity to unconditionally love others is a confirmation of one's authentic existence, including the capacity to feel and experience a wide range of positive emotions as a sentient and mindful person.

---

[2]Robert Thurman (2004) describes five transcendent virtues from a Buddhist perspective: "Transcendent generosity, justice, patience, creativity and contemplative serenity—acts, words and thoughts that express these transcendences shape your spiritual gene in ways that secure and empower your positive evolution, creating ever increasing stores of wisdom and merit" (p. 86).

The unconditional love of others enables ego-transcendence that releases psychic energy for the creative pursuit of optimal functioning.

4.11 Architecture of the Self: Self-Transformation and Identity Reinvention

> *Rebirth consciousness is the awareness that this moment is not the new moment. Nothing results. Nothing repeats. Nothing returns. Each moment is fresh, new, unique—impermanent.*
>
> *(S. Hagen, 1996, p. 45)*

In his studies of trauma survivors, Lifton (1993) described the process of transforming trauma as a protean task that all survivors face. In resilient and healthy survivors, the processes of self-transformation and reinvention are continuous and reflect self-actualizing tendencies, as well as blocks to their development. As a principle for living, the survivor recognizes the necessity of self-continuity on a daily basis that sustains active, self-directed processes of centering and grounding of the self. The creative decentering of the temporal, spatial, and emotional planes of the self is necessary in order to maintain organismic vitality. The natural consequence of centering and decentering the dimensions of the self is the reinvention of the core self—i.e., the subjective idiosyncratic inner sense of one's identity. This inner psychic process is continuous, dynamic, fluid, and continually active, although intrapsychic changes may not be evident in behavior that characterizes a sense of personal identity

> the conscious feeling of having a personal identity is based on two simultaneous observations: the perception of the self-sameness and continuity of one's existence in time and space and the perception of the fact that others recognize one's sameness and continuity. (Erikson, 1950, p. 50)

While there are clear threads of self-sameness and continuity that define individual identity based on *external* behaviors and the *qualitative* aspects of attempts at mastering experience, it is the inner world of psychological processes that are actively transforming the bases of the self and the perceptions that the person has of themselves, others, and reality (Kalsched, 1996). Nowhere is this more evident than for survivors who have "looked death in the eye" and faced the realistic possibility of their own death. Ultimate moments of the death encounter are epiphanous in their potential transformative power. At such moments, the specter of total annihilation and soul death are identical and transparent. The specter of nonbeing is itself a psychological experience of decentering and ungrounding of the core vitality of the self. Afterwards, the protean task of transformation is set into motion and persists until the symbolic or actual specter of "soul" death reoccurs during the life-span.

5 THE FOUR BASIC TRANSFORMATIONS OF PTSD IN THE SELF

The nature of transforming psychological trauma, especially the effects of PTSD and its associated features, can be understood within this framework. For example, the triad of core PTSD symptom clusters (reexperience [B], avoidance/numbing [C], psychobiological changes, hyperarousal [D]) have consequences for self-esteem and the capacity for intimate relationships. In a simplified way, one can identify four key areas of pathological impact caused by psychological trauma: (1) the self; (2) memory and consciousness; (3) emotions; and (4) relations with others. In the transformation process, these four areas shift in focus to comprise the four transformations of the self: (1) unity; (2) transcendence and integration of consciousness; (3) serenity; and (4) love. As a result of transformation, there is a unity of opposites into a new form, which is the foundation of personal transcendence. The distressing and painful memories of trauma are unified into a new perspective of life itself. The dysregulation and painful emotions associated with memories of trauma are no longer necessary or triggered in uncontrolled ways. Hence, serenity and calmness prevails. Problems of intimacy and being emotionally resonant through connectedness to others is transformed and the capacity to love others exists without fear. The four transformations of the core dimensions of traumatized states result in the unity of opposites, transcendence of the past, and the freedom for self-reinvention.

5.1 Spiritual Consciousness and Altruism

Just as treasures are uncovered from the earth, so virtue appears from good deeds, and wisdom appears from a pure and peaceful mind. To walk safely through the maze of human life, one needs the light of wisdom and the guidance of virtue.

(The Teachings of Buddha)

Trauma and the transformation of the self embraces the qualities of higher spiritual consciousness and altruism. These aspects of the healthy posttraumatic self are strongly linked to empathy, compassion, honesty, centering, grounding, and the maintenance of optimal states of psychological well-being. In a seminal paper written from the perspective of self-psychology, Kohut (1965) stated

> Man's capacity to acknowledge the finiteness of his existence, and to act in accordance with this painful discovery, may well be the greatest psychological achievement ... wisdom is achieved largely through man's ability to overcome his unmodified narcissism and it *rests on his acceptance of the limitations of physical, intellectual and emotional powers.* It may be defined as an amalgamation of the higher processes of cognition with the psychological attitude which accompanies *the renouncement of narcissistic demands* ... wisdom may thus be defined as a stable attitude of personality toward life and the world, *an attitude which is formed through the integration of the cognitive function with humor, acceptance of transience and a firmly cathected system of value.* (pp. 264–268; emphasis added)

Overcoming the psychic injuries injected into the fabric of personal identity, the posttraumatic self transforms negative emotional states associated with PTSD and existential angst through an altruistic orientation to life. While there are many portals of entry into higher states of spiritual consciousness, their common foundation rests on ego-transcendence, humility, and the creation of sources of meaning through prosocial behavior and altruistic actions.

6 CONCLUSION

The characterization of self-transformation in trauma survivors is, by definition, a composite set of traits of positive transformations that can and does occur in persons. Future studies are necessary to study the qualitative nature of personality processes that I have described for psychologically healthy trauma survivors. However, I have chosen to focus on the positive transformations that reflect the possibility of higher levels of human functioning and transcendence of some of the most powerful and threatening experiences to human life and the capacity to generate meaning. This personality description rests on 12 fundamental principles that characterize many trauma survivors in their quest to reinvent themselves and maintain meaning in life. Clearly, not all survivors embrace and manifest all of the principles nor are they limited only to those who achieve resolution and regain a healthy transcendent sense of themselves and their lives. Even the strongest and healthiest survivors sometimes mourn the loss of the self that they never had or the opportunity to experience a normal trajectory of life. Persons who suffer from PTSD or other posttraumatic emotional injuries manifest some of these qualities as well. Moreover, the history of research on posttraumatic coping and adaptation has largely focused on studies of psychopathology rather than positive coping. In this regard, the current literature is grossly unbalanced in its emphasis on psychopathology and understanding the adverse effects of trauma on the human psyche. In order to understand the nature and dynamics of the post-traumatic self in its entirety, it is necessary to know how individuals transform trauma, reinvent themselves, reconfigure their identity and self-processes, and forge new patterns of living with a sense of integrity, well-being, and wholeness. There is nothing easy in this task. The process of transforming trauma and maintaining a sense of personal integrity is ultimately the quest to be fully human. The scientific study of such individuals will enable discovery of the mechanism of self-transformation and the farther reaches of human nature. These people represent hopes for mankind, for the possibility of a tangible future in which love, generativity, and generosity prevail over evil, hatred, and despair. In essence, they are icons of the inner spirit of human nature across time, culture, and the generations, past and future.

REFERENCES

Agaibi, C & Wilson, J. P. (2005). Trauma, PTSD and resilience: A review of the literature. *Trauma, Violence & Abuse, 6*(3), 195–216.

Aldwin, C. (1994). *Stress, coping and development.* New York: Guilford Publications.

Aronoff, J., & Wilson, J. P. (1985). *Personality in the social process.* New Jersey: Lawrence Erlbaum.

Barton, A. H. (1969). *Communities in disaster: A sociological analysis of collective stress situations.* New York: Doubleday.

Campbell, J. (1988). *The power of myth.* New York: Anchor Books.

Campbell, J. (1990). *Transformation of myth through time.* New York: Harper.

Caputo, P. (1977). *A rumor of war.* New York: Holt, Rinehart & Winston.

Csikszentmihalyi, M. (1990). *Flow: The psychology of optimal experience.* New York: Simon & Schuster.

Dimsdale, J. (1980). *Survivors, victims and perpetrators.* New York: Hennisher.

Eitinger, C. (1975). Jewish concentration camp survivors in Norway. *Israel Annals of Psychiatry, 13,* 321–334.

Erikson, E. H. (1950). *Childhood and society.* New York: W. W. Norton.

Erikson, E. H. (1968). *Identity, youth & crisis.* New York: W. W. Norton.

Erikson, E. H. (1974). *Dimensions of a new identity: Jefferson lectures, 1973.* New York: W. W. Norton.

Erikson, K. (1974). *Everything in its path.* New York: Simon & Schuster.

Figley, C. R. (1985). *Trauma and its wake* (Vol. I). New York: Brunner/Mazel.

Foa, E., Keane, T. M., & Friedman, M. J. (2001). *Effective treatments for PTSD.* New York: Guilford Press.

Frankl, V. E. (1984). *The will to meaning: Foundations and applications of logotherapy.* New York: Meridian Books.

Friedman, L. J. (2000). *Identities architect.* Cambridge. Harvard University Press.

Friedman, M. J. & McEwen, B. S. (2004). PTSD, allostatic load and medical illness. In P. P. Schnurr & B. L. Green (Eds.), Trauma and healing: Physical consequences of exposure to extreme stress (pp. 157–189). Washington, DC: American Psychological Association.

Gleser, G. C., Green, B. L., & Winget, C. N. (1981). *Prolonged psychosocial effects of disaster: A study of Buffalo Creek*. New York: Academic Press.

Grinker, R. P. & Spiegel, J. P. (1945). *Men under stress*. Philadelphia, Pennsylvania: Blakiston.

Hagen, S. (1996). *Buddhism is not what you think*. San Francisco, California: Harper.

Horowitz, M. (1991). Person *schemas and maladaptive interpersonal patterns*. Illinois: University of Chicago Press.

Kalsched, D. (1996). *The inner world of trauma: Archetypal defenses of the personal spirit*. London: Routledge.

Kohut, H. (1965) Forms and transformations of narcissism. *Journal of the American Psychoanalytic Association, 13*, 243–271.

Krystal, H. (1968). *Massive psychic trauma*. New York: International University Press.

Krystal, H. (1988). *Integration and healing*. Northvale, New Jersey: The Analytic Press.

Ladner, L. (2004). *The lost art of compassion*. Boston, Massachusetts: Harper.

Lifton, R. J. (1967). *Death in life: The survivors of Hiroshima*. New York: Simon & Schuster.

Lifton, R. J. (1976). *The life of the self*. New York: Simon & Schuster.

Lifton, R. J. (1979). *The broken connection: On death and the continuity of life*. New York: Basic Books.

Lifton, R. J. (1993). From Hiroshima to the Nazi doctors: The evolution of psychoformative approaches to understanding traumatic stress syndromes. In J. P. Wilson & B. Raphael (Eds.), *International handbook of traumatic stress syndromes* (pp. 11–25). New York: Plenum Press.

Maddux, J. E. (2002). Stopping the "madness": Positive psychology and the deconstruction of the illness, ideology and the DSM. In C. R. Snyder & S. J. Lopez (Eds.), *Handbook of positive psychology* (pp. 13–26). New York: Oxford University Press.

Maslow, A. H. (1968). *Towards a psychology of being*. New York: D. Van Nostrand.

Maslow, A. H. (1970). *Motivation and personality*. New York: Harper.

Maslow, A. H. (1971). *The further reaches of human nature*. New York: Viking Press.

McCrae, R. R. & Costa, P. T. (2003). *Personality in adulthood: A five factor item perspective*. New York: Guilford Publications.

McEwen, B. S. (1998). Seminars of the Beth Israel Deaconess Medical Center: Protective and damaging effects of stress mediators. *New England Journal of Medicine, 338*, 171–179.

McEwen, B. S. (2002). *The end of stress as we know it*. Washington, DC: The Dana Press.

Parsons, E. (1988). Post-traumatic self-disorders. In J. P. Wilson, Z. Harel, & B. Kahana (Eds.), *Human adaptation to extreme stress: From the Holocaust to Vietnam* (pp. 245–279). New York: Plenum Press.

Peterson, C. & Seligman, M. E. P. (2004). *Character strengths and virtues: A handbook and classification*. New York: Oxford University Press.

Quarantelli, E. L. & Dynes, R. (1973). When disaster strikes. *New Society, 23*, 5–9.

Raphael, B. (1983). *When disaster strikes*. New York: Basic Books.

Sheldon, K. M. (2004). *Optimal human being*. Hillsdale, NJ: Lawrence Erlbaum.

Snyder, C. R. & Lopez, S. J. (2002). *Handbook of positive psychology*. New York: Oxford University Press.

Tangney, J. P. (2003). Humility. In C. R. Snyder & S. J. Lopez (Eds.), *Handbook of positive psychology* (pp. 411–422). New York: Oxford University Press.

Tedeschi, R. G., Park, C. L., & Calhoun, L. (1998). *Posttraumatic growth*. Hillsdale, NJ: Lawrence Erlbaum.

Thurman, R. (2004). *Infinite life*. New York: Riverhead Books.

Tolle, E. (1999). *The power of now*. San Francisco, California: New World Library.

Wilson, J. P. (in press). From crisis intervention to Croatia: The trauma maps of John P. Wilson. In C. R. Figley (Ed.), *Mapping trauma and its wake: Autobiographical essays by pioneer trauma scholars*. New York: Brunner-Routledge.

Wilson, J. P., Friedman, M., & Lindy, J. (2001). *Treating psychological trauma and PTSD.* New York: Guilford Publications.

Wilson, J. P. (2004) Broken spirits. In J. P. Wilson & B. Drozdek (Eds.), *Broken spirits: The treatment of traumatized asylum seekers, refugees and war and torture victims* (pp. 141–173). New York: Brunner-Routledge.

Wilson, J. P. & Drozdek, B. (2004). *Broken spirits: The treatment of traumatized asylum seekers, refugees and war and torture victims.* New York: Brunner-Routledge.

Wilson, J. P. & Thomas, R. (2004). *Empathy in the treatment of trauma and PTSD.* New York: Brunner-Routledge.

Wolfe, E. (1990). *Treating the self.* New York: Guilford Publications.

12

Transformational Principles: Healing and Recovery from Psychic Trauma

JOHN P. WILSON

1 TRANSFORMATIONAL PRINCIPLES

Those things which seem to take meaning away from human life include not only suffering but dying as well. I never tire of saying that the only really transitory aspects of life are the potentialities, but as soon as they are actualized, they are rendered realities at that very moment.

(*Frankl, 1984, p. 123: emphasis added*)

The extraordinary advances made in the field of traumatology during the past two and a half decades have pushed to new limits the frontiers of knowledge acquisition about posttraumatic stress disorder (PTSD), Trauma Complexes, and the effects of prolonged stress to the human psyche. History will record that these advancements were necessitated by the urgency to provide care on a worldwide basis to the millions who suffered from the adverse effects of massive psychic trauma caused by war, terrorism, natural catastrophe, and violence in its many guises, uniforms, and clothing. To suggest that the twentieth century and the first part of the twenty-first century were characterized as the Age of Stress and Trauma is eponymous and factually correct in terms of the unprecedented number of deaths and the scale of massive destruction caused by global traumas.[1] These events have spawned the birth of traumatology as a science and the collective mobilization of medical and mental health specialists to establish scientific journals and professional organizations. As part of the larger picture of the evolution of knowledge concerning PTSD, Trauma Complexes, and their allied conditions, there is an ever-growing set of controlled research studies that is pointing to commonalities in treatments, emotionally corrective experiences, and educational processes that facilitate healing and recovery. And while it is too early to have definitive data on psychotherapy outcome studies, randomized clinical trials (RCTs), innovative therapeutic treatments, teaching and educational programs, there is sufficient convergence of information to identify some of the major principles for healing and recovery. A similar position has been stated by Follette, Palm, and Hall (2004)

> Creative and flexible responding of treatment developers is essential in moving our interventions to the next level of effectiveness. Certainly, significant advances have been made in trauma therapy, particularly among behavior therapists. However, a number of our clients either do not respond to treatment or have additional problems that are not addressed by current protocols. *Instead of limiting our repertoire in responding to difficult client problems by repeatedly intervening in the same way, psychologists are accepting the current limitations of psychotherapy and investigating alternative ways to respond.* We expect no less of ourselves than we do of our clients. As scientist-practitioners, our lives stand for moving forward in ways that make a difference in the world. (p. 206; emphasis added)

In this chapter, I will discuss 10 principles for healing and recovery from psychic trauma. These principles are based on a holistic-dynamic view of personality dynamics and the psychobiology of prolonged stress-response syndromes: (1) trauma and living systems theory; (2) PTSD as degraded adaptive behavior in prolonged stress syndromes; (3) traumatic "mile markers" in life-span development; (4) Trauma Complexes and the striving for unity; (5) optimal congruence: restoring a sense of coherence to personality; (6) the power of continuity and connection; (7) transforming states of dissociability; (8) optimal resilience; (9) peak experiences, need gratification, and optimal integration;

---

[1]As this chapter was being prepared, the most destructive tsunamic natural disaster in history claimed the lives of nearly 200,000 people in Southeast Asia. Among the other problems in the wake of the disaster was the lack of preparation and international cooperation to cope with the aftermath of such an event at all levels of short- and long-term crisis response.

TABLE 12.1
Transformational Principles: States of Trauma and Prolonged Stress Syndromes to Integration in Personality

PTSD/traumatized states and complexes	Principles of transformation and trauma and integration
1. Dysregulated organismic functioning	Restore optimal organismic integration
2. PTSD as degraded adaptive behavior	Attentuate maladaptive stress response
3. Traumatic "mile markers" of trauma in life-span development	Identify traumatic "mile markers"
4. Trauma complexes and striving for unity	Unify trauma complexes in self and personality
5. Deintegration of self-dimensions	Restore optimal intrapsychic congruence
6. States of dissociability	Transform and integrate dissociative states
7. Loss of continuity and connection	Restore sense of continuity and connection
8. Insufficient organismic resilience	Facilitate development of resilience
9. Need deprivation, loss of optimal states	Facilitate peak experience of optimal need Gratification in hierarchy of needs
10. Loss of self-actualizing tendency	Facilitate optimal coping behavior and personality integration

Source: ©2004 John P. Wilson.

and (10) understanding the optimal adaptation of self-actualizing survivors.

Table 12.1 presents a summary of the 10 transformational principles and their relationship to PTSD, traumatized states, and Trauma Complexes.

The trajectory of research on PTSD and the sophisticated paradigms of empirical studies are now beginning to show areas of convergence concerning the depth and complexity of PTSD, posttraumatic injuries to the self and identity, and maladaptive behavioral consequences. This convergence of knowledge enables higher order patterns of understanding to materialize and begin to take shape more clearly, coming into a more refined resolution that reveals the underlying structural scaffold of the human stress-response system in its integrated psychobiological complexity. The focal resolution that is appearing on the epistemological screen of knowledge is similar to looking through a microscope at the organizational complexity of organic processes—i.e., the richly integrated structure becomes transparent, revealing hierarchically arranged suprasystems that characterize all living systems (Miller, 1978). In this regard, the study of the human stress-response syndrome has been the subject of intense study in behavioral medicine for over a century (Selye, 1976; Everly & Lating, 1995; Benson, 1993) and has commanded attention because of the relationship between psychological stress and a broad range of health-related phenomena such as heart disease, hypertension, diabetes, psychiatric illnesses, and problems in cognitive functions (Benson, 1993; Schnurr & Green, 2004). The study of PTSD as one form of prolonged stress-response reflects a continuation of scientific inquiry as to the nature of stress mechanisms and the limits of its capabilities. What distinguishes the early studies of Selye (1976) from current analyses of PTSD is the fundamental recognition that as a trauma-related stress disorder (as opposed to a stress reaction), the psychobiological mechanisms associated with PTSD persist in their actions, operating in relatively high states of continuous arousal "as if" traumatic stimuli were still present, rather than automatically shutting-off and terminating the response to external, threatening situations (Friedman, 2000; Wilson, 2004a). It is conceptually integral to the diagnostic status of PTSD as an "entity" that the episodic, prolonged, and continuous nature the stress-response causes impairments in adaptive behavior. There are clear, discernible, and measurable changes in behavioral functioning from the pretraumatic baseline, which has degraded in its adaptive quality. In essence, PTSD is degraded adaptive behavior at multiple levels of psychological functioning (e.g., memory, affect regulation, psychosocial capacities, self-reference, affiliative patterns, work capacity). However, not all aspects of psychological functioning are equally impacted by the dysregulated nature of the stress-response system, a fact which is apparent in the episodic nature of symptom expression in the tripartite diagnostic symptom clusters of reexperience, avoidance/numbing, and hyperarousal (i.e., the *DSM-IV*, B, C, and D diagnostic criteria). Moreover, the impact of prolonged stress-response patterns extends to self-processes (i.e., identity and self-dimensions) and to affiliative patterns of interrelatedness (Wilson, Friedman, & Lindy, 2001; Wilson, 2004a). Clinical interventions and treatment modalities developed for PTSD implicitly recognize this fact and target the maladaptive response patterns that have developed in connection with the stress disorder, whose existence causes clinically significant impairment in areas of behavioral functioning and to self-processes (Wilson, Friedman, & Lindy 2001).

The critical question that emerges from the convergent knowledge about the integrated psychobiological nature of PTSD as a prolonged form of stress-response is that of identifying the principles which enable the transformation of these dysregulated systems. What are the underlying principles that facilitate the restoration of the normal, if not optimal, capacity to adapt to overwhelming traumatic life-events?

2 PRINCIPLES OF TRANSFORMATION AND RECOVERY FROM TRAUMATIC LIFE-EVENTS

By adopting a living systems perspective of PTSD and Trauma Complexes, it readily becomes apparent that these forms of behavioral adaptation to trauma are hierarchically integrated suprasystems within the organism that have their own set of engineering mechanisms governed by the brain and nervous system (Miller, 1978; Schore, 2003; LeDoux, 1996; Friedman, 2000; McEwen, 2002). The organism is an extraordinarily complex system and traumatic impacts are multidimensional in their effects, operating on synergistic principles within subsystems of perception, affect regulation, memory, cognition, and behavioral dispositions. A holistic-dynamic understanding of the psychobiological nature of prolonged stress-responses evoked by traumatic stressors indicate that there are five distinct and interrelated symptom clusters: (1) traumatic memories and reexperience phenomena; (2) patterns of coping, adaptation, and ego-defensiveness that define an avoidance and numbing response to traumatization; (3) increased physiological reactivity, namely hyperarousal states, that reflect the continuity of nervous system responding "as if" the stressors were still present; (4) alterations in self-processes, personal identity, and ego-processes; and (5) alterations in patterns of attachment, affiliation, intimacy, and interpersonal relationships (Wilson, 2004a). These symptom clusters operate in a synergistic manner and there are marked behavioral changes from the pretraumatic baseline, reflecting a loss of adaptive capacity; a downward change from optimal levels that existed prior to the traumatic experience. The symptom clusters have reciprocal interaction effects as subsystems within the suprasystem of the integrated stress-response process governed by the brain and nervous system. The five clusters of PTSD symptoms (Wilson, 2004b) and the qualities of Trauma Complexes, reflecting organismic shifts in adaptive functioning, represent a new and scientifically measurable baseline (i.e., set point) of posttraumatic functioning. This new baseline can be discerned for each *DSM-IV* diagnostic symptom cluster (i.e., PTSD B, C, or D) or for the overall level of symptom severity, reflecting the magnitude of changes in the operation of the stress-response system (Wilson, 2004b). In this regard, the most severe damage in PTSD and Trauma Complexes occurs to the two core structures of the prolonged stress-response systems: (1) neurobiological responses of the adrenergic nervous system;

and (2) the structural components of self-processes (i.e., coherence, connection, continuity, autonomy, vitality, energy). Symptom patterns may be activated episodically through conditioned learning and evoke psychobiological response patterns of a generalized or specific nature, depending on the triggering stimulus and the nature of learning as encoded in memory and cognitive processes. From a living systems theoretical perspective, PTSD and Trauma Complexes reside in the nidus of the self as nested, in turn, within brain functions. *The treatment and transformations of these altered states of functioning recognizes this fact: it is the whole person who is impacted by trauma.* Thus, transformative principles of healing and recovery can be considered from a holistic-dynamic view of how trauma compromises the integrated wholeness of organismic functioning.

The 10 principles of transformation and integration that allow healing and recovery from the effects of trauma are discussed below.

2.1 Traumatic Impact to the Organism as a Living System

Principle 1: Restore optimal organismic functioning. Treatment approaches recognize that psychic trauma impacts the whole organism. Trauma affects the hierarchically integrated system as a whole. Trauma becomes embedded within the organism and, according to the dynamics of living systems theory, has synergistic interaction effects among all levels of system functioning.[2] The subsystems process the information of traumatic stressors in a wide range of situational contexts (e.g., parent–child relationships, warfare, natural disasters, technological disasters, political oppression, terrorism, etc.) and include: (1) input transducers; (2) internal transducers; (3) channels and networks; (4) decoders; (5) associators; (6) memory subsystems; (7) cognitive subsystems; and (8) output transducers. According to Miller (1978)

> inputs, internal processes, and outputs of various informational signals represent the *information metabolism* of such living systems. In all such systems *information flows through several subsystems, each one being a transmitter to the next one in the sequence, which acts as a receiver.* Then, after processing the information in its own special way, the second subsystem acts as a transmitter to the third ... living systems maintain their relationship with their environment or suprasystems by inputs and outputs of information. (p. 60; emphasis added)

---

[2]For a discussion of intracellular signal transduction and gene expression by stress-related phenomena, see Duman (1995).

In terms of PTSD and Trauma Complexes, traumatic stressors are received and processed by input transducers. Psychological perception and cognitive appraisal processes act as internal transducers which then distribute the information contained in the traumatic stressors (i.e., the individual subjective experience of trauma) to various organismic channels and networks which decode the information and then connect it to associative processes of memory and cognition where it is analyzed, processed, and activates both internal (e.g., neurophysiological) and external actions (e.g., avoidance behaviors) in the form of output transducers. For example, in presenting an overview of intracellular signal transduction pathways, Duman (1995) states

> Acute stress leads to activation of many brain signalling systems, including those for certain neurotransmitters and neuropeptides, as well as those for some new growth factors. The rapid actions of stress are mediated by amino acid neurotransmitters that regulate neuronal activity via gating off ion channels, and thereby directly inhibit or stimulate cell firing rate ... Regulation of these recorded messages represents the first step in a cascade of intracellular events mediated in most cases by protein phosphorylation ... Thus, these intracellular signal transduction systems represent the primary pathways by which stress, as well as other stimuli, regulate neuronal function. (p. 27; emphasis added)

Behaviorally, at a higher level of integrated organismic responding, the output transducers include ongoing perceptual mechanisms (e.g., hypervigilance to threat stimuli), cognitive decision-making processes (e.g., action strategies, ego-defenses, decision-making), and behavioral dispositions to execute a repertoire of coping activities.

A holistic-dynamic perspective of Trauma Complexes and PTSD enables treatment providers to see the "big picture" of how psychic trauma is embedded within the phenomenological field of a person. Trauma impacts the whole person and synergistic-interaction effects among subsystems is such that one can meaningfully describe *"cascade effects"* from one level of system functioning to another. In an overly simplistic example, the perception of threat evokes the fear response which activates cognitive attributional processes and behavioral dispositions to respond (LeDoux, 1996). The failure to successfully master threat situations results in memories of the event and creates a threshold potential to reactivate the fear response and the memories of the trauma encounter, which may have been emotionally distressing to the point of overriding existing coping responses, leading to states of helplessness and a wish to avoid memories and feelings associated with the traumatic encounter (Schore, 2003). The advantage of utilizing a holistic perspective of the consequences of traumatization is that it allows the treatment provider to assess the multileveled impacts and to identify their reciprocal relationships. It also enables identification of which subsystem (e.g., affect dysregulation, cognitive processing) of information processing and metabolism of the trauma was most severely disrupted. Indeed, from the perspective of psychological assessment, it would be useful diagnostically, and in terms of treatment planning, to have an accurate profile of how trauma has differentially effected subsystem functioning as related to symptom manifestation. In this regard, there is a need to develop multidimensional psychobiological profiles of PTSD and Trauma Complexes. These profiles could graphically represent specific forms of subsystem dysregulation caused by prolonged stress effects to the organism. As such, they would represent a meta-assessment of posttraumatic organismic states and enable treatments to more precisely target symptoms.

2.2 PTSD as Degraded Adaptive Behavior in Prolonged Stress Syndromes

Principle 2: Attenuate maladaptive stress-response pattern. It is now recognized that PTSD reflects allostasis as a stress-response syndrome (McEwen, 2002, 1998; Friedman, 2000). As a degraded form of adaptive behavior, PTSD reflects at least eight different allostatic processes, which include: (1) altered thresholds of response; (2) hyperreactivity; (3) altered initial response patterns; (4) altered capacity of internal monitoring; (5) altered continuous response patterns; (6) altered feedback based on distorted information; (7) the failure of the stress-response system to habituate and shut down and restore homeostasis; and (8) the resetting of the posttraumatic baseline of organismic functioning (Wilson & Thomas, 2004).

As part of a recommended complete psychobiological meta-assessment procedure to determine the nature of posttraumatic injuries, it is suggested that psychological and biological (e.g., neurohormonal assessment, neuroimaging, psychometric testing) assessment be placed into a comprehensive profile analysis for all organismic systems. The construction of a complete pre- and post-profile analysis based on multiple methods and techniques of assessment would enable a panoramic view of how organismic functioning was affected by severe trauma. In an analogical way, a complete psychobiological profile of posttraumatic assessment would be comparable to looking at the graphic summary profile for MMPI-clinical and validity scales, an MRI scan of a PTSD-diagnosed patient, or the psychophysiologial response patterns of a patient exposed to trauma-specific and neutral experimental stimuli (Kaufman, Aikins, & Krystal, 2004; Orr, Metzger, Miller, &

Kaloupek, 2004; Friedman, 2004; Knight & Taft, 2004; Buckley, Greene, & Schnurr, 2004). However, a comprehensive psychobiological profile configuration would constitute a meta-posttraumatic stress analysis without necessarily implying a diagnosis, but rather charting the specific ways that trauma led to a prolonged stress syndrome which, in turn, generated allostatic changes in adaptive behavior resulting in potential areas of degraded functioning from either the pretraumatic baseline or the optimal level criteria that had been established (see principle 10).

2.3 Traumatic "Mile Markers" in Ontogenesis

Principle 3: Identify traumatic "mile markers" in life-span development. Treatment approaches for PTSD confront patients at different ages in the life-cycle, from infancy to old age. The theory of trauma and the epigenesis of identity recognizes that traumatic events can strike at any point in ontogenetic development (see Chapter 3). There are traumatic "mile markers" that designate the age and stage during which trauma occurred. Traumatic "mile markers," like mile markers along a highway, indicate the nature, severity, and consequences of trauma on epigenetic personality and developmental processes. Traumatic events can have stage-specific consequences to a wide range of psychobiological processes, which include: (1) developing neurological systems (Schore, 2003); (2) ego and personality development; (3) emergent cognitive and intellectual abilities; (4) patterns of attachment, bonding, interpersonal identification, and affiliative patterns; (5) dissociative behavioral states and proneness to horizontal or vertical dissociative processes; (6) the emergent or existing structure of ego-identity (i.e., sense of continuity and sameness) and self-dimensions (e.g., coherence, autonomy, energy, vitality, connection, continuity); (7) physical health and the aging process; and (8) patterns of coping adaptation and ego-defensiveness, which include risk-proneness for psychiatric disorders, addiction, and acting out behaviors.

Ontogenetic and epigenetic perspectives of life-course development are critically important in the accurate assessment and treatment of PTSD and Trauma Complexes in several ways. First, they can establish the timeframe of traumatic injuries to the fabric of integrated organismic functioning. For example, they enable "analytic archaeology" to occur, to discover how formative identity processes were disrupted, impacted, or altered by trauma. Second, they enable assessment of developmental fixations, arrestations, dissociations, or psychosocial accelerations in psychoformative processes. Third, they enable identification of traumatic injuries to self-dimensions and narcissistic injuries which lead to various pathways of personality organization and defensive structures to protect areas of vulnerability (Horowitz, 1991). Fourth, they enable a therapeutic process of recapitulation of epigenetic development; to restore ego-strengths and capacities for mastery that were compromised by overwhelming experience. In this sense, the foundations of ego-strength can be restored in areas of psychosocial competence, including the restoration of good capacity for affect regulation and resilient coping. Similarly, dissociative tendencies can be identified, analyzed, and transformed into highly effective, integrative modes of adaptation in the face of future stressors that would tax coping patterns, maladaptive forms of psychological defense as well as counterproductive patterns of interpersonal relationships. Thought of somewhat differently, transformations of negatively impacted epigenetic processes can release conflicted areas of psychic energy that had been rendered unconscious, stored in dissociative, encapsulated ego-states or woven into complexly organized personality traits and syndromes, including those traditionally codified under the rubric of personality disorders (i.e., Axis II syndromes).

2.4 Trauma Complexes and the Striving for Unity in the Self

Principle 4: Unify trauma complexes in the self. Understanding the pathogenic and potentially growth-promoting effects of traumatization is useful in defining the total spectrum of traumatic impacts to the organism. Severe trauma can break the spirit and destroy the soul of a person. On the other hand, with nurturance, good guidance, and the reexperience of optimal and peak psychological states, even the most severely traumatized person can experience personal growth and self-transformations that result in posttraumatic character strengths and personal virtues.

Treatment approaches for traumatized individuals have tended to focus almost exclusively on the diagnosis of PTSD (Foa, Keane, & Friedman, 2001). While this is quite understandable since PTSD is a relatively new diagnostic consideration (first defined in 1980), and is a common form of psychological injury after trauma, it is limiting in scope and may lead to diagnostic myopia and a failure to see how trauma has affected the totality of organismic functioning and personality. Therefore, it is useful to identify the specific configurations of Trauma Complexes that develop in the wake of trauma.

Trauma Archetypes and Trauma Complexes are interrelated phenomena of unusual significance to complex mental processes. They stratify all levels of conscious awareness (LCA) and contain unique psychodynamic properties (Horowitz, 1991). As part of complex personality processes, Trauma Archetypes (as universal forms of experience) are the psychological soil from which Trauma Complexes evolve as unique constellations of psychically dissociative phenomena—meaning that they were split off from the ongoing stream of personality-governed adaptive processes. Trauma Complexes have their own identity and sets of characteristics, an encapsulated psychic constellation which evolves in the wake of trauma that generates fear states sufficient to give birth to the complexes in the first place. Trauma Complexes are not necessarily pathological in nature, although they can include PTSD phenomena and other psychiatric disorders. Trauma Complexes operate as a suprasystem within the hierarchically arranged set of organismic processes defined by living systems theory (Miller, 1978). Trauma Complexes are formed from the encounter with specific types of traumatic stressors that comprise the nature of the Abyss, Inversion, and Transcendent Experiences. The confrontation with traumatic stressors sets up posttraumatic processes in personality which include: (1) posttraumatic affect dysregulations; (2) individually constellated posttraumatic cognitive schemas; (3) posttraumatic personality processes (i.e., trait alterations); and (4) posttraumatic "cogwheeling" effects among other types of archetypically embedded experiences in the organism.

From a clinical perspective, there is much utility and value in understanding how Trauma Complexes function in posttraumatic states of personality. First, Trauma Complexes, formed out of the Abyss, Inversion, and Transcendent Experiences, reflect profound states of organismic vulnerability (i.e., fear, anxiety, dread, helplessness, hopelessness, etc.). Trauma Complexes mirror posttraumatic injuries to the self-structure, identity, and systems of meaning. The Trauma Complex, as a unique psychic constellation created by the trauma experience, represents the attempts of the organism to metabolize the overwhelming aspects of the trauma encounter as a form of prolonged stress-response. Moreover, the Trauma Complex reflects the inherent organismic drive towards unity in personality. This has been referred to by Horowitz (1986) as the completion tendency—a psychic drive towards the integration and synthesis of ego-alien trauma experience into a unified cognitive schema. In my view, the completion tendency exists as part of the larger drive and striving towards unity in personality and integration verses fragmentation in self-dimensions. In Jungian terms, this reflects the Unity Archetype, the tendency of the self to seek unification of opposites into an integrative whole; a drive towards balance within the psyche. In treatment approaches, it is important to recognize that the Trauma Complex is in continuous operation and is manifest in different ways: symptoms, motivational striving, symbolism, dreams, and value choices in daily living. The continuous operation of the Trauma Complex articulates dynamically with all systems of organismic functioning: PTSD as a syndrome; processes of memory and cognition; the functional operation of personality traits; the unconscious expression of conflicted aspects of personal identity, and more. At higher levels of organismic striving, the Trauma Complex contains motivational energy for self-transcendence—i.e., the awareness of higher levels of being, self-consciousness, and existence that can emerge from the metabolism of traumatic states of being and the reconfiguration of personality and the self.

2.5 Optimal Congruence

Principle 5: Restore optimal intrapsychic consequences between the inner world of experience and the external world. Trauma has the power to transform integrative states of psychological functioning at many levels which range from dissociative mental states to dissociability in psychic complexes, basic needs, and prepotent stages of identity formation in the course of the life-span. The principle of optimal congruence between external experiences and internal psychological schemas is important in the transformation of traumatized conditions into optimal and fully functional personality processes. *The transformational process requires converting trauma-evoked dysregulations in the core dimensions of personality (e.g., traits) and self-capacities into optimal states of integrated organismic striving.* These transformational processes reflect the inherent drive towards unity, as expressed particularly in the Unity Archetype and self-actualizing modes of organismic striving. In the purest sense, unifying experiences restore balance between external reality and internal modalities of experience. Need-gratifying experiences restore balance within psychoformative processes (separation vs. connection; movement vs. stasis; integration vs. disintegration), providing satisfaction to salient emotional needs (e.g., the need hierarchy), and subsequently release higher levels of adaptive functioning. Moreover, the principle of restoring optimal congruence between the inner and outer worlds of unifying self-experiences extends to identity and ego-processes, psychosocial competencies, and basic psychological processes (e.g., perception, cognition, memory, affect regulation) which provide the infrastructure to more complex forms of mental activity. Viewed in this way, we can understand how transformative experiences (e.g., psychotherapy, good love relationships, occupational success, peak experiences, somatic healing, etc.) help to restore congruence in personality (Wilson & Drozdek, 2004).

When optimal congruency facilitates the integration of unifying experience in the self, there are empirically measurable and clinically verifiable changes in personality and behavior. Stated simply, the nature of the traumatized state begins to dissolve and dissipate. Negative emotional energies are supplanted with positive affects and organismic vitality. In terms of self-dimensions, there exists the free use of autonomy, unencumbered by anxiety or depression. Equally important in terms of self-capacities, a sense of coherence returns to personality along with a renewed sense of continuity in daily living. The increased level of positive emotions, as well as physical and mental energy, is associated with an enhanced sense of well-being and life-satisfaction. Daily hassles and normal stresses of living seem less significant or difficult to manage. As these personality attributes emerge as renewed and revitalized there are feelings of meaningful connections to others as well as a willingness to connect with a wider circle of significant others in one's culture.

Restoration of optimal congruence between the outer and inner worlds of experience has positive effects on identity processes. A sense of self-sameness and continuity returns with a stronger sense of elasticity and integration to the core of being. Transforming the injuries of psychic trauma leads to a resynthesis and reconfiguration of the elements that constitute identity, restoring groundedness and centering in the planes of self-experience. As this process occurs, the ego sharpens its capacity for mastery and evidences more flexibility, assurance, and capacity for resilient adaptation. The revitalization of ego-processes has direct consequences for psychosocial functioning, which enables a wide spectrum of potential changes in integrative functioning. For example, new perspectives of personal meaning of the trauma experience develop and are placed within a life-span perspective of oneself as an active agentic process, walking the pathway of life's journey that began before traumatization and which continues afterwards. Similarly, new historical perspectives of one's life-experiences occur, shaping a sense of hope, purpose, and motivational goals. Feelings of self-esteem are strengthened and with it there is greater capacity for intimate relationships, work, and the enjoyment of life for its own sake. Survivors of extreme stress know that life can be destroyed, lost, or permanently scarred at any moment by unforeseen events or the hands of fate and destiny. But, as optimal congruence returns to organismic functioning, there is an increased awareness (i.e., consciousness) of living in the "now," enjoying life as it is, without unrealistic expectations for the future. Stated differently, learning to live authentically in the moment happens automatically for many trauma survivors who have had to face the specter of their own death or witnessed the death or profound suffering of others. Moreover, modern cognitive behavioral therapy has expanded its research and treatment of PTSD and trauma to include concepts of mindfulness, a concept inherent in Eastern religions and Buddhist teachings

> Mindfulness is based on the ability to focus on the present moment, with full participation in that experience and an attitude of nonjudgmental acceptance ... mindfulness has also been described as a metacognitive state of detached awareness. (Marlatt, Witkiewitz, Dillworth, Bowen, Parks, MacPherson, Loncozak, Larimer, Simpson, Blume, & Critchen, 2004, p. 264)

What this suggests is that restorative experiences of different types, including effective posttraumatic therapies, will facilitate the movement towards unity and positive, growth-promoting consequences to self processes. The clearest example of this phenomenon is seen in the lives of highly resilient survivors and those who have achieved the highest levels of posttraumatic growth and self-actualization (see principle 10).

2.6 The Power of Continuity and Connection

Principle 6: Restore a sense of continuity and connection to meaningful attachment. The power of psychic trauma to radically disrupt an individual's sense of continuity in living and meaningful connections to self and others cannot be overestimated. We know from clinical studies of survivors of the most extreme forms of brutalization imaginable (e.g., Holocaust and Hiroshima survivors; torture survivors; profoundly traumatized war veterans) that a critically needed sense of personal continuity and connection to sources of meaning can be destroyed, lost, or profoundly altered by extreme stress experiences.

The transformative principles of establishing positive continuity and connection within the self and to other sources of meaning and attachment is fundamental to healing and recovery from Trauma Complexes, PTSD, and damage to the inner self. As subparadigms of self-processes, the psychoformative modalities of continuity vs. discontinuity, connection vs. separation have important functions in terms of grounding and centering the structural and experiential dimensions of cognitive self-schemas.

First, a sense of continuity and connection helps to maintain emotional stability by providing threads of predictability and certainty to daily activities and the successful management of challenging life-events. Second, a sense of continuity and connection serves to confirm a positive sense of posttraumatic growth (see Linley & Joseph, 2004 for a review). Through continuity and meaningful personal connection with others, there emerges an existential awareness of the capacity to construct a new self; to literally reinvent the architecture of one's self

and life-structure. Third, a sense of continuity provides a constant reference point for feedback from others; to test the limits of one's newly
formed self and posttraumatic capacity for change. Fourth, an ongoing
sense of continuity and connection helps to maintain equilibrium, versus
organismic disequilibrium caused by trauma. Equilibrium in groundedness and centeredness is experienced as psychological integrity and
solidity of character. It is subjectively experienced as the constancy of
self-coherency which contravenes tendencies toward separation, isolation, purposelessness, distantiation, alienation, detachment, and psychic
numbing. Finally, a sense of continuity and connection represents
gyroscopic navigational tools for personal identity, charting the course
of life-experiences.

2.7 Transforming States of Dissociability

Principle 7: Transform and integrate dissociative states. Transforming
posttraumatic dissociability to integrated states of healthy functioning
is another principle in healing and recovery from psychic trauma. The
term "posttraumatic dissociability" has many different connotations
ranging from the psychiatric definition of an alteration in the "usually
integrative functions of consciousness, memory and identity (*DSM*,
p. 519) to dissociability in personality processes, a term used by Jung
(1971) to characterize *nonpathological complexes* which become constellated and split off from normal personality processes due to intrapsychic conflicts or the confrontation with traumatic events.

I am suggesting that the Trauma Complex is a unique form of psychological complex that is formed after a traumatic experience. Jung
defined a complex as

> [having] a powerful inner coherence, it has its own wholeness and, in
> addition, relatively high degree of autonomy, so that it is subject to the
> control of the conscious mind to only a limited extent, and therefore
> behaves like an animated foreign body in the sphere of consciousness.
> (1972, CW8, para 201)

The Trauma Complex, therefore, represents a complex form of
dissociability which has its own characteristics and qualities. Jung's
words "animated foreign body" are descriptively accurate and useful
when applied to the understanding of Trauma Complexes since these
complexes tend to function autonomously in accordance with their
own energy in the unconscious. In more behavioral terms, Trauma
Complexes are a set of dispositions to act in predictable ways based
on how personality and learned response tendencies were reinforced

by the trauma experience. The Trauma Complex is a superordinate concept which includes many forms of dissociation that can occur. In a simplified categorization this includes the following:

Organismically Based Forms of Dissociability

- Stage-specific forms of dissociation to the entire sequence of epigenetic development.
- Dissociated identity components associated with critical, age-related developmental tasks.
- Partial identity dissociation, i.e., fragmented elements of the configuration of identity as it exists at any point in ontogenesis.
- Horizontal (within-stage) and vertical (between-stage) dissociative phenomena (i.e., depersonalization, derealization, amnesia, DID) that occur at each of the stages of epigenetic development.
- Dissociated and encapsulated ego-alien personality constellations (i.e., non-DID) as part of the Trauma Complex.
- Pathological, split-off personality processes in response to trauma, abuse, and violence that incubate Axis II personality disorders or self-pathologies.
- Dissociated motive states in the hierarchy of needs (Maslow, 1970) which reflect dissociated states of safety, love and belongingness, esteem and self-actualizing tendencies.
- Dissociative psychosexual and psychosocial stages as emergent modalities of development with corresponding ego-states and identity configurations.

The recognition of the broad domain of dissociability associated with psychological trauma enables assessment of the many ways that deintegration has occurred. Clearly, deintegration is not an all-or-none phenomenon; there are degrees of dissociative processes in personality, a fact discussed extensively by Putnam (1997) in his DBS (discrete behavioral states) model which "seeks to account for symptoms, behaviors, physiology, and phenomenology associated with pathological dissociation and to provide insights into therapeutic interventions" (p. 13). Putnam notes that: "in a normal individuation, specific state-dependent senses of self are sufficiently integrated with one another that the individual maintains a sense of continuity of self across state and context" (p. 164). However, in trauma-evoked dissociative states, "DBS ... are widely separated in multidimensional state space from normal states of consciousness" (p. 173). Putnam (1997) suggests that in dissociative states of varying qualities and characteristics, there are four processes that constitute a hierarchically integrated subsystems: (1) *arousal* (e.g., heart rate, respiration, emotional state); (2) *memory* (e.g., the encoding, processing, and retrieval of information); (3) *structural connections* (e.g., information-processing pathways that have interlinks with dissociative and normal states); and (4) *metacognition* (e.g., knowledge of normal and dissociative states and the relative degree of articulation of them in an integrative structure). Consistent with the views presented in Chapter 3, Putnam (1997), states that "this function facilitates the integration and continuity of identity and behavior across daily fluctuations in behavioral states" (p. 174). Moreover, he notes "the DBS model implies that identity fragmentation seen in MPD and other disorders associated with childhood trauma is not a 'shattering' of a previously intact identity, but rather a developmental failure of consolidation and integration of discrete states of consciousness" (p. 176). This statement reflects stage-specific forms of dissociative processes in the course of epigenetic development, as described in detail in Chapter 3. Thus, one can meaningfully define horizontal (within-stage) and vertical (between-stage carryover effects) dissociative processes within an epigenetic framework for ego-processes, identity configuration, structural [self] dimensions (e.g., coherence, autonomy, vitality, continuity, connection, energy), and personality trait formation. Stated differently, a broad range of dissociative phenomena can occur developmentally which "cross-cut" emerging organismic capacities, strengths, abilities. and their higher order integration within personality. Further, various forms of the spectrum of dissociative phenomena can occur at any point in the lifecycle. However, their greatest impact is to the newly forming and emergent aspects of personal identity and the self. Conceptually, the Trauma Complex is similar to Putnam's (1997) DBS model, but larger in its dimensions and the manner in which it articulates with psychic constellations (i.e., normal, nontraumatic) and other archetypal phenomena.

In terms of restorative principles, the recognition of the array of dissociative phenomena enables therapeutic processes to establish sufficient trust and high empathic capacity (Wilson & Thomas, 2004). As a result, we can identify five primary processes to transform deintegrated (DBS) states into more optimal and integrative ones. First, it is necessary to engage in analytic archaeology to discover the specific types of DBS and dissociative phenomena. Second, encapsulated, dissociative states must be released by removing maladaptive ego-defenses and insufficient information processing of the original traumatic experience. Third, patterns of affect dysregulation that are uniquely constelled in DBS and Trauma Complexes need to be identified. Fourth, the patient needs to be helped to understand and increase personal knowledge as to the operation of DBS and normal mental states. Fifth, the hierarchical integration of deintegrated ego-states, identity configuration, and dimensions of the self must be facilitated. As these five interrelated processes of integration occur, there will be a natural and automatic set of changes in organismic functioning. As DBS dissolve, there will be a release of new energy and the capacity to supplant the previously pathogenic affective-cognitive modalities of functioning with more integrated ones. Stated differently, the hierarchically integrated system allostatically resets itself, terminating the maladaptive elements of prolonged stress syndromes (McEwen, 2002). Elsewhere, this process has been described as positive allostasis leading to natural healing and optimal levels of functioning (Wilson & Thomas, 2004).

2.8 Optimal Resilience

Principle 8: Facilitate the development of resilience. The transformative principles recognize the necessity to facilitate the posttraumatic development of resilience. In Chapter 10, twenty distinct characteristics of resilient trauma survivors were discussed. These psychological attributes comprise a profile of personality characteristics, behavioral styles, and coping patterns that distinguish highly resilient trauma survivors from less resilient persons. The identification of these qualities of psychological functioning in the face of extreme adversity are important for several reasons.

First, they identify repertoires of effective behavior that are *transsituational* in nature. Second, they suggest ways that these attributes can be learned through training, education, or psychotherapy. Third, they identify specific cognitive-behavioral processes associated with the appraisal and processing of extreme stress experience (e.g., not personalizing events, capacity to mobilize resources, sense of positive identity as a survivor). Fourth, they suggest specific types of coping behaviors that have a higher probability value for efficacious outcomes. Fifth, they identify belief systems and capacities for meaning-making in the wake of trauma. Sixth, they illustrate the role of positive emotions, the use of humor, prosocial behavior, altruism, mature ego-defenses, and a sense of kinship with fellow survivors. Finally, they demonstrate the value of perseverance, stamina, and continued striving to long-term mental health.

The idea of facilitating resiliency in trauma survivors is pragmatic, attainable, and capable of being taught in psychoeducational programs. A similar view was put forth by Putnam (1997) who stated

> To clinicians working with children across a wide range of settings, it is apparent that despite severe trauma and loss, many youngsters exhibit a remarkable natural capacity to restore order and function in their

lives. Resiliency is often overlooked in the evaluation and treatment of traumatized children. (p. 263)

In terms of transformational principles, it clearly makes sense to learn the lessons of healthy survival and life-long happiness from resilient survivors. Healthy, resilient survivors have demonstrated the capacity to overcome and, in many cases, transcend the experience of severe trauma. How did they do it? What can we learn from them about the fundamental principles of resiliency? Analysis of resilient survivors holds a key to understanding the mechanisms of effective coping with traumatic stress. By identifying the central mechanisms that make up the psychological profile of resilient survivors, we can gain insight as to the processes which can be facilitated in those emotionally impaired by trauma.

2.9 Optimal States

Principle 9: Facilitate need gratification and peak experiences. The transformation of traumatized states of psychological functioning into optimal ones raises questions of profound significance to the science of psychology. Understanding how individuals experience posttraumatic growth, ego-maturity, and self-transcendence, and how they transform narcissistic injuries is fundamental to good psychotherapy, the creation of archetypal healing ritual, eupsychian cultures, and therapeutic communities. It may be the case that knowledge of transformative processes (i.e., from psychic injuries that "hallmark" PTSD as a psychiatric disorder) into positive, optimal states of personality functioning is the archetypal expression of human striving towards unity, integration, individuation, and self-actualization. In that regard, posttraumatic striving concerns the essence of the human spirit; to seek the further reaches of personal evolution as a conscious being within a lifetime of epigenesis shaped by historical forces.

Optimal states of psychological functioning have been the focus of "positive psychology," behavioral medicine, transpersonal psychology, and studies of self-actualizing persons (Peterson & Seligman, 2004; Sheldon, 2004; Maslow, 1970; Rogers, 1951). While a review of this literature is beyond the scope of this chapter, it is noteworthy that there are a limited number of characteristics of optimal states of psychological functioning. These characteristics suggest a broad range of integrative processes that reflect organismic striving towards unity and efficacy in environmental transactions. As noted in Chapter 6, these attributes of personality overlap with the defining qualities of peak experiences as outlined by Maslow (1968) and as codified by Peterson and Seligman

(2004) in their taxonomy of moral character and human virtues. I am presenting them here as a focal point to contrast how optimal states of functioning differ from traumatized states. By establishing standards of optimal integrative states, we can then examine the question of how traumatized states can be transformed in the direction of greater degrees of psychological health and the restoration of organismic well-being.

Unique Characteristics of Optimal Integrative States of Psychological Functioning

1. A strong, positive sense of well-being. A prevalence of positive emotional states, a subjective sense of active mastery of experience.
2. A subjective sense of self-synergy and congruence between external reality and inner states of intrapsychic functioning.
3. A subjective, positive sense of identity, reflecting the potential for self-integration.
4. Spontaneity, naturalness, and the manifestations of inborn, pre-existing potentials in a relatively effortless state of being.
5. Higher levels of personal consciousness and holistic understanding of life as a process, an ability to see the "big picture" of things.
6. A tacit, deeper knowledge, wisdom, and intuitive understanding of oneself, capacity to identify empathically with others, and manifest altruism.
7. An inner sense of serenity, tranquility, peacefulness, centeredness, groundedness.
8. A subjective sense of "flow," synchrony, naturalness, autonomy, and resonance within self-processes.
9. Perceptual processes characterized by clear, accurate, focused, "enhanced," encoding of self, others, and nature.
10. A sense of personal connection to a Higher Power, the cosmos, or the raw power of natural forces in the environment.
11. Transcendent self-experiences in which there are altered states of awareness and episodic peak experiences characterized by perceptions of time, space, and normal ego-control processes over actions.
12. The experience of acute identity states that reflect and clarify innate self-actualizing potentials and capacity to master experience.

In traumatized organismic states, many, if not most, of these dimensions of optimal states are diminished, altered or nonexistent. At the organismic level, traumatized states cause the organism to "pull inward" in defensive ways in order to preserve as much adaptive functioning as possible in the aftermath of injury. As a hierarchically integrated living system, the organism reacts in direct response to the degree of threat to its integrated capacity for optimally effective transactions within the environment. However, as noted by McEwen (2002), Friedman (2001) and Wilson, Friedman, and Lindy (2001), prolonged forms of stress-response to traumatic events generate allostatic mechanisms of adaptation which reset the baseline of organismic functioning, shifting away from homeostasis to other modalities of adaptation in which psychobiological subsystems reset themselves in the service of integration and adaptation. The question of how they are reset to mobilize organismic energies towards optimal states can be analyzed from the perspectives of: (1) basic need gratification; (2) cognitive restructuring of maladaptive thought processes and patterns of information processing; (3) the restoration of wholeness and meaning to self and ego processes; (4) the facilitation of unifying self-experiences; (5) the deconditioning of hyperarousal states of affect dysregulation governed by right-hemisphere brain functions (Schore, 2003); (6) the release of somatically embedded trauma affects; (7) the facilitation of mini peak experiences; (8) facilitation of the reconstruction of self-dimensions (i.e., the architecture of the self); and (9) facilitation of experiences that generate basic need level gratification, thereby releasing higher levels of motivated behavior within a hierarchy of needs (see Chapter 6 for a discussion).

Maslow (1970) has argued that basic need gratification releases movement and growth towards higher states of motivation and the capacity for self-actualization. In traumatized persons, some, if not all, of the basic needs in the hierarchy of needs have been compromised (e.g., a sense of safety, self-esteem, capacity for attachments and intimacy). Although it is a truism, the facilitation of basic need gratification through psychotherapy (e.g., stable object relations, unconditional positive regard, safe therapeutic sanctuary), education, and occupational success has the potential to restore deprived or damaged need states. Based on the reciprocal principles of deficiency and growth motivation, gratification of the basic needs will automatically release higher order functioning, i.e., provide gratification of traumatically deprived basic needs for survival, safety, affiliation, self-esteem, identity, etc. As gratification occurs, it automatically frees-up preoccupation with lower needs and enables the traumatized person to pursue other, higher goals—in other words, to manifest a broader domain of competence in the mastery of experience.

A correlate of this position may be seen in the idea of facilitating peak experiences in persons suffering from PTSD and Trauma Complexes. As discussed in Chapter 6, peak experiences are reported by 79% of normal populations (Davis, Lockwood, & Wright, 1991) with about one third stating that the experience had a lasting effect that was beneficial and positive in nature. Since peak experiences have positive emotional consequences in terms of integrated behavioral states, it is useful to consider the potential role that they could play in the recovery from PTSD, Trauma Complexes, or other consequences of traumatization. Listed below is a capsule summary of the positive effects of peak experiences on core psychological dimensions.

Psychological dimension	Effects of peak experiences
1. Perception	Ego-transcending, holistic, fulgent
2. Memory	Clear, complete, accurate
3. Consciousness/awareness	Clear, transcendent, acute, meta-cognitive
4. Identity	Integrative, ego-less, "here–now"
5. Self-capacities	Unified, synergistic, functionally connected
6. Motivation	Effortless, self-directed, intrinsic
7. Affect	Positive, heightened (optimal), wonder, awe
8. Somatic (bodily states)	Sense of wholeness, increased tension, heightened proprioception

The above-listed attributes of the salutary effects of peak experiences all reflect greater degrees of integrated organismic experience. In optimal states the organism is functioning at a highly tuned, maximal level of efficiency and has the capacity for mastery of environmental challenges. Peak experiences are epiphenomenal experiences of organismic competence in the inherent potentialities of the system. In terms of PTSD and Trauma Complexes, a person whose emotional and defensive systems are governed by prolonged effects of fear has fewer degrees of freedom to attend to other uses of organismic potential. Ego-defenses predominate and are utilized to protect areas of psychological injury and to manage recurring states of affect dysregulation and distressing reexperience phenomena (Schore, 2003). Indeed, this is the basic paradigm of PTSD as a psychiatric disorder: trauma → prolonged stress reactions → dysregulated psychobiological systems → tripartite symptom function (reexperience, avoidance/defense, hyperarousal states) → behavioral consequences. In this sense, it is instructive to view PTSD and Trauma Complexes as organismic impairment in which the potential for optimal states of functioning has been compromised by the experience of clinically significant trauma.

Building on this perspective, a principle of transformation includes facilitation of mini peak experiences that help transform consciousness and somatic states to optimal ones in contrast to dysregulated posttraumatic conditions. We can summarize the positive therapeutic effects of mini peak experiences to PTSD and Trauma Complexes in a simplified format:

Mini peak experiences (PE) for basic psychological needs	Therapeutic effects for traumatized states
1. Physiological PE	Sense of organismic well-being; vitality
2. Safety PE	Freedom from anxiety and threat
3. Love and belongingness PE	Sense of meaningful connection to others
4. Esteem PE	Sense of self-efficacy
5. Self-actualization PE	Awareness of optimal states, capacity for creative potential

---

The idea of therapeutically facilitating mini peak experiences through a wide range of experiences (e.g., relaxation training, cognitive restructuring experiences, psychotherapy, music and art therapy, educational experiences, spiritual meditation, contact with resilient survivors, group identity and membership with healthy survivors, humor, athletic involvement, wilderness experiences) is a way of providing basic need gratification and evoking peak experiences which contravene the presence of persistent stress response patterns (Wilson & Drozdek, 2004). As the traumatized person becomes aware of the contrast in psychological states (i.e., traumatized PTSD state vs. peak/optimal states), the completion tendency is activated and the drives towards unity, integration, and self-transcendence will become stronger and manifest in psychosocial behavior (Horowitz, 1986). The idea of evoking/facilitating mini peak experiences is similar to the protocols of cognitive behavior therapy (CBT) in that repeated episodes of mini peak experiences would have positive accumulative effects of reducing the operation of maladaptive, prolonged stress response syndromes and supplanting them with more adaptive ones that release organismic striving towards optimal adaptive functioning. *Stated differently, the contrast between states of dysregulated emotions and tension in PTSD and the pleasures and positive euphoria of a peak experience helps the person become aware that there are desirable alternatives that are more adaptive and useful in daily living.* In other words, there are subjective contrasts in polarities of experience: freedom vs. defensive avoidance; spontaneity vs. constriction; positive mood vs. anxiety; future-orientation vs. past-fixation; etc.

The restoration of meaning and wholeness to personality following psychological trauma is, in itself, a process of unification in organismic functioning at the highest level. Restoring wholeness, however, has concrete meanings and is not simply an abstract therapeutic ideal.

First, there is the process of restoring wholeness to self-dimensions (i.e., coherence, continuity, connection, autonomy, vitality, energy). Integration in self-capacities means that they are functionally synergistic in the service of maintaining positive self-appraisals and the capacity for self-transcendence. Balance and groundedness within the self has many positive consequences which include the successful processing of posttraumatic shame and guilt (see Chapter 9). Second, there is the process of restoring wholeness to ego-processes (e.g., ego-strength, ego-flexibility, healthy ego-defenses, ego-effectance). Functional effectiveness in ego-processes is directly associated with the capacity to master experiences and the challenges of daily living. Third, restoring wholeness to personality involves the process of reestablishing balance and congruence between external reality and inner modalities of experience. In this regard, PTSD and Trauma Complexes always contain symptoms that have trauma-specific meanings and are manifest in trauma specific transference reactions in treatment (TST; Wilson & Lindy, 1994; Wilson & Thomas, 2004). Stated differently, posttraumatic symptoms are rooted in the experience of traumatic stressors that impact organismic functioning, generating alterations in affect regulation, memory, and behavioral dispositions. The transformation of these dysregulated psychological states results in the capacity to adequately modulate experience, leading to congruence between external reality and inner modalities of experience. Fourth, the process of restoring meaning and wholeness to personality has different patterns and structural forms: (1) acute, epiphanous transformations; (2) long-term gradual assimilation processes; (3) developmental, life-stage-evoked transformative processes associated with normative psychosocial crises of development; (4) transformations facilitated by the release of trauma embedded in somatic (bodily) states which generate psychosomatic manifestations of PTSD symptoms and Trauma Complexes. This includes mindful awareness of how fear responses generate character armor, psychic numbing, maladaptive anxiety states, and the overuse of defenses (Wilson & Thomas, 2004). The release of traumatically embedded states is a form of "letting go" of fear-based, conditioned reactions that no longer serve any adaptive function to the organism. Fifth, long-term or acute epiphanous transformations involve restoring wholeness and meaning to the self as the center of psychic life and spiritual centering. The process of self-reconstruction (i.e., reclamation) is that of helping the person to realize that they are the architect of their own identity, despite whatever injuries have occurred because of traumatization. Being the architect of one's identity is the ability to move beyond narcissistic injuries and feelings of being diminished in self-worth (Kohut, 1965). It is the recognition that the consequences of trauma only have as much negative meaning as one gives to them (Kalsched, 1996). Nevertheless, the posttraumatic effects to the self can be devastating when they occur at critical developmental stages, causing impairments in identity, regulating capacities, attachment tendencies, and emergent growth processes (Raphael, 1983; Pynoos & Nader, 1993; Goodwin, 1999). However, transformative experiences activate changes the experiential basis of the self. Resilient trauma survivors (see Chapter 10) personify the mantra: the past was, the present is! Resilient survivors know that healthy coping is an ongoing process of creating meaning and maintaining a sense of perspective about the big picture of life. Resilient survivors manifest a proactive, problem-solving orientation to life's stresses, facilitating effective coping as demanded by situational pressures. Resilient survivors appear to have a capacity to engage in healthy detachment, to rise above ego-involvement and unnecessary personal attachments. In Buddhism, this ability has been referred to as *transcendent detachment*. This capacity for healthy detachment and transcendence is both a cognitive ability and a realization of the limits of one's own ego. Generalizing from knowledge of resilient trauma survivors, the transformation principle of self-reconstruction is the realization that a fixation on the past is illusory and nonfunctional. Trauma remains pathologically active unless insight develops from positive experiences that trauma only has the power to limit optimal strivings when encapsulated in ongoing psychic states of traumatization. The posttraumatic realization that one is, in fact, the architect of one's own identity restores autonomy. This insight inevitably creates the potential for change in striving towards optimal levels of self-actualization. The paradox of this insight is that to become the posttraumatic architect of one's identity involves the surrender of the ego and narcissism, a fact noted by Kohut (1965).

2.10 Self-Transformation and Resilience

Principle 10: Facilitate optimal coping behaviors and personality integration. What constitutes psychological health and posttraumatic growth after trauma? This question is not only important to answer from a clinical and developmental perspective, it belies the depth to which profoundly traumatic life events can alter the inner world of psychological experience and the outer world of actions, i.e., the process of Being-in-the-world.

Is recovery from psychological trauma simply the "return to normal," in whatever context that might have meaning? What is "normal" psychological functioning following extreme stress and life-altering events? What, for example, does it mean to be "normal" after surviving the Holocaust, the atomic bomb at Hiroshima, a year of combat in

Vietnam or Iraq, or the ethnic cleansing which killed tens of thousands of persons by murder, torture, or starvation in countries such as Rwanda, Sudan, and Bosnia? What does it mean to be normal in the aftermath of the terrorist attacks in New York on September 11, 2001? When a person or nation can be rendered vulnerable to the core, stripped psychically naked by massive trauma such as the attacks on September 11, 2001, what constitutes "normality" at the individual and collective (e.g., national) level? Do nations, as collectively organized social entities, suffer from symptoms of PTSD and Trauma Complexes? In the U.S., for example, is the post-9/11 establishment of new security measures (e.g., Office of Homeland Security, Transportation Security Agency, the Patriot Act of the federal government to legally detain and interrogate suspected subversives), a manifestation of symptoms of PTSD, born out of the helplessness to interdict and take effective countermeasures against the terrorists and attacks which might occur in the future? How does the national psyche of a people return to "normal" in the wake of unprecedented terrorist attacks? Is being "normal" simply the absence of preoccupation with the effects of trauma? Is it that a subtle and perhaps necessary form of psychological denial and disavowal of vulnerability and injury? Is "normal" defined as resuming the same pattern of living that existed prior to traumatic exposure? Is "normal" being able to manage symptoms and carry out role responsibilities deemed necessary by society? Is "normal" defined normatively by conformity to acceptable behavior by society? For example, in the wake of the Nazi Holocaust in post-World War II Germany or in U.S. culture following the September 11, 2001 attacks, what if it were considered "normal" to actively avoid conversations, moral reflections, situations or reminders of these unprecedented historical events and instead engage in ritualized social drinking of alcoholic beverages, mind-numbing absorption of watching television entertainment or, engaging in other forms of distraction or escape from unresolved and omnipresent tensions generated by involvement in the events? Are culturally avoidant and counterphobic reactions to trauma normal in the sense of optimal mental health?

These questions serve to highlight the complexity of defining "normality" in the recovery process in the context of a posttraumatic event. Moreover, the question of defining normality in the field of psychiatry is not a new controversy (Offer & Sabshin, 1984) and many of these same questions have been posed in terms of defining mental illness versus normality. Clearly, one can see that these questions quickly come "full-circle" in terms of establishing adequate criteria by which to define posttraumatic growth and the recovery from states of traumatization. However, the relevance of the question of posttraumatic "normalcy" serves to clarify that it has multiple meanings which include the following. (1) The absence of maladaptive PTSD and other psychiatric symptoms. (2) The return to physical health and the reduction or absence of hyperaroused states reflecting dysregulated, prolonged stress-response patterns. (3) The resolution and metabolism of the major posttraumatic effects that altered psychological, social, and occupational functioning. Usually, this criterion implies that the trauma survivor has cognitively metabolized the nature of the traumatic experience and integrated it into existing cognitive schemas (Horowitz, 1986). (4) The reduction of clinically significant distress or impairment in social, occupational, or other areas of functioning (i.e., the *DSM* criteria for "disordered" impairment caused by a clinically defined syndrome). The *DSM-IV-TR* (2000) instructs in the use of a "Global Assessment of Functioning (GAF) Scale" in connection with psychiatric diagnoses which "is to be rated with respect *only to psychological, social and occupational functioning*" (p. 32; emphasis added). But what if the posttraumatic impairment is to one's capacity for morality and moral judgment or the quality of social justice, freedom, and life in a culture, nation or the world in the wake of massive trauma? What of the loss of one's spiritual essence and soul, the capacity for full humanness? If the trauma survivor can go to work, earn an income, socialize normally (i.e., superficially) and maintain a functional role in a society, are they "normal" even if they are destroyed in their human essence? These themes and crises have been depicted in cinematic productions such as *The Unsaid, The Pawn Broker, Jacob's Ladder, The Prince of Tides, Nuts*, and *Sophie's Choice*. Survivors of horrific trauma may "walk" through life in a seemingly "normal" way and yet harbor horrific inner scars to their identity, sense of selfhood, spiritual essence, and human integrity.

By examining the four sets of criteria presented above, it becomes apparent that healing and recovery from trauma is more than the reduction of posttraumatic symptoms that produce impairment in psychological functioning. Posttraumatic growth and self-transformation is more than a return to normalcy, in whatever sociocultural context it is defined. The transcendent posttraumatic self has evolved and changed in profound ways from the nature and organization of the pretraumatic self. The whole person, as an integrated organism, has changed. The way the person perceives situations, regulates their emotions, and relates to others has altered in discernible and operationally measurable ways. The inner self has changed—the configuration of identity, self-dimensions, and ego-processes—and functions in a qualitatively different manner. In a metaphorical sense, one consequence of the trauma experience is that it has altered the prism by which the survivor filters experience. *In the transcendent posttraumatic self, the world is viewed through the eyes of human kinship, recognizing the beauty and fragility of others and life itself.* Transcendent trauma survivors possess many of the B-values described by Maslow (1968) for self-actualizing persons. They manifest concerns for justice, fairness, beauty, freedom, equality, respect, higher moral reasoning, love, compassion, altruism, creativity, "here-now mindedness," naturalness, and so on. They are autonomous self-directed persons who view life (as a product of the death-encounter or trauma-tization) in-the-moment. They live in the present, not the past. They exhibit mindfulness and acceptance without solipsism or nihilistic attitudes. They participate in the fullness of life on a daily basis, without holding expectations for life-in-the-future. Trauma teaches that life can be dictated by the whims of fate and unpredictable historical circumstances. The self-transcendent trauma survivor knows that meaning to existence is created by choice and mindful consciousness of the moment. Posttraumatic growth and self-transcendence reflect changes in levels of conscious awareness in the self and the world at large. These changes in capacity for higher levels of consciousness are part of a wider set of changes in cognitions and patterns of beliefs and personal valuing. As such, they reflect changes in the inner world of intrapsychic function-ing. At the highest levels of self-transformation following trauma, the person understands that they are the architect of their identity—the central guidance mechanism located in the core of self-dimensions and personality processes as a whole.

3 BEYOND TRAUMATIZATION

Our knowledge of healing and recovery from states of traumatization can be advanced by careful analysis of the qualities of resilient and self-transcendent trauma survivors. In behavioral terms, these are autono-mous persons and relatively independent of cultural influences. They exhibit attributes of optimal functioning, posttraumatic growth, and healthy psychosocial adaptation. In empirically measurable ways, they are the behavioral "gold standard" of posttraumatic adaptation and the capacity for optimal levels of functioning. If life is thought of as a controlled experiment which exposes persons to a wide range of traumatic situations, life-threatening environmental tests, and difficult "hurdles" to pass, they emerge as the best performers across a wide range of psychological criteria that define positive outcomes and adaptation to environmental demands. In this sense, they are "best of class," the survivors of extreme challenges to mental and emotional functioning posed by traumatic stressors. Having overcome the chal-lenges to organismic functioning, they display qualities of behavior that differentiate them from other survivors, who can be placed on a continuum from severe pathology to conventional adaptation to self-actualizing states (see Chapter 2). The effectiveness of posttraumatic functioning in resilient and self-transcendent survivors thus provides clues to their success but also to the therapeutic and educational techniques that might assist others in achieving optimal levels of posttraumatic functioning and setting the stage for higher forms of posttraumatic growth and self-individuation. By studying the healthiest, strongest, and most psychologically integrated trauma survivors, we can come to understand what "went wrong" for those who were less fortunate and suffered from debilitating PTSD, psychiatric disorders, and self-pathologies.

We can briefly summarize the core qualities of trauma survivors who have transformed the negative effects of trauma to organismic well-being and integrated them in new ways in the posttraumatic self. First, they have discovered how to create positive emotional states to contravene the psychobiological effects of PTSD, nonpathological prolonged stress-response syndromes, and Trauma Complexes. Positive affective states replace negative affect tendencies towards depression, anxiety, generalized fears, and low self-regard. Second, physical and mental energy is restored to near-optimal levels providing a deep sense of spiritual vitality against apathy, stasis, resignation, indifference, and despair. There is a desire to create meaning and to live life with joy and serenity. Mindfulness becomes a priority (i.e., part of daily consciousness and the need to live in the moment). Third, there is an inner sense of connection and continuity to self, others, and a higher sense of purpose to life. The beneficial power of having a sense of meaningful connection and continuity is associated with altruism and the need to give back to others with gratitude and humility. A sense of connection, continuity, and altruism is integral to the creation of a health-sustaining environment.

To illustrate the principles of learning from resilient and self-transcendent trauma survivors, Table 12.2 presents a summary of the 20 dimensions of resilient trauma survivors and the 12 principles that characterize self-transcendent individuals. The table illustrates where there are overlaps (i.e., correlations) between the 20 dimensions that characterize resilient survivors and the 12 categories that define self-transcendent individuals (see Chapter 11 for discussion).

Examination of Table 12.2 enables analysis of the qualities that define resilient and self-transcendent survivors. Consideration of these factors is germane to the identification of transformative principles amongst trauma survivors. Inspection of Table 12.2 reveals that there are strong overlaps between the specific characteristics of resilient survivors and the principles by which self-transcendent trauma survivors live. In a categorized analysis, the following questions can be discussed from the reviews presented in Chapters 11 (transformation of the self) and 10 (the resilient trauma survivor) and study of Table 12.2.

TABLE 12.2
The Interrelationships Between the Characteristics of Posttraumatic Resilience Self-Transformations

Twenty characteristics of resilient trauma survivors	Twelve principles of posttraumatic self-transformation[a]											
	1	2	3	4	5	6	7	8	9	10	11	12
1. Extraversion (personality)	*		*	*	*	*	*	*	*	*	*	*
2. Positive identity as survivor		*	*	*	*	*	*	*	*	*	*	*
3. Group identity as survivor	*		*	*	*	*	*	*	*	*	*	*
4. Prosocial behavior and altruism	*		*	*	*	*	*	*	*	*	*	*
5. Mature ego-defenses			*	*	*	*	*	*	*	*	*	*
6. Affect balance			*	*	*	*	*	*	*		*	*
7. Autonomy	*		*	*	*	*	*	*	*	*	*	*
8. Accurate appraisal of stressors	*	*	*	*	*	*	*	*	*	*	*	*
9. Cognitive efficacy		*	*		*	*	*	*	*	*	*	*
10. Human kinship	*		*	*	*	*	*	*	*	*		*
11. Capacity for meaning	*	*	*	*	*	*	*	*	*	*	*	*
12. Humor	*		*				*					*
13. Flexible coping			*	*	*	*	*	*	*	*	*	*
14. Problem-solving			*		*	*	*	*	*	*		*
15. Positive ideology and values		*	*	*	*	*	*	*	*		*	*
16. Transcendent detachment			*	*	*	*	*	*	*	*		*
17. Lack of personalization	*	*	*	*		*	*	*	*			*
18. Low guilt			*			*	*					*
19. Mobilize resources		*	*	*		*		*	*	*	*	*
20. High energy						*	*		*	*	*	*

Source: ©2004 John P. Wilson.

[a]1 = Vulnerability and illusions; 2 = pain, suffering, and transformation; 3 = humility and limits to ego; 4 = continuity and discontinuity in life; 5 = connection to sources of meaning; 6 = balance and groundedness; 7 = empathy, compassion, and fresh appreciation; 8 = honesty and gratitude; 9 = love and generosity; 10 = self-transformation and reinvention; 11 = spiritual consciousness and altruism; 12 = acceptance of life's unequal playing field.

What set of personality attributes do resilient and transcendent trauma survivors share in common? What characterizes the uniqueness and effectiveness of their coping styles across different types of traumatic situations? How do they appraise and process stressor experiences? How are their stress-appraisal processes related to affect regulation as part of the stress-response syndrome evoked by traumatic stressors? What is the nature of their cognitive appraisal processing. In terms of living systems theory (Miller, 1978) how do internal transducers link the perceptual processes of traumatic experiences to associative, higher order cognitive processes, information storage, and memory? What are the qualities of interpersonal processes that enable resilient and self-transcendent survivors to mobilize resources (personal, social, economic, etc.) to aid in adaptation? What belief systems, values, and systems of meaning characterize resilient and self-transcendent individuals? What is the relationship between their ideological and value-orientation to personality processes, ego-capacities (e.g., strength, flexibility), and dimensions of the self? Finally, in terms of the proposed comprehensive psychobiological meta-assessment profile for trauma survivors, what factors, variables, or attributes distinguish the pre- and posttraumatic characteristics of the most resilient and psychologically healthy survivor?

The answer to these and related questions will require empirical studies, especially longitudinal ones to understand the dynamic mechanisms which underlie the processes that differentiate resilient and self-transcendent survivors from those who suffer debilitating consequences. Nevertheless, there can be no question that knowledge of these processes holds an important key to identifying the ways in which ordinary persons achieve extraordinary transformations in the face of some of life's most difficult challenges. Beyond doubt, transcendent trauma survivors have already unlocked the door to this knowledge, and the treasures of humanity lie awaiting discovery on the other side.

REFERENCES

Benson, H. (1993). *The relaxation response*. New York: Morrow.

Buckley, T., Greene, B. & Schnurr, P. (2004). Trauma, PTSD, and physical health: Clinical issues. In J. P. Wilson & T. M. Keane (Eds.), *Assessing psychological trauma and PTSD* (2nd ed., pp. 441–466). New York: Guilford Publications.

Davis, J., Lockwood, L., & Wright, C. (1991). Reasons for not reporting peak experiences. *Journal of Humanistic Psychology, 31*, 86–94.

Duman, R. S. (1995). Regulation of intracellular signal transduction and gene expression by stress. In M. J. Friedman, D. S. Charney, & A. Deutsch (Eds.), *Neurobiological and clinical consequences of stress* (pp. 27–43). New York: Lippincott–Raven.

Everly, G. & Lating, J. (1995). *Psychotraumatology: Key papers and core concepts in post-traumatic stress*. New York: Plenum Press.

Foa, E., Keane, T. M., & Friedman, M. J. (2001). *Effective treatments for PTSD*. New York: Guilford Press.

Follette, V. M., Palm, K. M., & Hall, M. L. R. (2004). Acceptance, mindfulness and trauma. In S. C. Hayes, V. M. Follette, & M. M. Lineham (Eds.), *Mindfulness and acceptance* (pp. 192–209). New York: Guilford Publications.

Frankl, V. E. (1984). *The will to meaning: Foundations and applications of logotherapy*. New York: Meridian Books.

Friedman, L. J. (2000). *Identities architect*. Cambridge. Harvard University Press.

Friedman, M. J. (2000a). *Posttraumatic & acute stress disorders*. Kansas City: Compact Clinicals.

Friedman, M. J. (2000b). *Post-traumatic stress disorder: The latest assessment and treatment strategies*. Kansas City: Compact Clinicals.

Friedman, M. J. (2001). Allostatic versus empirical perspectives on pharmacotherapy. In J. P. Wilson, M. J. Friedman & J. D. Lindy (Eds.), *Treating psychological trauma and PTSD* (pp. 94–125). New York: Guilford Publications.

Friedman, M. J. (2004). Psychobiological laboratory assessment of PTSD. In J. P. Wilson & T. M. Keane (eds.), *Assessing psychological trauma and PTSD*, (pp. 419–441). New York: Guilford Publications.

Goodwin, J. M. (1999). The body finds its voice (Part IV). In J. Goodwin & R. Attias (Eds.), *Splintered reflections* (pp. 281–283). New York: Basic Books.

Horowitz, M. (1986). *Stress response syndromes (2ⁿᵈ Ed.)*. Northvale, New Jersey: Jason Aronson.

Horowitz, M. (1991). *Person schemas and maladaptive interpersonal patterns*. Chicago, IL: University of Chicago Press.

Jung, C. G. (1971). The collected works (Bollingen series XX, 20 vols.). Trans. R. F. C. Hull. In H. Read, M. Fordham, & G. Adler (Eds.), *Psychological types* (CW 6). Princeton, NJ: Princeton University Press.

Jung, C. G. (1972). The structure and dynamics of the psyche. The collected works (Bollingen series XX, 20 vols.) Trans. R. F. C. Hull. In H. Read, M. Fordham, & G. Adler (Eds.), *Psychological types* (CW 8). Princeton, New Jersey: Princeton University Press.

Kalsched, D. (1996). *The inner world of trauma: Archetypal defenses of the personal spirit*. London: Routledge.

Kaufman, J., Aikins, D., & Krystal, J. (2004). Neuroimaging studies in PTSD. In J. P. Wilson & T. M. Keane (Eds.), *Assessing psychological trauma and PTSD* (2nd ed., pp. 344–389). New York: Guilford Publications.

Knight, J. F. & Taft, C. T. (2004). Assessing neuropsychological concomitants of trauma. In J. P. Wilson & T. M. Keane (Eds.), *Assessing psychological trauma and PTSD* (pp. 344–389). New York: Guilford Publications.

Kohut, H. (1965) Forms and transformations of narcissism. *Journal of the American Psychoanalytic Association, 13*, 243–271.

LeDoux, M. (1996). *The emotional brain*. New York: NYU Press.

Linley, P. A. & Joseph, S. (2004). Positive change following trauma and adversity: A review. *Journal of Traumatic Stress, 17*, 1–21.

Marlatt, G. A., Witkiewitz, Dillworth, T. M., Bowen, S. W., Parks, G. A., MacPherson, L. M., et al. (2004). Vipassana meditation as a treatment for alcohol and drug use disorder. In S. C. Hayes, V. M. Follette, & M. M. Linehan (eds.), *Mindfulness and acceptance* (pp. 261–288). New York: Guilford Publications.

Maslow, A. H. (1968). *Towards a psychology of being*. New York: D. Van Nostrand.

Maslow, A. H. (1970). *Motivation and personality*. New York: Harper.

McEwen, B. S. (1998). Seminars of the Beth Israel Deaconess Medical Center: Protective and damaging effects of stress mediators. *New England Journal of Medicine, 338*(3), 171–179.

McEwen, B. S. (2002). *The end of stress as we know it*. Washington, DC: The Dana Press.

Miller, J. G. (1978). *Living systems*. New York: McGraw-Hill.

Offer, D. & Sabshin, M. (1984). *Normality and the life-cycle*. New York: Basic Books.

Orr, S. P., Metzger, L. J., Miller, M. W., & Kaloupek, D. (2004). Psychophysiological assessment of PTSD. In J. P. Wilson & T. M. Keane (Eds.), *Assessing psychological trauma and PTSD* (pp. 289–344). New York: Guilford Publications.

Peterson, C. & Seligman, M. E. P. (2004). *Character strengths and virtues: A handbook and classification*. New York: Oxford University Press.

Putnam, F. (1997). *Dissociation in children and adolescents*. New York: Guilford Press.

Pynoos, R. & Nader, K. (1993). Issues in the treatment of posttraumatic stress in children. In J. P. Wilson & B. Raphael (Eds.), *International handbook of traumatic stress syndromes* (pp. 527–535). New York: Plenum Press.

Raphael, B. (1983). *When disaster strikes*. New York: Basic Books.

Rogers, C. (1951). *Client centered therapy*. New York: Houghton-Mifflin.

Schnurr, P. P. & Green, B. L. (2004). *Trauma and health: Physical consequences of exposure to extreme stress*. Washington, DC: American Psychological Association.

Schore, A. N. (2003). *Affect regulation and repair of the self*. New York: W. W. Norton.

Selye, H. (1976). *The stress of life*. New York: McGraw-Hill.

Sheldon, K. M. (2004). *Optimal human being*. Hillsdale, NJ: Lawrence Erlbaum.

Wilson, J. P. (2004a) Broken spirits. In J. P. Wilson & B. Drozdek (Eds.), *Broken spirits: The treatment of traumatized asylum seekers, refugees and war and torture victims* (pp. 141–173). New York: Brunner-Routledge.

Wilson, J. P. (2004b). PTSD and complex PTSD: Symptoms, syndromes and diagnoses. In J. P. Wilson & T. M. Keane (Eds.), *Assessing psychological trauma and PTSD* (pp. 7–45). New York: Guilford Publications.

Wilson, J. P. & Drozdek, B. (2004). *Broken spirits: The treatment of traumatized asylum seekers, refugees and war and torture victims*. New York: Brunner-Routledge.

Wilson, J. P. & Lindy, J. (1994). *Counter-transference in the treatment of PTSD*. New York: Guilford Publications.

Wilson, J. P. & Thomas, R. (2004). *Empathy in the treatment of trauma and PTSD*. New York: Brunner-Routledge.

Wilson, J. P., Friedman, M. J., & Lindy, J. D. (2001). An overview of clinical consideration and principles in the treatment of PTSD. In J. P. Wilson, M. J. Friedman & J. D. Lindy (Eds.), *Treating psychological trauma and PTSD* (pp. 59–94). New York: Guilford Publications.

Index

Numbers in italic indicate entries in illustrations.